GLOBAL MISSION

GLOBAL MISSION

H.H. ARNOLD

MILITARY CLASSICS SERIES

FIRST TAB EDITION
FIRST TAB PRINTING

Copyright © 1949 by H. H. Arnold
Photograph insert © 1989 by TAB BOOKS Inc.

Letter to Saint Peter by Elma Dean is reprinted by permission of The American Mercury.

Library of Congress Cataloging in Publication Data

Arnold, Henry Harley, 1886-1950.
    Global mission / by H.H. Arnold.
        p.   cm.
    Includes index.
    ISBN 0-8306-4004-5
        1. Arnold, Henry Harley, 1886-1950. 2. World War, 1939-1945-
-Aerial operations, American.   3. United States.   Army Air Forces-
-History—World War, 1939-1945. 4. World War, 1939-1945—Personal
narratives, American.   5. Generals—United States—Biography.
6. United States. Air Force—Biography. I. Title.
D790.A9   1989
940.54′4973′0924—dc19
[B]   88-37504
                                                         CIP

TAB BOOKS Inc. offers software for sale. For information and a catalog, please contact TAB Software Department, Blue Ridge Summit, PA 17294-0850.

Questions regarding the content of this book
should be addressed to:

    Reader Inquiry Branch
    TAB BOOKS Inc.
    Blue Ridge Summit, PA 17294-0214

Front cover: U.S. Air Force photograph.

Military Classics Series

The U.S. military today is enjoying a renewed popularity with the American public. To help serve this burgeoning interest, TAB is proud to present the *Military Classics Series.*

This series will bring back into print quality, hardcover editions of many of the most famous books by or about key figures in U.S. military history. Whenever possible these will be firsthand accounts—the autobiographies of noted military figures or the memoirs of journalists who were at the front. Some will be biographies written by knowledgeable friends and associates of the subject. All will provide the closest possible insight into the events that have shaped our military history.

The series will span the length of American military history—from the Revolution to Vietnam. Although the series will be limited to the wars and conflicts in which the United States participated, it occasionally will include an outside perspective through the autobiographies of allies and enemies alike.

These books have long been unavailable in hardcover for both readers and collectors. The *Military Classics Series* will present them in an affordable personal-library format for military enthusiasts.

ACKNOWLEDGMENT

I want to express my thanks and sincere appreciation to my good friend William R. Laidlaw, formerly Lieutenant Colonel, Eighth and Ninth Air Forces, for his great assistance during the writing of this book. For more than a year, Bill Laidlaw has helped me wrestle with the countless problems presented by the compilation and editing of the vast material involved.

This book is dedicated to the officers, men and women of the United States Air Force, 1907–1949, and to the men and women who follow them.

It is dedicated to all those, living and dead, whose efforts and sacrifices in the past forty years have built American Air Power into one of the determining facts in maintaining world peace today; to the first "Military Aviators," to the men in the Jennies and DH's; to those who fought over Europe, the Atlantic, the Mediterranean, Africa, Asia and Japan. It is for those who flew in the cold of the Arctic, the heat of the tropics and over the lonely stretches of the Pacific, and for those who helped them fly; for the workers in the factories and scientific laboratories, and those guarding the coasts of our own hemisphere.

It is especially dedicated to those American airmen and airwomen who gave their lives, in combat, in the line of duty in Occupied Germany and Japan, and on the unknown battlefields at home.

H. H. ARNOLD
General of the Air Force.

CONTENTS

GLOBAL MISSION

☆ *1* ☆

The first airplane I ever saw was neither flying nor sitting on the ground. It was suspended above the middle of a street in Paris, near the Place de l'Opéra. That was in the late summer of 1909. I was a young Second Lieutenant, two years out of West Point, on my way home to the States from my first assignment in the Army, an unexpectedly exciting tour of duty in the Philippines. During the long months when we had been cutting our way through the Island jungles on our mapping expeditions we hadn't had much chance to spend money. Hence, my $116.66 a month (plus 10 per cent for foreign service) was allowed to grow into a little pile, big enough to pay off the debts for equipment dating back to graduation and to leave a bit over. Out of the saved-up dollars had come this fine roundabout return to New York: Hong Kong, Singapore, the Suez Canal, Alexandria, Cairo, Shepheard's Hotel, and the pyramids. Then the Mediterranean and Genoa, where I had debarked from the S. S. *Grosse Kurfuerst,* said good-by to the friendly British officers coming home on leave from India and Burma, to the British career diplomat returning from thirty years' service in the Far East, and to the cocky German officers bringing their battalion of infantry home from Tientsin. I had shaken hands with the fellow-passengers who had helped me wind up the first real adventure I had known, the American school teachers, each with her Baedeker, the Dutch father who had guarded his twenty-four-year-old son so anxiously ever since the two red-light "ladies" had come aboard at Singapore, the rich young Austrian officer who loved to tell everything he knew, and the Italian count to whom even the relief money which America was sending the victims of the recent Mt. Etna volcano just then seemed a Machiavellian gesture of Uncle Sam's. I had bowed to the sister and brother, "Who," the captain of the ship an-

I

nounced in his loud English accent, "if they *are* brother and sister are the most peculiarly acting brother and sister I have ever seen!" And finally, with a last derogatory remark about America from the captain himself, I went ashore at Genoa, and on to Switzerland.

A few weeks later I was walking along, taking in the sights and sounds and smells of Paris, and, all of a sudden, there it was, a queer contraption hanging overhead.

Reading the sign below it, and listening to what other onlookers said, I managed to find out with my best West Point French that this was the flying machine in which Monsieur Louis Blériot had, on the 25th of July, 1909, only a few weeks previously, flown from Calais, across the English Channel to Dover.

Thousands of other Americans (and Frenchmen and people from other lands) have seen Louis Blériot's monoplane since then. For more than a generation, a frail, heroic freak, it has been on exhibition in the Museum of the Invalides. But it can scarcely have looked to the Invalides' visitors quite as it looked to me; not even to Lindbergh when he was conducted there ceremoniously to pay his respects to it, following his own landing in Paris, in 1927. Even by Lindbergh's time Blériot's monoplane, with the Wright brothers' first aeroplane, or Glenn Curtiss' first flying machine, had assumed meaning. Like Caxton's printing press, or James Hargreaves' first spinning jenny, it had come to be looked upon, at least by the outbreak of World War II, for what it was—the forerunner of a human instrument that, for good or evil, in war and peace, was to change the face of the earth.

I'll confess I hadn't any blinding vision of the future of Air Power at this moment, but one thought I did have was probably as good as anybody else's who looked at Blériot's plane that summer. I thought: "If one man could do it once, what if a lot of men did it together at the same time? What happens then to England's Splendid Isolation?"

That was no clairvoyant vision, either. If Blériot's flight hadn't happened to be across the English Channel I probably wouldn't have thought even that much about his flying machine. But the Channel, and England's isolation, had been the refrain of my whole trip from Hong Kong to Genoa, night after night. I was no sooner aboard the *Grosse Kurfuerst* than the topic of Japan's intended invasion of the Philippines, our nightly theme in the Islands, had given way to the question of war between Germany and England. Every time the British and German officers met in the ship's smoking room or on deck, little tensions would occur. The last few months had seen the Bosnia-Herzegovina ferment and other frictions inflaming the European crisis, with England and France tentatively engaged on the side of Russia against Germany and Austria-Hungary in the diplomatic juggling. The German officers loved to bawl out toasts and songs in the dining salon, indicating their impatience for "Der Tag" and their wish to be sailing against England immediately. The British officers were made uncomfortable by this, not for direct reasons but because the "bloody Germans" were making a scene.

But later at night it was different. Then, crossing the Indian Ocean, where the monsoons with their furnace-like trade winds made it too hot to sleep in the unventilated bunks, all of us bachelors and some of the married men used to sit on the top deck and talk. Both the Britons and the Germans discussed their past service—and the future. It was an interesting experience for a young American officer, whose own country was seldom mentioned. Up on that deck, after two or three drinks, the Englishmen became as rude as the Germans. Everybody knew a war was coming, and both British and German knew he couldn't lose it. Every phase of the thing was discussed and hashed over again, except the fact that the United States might be a factor, and that nobody ever suggested that this still uncommenced war might be prevented altogether.

To the barking of the German officers regarding the superior condition of their Army, the British officers, exchanging smiles, would inquire ironically: "What about the Royal Navy?"

This question always made the Germans purple. It was as if the renowned sensitivity of the Kaiser regarding the British Fleet had trickled down through channels into the veins of the youngest German *Unteroffizier*. All very well about "sailing against England" and all that, said the British officers calmly—but just how were you going to do it? What had defeated Napoleon, actually? Waterloo? Nonsense. 1812 in Russia? Not at all. Desperate aftermaths, those. Even if he'd *won* Waterloo, it would only have been a temporary business. Britain would still have been there, rebuilding every day, controlling the seas of the world. And that would have meant, as it did mean after 1804, that "Old Boney's" Empire wasn't secure at all. Just waiting for "The Day" again. Trafalgar was the real thing. Didn't Napoleon himself make plans to sacrifice half the French Fleet, so that he could have the other half free for a precious twenty-four hours' invasion escort? Didn't get it, did he?

The Germans would explode. "The British Navy was only a big bubble," they would say. "One prick and it was gone forever! All this silly English emphasis on Sea Power!" But I saw they had an uneasy belief in it.

A year before, living in a state of war-jitters-with-Japan which seemed not even to be thought about at home, we had seen in the Philippines the effect which Admiral Bob Evans' American Fleet had had as it came round the world through Manila, making its "friendly visit" to Tokyo. Differences between our Army and Navy then, and there were many, were not based on any lack of appreciation of "Sea Power." Apparently it was the same with the British, whose naval supremacy at that time undoubtedly influenced their enthusiastic reception of Mahan's theories even before we ourselves were unanimous about them. The great naval theoretician (who incidentally was born at West Point) had published *The Life of Nelson,* the third volume of his classic trilogy, only a dozen years before, but it was already gospel to all those who thought in terms of "World Power." A strategic force, affecting, but far surpassing, the results on any battlefield, its effects might not be immediately evident; but its ultimate control, economically and geographically, and hence militarily, was finding renewed recognition not only in the United States, and Nelson's Britain, but even in France and Italy, and strenuously in Wilhelm II's Germany. History had proved that the most grandiose land conquests, even on the continent of Europe, must finally face it. And obviously no weapon on earth could defeat sea power except a stronger naval force.

Those German Officers, arguing in the hot darkness on the top deck of the *Grosse Kurfuerst* in 1909, understood all that, underneath, I'm sure. The sharpness of their irritability in discussing the British fleet was proof of it. And, also, the manner in which they reverted to alternative arguments against the permanent impregnability of the British Isles, fleet or no fleet. Everything, from Napoleon's desperate conjectures about the use of balloons, to his (and the then still prevalent) theories about building tunnels under the English Channel, was brought up.

No wonder that, as I looked up at Blériot's monoplane, I thought of Britain's isolation. And, also, of Napoleon's balloons.

At West Point, we cadets had witnessed a flight above "the Plain" by a balloonist named Lieutenant Frank P. Lahm. There was an imaginative picture somewhere, at the Academy or in some museum, in which an eighteenth-century artist had gone hog-wild, no doubt influenced by the cross-Channel feat of the eighteenth-century balloonist Blanchard, or Rozier, or one of them. The painting showed an imaginary invasion of England from the air, the sky over the Channel full of balloons and queer soaring devices, men flying independently with wings not unlike this monoplane of Blériot's.

And that, I think, was about the extent of my first contact with the airplane.

I was occupied with a more personal problem. It looked as if here and now the adventurous life was over. A few days more and I would be fulfilling the routine duties at my new post at Governors Island, New York City. Probably the dullest garrison job in the Army, I thought.

Perhaps this is as good a place as any to note down a few earlier events.

I was born on the 25th of June, 1886, at Gladwyne, at one time called Merion Square, Pa.—a little place near Lower Merion on the "Main Line." My family, on both sides, had been living in the vicinity of Montgomery County since before the American Revolution. My mother, a staunch member of the Montgomery County D.A.R., steadily reminded us that a number of our ancestors—four on her side, and three on my father's—had taken part in that war. . . . The earlier Arnolds were chiefly connected with the iron foundries of the district, and my grandfather, Thomas G. Arnold, who had fought at Gettysburg, had a local fame as a nail maker. His son (my father), H. A. Arnold, had chosen to study medicine instead, so I grew up in one of the happiest environments an American boy could know in those days. I was "the Doctor's second boy." My Dad was the local general practitioner in an area embracing a sizable community of farms and country people, but also close enough to the county seat at Norristown, and even to Philadelphia, to keep life interesting.

Unless the winds blowing from Brandywine and Valley Forge have a special virtue, there is no great reason why the climate in that gently rolling farming section of Pennsylvania should be conducive to a military career. We boys did feel that Winfield Scott Hancock, sitting on his iron horse in the square at Norristown, was undoubtedly the greatest hero of the Civil War, but all over America other favorite sons were held in the same esteem. Yet it is surprising how many of my lifelong service friends have hailed from Pennsylvania, including George Marshall and Tooey Spaatz, and the late Uzal Ent, whose own conduct over Ploesti is now as proud a part of American history as Hancock's in front of Pickett's charge. Hubert Harmon was born at Chester; Lewis Brereton and Joe McNarney were born farther west in the state. Even Admiral Bill Halsey, though properly a New Jerseyite, had the good sense to come across the line and go to school at Swarthmore, just down the road.

The immediate military example in our family came not from the tranquil Pennsylvania countryside, but from my father, who in 1898 put aside his practice temporarily in order to serve as Lieutenant and Surgeon of the Pennsylvania Cavalry in Puerto Rico. Thereafter, my father wished to have one of his sons go to West Point, and he was able to bring a bit of influence to bear toward procuring an appointment. It was not I, however, who was designated as the future Cadet and Army Officer. That was to be my older brother, Thomas. A different kind of cloth was intended for me. After a suitable curriculum at Bucknell College, I was slated to become a minister of the gospel.

I have never understood why my friends laugh when I tell them this. As my career did work out, it came to require quite as much sheer faith as any preacher's. Or perhaps I should say, as any other preacher's, since it actually took as much evangelism, and maybe more years, to sell the idea of Air Power as it would ever have taken me to sell the "Wages of Sin."

Still, I can't think of much that forecast the future of any of us: my sister, Elizabeth, my older brother, Tom, my younger brothers, Clifford and Price, or me. Only one childhood scene comes to mind that might be linked up with the half scientific, half casually lunatic approach that went with the development of flight. One morning in the summer of 1889, in Gladwyne, I see a frightened mother staring at her two small sons. The younger boy, three, is gasping a little, dripping, soaking wet from head to waist, but bone-dry below. His brother, five, with only a few splashes on his clothes, explains calmly, "Harley was trying to swim a horseshoe in the rain barrel. When he went in after it, I had to go in after him."

In a way no less decisive, it was my brother, Tom, who altered my destiny again. When the time came for him to go to West Point, he simply announced, with the same calmness with which he had effected my rescue from the rain barrel, that he wasn't going. He had decided to continue at Penn State instead, and be an electrical engineer.

Even my father could not alter that. But since Dr. Arnold had requested that a son of his be permitted to take the Academy's competitive entrance examination, you could bet that one of his sons would be there to take it. Also, regardless of the discouraging prophecies of my high school principal, you can guess what happened.

Despite the legends about it, the Point was not nearly so tough a place from which to graduate then as it is today. If I had had to do the things and take the courses that my three sons have been required to complete since Hank, our first son, started his Plebe Year in 1936, I wouldn't have had half so much time for mischief. The quality of leadership in all branches of the Army in both World Wars is ample proof of the fact that the Academy, then, as now, was doing a good job of training future officers. But, like all life, the approach to the military education was simpler then. We lived, I should say, in conformance with a code, and with daily routines which had not changed strikingly (except for the introduction of the football season) since Grant was a Cadet. After I had once learned how to study in my Plebe Year, in 1903, I skated along without too much effort in a spot just below the middle of the Class— seldom standing higher than sixty-second in a Class of one hundred and ten, nor lower than sixty-sixth. I had time to play football as a substitute fullback and halfback, to play on the polo squad, place in the shotput at interclass track meets, and with the rest of the Cavalry fanatics ride furiously, not only at drill, but in the Riding Hall and over the reservation on our own.

My diary, like the memory book I kept, is full of old reminders of events and of friends and off-the-record projects, but scanty in regard to my military progress. (I never even made Cadet Corporal.)

My Academy memory book is loaded with slips requiring Cadet Arnold to report immediately in order to explain why he was "entering barracks at 3:45 A.M.," or "found in front of barracks at 4:15 A.M.," etc. These nocturnal sorties were not the kind to trouble the Chaplain. They were the obligation of membership in the "Black Hand." This special society, handpicked by itself, operated only in the dark, and was a model of self-imposed discipline and efficient coordination.

The greatest success of the Black Hand involved smuggled fireworks, and surpassed the most optimistic hopes the organization had ever had. In the exploding glare which rose over the whole Academy, bugles blew, sirens sounded, officers and men tumbled from their beds, the whole reservation was alive! In the center of it all, atop the Barracks, I touched off the pièce de résistance. ".1907," my pinwheels spelled out; "Never again!" At that moment, disaster. Through bad luck I was left alone, silhouetted against the light of my own handiwork, in full view of the entire Corps. It was in connection with this incident that when my future wife made her first visit to the Academy, I happened to be in solitary confinement.

But, work or play, the thing that dominated the Cadet lives of one little group of us at least was—the Cavalry! That was why we were here! It was what we lived for—our whole future!

The Horse Cavalry! It was the last romantic thing left on earth. The galloping charge! Indian fighting! When we speculated on the stations we would draw, we were not always sure whether the ones we named were inside now peaceful Indian reservations or on the frontier, but it didn't seem to make much difference. We rode, we thought about horses all the time. My diary's most serious note is a running discussion of such matters as, "Ordered to submit views on newly adopted method of holding reins, etc." We knew the name of every Cavalry hero; and outside of drill, on our own time, we tried to emulate and beat every riding stunt on record. We jumped and mounted over two other horses to a third, rode in pyramids, schooled our horses at high jumping, and a hundred other things. And in between mounts, we cussed and swaggered, and even occasionally chewed surreptitiously, as Cavalry troopers were supposed to do.

We dreamed night and day of being Cavalry officers, and the nearer graduation came, the more we dreamed. As my last June Week drew near, I still didn't know what two brothers named Wilbur and Orville Wright had done at a place called Kitty Hawk in North Carolina on December 17th of my Plebe Year. I doubt if any officer or cadet on that whole reservation, except one, had paid much attention to that flight when it happened. That one was a young Math instructor, Lieutenant Tom Selfridge, who was to be the first man ever to die in an airplane crash.

At graduation, with true Cavalry swank, I did what all of us soon-to-be-troopers naturally did—ordered my new uniform, not with the prescribed trouser stripe of an inch and a quarter, but with one inch and a half wide, to stress the glorious Cavalry Yellow. Then I went home for a short, happy leave to wait for my first assignment.

I remember distinctly the morning my Commission came. I was sitting alone with my mother at breakfast, and I tossed it to her gaily without looking at it. Does a World Champion Rider, after all, carefully inspect the inscription on his trophy when they hand it to him?

Mother took it and read it slowly, then lifted her eyes to mine. "You'd better read this, Harley," she said. I did, and my world collapsed. "Henry H. Arnold . . . 2nd Lieutenant of . . . Infantry!"

I think before the train passed Havre de Grace, my Congressman, Mr. Wanger, and Senator Penrose already regretted their agreeable willingness to oblige my ex-Cavalry father. Listening to my outbursts, they looked at one another and cautioned me to stay at the hotel and not to join them at the War Department until 10:30 the following morning.

When I arrived, they had already been in conversation with The Adjutant General. In the presence of Senator Penrose and Representative Wanger, this pompous individual admonished me gravely that I was now a second lieutenant in the United States Army; that as such I ranked at the very bottom of the commissioned hierarchy, and that as a second lieutenant I would do what everyone in the Army, including himself, The Adjutant General, had to do—carry out the proper orders of my lawful superiors and accept whatever assignments I was given.

Well, I was twenty-one years old, and I had just received the worst hurt of my life. "No, Sir!," I said. *"No, Sir!* I am *not* a second lieutenant in the United States Army! I haven't accepted my Commission yet!"

The senior Senator from Pennsylvania at once took my arm and ushered me from the room. Then he returned and I suppose he told The Adjutant General that such fiery spirits ought to be harnessed for the good of the service. Anyway, that's what *I* would have told him. Besides, it was true. There was no commitment then requiring a West Point graduate to stay in the Army. And I *hadn't* signed my acceptance.

Presently they let me come back and The Adjutant General, with grave patience, repeated what he had said, adding that nobody could change my situation except the Secretary of War himself, and he was at present in the Philippines. If I cared to select a particular Infantry station, however, he, The Adjutant General, would see what could be done about it.

Infantry station! What Infantry station could I name? The Forts I knew were Wingate, Custer, Apache, Crook, Riley! Even my second and third choices at graduation had been Cavalry stations. But The Adjutant General had mentioned the word "Philippines" and said the Secretary of War was there. There might still be a chance.

I blurted out that I would like to go to the Philippines. The Adjutant General, still with remarkable forbearance, said he thought that could be arranged, and nodded my dismissal.

On November 7th I was on my way to Manila, complaining, according to my diary, because a couple of days after sailing from San Francisco we were "still on the briny deep. Can't even get sick to vary the monotony."

As I sailed across the Pacific I was carrying with me three other severe handicaps besides my own impatience. I was aware of the first, but not yet of the other two. The first was the unwelcome responsibility of a huge amount of money, entrusted to my care, cash funds belonging to the Philippine Government, packed in boxes, stacked in a stateroom with a sentry on guard. The second, still unknown to me, was the fact that I, the erstwhile Cavalry desperado, was being sent—either through chance or highly placed malice—to join an infantry regiment which consciously and articulately, scorned the Cavalry, above all things. There was a bonus disbursed to cavalrymen in those days, called "Mounted Pay" which aroused almost as much bitterness among walking soldiers then as Flight Pay was to do among all ground forces later. My scene with The Adjutant General had leaked into print in the Army and Navy weekly service papers and the officers of my new outfit had seen it. The 29th Infantry was lying in wait for the would-be cavalier. The third handicap I carried not so much with me, as on me. It was my O.D. woolen uniform. Extremely low on cash, I had thought to postpone the purchase of a tropical outfit until I reached the Islands, where cheaper price, and the money I had been able to save during the voyage would combine to make a better deal. I never made a worse mistake in my life. As we sailed deeper and deeper into the hot latitudes, that woolen uniform, the only garment I had to wear, became not only a torture of hot scratchiness to me, but, I have an idea, an affront to all on board. By the time we neared Manila, it had given me such an inferiority complex that I scarcely dared to enter the dining room.

On the night of December 6, 1907, the ship lay at last in Manila harbor, but I did not go ashore with the others. I was still in my cabin, and also still perspiring in the unwholesome woolen uniform, guarding the money. Veterans of Philippine service, obviously with the "best intentions in the world," had assured me, with solemn faces, that my difficulty in making arrangements for landing the Philippine Government funds would be only the beginning of my troubles. I would undoubtedly lose the money boxes to robbers by the following noon. Thirty-four years later, to the minute, back in California, I was again sleepless about things in that part of the world, and a good deal more seriously. But if anybody had told me then, that night in 1907, that life could be blacker, I would have been incensed. Not only the money—and the danker and danker uniform—but, also, word had come over the cables that Navy had defeated Army, 6–0!

The actual landing of the money next day was indeed almost the last straw. On the strange, babbling pier, carabao carts, driven by the most villainous looking men I had ever seen, were waiting. Before I could finish my halting instructions in West Point Spanish, the first Filipino driver suddenly started away with about ten of the money boxes. I started to run after him, but looked back, and other money chests were being driven off in apparently different directions. This was the worst jam I had ever been in. Hours later, after I had searched desperately for the cart drivers everywhere in the city, I found that in their phlegmatic fashion they had all calmly delivered the money boxes to precisely the right place, and in my name. I received my receipt and all was well again, except—that uniform!

Arriving at Fort McKinley, I took one of the busses used as a carryall from the trolley station to the Post. There was a baseball game and track meet on at the Fort, so I couldn't find either the C.O. or the Adjutant to report to. As I staggered with my bags, unguided, to the Bachelor Officers' Quarters, I was suddenly confronted by a Filipino houseboy, with a great toothy grin. "Señor," he exclaimed, "you need a bath!" Whereupon he thrust me into an empty room, stripped away the woolen uniform forever, pushed me into a beautiful fresh shower, and by the time I returned, he had "borrowed" for me a cool, tropical uniform from an unknown officer exactly my size—every button and insignia in place. Major General "Jake" Fickel of the Air Corps (then a Second Lieutenant of Infantry) still insists I never returned the buttons.

Soon after that I went to work, for the first time in earnest, at my profession. The Philippines were a whole new world. Even such routine duties as being officer in charge of the prisoners' stockade for a day put a new young second lieutenant face to face with men and problems that were not seen back home. It was not merely the so-called "exotic" atmosphere of foreign service, nor the increased directness between officers and men once we went out into the *bosque,* but a sense of some imminent mess in which we, the navy people as well as ourselves, seemed about to be involved. It was in this same year of 1908 that Homer Lea was writing his *Valor of Ignorance.* The great little dwarf published his prophetic work about the Japanese-American future a few months later; in fact, just about the time I was looking at Blériot's plane in Paris.

We really expected Japan to invade the Philippines at any minute. We were ready to hike to Baguio and make a last stand. Men slept with two hundred rounds of ammunition at the foot of their beds. This feeling was not the hysteria of greenhorns or recruits (many of the soldiers who felt it had grown brown in the Philippine service), nor was it whipped up by any propaganda trend. The Japanese, methodically and almost openly, *were* making war preparations all around us.

My first assignment out in the *bosque* was with the Engineers, working on a topographical military map of the Island of Luzon. In our work, we established triangulation stations in the valley of Luzon from

Lingayen Gulf to Manila, using levels and transits to fill in the detailed topographical features. All along the way, across the plain, in the hills, and as we hacked our way through the jungles, we seemed to be accompanied or met by Japanese photographers, itinerant Japanese "peddlers" or Jap botanists solemnly absorbed by the flora of the Island—whose best specimens always happened to be growing just where we had set up our instruments. The climax came when one of our crews, turning their theodolite back on a triangulation station they had just left, saw some strange people working there. It turned out they were Japs also making maps, and using our own stations—the ones we had labored so hard to establish.

When the Luzon Valley mapping project was finished, I was assigned to make the map of Corregidor. Corregidor, even then, was planned to be a fortress as impregnable as Gibraltar. Again, for days and weeks, we cut paths and swaths through the jungle, ran level lines to get elevations, transit lines to get directions. The hulking volcanic rock might be attacked at any minute! Thirty-three years later, when it finally was, and the American flag had to come down after that great "beaten but unashamed" stand of Wainwright and his men, I wondered how much my maps had helped to defeat them. In 1909, I'm sure, the Japanese were getting hold of those plans, too, as fast as we sketched them.

The personal associations of those two years were in themselves a tremendous professional advantage. In addition to having his horizon constantly widened by contacts with British, German, French, Chinese, Russian, Japanese, Filipino, and other officers and nationals, a young officer could become far better acquainted with his own seniors and with naval officers than would have been possible at home.

A couple of weeks after I saw the Blériot plane in Paris, I reported for duty at Governors Island, New York.

My worst fears were immediately realized. Governors Island was so flat that it wasn't even fun to ride a horse on it, when a second lieutenant could get one, and the life there was flatter than the terrain. The attitude of our hardboiled 29th Infantry, back from the Philippines, is best expressed by the action of my Company Commander after an unsatisfactory company inspection one Saturday morning. "Sergeant," said the Company Commander grimly, "re-form the company in twenty minutes in civilian clothes."

The First Sergeant had had many strange orders before, but none like that. However, he saluted and gave the necessary commands. In twenty minutes, there we were back again, as sad an assemblage as the

Army had ever called together. Sheepish jungle fighters in top hats, straw hats, spats, and tails, men in derbies, sports suits mixed with leggins, and dinner vests. Here and there was a cane. The Company Commander solemnly opened ranks and inspected his veterans. At the end, he stood out in front again. "I am very glad," he said, "to see how well the men of this company are prepared to perform their arduous duties in the city of New York."

But apparently the flatness of the land had a virtue. Governors Island was New York's first "airport." Presently the great inventor, Wilbur Wright, appeared on our island, in connection with the Hudson-Fulton Centennial, to set his "airplane" up for a "record-breaking attempt" up the Hudson River, around Grant's Tomb, and back. Actually, we had heard stories about this remarkable man before. He was just back from a tour with his stunting gadget in France, where King Edward VII was supposed to have gone to look at him and his machine at Pau. They said there was a direct connection between him and the girls now mincing along Fifth Avenue in tight gowns. It was understood that those so-called "hobble skirts" had started when a lady had taken a ride in his "airplane" over there, and her husband had gathered her long skirt together with a rope to keep it from blowing. Some fashion designer or other had seen her walk away afterward with the rope still on.

Wright was a modest, quiet man, and after making a trial pass around the Statue of Liberty the day before, flew up around Grant's Tomb and back, as previously scheduled.

Then—to win the $10,000 prize offered by the *New York World*— another inventor named Glenn Curtiss landed on our flat island, having flown down the Hudson from Albany to Spuyten Duyvel, where he had come down in order to refuel. I still have a wonderful photograph of Curtiss' plane passing West Point. The older buildings look just as they do today. Only the plane itself suggests the changes that were to come, not only in the lives of future cadets, but for a number of those attending the Academy at that moment.

In the fall, perhaps because of these events, perhaps by accident, some of us went up to Belmont Park to see "the first international air meet ever held in America." There they all were—the great Brazilian, Santos-Dumont, whose fleet of dirigibles, said to roam above the streets of Paris between the buildings, was promised to France for war against any country in the world except America; Hoxey, Johnson, Ely, Grahame White, Willard, and young Walter Brookins, the nineteen-year-old dare-devil of the Wright flying team. The companies, like Wright and Curtiss, had exhibition teams to pit against each other, and there were individual stars as well. The crowd—packed with small boys, the eternal backbone of aviation—gaped at the wonders, the exhibits of planes from home and abroad, secure in the knowledge that nowhere on earth, between now and suppertime, was there such a good chance of seeing somebody break his neck. The crash of young Walter Brookins in his special little Wright "speedster" (he walked away from it, fortunately) was the beginning, though we couldn't know it then, of the particular meaning of speed in the development of the military "fighter plane." While professional judgments were being exchanged in one part of the grandstand, over another part of the field, perhaps, Brookins would be completing the quickest 360-degree turn ever made in a plane. Down below were foreign aviators dressed in costumes worthy of Superman, and among them, talking quietly, the Wright brothers and Curtiss in ordinary business clothes. Beyond the stands where the flamboyant posters and newsstands, with their aviation magazines, advertised every sort of aerial feat, I saw for the first time the announcement in red letters that "Horace Hot Shot Kearny, Death-defying Daredevil of the Air, is Open to Any and All Engagements at Any Time!"

Well, it was fine. It was interesting to hear that all through the country, at places which were no more than cow pastures, men who were willing to take chances could make $1000 a day this way. It was vaguely interesting to hear that our own service, the Army, was now involved in this "flying game." Since 1902, we heard, though the interest in ballooning which General Greely had encouraged had languished, and though the last unsuccessful trial of the Langley plane had been a setback, new aerial steps were being taken by the Army.

Lieutenant Frank Lahm, by winning the first Gordon Bennett International Balloon Race in 1906, had helped to restore the War Department's interest in flying. Of course, no one thought of the flying machine as a weapon, but it seemed that it might be a more efficient "carrier pigeon," not to say a more mobile observation point, than balloons had been before. We heard that in 1907, to further such a possibility, a so-called Aeronautical Division had been established, naturally in the office of the Chief Signal Officer, at that time Brigadier General James Allen. We also heard that Lahm and three other officers were at the present time undergoing training in the operation of airplanes, and that a main consideration on the part of such aircraft builders as the Wrights and Curtiss was to interest the Army and the Navy. We were reminded that in 1908 the first man ever to be killed in a crash of a heavier-than-air machine had been Lieutenant Thomas Selfridge of the Field Artillery.

Personally, I was completely engaged in a project at that moment which took all my time. It was a plan that has occupied every second lieutenant since the beginning of armies. I was trying to get to be a *first* lieutenant. In those days in the Regular Army your chances for remaining a second lieutenant for six or seven years at least were very good unless you had an angle—and I thought I had found such an angle. The Ordnance Department had no second lieutenants in it—first was the lowest—and Ordnance vacancies had been announced. I was busy boning up at Sandy Hook for the competitive examinations. It was a very stiff business. I remember, for example, the question which required us to imagine a three-inch artillery shell half empty, the other half filled with water, fired into the air at a certain angle. We were then to estimate all the stresses and strains within and without this shell at the peak of its trajectory.

I had just taken this exam and was awaiting word of whether I had passed it, when out of the blue an official letter arrived from the War Department. Would I be willing to volunteer for training with the Wright brothers at Dayton as an airplane pilot?

Puzzled, I took the letter to my commanding officer. After reading it, he said, "Young man, I know of no better way for a person to commit suicide!" It was a challenge. Gone were all thoughts relating to the Ordnance Department.

Thus it was that on a night in the third week of April, 1911, I found myself on a train bound from New York to Dayton. In my pocket was a copy of War Department Special Order 95, dated 21 April, 1911. In accordance with paragraph 10, "The following named officers are detailed for aeronautical duty with the Signal Corps, and will proceed to Dayton, Ohio, for the purpose of undergoing a course of instruction in operating the Wright airplane:

2nd Lt. Henry H. Arnold, 29th Infantry
2nd Lt. Thomas DeW. Milling, 15th Cavalry

The travel directed is necessary in the military service."

☆ 2 ☆

Back in the early 1900's, when the area surrounding Dayton, Ohio, was not so thickly populated as it is today, there were many small farms—one in particular located about nine miles out of town at a place called Simms Station. Later, it was sometimes called Huffman Field after the well-to-do citizen who had allowed the Wright brothers to use it free of charge for their experiments. It was a cow pasture, not very different from hundreds of other fields in the vicinity. It had a large thorn tree at one end, and at the other end a fairly large wooden shed. The balance of the field was clear of trees and bushes.

Every morning a man would arrive in a wagon, coming along the old Springfield Turnpike. He'd hitch his horses alongside the fence around the cow pasture and sit there and wait in the wagon until noon and then he'd get out, untie his horses, turn them around, and, slowly shaking his head, solemnly drive back to Dayton. The man was a local undertaker.

"Go out to Dayton," a wire from one of our foremost scientific papers had said to a representative only a couple of years before my arrival at Simms Station. "Interview some of the prominent citizens of that city. Get the truth about this flying story. Put an end to this Wright hoax. We know Man cannot fly."

When I arrived at Dayton I went first to the Wright factory, not to "the field." There was nobody at Simms Station except, perhaps, a mechanic working on one of the two planes, because it was only in the early morning or in the evening that one could try to go up—the rest of the time there was too much wind.

Wilbur and Orville Wright, as well as Frank Russel, who was the first person I met in the corridor of the factory, gave me a warm welcome. Immediately I was in the midst of a fine crowd. Nineteen-year-old Brookins, who had worshiped Orville Wright since he was four and was the first pupil Orville had trained to fly, was there—the only member of the original Wrights' exhibition team still around, since Hoxey and Johnson had recently been killed. (It was not long after this that Walter Brookins made his famous remark, "I would rather be the oldest living pilot in America than the best.")

Cliff Turpin, Al Welsh, Frank Coffyn, and Phil Parmalee were still flying for the Wrights then, some of them away competing at exhibitions, others teaching Army and Navy officers and civilians to fly at the schools. In addition to Lieutenant John Rodgers, the first Naval officer to learn to fly a Wright plane and who was fairly well along in his instruction when Milling and I arrived, various civilians were trying to qualify as members of the Wright Flying Team, enthusiastic, chafing to get on the road and pick up some of that easy exhibition money. Among them were Leonard Bonney, who flew with the Wright Team only a short time; Howard Gill, killed within a year; and Oscar Brindley, who subsequently became an instructor in the Army Flying School and was killed testing out the first of our DH's in 1917.

While I was there, Harry Atwood was to come from Boston, later making aviation history with his long cross-country flights. He was the first man to fly (not nonstop, of course) from St. Louis to New York. And soon after I met Calbraith P. Rodgers, a cousin of John (and therefore called, not "Rodgers," but "Uncle Cal," to keep them separate). He made the first transcontinental flight from New York to Los Angeles. It took forty-nine days to complete, with a train bearing a traveling machine shop following along across the continent and making repairs on the plane each night.

Milling and I were soon grateful for the days spent in the factory, for in addition to learning how to fly we found we would have to master the construction and maintenance features of the Wright machine well enough to teach our own mechanics the ABC of a ground crew's job when we went to our first station; there were no crew chiefs nor aircraft mechanics in the Army in those days.

Our primary training also took place in the factory. Almost as soon as we arrived, Orville and Wilbur Wright, Cliff Turpin, who was to be Milling's instructor, and Al Welsh, who was mine, took us out to a back room of the shop where an old plane was balanced on sawhorse supports so that the wing tips could move up and down. No two types of controls were the same in those days, and from the student's point of view the Wright system was the most difficult. Curtiss, for instance, adopted controls the movement of which corresponded to the movement of the plane. For fore and aft control he used a wheel. When pulled backward or forward the nose of the plane would go up or down. The wheel also had a rotary motion which corresponded to an automobile wheel for turning the rudder and, thus, the plane. The lateral controls were hitched to a shoulder yoke. To drop the right wing, the pilot leaned toward the right side; to drop the left wing, he leaned toward the left side. These were natural motions, and easy to learn.

The Blériot machine, of which I have previously spoken, also had a wheel control, but for turning his plane, Blériot used the foot pedal.

The Antoinette control was entirely dissimilar. It had two wheels mounted on the sides of the frame fuselage. A forward movement of one wheel dropped the nose of the plane, while a backward movement pulled up the nose. The wheel on the other side had a motion just as unnatural as the Wright control. Forward and backward motions of the wheel moved the wing tips up and down. Foot pedals were used to turn the plane. There were almost as many other systems as there were inventors.

In the Wright plane, after crawling under wires which crossed in front, one sat on a hard seat located on the leading edge of the thin lower wing. The airman's feet rested on a slender bar before the wing. (Here the Curtiss plane was the same, except that it placed the aviator alone, and entirely out in space, on a little board ahead of the wing.) For the elevator, the Wright pilot moved a vertical stick in the conventional manner of the present type of control. There were two of these sticks, one outside each seat, for whichever pilot happened to be flying the plane, but there were not two complete sets of controls. The third stick, between the two aviators, though it also moved fore and aft, was for lateral balance and rudder. The top portion of this middle lever was hinged to rock laterally, and was connected by a rod to a quadrant on the same shaft as the warp control. The rudder could be moved either in combination with the warping or independently. (Today, of course, ailerons are used in lieu of the twisting of the wings.) Operation of the warp-rudder lever as a whole warped the light wings and simultaneously moved the rudder the correct amount for maintaining straight flight during adjustment of lateral equilibrium. A right turn, for example, was achieved by pulling the lever back to lift the left wing and simultaneously rotating the hand grip an appropriate number of degrees to the right for right rudder. After the turn was started, the pilot eased back to normal attitude for level flying. This scarcely instinctive procedure had to be mastered before one could go into the air as a Wright pilot. The old plane mounted on a sawhorse was how you began.

The lateral controls were connected with small clutches at the wingtips, and grabbed a moving belt running over a pulley A forward motion, and the clutch would snatch the belt, and down would go the left wing. A backward pull, and the reverse would happen. The jolts and teetering were so violent that the student was kept busy just moving the lever back and forth to keep on an even keel. That was primary training, and it lasted for days; in the meantime, actual flying instruction was received in an airplane out at Simms Station.

I still have the official summary which Al Welsh turned in to the Wright Company on my training. The first date is May 3, 1911. The number of the machine was "B2." "Time of Flight" and "Wind Dircn Vlcty" are not filled in, but in the line reporting Lesson No. 1, Al notes that the flight lasted seven minutes, and that he carried Lt. Arnold as a pupil. "Rough," he says under "Remarks," "just rode as passenger."

The next lesson lasted only five minutes; the "Remarks" were the same. But the day following, with twelve minutes in the air, my first operational experience was described, "Hand on elevator." Lesson No. 4, and I "had charge of elevator part of the time." Then four more tries, each lasting from seven to fourteen minutes, and Welsh could report that during Lesson No. 9 I "Had charge of warping lever part of the time." After flight No. 10—really two hops lasting fourteen and three minutes each—there is the notation, "To Shed." I had taxied the plane myself.

Beginning with Lesson No. 12, Al was "teaching landing." And after being charged with his first aerial mission—"To get photos of two machines in air," Lt. Arnold, at Lesson No. 19, "Landed without assistance" and "To Shed." The flights that day were four minutes and one minute long, respectively. Thereafter, it went rapidly. Following five minutes in the air on Lesson No. 26, I "landed without assistance." At the end of Lesson No. 27, I "Landed without assistance," and as we came in from Lesson No. 28, I again triumphantly "Landed without assistance." I could fly! I was an aviator! Al wrote at the bottom of my report, "Number of flights, 28. Total time in air 3 hours 48 minutes. First lesson 3 May, finished 13 May—10 days learning. Average 8 minutes." (The actual elapsed time was eleven days, since the Wrights didn't fly on the Sabbath.) Without filling in the blanks for "Gasoline and Oil used," Al signed it "A. L. Welsh, Teacher," and turned it in. He had taught me all he knew. Or, rather, he had taught me all he could *teach*. He knew much more.

All those early aviators knew more than they could tell anybody. But what was it they knew, or knew they didn't know? Things happened, that was all. The air was a tricky place. The best laws, discovered and formulated by the best aeronautical brains, could still be upset, it seemed, in a second. "It" could still happen to anybody's plane Well, not "anybody's," of course. Despite the serious, mysterious talk of "holes in the air," and so on, the personal factor was continuously stressed. If Joe crashed, he must have done something that you would never do. You and the other flyers talked it over and eventually "decided" what it was. The fact that one of your own number presently joined the casualty list did not alter this dogged credo. *He* had done something else, now, that none of the rest of you would do. It is interesting that in that day, when there was none of our modern standardization of planes, controls, or flying equipment, it was seldom the plane, or an unknown quantity in the air, but almost always the pilot, who was blamed for being in error. You *had* to believe that to keep up your morale. Even today, when the airplane is 90 per cent of flying, and the pilot less than 10 per cent, you will find young airmen who insist "Joe must have done something special." All this influenced the subsequent "seat of the pants" flying tradition much longer than it should have. It also made aviators who had advanced well enough so far—as they were doing—hostile to technical innovations. (Another tradition which was still not dead in World War II.)

In those days, the primitive method for determining whether the engine was turning up fast enough seemed satisfactory. You just used a revolution counter on the propeller shaft, and took time with a stop watch. If the engine crankshaft was accessible, that was used. If you wanted to be really scientific about testing the engine, the flying machine was hitched to a rope, the rope to a spring balance, and it, in turn, was tied to a stake in the ground. Then, by reading the scale on the spring balance with the engine running full-out, you determined the actual propeller thrust. The only instrument used on airplanes when I began to fly was a piece of string tied to the front crossbar on the skids. When it stood out directly to the rear, everything was O.K.—the pilot was flying correctly. When it drifted to one side or the other, the plane was in a skid. That piece of string was a wonderful instrument. However, in time, the inevitable happened. Someone came out with an electrical tachometer to indicate to the pilot in his seat the exact speed of the engine expressed in "revolutions per minute." Would the aviators accept such a thing? Not a bit of it! Such devices would make them "mechanical" pilots. They had been flying by the "seats of their pants" so far, and they didn't want any change. On the other hand, devices to improve personal safety were less frowned upon.

The safety belt came along as an airplane accessory by accident. The then Lieutenant—now Admiral—Jack Towers was thrown from his seat on an old Wright plane. The pilot, Lt. Billingsly, was tossed clear; since he had no parachute, he didn't have a chance, and dropped like a rock into the ocean. Towers, rattling around between wings, struts, and wires, managed finally to grab a wire and hang on until the plane hit the water. He remained conscious, lashed himself to a pontoon with his belt, and was picked up soon afterward. Subsequently, he spent several weeks in a hospital. After that, we all used safety belts, and Milling devised an improved version which is practically the one in use today.

The first goggles worn by Army airmen came as the result of a bug's hitting me in the eye as I was landing my plane. Prior to that time, our custom was simple. We merely turned our caps backward and were all dressed to sit on the lower wing and start flying. On this particular flight, soon after I left Simms Station, I was coming back into the field when a bug hit me in the eye and left one of its transparent wings sticking to my eyeball. The pain was terrific; blinded by tears I could scarcely see to make my landing. As a matter of fact, it was some days before the doctors were able to find that transparent wing and remove it. The possibility of being rammed dead by a bug had not occurred to us before. After that we wore goggles.

The "hangar flying" during those hours in the shed at Simms Station, while Milling and I waited for the weather to become calm enough to fly, covered everybody and everything that the most encyclopedic aviation editor could have dreamed up: stories of men who had put the most zealous imagination—and often their last penny—into abortive aeronautical designs, freakish flying machines that wouldn't fly: how the great Hoxey and Johnson had died, and always, of course, since Orville Wright had been the pilot of that plane, how Lieutenant Tom Selfridge, the first Army flyer, had been killed. We heard more about the exploits of airmen from all parts of the country. Charlie Hamilton, whom I had seen fly at Belmont Park, was typical. He had become the most famous aviator in the country a few months before with his record-breaking round-trip flight from New York to Philadelphia. Laughing, the men in the hangar told me a story from Philadelphia. A teacher had asked her

young class, "Who was Alexander Hamilton?" Immediately the hand
of every small boy was raised. "The aviator," said one eagerly, "who
just flew from New York and back!"

"Kids are the same everywhere," the Wright flyers said. If everybody
in the country were as smart as the small boys about aviation, there'd
be nothing to worry about. The kids weren't like the city of St. Louis,
for instance, which still had legislation barring flying machines on or
over its streets. This law had been passed after a balloon on the ground
had frightened some coach horses and caused an accident. Nor, the boys
in the hangar would add, winking at each other and looking at Milling
and me, were the kids like the old moss backs in the United States Army
who had been rejecting the Wright brothers proposals for five years.

Milling and I would rise to the bait and protest—more strenuously
than we might have a bit later. What were they talking about! Wasn't
our presence there proof of the Army's interest? Hadn't the Signal
Corps formed an "Aeronautical Section" as far back as 1907? Hadn't
the specifications which the Signal Corps had announced in requesting
bids for a "military airplane" that same year, been pretty forward-
looking? "Must be tested in the presence of Army officers; must be able
to carry for one hour a passenger in addition to the pilot, the two
weighing not less than 350 pounds; must show an average speed of forty
miles an hour in a ten-mile test, and carry enough fuel for 125 miles.
Also, the machine must have 'demountability'"; that is, it should be
built in such a way that it could be taken apart and later reassembled
without too much difficulty, in order to fit into an army wagon when it
had to be transported. Nothing unimaginative about that! Indeed, the
New York *Globe* called it a delusion. "One might be inclined to assume,"
said the *Globe,* "from the announcement, 'the United States Army is
asking bids for a military airship,' that the era of practical human flight
had arrived, or at least that the Government had seriously taken up the
problem of developing this means of travel. A very brief examination
of the conditions imposed and the reward offered for the successful
bidders suffices, however, to prove this assumption a delusion."

Even the "professional" *American Magazine of Aeronautics* had suggested in an editorial in January, 1908, that, "Perhaps the Signal Corps
has been too much influenced by the 'hot air' theorizers, in which aeronautics unfortunately abounds . . . talk is their stock in trade . . ."

As a young Cavalry and an Infantry lieutenant on Detached Service
to learn how to fly, neither Milling nor I could know anything then about
the way Secretary of War Taft had circumvented the absence of any

regular War Department appropriation to cover the procurement of that first plane for the Army in 1908; how he and President "Teddy" Roosevelt, who had not forgotten his flight with Arch Hoxey at St. Louis in 1910 and who hated red tape anyway, had found a way to dip into some special Presidential funds that could meet this "emergency."

We all knew how the Army had reacted to the crash that caused Selfridge's death. Because Orville's test plane had behaved well until then, they had told the Wrights to try again. Other officers—First Lieutenants Frank P. Lahm of the Cavalry (that same balloonist Lahm), Frederic E. Humphries of the Engineers, Benjamin D. Foulois of the Infantry, and Oliver A. Dickinson, another infantryman who had shared in the experiments with dirigibles, had presently been detailed for flight instruction by the Wrights. When Curtiss opened his winter flying school on North Island at San Diego, and offered to give free instruction to one or more officers each of the Army and the Navy, it was said that at least thirty Army officers in California promptly volunteered. The three selected—Beck, Walker, and G. E. M. Kelly—had gone to join Foulois and the other Wright students in San Antonio, Texas, where Kelly was later killed, the second fatality in Army flying. Despite this tragedy at Fort Sam Houston in San Antonio, the enthusiasm had risen so high among young Army officers that eighteen more had volunteered and were eagerly awaiting a chance to fly—a fact that had led Major Squier of the Signal Corps to inaugurate a provisional "Aero Company."

If anyone thought that "flying" was not attracting keen interest among Army people, he had only to note the recent zeal of my friend, Lieutenant Jake Fickel of the 29th Infantry at Governors Island—the same Fickel who loaned me my first tropical uniform in the Philippines. Jake, inspired by Major Sam Reber, a Signal Corps officer at Governors Island who had great faith in aviation, had gone over to the Sheepshead Bay Air Meet, Long Island, in August, 1910. There he had prevailed on Glenn Curtiss and Charlie Willard to carry him several times, at an altitude of 100 feet, over a target on the ground, which Fickel had then proceeded to shoot at with a rifle. Jake had hit it, too, despite the misgivings of Curtiss himself, whose previous passengers had always been supposed to use both hands to hold on with. (There was no real seat for a second aviator, as in the Wright plane.) Furthermore, Curtiss had worried lest the recoil of the rifle might upset the plane's flying equilibrium. It seemed to Milling and to me that the Army was showing plenty of interest. By the time the Army had reached the stage where they were willing to accept Glenn Curtiss' invitation regarding the San

Diego school the Navy already had a man flying at Hammondsport, New York—a Lieutenant T. E. "Spud" Ellyson—just as John Rodgers had preceded us here at Dayton. The Navy was on its toes. They told us how Glenn Curtiss himself had been the origin of Navy interest in heavier-than-air flying, with his first flight from shore to a ship, when he had landed beside the battleship *Pennsylvania,* moored his plane, and after a short visit aboard, flown back to shore again. In 1909 another Curtiss pilot, Eugene Ely, had been the first man to land on the deck of a warship, the cruiser *Birmingham.* And just this past January (1911) Ely had not only landed on the *Pennsylvania* in San Francisco Bay, but had taken off again and flown back to shore. The arresting gear used at that time on board the *Pennsylvania* was very similar in principle to that used on carriers today, sandbags, instead of the modern mechanical attachments, providing the tension at the end of the cables.

It was interesting to see that despite the real bitterness which the pending patent suits of the Wrights against Curtiss had generated between the two competing camps, the rival flyers kept track of each other's achievements and were always ready to grant recognition when it was clearly due. Thus, in the same way, we knew about men we hadn't met— like Glenn Martin and Lincoln Beachey, for instance—and saw in the red-lettered advertisements of the aviation journals that such dare-devils as "Hot-Shot" Kearny were still "open to any and all engagements at any time": we could also keep abreast of the progress of the Army students at San Antonio. Lieutenant Paul Beck, especially, was apparently a fireball of enthusiasm. He had been infected with the air bug at the first aviation meet he had witnessed at Los Angeles, thereafter plaguing his superiors for detail as an "observer" at such exhibitions whenever they were held on the West Coast. As a flyer he was said to be not only eager, but to possess the kind of "pilot's luck" that impressed even such phlegmatic pioneers as our instructors. A few days before Kelly was killed, Beck had crashed in the same plane at San Antonio, and though he had come out of the accident dazedly wandering around on the ground, with the plane in a tree and the control wheel still in his hands, he had been otherwise unhurt.

Earlier, he had been mixed up with the enterprise of Second Lieutenant Myron T. Crissy, whose suggested project, at an air meet in San Francisco in 1910, had not only won the instantly fascinated collaboration of Phil Parmalee, the Wright exhibition pilot, but had fairly dwarfed the stunt of Jake Fickel with his flying rifle at Sheepshead Bay, and with an airborne pistol at Boston. Crissy and Beck had gone to San

Francisco, obtained some two-and-a-half-inch pipe, and made a bomb. They also put fins on a regular three-inch artillery shell. They then flew over the Tanforan race track where the air meet was held. Crissy tossed them down on the field and they exploded! The first live aerial bombs!

Take that, and things like the successful radio message which Pilot J. A. D. McCurdy had sent from his plane to the ground at Sheepshead Bay Meet, and you could see the flying machine was beginning to have complicated possibilities. None of the four officers taught by the Wrights ahead of Milling and myself had really completed their training. With its typical "holier than thou" policy, the Corps of Engineers had recalled Humphries because he wasn't "performing Engineering duty." (In disgust, he presently resigned from the Army.)

Following a report that Lahm had taken a woman into the air, he had been relieved from aviation duty and sent back to the Cavalry. Dickinson, despite his fine balloon background, had never really started flying. That had left Benny Foulois, with the one much-battered and repaired Wright plane, who had been sent south to San Antonio on his own. There, with the maintenance aid of only a few student mechanics, the regular post carpenter, electrician, etc., and a maintenance fund so small that he had to supplement it with money from his own pocket, he had tried to carry on. The Curtiss trio were sent to join him and finish their training at Fort Sam Houston, but before that, Foulois had become the first Correspondence School pilot in history.

Before he was sent to San Antonio, Foulois had learned how to take off and fly reasonably well in the air, but he had not had a chance to master landings. Accordingly, he would take off time after time, and fly successfully, only to come back to the field and crash. Then the plane would be repaired while Ben wrote patiently to the Wright Brothers, explaining what he thought he had done, and presently would receive in the mail an analysis and suggested procedure for the next flight. Finally, the Wrights had taken pity on him and sent Phil Parmalee down to San Antonio to give him additional instruction. After that, Frank Coffyn succeeded Phil Parmalee as the Wright instructor at the San Antonio field, and Foulois made some real pioneering contributions. He flew in winds as strong as fifteen miles an hour (a formidable feat in those days) and made cross-country flights along the Mexican Border, which impressed the Army with the airplane's reconnaissance and communications value.

The best times of all in that Simms Field "hangar," of course, were when the Wright brothers themselves joined us. There was a saying among early airmen that when the Wrights were on the ground—quiet Orville in his derby and business suit, the even gentler Wilbur in plain cap—you never recognized them, but when they were in the air they could be spotted miles away.

Their presence in the hangar always made the sessions different. Despite their mild, retiring way of listening until everyone else had made his speech about this incident or that phenomenon, or what the exact future of an air development would be, you always felt them there. They were usually so courteous, almost diffident, really. Wilbur, for example, often hesitated to give an opinion without first consulting the little black notebook of aeronautical data he always carried with him.

Once, I remember well, a loud argument was in progress about just how the loop would be accomplished—a time we hoped was not far off. Opinions differed as to whether it would be done from "the inside" or "the outside"; as to just how the airplane would behave. The Wright brothers listened with interest, never saying a word. Then, as everyone was laying down the law about this or that approach, Wilbur quietly attracted our attention and pointed overhead. In the slightly windy air far above the top of the shed, a lark was fighting hard to fly straight upward, and as we watched, the bird struggled over on its back and curved down again, coming out in level flight from a crude but indisputable loop.

The Simms Station shed is gone today. In later years when it was taken down I tried vainly from a distance to save it because it would have been a fine exhibit in the midst of what is now sprawling Patterson Field, with Wright Field just over the hill—virtually in the center of the modern United States Air Force's technical proving ground.

The national monument to the first pioneers of flight looks squarely down on the site where the old shed stood. Another building—in fact two—which meant a lot to Milling and me during the time of our flight training may still be seen, not in Dayton ,any more, but in the museum at Dearborn, Michigan, to which Henry Ford, with a just appreciation of historical worth, had them moved. Along with the bicycle shop itself, the little white house at No. 7 Hawthorne Street, with the steps set in the corner of the front porch (the Wright brothers built that porch themselves when they were kids) has been transported intact to Michigan and set up as an American shrine.

Every Sunday the Wrights would invite Tom Milling and me to their home for dinner. The food and hospitality were more than welcome to a couple of young second lieutenants who found their boarding-house fare rather lean fuel, but the nourishment which all four of the Wrights gave us went far beyond the good full plates. I say "all four" because not only Wilbur and Orville, but the old Bishop and their sister Katherine were part of it, too. On some Sunday afternoons Lorin, their older brother and business representative, would come in after dinner and make it five.

I always felt their father, the Bishop, gave the stimulus of the flying idea to the boys with a toy helicopter he once bought them. At least, they were always referring to it. Later on, the Bishop—and generally Katherine and Lorin—gave unflagging encouragement as their work progressed. The year before, the old gentleman had made his only flight at the age of eighty-two, staying aloft for almost seven minutes over Huffman Field at an altitude of 350 feet and exclaiming eagerly to Orville, "Go higher, higher!"

Katherine and Lorin never doubted, either. Indeed, Katherine gave not only her constant moral and financial aid, but most of her life to her brothers' work. She had always been ready, at the drop of a hat, to turn from her own interests to help them, as at the time when the first great news came from Kitty Hawk, and she rushed home, abandoning an important college meeting at Oberlin, to be on the receiving end of their messages. When the indifference of our own country to their offers had carried their affairs to France, it was Katherine, with her knowledge of French, who was the translator and adviser of their correspondence. When she was away, and especially when the brothers were engrossed with a new trend in the shop, they confessed sheepishly, vital things were apt to be left hanging. Also, the French used funny stationery. Once, when Katherine was absent, a seedy looking brown envelope, apparently made of butcher's wrapping paper, arrived, and they tossed it aside, unopened, discovering only on their sister's return that it contained the kind of invitation from the French Academy of Sciences that many men wait for vainly during a lifetime. Wilbur and Orville laughed hard when they told us this story.

They never took themselves half so seriously as we took them. Still, to Milling and me, sitting at their Sunday dinner table and listening to their quiet stories what they had done was a miracle—and it is a miracle to me today. Without any formal scientific training whatever, two "ordinary" young Americans from an ordinary town in the state of Ohio had not only grasped and advanced the whole known science of aerodynamics—they had become its admitted masters, even more appreciated in Europe than at home.

Take alone the classic case of "the crossed bicycle chain." After the patient years with the kites and gliders at Simms Station and Kitty Hawk they had built the first actual flying machine, and after various trials, decided to link the propellers to the engine with bicycle chains. To obtain counter-rotation of the two props they simply crossed a chain to one of them. Well, you *can't* cross a bicycle chain! It will break; it *must* break. Certainly, of all people on earth, two bicycle manufacturers ought to be the ones to know that! But they *did* cross it, and it *didn't* break! And in all my own experience with the Wright plane, I never knew or heard of a single one of their crossed chains that did.

Again, when they came to the problem of an engine, they couldn't find one light enough for the plane to lift, so they went ahead and designed one of their own—a little box with four cylinders looking like tomato cans on top—which, among other features, happened to include the principle of direct fuel injection, a factor hailed as ingenious when it reappeared during World War II. More than anyone I have ever known or read about, the Wright brothers gave me the sense that nothing is impossible. I like to think—and, during World War II, often did—that the Air Force has rooted its traditions in their spirit.

It is a temptation to repeat more of their stories here, but the saga of the Wrights would fill a separate volume, and has been well told elsewhere, in the authorized biography by Fred C. Kelly. Even the phase which Kelly reviews in a chapter called, "The Army Wasn't Interested" needn't be gone into in this book. No references to the shrewdness of hindsight can excuse that sad tale of bureaucratic rebuffs—two discouraging letters from the War Department, dated a year apart, began with the identical meaningless phrase.

By 1911, as far as the Wrights were concerned at least, the War Department had stirred, if not quite awakened. The original Wright "military" plane was going to the Smithsonian Institution. Two more had been ordered by the Army, the first of which Milling and I were about to take to College Park, Maryland, where the Signal Corps' first aviation school was to be established. The Army admitted now that the airplane could fly, even if it didn't know yet quite what to do with it.

With their gentle smiles, the Wrights remarked dryly that maybe Milling and I would have to prove helpful in that respect. It seemed that there had been a still further depletion of the Army's air ranks—a new start would have to be made. The Wright plane which Benny Foulois had been flying in the south (not the Smithsonian plane) did not belong to the Service at all—it had only been loaned by Robert J. Collier, the

publisher and aviation enthusiast, as a stopgap. It was being returned
to its owner, and, surprisingly, Benny Foulois himself was being recalled from flying duty in July for a new assignment in Washington.
Of the Curtiss-trained pilots, Walker had been relieved, the numerous
new volunteers had not been taught as yet, so only Captain Paul Beck
remained. Beck's own status as a pilot was doubtful, as was that of
many Curtiss-trained airmen at that time; this, because of the method of
instruction used. Instead of being methodically checked out in the air
under the watchful eyes of a flying instructor, the student began by
taxiing a low-powered plane, was promoted to one that had just enough
power to rise a few feet, and then sank back to the ground, and at last,
if he seemed to be doing all right, was given a machine with enough
power to stay airborne for a few hundred feet, and in which he could
make gradual turns. The instructor continued to watch him from the
ground. The complete aviator's tests being rather simple at that time,
there was no real way of telling how good a pilot was, so long as he
did not have too many accidents. Beck had not been doing much flying,
and had had a couple of bad crashes, so he might or might not be counted
as a graduated military pilot.

Otherwise, Second Lieutenant Tom Milling and I actually were the
only two qualified pilots in the United States Army.

★ 3 ★

Milling and I sent our Wright plane to College Park by train, partially dismantled, in a box car. College Park was not only the first "regular" Army air base but a civilian field as well. We found the inventor, Rexford Smith, set up there, together with other pioneer aviators. The Signal Corps Aviation School consisted of four hangars near the B. & O. railroad tracks, a small administration building, and an emergency hospital tent under the alert direction of Lieutenant John P. Kelley, our medical officer, who was probably the first "flight surgeon" in history.

We didn't live at the field, but commuted the seven miles to and from Washington either by railroad or by car. Quiet air was still a requirement for training. Normally we would arrive at College Park at about 7:00 every morning, fly until about 9:30, go back to the War Department to work at desks in the Office of the Chief Signal Officer, and return for the calmer period that set in about 3:00 or 4:00 in the afternoon. In the long twilights of the summer months, we would sometimes stay out there practicing take-offs and landings until dusk. Other days we would remain at College Park all day, doing the one hundred and one things necessary to start our aviation school.

Our first job was to teach our immediate superiors how to fly. My pupil was our Commanding Officer, Captain Charles de Forest Chandler, a former balloonist with Lahm, who was not only Commandant of the Aviation School but head of the Aeronautical Division in the Office of the Chief Signal Officer. Tommy's student was our Adjutant, Lieutenant Roy C. Kirtland. Both men were quick to learn, and when the wind stayed down around five miles an hour we made many practice flights.

We soon had all four of our hangars occupied. Our Number 2 Wright plane, a Burgess-Wright model, and the demolished Curtiss plane in which Kelly had been killed at Fort Sam Houston, and which

Captain Paul Beck had brought to College Park to be rebuilt around its nameplate, were our full complement of planes for several weeks. Then the War Department purchased a short-hopping Curtiss trainer in which the student learned the fundamentals before flying the full-fledged Curtiss article.

We still weren't exactly sure what our mission was. The lessons to Chandler* and Kirtland were clear-cut enough, and there was no trouble there, except the fact that Milling and I had both been trained entirely in the left seat of the three-stick Wright plane. Thus, our first pupils became specialized "right-seat" pilots, taught to depend on their left hands for warping and steering, and on their right for changing altitude. There was another disadvantage to right-seat piloting: the pilot's position threw the plane out of balance so that he could not fly it alone; consequently, he was forced to carry a passenger with him on all flights.

In general, however, our purpose had to be the vague one—as we had anticipated at Dayton—of developing the airplane into a military weapon as best we could, for we certainly received few, if any, suggestions from the War Department. It was a routine of flying a bit higher or a bit farther, or mounting some communications gadget or weapon on our flying machine in an endeavor to give the airplane a military value. The Signal Corps had already admitted that the power-driven flying machine was a more mobile observation platform than the balloon, and that was as far as the War Department pamphlets definitely went. Without radio air-to-ground communications, the rapid delivery of intelligence still depended largely on horsemen. We, the airmen, were to jot down what we saw on brightly colored pieces of paper and drop the weighted paper to the ground, where a cavalryman, galloping hell for leather, would pick it up and take it back to the Command Post.

At first, every flight from the field was notable. Tommy hopped over to Washington Barracks with Kirtland—a distance of eight miles —to pay a visit on some officers there, and it was publicly described as a "cross-country" flight. That same afternoon—being Officer of the Day at the field, I couldn't leave College Park—I put in the time breaking the United States Army's altitude record—or setting it anyway, for there was nobody ahead of me.

In August there was a "dual cross-country flight" to nearby Fort Myer and back. Paul Beck flew to Fort Myer in his Curtiss plane, and as Chandler and I took off from College Park for the same destination,

---

* For further details of the period prior to 1914, and of the Army's earlier experiments with balloons, dating back to the Civil War, see Brigadier General Frank P. Lahm's and the late Colonel Charles deForest Chandler's definitive *How Our Army Grew Wings*.

Beck started home again. We had agreed that for safety's sake we would fly at 3000 feet. That would give us gliding room for a dead-stick landing in some open field in case our engines cut out. The sight of the two airplanes passing each other over the city was considered worthy of the Washington front pages next morning.

It was the same way when Harry Atwood landed in the White House grounds, where he stepped from his plane to the east portico to be decorated by President Taft for a record cross-country flight, originating in St. Louis.

Another time, as I was checking Chandler out for a solo flight, he and I were ordered to visit the encampment of the District of Columbia National Guard, near Frederick, Maryland. We took off at 6:34 A.M. and arrived over Camp Ordway at 7:23 A.M., covering the forty-one miles without incident. All Frederick had arranged a holiday just to see us. Lookouts were waiting, factory whistles blew, and as we came in sight, even the fire department abandoned work. At the end of a triumphant day, Charlie Chandler and I were awarded engraved cigarette cases by the mayor at a civic ceremony. Unfortunately, on the way home we ran into head winds and had to make a crash landing, continuing on to Washington by train. All that evening the phone in my Dupont Circle apartment kept ringing with calls from reporters who asked if I happened to know "how those two boys on the big flight to Frederick made out."

Popular interest in our new Army flying field was at times embarrassing. Washington was still a relatively small town in those days. Milling and I would be pointed out in restaurants as if we were celebrities. We would hear people behind us say: "There they are! They're the ones!" The glamor part of the early flying days was enough to spoil a man if he let it, and I must admit that at the outbreak of World War I I saw a few of the "Early Birds" do things that helped to establish a long-lasting prejudice in other parts of the service against airmen.

It was during this first summer that the famous "Atwood Hoax" occurred. With Charlie Hamilton as a passenger, Harry N. Atwood had started a great cross-country flight from Squantum, Massachusetts, to Washington. After various mishaps and changes of planes, they finally reached Baltimore, and were expected to appear over Washington at any minute. The sky was being watched, a special luncheon in Atwood's honor had been arranged by the Chamber of Commerce, the important guests were waiting to be alerted by phone. At about that hour, on a routine training mission, Kirtland and I happened to pass over Washington at 2400 feet. At once it was assumed in the city that we were the famous Atwood and Hamilton. Roofs were crowded, sirens blew, thousands of people rushed by every available means to the Monument grounds where Atwood was expected to land. Vice President Sherman banged his gavel and adjourned the Senate so that the senators could join the rush. I was pleased later to learn that among those who dropped the nation's business to hurry out was my former disapproving mentor, Senator Boies Penrose, of Pennsylvania.

During those early aviation days, the press kept reporters stationed daily at the field, notably J. Daly of the *Washington Post*, John Mitchell of the *Star*, and Dick Richards of the *Times*. Though we knew that they were there primarily to await the newsworthy accident that was bound to occur sooner or later, they became our friends and the first regular "aviation writers."

We now had a definite set of standards which the student-officer must meet to qualify as an *Army* pilot. They were the regular tests prescribed by the F.A.I. (Fédération Aeronautique Internationale). The Aero Club of America, as the sole representative in this country for the F.A.I., issued all qualification certificates to the pilots of airplanes, airships, and spherical balloons. The Contest Committee of the Aero Club facilitated the tests at College Park by appointing Captain Chandler as their representative to observe and report qualifications of officer candidates. Milling and I both passed the test on July 6th, he receiving Certificate Number 30; I, Certificate Number 29. On the landing test, Tommy put the plane down only five feet from the designated mark. Beck, in the rebuilt Curtiss ship, got Certificate Number 39 on August 3rd. Kirtland, in the Wright plane, passed on August 17th, and Chandler on September 20th, receiving licenses 45 and 59. There were no special Army pilots' insignia as yet. These F.A.I. certificates we received were the first Army "wings." They remained that equivalent until the following year, when the tougher tests for the "Military Aviator's Badge" were inaugurated. Tommy and I had no more pupils at College Park during 1911, but in August Beck began to check out Lieutenant Frank M. Kennedy, 10th Infantry, who became our second Curtiss pilot, soloing in October.

Meanwhile, Tommy Milling and I were advancing another important training program. We had had a long serious talk about it before we left Dayton. Who was going to service these planes? We couldn't do it ourselves. Yet we had been trained in the Wright factory by the mechanics there. Should we be content to supervise the work of our mechanics at the new station, or should we *show* the best of them a uniform system, starting from the ground up? We decided on the latter course. Our first act was to take a large, clear photograph of the Wright and Curtiss planes and label, in ink, every section, part, nut, bolt, and gadget on it. Thus was established the first system of nomenclature for airplane parts.

Our first mechanics were excellent Signal Corps enlisted men who learned the technique of airplane maintenance and repair very rapidly. Soon some of the veteran mechanics from Lt. Foulois' detachment at San Antonio arrived for duty. This was a great help because these men had worked on both the Wright and Curtiss planes at San Antonio. They formed the nucleus of today's vast Air Force maintenance machine. As a senior mechanic, there was a civilian employee of the War Department, Mr. Henry S. Molineau, at first the only man we had who understood the technique of operating machine tools.

We were constantly trying out experiments. Riley E. Scott, a former Army officer, brought an invention of his to the field which he called a "bomb dropper." It could carry two bombs, had a telescope to measure the speed of the plane, and a table of figures that gave a more or less correct setting for speed and altitude. Lying flat on the lower wing, Scott would look through this thing, and from about 400 feet was able to drop a "bomb"—a regular three-inch artillery shell with fins on it—with considerably more accuracy than was achieved by just tossing it overboard.

I wanted to be the test pilot on this tryout, but with my weight—160 pounds at the time—the plane carrying the bombsight would not rise from the ground. With Tommy at the controls—he weighed 140—the experimental bomber took off with difficulty. We thought Scott's bombsight was well worth developing—putting on planes to give them power of destruction—but nobody in the War Department seemed interested. In fact, nobody at all—that is, nobody in our own country.

The next year, Riley Scott took his instrument to France, where, over Villacoublay airdrome, using fifteen-pound bombs, he first hit a 60-foot square twelve times out of fifteen from 656 feet, then smacked a 375 × 124-foot target eight times out of fifteen tries from an altitude at 2624 feet. His demonstration won the Michelin Prize of $5000 and aroused the interest of the French and German General Staffs. During World War I, before we had bombsights of our own, a further development of this American invention was employed by the Germans with good effect against American troops.

During 1911 we were encouraged to attend the civilian air meets, where we not only renewed aviation acquaintances, but took part in the events. When Jake Fickel again fired his rifle from the air at Nassau Boulevard—his picture "proving the practicality of the aerial rifle" was already on the cover of schoolboys' copybooks—I was his pilot. We flew —and fired—in competition with the English team of Campbell and Sopwith, both famous later in the fields of auto racing and international yachting. Jake's six hits on the tin dinner plate that was our target as we flew over at a couple of hundred feet gave him a clean-cut victory. Following one of these affairs at Nassau Boulevard, I picked up a few extra dollars by acting as the first flying "double" in the movies.

Army and Navy pilots were required to pay their own expenses at these meets—not always easy on $124.00 a month. Once, after a show at Nassau Boulevard, I was so broke I didn't even have enough money to get back to my hotel in New York. It was beginning to rain. I arranged for a tall, lanky friend of mine—he was six feet three, and had a voice like a Coney Island barker—to move through the crowds, calling: "Flights can be arranged here with Lieutenant Arnold! Flights can be arranged here with Lieutenant Arnold!"

A regular queue began to form. The people were not discouraged to hear that the price of a ride would be fifty dollars. The first man climbed in, and I took off. But the rain ahead was getting heavier, and when I turned, it was heavy in that direction, too. I therefore swung back to the field and landed, taxiing right into the hangar to get out of the rain. All the time I was wondering whether or not I could ask payment for such a short hop. However, when my passenger extended a hundred dollar bill and said, "It's the usual price, I presume?" I was so broke that I didn't refuse. My tall friend ran to a hotel a mile away, through the rain, to get change. I gave my passenger back fifty dollars, paid my friend his agent's fee, and took the train to New York. Seventeen years later, at a cocktail party in Washington, I thought I saw a familiar face. It was my former passenger at Nassau Boulevard—Congressman Bacon, of New York, I was informed. We were introduced, and the Congressman instantly remembered. He turned excitedly to his friends and told them a story about a wonderful but dangerous flight. As I listened, I quietly put five ten-dollar bills back into my wallet. "I was going to pay you back that fifty," I told Bob Bacon. "It's bothered me for years. But after hearing your story of that flight, I realize it must have been worth every cent of it."

That fall we followed an example already established by the Wrights and Curtiss, and moved our Army Flying School for the winter. At about Thanksgiving time, after extensive search and consultations with the best meteorological advisers—for there must be no freezing temperatures, nor winds in excess of four miles an hour—we took off in a nine-car train for "Barnes' Farm," on the Savannah River, just outside Augusta, Georgia. The two Curtiss pilots, Beck and Kennedy, were detained in Washington until January, but we took all four planes along, plus the United States Air Arm's full remaining complement of six officers (including Dr. Kelley) and some twenty enlisted men. We quickly set the four planes up in tent hangars and prepared to take advantage of the balmy southern air. Almost at once a blizzard, which would have done credit to Alaska, descended on our camp. Icy winds howled, the tents were buried and collapsed, the four aircraft were knocked completely out of commission and had to be repaired.

The old-time residents, with true local pride, insisted it was the first snow they had had since the soldiers were there in '98!

A couple of months later, when Beck and Kennedy joined us, the planes had been set up again and we were ready to resume training. Trouble again—this time heavy rains. The gentle Savannah River burst its banks and rushed down on us, flooding our field like a lake, forcing us to prop our aircraft up on boxes and wade out to attend them. Nevertheless, perhaps because of a psychological attitude toward "the southern climate," we did get in many hours of flying. We were more experienced now, and flew in winds which were often stronger than those that had kept us on the ground at College Park. Sometimes they blew our Wright planes straight backward over the ground. Beck, not realizing this, and seeing Milling and me take off one day, took off after us and ended up with his Curtiss plane in pieces in a tree. It was one of two serious crashes he had at Augusta, but he seemed to live a charmed life and escaped from both without a scratch.

Nobody in the Army had been killed in an airplane since George Kelly's death a year before. In February, Kennedy had had a bad crash in the Curtiss plane. He wasn't killed—his life being saved by the special new leather helmet we were then wearing—but his head plowed a hole in the ground five inches deep, and though he served well in balloons during World War I, he was never able to fly an airplane again. Soon after that, a lieutenant named Leighton W. Hazlehurst, Jr., joined us; then a lieutenant colonel of the Ohio National Guard, named Charles B. Winder, who had obtained special permission; and in March, just before we moved north again, First Lieutenant Harry Graham, 22nd Infantry, reported at Augusta. Meanwhile, we tried out the little airborne radio that Benny Foulois, still interested in flying, had been working on back at the War Department.

During the winter at Augusta, Wilbur Wright came down to see how we were getting on, and we gave him a happy dinner at the country club. On the 30th of May, Memorial Day, 1912, a few weeks after our unit's return to College Park, we were shocked to receive a telegram from Orville, in Dayton, saying that Wilbur had died that morning of typhoid fever.

After that, deaths became more frequent. Only twelve days later my old friend and instructor, Al Welsh, came to College Park to help us lick the challenge of carrying an increased load, up to 450 pounds. This was a good problem to combine with the weight of Lieutenant Hazlehurst, who volunteered as an enthusiastic passenger for the test. Late on the afternoon of June 11th, the air over the field was exceptionally calm. Al took off with Hazlehurst as passenger, and when he had climbed to about 200 feet, dived as he had often done before, to get momentum for the initial climb. Apparently the sharp "pull out" caused the plane to crumple and crash. Both men were killed instantly.

Across the world the lethal possibilities of the airplane for others besides those flying in it were being, if not quite demonstrated, certainly suggested. In the Balkan War, guerilla volunteers of various mercenary nationalities including the American Bert Hall, who fought for both Turks and Bulgars, were arriving with planes. Bombs were being dropped, some already perhaps with Riley Scott's device. The first combat aviator in the modern world seems to have been a Russian named Sakoff, hired by the Bulgarians, who dropped a couple of bombs, got a couple of bullets in his plane and returned to his own lines otherwise unscathed. It was part of my desk job in the War Department to keep track of these reports, translating some of them from French and German, and evaluating them.

One day a sharp-faced, eager young captain of the General Staff came in to see me. He was not a flyer himself, but was working on a paper concerning the military future of aviation which he intended to present to the Army War College. He had recently returned from Alaska, where he had apparently put in a highly interesting and most observant tour of duty. Afterward he had been in Japan where he had had a look at the Japanese Army. He said the Japanese Air Force was bigger than ours—it had ten planes. His questions about the air were intelligent and to the point; in fact, it was he who did most of the talking, asking questions only to get concrete facts and accurate data. It seemed that as far back as April, 1906, he had written in the Cavalry Journal that "Conflicts, no doubt, will be carried out in the future in the air, on the surface of the earth and water, and under the earth and water." When he left, I had completed my first conference with Billy Mitchell. At thirty-two he was the youngest officer ever to have been appointed to the General Staff.

In June, Colonel Isaac N. Lewis came to College Park for an airborne test of his famous machine gun. Milling and Chandler flew several times over a cheesecloth target on the field, with Charlie getting some excellent hits. We were delighted with the gun, which was fed by a compact cylindrical drum (the Lewis gun was, of course, the standard armament on almost all Allied fighting planes in World War I). The test led to eager press queries at the War Department about the possibility of the airplane's becoming a weapon. Older officers said No, no, there was no such idea. The plane would remain a reconnaissance vehicle. The War Department did approve the experiment in principle. But it said that, instead of the Lewis gun, we must accept the Benet-Mercier machine guns which the Ordnance Department already had on hand as standard equipment for the Army. The Benet-Mercier was a very satisfactory weapon—on the ground. As an aircraft weapon it was impossible. With the Benet-Mercier mounted aboard, the controls of the Wright airplane could not be operated and the movement of the Curtiss wheel yoke was interfered with. The ammunition feed of the Benet-Mercier gun was a long metal chute projecting about eighteen inches to one side. The ejector slot was a chute projecting the same distance on the other side. Thus, whichever seat the gunner sat in, one chute or the other blocked the control sticks of the airplane. Nevertheless, the War Department ruled that it would be the Benet-Mercier or nothing, because it was the standard weapon of the Army.

More students were coming to College Park continually. Among them was a West Point classmate, Lewis C. Rockwell, who, recuperating from a stretch in Walter Reed Hospital, came over for a ride with me, and after that wanted to be a pilot himself.

In the late summer of 1912, Kirtland and I flew up to the Burgess-Wright plant at Marblehead, Massachusetts, to take delivery of the Army's first tractor plane, i.e., the first plane with an engine that pulled instead of pushed. The engine instead of the pilot was out in front. This was a revolutionary step in aviation. We had been buying a few aircraft engines abroad, such as the 103 h.p. Renault which held the world's endurance record, the 120 h.p. Austro-Daimler which held the world's altitude record, and the 160 h.p. Gnome which held the world's speed record. As Engineering Officer, I made the tests of these engines on the stands, but with difficulty. The United States Bureau of Standards had no dynamometer which could absorb more than 100 h.p., and after a fruitless search throughout the entire East I was forced to improvise by connecting an electrical dynamometer to a water dynamometer. Such a situation is rather difficult to imagine in these days of 4000 h.p. airplane engines and 200 h.p. automobile engines.

At Marblehead I found that this first American tractor aircraft (designed as a military plane) was not too difficult to fly once you had accustomed yourself to the cut-down visibility forward. This craft, with a 70 h.p. Renault engine, had been thoroughly checked out by pilots of the Burgess company, but had not completed the Army acceptance tests. Burgess, who had been licensed under the Wright patents to build their planes, was an interesting man, a dreamy sort of fellow who was, nevertheless, capable of sudden intense enthusiasm. On a dock at his plant at Marblehead harbor one day—a cold, raw day in midwinter—he was showing me a lightweight airman's life preserver he had invented, which was slipped on like a coat. "Will it really keep a man afloat?" I asked. "Afloat!" he cried, and leaped at once into the frigid bay, drifting about at his ease, unmindful of the cold water, and enthusiastically calling my attention to the good points of his device. This was the first Kapok life preserver ever made in the United States for airmen.

The Burgess-Wright tractor was supposed to be ready to take part in ground maneuvers in Connecticut in July, 1912. Accordingly, after I had completed the Army test flights, the plane, still equipped with floats, was loaded up to take off for a nonstop flight from Salem, Massachusetts, to Bridgeport, Connecticut. Had that flight been completed a world's record would have been made. We took off confidently, but the weather became so rough we were soon forced to land near Plymouth, Massachusetts. After spending the night at South Duxbury, we pumped the water out of the floats and, with the tide coming in smooth as glass the next morning, tried to take off again. With the smooth water, the overload on the floats—anchor, ropes, tools, suitcases, two people, and tanks full of gasoline—was too much for that 70 h.p. engine. We managed to get airborne but were headed directly toward the steeples of the town. I tried to turn; the plane slipped, and we dropped into the water like a stone. A float broke off, a wing crumpled. We started to drift out to sea, my irritation increased by the fact that my head was cut, my tongue half bitten off, my thumb dislocated, and that I was bleeding like a stuck pig. As we floated away toward the Atlantic, a sailboat came out manned by two veterans from the Soldiers' Home at Plymouth. They approached the plane so closely I could almost touch them from my position on the tip of the wing, where I was trying to keep the half-floating aircraft from losing balance and going to the bottom of the bay. They sailed around us without a word, and then calmly sailed back to their dock. Some time later the Coast Guard picked us up and towed the wreck back for what we called, "The Second Landing on Plymouth Rock," exactly on the spot where, according to the monument, the Pilgrim Fathers had landed. The plane was rebuilt and shipped to College Park.

On September 28, the weather was fine and we had an informal exhibition of flying at the field, attended by Colonel George P. Scriven, Acting Chief Signal Officer of the Army. Rockwell, who was considered one of our best pilots for the length of time he had been flying, started to let down for a landing in front of the hangar-line. Suddenly, his engine went to full power; the plane dived to earth. When we reached it, both Rockwell and his passenger, Corporal Frank S. Scott, were dead. Corporal Scott, for whom Scott Field is named today, was the first enlisted man to be killed in an Army air crash.

Again, a close friend of mine. Again, for all of us—Why? Like Al Welsh, Rockwell had been a good pilot. What had happened?

In October, in connection with maneuvers involving a forty-five minute search for troops on the ground and certain other prescribed tests, I won the first Mackay Trophy. That summer the new, strictly Army tests for the "Military Aviator's Badge" had given us our first actual "wings" to wear.

In the fall of 1912 I had an interesting little experience of my own. Captain Hennessy, a new student, Milling, and I had been sent on temporary duty to Fort Riley, Kansas, for experiments in observing the effects of artillery fire from the air and reporting the results to the batteries. Hennessy, as a field artillery officer himself, coordinated the work. Milling and I flew the two Wright "C's," dropping our observations on colored cards weighted with iron nuts for mounted messengers to pick up. To keep them from sticking on the wings or wires we dropped them through a stovepipe, thus clearing the wires supporting the landing gear.

In one plane we also had a crude, one-way radio—a sending set devised by Lieutenant (later Major General and Chief Signal Officer) Joseph O. Mauborgne—good up to fifteen miles. The artillerymen sent messages to us from the ground with panel code.

In the other plane we used a smoke signal set with a Prest-O-Lite tank of air under pressure. When the air was released it blew through a can of lampblack and we were able to throw smoke clouds into the air—large clouds for dashes, small ones for dots. Unfortunately, the slip stream sometimes blew our smoke clouds away before they could be read from the ground. Flying over Fort Riley after one of these operations, my observer, Lieutenant A. L. P. Sands, Field Artillery, and I were watching the men from the cavalry and artillery regiments line up below us for pay when suddenly something happened. The plane spun completely around in a small 360-degree circle. As we started to plunge down I looked back quickly, thinking one of the propeller chains had broken. It hadn't. Now in a whistling vertical nose dive, I took in everything, as you do at such a time. Everything was all right, nothing broken, my hands doing all the right things on the controls. Nevertheless, we were diving straight down—without a chance. My observer didn't realize this and was taking photos. Somehow, after every frantic yank and twist I could make, just a few feet over the ground I managed to pull the plane out of the dive. As soon as we had rolled to a stop I climbed down and said shakily, "Come on, Sandy, let's walk over to the barracks."

"Walk?" Lieutenant Sands said, "Aren't we going to ———?" Then he must have seen my face for his own turned green. Just then we heard the sound of hundreds of feet running. We turned around, and out of the woods appeared the men who had been in the regimental pay lines and had seen us disappear, plunging straight down behind the trees. They ran silently, expecting to find us dead.

The artillery-air experiments continued, and upon their completion, about December 1, 1912, we returned to Washington. Charlie Chandler took the schoolmen and planes to Texas City, and I was made assistant to Major Russell in charge of aviation in the Office of the Chief Signal Officer. I had become a desk officer.

Almost at once the tense situation with Mexico led to the formation of the "Provisional 1st Aero Squadron" at Texas City, on the Border. At first, Captain Charlie Chandler was in command. The squadron was made up of tthe few planes and still scanty personnel from the school. As time passed I became aware that there was discontent among our pilots. The increasing number of Army flying accidents, too many of them fatal, had set off a feeling of pessimism among the airmen which in part was just low morale, but beyond that was a resentful feeling that they should be commanded at the top by men who understood flying.

There had already been recognition in Congress of the casualty rate in agitation for some kind of "flight pay." At the end of 1912 this resulted in an original bonus of 35 per cent of base pay, which the flyers said grimly was none too much since their fatalities would probably increase to 50 per cent before long.

One day, Brigadier General Scriven, then the Chief Signal Officer, called me in. Unhappily, he handed me a paper. "What are we going to do about this?" he asked.

I looked at it and my eyes popped. Here was not a request, not a recommendation through channels, not even an angry communication to the Inspector General. It was a round-robin letter direct to the Chief Signal Officer from the pilots on the Border, stating their *demands!* The demands included changes in top aviation personnel in Washington, changes at Texas City, changes at the school at San Diego, and even stated who was to be put where!

"What are we going to do about it?" the Chief Signal Officer asked.

Those officers were my friends and it was a tough question for me to answer, but I said that if it were my decision to make, every man involved would be taken off aviation duty and sent back to his regiment.

"We can't do that!" General Scriven said. "Then I wouldn't have an Air Service. We're going into Mexico and I must have an Air Service."

"Sir," I said, "You haven't got an Air Service now."

It was ironed out. Most of the demands were granted. But the interesting thing is that a few weeks afterward I found myself a witness at a congressional hearing (Committee on Military Affairs, H. R. 5304) at which the setting up of an independent Air Corps was seriously debated. All the leading air officers were present, but only Beck, who we all believed had inspired the bill himself, came out in favor of the proposal. General Scriven talked sympathetically about it but did not think the time was ripe. Milling and I testified, pointing out the failures to date but certainly unable to see how the time for this change was ripe either.

I was questioned about the "air power" of foreign nations, on which I was the War Department's "expert." A bit of the future was foreshadowed by the appearance of Captain Billy Mitchell, not as an airman —he was still neither a flyer nor in the Aviation Section—but as a representative of the Signal Corps on the War Department General Staff. As at his own court martial later, Billy's thoroughness was exhibited, but the brilliance he showed, in conversation and in print away from such hearings, was not. A researcher will see that page after page of the transcript of Billy's testimony continues without any interrupting dialogue—there is only Billy's speech. He went back to early Europe, Bull Run, Gettysburg, and Admiral Cervera for examples, while the Committee members fidgeted restlessly.

At this hearing, in answer to a question from the chairman (Rep. James Hay, of Virginia), I verified that I was about to be relieved from aviation duty, at my own request. Eleanor Pool and I intended to be married in September; and in those days, you didn't plan to continue flying after you were married—unless you were an optimist.

At the hearing of the Military Affairs Committee, Mr. Hay was particularly interested in our high casualty rate, compared to foreign countries. I replied it was because, compared to them, we were still in the "instructional phase."

The Chairman: "And how long do officers generally stay in the service?"

Lt. Arnold: "That depends upon the temperament of the officer. Lt. Milling has been in the service for some time. He started at the same time I did and it has not affected him as far as I can see, but his length of service has made him more cautious, that is all. Some other officers find that it gets on their nerves and they become practically worthless as aviators."

Soon afterward, General Leonard Wood, the Chief of Staff, had me in for a little chat about flying duty for married officers and the question of young lieutenants being in Washington at all. As a result of that conversation, after two very pleasant months with the 9th Infantry at Fort Thomas, Kentucky, my wife and I presently found ourselves on the way to join the 13th Infantry in the Philippines, in December, 1913.

In 1912, after his return to aviation duty, Lieutenant Frank P. Lahm had started up a small flying section in the Philippines, including schools in Manila (at Fort McKinley) and on Corregidor, where hydroplanes were used. This effort to establish aviation there reached a peak of three planes, resulted in the reassignment of Charlie Chandler and the detail of Lieutenant H. A. Dargue as a student, and culminated in the death of Lieutenant C. Perry Rich. After that, aviation in the Philippines struggled along for over a year until the 2nd Aero Squadron arrived from the States.

Just prior to the outbreak of World War I in 1914, Admiral Graf von Spee visited Manila with the Far Eastern squadron of the German Navy, which the Royal Navy was to sink off the Falkland Islands a few months later.

About that time we held some big maneuvers, with the force of which my regiment was a part simulating a Japanese landing at Batangas, and the rest of the United States and Philippine troops defending the city of Manila.

Later, there were maneuvers for the defense of Corregidor, in which Captain Harrison Hall, F.A., after some fierce argument, received permission to move a few of his larger guns, by hand and mule, up to the supposedly impassable ridge on the north side of the entrance to Manila Bay. Not a man nor a mule, much less a gun, was ever seen by the "defenders" until it was too late. Hall set his batteries up and actually fired on Corregidor, getting hits on its gun emplacements that sadly proved their real vulnerability.

In the Batangas maneuvers, I had my first opportunity to see a future good friend in action as a super staff officer. My company of Infantry was moving up to make an attack when we halted to rest on a trail. Under the shade of a bamboo clump lay a young lieutenant with a map spread before him. It developed that he was dictating the Order for the attack that was to break through the defenders' line. This youthful officer was our side's Chief of Staff for the maneuvers, a job any lieutenant colonel or major in the outfit would have given his eyeteeth to have. Following out the young lieutenant's plans, we won.

When I returned from the maneuvers, I told my wife I had met a man who was going to be Chief of Staff of the Army some day. He was, too. The young lieutenant was George Catlett Marshall. The day he was appointed, my wife reminded me of my prophecy.

In 1915 our first child, our daughter Lois, was born in Manila.

By then the war in Europe was a year old. From across the world, we all looked toward it tensely, and I remembered many of the things that had been talked about during my first tour in the Philippines. In those days, by the way, George Marshall's strategic and tactical observations were as interesting as his interpretations during our maneuvers had been, and as accurate. We wondered what was going on at home. We understood that my old friend Billy Mitchell was a major in the Aviation Section himself—now, in fact, its Executive. During the winter of 1915–16 we also heard that he was learning to fly, at his own expense, at the Curtiss school in Newport News, Virginia. He was then thirty-six years old.

We were at sea aboard a San Francisco-bound transport in the late winter of 1915–16 when I received a radiogram from the Adjutant General as abrupt as my original invitation to flight training had been. Would I volunteer for duty in the Aviation Section? Or if so detailed, would I object? Naturally, I sent back a reply asking what that meant. Immediately I received another message: "If you apply for detail in the Aviation Section, Signal Corps, you will come in with the rank of Captain. If not, you will be detailed and come in with the rank of First Lieutenant." I knew at once that my old friend Billy Mitchell was on the job in Washington.

After two winter months with an infantry outfit at Madison Barracks, New York, I was assigned, in May, 1916, as Supply Officer of the newly formed Aviation School at Rockwell Field (North Island), San Diego. Big changes had taken place in what was now known as the Aviation Division of the Signal Corps.

There were 23 Military Aviators (including Junior Military Aviators, a new rating since my time) and 25 aviation students, plus one nonflying officer. The planes were now all modern tractor types, the Burgess-Wright "C" itself a thing of the past, and the Curtiss JN (the famous "Jenny") the most active service model.

Though the mountains of Mexico had furnished hazards, and the dry climate had caused wooden propellers to fly apart, "military" aeronautics was playing a recognized part in the pursuit of Villa, carrying mail and messages and flying reconnaissance and photographic missions. Compasses were still not too good, maps only fair, but the desire to fly cross-country was acute, as one incident at San Diego illustrates.

Lieutenant W. A. Robertson, accompanied by Colonel Harry Bishop, F.A., took off from North Island, San Diego, for El Centro, California—a distance of approximately 100 miles. They ended up on the coast of the Gulf of California. Even after they had landed, the two airmen thought they were on the Salton Sea. They did not suspect their actual location until, after walking up the beach for some time and returning toward their plane, they found their footprints completely obliterated by the incoming tide. Then they realized where they were. Taking two sandwiches, two oranges, and a can of water, they started a long trek northward on foot across the deserts of Baja California, and were finally rescued, more dead than alive, near Wellton, Arizona, some nine days later.

Much hot criticism came from flying people about the way the Army handled this rescue search, and charges and countercharges were made by officers at the School. The permanent staff divided into two parts— those who thought the Commanding Officer might have backed a far more aggressive search for the lost airmen, and the headquarters staff, who were inclined to let nature take its course, and assume no responsibility. The younger airmen were almost wholly in the first group. They could not understand why a couple of days were allowed to elapse before any actual search operations were begun. I naturally was one of the group who were eager to start flying at once over the route of the lost plane.

In the end, this search, the many narrow escapes of the searchers flying cross-country, and the close call of the two principals, Bishop and Robertson, called forth an investigation by the Inspector General's office. Some young airmen were relieved from aviation duty; others, of whom I was one, came through with nothing worse than a black mark on their records.

The first American pilots to fly against Germany had already started overseas. The famous Lafayette Escadrille, "Nieuport 124" of the French Army was formed.

In our own Aviation Division it was announced that there would be seven "Aero Squadrons."

The 1st Aero Squadron was to be stationed at San Antonio, Texas; the 3rd, 4th, and 5th at various points in the United States; the 2nd in the Philippines; the 6th in Hawaii; and the 7th in Panama. This was the real foundation of the Air Arm of the United States Army. I was selected to command the 7th Aero Squadron, primarily, I believe, because after the Robertson-Bishop episode and its consequent ruckus, my superiors wished to get me as far away from San Diego as possible.

The day before my departure, our first son, Henry H. Arnold, Jr., was born, on January 29, 1917.

Upon reporting to the Commanding General in Panama—Major General Clarence Edwards—I told him my assigned task was to locate a suitable site for an air station, and then bring down a unit, the 7th Aero Squadron, to occupy it. General Edwards gazed at me gloomily. "Have you seen your San Diego efficiency report?" he asked.

"No Sir," I replied. "Why?"

"It's so bad it makes you stink," he said.

"Thank God, they were not all that bad!" I said, reflecting on the troubles we had had in our search for the missing men in Mexico.

Everybody down there—the Navy, the Signal Corps, the Coast Artillery, and the Air Officer—had different ideas about where the new squadron should be located. The Panama authorities could not decide, so the Commanding General told me I had better go back to the United States and take the matter up with General Leonard Wood himself, the Commanding General of the Atlantic Department under which Panama came, and then go to the War Department and take it up with the General Staff.

I was on a ship between Panama and Cuba when our radio operator received the news that the United States had declared war on Germany. We had read about darkened ships, lifeboats, and all that, but our skipper hadn't had any first-hand experience with wartime sailing. He turned out all lights, swung our lifeboats, and the ship crept on to New York. It was an eerie feeling, but at the same time a relief. Now we really knew where we stood as far as Germany was concerned.

I had no intention of going back to Panama if I could help it. As fast as I could, I wanted to get command of another squadron and take it overseas.

☆ *4* ☆

My ambition to take an air outfit to France was never realized. In a sense, it remains a disappointment to this day. During World War II, in Washington, I deliberately deprived myself of the aid of a whole series of fine Chiefs of Staff and valuable topflight advisers so that these men would not miss out on wartime experience that I never had.

From the start of World War I until the Armistice, I was always asking for transfer overseas, but my requests were always turned down. I remained stuck in an assignment which left me, for most of the war, the second-ranking officer in the War Department's Air Division, and, for the greater part of those eighteen months, the senior officer in Washington with wings. Promotion came rapidly in wartime—especially in an Air Force in which only a few relatively junior officers knew how to fly. By August, 1917, I was a full (though temporary) Colonel, the youngest one in the Army. My wife and I looked at those eagles on my shoulders, and though we were certainly pleased to see them there, they seemed unreal, even embarrassing. Youngsters, in those days, just didn't get to be colonels. At first, I used to take back streets when I walked to the War Department from my house, imagining that people would be looking at me incredulously. There had been thirty-year-old colonels in the Civil War, but that was before my time.

It was the first war, however, in which "Production" was regarded openly as a combat weapon instead of just something that came through the Quartermaster as "Supplies." Farms and factories were suddenly seen to be just as critical in the fight as infantrymen at the Front.

Two weeks to the day after President Wilson's War Message, Balfour's British mission was already in Halifax, bound for New York. On the 24th of April, former Premier Viviani and Marshal Joffre arrived in Washington from France, followed quickly by missions from Italy, Belgium, Russia, Rumania, and Japan. Almost at once, the foreign loans which were ultimately to pile into a total of $9,500,000,000 began to be voted. This seemed to be taken as a success in itself, only a small part of the public recognizing the fact that the loans were intended primarily to buy American materiel and supplies which didn't, as yet, exist for the equipment of our own Army and Navy, much less for our Allies. In the same way, the competitive recruiting posters, and the voices of Marine Master Sergeants, Navy C.P.O.'s, Army Top-Kicks, or pretty girls, urged every man to join up. We had a few pretty good posters of our own. "Be an American Ace!" one invited. "Enlist in your Country's Air Service!" The national spirit behind this rush to get into uniform was commendable, but those in charge of the allocation of draft quotas soon found out it had to be more sensibly harnessed.

Major Billy Mitchell had already sailed for Europe. A week before war was declared, he had landed in Spain, on his way to Paris as one of the first four American air observers. He had, perhaps inadvertently, speeded his own departure from Washington by some outspoken criticism of the way aviation preparations were being handled. The suggestion that we develop air units for the militia component when we still had practically none in the regular service, particularly irritated him. His public remark, "To Hell with the National Guard!" did not go down well, and caused Secretary of War Baker to make a corrective statement.

Within a few weeks, however, Billy Mitchell had already grown into one of the most popular American heroes of the war. He had become the first U. S. Army officer to fly over the enemy lines, had received his first Croix de Guerre, and despite the protests of the French General Staff, had spent ten days in the frontline trenches. He had seen Pétain, who put aside his pressing work to talk to him about American aid, and was sending home a steady flow of reports on every subject from bombs to the effectiveness of German parachutes. Our airmen, too, could have had parachutes by then, but they were turned down as useless until after the Armistice—not by the War Department, but by flying officers themselves.

As for the Allied bombers, dropping a few one hundred-pounders on trenches and villages now and then, Billy reported in his enthusiastic style: "The bombardment people are sure that if they are given enough planes and explosives, there would be nothing left of Germany in a short while." He was impressed by the fact that "we could cross the line of these contending armies in a few minutes in our airplanes, whereas the armies have been locked in the struggle, immovable, power-less to advance for three years."

On May 24, 1917, exactly forty-eight days after President Wilson's War Message to Congress, the War Department had a virtual bomb dropped in its own lap. The famous cablegram of Premier Ribot arrived from France, outlining coolly what our immediate program should be. It recommended that America plan to send to the French Front, by the spring of 1918, 4500 airplanes, 5000 pilots and 50,000 mechanics, with the necessary accompaniment of personnel and materiel. It stated that 2000 planes and 4000 engines would have to be constructed each month and that, during the first six months of 1918, 16,500 planes and 30,000 engines (training planes and engines not included) would have to be built.

Forwarded from the White House to the Joint Army and Navy Technical Board, the French proposal received the approval of that body on May 27th. It was approved by the Secretaries of War and Navy the same day. We were told to prepare a Bill for Congress. Our understaffed Airplane Division in the War Department received the news with great interest. It was our first program. The total strength of the American air arm at that moment was 52 officers and 1100 men, plus about 200 civilian mechanics. Out of a total of 130 so-called pilots, only 26 were really qualified. Altogether, we had 55 airplanes, 51 of them obsolete, 4 obsolescent, and not one of them a combat type.

This, too—the cable from Premier Ribot to President Wilson—was Billy Mitchell's handiwork. A few of us recognized it at once. Later, Billy, himself, jubilantly confirmed our guess. "I decided," says an entry in Mitchell's diary, early in May, "it will be a good thing to get the French Government to exert pressure on ours." His biographer, Isaac Don Levine, describes the way in which Billy called at the French General Headquarters and cooked up a communication which, on May 6th, went up from the commander of the French armies to the Minister of War, outlining the size of the air force which the United States should be requested to furnish "for obtaining and keeping control of the air." This memorandum called for 8000 planes on the line by May 1, 1918, out of a total of 20,000 machines, to be serviced by 38,500 mechanics, in addition to a heavy monthly output of engines. Shortly thereafter the Ribot cablegram was dispatched to President Wilson.

At this time we "ranked fourteenth among the nations of the world in terms of aviation." Actually, it was worse than that. Statistics aside, we had no air power at all. In the raw, the country's manpower, industrial strength, and the national know-how in general, assured the building of any kind of military force we wanted—*if* there was a realistic organization of the energy and materiel, and *if* there was time. Was there time?

On May 1, 1917, through the French Commission, we had received confidential word that the Germans had attained superiority in the air. The ground forces themselves realized that it would be a year at least before their part of the American war effort could really be felt in France. Apart from the complete absence of airplanes and equipment, it took six to nine months to train an airman, as against three for a ground soldier. How long would it be before we could put an American flying force on the Western Front, "obtaining and keeping control of the air?"

The Navy was in far better shape. Since the Spanish-American War, and more so since Mahan's sea doctrines were published, the American public, and Congress, had been inclined to accept the Navy's function, organization, and recommended size in a way it would never accept a large standing Army. Also, the Navy had followed the ball of public opinion warily, letting no chance pass to sell their "bill of goods" to Congress and to the American public.

The Navy had another advantage which the Air Force always has had too, even if it took a while to be recognized. In peace, sailors keep their skills sharp on a real adversary—the sea. In the same way, every airplane that takes off, shooting or no shooting, is up against the hazards of the air. Except for a few well-trained regular units with special foreign service, such as those who had been in Mexico, the peacetime Army had to make a case for new equipment or increase in size from simulated maneuvers, or await an actual war threat.

The Navy did not need a war to teach it that ships at sea are not by themselves sea power. Though it had to be greatly expanded, the nucleus of a realistic naval system—shipyards, shore bases, plans for the steady replacements of ships and supplies, of skilled personnel as well as ordinary seamen—was already in being. When the real thing came, the Army had farther to go. It was their first actual experience with modern war.

As the tar-paper barracks sprang up in 1917, and Liberty Bond drives, the draft, the recruiting posters about the "Beast of Berlin," and excited enlistments swept the country, the War Department was too busy to give more than hurried attention to our Army's Air Arm. Our superiors were thinking about infantry divisions, field telephones, Yaphank and

Spartanburg, muleskinners, horse artillery, trench helmets, campaign hats, gas masks, canvas leggings, shipping priorities, French .75's, duckboards, and everything else Pershing needed right away. In the Airplane Division, we couldn't do much about it either, for even when we did get the rare chance to give advice, our lack of experience prevented our making clear-cut, conclusive recommendations. Our Signal Corps superiors, though they didn't always listen to us, certainly listened intently to the comments and criticisms of those foreign commissions. The British, French and Italians naturally wanted everything we could send immediately—men and machines—and all of them disagreed on every point except one: we, the American airmen, didn't know anything. They had been fighting the war, and we hadn't. Therefore, we should do as they prescribed. In 1942 we ran into this again, but with a difference. The American Air Force by then had some solid theories of its own, even if they had been tested only in peacetime and by observation on the battle fronts abroad.

In "the Great War" it was entirely different. We had no theories of aerial combat, or of any air operations except armed reconnaissance. Despite Billy Mitchell's eagerness to blow up Germany, we hadn't a single bomber. Such things as formation flying, a new German development appearing on the Western Front that spring, were unknown to us. It was quite a shock to look helplessly at Europe that year and remember that ours was the country of the Wright brothers and Curtiss, also the country of Riley Scott's bombsight and of the Lewis machine gun. It seemed more than three years since Germans and Frenchmen had fired pistols at each other as their planes passed in the air. The handfuls of fluted darts which both sides had dropped on marching troops in 1914, hoping to pierce the infantrymen's steel helmets, had given way, first to bombs made from finned artillery shells, and then to more scientific missiles. The aerial riflemen who had succeeded the pistol-duelling pilots had become aces firing machine guns, which, ever since Anthony Fokker completed his designs in 1916, had been synchronized to shoot through the propeller. These new weapons had evolved new air tactics, but until the Ribot cablegram came in May, our Army superiors were not especially interested in the airplane as a shooting weapon.

Our first projected task was to provide every two ground divisions with one squadron of aerial reconnaissance and one balloon company. For the moment, a complete lack of combat experience had left American military aviation behind.

Just prior to our entry into the war, the Government had created a

Bureau of Aircraft Production, directed by Howard E. Coffin, the automotive engineer. Coffin was a remarkable production expert, as well as engineer, but knew nothing of airplanes or their construction. By pooling all aviation patents, paying the patentees—Wright, Curtiss, Blériot, etc.—a thousand dollars apiece as a consideration, it was hoped that jealousy regarding patent rights would be eliminated, and teamwork between all airplane manufacturers would be secured. This patent pool was to be involved in trouble later, none of it logical nor, to the best of my knowledge, caused by any leading designer of airplanes or aircraft components.

The Bolling Mission landed at Liverpool on June 26th, only eighteen days behind Pershing. Headed by Colonel R. C. Bolling, an Air Reserve officer, and consisting of eleven Army, Navy, and civilian technical experts, its job was to confer with the Commander of the A.E.F. and to find out in England, France, and Italy how the American air effort, as regarded training, airplane production, and combat organization—in short, as defined by the Ribot cablegram—could best be coordinated with that of our Allies. Joint training plans were discussed, as well as a mutual program for aircraft procurement.

General Squier, Chief Signal Officer, had invited foreign air missions to the United States before we were in the war. We had already sent one of our own to Canada.

In the Aviation Section of the War Department we came out of our huddle over the appropriations which the Ribot proposal would require, and they almost staggered us. What the effect would be on the War Department, we could only guess. There had been enough raised eyebrows among our superiors in the Signal Corps when the so-called "54 Million Dollar Program" had been submitted to the Secretary of War on March 29th, calling for a force of 1850 aviators and 300 balloonists, with the requisite equipment—16 reconnaissance squadrons and 16 balloon companies in all. This program had been based solely on air reconnaissance units for the number of infantry and cavalry divisions the Army contemplated using, and still visualized no bombing or fighting planes. It was later reduced to $43,450,000, and became a law on June 15th, three months after war was declared.

Before this, from the time the Aviation Section had been established in 1907, only $900,000 had been appropriated for all Army air development, $500,000 of that sum being approved to aid Pershing's Mexican expedition, and the whole average since my graduation from West Point amounting to about $100,000 a year. Now, we presented a real program.

Even after having pared things down as well as we could, we submitted a bill calling for 22,600 airplanes, 45,000 engines, a procurement, construction, and maintenance cost totalling $707,541,000. Somebody above can always cut it some more, but in the end, no matter how it was sliced, it came out as a necessary $639,241,452. Our immediate superiors were aghast; the War Department General Staff could not understand it. But the Allies were awaiting an answer.

With the bill not approved by the General Staff by July 4th, the Secretary of War, upon recommendation of General Squier authorized its submission to the Appropriations Committee of the House of Representatives. It was introduced on July 6th, reported unanimously out of the House Military Affairs Committee on July 13th, was debated in the House on the 14th, and passed the same day. On the 16th, the famous "640 Million Dollar Bill" was reported to the Senate and referred to the Committee on Military Affairs. On the 21st it was passed by the Senate, and on July 24th, the President signed it. As far as I know, it has never, up to the date of this writing, had the approval of the General Staff of the Army.

Now we had the money. We had the eager young men joining up by the hundreds, and then the thousands. But we had only the beginning of a system of training fields—eight in all America by midsummer. We lacked everything from hangars and transportation to mess kits, and we still had no combat airplanes, and worse, no practical administrative setup for providing them.

"The basic task we faced," wrote Colonel Gorrell, who, in addition to being its definitive historian, was successively Chief Engineer, Assistant Chief of Staff, and Chief of Staff of the A.E.F. Air Service, "was that of training men. . . . Our experience was that materiel for a larger A.E.F. Air Force was generally available. . . . *The limiting factor was, trained personnel.*"

This may have held true in the A.E.F. locally, or at least seemed to have been true when Gorrell wrote. In the larger picture, however, we found the trouble to be exactly the reverse. Our main headache in trying to create an American Air Service that would halfway meet the Ribot plan was almost entirely due to shortages, in many cases the complete absence, of materiel, especially airplanes. The manpower was there, the know-how soon began to be there, but the facilities—the physical plant and the machines—were not. At the end of the war, thousands of keen young men, practically all partially instructed and many of them fully trained, were still standing around on the ground in the United States, with no airplanes for them to fly, and no personal equipment, squadron upplies, or shipping facilities ready when we organized our combat units.

In 1917, as in 1942, special circumstances put American airmen in a more vulnerable spot to be grabbed as individual replacements for our Allies' forces than any other category of U.S. soldier. Since we had no service-type airplanes, but did have the right kind of men, and since the British, French, and Italians were desperately short of men but pressed the fact that they had training facilities and airplanes standing idle, it was agreed that until we had procured our own combat planes, we would give our flying cadets the best primary training we could, and then send them overseas to complete their advanced courses in the schools of our Allies. The Bolling Commission, the British, French, and Italians and we in Washington, all saw eye to eye on this, but apparently for different reasons.

As a few of our half-trained pilots began to trickle overseas in August, 1917, it was seen that the picture was not quite the rosy one that had been painted for us in Washington. Gorrell himself who, as a member of the early Bolling Commission, had reason to be impressed by the asserted excess of materiel over manpower abroad, wrote presently that actually the "crowded situation in the European schools was a serious setback to our air program." Also the situation in Europe had "so changed that we found in the fall of 1917 that prospective places available in the summer of 1917 for training our men when they weren't there, became too often unavailable by the time they did arrive."

The first American Squadron to arrive on the Western Front, other than the Lafayette Escadrille, formed in 1916 and later brought into our service as the 103rd Pursuit Squadron, was an observation outfit (the 1st) soon sent behind the lines for gunnery training. The first fighter unit to get into action was the 94th Pursuit Squadron, subsequently celebrated as "Eddie Rickenbacker's Hat-in-the-Ring Squadron." This was not until April 14, 1918. Nevertheless, before we finally had our air units operating with our armies, we had to convince all our major Allies that we meant business when we said that American airmen would stay not only in American uniforms, but in American squadrons.

At home and abroad, if the question had only been one of available instructors and eager manpower, we could have had our training program set up in no time. In the rough, our goal of 41 flying schools—25 in the United States and 16 in Europe, including the great center at Issoudun, which was really a complex of 14 entire fields—was soon on its way to achievement. Aided by the colleges and universities—California, Cornell, Georgia Tech., Illinois, M.I.T., Ohio State, Princeton, and the University of Texas—we were establishing ground schools, 28 mechanics' schools, two and then four photo schools, schools for engineer officers and for adjutants. An Artillery Observation School was set up at Fort Sill. Our ground schools were modeled on the ideas our Air Commission to Canada had brought back—the course to run for three months, graduating 200 men a week.

Phrases like "Knights of the Air," "War Birds," "Richthofen Circus," "Shot Down in Flames," and "Fighting Aces" filled the newspapers. The scores of the German planes shot down by the Guynemers and René Foncks were followed as eagerly as those of such U.S. champions as Rickenbacker and Lufbery later. The triumphs of the original Lafayette Escadrille headed by the French Captain de Laage—Norman Prince, William Thaw, Victor Chapman, Kiffin Rockwell, Bert Hall, Elliot C. Cowden, and James McConnell (some of the first ones lasted long enough to transfer to the American Air Service in 1918, but only Thaw and Hall survived the war)—were celebrated in New York and Washington and on small-town Main Streets.

As early as 1916, the sense of the Air Service as a sort of *corps d'élite* was shown by the zeal to form private groups like the Yale or Harvard "aero clubs," volunteer militia squadrons which learned to fly at their own expense, and were donated the estates of wealthy Long Islanders as "training camps." A certain number of the best officer candidates at Plattsburg were eager to be pilots. The "Aerial Reserve Corps" which President Wilson had authorized on July 13, 1916, proposed that the would-be flying officers pay for their own primary training at the rate of about $500 apiece before being advanced to a six-month Army flying school. When Lt. Col. George Squier returned from Military Attaché duty in London later in 1916 to head the Aviation Section of the Signal Corps, his recommendations did away with the self-payment plan and provided for an annual output of 500 new pilots from civilian life whose whole training course would be supplied by the Army.

The glamor of these first war months did not penetrate to the inner halls of the War Department where the long days were now filled with feverish work in an attempt to meet, equip, and start the training of the swarm of air recruits.

I say "halls of the War Department" as a figure of speech, for as the year wore on the personnel of the Air Division could be found scattered all over Washington. It may be noted that in this chapter there is reference to the "Aviation Section," the "Aeronautical Division," the "Air-

plane Division," the "Air Division," the "Air Service Division," and
so on. These designations all refer to the same old "Aviation Section of
the Signal Corps," which, typical of the confusion, was renamed half a
dozen times, but was still the same suboffice until we were finally pulled
out from under the Signal Corps as a separate "Air Service" of the
"National Army" in May, 1918.

Originally, the Aviation Section did all its own work, handled its personnel requirements, its training and operations, and the design and
development of its own airplanes. During 1917, most of these functions
were taken away from the Aviation Section, one by one, and made
independent divisions heading up directly under the Chief Signal Officer
who was, in theory, to coordinate their activities.

On the administrative side, it is worth noting that our rapid expansion
to an ultimate enlisted strength of 148,000 was facilitated by no such
reservoir of reserve officers who could be called to active duty as was
available in World War II—we had 50 altogether. Nor did anybody
seem to hit on the idea—it needed 1917–18 to teach us—that thousands
of experienced men might be commissioned directly from civilian life
and trained quickly for this function, as was done in 1942. We first
turned to the Regular Army, offering increased rank of one or two
grades to officers from other branches brought into the Air Service by
the 5th of September. Then we turned to civil life to get men with
special training and experience for particular jobs.

The separation of functions caused by the everchanging channels in
the Signal Corps was the worst problem of all. Now Mr. Coffin's Aircraft
Production Board decided all policies for numbers and types of planes
and their supply, and all engineering matters from tests to spare parts.
As there was no practical airman on either this Board or the Chief
Signal Officer's Staff, procurement was handled by the Production
Division—a serious organizational split. U.S. airmen were used in an
advisory capacity only on production and engineering matters. It was
not an organization that was to inspire confidence among the men who
had to fly the planes.

Before mentioning in more detail the greatest American air headache
of World War I—aircraft production—it should be emphasized that
the matters described here did not end up in failure. Our national air
effort fell below what it could have been, even starting from our state
of unpreparedness and of technical infancy in 1917. On the other hand,
fanciful statements were made by people in authority, including the
Secretary of War himself, about the air strength with which we were

going to deluge the Western Front. "If we start immediately, we can put ten thousand aviators on the French Front by this time next year . . . Twenty thousand engines for airplanes will be delivered monthly, beginning in November, 1917! . . . We can make the Kiel Canal, itself, useless!" No wonder that the *Saturday Evening Post* felt fired to head a 1917 article by Howard Coffin: "Fifty Thousand Open Roads to Berlin!"

A chief result of all this loud proclaiming was that the Germans immediately launched what they called their *Amerikaprogramm,* and built and redoubled their air strength on the Western Front before we had a plane there. The actual commitments of our Air Service regarding manpower and American-built planes were not realized, except in fractional terms. But in the last six months of the war—the only period in which Americans took a full fighting part—squadrons of the U.S. Air Service were present, not only doing admirable work, but revolutionizing tactics. Our first fighting air outfit arrived on the Western Front on April 14, 1918, a full six weeks before the American counterattack at Cantigny. Cantigny, starting the break-up of Ludendorff's last great offensive, was the first time American military strength was felt with its full power in the war. Prior to 6:45 A.M., May 28, 1918, when the First Division started to move forward, Pershing's few units in France were more of a bone of contention with our Allies than a threat to Germany. Thereafter, they were the spearhead—indeed, the front of victory.

It was Hindenburg, not Pershing, who said, grimly, in November, 1918: "The war was decided by the American Infantry." In those battles, and in the first tactically massed air strength in history at St. Mihiel and again on the Meuse, the American Air Service flew hard and well in support of that infantry victory, and this, in spite of Monday morning quarterback tales, was its only function. What might have happened had the finger been pulled out of the dyke at home, as some historians like to say, and had our air manpower and our aviation production achieved the massive output that might have come if the war had lasted a year longer, is beside the point. American troops dominated the final Allied advance, and American aviators, in proportional numbers, were part of it.

Our harassed little Aviation Section Headquarters in Washington was the nerve center of something growing bigger all over the country every day. Its continual changes in personnel would not make exciting reading, though they changed our lives almost weekly. The airmen who came to join us were only transients in their own eyes. They wanted to get over there, and as each one went, I wanted to go with him. Nothing doing.

In February, 1917, Lieutenant Colonel John B. Bennett, another non-flying officer, took over the post of head of the Aviation Section of the Signal Corps, until Major Ben Foulois, quickly a Brigadier General, succeeded him in September. In my own dozen-jobs-in-one, I was first technically head of the Information Section, then Assistant Executive, then Executive Officer of the Air Division. Despite my awe at my own eagles then, in World War II this would have been the three-star job of Assistant Chief of the Air Corps—perhaps a fair measure of the strides American air power made in the intervening years. When Benny Foulois went overseas, I remained Executive—presently "Assistant to the Director of the Aeronautical Division"—and the senior man in Washington with wings. A staunch old cavalryman, Brigadier General Alexander L. Dade, was placed in charge of the Air Division. So long as discipline proceeded along true and tried Cavalry lines, he made no objections, but the Wright brothers did not seem to have impressed him much. Once as we were driving across Washington in our big old Staff car, he said to me with a concerned expression: "Arnold."

"Yes, Sir."

"I think when we ride in this thing it might not be a bad idea if we observed the protocol the Navy uses for small boats."

"Sir?"

"You know how they work it. Getting into a small boat, Junior Officer always goes first. Getting out, Senior first. See what I mean?"

"Yes, Sir."

If the Aviation Section was in a fog at times, so was the whole Army. Take the case of the 1st Aero Squadron, ordered to accompany the 1st Infantry Division overseas. By the end of May, the Squadron was all packed up, ready for transportation from the Mexican Border to the Port of Embarkation. The 1st Division sailed in June, and in so far as the theoretically secret details of that troop movement were known by the General Staff, the 1st Aero Squadron was with it. But according to plaintive messages received from the 1st Aero Squadron itself, it was with nobody—it was still left behind, with all its goods and chattels packed and crated and on the railroad sidings and platforms—at Nogales, Arizona. It had nothing to do and was getting bored. The Commanding Officer sent in one telegram after another about its plight, but it required several to convince those on our General Staff in charge of the movement of the 1st Division that the 1st Aero Squadron was not in France.

They couldn't, and wouldn't, believe it. It was August before the Squadron sailed to catch up with the 1st Division.

Another incident, in the fall of 1917, shows the lack of both materiel and administrative coordination at that time. The French were in a bad way for manpower, and made a formal request for 332 officers and 4000 enlisted men to be put into their automobile factories in order to release the same number of Frenchmen for work as mechanics in aircraft plants. We immediately formed four motor mechanic regiments of about 1000 men each. Special construction at Camp Green, South Carolina, was provided for them. Each regiment was to be administered by a Colonel with Regular Army experience, and to have for its second in command a technical officer who understood production, repair, and assembly of automobiles.

Lieutenant Colonel Henry Joy, who had been president of the Packard Motor Company, was selected to assemble this personnel, and was second in command of the first regiment to go overseas. Its sailing date came, but it could not go. The outfit's training and organization were complete, but such items as spoons, mess kits, and shoes were still lacking. As renewed pleas came from France, the Chief of Staff, General Tasker Bliss, called me to a conference to ask WHY the motor mechanics had not been shipped as promised. I was armed with a list of the shortages, and General Bliss sent me at once to General Goethals, who, at that time, had taken over all procurement, supply, and transportation for the Army.

My interview with General Goethals was short but not very sweet. "What do you mean, not equipped!" he growled. "Of course they're equipped! Stick to your bacon, young man, stick to your bacon!" But when I showed him the reports from the commanding officers themselves, he said: "Here, give me those lists. That is all." Within a couple of weeks, all four of the motor mechanic regiments, fully equipped, had started on their way.

It was apparent by September 1st, as our recruiting grew, that there would be a serious shortage in many key specialties. Accordingly, the War Department decided that all voluntary enlistments would be stopped by December 13th, the draft, with its ability to allocate manpower where needed, to take over completely.

However, the Air Service was ready with its new schools, and needed a large number of enlisted men to man them. Furthermore, for various reasons, Air Service enlistments, as presently admitted by Secretary of War Baker in October, had slumped. One reason was that we probably kept our qualification standards too high for wartime. In any case, a big Air Service recruiting drive, with a deadline of December 13th, was approved by the War Department. I selected Colonel E. Z. Steever to promote this work and brought in H. M. Byllesby, a prominent business-man from Chicago, who was commissioned a Lieutenant Colonel. A nation-wide campaign ensued, with posters, newspaper ads, speeches, and motion picture publicity. Though the campaign never finished, the number of enlisted men in the Air Service jumped from 22,000 on November 1st to 87,000 on January 1st, 1918.

Army regulations required all new volunteers to go through the established Army recruiting stations under the Adjutant General. Dur-ing November, over 50,000 were received in one bunch. The recruiting stations were unable to take care of such far-above-normal numbers. Town halls, churches, schools, private homes, Chamber of Commerce buildings, auditoriums—any sort of shelter was called upon that would house the men while they waited to be processed. This confusion came in spite of careful advance conferences between the Adjutant General's Office and the Air Division. Our recruiting drive had to stop cold. There was no place even to feed the enlistees, and no place for them to sleep. Many thousands were sent home and told to report again weeks later. The last of these recruits did not reach their Air Service stations until three or four months afterward.

The effect of this on thousands of eager young Americans who had dropped whatever they were doing, said good-by to friends and families, and rushed to enlist, was clear. They trooped to us singing that the Yanks were Coming, "Good-by, Broadway, Hello, France!" and so on, and all we could do with them was tell them to go home and take it easy for awhile.

In the same way, as the British, French, and Italian advanced flying schools were increasingly unable to meet their schedules, owing to lack of airplanes, the men who had finished their primary flying training in the States had to be assigned to other than flying duties. When the equipment situation started to clear up a bit in France, the bad weather of the fall and winter of 1917–18 settled down on Europe as well as at home, and we had thousands of primary pilots on our hands with noth-ing to do—at least nothing in the way of flying. The morale of these men dropped gloomily. Their parents wrote their congressmen and the War Department demanding to know why their sons were not flying as they had joined up to do. Why was Willie only doing ground exercises?

However, by the time the Armistice came, we did have 2768 completely trained pilots and observers on the Western Front. Out of 20,000 officers and 149,000 enlisted men in the Army Air Service at home and abroad, almost 40 per cent of the officers and nearly 50 per cent of the enlisted men were in France or at advanced training bases in England. Many more would have been there if there had been airplanes for them.

After World War I the lesson of the failure of aircraft production in 1917–18 remained uppermost in my mind. It can be, and still is, argued that it was not a complete failure. On the side of aircraft components, notably engines, there was marked success. The story of the Liberty engine, for example, has been told and retold. The Liberty engine was not only designed and put into production in what we like to think of as the typical American way, but was so good that it was soon requested in large numbers by our Allies for use in their own planes.

Among the civilian engineers and other experts who came to Washington to help us out, accepting commissions in the Army, were men like Howard Coffin, E. A. Deeds, Robert Montgomery, Harold Emmons, L. S. Horner, and Sidney Waldron, and experienced aircraft engine builders like E. J. Hall (of the Hall-Scott Company) and J. G. Vincent, of Packard.

Normally, two years were required to produce an engine of the type desired. Deeds (Colonel Deeds by then) exercised rare judgment early in 1917 when he decided that the United States should concentrate on one type of engine, if possible, to meet the requirements of all types of combat airplanes. Colonel Waldron, Lieutenant Colonel Vincent, and Lieutenant Colonel Hall agreed. The tale has been told many times of how Deeds practically imprisoned Hall and Vincent in his room at the Willard Hotel in Washington for two days, at the end of which they came downstairs with the design for the Liberty engine, a fact. At first, it was believed that an 8-cylinder engine with 225 h.p. would meet all requirements for the spring of 1918. A 12-cylinder engine with 330 h.p. was visualized for action in 1919–20.

The men met in Deeds' room on May 29th. On June 4th their plans had been approved by the Aircraft Production Board, the Joint Army and Navy Technical Board, and by Colonel Bolling's recently returned Commission, including Colonel V. E. Clark and Lieutenant Colonel Howard C. Marmon. Ford swung into action with his miraculous belt line.

Production difficulties, not inherent in the Liberty's design, were to ensue. Combat experience abroad was to show that the 8-cylinder model was inadequate, and that it must be discarded in favor of the stepped-up 12-cylinder version. Still, despite the initial confusions about the Liberty engine at home and in Europe, it was the most satisfactory venture up to that time in high horsepower for airplanes. There was unwarranted optimism in this matter, too. Original production schedules had to be sharply reduced. But the first 8-cylinder Liberty was delivered on July 4th. The first 12-cylinder model made its appearance on August 25th. The power of the Liberty jumped rapidly from 330 to 375, and finally to 440 horsepower, a truly remarkable feat. A year from its conception, 1200 were delivered to the services. By the time of the Armistice, 15,500 were in the hands of our Army, our Navy, the French, British, and Italians.

At the same time, the American automotive industry had continued to turn out the OX and Hall-Scott, and, under license, the French Le Rhone and the Gnome and Hispano-Suiza—a total of 32,000 aircraft engines produced in the United States in little more than eighteen months. It was unfortunate that our industry was not able to produce combat planes with the same ease and in the same numbers.

In other directions, American ingenuity was not only successful in producing aircraft components, but made innovations of high importance. One of these, to be mentioned presently, was an air weapon of the future, which seriously affected our Air Force deliberations on the eve of World War II, was used desperately by Hitler after D-Day, and is a subject of international planning today.

The shortage of spruce—the most desirable of woods for aircraft construction at the time because of its light weight and strength—was overcome in the summer of 1917 in true pioneering manner. Under command of Colonel (later Brigadier General) Brice P. Disque, Spruce Production Regiments were organized, which bought forest areas with large stands of fir and spruce, and moved out into the woods. Ultimately, the "U.S. Spruce Production Corporation" was set up with a capital of $10,000,000. The Army built railroads, established logging camps, and started wholesale production of lumber. Of all the production activities in World War I, this was the only one that resulted in a profit to the U.S. Government.

Other American inventions included an oxygen mask equipped with telephone connections; electrically heated clothing; radio telephone for air-ground communications; an automatic camera; helium gas for balloons; an armored pilot's seat; the introduction of eight-machine-gun armament for ground strafing; instruments aiding aeromedical research, and experiments and progress in the whole new field of aviation medicine.

It was in trying to produce the airplanes themselves that we met our real setback. Young Americans today, familiar only with the story of World War II, have a right to feel that the phrases "American" and "Aircraft Production" go together automatically. It was not like that in 1917–18. No American-designed combat plane flew in France or Italy during the entire war. The foreign planes built in this country failed to arrive in Europe either on schedule or in the promised numbers, until what had started out as a triumphant exhibition of American know-how turned into a humiliating series of Congressional and other investigations.

In April, 1917, twelve aircraft factories, ranging in size from medium to small, existed in the United States. In all the years before 1917 they had been given orders from the Army for a total of 154 "military" planes. During the previous year, all of them together had received orders from all sources, military and civilian, totaling but 366 airplanes. Nine of the twelve factories were capable of producing 90 per cent of the whole output. None, on America's entry into the war, had any experience at all in building combat type airplanes, although the Curtiss "Jenny," with its OX engine, was recognized as an excellent primary trainer.

To make the required expansion in aircraft production a reality, it seemed natural to turn to the highly organized American automotive industry. Hence, Howard Coffin and his associates had been brought to Washington, and the Bureau of Aircraft Production set up. Despite the two and a half years of warning Europe's example had given us, and our own not altogether useless experiences on the Mexican Border, no design for a U.S. combat plane had even been broached by the War Department. Thus, it was necessary to select quickly some proven combat plane, or planes, already in use by our Allies for production in the United States. This had been a primary objective of the Bolling Commission when it went abroad in June.

☆ 5 ☆

Colonel Bolling and his associates had sailed for Europe with the competitive cries of the Allied Air Commissions in Washington beating in their ears like sledgehammers, and we who stayed behind had to stand up under it every day.

The contentions about training methods were bad enough—the English with their Gosport system being about 180 degrees opposed to the Penguin approach the French battled for, and the Italians having still another. No wonder one foreign officer, watching us try to mold the best of all these systems into one of our own, observed: "The British tell them to go North, the French tell them to go South, the Italians tell them to go West, so they usually do what they think best, and go East."

The international disputes about what kind of combat airplane the Americans should build were even hotter. The French pressed for their single engine Spads and what not, the British for their SE-5's, the Italians for the Pomilio. The British and the Italians argued the Handley-Page bomber against the Caproni, with the French throwing in the Breguet. And so it went. The average young air veteran of World War II may not realize that, despite the infancy of combat aviation then, there were probably more different types of fighting planes in that first World War than in his own. Actually, "the British put into service over forty different types; the French put into service over fifty types; the Italians over thirty types, the United States nine types which we purchased in Europe, and the Germans over thirty types of combat planes during the war.

"The airplane" (concludes the final official record of 1917–18), "is one of the most short-lived of all implements of war !"

In the midst of all this, the Bolling Commission chose exceptionally well. They selected two types of combat planes to be built in America. The first was the British De Havilland-4, a two-seater ship which indicated that it would be efficient not only as a reconnaissance plane but possibly as a day bomber, and, it was hoped, as a two-place fighter. The other type chosen was the single-seat French Spad, which was not only showing up well in combat on the Front, but improving its models as the war progressed.

The first sample Spad was not shipped to us from France until August 28, 1917, and by that time, it was approaching obsolescence. At about that date, however, General Pershing sent word that we should forget about the production of single-seat fighters in America, leaving that to France; we should concentrate on two-place aircraft. Thus, although American pilots fought in it at the Front, our share in producing the Spad, except for a thousand subsequently ordered from Curtiss for training in the States, was limited to those produced by the French technicians whom our motor mechanic regiments had released from the French automotive factories. We also built 14 SE-5's, though they were never sent overseas. Not heeding Pershing's decision, proponents of the English SE-5 kept hammering at us, and an Italian Commission hurried over and practically demanded that we get to work on the Pomilio.

This left us with the DH-4. The first airplane of this type for production drawings appeared in Washington, July 27, 1917, and arrived at Dayton on August 13th. It came without an engine, without armament, and without any of the accessories essential to combat types. It also came with all its measurements carefully set down in the metric system, and all those meters, centimeters, and millimeters had to be reworked into our feet and inches before we could even start. Memory of the headache of that operation alone caused me to hesitate about American manufacture of the British Mosquito and certain other types in World War II.

The DH-4 was a good airplane. For that day, its performance was excellent. It could stay in the air for about three hours; had a ceiling of 19,000 feet; could climb to 10,000 feet in fourteen minutes, and it had a speed of about 124 m.p.h. In addition to that, it carried a live load of about 1200 pounds. It had, however, one bad drawback, a thing which, with a little more experience, could have been foreseen when it was designed. This was the construction flaw which led to its becoming known ominously all through the American Air Service as "The Flying Coffin." The observer did not sit directly behind the pilot, but was separated from him by a large gas tank. The position of this gas tank, either when it was hit by incendiary bullets, or involved in crashes at home (there were no parachutes then), frequently caused a fire of such raging suddenness that both pilot and observer were doomed. In my long experience with airmen and airplanes, I have learned that if the flyers themselves come genuinely to believe that a certain plane is a "Flying Coffin" or a "Man Killer," then it is definitely a "Flying Coffin," or a "Man Killer" until they have been convinced otherwise.

Later on, it will be seen how two of the best fighting planes of World War II—the B-26 and the P-38—fell into this unwholesome category, until, in one case, with the help of Jimmy Doolittle, and in the other, through the coolness of a formation of Sergeant Pilots each flying on one engine, I got the boys to see the light. After 1919, when the DH-4 became the DH-4B, with that gas tank moved back and the pilot and observer sitting directly behind each other, it wasn't called the "Flying Coffin" any more.

The first DH-4 was ordered into production on October 18, 1917, by which time we had been at war more than six months. The first one to reach France was not to get there until May 11, 1918, and it was July, with the A.E.F. at last in full action on the Marne, before we were able to ship the DH in any quantity. The engines were also taking months longer to turn out than we had expected.

There were many complicated reasons for the lag in production. National unpreparedness, and the fact that even the best aircraft manufacturer in America had to cut his eyeteeth when it came to producing combat planes, were fundamentals. Real Air people were not running the show—either in industry or in the Army. Overseas, General Foulois, commanding the A.E.F. Air Service, was up against a similar problem. Colonel Mitchell asserted publicly and pointedly that not a single American commander in France, except General Hunter Liggett, Commander of the First Army Corps to which Billy was attached, understood the first thing about the employment of airplanes. However, up to the end of 1917, there was no employment of American airplanes to understand.

One day I was talking with Howard Coffin, who had certainly worked hard to push the production of both training and combat planes. "Just think," he said, "we now have orders for over 40,000 airplanes in our factories, and by this time next June they will have them built!"

"That's fine," I said. "How many spare parts have you ordered, Mr. Coffin?"

"Spare parts?" he asked, apparently startled. "What do you need spare parts for?"

The answer was soon clear in the way our training was held back. Before long the production figures meant nothing, because so many aircraft had to be cannibalized for spare parts to keep others flying that we never could really say how many airplanes we had available.

Later in the year Colonel Lee of the Royal Flying Corps inspecting the R.F.C. Texas installations, was greatly disturbed to discover he could not get spare parts for the R.F.C. training program. I suggested to him that he make a tour of *all* our fields, and send wires from each base to the still unconvinced Aircraft Production Board concerning his findings. He did, and at the end of a subsequent meeting of the Board during the winter, the Chairman of the Board, asking if there was anything further to be discussed, was suddenly confronted with the pile of Colonel Lee's telegrams.

There was immediate consternation. These criticisms were from a British expert—not from some U.S. Army officer who might be ignored. The Chief of the Aircraft Procurement Section arose and said, "Now, this is not a matter for the War Production Board; this is something we can talk over and solve among ourselves later." He was not prepared for my reply: "For four months we have been talking this over and getting no results. If we are to continue our training we must have action now." The meeting broke up in a row, but we soon began to get spare parts for our training planes, two-thirds of which had been laid up without them.

Such outstanding U.S. Army pilots as Lieutenant Colonel B. Q. Jones, who had been the first man to experiment with deliberate spins, were not even permitted to fly the foreign aircraft types that came over. It was implied, if not said in so many words, that our people just weren't good enough to be trusted with such valuable equipment.

I well remember a day when a British pilot was stunting over Washington, and high-ranking officers of the Army and Navy were assembled on the roof of the War Department building to watch him. It was one of our own senior Signal Corps officers in charge of Aviation who kept exclaiming: "There you are, you see! Nobody but a foreign airman in a foreign airplane could ever do such flying as that!" This made me so angry that I went down and telephoned to Dayton for Captain A. D. Smith, one of our hottest pilots, to come to Washington. After getting his instructions, he went to pay a call on the English aviator, who finally agreed to let Smith borrow his plane the following day. He didn't know that I had urged "A. D." to kick it, roll it, climb it, dive it, and otherwise put on the prize performance of his life. I found a pretext for getting the same group of Army and Navy officers up on the roof again the following afternoon. They were thrilled and our Signal Corps boss started again: "Marvelous! Wonderful! He gets better every day! Nobody but a foreign . . . !" The funny part is, when he learned it was an American pilot who was throwing that plane around up there, his enthusiasm suddenly collapsed.

There was also that day the following winter when at a senatorial hearing the Chief Signal Officer asked casually: "How many combat airplanes have been shipped abroad?"

Instead of answering outright, the production people went into a hasty huddle from which they emerged agitatedly to say: "We can't answer that question now. We'll answer it tomorrow." Immediately on returning to their office they began to burn up the wires trying to get the *one lone DH-4*, which at that time was flying at Dayton, shipped to New York by express. It arrived next morning, was hurriedly trans-shipped to the dock, and by the time the hearings reopened, had sailed. Proudly the report was made to the Senatorial Committee: "We have shipped combat airplanes to France."

Ironically, the ship carrying that first DH airplane was torpedoed off the Azores, so the statement, "American-built combat airplanes have arrived in France," could not follow. This affair caused much criticism during the later congressional investigations.

So did the matter of aircraft tests. Because those in charge lacked the aviation know-how, when the DH-4 did start to go overseas, it still had not been properly tested. In the first genuine air test of the DH-4 military prototype with the Liberty engine at Dayton, in May, 1918, it went into a spin and killed Colonel Henry J. Damm and Oscar Brindley, the famous civilian instructor who had been a fellow flying student with me at Simms Station, in 1911.

By the end of the war, about 4500 DH-4's had been built in this country. Of the total of 1216 American-built planes to reach the Western Front, all but three—two LePere's and one experimental DH-9—were this same De Havilland model.

The LePere, incidentally, a plywood machine, designed by the French aeronautical engineer around the U.S. Liberty engine, had a speed of about 136 m.p.h. and was a much better all-round plane than either the DH-4 or the DH-9. Only 25 LePeres were ever built.

U.S. production of a night bomber type was seriously discussed. The British were confident that the Handley-Page had no Allied equal in this field. The Italians, who had a little the better of the argument as far as performance was concerned, thought the Caproni was the best night bombing plane available. However, the Handley-Page bomber was much simpler in construction and did not present the production problems. Both were considered and both accepted.

Captain D'Annunzio, the soldier-sailor-poet-aviator of Fiume fame, arrived at the head of a commission of fourteen Italian experts to start guiding the production of the Caproni triplane with three Liberty motors. Normal difficulties with the Italian language, and the inability of American engineers to read the Italian blueprints caused postponements. Only one Caproni was built in the United States prior to the Armistice.

If the detailed blueprints and drawings of the Handley-Page had not taken so many months to follow up the general drawings which arrived in August, 1917, and if the so-called "Handley-Page Agreement" had ever been implemented, our Air Corps might have had a striking force of great power ten years ahead of time. The Handley-Page was too big to be shipped intact, and no planes, of course, could fly the ocean in those days. Thus, it was proposed to fabricate the small parts and subassemblies in the United States and ship them to England for final assembly.

In December, 1917, Colonel R. C. Bloomfield, of the Royal Flying Corps, arrived to join the British Mission in Washington, bringing with him the advanced copy of the Handley-Page Agreement, signed by Air Minister Rothermere for the British, and by Foulois for the Americans. This was a rather far-seeing document, and one of the most realistic ones we had dealt with yet. It envisaged the shipment to England of the parts for 300 Handley-Page airplanes, with the necessary Liberty engines, during the months of May, June, and July, 1918, and thereafter forty sets of parts to be sent each week. Further, that 30 U.S. squadrons be formed for flying Handley-Page airplanes, ready to operate by September 1, 1918. Three thousand bricklayers, carpenters, and general laborers were to be dispatched to England at the earliest possible moment to get the fields ready. In a revolving pool, 1500 American mechanics would be kept training in Britain at all times. A balanced plan like this calls for an integrated kind of teamwork which was not ready then. The parts for 101 Handley-Pages were finally shipped.

As it developed, only the mechanics were on time, and since they were held in England in accordance with the terms of the Handley-Page Agreement, actually the only result was that the American air outfits in France were deprived of their needed services. Our troubles with the foreign types convinced everybody that at the earliest possible moment we must start to produce combat planes of our own.

In the fall of 1918, Glenn Martin brought out plans and finally, a complete night bomber, the "MB," equipped with two Liberty-12 engines. The Martin bomber was about the same size as the Handley-Page, carried a useful load, and gave about the same performance as the British plane. It never reached quantity production before the Armistice, but it was the standard heavy bomber of the Air Force in the years that followed World War I.

The general lack of confidence in the United States air effort had begun back in 1916 with editorial criticisms from such public sources as the *New York Times*. Some of the same writers who ten years before had laughed at the Wright brothers, now complained because we were trailing Europe so badly in aviation developments. There was rising dissatisfaction in Congress. Our casualties in training—still about the only American war casualties—were not helping matters. We hoped that instructions for the Army to inaugurate the first air mail service between New York and Washington early in 1918 would increase public confidence in our ability. I was particularly pleased, having been one of the first airmen to fly air mail in 1911 from Nassau Boulevard to Garden City, Long Island, a distance of five miles. Public confidence would not have been so bright in this respect either if a true report of the first Washington–New York air mail flight had ever reached the newspapers. The young pilot selected by the Postmaster General for the trip was the relative of a high government official connected with the post office, but he was not our best navigator. He took off from Washington with the mail sacks in fine style amid the farewells of a distinguished group, including the President of the United States, members of the Cabinet, a band, his relatives, and fanfare from the press, but when he telephoned me that night that he was down, I realized at once he wasn't speaking from New York.

He was grounded at Waldorf, Maryland. Unhappily, I immediately got in touch with the Postmaster General and told him what had happened; I also informed him that I was going to select another pilot for the next day's trip. "Now don't be too hard on the young fellow," said Postmaster General Burleson. "Give the young man a chance."

Against my better judgment I did, but this time I had Major Reuben Fleet, later President of Consolidated Aircraft Corporation, lead the new pilot along the four-line Pennsylvania Railroad to the Susquehanna

River crossing. I knew he could not go wrong from there. Fleet returned, and, coming into my office, reported everything O.K. He had scarcely completed his report when the telephone rang. It was the mail pilot, who was down at Cape Charles, Virginia. After Fleet left him, he had flown away from the railroad tracks and followed the shoreline of Chesapeake Bay in a semicircle to Cape Charles. When he had run out of land to guide him, he had brought his plane down and telephoned. Actually, the mail went to New York by plane on the third attempt, with another pilot at the controls.

It will be noted that no strict chronology has been observed for the events of 1917 insofar as the Aviation Section is concerned. Until the spring of 1918 our situation, despite constant minor changes, was more a state of affairs than a chain of events.

The initial Washington program of July, 1917, calling for an ultimate of 345 U.S. squadrons on the Western Front, and soon upped by the A.E.F.'s request to a projected 386 squadrons, was reduced on January 4, 1918, to a goal of 100 squadrons by December 31, 1918. In November, 1918, when optimism had climbed high again and the end of the war was only three days distant, the A.E.F. had still asked us for only 210 American squadrons by July 19, 1919. It made little difference, for we continued training pilots, gunners, mechanics, and other men as fast as our equipment permitted. Then we formed new squadrons as rapidly as squadron equipment became available. That was really the only program we had.

We heard that Mitchell wasn't getting on with Pershing, and then again that Pershing thought Mitchell was wonderful. There was a rumor that there were frictions between Billy's "Get It Done" ideas and the more conservative methods of Foulois, his A.E.F. Air Service superior. One courier reported the British and the French were enthusiastic about the primary pilots we were sending them; another that the British and the French were shocked by the fact that most of the primary pilots we were sending had never fired a machine gun in the air. Everybody— British, French, Italians, and couriers from the A.E.F.—asked anxiously when more American squadrons and more American-built DH-4's were coming.

The various reorganizational plans which were always in progress in the Air Division do not require much comment, for so long as we were left under the command of Signal Corps officers who were not themselves airmen, the results could not have been basically different.

During the winter, we understood that General Dade was to be relieved as head of the Air Division, and requested that, assuming he could not be replaced by an Air Officer, General William L. Kenly be recalled from the A.E.F. to succeed him. General Kenly was a mature officer who had taken the "Get Rich Quick" flying course at San Diego, California, had spent much time with the Royal Flying Corps since going overseas, and had a good grasp of the problems we were up against. The suggestion that we be placed under a real air officer was again disapproved and General Kenly was ordered home. Much to his surprise, however, he was not put in charge of the Air Division until April, at which time the President issued an Executive Order taking the Air Service away from the Signal Corps and placing the operating end under General Kenly and production matters under Mr. J. D. Ryan.

During World War II I used to look back to those days and see the present in miniature—like reversing a pair of binoculars in a familiar room. This was especially true of the civilians who aided us. There was a direct connection between the services that some of those industrialists, scientists, engineers, and other professionals rendered during World War I and my efforts to enlist their aid, and the help of other men like them, in the 1940's. Donald Douglas, the aircraft manufacturer, was a staff member of our Section in 1917–18 as a civilian engineer. The people on the National Advisory Committee for Aeronautics and the Aviation Committee on the Council of National Defense, though limited to research and advisory functions, constantly broadened our horizons. The astonishing Henry Ford, whose magic belt line was finally turning out cylinders for those complicated Liberty engines so fast they were stacked up at his Detroit factory like cords of wood, was an enlightening contact for any young Army officer. For an Army officer whose military specialty was then, and forever, as dependent on that kind of efficiency as on trained soldiers, Ford's way of doing business was a revelation. It was also at the River Rouge plant in 1917 that I first met Bill Knudsen. The big project in the factory then was the construction of Eagle Boats with which the Navy hoped to beat the German submarines. Bill was running it in the way only he could, showing the same kind of energy and brainwork that was to enable him to help quadruple the output of our World War II aviation industry after 1942.

J. D. Ryan, Sidney Waldron, W. C. Potter, C. W. Nash, McCauley, and Vincent, who did such wonderful work in connection with designing the Liberty, Captain LePere of the French Army, and also of Packard—these men and many more, some in uniform and some in civilian clothes, not only contributed to the victory in 1918, but sowed the seeds then of a contact between the Air Force and a number of skilled civilian fields which I tried, for the rest of my career, to keep growing.

One of the men with whom I became acquainted and from whom I secured advice was Bernard Baruch. He stood high among the advisers to the administration, but could always find time to help out the little fellows. Years later, in World War II, when I needed experienced counsel and advice so badly, his aid to me was invaluable.

Charles Kettering, of Delco—"Ket"—was another man who did all kinds of "impossible" things. It was he who took the "spark knock" out of gasoline. Whatever the problem, he made it seem simple. When a group of young men asked him, "What new development or research is left on earth for our generation?" he replied with a typical Kettering remark: "Find out what makes the grass green!"

Once he asked a group of scientists, "Why can we see through glass?" Somebody answered, "Because it's transparent." "O.K.," said Ket, and took down a dictionary. "Let's see what that means. 'Transparent—admitting clear view of objects beyond.' Then we can see through it because it can be seen through." For two days the scientists filled blackboards and papers with equations, symbols, and figures, but in the end, they had to admit we can see through glass because it is transparent.

Twenty-six years later, exactly one week after Eisenhower's troops hit the Normandy beaches on D-Day, the world was horrified by the sudden appearance over London of the first V-1's, the gruesome pilotless buzz bombs. A number of people in this country, including Ket, were not surprised, for he and our own Air Force had fathered, if not invented, this weapon back in 1917.

Early in the fall of that year, working with the Sperry Company, and with Ket's Delco firm, we had developed—not merely experimented with, but successfully tested—two pilotless planes. One was a full-sized airplane, but equipped with complete gyroscope controls, built at Sperry's Long Island plant. Further tests in the spring of 1918 showed that this flying bomb was sufficiently accurate to reach a point within a hundred yards of its target after a forty-mile run, but the necessary precision devices, man-hours to be expended, and so on, made it too expensive to pursue in terms of quantity production. Under Ket's direction, we then devised a pilotless airplane—or bomb—which we called the Bug. It was a complete little airplane built of papier-mâché and reinforced with wooden members, its smooth cardboard wing surfaces spreading less than twelve feet. Its fuselage held 300 pounds of explosives, and it weighed, unloaded, 300 pounds itself. It took off from a small four-wheeled carriage which rolled down a portable track, its own little two-cycle, 40 h.p. engine, built by Henry Ford, meeting the requirements for both pressure and vacuum necessary to operate the automatic controls. The actuating force for the controls was secured from bellows removed from player pianos. They rotated cranks, which in turn operated the elevators of the rudder. The direction of the flight was insured by a small gyro, elevation from a small supersensitive aneroid barometer, so sensitive that moving it from the top of the desk to the floor operated the controls. This kept the Bug at its proper altitude. At first we relied only on the dihedral of the wings for lateral stability, but later, more positive directional controls had to be installed with orthodox ailerons. Including the $50 gasoline engine built by Ford, the entire device cost about $400.

To launch the Bug, tracks were pointed toward the objective. The distance to the target, and wind direction and intensity, were figured out as accurately as possible. The number of revolutions of the engine required to take the Bug to the target was then figured, and a cam set. When the engine had turned exactly that proper number of revolutions, the cam fell into position, the two bolts holding on the wings were withdrawn, the wings folded up like a jack rabbit's ears, and the Bug plunged to earth as a bomb. (In 1944 the German V-1's flew to their objectives on similar principles, insofar as range was concerned.)

Our first tests being highly successful, we decided to demonstrate the Bug to the top Washington brass, and invited them to Dayton, Ohio. With the care that goes with such occasions, it was decided that only enough gasoline would be put in the tank to allow the Bug to leave the track and make a straightaway flight of two or three hundred yards at most. Unfortunately, not even Kettering realized how little gasoline the Bug needed to operate. After a balky start before the distinguished assemblage, it took off abruptly, but instead of maintaining horizontal flight, it started to climb. At about six to eight hundred feet, as if possessed by the devil, it turned over, made Immelmann turns, and seeming to spot the group of brass hats below dived on them, scattering them in all directions. This was repeated several times before the Bug finally crashed without casualties.

Ket put ailerons with proper controls on it and a second show was set up. This time, we believed the Bug would fly straight for a mile or so at about 50 miles per hour, so we loaded the high-ranking visitors into automobiles to follow it and be present when it crashed. Everything looked perfect for the test. The efficiency of the flying bomb was now a certainty. Our one fear was that information about it might leak out to the Germans. Again it got away, but this time only because it was too fast for the automobiles to keep up with. However, instead of flying straight, it made a circle around the city of Dayton. We had to get to that wrecked Bug before anyone else. In the vicinity where we thought we had seen it come down, we came upon some excited farmers. "Did you see an airplane crash around here?" we asked. One farmer said, "Right over there! But strange thing, there's no trace of the pilot!" Colonel B. J. Arnold, the Army officer in charge of the project, remembered quickly that we had a flying officer in a leather coat and goggles in the car. "Here's the pilot," he said. "He jumped out in his parachute back a piece. Let's go pick up that wreck." Our secret was secure. The awed farmers didn't know that the United States Air Corps had no parachutes yet.

By mid-1918, the development of the Bug had proceeded so favorably that we decided to tell General Pershing and the Commanding General of the Air Service in France what we were doing. We were sure we would be ready to send some of the pilotless bombs overseas within a few months. A proposed Table of Organization was drawn up showing the number of officers and men that would be required in each Bug squadron, and an estimate was prepared showing the number of Bugs each squadron would be able to launch in twenty-four hours. It was planned to launch thousands every day against German strong points, concentration areas, munition plants, etc.—which would certainly have caused great consternation in the ranks of the German High Command at least.

The Bug was twenty-five years ahead of its time. For all practical purposes—as a nuisance weapon—it compared very favorably with the German V-1. It was cheap, easy to manufacture, and its portable launching track would have permitted its use anywhere. Considering the trends in air weapons today, and that the first German V-1 was not launched against Britain until the fifth year of World War II, it is interesting to think how this little Bug might have changed the whole face of history if it had been allowed to develop without interruption during the years between the two wars. It was not perfect in 1918, of course, and as new gadgets and scientific improvements came out they continued to be incorporated into the Bug until the economy wave of the mid-twenties caused it to be shelved—to be dusted off, as we shall see, in 1942.

Meanwhile, in World War I the Bug accomplished at least one thing: it finally got me overseas. That trip, however, didn't materialize until nearly the end of the war, in October, 1918. Long before that, in the spring, as if all the fuses had been set for April and May, things began to happen in the air overseas.

First, on Sunday, April 14th, the word flashed that the U.S. 94th Pursuit Squadron had banged into combat to start the ball rolling. Two freshman pilots, Lieutenants Alan Winslow and Douglas Campbell, took off as part of the first American patrol, to head off two German planes reported approaching through clouds. As the Germans swept into the clear, with thousands of American, British, and French soldiers looking on from below, Winslow and Campbell closed on their tails, and in exactly four and a half minutes shot them down. Both German pilots bailed out behind our lines, and turned out to be experienced and somewhat surprised veterans.

From then on, it looked as if the long dreary months of preparations and attempts at preparations at home and abroad might pay off. Our pilots and our squadrons were in the war, and in a few weeks not only the Rickenbackers and Lufberys, or the old-timers of the Lafayette Escadrille, but a whole string of new names were to become American aces. And new names were becoming familiar among the young colonels, majors, captains, and lieutenants, some of them to be still more familiar in World War II as the names of Air Force generals.

Colonel W. G. Kilner who commanded at Issoudun was the same officer who headed the Kilner-Lindbergh Board in 1940, setting up the B-29 and other planes. His training officer was Major Tooey Spaatz, who shot down two German planes himself before he came home. There were Ted Curtiss, Spaatz's Chief of Staff in World War II; Lieutenant Everett Cook and Bill Stovall, to be two of his USSTAF Deputies in 1942-45; Lieutenant "Monk" Hunter, who years later was to bring the Eighth Air Force Fighter Command to England; Captain "Vic" Strahm, a future Chief of Staff of the Ninth Air Force; Lieutenant Harold Lee George, World War II Commander of ATC; the future General Ralph Royce, then the first U.S. squadron commander ever to receive a field order; Captain Clayton Bissell, who shot down five planes in that war, but had a tougher fight with Chiang Kai-shek in the second one—the list is too long to cover.

Another new name appeared for the first time that April—the R.A.F. The British merged their Royal Flying Corps of the Army and most of their Royal Naval Air Service into a separate Royal Air Force with its own Air Ministry in Whitehall. A small "Fleet Air Arm" was retained by the Royal Navy. The new independent R.A.F. was put under the command of Hugh Trenchard, now styled "Air Marshal," a forty-five-year-old pilot who, in the expansion of the R.F.C., had risen from Major to Major General within a year. Like Billy Mitchell, Trenchard had learned to fly in middle age (in 1912 when he was thirty-nine) and like Billy, he fought not only against the Germans but also for the cause of air power at home. He believed fanatically in the destiny of aviation in general, in peace, and in war.

All the air news received at home during that active April–May period was not good by any means. In fact, one reason for the reorganization of our Air Division into the "Air Service Division" in April, 1918, was a general dissatisfaction with the achievements of the Air Service, stemming from President Wilson on down. The appointments of J. D. Ryan to succeed Howard Coffin in charge of Aircraft Production, and of General Kenly to take over the Aircraft Division, were healthy in themselves. But it was ironic that just as our efforts to put a fighting American Air Service on the Western Front were beginning to click, the backlog of troubles finally attracted national attention, almost at the moment when they were being licked. The congressional investigations of the aircraft industry, another headed by my friend, Gutzon Borglum, another by Charles Evans Hughes, were pressed forward, with an understandable decline not only in public confidence but in the morale of everybody in the air picture.

Most aircraft manufacturers during the war I knew were intelligent, conscientious, and hard-working men, whether they were of the old "cut and try" group that had created and grown up with the industry, like Orville Wright, Glenn Curtiss, and Glenn Martin, or the younger men who had come into the industry or had become air-minded during the war. Among the latter, for example, were Donald Douglas and Jack Northrop with their M.I.T. backgrounds, Chance Vought, Reuben Fleet, Dutch Kindelberger, Phil Johnson, Guy Vaughan, and Don Brown who had come from technical or automotive industries in which precision manufacturing and working with special metals was an everyday affair.

World War I was a hard proving ground and practical school of experience for the men who years later were to build the foundation of our enormous aviation industry of the 1940's. In 1917–18 they tackled their own separate problems, developments in a dozen component fields, with zeal and initiative. There was a single over-all Air Force plan, but the daily coordination of that plan was lacking. Close integration by responsible air officers of actual combat and training operations with production was unheard of. The equipping of training planes to meet the requirements of our flying cadets; the timed switch of training-plane production to combat-plane production as the number of graduated cadets increased; the readying of equipment for training mechanics and other ground auxiliaries for the new squadrons; the assured presence of equipment, transportation, supplies; the proper replacements in men, planes, and materiel to insure that the outfit maintained its planned strength and location regardless of losses—all this was lacking; yet all these factors, and more, had to be in exact balance, or at the critical moment the planned Air Force would turn out to be made of paper.

In the midst of all this confusion there was an increase in the strength list of the family. William Bruce Arnold arrived on July 17, 1918.

A month or so before that event there had been a sudden step toward Air Force autonomy. General Squier had been ordered to confine his authority to Signal Corps duties. General Kenly, as "Director of Military Aeronautics," was to work directly under the Chief of Staff. Coequal with him was the "Director of Aircraft Production," Mr. Ryan.

Following up the terms of the Overman Act, the "Air Service of the National Army" was authorized on May 29th, "under presidential direction . . . the strength of the Division of Military Aeronautics to be 9807 officers and 109,801 enlisted men; that of the Bureau of Aircraft Production not specified in numbers." After further congressional action and War Department orders in June and July, the two parallel divisions were placed under the single authority of Mr. Ryan as Second Assistant Secretary of War and Director of Air Service, on August 28, 1918. Thus, the head of the first U.S. Army Air Service to stand on an "equal" footing with the other branches was neither an airman nor a soldier, but a highly capable civilian.

In France, where the air arm of the A.E.F. had already been called "the Air Service" for some time, there was an even more critical command snarl that spring. Colonel Billy Mitchell, with his dynamic personality, his colorful dash and determination to get things done, had just about assumed command of all American aviation in Europe by the time General Foulois, the appointee of the Secretary of War, arrived to take charge.

Mitchell had created splendid relationships with the French and the British, had made arrangements on his own to secure equipment that was not forthcoming from the United States, and without portfolio had established himself as the leader of the American Air Force in the war. Arriving nearly a year after Mitchell, Foulois, with a much more studious, careful, mechanical-minded experience of his own, dating back to the Army's first airplane, still had to make such contacts.

Pershing himself was dissatisfied with the slowness in getting American airplanes into combat. He was pleased only with the balloon setup. A clash between the red-tape-cutting Mitchell and General Foulois was bound to come, and come it did. Which man would the Commander of the A.E.F. select as his Air Chief?

Pershing selected neither. In a decision that affected the development of the American Air Corps for the next decade, he sent instead for an old West Point classmate, Brigadier General Mason M. Patrick of the Corps of Engineers.

"In this Army," he told Patrick, "there is but one thing that is causing me anxiety, and that is the Air Service. In it are a lot of good men, but they are running around in circles. Someone has got to make them go straight. I want you to do it."

Foulois was placed in command of the Air Force Services of Supply and Schools, in the rear area, with headquarters at Tours. General Billy Mitchell was placed in charge of all American Air Service Units under General Pershing. Colonel Thomas DeWitt Milling was in command of the Air Service Units of the First Army, which was commanded by Lieutenant General Hunter Liggett, and Colonel Frank P. Lahm was in charge of all Air Service Units in the Second Army which was commanded by Lieutenant General Robert Lee Bullard.

Cantigny came, with the British Fifth Army practically disappearing in shreds before Ludendorff's spring offensive. Pershing had already volunteered to throw his American units in wherever they could help, regardless of their state of training. Late May, and the Germans, who a few days before had been exultantly advancing, were falling back by bitter miles before those same untrained American troops. What part the Air Service was really playing in it was still hard to tell, though we knew they were not only carrying out constant reconnaissance missions, but fighting daily duels with German aces, mostly in French Spads and Nieuports, and British Sopwith Camels or SE-5's.

As the Second Marne developed, and Château-Thierry and Belleau Wood became household words, our air losses, like the Infantry's, were heavy. So were the German losses, though they still held a numerical air superiority.

So far, bombing had been mostly an enemy activity. Their Zeppelins, as well as a few of their airplanes, had carried it to England, though the Zeppelin offensive was rather disrupted, not by our planes or ack-ack guns but by nature, when on a single morning eleven of them returning from England were blown all over Europe by a storm, crashing or being captured from the North Sea to Africa. Out of the air fighting around Château-Thierry, however, had come a lot of hard experience for our flyers. Between mid-July on the Marne, and September in the Meuse-Argonne, there were two American air triumphs, if not four, which may have altered the course of the war. First, on the morning of July 15th, a critical reconnaissance mission was flown by Billy Mitchell himself, which discovered the German army starting to move south across the Marne on five pontoon bridges east of Dormans (all the bridges were supposed to be down). Mitchell gave Pershing's headquarters exact knowledge of the whole German push. Our airplanes also helped in breaking up the enemy offensive.

Three days later, on the 18th, another brilliant and perilous reconnaissance mission, carried out by Major Lewis Brereton, with Major Elmer Haslett as an observer, showed the Germans to be in full retreat at a moment when Pershing's staff were still unaware of it and reluctant to counterattack. On the basis solely of his air intelligence, the A.E.F.'s commander grabbed opportunity by the horns (or tail). The last, long, very tough pursuit began.

The air offensive which Mitchell laid on in the Meuse-Argonne in September was the greatest thing of its kind seen in the war, although the Germans had done it on a smaller scale. Billy himself had tried it on about one-fifteenth of the scale in the July fighting on the Marne. But the air attack that he launched as part of the American advance in the Meuse-Argonne between September 12th and 16th, 1918, was the first massed air striking power ever seen. Until then, the air fighting had been chiefly between individual pilots. With his mind full of what stronger, more coordinated numbers might have accomplished around Château-Thierry in July—with the successful bombing of the enemy supply center at Fère-en-Tardenois as an encouragement—he sold Pershing and the Allied High Command the idea, and early in August began assembling a force of 1500 combat planes—American, French, British, Italian, Belgian, Portuguese—every kind he could get his hands on. When the American ground forces—400,000 strong—struck, Mitchell struck ahead of them through the air.

In relays of 500 planes at a time, he hit the Germans' St. Mihiel salient on one flank, then on the other, then on both, then cut around both flanks, and hit them in the rear—the first attempt to apply the theory of "the isolation of the battlefield."

In one instance, Billy reported that 170 of his planes defeated a German counterattack by themselves. The accuracy of the enemy's artillery was repeatedly upset by the destruction of Ludendorff's observation balloons, a specialty of the American ace, Frank Luke, until he was killed. This was a reversal of the picture of recent months when it had been our own balloon observers who had had to bail out of their baskets three or four times a day with the burning bags collapsing above them.

The commander of this rugged type of observation work in France was my old friend, Colonel John Paeglow. In 1906, Paeglow had been a retired Army Sergeant serving as a Captain of the Philippine Scouts when he met General Pershing. Out in Jolo, Paeglow captured an outlaw, cut off his head and carried it in a sack to Pershing's headquarters on Christmas Day. This was the first Christmas Day after Teddy Roosevelt made Pershing a Brigadier General directly from a Captain, over the heads of 862 senior officers. General Pershing, looking over his gift, invited Captain Paeglow to have Christmas dinner with him. As Paeglow had only the clothing in which he had been crawling, climbing and hiking through the bosque, Pershing lent him a uniform of his own. So they ate Christmas dinner together, and they had been close friends ever since. When the war came, Paeglow had quickly volunteered for air duty after special training. He was sent overseas at once in charge of the Balloon Command.

There he soon had to be as relentless as with the machete in Jolo. Up in those balloons, aside from the fact that you might be burned up, or have a hole shot in you, or have to parachute down, it was cold, damp, rainy, foggy; missions lasted day and night, and you seldom saw anything. "Why," the balloon officers asked themselves, "reel out that 3000 to 4000 feet of cable for nothing all the time?" Paeglow knew this. In front of his billet he placed a center stake. Radiating from that center stake he set up five, six, or seven more stakes, depending on the number of balloon companies on duty at the Front at that particular moment. Then Paeglow would stand to the rear of the center stake and sight along each one of the outside radiating stakes to see the point at which every balloon should be. If any one was not up, all Paeglow had to do was go to the telephone, and then hell would begin to pop. Soon the troops in the surrounding area would see the missing gasbag rise rapidly toward the sky. Those balloon companies of Paeglow's did a great job, carrying out close-up reconnaissance from the Battle of Château-Thierry to the Armistice. In the early fall of 1918, it was good to know that our own new air superiority was giving them a much better chance of survival.

Indeed, in September, Mitchell assured General Pershing that the enemy could no longer carry out reconnaissance missions over our lines.

In World War II such a promise would have been impossible even at the most victorious moment. The great speed of World War II photo reconnaissance planes on both sides, operating at altitudes of 35,000–45,000 feet, made it impossible to intercept them surely even after the otherwise complete attainment of air superiority. Billy's promise to Pershing, however—who seems to have been convinced at last by the significance of his own air reconnaissance in the campaign, and therefore was anxious to keep enemy aerial observation away—was apparently justified.

After the war, Mitchell loved to tell the story of how he was walking toward his headquarters with Pershing himself one day when a German observation plane did appear at about 20,000 feet, miles behind the Allied Front. Pershing said nothing, but his face took on a look of concern. Our troops were starting to move into the big push, so far, it seemed, without the enemy's being aware of it. Mitchell knew, of course, that anywhere from two to six of our own Pursuits would be up to head off the intruder, but instead of saying so to Pershing, he waited until they reached his office. Picking up the telephone, he called an operational field and "ordered" that Pursuits be dispatched to intercept the German plane. Almost before he could hang up, the phone rang back. Billy took it, and turned nonchalantly to General Pershing. "Enemy reconnaissance plane going down in flames five miles southwest of Chaumont, Sir," he said. "Care to step out and look?"

Such stories from France redoubled and quadrupled my itch to get over there. The memorandum of May 21st, however, seemed to have killed my last chance. It had designated me as Assistant to the Director of Military Aeronautics. That job—No. 2 man in the Washington headquarters of the newly authorized Air Service—may have looked very good for the moment, but I was convinced that without combat experience my future in the air arm was limited.

When I was informed in September that General Pershing was interested in the possibilities of the Bug I decided to take over the details immediately to demonstrate it to him. Arriving in New York in the midst of the influenza epidemic, I boarded the S.S. *Olympic,* ostensibly as Commanding Officer, but actually coming down with pneumonia.

Before I passed out of the picture completely, I had just time to call the conscientious Major Reuben Fleet to my cabin and explain to him hoarsely that a telegram had been received from General Pershing stating that of all the troops moving overseas, the Air Service officers and Chaplains presented the worst appearance and were the most undis-

ciplined. This must be corrected. Exercises, drills, and training would be
given by Major Fleet on the broad decks during the voyage. There must
be no such report on Air Service troops and Chaplains disembarking
from the *Olympic*. Nothing more, officially, was brought to my attention.

The next thing I remember clearly was being put into an ambulance
on the Southampton dock with three other men at ten o'clock at night,
in a drizzling rain, and starting for a hospital at Hersey Castle, right outside Winchester. There wasn't a sign of a light anywhere. A fine, pene-
trating rain was falling, and it was cold as it can only be in England. Not
a sound was heard until a faint murmur reached us from ahead. As we
drew closer the sound became more distinct. It was Major Reuben Fleet,
marching his Chaplains and Air Corps officers from Southampton to
Winchester, at attention, in the rain, in the dark, at eleven o'clock at
night. "One, two, three, four. Damn you, Chaplains, keep in step! One,
two, three, four. Damn you, Chaplains, keep in step!" It is about twelve
miles from Southampton docks to Winchester, but he was making
soldiers out of them.

Convalescing at Hersey Hospital, a makeshift building whose old-
fashioned coal stoves smoked up a fresh epidemic of coughing among
the pneumonia-bronchitis-laryngitis patients each morning when the fires
were started, I was visited by all sorts of people who told me what was
going on outside. They warned me I'd better hurry if I wanted to see
any of the war. It was almost over.

By the time I was released from the hospital and got over to the headquarters of the First Army, I heard that preliminary discussions leading
toward a truce were already under way. As an armistice was scheduled
for November 11th at eleven o'clock, and as the weather was too bad
for me to fly over the lines, I decided I would go up to the Front with
the infantry. Accompanied by a Colonel Hunter of the 31st British
Lancers, I drove through Verdun to the Argonne, where we joined
the 103rd Infantry. There we saw the last of the war, and I found myself—the only time I ever saw any fighting in World War I, and then
I didn't see much—back with the doughboys.

During my stay at First Army Headquarters, I again met George
Marshall, who was running General Liggett's Plans Section. I hadn't
seen him since the Philippines in 1914.

It was too late to put over the Bug, of course, but the inspection
tour I made of our air installations in France—everywhere I went I
seemed to come on another U.S. Army Air Service training field—was

an illuminating experience, some parts filling out the picture in a wonderful way, other parts of it disappointing.

At Chaumont, General Patrick invited me to express my full and most critical reactions to all air installations without hesitation. I did so, and in later years, when General Patrick was in Washington as Chief of the Air Service, and I as one of his staff officers, I had time to wonder if this had been an altogether wise thing on my part.

At Chaumont, too, as at many of the bases, I had the unique experience of seeing "the other end of the line"—that is, just what had come out of the horn we had been filling all those eighteen months back home.

Billy Mitchell was on top of the world at that time. In his headquarters at Souilly, it was plain that the stories about Brigadier General William E. Mitchell had not been exaggerated. Laughing and constantly talking, wearing that blouse with the outsize patch-pockets, and the famous pink breeches (the decorations that dazzled Washington were not in evidence, though his sister said later they were in his pockets), Billy practically held court. American, British, and French airmen—and generals— streamed in to see him. The flyers around him would have done anything for him, and so would the boys out in the squadrons. On the night of the Armistice in Paris, he had to be rescued by the police from a joyful mob of French pilots cheering, *"Vive nôtre Général Américain."* Billy was as clearly the Prince of the Air now as the Prince of Wales (whom he shortly took for a ride in his plane without anybody's permission) was the heir to the throne! He had his personal planes, two automobiles— one a gift from the French Government, the other a rakish Mercedes said to be the fastest car in France, which he drove himself at breakneck speed around the countryside with his chauffeur sitting behind—he had two American aides (the outstanding combat airmen Winslow and Haslett, both of whom had been shot down and captured, rejoining him after the Armistice)—and he had a French aide. All were kept busy. Upon meeting a French officer, Billy would start his enthusiastic French, run out of French words, and without pausing, continue rapidly in English. But in whatever language he spoke, everybody seemed to understand him. Not only airmen like Trenchard, who had called his Meuse-Argonne offensive "the most terrific exhibition I have ever seen—you have cleaned out the air," but Allied ground force officers listened attentively as Billy expounded Air Power.

Mitchell received Pershing's tacit approval before November 11th arrived for a very special project of an even greater concentration of

Allied airplanes than the September force. It was to include night bombers for day operations and was to see the beginning of a heavy bombardment offensive against Germany's homeland. Had Metz held out, he had prepared in detail plans for an operation which called for the dropping of a strong part of the 1st Division behind the German lines by parachute. That operation, as it was worked out, was a complete example of modern paratroop tactics, long years before the Germans, Russians, or British even thought of them.

In a sense, for Billy, the Armistice was an untimely interruption—as if the whistle had ended the game just as he was about to go over the goal line.

Watching him and listening to him, I realized how much we needed him back in Washington. There, a different kind of war was going to continue. Ryan had asked to be released as soon as possible in order to return to his business. There would be a new Chief of Staff in Washington now, and of course it would be General Pershing. Following the tradition of all returning battlefront commanders, he would certainly bring his own staff to the War Department. The Air Service needed Billy back home, fast, and with every argument I could muster I tried to convince him of this fact.

Why shouldn't he capitalize on his war record and be the new Air Chief? Could he swing it with Pershing, I asked him. Taking off the necessary percentage which one had always to subtract from Billy's enthusiasm—for instance, the "destroyed" railway station at Metz-Sablon was still in good shape when I saw it, the trains running in and out on schedule—there was still nobody who could possibly move into the Air Service job at home in the way that General Mitchell could and undoubtedly would. He, above all others, had the background, the reputation, the personal courage, the knowledge of air operations to do the job. He should be the Chief.

Billy smiled and said, "No." At least, he insisted firmly, "Later. My boys are going into Germany, and I'm going with them. I want to see this thing through."

He wanted to drive that fastest Mercedes in France down Unter den Linden.

I said good-by, and while he and Tommy Milling prepared to go to Germany via Belgium, I went back to Paris for a few days before returning home.

About two nights before I was scheduled to leave, the phone in my hotel room rang with a long distance call. It was Billy calling from a small town in Flanders. "Listen," he said, "as soon as you get back there, have orders issued getting me home. I want to get home as fast as possible. Right away. Can you do that?"

I thought I could. Something must have changed his mind up there. "O.K., Bill," I said, and started for England and home the next day.

☆ *6* ☆

When I returned from Europe, I had no trouble in getting Billy Mitchell's orders cut, but I found I had worked myself out of a job. In January, 1919, I was ordered from Washington to Rockwell Field, North Island, San Diego, California, as District Supervisor, Western District of the Air Service.

The Rockwell Field I found when I arrived there from Washington was not the one I had left when I went with the 7th Aero Squadron to Panama in 1917. Old North Island, which had begun its aviation career when the Spreckels Company had offered it to Glenn Curtiss as a site for a flying school in the winter of 1910–11, was now occupied at one end by the Navy, at the other end by the Army.

My chief problem involved personnel. The Army station on North Island, Rockwell Field, had been a gunnery school. It consisted of the home station on the island itself, and two outlying stations farther down the bay. There were some 375 officers there and about 8000 enlisted men. They were all excellent men and included some first-rate pilots, most of whom had been ready, as far as training was concerned, to go overseas for combat, but as an outfit they were not happy.

All over the country in 1919, of course, our air arm was a mixed-up world for those of us who had to keep it going. Although the League of Nations had already been practically rejected in Washington, the popular postwar feeling of disarmament and no-more-war-forever was strong in America. Even before the ink on the Armistice of 1918 was dry, the armed forces of the United States were ordered to shrink themselves down to an irreproachable minimum, and shrink down fast.

The position of the Air Force in this matter was rather peculiar, for it was entirely a wartime creation. It couldn't very well go back to the

16 planes and 26 pilots that had started on the Mexican Border in 1916. The 700 pilots, observers, mechanics, and other personnel who had hoped to remain in the Air Service as a career had achieved their status only after April, 1917. If the Air Service was reduced now in proportion to the rest of the Army, it would disappear entirely.

My job as Commanding Officer was to discharge officers and enlisted men as rapidly as I could and at the same time comply with War Department regulations relative to separations from the service. But that was not as easy a task as it may seem, for there were many officers and enlisted men who could not make up their minds whether they wanted to continue in the service or wanted to get out. Meanwhile, those who did stay in had to continue their training and we had to supply the necessary airplanes and instructors for that purpose.

It was at this time, for instance, that Captain A. D. Smith led a group of five JN's from their home station in San Diego across the United States to Florida and back. It was quite a feat, for the Jenny was far from a cross-country airplane.

About the same time I was ordered to have two airplanes fly from San Diego to Phoenix to take part in a Victory Loan drive. I remember the pilots well. They were typical of the entire group of war pilots, cocky even in their disregard of instruments and maps. Why worry? They could fly anywhere, any time. Like many others in those early days after the war, they were content, despite my instructions about maps, to rely principally upon the "iron compass"—the railroad tracks.

Somewhere out in the desert wasteland one of the JN's ran out of gasoline and had to make a forced landing.

Soon the other pilot came back to look for him and saw his friend on the ground. In landing on the soggy stretch of ground, the second pilot turned his plane upside down. Neither the pilots nor their two passengers had the slightest idea where they were. None of the airmen had even taken a careful look at the ground before they set their planes down.

As a last resort, they decided to take the gasoline out of the nosed-over plane and put it into the first one. Then they would fly two men out and get help. The transfer of gasoline was completed, but in front of the airplane with the gasoline was a small swamp. That made no difference to those boys. They were good. They were so good they could run the Jenny along the ground, get up speed, and bounce the plane into the air; cross the swamp, hit the wheels on the other side, and take off. Well, presently there were two planes on their backs and four men stranded, looking at the wrecks. Fortunately, no one was hurt.

For nearly a week the discomfited and hungry airmen lived on grasshoppers. Then an owl attracted their attention and they shot it. Then, much to their astonishment, they came upon some cattle and killed a steer. The men were resourceful; they took a piece of the metal side of the engine cowling and made a pan and stewed some of the steer meat in it. During the night, however, a coyote came, took the meat from where it was hanging on the wrecked plane, and cleaned the steer's bones. Two days later, while looking for another steer, they met a cowboy. At that time, because of relations between Mexico and the United States, all airmen were suspicious of everyone they met along the Border, so these men immediately drew their revolvers. The cowboy told them in no uncertain English to put their guns back in their holsters. He then took them to a ranch house—less than half a mile from the spot where they had landed.

All our lost airmen, however, did not have the same luck. A tragic case was that of Lieutenants Waterhouse and Connolly. They were flying from Yuma to San Diego in a DH. It was a common thing in those days to hear an airman say, "My compass went bad." It was hard to make them realize that if properly checked and "swung" at regular intervals, the compass was their best friend.

It was many weeks before we found the story of Waterhouse and Connolly scratched on the side of their airplane far down along the Gulf of Lower California: "Came to the Pacific; turned right to go north."

As a matter of fact, after getting lost in storm clouds, they had turned completely around, and instead of reaching the Pacific Ocean, they had gone to the Gulf of Lower California. There they turned right, and had flown south.

"Flew for four hours and twenty minutes until we ran out of gas, then landed on the beach," read the scratched message. The search for Waterhouse and Connolly was one of the greatest in history. We had a hunch they were somewhere in Lower California and drew circles ten miles apart across a map of Lower California, starting at the Border. Each day we would take an additional ten-mile circle and comb it from coast to coast, and just as we were about to go into the final area—the one in which Waterhouse and Connolly and their plane were finally found—the search was called off as useless.

These two young men had tried to walk out, then returned to their plane. They had lived for days on water from the radiator of their plane and on fish caught with improvised tackle. It was later established that they were so weak from thirst and hunger that they could no longer protect themselves, despite the fact they still carried their service pistols. A Mexican had beached his boat near them and picked them up. He told the airmen he would take them south to a spring. There he had murdered them.

About this time I met a man who was to be a lifelong friend. One day my Adjutant came in and said, "Colonel, there is a man down at Ream Field whose conduct has been so bad it requires your personal attention." I asked who this man was. "Chap by the name of Doolittle," replied the Adjutant. "Second Lieutenant James H."

It seemed that Doolittle, Second Lieutenant James H., had been sitting in front of a hangar, bored. Another pilot was about to practice landings and take-offs. To the man sitting beside him, Doolittle said, "I'll bet you five bucks I can sit on his landing gear while he lands." His friend laughed, but on seeing that Doolittle was serious, quickly took the bet. Doolittle approached the unsuspecting pilot and asked if he would take him up for a ride. The pilot replied, "Sure, hop aboard." But as soon as they had leveled off in the air, the pilot's good nature was turned to consternation as he saw his passenger climb down to the lower wing then underneath to seat himself on the cross bar between the fixed wheels of the landing gear. Nothing he could shout through the roar of the engine seemed to reach Doolittle; none of his frantic gestures attracted Doolittle's attention. There Doolittle sat until the sweating pilot had to land. When the plane rolled to a stop, Doolittle walked over to the group of open-mouthed spectators and said to his friend, "Pay me."

I knew there was only one sort of punishment that would impress that kind of man, and I grounded the chap by the name of Doolittle for a month.

The officer most responsible for the progress of the Air Service, for maintaining the interest and morale of its personnel in those lean years, was General Billy Mitchell. He was badly disappointed when he came home from Europe and found he was not to command it and that he was to serve as Assistant Chief of Air Service and Director of Military Aeronautics, under Major General C. T. Menoher, a former commander of the 42nd (Rainbow) Division, who had been appointed, without any aviation experience or qualifications, Chief of the Air Service in December, 1918. Mitchell at once began the running battle which was to increase the Air Arm's vitality and lead, in the end, to his own elimination from the Army. By the middle of 1919 he had been instrumental in setting up a series of projects which quickly began to snap our pilots out of their doldrums and put them on their toes, develop the possibilities of the airplanes and their crews, and attract a certain amount of popular attention. They also began a new pattern of national usefulness in peacetime.

In June, 1919, my job as District Supervisor of the Western District was abolished and I was ordered to San Francisco on the staff of General Hunter Liggett where I was given charge of all aviation in the western part of the United States. I was happy to serve under General Liggett, who had commanded the First Army in France, for I had known him years before.

We were trying to find ourselves during this period—trying to find out how the airplane could be used and what value it might be to the public. Out on the West Coast we carried on an innovation strictly our own. That was aerial Forest Fire Patrol. I set it up in June, 1919, and it was continued by the Army Air Service for some years until the Forest Service was able to take it over with planes rented from civilians. We made air patrols over the forests in the West from the Cascade and Olympic Mountains, along the Sierra Nevada and Coast ranges down to the Sierra Madre. Our purpose was to find out if the airplane could detect and locate fires and direct the fire fighters in their suppression work. The Forest Fire Patrols operated from bases in the valleys and flew over mountain peaks and the high points in the ranges. This service not only reduced the actual fire damage in the timberland to a marked degree and thus saved millions of dollars in timber, but it also accustomed our pilots to some of the most difficult cross-country flying in the world.

In the fall of 1919, Mitchell, in order to stimulate interest in aviation and open up airways across the country, made plans for the first transcontinental air race. This was not a mere sporting event, any more than was the later speed competition for the Schneider Cup, which ultimately led to the creation of the Spitfire, so effectively used in the Battle of Britain. Although an Army Air Service affair, the transcontinental race was, in fact, the foundation of commercial aviation in the United States.

Prior to that, there were no established air routes, no communications facilities, no system of linked air bases in this country. Not a single commercial air line was in operation. Our little five-mile hops with the first air mail from Nassau Boulevard to Garden City, New York, in 1911, had suggested that someday mail might be carried in planes. The Washington-to-New York air experiment started in 1918 was an effective attempt by the Air Service to give the Post Office Department a shot in the arm. After the Armistice, several hundred independent pilots had bought war surplus Jennies and DH's and had started barnstorming around the country, offering rides and participating in local fairs and air shows and trying to start small businesses of one kind or another, but they had no organized contact. They flew anything and anywhere to gain an honest dollar, but followed no regular cross-country routes.

It was always Billy Mitchell's idea that aeronautics could establish air bases and airways anywhere in the world, and that wherever air power could operate it could dominate sea lanes against navies, land areas against armies, and connect various population centers, even the most inaccessible points, with rapid lines of communication. He felt that if military airways were set up to pave the way, commercial air expansion would quickly follow with a resultant exchange of passengers, goods, and services.

Early in 1919, he had prophesied in the magazine *Air Service* that in another few years commercial air passengers would be as familiar a sight as travelers on trains; that distances between, say New York and Chicago, would be figured in terms of hours, not miles.

In the transcontinental air race, the plan was for thirty pilots to take off from San Francisco for New York, and return, while simultaneously, thirty other Army pilots took off from New York for San Francisco and return, the winner to be the first pilot to complete the round trip. When Mitchell planned the transcontinental race there were no facilities along the way to take care of the competing aircraft, so our first task was to provide them. The top speed of the planes that would participate, mostly DH's, was under 130 miles per hour. None of the planes could fly more than about 300 miles without landing to refuel, and none was equipped to fly at night. Consequently, some of us went out as advance officers to visit the city fathers in the various communities where we wished to put the landing fields. In general, both city fathers and ordinary citizens were highly interested, not only in the idea of having planes come in and out of their towns, but in the race itself.

The string of airport facilities located about 200 miles apart—with emergency fields sometimes only 50 miles from each other—all properly staffed with mechanics, fuel, and spare parts, in touch with each other by telephone, telegraph, and sometimes even radio, sprang up rapidly from west to east, from east to west, making a 3000-mile course across forest, farm land, desert, mountains, and rivers.

The difficulties encountered were many and different in each section of the country. In one case, it might be the creation of a flying field in the mountains at an altitude above 7000 feet; in another, the building of landing strips at the bottom of a deep valley.

The race demonstrated that it was possible for airplanes with average pilots to fly across the United States, regardless of topographical features, if suitable bases and communication facilities were available and proper navigational aids employed. It also paved the way for what later was to be the air-mail service across the continent, though until 1923 the air mail traveled by plane only in the daytime, being transferred to trains at night. In 1919 and 1920, however, as increased acquaintance with airplanes and wider experience with cross-country navigation built up confidence, Air Service officers were already regarding night flying as a necessary qualification for all pilots.

Prior to the transcontinental race, Mitchell had sent Lieutenant Colonel R. S. Hartz and Lieutenant E. E. Harmon and their crew in a Martin M-2 bomber around the boundaries of the United States, a distance of 9000 miles. Such flights as Hartz's and those of the transcontinental flyers fired the imagination of our pilots and made flying a practical affair.

The Cal Rodgers flight in 1911, requiring fifty-nine days from coast to coast, had really been only a stunt. Commander A. C. Reed, the only pilot to finish the flight of the Navy's NC-4's across the Atlantic to England by way of the Azores and Portugal in May, 1919, had proved the great skill and fortitude of his crew. Alcock and Brown, who flew a British bomber from Newfoundland a month later and crash-landed in an Irish field, also had great skill and great bravery. But none of these flights indicated that the airplane had yet reached the stage where it could be used on regular transcontinental and trans-Atlantic flights. Most of them were freak flights, depending on the determination and will-to-do of the flyer.

As time passed, men like Byrd and his crew, and Clarence Chamberlain, and young women like Amelia Earhart surpassed the flights made by their predecessors. But events like our first transcontinental air race were of real benefit in the future development of civil aviation and commercial air lines.

Another operation that kept our airmen busy was the Border Patrol, started by Mitchell. The troops along the Mexican Border had not yet disbanded. Villa's raids had not been forgotten and there were still petty disturbances. To help the Internal Revenue Department prevent illegal crossing of the Rio Grande—in those desolate wastes a walking man could be seen for miles from the air—and also to maintain a show of military force, the Air Service set up a regular patrol from Brownsville, Texas, along the Rio Grande to El Paso, and then westward, following the border to San Diego. Our airdromes were located in little towns along the route about 150 to 200 miles apart. The patrols flew twice daily, both eastbound and westbound.

Operations along these hundreds of arid miles soon proved at least as toughening for the pilots as the missions over the mountains on the Forest Fire Patrol. We learned a lot of things the hard way, especially regarding navigation and the need to secure accurate flight plans before taking off. Our staffs learned the mechanics of supply and administration for small units covering areas of 2000 miles. For instance, my own domain extended from a point in Arizona along the Mexican Border to San Diego, and then north for 1400 miles to the Canadian Border.

It was in connection with the Border Patrol that I first saw Billy Mitchell after his return from Europe. He flew down to the Border and ended up at El Paso just to see how things were getting along, and on the Fourth of July, 1919, I went down there to meet him. I remember the exact date very well because it was the day an almost unknown heavyweight named Jack Dempsey took the championship away from the giant Jess Willard in less than four rounds.

Our host was a tough, bewhiskered old Cavalryman, Colonel Tommy Tompkins, who expressed admiration for the air Border Patrol, and said what a good thing it would be if we could fly right across the Border down to Chihuahua, Pancho Villa's own province, to take a look at the new trouble which was rumored to be stirring up down there at that moment.

Without waiting a second, Billy Mitchell said, "Well, come on. What are you waiting for? Let's do it!" Tommy Tompkins was a Cavalryman from his misshapen campaign hat to his boots and spurs. He lived to ride the plains, patrol the Border, and run down renegades, but this abrupt defiance of international protocol apparently horrified him for a moment. "Why, we can't do a thing like that," he exclaimed. "The hell we can't," said Billy. "Come on, let's get moving. Here's the airplane."

Billy piloted the plane himself. I can still see old Tommy Tompkins with his whiskers blowing out from both sides of his face when he took off on his first, and perhaps his only, airplane ride—one that was completely against regulations.

I remember well when I wanted to establish a base line along the Border to take photographs. I figured that from a high altitude I might photograph a strip ten miles wide south of the Border, so we put in white concrete markers every ten miles or so along the Border—circles, squares, triangles, crosses, or anything that would be distinctive. Then we started taking photographs. From the results, one might well have thought that we were invading Mexico. United States Army Inspectors appeared from all directions to learn why we had violated War Department regulations. We received letters from the Corps Area and from the War Department directing us to explain our conduct. As a matter of fact, I doubt if any of our photo planes were ever more than two miles south of the Border, and furthermore, no one on the ground could have possibly told whether we were north or south of the Border; but that was the way we did business in those days. So I leaned over backward to play safe.

I could see a change in Billy Mitchell that summer. He was sharper, more alert than ever. I knew him well, and I could see he felt his office in the War Department was not the gay, triumphant headquarters he had had in France during World War I. Billy had always been an eager preacher of the possibilities of air power, but now his experiences in France and perhaps the things he was encountering in Washington had given him an undercurrent of angry impatience. He seemed to brush aside the possibility that a lot of people still might not understand his theories, and he could not be convinced that air power was not being blocked by deliberate and well-organized enemies.

Billy said it was primarily the Navy, the entrenched Admirals "unable to face the fact that sea power was done for." Old-fashioned generals in the War Department were a big part of it, too. Billy's feeling about profit-seekers at that time was largely directed against the heavy industries behind the battleship. His main thought when I saw him in El Paso that summer seemed to be to show them—with activities like the transcontinental air race, the Border Patrol, the Forest Fire Patrol, and now with a mass flight to Alaska and a mass flight around the world— and above all, to sink those damned battleships!

Again and again, he pressed for a chance to show the Navy and the world what airplanes and bombs could do to the best battleship ever built. The United States Navy then had some of the former German warships in its possession, including the big battleship *Ostfriesland*. They were no good to anybody, but would the Navy give the Air Force a chance at them? "Hell, no!" said Billy, with a grin on his face. "Can you guess why? Well, we'll see. Keep going the way you are. We're going to get them and we're going to sink them."

Soon after I got back to San Francisco he wrote me again: "I am very anxious to push through this flight to Alaska with land planes. Better get oriented along that line as to the possibilities from your department north. This might develop into a round-the-world flight."

In the summer of 1919, Assistant Secretary of War Crowell headed an investigating board to go to Europe and look into the various air organizations and make recommendations about what we should do in the United States. On its return, the Board was so inclined toward Mitchell's views that Admiral Benson, Chief of Naval Operations, was stung into telling Howard Coffin, one of the Crowell Board members, that he was wasting his time, and "furthermore," Benson said, "I cannot conceive of any use the fleet will ever have for aircraft." Later the Admiral told Mr. Crowell, "The Navy doesn't need airplanes."

When Billy Mitchell learned that Admiral Benson was about to issue an order abolishing the Naval Air Arm, it was right down his alley. However, he didn't have a chance to say much, for the Assistant Secretary of the Navy, Franklin D. Roosevelt, immediately came out with a statement that it wasn't so, and anyway, if it were so, he hadn't heard about it. Mr. Roosevelt, whom I had known slightly in Washington during World War I, and whom I was to know in far closer friendship some twenty years later, felt very differently about the Air Arm.

When he was asked by Senator Wadsworth, Chairman of the Military Affairs Committee, if it might not become the principal factor in the Navy or the Army, Mr. Roosevelt replied, "It might conceivably, in the Navy, become the principal factor. I don't know whether the Chief of Naval Operations will agree with me, but I might say that later on, in the future, aviation might make surface ships practically impossible to be used as an Arm."

Those who visited Billy Mitchell in his office in Washington those days were immediately led to a globe, and Mitchell would run his finger from Alaska down to Natal, off the coast of Brazil, then up to the islands at the mouth of the St. Lawrence River. He would tell all who would listen to him or read what he wrote, that air power made these locations "the three-pronged suspension of our real national defense"; that other fortifications, including the Navy, were obsolete.

He wrote articles on the subject for magazines, and before a Senate committee in October, 1919, with one of those impetuous but somehow accurate gestures that were so characteristic of him, he even changed the third point—the mouth of the St. Lawrence River—and shoved his finger across the Atlantic to Iceland. On this occasion, as was happening more and more often, he lashed out with one of those impatient criticisms which, like a ringmaster's whip, would crack at some complacent performer in the government who, until then, had never thought of himself as having anything to do with air power. This time it was the State Department.

In 1916, Grinnell Land and Grant Land, originally discovered by our American General Greely, had been traded to Denmark for the Virgin Islands. "Had the advice of any airman been sought when this transaction was taking place," Billy told the Senate committee, "decided recommendations would have been against giving up this land which would form an ideal air base for commercial air traffic to Europe and Asia in case of war."

The first flight to Alaska, under command of Captain St. Clair Streett, took place in July, 1920, starting from Mitchel Field, Long Island, New York, in DH's. It was a great achievement for that day, and in those airplanes, for any day. It may seem strange that, two years after the war, this top priority mission was entrusted to the same old DH's that had been the subject of so much criticism during the war.

Despite Mitchell's hammering on the theme that airplanes, especially a military airplane, became obsolete the minute you began to build it, no one in authority from the President down to the War Department, nor members of the Congressional or Senate committees, paid much attention to Billy's warnings of the danger of the static equipment situation then existing.

There were hundreds of Liberty 400 h.p. engines still in storage. The fact that the DH's could accomplish such a remarkable mission as Streett's Arctic flight simply proved in the eyes of Congress and the War Department how durable they were.

There were many other records set with the DH's in those early days, not because it was such a wonderful plane, but because it was all we had.

The special sort of "outlaw" status of the Air Force was felt even in faraway California, and not just because of the Mitchell controversy. The National Defense Act of 1920 created once and for all an air service on a par with other branches of the Army, and gave us the power to procure our own equipment, which caused considerable grumbling in the ground forces. It was this provision, I believe, rather than the 1514 officers and 16,000 enlisted men, that caused so much comment, for it constituted a theoretical threat to the budget of other parts of the Army. The fact that the rating of "Airplane Pilot," a new designation, now established permanent flight pay of 50 per cent, was another grievance.

It was while I was at General Liggett's headquarters, in 1920, that we lost our temporary war rank and reverted to our permanent status. Major "Tooey" Spaatz, my assistant, had won his temporary rank in combat and so retained it by law. I went from the rank of Colonel to Captain. On the morning the orders came through, I arrived at the office first and moved all of Tooey's stuff into my desk in my office, and vice versa.

When he arrived, he was aghast. "What the hell is this all about?" he exclaimed. I explained that he was in command now and I was his assistant and ready to carry out any orders he cared to give me.

I said, "Look, Tooey. Law is law. You are in command now and you can't change it." Tooey looked at me for a moment and then left the office. A few minutes later he returned and said, "Well, everything is fixed up." It soon developed that he had gone straight to General Liggett himself, had submitted the case to him for a Solomon's judgment, and had gotten orders out having himself transferred to Mather Field rather than take my job away from me. So, because of Tooey Spaatz' Pennsylvania Dutch stubbornness, I was left in charge as West Coast Air Officer, as a Captain. A few months later I was made a Major.

Billy Mitchell came out to the West Coast again in 1920 to attend the American Legion Convention and, as usual, the ovation that greeted him was tremendous. A flight of 24 Navy planes had also headed for the celebration at San Francisco, but because of bad weather, were spread all over California. To the newspaper reporters eagerly waiting for just such a remark, Billy cracked, "What more can you expect from the Navy than that?"

Nevertheless, the naval allies who came to Mitchell's side in this argument that was rapidly becoming a battle were surprising. Not only Admiral William S. Sims, our own brilliant C. in C. in European Waters in World War I ("The average man suffers very severely from the pain of a new idea. . . . It is my belief that the future will show that the fleet that has 20 airplane carriers instead of 16 battleships and 4 airplanes will inevitably knock the other fleet out.")—not only Americans like the great naval inventor Admiral Bradley Fiske, and quite a few others—but some of the very fathers of the battleship in Britain spoke out as if they themselves were airmen. Admiral Sir Percy Scott, the pioneer of modern naval gunnery, asked the London *Times:* "What is the use of the battleship?" And Admiral Sir Jack Fisher, First Sea Lord of the Admiralty, gave what Isaac Don Levine in his biography of Mitchell describes as a Biblical warning. "By land and by sea the approaching aircraft development knocks out the present fleet, makes invasion practicable, cancels our country being an island, transforms the atmosphere into a battle ground of the future. There is only one thing to do to the ostriches who are spending these vast millions on what is as useful for the next war as bows and arrows. Sack the lot. As the locusts swarmed over Egypt, so will aircraft swarm in the heavens, carrying inconceivable cargoes of men and bombs, some fast and some slow. Some will act like battle cruisers and others as destroyers. All cheap and—this is the gist of it—requiring only a few men as crew." Our own Admiral W. F. Fullam concluded an exhaustive analysis at this time with the statement that henceforth "Sea power will be subordinated to or dependent upon air power."

So Mitchell's fight with the Navy over the battleships was not just a simple fight between the Army, the Navy, and the little Air Service. It was really a battle of ideas, involving air-minded people and non-air-minded people in both services. But Mitchell's constant use of the press to put his ideas across oversimplified the question. His hot pressure to get a crack at sinking the German battleships, and the extreme opposition of such key figures as Secretary of the Navy Josephus Daniels made it seem like a straight fight between the Air Service and the Navy. A lot of people never realized that we were finding more of an obstacle, or at least just as much of an obstacle, in the Army itself. Our Chief, General Menoher, was not only unable and wholly unwilling to cope with Mitchell's ideas, but he could not handle Billy Mitchell. Also, to make matters worse, he did not fly much.

Regardless of where they were, all air officers did what they could to keep the Air Arm before the public. Once, for example, in 1921, I flew a race against pigeons. Radios then were not in general use for air-to-ground communications except at very short range. We still released carrier pigeons from our airplanes over longer distances.

A newspaper in San Francisco started an argument by speculating which could fly the faster—pigeons or airplanes. I accepted the challenge for the airplane and the Signal Corps accepted the challenge for the pigeon, and soon I was carrying a coop of pigeons—famous pigeons—with me to Portland, Oregon, from whence the race was to start to San Francisco. These pigeons were all known by name, rank, and serial number, and some of them had distinguished combat records.

The Governor of Oregon, Ben Olcott, was an aviation enthusiast and always wanted to accompany me on my trips. I picked him up at Salem and took him on to Portland. Early next morning, with much publicity, the birds were released. They took it in a routine manner, making a broad turn over the field, then taking off for their coops in San Francisco.

Unfortunately, airplanes did not have self-starters then, as the pigeons had. The weather was cold, and the Liberty engine was hard to start. I had had to drop off my mechanic when I picked up the Governor, so I had no one there who knew the engine as he did. This business of pulling the propeller of a Liberty engine "through" was no task for a small boy. To make a long story short, even using the Governor to pull —and everybody else on the airport—it required forty-five minutes to start the engine. This gave the pigeons a good forty-five minutes' lead, so when we finally took off, they were out of sight.

There were few radio broadcasts in those days, but the newspapers sponsoring the flight pasted bulletins on their windows, and crowds on San Francisco's Market Street blocked all traffic for hours, awaiting the outcome of the race. The excitement was terrific. Betting was taking place just as at a race track. There were even "bookies" there offering odds on which would win—the pigeons or the airplane.

Certainly somebody with remarkable eyesight, who apparently could identify a pigeon by name at a couple of thousand feet, must have kept the newspaper abreast of the race, for the reports kept coming in: "Miss America is flying over Albany"; "War Bird is flying over Salem"; "Columbia is now over Roseburg"; "Diamond Head is over Eugene." Miss America, for instance, was over Red Bluff before my plane reached Medford, Oregon, to refuel.

As pigeon after pigeon neared its home coop, Governor Olcott and I munched sandwiches and refueled at Medford, practically ready to concede the race. But apparently pigeons, as well as pilots, make private plans in flying their cross-country missions, for none of the feathered war heroes reached their home base until forty-eight hours later. The Governor and I had completed our flight in about seven and a half hours.

Our Air Force was small in those days, but the pilots were good. I think it might well be said that any one of our boys, picked at random, could have made nonstop flights across oceans or continents had the planes been available. I am thinking now of Lieutenant W. D. Coney who always had ambitions to make a transcontinental flight. In 1921 he came to me with the idea of putting extra tanks on his DH which he thought would enable him to fly nonstop across the country.

Prior to getting ready for that flight, one day at Eugene, Oregon, he went up to make one of the first exhibition parachute jumps that the Army Air Forces had ever made. His chute suddenly opened by mistake. It could well have pulled him out of his seat, and the pilot, Captain Lowell Smith, also, for Smith had reached around to grasp Coney. The whipping chute streamed out like a string and blew across the tail surface. Smith soon realized what would happen if the chute opened, so he released Coney to save both of them from being pulled through the horizontal stabilizer.

Breathlessly, the crowd below watched as Coney crawled calmly out of the cockpit, down the steps, and took hold of the control wires. He then dropped, hanging to those wires with his bare hands. In a ninety-mile-an-hour wind, along that thin wire, sharp as a knife blade, Coney pulled himself hand over hand, with Smith skidding the plane, trying to toss the chute free.

Finally Coney dropped. He opened his emergency chute and came down safely, but with his hands sliced through to the bones.

Soon after this, Coney started on his long-planned cross-country flight. He made it from Rockwell Field to Jacksonville in 22 hours and 27 seconds flat. On the return trip, in a storm over Louisiana, he ran into a tree and was killed.

In the meantime, back east great things were going on. In June and July, 1921, Mitchell finally did bomb battleships. The story has been told a thousand times by now, but the page of history that was turned still can't be overemphasized.

On every sort of pretext, all kinds of people had tried to stop the tests. Strong pressure was brought to bear on President Harding and on Congress to withhold permission to designate the German ships as targets and thus block the experiment. But Mr. Harding liked the way Billy Mitchell did things, or in any case sensed, with a good instinct, Billy's appeal to the American public. Mitchell said, after the President's death, that one of the things Harding had promised to keep at the top of his list as he left on that last fatal journey to Alaska, was the matter of air bases up there. Also, Billy had many friends in Congress.

Former Secretary of the Navy Daniels didn't try to stop the tests at the end, but on behalf of the Navy flared forth unequivocal defiance. He said he would stand bareheaded on the bridge of any battleship during any bombardment by any airplane, by God, and expect to remain safe! He only regretted that the eager airmen could not be allowed to attack under actual combat conditions to learn how fast the would-be bombers would be shot down by battleships in a real war.

Instead of this blast of the ex-Secretary's having a merely rhetorical effect, it at once made the pilots in the Air Service besiege Mitchell with the request that the Navy be allowed to shoot back at them while they sank the battleships.

"Let's do the thing right," they said. It was probably the closest thing to undeclared civil war since the Whiskey Rebellion in my home state in 1791.

Official international observers on the U.S.S. *Henderson* didn't watch the performance any more closely than we did out on the West Coast and from every air station in the country. First, the German submarine *U-117* went down almost too quickly to count, on the 20th of June. The zealous training time of Mitchell's boys on the hulk of the old *Texas* in Chesapeake Bay had been well spent. Navy flyers hit the radio-controlled *Iowa* with dummy bombs on the 29th, scoring only two direct hits, but strongly reviving the unhappy discussion of the Navy's effective off-the-record trials on the *Indiana* with live bombs a short time before.

The Navy had kept the results of that experiment a secret. Mitchell and a few others had pulled it into the open after pictures of the battered *Indiana* had appeared, without identification, in England. In the same way, sixteen years later, Bob Olds' beautiful pin-pointing of the U.S.S. *Utah* off the California coast in 1937, through bad weather, and the bombing of her decks with water-filled bombs, was to remain a matter of Navy "security."

On July 13th, the official and mostly skeptical observers on the *Henderson* saw the German destroyer *G-102* sent below the waves with alarming ease. On July 18th, the cruiser *Frankfurt* was the anchored target. The first attack of the Navy planes and Army aircraft carrying light bombs raised the hopes of the Admirals and their Army friends. Then Captain W. R. Lawson appeared, leading six Army bombers loaded with 600-pounders. But he was made to stand by, circling around, while the observers from the *Shawmut* went aboard the *Frankfurt* to inspect the earlier damage. There was talk now of sinking the *Frankfurt* with Navy gunfire—the only thing that enthusiastic Navy officers said could do it.

Meanwhile, Captain Lawson was getting impatient and he radioed: "Must begin bombing in fifteen minutes; fuel limited." The observers retired from the target ship to watch while the Navy guns were made ready. They were never needed. After Lawson and his planes had finished bombing, the *Frankfurt's* main mast snapped, the bow settled. Eleven minutes later she dived out of sight.

But it was the battleship *Ostfriesland,* veteran of Jutland, the unsinkable dreadnaught, that was the main thing. Not only the press, uniformly on Mitchell's side, but other factors had heightened the public's interest in the fate of the *Ostfriesland.*

The first attempt then came on the evening of July 20th. Not understanding the rules limiting him to 600-pound bombs, the observers off
the Virginia Capes thought Mitchell had failed because he did not sink
the ship. It was no more than they had expected! The former German
flagship had four separate skins of steel and every sort of unsinkable
bulkhead. During the war she had not only withstood the heaviest naval
gunfire in the Battle of Jutland, but had made port after a mine had
exploded directly under her.

The weather off Hatteras was inclined to be rough and some of the
observers had become seasick. General Pershing and Secretary of War
Weeks did not think it worth their while to return the next day. Thus
it was that, sitting comfortably ashore the following evening, they only
heard the distant rumbling of the explosions as the *Ostfriesland* went
down.

Rules or no rules, Billy Mitchell had been out to sink that battleship.
His first wave of eight Martin bombers were loaded with two 1000-pound
bombs apiece, and after a few hits the ship went down. The rest of the
planes had nine bombs still unreleased. They went home, dropping their
bombs in the water as a safety measure. Within a matter of hours, the
Navy had protested against Mitchell's tactics. The protests, however,
were drowned in the wave of excited headlines. Billy Mitchell had proved
his point! His bombers had done what he said they would do.

Everybody throughout the Air Force celebrated; at Langley Field
they put planes in the air to meet the returning bombers; and every man,
woman, and child was down at the line to meet the men as they got out
of their planes. General Menoher, from his position as observer on the
Henderson, sent Mitchell a congratulatory telegram. I wondered whether
Colonel Tommy Milling, who was Mitchell's Executive for the operation, remembered that first bombsight of Riley Scott's back at College
Park. But maybe he didn't, because everybody in the Air Force was
looking ahead that night—not back.

In the meantime, General Menoher, who had not been getting along
too well with Mitchell, made a request to Mr. Weeks, the Secretary of
War, that Mitchell be relieved from his job. Mr. Weeks probably would
not have minded such a change very much. He was getting fed up with
Mitchell's activities and complained at a Washington press conference
that Mitchell "had greatly annoyed the Navy on numerous occasions."
But nobody in Washington, least of all Mr. Harding's Secretary of War,
wanted to tangle with the popular Billy Mitchell. At the first rumor of
the relief from command, the press roared, practically unanimously,

that maybe other changes were needed instead. Menoher, for example, was the "spokesman of the Army and the Navy conservatives." General Mitchell was being persecuted, not only for his up-to-date ideas, but more especially for his pressure for a unified Air Force.

Mr. Weeks, as he was getting into the habit of doing, reprimanded Billy once more for his undisciplined way of saying things, and prevailed upon General Menoher to withdraw his request.

In August, 1921, the International Conference on the Limitation of Armaments convened in Washington. Mitchell was the American air representative. At that particular moment the Joint Army and Navy Board issued its findings in regard to the bombing tests. There were editorial comments on the fact that this report did not bear the signatures of several members of the Board of Army and Navy officers who had prepared it, but was signed only by General Pershing. The report stated that nothing conclusive with regard to air power had been proven. Planes were a valuable auxiliary, but not to be depended upon by themselves. The battleship was "still the backbone of the fleet and the bulwark of the nation's sea defense."

The press and members of Congress snorted at this verdict.

Then suddenly, somehow—no one quite knew how—a report of Billy Mitchell's, believed to be safely pigeonholed in General Menoher's confidential files, was published throughout the entire country. It mentioned no names, but it tore the battleships, the Admirals, and the Pershing report to shreds. General Menoher resigned as Chief of the Air Service.

For a few days there was excited newspaper speculation over whether Billy would now be completely vindicated by being appointed to succeed Menoher. I will state here that no one in the Air Service (except some of the younger pilots) believed such a thing was possible, though we all hoped that it might be. Following General Menoher's request to be relieved, Mitchell, in view of the circumstances, offered his own resignation, but no one took that very seriously.

On October 5th, a couple of weeks after Menoher stepped down, General Mason M. Patrick was sent for again. Pershing's classmate, the old A.E.F. Commander, was again in the saddle. He was not a pilot, though he presently acquired wings during a trip out to the West Coast. But the newspapers all noted that he was Mitchell's friend and former boss—an experienced friend of air power.

We all recognized that the new Chief's experience with air power was a secondary consideration in his appointment. In the eyes of the General Staff, it was experience with General Mitchell that counted. If there was any officer in the Army who should know Mitchell's way of doing business and be able to control him, Patrick was the man. Indeed, according to the story, he started off toughly enough. Billy insisted that, after all that had happened, he be given command prerogatives as the senior flying officer in the service. Patrick was sympathetic, but adamantly insistent that if he was in command, he was damned well going to command.

Mitchell said that left him no choice but to resign from the Army. Patrick answered by escorting him directly to the office of General Harbord, the Deputy Chief of Staff, who had turned down Billy's resignation a few days before, but who now stated that if it were submitted again it would be accepted immediately. Harbord hadn't been in on Saturday when they first called, and Billy had the week end to think it over. For once in his life, he backed down and agreed to Patrick's terms.

The affair of the *Ostfriesland* and its aftermath was invariably written up as a turning point in air power, which, of course, it was. Along with the technical demonstration there was hard prophecy in Billy's verbal bombardment of the Pershing report as well. If he could attack the signature of the Chief of Staff of the United States so bluntly, and a Chief of Staff who was General Pershing at that, it was plain it was going to take a lot to stop Billy Mitchell.

Along with constant speed tests, attempts to build and fly larger airplanes with larger pay loads, etc., important strides had been made in equipment for airplanes—equipment that made night flying as safe as day flying. These were stepped up by a series of night cross-country flights from Bolling Field to Langley Field. They were started by Lieutenant Clayton Bissell and maintained, in general, by him. On June 16, 1922, Captain Stevens set another record by jumping in a parachute from a Martin bomber at 24,200 feet. And so it went. Such achievements made people feel that very soon nothing would be impossible in the air. Bigger planes, bigger pay loads, and in a short while airplanes would be produced that would be able to go anywhere in the world at any time.

As I have said before, the only planes available for the airmen to fly were the old DH's and the JN's. It is true that a few pilots—like those in Washington and at Dayton—had special planes. I was very fortunate in having one of the LePeres. The LePere was a much more modern plane than the DH, streamlined and about ten miles per hour faster, but it had gasoline capacity to fly only for about an hour and a half. Accordingly, I installed four additional gasoline tanks.

It was while I was landing this plane as Rockwell Field, in 1919, that I had a major wreck, one that threw me forward on the belt buckle and injured me internally—an injury that was to send me to the hospital and force me to give up my job in San Francisco in the fall of 1922.

Meantime, the LePere was flown all over the West Coast and finally ended its career on a trip I made from San Francisco to March Field, near Riverside, California. The air that day was particularly rough, and over the Tehachapi Pass I felt a bad jolt and noticed that the control wires to the tail surface had tightened. I looked around but could see nothing wrong. Anyway, I had no parachute, so I kept on going. Then, while flying over the Mojave Desert at an altitude of 7000 feet, I felt a draft. I looked down and saw the bottom of the LePere's wooden fuselage had cracked wide open and apparently was opening more.

I flew that airplane very carefully, taking no liberties with it, and landed at March Field as if the plane were loaded with eggs. But when I gave her the gun to head for the hangar, it was too much. The tail skid held fast, the engine kept on going, and the fuselage split in half directly under my feet.

I had flown that old LePere all the way from Tehachapi Pass to March Field with nothing holding the fuselage together but the control wires. That was the last of the LePere. However, its effect on me became manifest in the fall of 1922, and after a tour in the hospital I was relieved as Western Air Officer and sent to Rockwell Field, San Diego, as Commanding Officer.

The Air Depot at Rockwell Field was not new territory to me. I was acquainted with its change from a flying school to a depot. There were about 800 civilians, a handful of enlisted men, and nine officers, including myself. Nevertheless, we had a baseball team, a trapshooting team, and a rifle team in the outfit.

At Rockwell Field, I had brought home to me the difference in the War and Navy Departments' postwar policies regarding surplus supplies and property. The War Department policy was to get rid of everything regardless of what use it might have in peacetime operations; the Navy always kept quantities of building supplies, paints, etc., for the peacetime period. At Rockwell, out of its abundance, the Navy gave me paint, lumber, and other necessities to meet our own needs.

Living close to the Navy as we did there on North Island in 1922, being associated with them practically all the time, going to civic functions with the admirals and the captains time and time again, I saw plainly the need for a consolidation of the two services, a standardization of their activities, a more uniform distribution of funds. For instance, why should officers in the Army at one end of the Island be living in old latrines that had been sawed in half and remodeled into officers' quarters while at the other end of the Island, Navy officers were living in new buildings put up expressly for them? It didn't make sense. There was just one answer: Unification of the services—one standard for all in order to obtain the maximum efficiency for the Army and the Navy with the least expense to the taxpayer.

There were not many airplanes flying around in those early days and the accidents that occurred made far greater impressions than they do today, probably because we knew most of the people who were lost. Out in the wilderness of the West where there were not many farms and settled areas, too often our airplanes failed to return from their operations. Sometimes, in the vastness of the desert and in the mountains they simply disappeared.

One day, Colonel F. C. Marshall, Assistant Chief of Cavalry, came to Rockwell and asked me for an airplane to take him to Phoenix. The next day I sent him off with Lieutenant "Bridgie" Webber, one of our better pilots. I even flew part of the way over the mountains alongside them to make sure the weather was O.K. before I waved good-by and turned back to Rockwell Field.

We received no telegram of their arrival at Phoenix that night and when we called to check and find out where they were, they were still unreported. A search was begun immediately, and by the next day involved over one hundred airplanes. It continued for weeks. With headquarters pressing us for results, we even sent out ground-searching expeditions in automobiles to ask people along the roads if they could give us any clues to where the airplane might be.

Even crystal gazing came into it. A fortuneteller in San Diego called me and said it was on her conscience because she knew exactly where the lost airplane was. She told me how she could see the big man now, walking around (that would have been Colonel Marshall), with the little man lying on the ground, hurt. She described a large body of water where a river was coming in, with a cliff and a sandy beach below. She even described an umbrella-shaped group of trees on a small plateau.

I asked her if she had ever been in Mexico where the Colorado River flows into the Gulf of Lower California. She said she had not. I told her she had described the place accurately. I sent planes over there and we found everything just as she had pictured it—except the lost airplane.

February passed, with the accident almost forgotten. When the first of May arrived, some of us went trout fishing in the mountains back of San Diego. That night, lying in my bunk, I had a dream. I saw Colonel Marshall and Lieutenant Webber come into my office at Rockwell Field, and I asked, "Where have you been?"

Their answer was, "Well, we landed on the coast of Lower California and we couldn't get off for a long time. Then a sailing vessel came along, but it had no radio. They took us to Australia with them and we just got back."

That dream was so vivid that I told it the next morning at breakfast. Two days later, a cowboy hunting cattle came upon the wreck of the Marshall-Webber plane, and the bodies were found less than half a mile from the place we had slept that night.

In 1923, through the ingenuity of my Engineering Officer at the Rockwell Air Depot, Captain Lowell Smith, we put on a demonstration of the first refueling in the air. Captain Smith had come to me with the idea in about June of that year. His equipment for the venture consisted of—besides the skill of himself and his companion, Lieutenant J. P. Richter—a regular gasoline hose, standard except for its extended length of about forty feet, and a piece of rope with which the refueling plane could pull the hose back up after the delicate job was done.

In short order, Smith and Richter established two endurance records using this technique—a technique that soon became familiar to newsreel-goers from coast to coast, and is used today when it is desired to keep a plane in the air longer than it can stay with the gasoline carried in its own tank.

Mitchell was constantly pressing our engineers and designers at Wright Field to get out more and better airplanes. As a result of this, a number of new types came out, with some of which our Army Air Forces set new records. In 1923, the Army purchased the original T-2. The T-2 was designed by a Dutchman, Anthony Fokker, who had created the Fokker plane that flew so well for the Germans during World War I. It was a large transport of the monoplane type, built around a single Liberty engine. It carried a useful load of about 3000 pounds, including eight men. It was in this plane, on May 6, 1923, that Lieutenants Kelly and Macready, after two bad tries—one due to bad weather, the second to a cracked water jacket—made the first nonstop flight across the continent, arriving at Rockwell Field, San Diego from Mitchel Field, New York, in 26 hours and 50 minutes.

The same year saw Billy Mitchell's biggest attempt at a long-range, load-carrying heavy bomber—the Barling, the largest plane built up to that time in the United States. During the time of its construction there were many raised eyebrows, because not only did the bomber itself cost somewhere near $500,000—a lot of money for those days—but it required a hangar for its erection and assembly which cost another $700,000.

Theoretically, the Barling would carry a pay load of about 10,000 pounds, and had a cruising radius of about 1000 miles. Actually, its performance did not come anywhere near those figures. This bomber, with its six Liberty engines, was first flown by Lieutenant H. R. Harris on August 22, 1923. Harris was one of the few people who ever flew it. The Barling was soon abandoned, for when it was desired to take it the mere 400 miles from Dayton to Washington to exhibit it, they found that when loaded with enough gasoline to make the trip, the enormous plane could not climb over the Appalachian Mountains. So the Barling Bomber was first held at Dayton for study, and then became an obsolescent object of curiosity. Later it was dismantled and destroyed.

People generally do not understand that a plane like that cannot be classed as a one hundred per cent failure. It is true, the Barling itself failed to fly as planned, but many aeronautical engineering problems were solved by it. Records from wind-tunnel tests, theoretical analyses of details of assemblies, and newly devised parts on paper are all right, but there are times when the full-scale article must be built to get the pattern for the future. The B-19 and the B-15 are other examples of this method of securing data. The big wooden airplane of Howard Hughes is still another. The positive progress gained from such "abortive" experiments is always more important than the negative lessons learned from paper drawings. The Barling, if we look back on it without bias, certainly had some influence on the development of the B-17's that bombed Germany and the B-29's that bombed Japan.

The idea of successfully employing bombers in mass formation to attack key industrial plants in the heart of enemy country was still far in the future. Our national policy then, and for a long time afterward, was simply to defend our own shores, the real meaning of even that idea not yet being apparent to our statesmen or to many of our high-ranking military or naval officers.

The first missions against the *Ostfriesland,* and, a few weeks later against the U.S.S. *Alabama,* were the real beginning of precision bombardment. The later trials off the Virginia Capes against the battleships *Virginia* and *New Jersey* in September, 1923, were a further development of the idea that we must seek out a tiny target with accurate navigation and then bomb it, the little target itself, since hits in the surrounding (sea) area would be of no value. The War Department required that the 1923 bombing tests, in which we used for the first time the 2000-pound bomb, be made from 10,000 feet. Much to the surprise of many airmen themselves, this was done, a feat made possible by Dr. Sanford Moss' supercharger, which from then on became standard equipment for our bombing planes.

I managed to get back east during 1923 and have a chat with Billy Mitchell in Washington. He was down in the dumps. Despite all his fighting, writing, flying, and daring speeches, he said, "Air power doesn't seem to be getting anywhere at all." The public was interested, but the individual leaders in Washington who could do something about it were not. It was true, there were a few new airplane types coming out, but nothing to speak of—not what he wanted. And there was that constant fight for funds. He was always defending himself against the Navy, the War Department, or some "idiotic" committee with an axe to grind about the accident rate or something like that, but so far as funds were concerned the Air Service had to work through the War Department budget, then through the Federal budget, and then the House would trim it even if the Senate did eventually give us a little back. All in all, it was a very thankless job.

That didn't mean Billy had quit fighting. Far from it. He was simply more zealous than before. Also, since I had seen him last, he had made himself a new and rather potent adversary. Calvin Coolidge, who had succeeded the late President Harding in the White House, was not particularly enthusiastic about the flying machine, and he certainly didn't relish Billy Mitchell's unorthodox methods of promoting it. Indeed, President Coolidge's whole view of life was almost exactly opposite to that of the flying men, and there can have been few of his fellow citizens who aroused a testier feeling in him than Billy seemed to do personally.

As far as the Air Service was concerned, the year 1924 came in with a bang—the first round-the-world flight. This was made with a plane, especially designed by Donald Douglas, that could carry heavy loads and at the same time acquire a fairly high speed.

Major Frederick L. Martin was selected as commander of the flight, with Captain Lowell Smith, as his second in command. When Major Martin was forced down in the mountains of Alaska out near the Aleutian Islands and was compelled to make his way with his mechanic to Port Moller on foot, Smith took over command.

This flight had required long and careful planning. From Santa Monica, California, to Seattle, the planes flew as land planes. There they had floats installed and flew as seaplanes until they reached Calcutta. At Calcutta, the floats were removed and wheels were put on again and they flew as land planes until they reached north of Scotland. Here, once more, floats were put on and they flew across the North Atlantic as seaplanes, finally ending their flight again as land planes. All this meant that advance officers and crews had to be stationed around the world.

Everything went well with the three planes after Martin's accident until, crossing the North Atlantic, Lieutenant Lee Wade's plane went down with trouble and he was out, his plane being picked up by a naval ship. Smith's plane nearly got lost between Greenland and Labrador when the gasoline pump went out and Lieutenant L. P. Arnold, his passenger, had to pump the gasoline by hand during the whole trip. (His arm was practically useless for many days thereafter.) Both Smith's plane and the plane flown by Lieutenant Eric Nelson completed the flight, arriving in Washington, then flying on to Santa Monica, where the flight had originated.

Another outstanding flight occurred in August of that year, when Lieutenant Jimmy Doolittle made a record-breaking trip from Jacksonville, Florida, to San Diego, California. He was still flying a wartime DH.

In the fall of 1924, shortly after the round-the-world flight of the Douglas Cruisers started, orders came transferring me to Washington to attend the Army Industrial College.

This was an interesting assignment. It seemed to me that in its planning the War Department was making a grave mistake in relying upon the automobile industry as the prime contractors for manufacturing airplanes. Nothing in my World War I experience had served to convince me that any automobile manufacturer could take the plans for an airplane from an aircraft manufacturer and, without knowing anything about the techniques or employment of aircraft metals or the small tolerances and other difficulties, build airplanes in quantity without unnecessary loss of time or long periods of schooling for metalmen. We discussed these things at great length during my course at the Industrial College, and finally agreed that the best idea would be to have the aircraft manufacturers as the main contractors—perhaps even depending on them for the jigs, dies, fittings, and special fixtures—and let them go to the automobile industry, or any other industry for small parts, subassemblies, and so on, even subletting contracts where necessary. This experience in planning was to stand me in good stead in later years.

Upon completion of my tour at the Industrial College, I was made Chief of the Information Section under General Patrick. I held that job during the last year of Billy Mitchell's service in Washington, and for a period just beyond the termination of his court-martial.

That circus whip of Billy's was now cracking in a manner which many quarters in Washington noticed. I saw that half the time it wasn't what Billy said, but the way he said it that made him enemies. Even General Patrick, though scarcely the most sweet-tempered of commanders (he certainly never seemed to forget that I had accepted his invitation to criticize his air command in France), frequently stuck his neck out to back Billy up.

Billy and I used to talk over the developments in flying and the men who were responsible for them. We both agreed there was one outstanding young man who would make a name for himself and be present in a big way when Air Power really came into being. His name was Doolittle.

Jimmy seems never to have been absent when something big was happening in Air Power. His dissenting opinion as a member of the Baker Board, in 1934, in which he stressed the need for a unified service with an independent Air Force, is as historic as the story of his operational commands. It is interesting that Billy Mitchell, describing the night after the court-martial finally found him guilty, mentions only one name. "But the implications of my trial were overshadowed, in my mind anyhow, by one great event which no one seemed to associate with my predictions. It seemed to be lost in the sweep of happenings of the time. It had taken place as my court-martial approached its climax. Lieutenant James H. Doolittle, the champion aquatic aviator of the Army, had set his fourth world speed-record for seaplanes at Bay Shore Park by flying four times over a measured course at an average speed of 245.715 miles per hour.

"I was interested in Jimmy because, for one thing, he knew Alaska. Previously, that year, Jimmy, who was to become one of the most scientific flyers in the world, had won the Schneider Cup Race. With cold and deadly accuracy he had written in the sky the answer to my conviction!"

I said to Mitchell again and again: "Billy, take it easy. We need you. Don't throw everything away just to beat out some guy who doesn't understand! Air Power is coming! Calm down, Billy. Get a balance wheel in your office! Let him look over some of the things you write before you put them out! Stop saying all these things about the independent air arm that are driving these old Army and Navy people crazy!"

But he would always reply: "When senior officers won't see facts, something unorthodox, perhaps an explosion, is necessary. I'm doing it for the good of the Air Force, for the future Air Force, for the good of you fellows. I can afford to do it. You can't."

During that year I myself got mixed up in something that almost caused me to leave the Service. It is not generally realized that that great international air line, Pan American Airways, was not started by any rich and powerful business combine, but actually was founded by three young Army officers and one ex-Navy officer without a dime between them.

In a sense, the formation of Pan American Airways turned out to be the first countermeasure the United States ever took against Nazi Germany, though Hitler was unknown in America then, and in jail at Landsberg-am-Lech as a mild punishment for his Beer Hall Putsch at Munich the previous November. (The airfield at Landsberg was to be a target for our Eighth Air Force bombers twenty years later.)

In my job as Information Officer, I saw reports from the military attaché in Colombia which gave repeated data about a German air line, Scadta, run by a Captain von Bauer, and operating between Barranquilla and Bogotá. All pilots, mechanics, and equipment of this line, running up the Magdalena River, and far too close to the Panama Canal to be ignored, were German. Then I received information that Captain von Bauer wanted to expand his successful air line, pushing it up not only to Panama itself, but extending it through the Central Americas to Cuba and the United States to carry mail and passengers.

That was the last straw. I immediately went to see G-2 of the War Department, and after that I called on Postmaster General New. I asked the Postmaster General whether, if Captain von Bauer arrived in Washington and requested authority to carry U.S. mail from the United States to Barranquilla and Bogotá, under the law he would have to give him the contract. Mr. New thought it over for a while and said he thought he would, unless there was some other line, preferably an American line, that could perform the service. I asked him whether the American line must be "in being" or if it could be one in the process of organization. He said he would have to wait and see just what I meant by that.

I went back to my office, took a map, and drew a sketch of an air line operating from Key West to Havana, to the Western end of Cuba, to the northeast point of the Yucatan Peninsula, down through British Honduras, Guatemala, Nicaragua, and to Panama. I then called in Major Spaatz and Major Jack Jouett. We talked it over for hours, and finally we called in an ex-Navy man by the name of John Montgomery. Together, we drew up a prospectus of such an air line and how it might make money. Then we sent John Montgomery to New York. Montgomery interested some moneyed people and funds were set up for an air line operating between Florida and Cuba and Panama. We found out that the Standard Oil Company had to send supplies to Havana, Key West, and to the Central American ports, and the freight charges and the funds received for carrying the mail between Key West and

Havana would pay for the operating expense of that part of the line. We also found out that most of the ports where we were going to land had ships arriving but once every thirty days. We figured that we would start out by giving these ports airplane service once a week, and later on, give them service twice a week, which would save from thirty to forty-five days in delivery of goods.

With that information, and knowing that the capital in New York was interested in the line, we went back to Postmaster General New and told him just what had happened. When Captain von Bauer made his final appearance and applied for permission to run the Scadta Line from Barranquilla to Panama and to the United States, he was refused.

Very few people in the War Department, or in Panama, knew that at the moment, jobs had been offered to Spaatz, to be operating director of the new company; to Jouett, to handle all personnel; to Montgomery, to be field manager on the line when it was in operation; and to me, to be president and general manager of Pan American. Just what would have happened had my tour in Washington remained unbroken, I do not know.

In February, 1925, General Patrick was reappointed Chief of the Air Service. General Mitchell, to the surprise of numerous editorial writers but not of everybody in Washington, was not redesignated as his assistant. Billy was ordered to Fort Sam Houston, Texas, as "Air Officer" where he reverted to his permanent rank of Colonel, being succeeded by Lieutenant Colonel (soon Brigadier General) James E. Fêchet.

We naturally mourned Mitchell's departure though we scarcely regarded it as permanent. For the time being, no more warm gatherings at the house in Middleburg, no more of those flashing statements in the morning papers like the very ones he left us with: "Neither armies nor navies can exist unless the air is controlled over them. The evidence shows plainly that the United States has adopted no modern plan of organization for meeting the general world movement in the organization of world power . . . [and] . . . I found it impossible to do anything in the War and Navy Departments on the matter of air defense. So I took it to Congress and the people, and will continue to take it to them until it is recognized. . . . I have not even begun to fight!"

The farewell luncheon for Billy at the Racquet Club which I arranged went off well enough, with both Patrick and Fêchet present to help give him the kind of send-off he deserved. The memorable barbecue party that night, however, had an unfortunate aftermath. I had gone in to invite General Patrick, who was undoubtedly troubled by special pressures at the moment, and who, in any case, had an irritable habit of interrupting the explanations of subordinates with the interjection: "Yes, yes, I know! Yes, I know, I know . . . !"

"Sir," I said, "We are having . . ."

"Yes, yes, yes, I know!"

"And we would like . . ."

"Yes, I know, I know!" he said, not listening.

"We would like, sir," I said . . .

"All right, I know, I know!" General Patrick said. So I thought, well, maybe he does know. Anyway, I left, respectfully, but without establishing the invitation.

It was quite a party, but General Patrick wasn't there.

Next morning he summoned me in a wrath, and demanded to know why he had not been invited to this gathering of goodwill for Mitchell. When I could get a word in, I finally said: "Sir . . ."

"Yes, yes, I know!" he began, and then, as if he suddenly realized everything, stopped speechless, picked up a paper weight from his desk and threw it. The interview was over.

So Billy went off to Texas, where they still called him "General," and for a time there was relative silence, though occasional remarks still got into print from down there, and once he and his observer were nearly killed in a crash from which he walked away, saying casually: "It's all in the day's work."

From time to time he would write me sharp little notes, sometimes only a sentence or two long, referring to some incident that illustrated a previously expressed view of his. Once a note came which simply repeated that conspiratorial phrase he had used down on the Border: "Things are coming along well. Keep going as you are."

Actually, at this time our plans for Pan American had progressed so well that I had made up my mind to resign from the Army. Then on September 1st and 3rd, two things happened in rapid succession. First, my old friend, Commander John Rodgers, and the crew of four with whom he was trying to fly from San Francisco to Honolulu, were reported missing in the Pacific. As the great and finally successful search for them by planes, ships, and submarines went on, publicity was given to the fact that their gas supply had not been sufficient if they should encounter headwinds—as they did on the second day. Mitchell went on the air in San Antonio and called them "martyrs." While they were still missing on the 3rd, the tragedy of the *Shenandoah* occurred.

For some time past, because of an agreement giving the Navy responsibility for rigid lighter-than-air craft, and putting the Army in charge of the development of nonrigid blimps, dirigibles had not been a concern of the Air Service. On September 3rd, two of the Navy's finest experts in this field, Commander Zachary Lansdowne and Commander Charles Rosendahl, took off from Lakehurst, New Jersey, with a crew of 42 for an exhibition cruise over the Middle West. (Commander Rosendahl, incidentally, who is still an airship enthusiast today, was as zealous about lighter-than-air as Mitchell was about air power.)

Before dawn next morning, over Ohio, the *Shenandoah* ran into a bad line-squall. Despite a desperate battle to get the medium-sized airship out of the storm, she was torn into three parts. Commander Lansdowne and 14 men fell to their deaths. Rosendahl, in an outstanding display of courage and airmanship, managed to maneuver one section of the dirigible as a free balloon and bring it safely to the ground, saving the lives of 27 men besides himself.

Coming only two days after the disappearance of John Rodgers and his crew, this second disaster to the Naval Air Arm raised a storm of questions all over the country. What was this rumor that Commander Lansdowne had protested against making the flight because of uninvestigated weather conditions, and had even predicted his own death to his wife? What about the charge that for "economy" reasons the *Shenandoah* had been underequipped with important valves?

It is interesting that to Secretary of the Navy Wilbur the two tragedies seemed to indicate, more than anything else, that the country had nothing to fear from any invading air power. "The Atlantic and Pacific are still our best defense," he said. Perhaps those words had something to do with the remarkable statement—and a prepared press statement at that—issued at San Antonio, Texas, on September 5th, which startled both Services.

It was 6000 words long, and starting off with one more of Billy's challenges that if this meant court-martial they could make the most of it, it said that such "terrible accidents to our naval aircraft . . . are the direct results of incompetency, criminal negligence and almost treasonable administration of the national defense by the War and Navy Departments." Looking at the "disgusting" record was enough "to make any self-respecting person ashamed of the cloth he wears."

Mitchell pointed out that all aviation policies were made by non-flying men, that Congress treated the Air Arm as if it were nothing but an organization created for the benefit of the two departments; blasted at the fact that we still had to fly the old "Flying Coffins"; said we, the airmen, were so bluffed and bulldozed that we dared not tell the truth for fear of ruining our careers; and spoke of bureaucratic superiors who "either distort facts or openly tell falsehoods about aviation to the people and to the Congress."

He went on from there, ending with the thought that he personally desired no advancement, had had the "finest career that any man could have in the armed service of the United States . . . I owe the Government everything, the Government owes me nothing. As a patriotic American citizen, I can stand by no longer and see these disgusting performances by the War and Navy Departments at the expense of the lives of our people, and the delusion of the American public."

A couple of days later, a press aide at the White House replied to the eager Washington correspondents, "Yes, there will definitely be a court-martial."

Billy wrote me right away, and then wired me, outlining the records and papers he was bringing with him and establishing me as his liaison man. The night he and Betty arrived, I drove down to Union Station to meet them. The word had spread, and a fife and drum corps of the American Legion were down at the station, with a large, pressing crowd. I had a tough time getting the Mitchells away in my car.

Affairs were complicated by the fact that before Billy, now relieved from duty, faced his own court-martial, he was supposed to be an ace witness before the Morrow Board, then sitting at the President's request to deliberate on the status of American air power. It seemed to many that the real purpose of this Board was to head off the year-long investigation headed by Congressman Lampert, so favorable to Mitchell's air power views as to be alarming.

The Morrow Board had, in addition to Dwight Morrow himself, some very reputable citizens on it, including General Harbord and Admiral Fletcher, my old associates Howard Coffin and Senator Hiram Bingham, Congressmen Carl Vinson and James S. Parker. Unfortunately, American air power received little benefit from the formation of this body, and very little from Billy Mitchell's appearance before it.

I can still remember how we all crowded into that room, with our wives, listening while Billy's expert testimony turned out to be not the brilliant defiance we had looked for, but a dry reading to the Committee of his own book, *Winged Defense*. It took me back to that other committee room years before, in 1913, when Billy had gone on lecturing and lecturing without noticing whether his hearers were interested or not.

We of the Air Service practically squirmed, wanting to yell: "Come on, Billy, put down that damned book! Answer their questions and step

down, that'll show them!" But he read on and on like a schoolmaster
until at last Hiram Bingham, friend of air power and former air officer
though he was, became so restless that he said: "Colonel, in view of the
fact that each of the members of this Committee has a copy of your
book and has read it . . ."

Billy said sharply: "Senator, I'm trying to make a point!"

And that was that. Afterwards, I think Billy found most unforgivable
the Morrow Board's curious finding about the relation between our Air
Service and the maintenance of an American aircraft industry. (That,
and the whitewashing of the DH's.) "The Board urges the encouragement of civilian aircraft," said its final report, "and the sale of planes
to foreign countries so as to *lessen the number* of planes which the
Government must order to keep the industry in a strong position.

The court-martial was better, perhaps because everybody realized
that a good showing was the best that could come of it. Billy was licked,
of course, from the beginning. No matter what was said about "Air
Power being on trial"—as it was, at times even in the eyes of the
prosecution—the thing for which Mitchell was really being tried he was
guilty of, and except for Billy, everybody knew it, and knew what it
meant.

I have tried to think what new light I might be able to shed on that
famous court-martial, but I'm afraid there isn't any. It has all been pretty
well told: how Major General Charles P. Summerall, originally president of the Court, was challenged by Billy on the grounds of bias and
asked to be excused, shaken by the "bitter personal hostility" of Mitchell's
confidential report on Hawaii; the brilliant efforts of Congressman Reid,
Billy's defense attorney; the bellowing of Major Gullion as prosecutor;
the way the nine Generals of the Court, now headed by General Howze,
listened to the smallest argument in Mitchell's behalf.

Sometimes Billy and Betty would have gone riding before Court
opened, coming in gaily and greeting the judging officers before they
sat down (after all, most of the generals were old friends). MacArthur,
and his alleged final vote on Billy's side; Frank McCoy, Blanton Win-
ship, and all the others; the Air, Army, Navy, Press, and just Washington friends who jammed into that dingy old hall—it all was described
daily then, and has often been pictured since. The thing I remember
best is the way veteran airmen who suddenly appeared there at Billy's
side from all over the country played up to him like an alert football
team up against big odds but following the ball for the breaks. Before
Gullion or Moreland, the other prosecutor, could even say "I object!"

Spaatz or Herbert Dargue, Bob Olds, Gillmore, Schauffler, Gerald Brant, Horace Hickam, or one of us would have jumped in with the statement the prosecutor didn't want to hear. "What (question to Brant) would happen to Hawaii if such a refusal (referring to lack of co-operation between the Army and the Navy) came in time of war?" Quickly: "It would result in the capture of Pearl Harbor!" ... "So you believe (to Spaatz) that the organization of the tactical units of the Air Service is being retarded by the War Department?" Promptly: "I do!" ... To make sure they were backing up Billy's ideas, they wouldn't even paraphrase his words. General Howze asked Bob Olds somewhat sarcastically: "Do you think the General Staff should always listen to your recommendations?" "As the General Staff is now constituted, I do!" Bob replied. "How would *you* constitute the General Staff?" General Booth demanded. "On Colonel Mitchell's plan!" Bob answered quickly. The prosecution dismissed the witness.

Billy himself was in strong form at the trial, often putting the prosecution and even the Court on the defense. It was nothing like the Morrow Board. He could be as affable with a foe or a judge as with a friend, but he was a hard man to make peace with. He was a fighter, the public was on his side, he was righter than hell and he knew it, and whoever wasn't with him a hundred per cent was against him. Nights, we would adjourn to his apartment in the Anchorage where, with our wives, we would "plan the next day's strategy and talk things over."

The small gains—the only kind possible for any military expansion in those years of disarmament, he regarded as a contemptible compromise. Yet military aviation really couldn't have amounted to very much then, even if everybody had agreed with him. Planes with performance, engines with reliability and the navigational aids were lacking. It was the man—the pilot—who was driving the plane to new records. The time of airplane performance, in fact, had not yet arrived. Air Power was still ahead of us.

Everybody knows how it ended. To find the sentence it wanted, the Court had to go back to post-Civil War days to the punishment of another military firebrand, George Armstrong Custer, who was also "deprived of his command and given half of his pay for a period of years." Billy's sentence was, of course, worse, since he was suspended from all military duties as well. He could scarcely serve under such conditions, and that President Coolidge would uphold the sentence was certain. There was nothing left for him to do but resign from the Army.

We all knew there was no other way—in accordance with the Army code, Billy had had it coming. But at the time we didn't think these things out. As the testimony of any of us who were called to the trial shows, the whole Air Service was angry. The first ones to try to keep the battle going were Major Herbert Dargue and myself. After such long service in Washington we had many friends, in Congress and in the press. We continued going out to Billy's house in Middleburg, and also over to Capitol Hill, and writing letters to keep up the fight.

At once the boom was lowered with a bang. After all the trouble with Billy Mitchell—and the case unpopularly closed—there was no thought of allowing small fry to keep it going. It was understood now that President Coolidge himself had been the prime accuser. We were both called on the carpet to answer for our "irregular" correspondence relative to changes in Air Service status. Dargue got off with a reprimand. I was, as the Press announced, "exiled!"

That was the end of my plan to resign and become president of our newly founded Pan American Airways. I couldn't very well quit the Service under fire. I was to be C.O. of the 16th Observation Squadron, at Fort Riley, Kansas.

In retrospect, I do not believe that the War Department, as an agency, profited much, if at all, from the Mitchell "period of influence on air development." They seemed to set their mouths tighter, draw more into their shell, and, if anything, take even a narrower point of view of aviation as an offensive power in warfare. Our Navy, on the contrary, made a study of the entire affair and of all the incidents relating thereto, and became air-minded in a big way. They even went out of their way to find new means of using aircraft in naval operations.

I can remember the train going out; discussing Fort Riley where I had flown in 1912, and the fact the Commanding General was a stern old cavalryman named Ewing E. Booth who had been a member of Mitchell's Court; my wife getting the children around her and telling them this was going to be rough. They'd have to take it. There were bound to be fights with those Fort Riley Cavalry children who would be laying for them. Hank, who was nine then, wasn't impressed. "Will they be tougher than those Navy kids in Washington?" he asked.

The night we pulled in to the Post railroad station at Riley we were met by a solitary officer, Captain Fabian Pratt. Pratt was a Flight Surgeon—a wonderful one as I was to find out—but this night he was more. In fact, he was everything. He explained that at the moment he was Acting Commanding Officer of the Squadron, he was Operations Officer, and was holding down all the other jobs. All the other officers were officially absent. One was on duty at Kansas State College, two were on the West Coast getting airplanes, two officers were sick, and that left only him.

When the children were in bed in our new quarters, Bee and I started the uncomfortable walk to General Booth's house for our first official call. The house was all lighted up. As we were admitted we saw the Commanding General was having a card party. The living room was full of people. We stood there, and General Booth looked across the room and apparently recognized me. He rose and came toward us. Then he held out his hand and put the other on my shoulder with sincere hospitality. "Arnold," he said cordially, "I'm glad to see you. I'm proud to have you in this command." And then, so that everybody could hear, he added: "I know why you're here, my boy. And as long as you're here you can write and say any damned thing you want. All I ask is that you let me see it first!"

I had not been at Fort Riley long before I found out that my duties there were not only to be Commanding Officer of the 16th Observation Squadron, but also to furnish airplanes for aerial work with the Infantry and Cavalry units in the Seventh Corps Area, which consisted of North and South Dakota, Minnesota, Wisconsin, Nebraska, Kansas, and Arkansas. In addition, I was to be the senior air instructor at the Cavalry School.

To do this work I had one squadron, manned by about eight officers and equipped with five DH's which had long, long since outlived their usefulness, and some eight or ten Jennies which were used mainly to train reserve officers in the summer camps. A short time after my arrival, however, we did start to get some of the newer and better observation planes.

Fort Riley was the Cavalry School. Through Riley came a steady stream of officers of all ranks for horsemanship instruction, colonels taking refresher courses, lieutenant colonels and majors taking field officers' courses, and captains and lieutenants taking the company officers' courses. The number in the student body ran as high as 250 to 300. Here, it seemed to me, "exile" or not, was a wonderful opportunity to indoctrinate ground officers all through the Army with the possibilities and capabilities of the airplane and we decided to take advantage of it.

With that in mind, I sold the Commanding General of the school the idea of an indoctrination course in which we would take these various officers from the Cavalry, Field Artillery, or any other branch who happened to be there, as observers in our planes, fly them to various localities, pick up salient features, items of military importance, and information, letting them learn in practice the many ways the work of a corps or division G-1, G-2, G-3, or G-4 could be aided from the air. The Commanding General was very enthusiastic and such instruction was soon included in the Cavalry officers' course—and it gave us more to do.

It is true I had a certain amount of trouble convincing all my pilots that the course was designed for military usefulness, rather than to discover whether or not the Cavalry officers could "take it." From one such mission a pilot known as "Irish" O'Connor returned with a cavalryman in his rear cockpit who could scarcely sit up. His face was literally green. From O'Connor's landing gear hung at least 300 feet of telephone wire. I looked at the Cavalry officer and when the pilot had climbed down I said, "O'Connor, what have you been doing?" He said innocently: "Nothing." "Where did you get that telephone wire on your landing gear?" I asked him. He said, "Somebody must have picked it up on the last flight, and I took off without noticing it." "O'Connor," I said, "You know as well as I do that you can't take off with 300 feet of telephone wire hanging on your landing gear. Where did you get it?" "I haven't the faintest idea," he said. I looked again at the unhappy cavalryman gradually coming to, and I said, "O'Connor, we're trying to build up a little cooperation here! Hereafter, you stay up above 3000 feet where you belong! Don't ever let me catch you flying low like that again!" "Yes, sir," O'Connor said.

A short time later, after a similar practice tour over Marysville, about fifty miles north of Riley, I landed back at the field with my own Cavalry passenger and asked the Operations officer if everybody was in. "Everybody but O'Connor," he said. I had seen O'Connor finish his mission over Marysville before I did, and he should have been home well before me. We wondered if he had had a forced landing. Finally we saw him coming, or at least saw a plane so high in the sky that you could barely identify it. Slowly circling, losing altitude, the plane landed at last, and O'Connor taxied up. In the rear seat was the same cavalryman. He was not green this time. He was blue and still. In his thin summer flying suit he looked nearly frozen to death. "O'Connor," I said, looking at his numb passenger, "what in the hell have you been doing to that poor cavalryman this time? What were you doing way up there?" "Well," O'Connor said in an aggrieved tone, "you told me never to fly low. All I did was to fly high enough so that there would be no criticism."

Sometime later we started tests to determine from what formation cavalry and artillery could get off the road most quickly in case of attack by low-flying aircraft, and reach positions where their losses would be at a minimum. Tests were so realistic that only ten seconds were allowed for the men and horses to reach their positions off the road. Their positions were then marked with stakes, which later were replaced by full-sized targets. Then airplanes would come along, flying low, and sweep over the area with machine guns and fragmentation bombs to show what damage might have been inflicted had it been real combat instead of an exercise. These exercises, continued over a period of many months, were of inestimable value to both the Air Force and the Cavalry, and the officers in both branches were enthusiastic.

During the time I was at Fort Riley, the Air Corps combat groups made great progress in the technique of operations and the development of tactical operations. We grew up. We had started thinking in terms of Squadrons; by now we were thinking in terms of Groups and Wings. We were training Group Commanders, Wing Commanders, and staffs for higher units. We had the first of our big maneuvers—maneuvers that moved from one school to another: the Command and General Staff School at Leavenworth; the Artillery School at Fort Sill; the Cavalry School at Fort Riley; the Infantry School at Fort Benning. We put on demonstrations with bombardment, attack, and fighter planes. The training afforded by the maneuvers in supplying, moving, handling, and employing large numbers of planes, was of course invaluable.

During the excitement and furor of all the air operations at Fort Riley in 1927, once again there was a pause, for the Arnold family had another increase—David Lee Arnold was born.

In the late Spring of 1927, I received word to go to North Platte and from there to Rapid City, South Dakota, there to confer with Colonel Starling of the White House Secret Service. I didn't know what was going on, but when I reached Rapid City and met Colonel Starling, I learned that President Coolidge was coming up to the Black Hills for his vacation, and while he was there, my outfit was to carry the mail for the President from North Platte to Rapid City, the regular airlines carrying it from Washington to North Platte. There was a schoolhouse near the President's summer camp, and on the desk in that schoolhouse, every Tuesday and every Thursday morning, Mr. Coolidge would expect to find his mail waiting. There was to be no slip-up, ever.

We quickly learned one thing, and that was that President Coolidge was adamant about his mail. It made no difference whether it was raining between Washington and Chicago and the mail couldn't get through, or whether there was fog on the ground between Chicago and North

Platte. President Coolidge demanded his mail! He had to have his mail!

Secretary New was called into the second conference, and he and the Corps Area Commander both told me in no uncertain terms that I had to get the mail through. Naturally, I didn't want to risk the lives of my men, but I meant to satisfy the President if it were humanly possible to do it. Thereafter, things were arranged so that every Tuesday and Thursday there was always a package of mail on President Coolidge's desk when he arrived at the school, regardless of what the weather conditions were, or whether our planes got through or not.

One of the pilots who carried the mail to Rapid City for President Coolidge was Lieutenant Jack Munson who came from a small town in Iowa and was very shy and silent. Carrying that important mail, he conceived a desire to see the President. Accordingly, on one of his trips, he went to the school and asked the guard how he could get a look at Mr. Coolidge. The guard said, "Wait right here." In a few minutes he returned with Mr. Sanders, the President's secretary.

"Do you want to see the President?" he asked.

Munson replied, "I would like to get a look at him. I have been carrying the mail now ever since it started."

"Come with me," said Sanders.

Before Munson knew what was happening, he was in the President's office. Just what those two silent men talked about, history will probably never know, but Munson was in there for over forty-five minutes.

During World War II and later, Munson was pilot for General George Marshall.

There were a lot of great, or near-great men coming and going through Fort Riley in those days and my boys and I found ourselves running what was practically an air taxi service. Some of our passengers were considerate, but others would ask us to fly them to some town a long distance from Fort Riley and then jump out of the airplane and drive off without so much as saying "Thank you."

One who was entirely different was Will Rogers. Will came to Fort Riley one day and asked me if I would take him up to Des Moines. I said I would be glad to. When we arrived there he said, "What are you going to do now?"

I said, "I'm going back to Fort Riley."

"Aw, no," he said, "Come on in and have lunch with me."

I said, "Will, you're busy. You have a whole flock of people who want to see you."

"Aw," he said, "Come on."

So we went into town and had lunch and it was a very enjoyable meal. While we were there the Mayor of Des Moines came in, and Will Rogers introduced us and the three of us sat down and chatted. When I got up to go, Will said, "What are you going to do now?"

I said, "I'm going back to Riley."

"I'll ride out to your airplane with you," he said.

I said, "What for? You have the Mayor here, and all these people who want to see you, and the papers want you to give them an interview. You have work to do."

But he said, "Listen, I want to talk to you. I'm going out to the airport with you."

So we drove out together, talking over civil and military air matters on the way. After a while, he said, "Say, you have some kind of a fund or other for the enlisted men, haven't you?"

I said, "Sure, we have a squadron fund."

"Well," Will said, "I want to do something for the boys. Put this in the squadron fund," and he slipped something into the pocket of my blouse. When I got back I found it was two hundred dollars.

The years 1920 through 1929 have been called "The Golden Age of Aviation," and probably rightly so. There were many long-range flights made over the oceans and over the North and South Poles that necessitated far better and more accurate instruments for navigation. There could be no more flying by the "iron compass." For, from the military point of view, if it were possible for a commercial or any other kind of airplane to fly across the Atlantic or from Oakland to Honolulu, an Army bomber could and must do the same thing.

When airmen wanted to fly across the Atlantic in the 1920's, they couldn't get the kind of weather information they wanted from the Weather Bureau. The Weather Bureau was still thinking in terms of forecasting for people on the ground, or at sea. One of the foremost weather prognosticators was Dr. James Kimball, meteorologist, and it was to his office in New York that most of the trans-Atlantic airmen, realizing the need for a different kind of weather service, went to get predictions about the kind of weather they might encounter on their ocean flights. As the air operations of the Army and the Navy spread over the continents and oceans it became essential for every Army and Navy air station to have its own weather service, so that hundreds of airplanes could be moved when necessary without having to wait for weather reports from some distant place.

For several years now I had had in an application to go to the Command and General Staff School at Fort Leavenworth. Each time, for some reason or other, I was doing some job from which I could not be spared for the moment. But in 1928, it was decided by my Chief, General Fêchet, Chief of Staff Summerall, and Assistant Secretary of War F. Trubee Davison, that I could go to the school at Fort Leavenworth.

I was told afterward that General Summerall had sent a wire to the Commandant at Fort Leavenworth asking whether an additional officer could be taken care of. The reply came back, "Yes, who is he?" My name was submitted. A second reply came back stating that they didn't want me, but if I did come I would naturally be accepted. Until that time, however, I was unacceptable. In a private letter to General Fêchet, the Commandant at Leavenworth wrote that if I came to Leavenworth as a student I would be "crucified." However, I was determined to go. I also remembered that the commandant of the school had served on the Court that had tried Billy Mitchell, which probably had something to do with his feelings. In spite of the lack of cordiality in his letter, I found the course there of great value. I did not get into many difficulties and I did not find the going very tough. Naturally, I did not agree with many of the school's concepts relative to the employment of aircraft and I thought the course, as far as the Air Arm was concerned, could and should be modernized.

Upon completion of my course in June, 1928, I went to Fairfield, Ohio, for station. There I was placed in command of one of the largest depots, where airplanes, engines, instruments, and accessories were repaired and overhauled.

While walking through a warehouse after arriving there I came upon the old Barling Bomber, still lying around, still carried on paper, of no value to anyone. When I asked why it had not been surveyed, I was told that every time a Report of Survey was put in, it came back with the note, "No action will be taken on the Barling Bomber at this time." I could see no reason why the old Barling should be kept, although I realized that the recurrent congressional interest in its fate—an interest prompted by the tremendous original expense of the bomber and its hangar—made the Chief of the Air Corps understandably reluctant to destroy it. But the bomber itself was a wreck, lying around disassembled, and the hangar badly in need of repair. I had another Report of Survey prepared, but instead of calling it the Barling Bomber, I referred to it by its technical name—"One Heavy Bomber," and then gave it an "X" number—for instance X-32, or whatever the experimental number happened to be—and sent it in to Washington. Without the name "Barling" on the survey, it came back, approved. So that there would be no undue criticism or fuss we immediately took the big ship out to the dump pile, where it was consumed in fire with the other obsolete, broken, and crashed airplanes. And that was the end of the Barling Bomber.

While we were at Dayton, many of the modern improvements made their appearance on the airplane, including the first brakes and the first adjustable pitch propeller, designed and invented years ago for that purpose. The DH airplane finally disappeared from our Army Air Corps, and new airplanes of all types became available. The first all-metal, all-American-made airplane came on the market, and the first all-metal pursuit plane made its appearance before I left Dayton in 1931. Plans, specifications, and requirements were being prepared for the first 200 m.p.h. bomber—the Martin bomber which came out in the early 1930's as the B-10.

The Guggenheim Foundation started its investigations about that time to produce safer and more reliable airplanes. They developed their gadgets and devices to such an extent that Jimmy Doolittle, in 1929, was able to make the first totally blind landing under a hood. He took off under the hood, flew for fifteen minutes, and landed with the hood still down. All these developments tended to improve the performance of both planes and pilots in all kinds of weather, at night as well as in the daytime. Flying became more general, more airplanes were used on the airways, and the beacons and beams were improved.

As I have said, all Air Corps stations were crossroads in those days. One time, General Fêchet came through accompanied by General Preston Brown, one of the Assistant Chiefs of Staff. The weather was too bad for them to continue on, so they came up to the house and started playing cooncan. All during the game they were arguing that classic debate—who should be considered in command of an airplane, the pilot or the senior officer aboard? Flyers themselves had settled that question long before, as definitely as sailors had established a century back that the actual skipper of a ship must command it, no matter what exalted passengers he carried. General Fêchet, the airman, naturally took this side. The pilot was always in command of his own aircraft. General Brown said No; the senior must always be the senior, on the ground or airborne. "What would you do," Jim Fêchet pressed, "if you were in an airplane and there was a bad thunderstorm ahead, and the pilot instead of heading into it turned around and headed back towards his home station, even though you thought he should go through the storm? What would you do?"

"I would *order* him to do it!" cried General Brown slapping down his cards.

"Supposing he still wouldn't do it?" Fêchet asked. "Then what would you do?"

"I would *make* him do it!" said General Brown.

"How?" asked General Fêchet.

"I would order him to do it," General Brown replied. "And if he didn't, I would shoot him!"

"Well, what then?" asked General Fêchet. "You would sure look silly as hell up there without a pilot in your plane!"

This conversation may have led to the fact that General Brown soon afterwards enrolled in a pilots' course and learned to fly his own airplane.

On still another occasion General Brown, stopping over for the night, said he would like to have me prepare an ornament to be placed in the center of the table used by the War Council in the War Department. Following his instructions, I prepared a cube of wood about six inches on a side. It was smoothly finished and highly polished, and on one side, in gilt letters, was the legend: "Lord forgive them for they know not what they do."

In the early spring of 1930 we had our grand maneuvers at Sacramento, California, with General Gillmore in command. Taking advantage of the best weather it is possible to get in the United States, we had one of the largest and best maneuvers ever held up to that time. Two hundred and fifty planes were engaged, and as G-4 of the whole operation I soon found out it was the transportation, supply, and maintenance of such an air armada that decided, in the first place, how much of the listed "air strength" would ever get into the air at all. After the maneuvers we flew from Sacramento in massed flight over San Francisco and then Los Angeles, where the formation broke up and the individual groups went back to their stations.

The following year, 1931, we repeated these maneuvers at Dayton, assembling nearly 700 airplanes, from all parts of the United States.

General Foulois, who had gone to Washington as Assistant Chief of the Air Corps under General Fêchet, was in command, and once again I was G-4.

The maneuvers were principally to get experience in supply, operations, and command. Supply, as we were to learn, meant more than merely furnishing gasoline and oil. It meant preparation of the airdromes; providing airdrome space for parking; providing shops and temporary buildings for maintenance and overhaul at all the minor airdromes; sleeping accommodations and messing arrangements for the men (1400 officers and men were involved); it also necessitated securing communications of some kind or another, mainly telephone, between each Group and the next higher headquarters. But above all, supplies had always to be available when they were needed.

In order to have suitable accommodations and airdrome space so the airports would not be overcrowded and so we could get the airplanes off in time to participate in the operations, the various units had to be scattered pretty well all over central Ohio. That gave us some idea of the area we must contemplate using in time of war when we talked of concentrating 1000 or 2000 airplanes.

When General E. L. King, who had been my Commanding Officer at Leavenworth, arrived for these maneuvers in 1931, he surprised me by saying he appreciated very much the paper I had submitted when I left Leavenworth, outlining my ideas of the proper instruction in air operations at the Command and General Staff School. He also congratulated me on the way I had handled my job as G-4. This, from the man who had not wanted me at Leavenworth and who had said he would crucify me if I went there, made me feel good.

In spite of all the advances we were making, in my opinion, it wasn't until 1935 that we had the airplanes, accessories, installations, the gadgets the technique, and the know-how necessary to provide Air Power for the United States. It was true, however, that with a bit more encouragement and more funds, the date might have been advanced a few years. The operations of the Air Arm throughout the 1920's and early 1930's should have given an indication of its real value and should have created greater interest in its development as part of our national defense machinery. The surprising thing to me, in retrospect, is that so few saw the air's real possibilities. The Crowell Board did make a few positive recommendations. Then followed the LaGuardia Board, the Lassiter Board, the Select Committee of the House of Representatives called the Perkins Committee, the Morrow Board, the Howell Board, and the Baker Board.

Except for Jimmy Doolittle the Baker Board, which met in 1934, by which time aviation was certainly coming into its own, was unanimous in stating, "Independent air missions have little effect upon the issue of battle and none upon the outcome of war."

Douhet's theory came out in 1933, and was studied by airmen all over the world. It came very close to conforming to the theory we had worked out from our bombing and our operations on maneuvers. But not until March, 1935, was the principle of Air Power finally recognized by the War Department. Before that, in the fall of 1931 I was relieved from duty at Dayton, Ohio, and ordered to take command of the Air Corps station at March Field, Riverside, California.

My immediate job on arriving at March Field on November 26 was to transform a primary flying school into an operational base consisting of two Groups, one a bomber, and the other a fighter outfit. Among the excellent officers who had already started work on the transition were a number of old friends. Major Joseph T. McNarney, who had commanded the pilot-training school, requested that he be assigned to the Bomb Group, and I was happy to have him in that capacity. The Fighter Group was put under the command of Major Frank O'D. ("Monk") Hunter, a World War I ace with four clusters on his D.S.C., who knew fighting planes and was a natural-born leader. Major Carl ("Tooey") Spaatz, who had served with me off and on ever since he joined the Air Corps, became my Executive Officer in general charge of operations. It was a strong team.

We immediately started doing all the things necessary to form a couple of combat units. A small increase in personnel recently authorized by Congress made the organization of such units theoretically possible, but, it was not that easy. We had a few old-timers, officers and enlisted men as a nucleus, and many of our mechanics had recently been graduated from the Technical School at Chanute Field, but mostly, our personnel was made up of raw recruits. Most of our pilots were recent graduates from the Advanced Flying School at San Antonio. As for aircraft, we had a small number of Curtiss "Condor" B-2's, Keystone B-4's, B-5's and B-6's for bombers, and a miscellaneous collection of planes for our Fighter Group; mostly P-12's.

From the flying point of view, there was the advantage of California and of the West in the large expanses of terrain; the long distances available for flying exercises. With such bombers and fighters as we had, we were able to carry out "interception" missions that taught us tactical lessons. These were developed into an air defense doctrine that was constantly modified, but never abandoned, through World War II.

Flights starting from the baked plains of March Field could soon be over hot deserts, the high mountains, the great salt flats, and the Pacific Ocean. Thus, we were able to take advantage of rugged training conditions impossible in the East. During the next four years I put crews, and whole squadrons, on airdromes away from their home stations for weeks at a time, under field conditions which no other American airmen were to know until Brereton's units joined Tedder and Coningham in time for Alamein.

I think that one episode during the winter of 1932–33 makes it possible for us to take credit for having staged a dress rehearsal for the great Berlin Airlift ("Operation Vittles") fifteen years later. That winter's unprecedented blizzards swept over New Mexico, southwest Colorado, south Utah, and northern Arizona, and the isolated Indians in the villages faced starvation. I was asked if we could help from the air. We had never been confronted by such a problem, but I said, "Yes."

Our first question, as we took on this job, was not how to cope with the weather over that mountainous territory with its high winds, but how to pack the sugar, flour, potatoes, etc., so that the bundles we dropped wouldn't break on the frozen ground and spill their contents. The use of standard parachutes was out of the question. Captain Charlie Howard, with his famous 11th Bombardment Squadron of "Condors," made one test after another at March Field. Finally, we were able to pack the different commodities so well that, as one of my sergeants said, we could "drop a dozen eggs without breaking a damned one." Our bombers operated from various airports along the TWA line from Kingman, Arizona, east to Amarillo, Texas, and for several weeks, at the direction of the Indian agents, we located the scattered villages and hogans buried in the deep snow and bombed them with food.

Between 1931 and 1933, our little fighter and bomber units concentrated on night missions and altitude flying. Actually, the crews found it was easier to fly at night than in the daytime. We continued our individual, flight, squadron, and group training and were highly pleased when we got engines with superchargers—the superchargers that had made it possible for Mitchell to bomb the *Virginia* and the *New Jersey* from 10,000 feet. These superchargers now enabled us to fly high enough to clear the tallest mountains in the southwest.

The keenness of officers like Spaatz, McNarney, Hunter, Clarence Tinker and Ira Eaker, pushed everything ahead rapidly. There was a famous story on the base about the omnipresence of "Tooey" Spaatz. An ailing rookie was being examined by the doctor in the hospital. "Do you see spots before your eyes?" the medico asked. "My God!" groaned the soldier. "Do I have to see him in here, too?"

But even such alertness left us unprepared for the shocking report dumped in our laps one morning by the District Attorney of San Bernardino, who, with the Sheriff, called upon me in my office. Like everyone else, I had read stories in the newspapers and magazines of subversive activities—Reds, Communists, and what not—and I knew there had been recent disturbances in San Bernardino. It developed, however, that not only did the Communists have the railroad town of San Bernardino thoroughly organized, with various cells and weekly meetings, but we at March Field were one of their prize targets!

The District Attorney handed me documentary proof. He and the Sheriff had kept track of the Communist meetings, regarding them not as particularly harmful, but still as sufficiently important for one of their own men to join the Party, sit in on things, and make stenographic notes. Now the transcriptions of these notes were handed to me, covering a period of several months. At first, the reading was dull. Then my eyes popped out! Comrade Nelson reported proudly on the chain of "study classes" he had started at March Field! They were headed by a Technical Sergeant, with a Staff Sergeant regularly present. Comrade Dynes reported: "We no longer need fear the machine guns, nor the bombs, nor the airplanes at March Field. We have taken care of that!" The District Attorney and the Sheriff left me with the notes to think it over.

I was dumbfounded. Just what could I do? Who were the Reds in the Army at my station? How could I find out? My experience with such problems was about zero. I thought over my officers and selected Lieutenant Jack Stone. I told him I had a very unpleasant job for him. It could be dangerous; but it was essential to find out who the two men were who were coming to the base to conduct the "Red" classes—one described as "Comrade Dynes," the other, as "Comrade Nelson." I wanted to know what they looked like and the numbers of their automobile licenses so that they could be identified as they came on the Post.

Through arrangements of the DA and the Sheriff, Lieutenant Stone actually accompanied the Party leaders to a big rally. When he started to take photographs of Dynes and Nelson, his camera was grabbed and broken, he was manhandled and badly mussed up, but managed to get away without serious injury. By that time he knew enough about our two subjects to enable us to watch Dynes and Nelson on the Base until the soldiers attending the "Red" classes were identified.

It is rather difficult, now, to realize the "don't care" attitude of the United States, and that includes the War Department, concerning subversive activities at that time. Actually that attitude was not much different from the foreign policy of appeasement and compromise which we followed with Japan and Germany for the next several years. There was not much that I could do other than transfer the enlisted men, discharge those who were due, and keep others under strict surveillance. A court-martial, under the circumstances, was out of the question.

After that, I sent one of my brightest young men to Los Angeles, where, by careful conniving, he eventually managed to sit in on the meetings of the Communist "inner circle," and was able to keep our March Field Intelligence up to date on their activities.

We felt more and more our lack of both a real bombing range and an aerial machine gun range. We had none but the Pacific, and our Navy said "taboo" on using that. It was duck-boarded for their operations. We had to look elsewhere.

To the north of us, just over the San Bernardino mountains, was the Mojave Desert; large, unsettled; not good for anything but rattlesnakes and horned toads, or where there was water, for the establishment of desert colonies for the idle rich. It was ideal for a bombing range. A map from the land office indicated that most of the Mojave belonged to the United States Government. The main exception was a strip ten miles wide along the Southern Pacific Railroad. There the land ownership was checkerboarded. The Government owned a square mile, then the Southern Pacific, a square mile. There was also a small amount of so-called "school land" in the desert, owned by the state of California.

We had to make a personal reconnaissance of the land to be sure it really did suit our purpose, but we knew that the minute people learned the Army was interested, the price asked for that wasteland would go sky high; lease clauses of miners, prospectors, etc., would come to be involved, and we probably would never get our bomb and gunnery ranges. And those ranges were just as important to us as the equipment in our hangars at March Field.

Friends in the Automobile Club of Southern California agreed to help, and one morning at three o'clock we set off—two men from the

Automobile Club, and three Army officers in civilian clothes. At six
A.M. we reached the little town of Muroc, adjacent to a big dry lake,
fourteen miles long, seven miles wide, with a hard surface as smooth as
glass. The texture of the soil was the finest kind of clay—a clay they
were harvesting for women's face packs, and for oil men to use on their
bits while drilling. It made about the best and smoothest landing field
imaginable. It was a "natural" for a bombing range. Taking off from
this dead lake, thousands of young men were to learn how to send their
bombs down accurately on Berlin, Tokyo, Rome, Tobruk, and remote
places from New Guinea to the Polish port of Gdynia. Also, it was
here that man first would break through the supersonic barrier.

In the half dark, we woke up the one man who lived in the town, ran
the general store, and was station agent. He emerged with understandable irritation. Our friends explained cooperatively that we were a party
from the Automobile Club looking over routes and signs, and would
appreciate his comments or suggestions, if he had any.

To the delight of the Army contingent he at once expressed enough
comments on the Automobile Club to fill a book—had they been print-
able! But interlaced with the abuse were valuable answers to our questions. Returning to March Field with a boiling radiator in our car, we
started a title search at the County Courthouse, covering a piece of the
Muroc desertland about nineteen miles long by nine miles wide.

That project looked like a simple one to carry out; the land was
cheap, and most of it was owned by the U.S. Government. Nevertheless,
though we used certain sections of the government land earlier, it was
three years after I went to Washington (1939) before we got legal title
to that bombing range. Muroc was, and is, one of the finest bombing
and gunnery ranges in the world. The clay-covered lake is so smooth
that the early pilot had to receive special instructions before going in
to land. A speed of 100 miles an hour on it seemed slower than 50 miles
an hour on a normal field. It is so vast that there was no way the pilot
could tell whether he was rolling straight ahead on landing, or turning,
unless he was careful to pick out checkpoints on a mountain from five
to seven miles away. This caused one ground loop after another until
finally our pilots learned. Today Muroc is one of our most important
experimental stations, and supersonic airplanes land on that same lake
at speeds of 150 miles per hour with the reliability of standard planes
at normal speeds.

Muroc was close enough to March Field for us to start bombing or
shooting in a matter of minutes, so live bombing, and air-to-ground, as

well as air-to-air, gunnery became part of our daily training schedules. We were also fortunate in being able to carry on maneuvers all over California, and, later, throughout the whole West. In March, 1933, I took over command of the 1st Fighter Wing, including units at March Field, Rockwell Field, and at Hamilton Field, near San Francisco. In November I was ordered to assume command of the 1st Bomb Wing, composed of the bombardment outfits at the same three fields. Thus the establishment of the "1st Wing of the G.H.Q. Air Force," in 1935, required no real organizational changes.

Our exercises were planned to cover every phase of air operations in combat that we could realize, from the training of the individual pilots in fighters at separated spots, such as Long Beach, the Imperial Valley, or the top of Tehachapi Pass, whence they made contact with the home station by radio, to the mass training of groups and squadrons. We were especially interested in developing radio and navigation, and in the use of air-ground radio for communications and command purposes. However, our radio operators had to be selected with great care, for our radio equipment, though terribly expensive, was intricate and unreliable. If there was any sort of mountain in the way, reception usually failed.

I remember the surprise of Major Ira Eaker and myself about that time, when we were fishing in the Sierras with some U.S. Foresters who had brought a radio along on the back of a mule so that Ira and I could keep in touch with the outside world. All day that old pack mule went kerlank, kerlank, kerlank, up and down the mountain trails. We were so busy making our camp that night that I forgot about communications. Then a ranger who had been wrangling mules all day and who was, for the moment, cooking trout, suddenly said, "My God! I forgot the radio!" He rushed over to a beaten-up box, took out the antennae, ran a wire between two trees, opened up the set and called into the transmitter: "Hello there, Porterville, is that you? This is Bill talking. Have you got any messages for the boss?"

The answer came through immediately, although there was a 10,000-foot mountain between us and Porterville. Eaker and I sat there with our mouths open. "How much does that thing cost?" I asked. The old muleskinner said it cost about $600. The Air Force sets cost $2500 apiece, and were supposed to be the finest money could buy! Neither Ira nor I could understand it. For seven days we had radio communication with the outside world in terrain that would have kept our beautiful sets, with our highly trained radio men, silent.

That spring, March Field made friends with a man who was to be an important contributor to the Air Corps' development in World War II. I had worked with him in World War I and knew his wonderful ability and technical knowledge. This was Dr. Robert Millikan, of the California Institute of Technology. He came to me to ask if I would help him with his cosmic ray experiments. I said, "Yes, of course," and then asked him what it meant.

He said the experiments would involve flying a lead sphere, weighing five to six hundred pounds, to various altitudes. Within this metal ball were all kinds of instruments which measured the intensity of the cosmic rays. Since none of our bombers were equipped to carry such a machine, our squadron mechanics devised a special rack for the lead ball. We made many altitude flights with this lead ball until Dr. Millikan's air experiments were successfully concluded. The noted scientist then took his lead sphere to the bottom of a limestone mine, five hundred feet below the earth's surface, to see if the rays would penetrate there. His first mishap came when, wishing to measure intensities on various mountaintops, he carried his cosmic ray machine to Lake Arrowhead to load it into a somewhat flimsy boat. The heavy lead ball plunged through the bottom of the boat as if it were paper, and disappeared in thirty-five feet of water. The next time I saw him, I called him "Admiral."

There was a powerful "will to do" in that First Wing, regardless of the task to be performed. At March, Rockwell, and Hamilton Fields, the sparse equipment seemed only to increase the esprit de corps. The bitter months of the air-mail tragedy, soon to be upon us, were met with the same "Can Do" spirit which later beat Germany and Japan. Whatever went wrong, the men were never found wanting. An unforgettable example was the case of Captain Donald W. Buckman and his transport plane at Bakersfield.

One day Buckman was flying one of the earliest Army transports from March Field to Bakersfield with six enlisted men for passengers. Some while before Buckman's estimated time of arrival, we heard him calling the Bakersfield tower. He said he believed he was having a heart attack; the pain was very bad and he didn't know whether he would be able to make it or not. He would do everything he could, but in case he blacked out, he wanted us to know what had happened.

We sent him such encouragement as we could by radio, and waited for him, with an ambulance and the crash wagon standing by. Everybody knew that in that plane, a monoplane, the pilot sat alone, in front, without any possible communication with the people back in the fuselage.

At last the plane appeared. It came in a little uncertainly, making a more abrupt approach than usual, but it leveled off all right, touched its wheels, and rolled to a stop. With great relief, we hurried out to meet it, and, as we drove up, saw the enlisted men climbing down casually, unaware they had been in any danger. Then we looked into the cockpit. Captain Buckman was sitting at the controls, dead.

In the spring of 1933, I had one of the biggest thrills of my life. We were to have maneuvers at March Field, with airplanes flown in from every part of the country. General Oscar Westover, then Assistant Chief of Air Corps, was to be in command, and I was to be Chief of Staff during the operations. In my long years of service I had held practically every job in the Air Corps, from a squadron pilot to "high-ranking" staff officer, but I had never been a Chief of Staff, and looked forward with interest to the work. These maneuvers were to develop further the technique of combined bomber and fighter operations in combat. There were to be no interruptions. We had the entire West Coast region in which to operate, and the newly acquired Muroc Lake area in which to drop bombs.

In due season the visiting units began to pour in, until we had about three hundred airplanes at March Field. The visiting enlisted men and officers were billeted in tents, barracks, bachelor officers' quarters, or wherever else we could find room. Even as late as 1933, we were still using many of the tar-paper barracks thrown up at March Field in 1917.

The maneuvers started very successfully. We carried out one exercise after another, over ocean, mountains, and desert.

Then, right in the middle of it, in May, 1933, I received a telegram from the Corps Area Commander: "Can you take care of 1500 CCC boys at your Station, effective next week?" Naturally, I wired back: "We are having maneuvers here now. All the combat type airplanes in the U.S. Air Corps are engaged. Cannot take care of CCC boys at present." At that moment my idea of the CCC program was sketchy, to say the least; but I learned rapidly—the hard way.

Within twenty-four hours came the reply: "You probably do not understand. This is an Executive Order of the President who says that CCC camps will be established and will be administered by the U.S. Army. Can you take care of 3000 CCC boys effective immediately?"

There went my short career as a Chief of Staff. I informed General Westover I was sorry, but that I, and most of my officers, would have to stop the maneuvers in order to go on immediate CCC duty. Wet blanket as it seemed at the moment, we were to know two years later that this sudden order sending us the Civilian Conservation Corps gave us practical experience of a kind that was badly needed.

The CCC boys began to arrive. They came in by railroad train, by bus, by truck, thumbing rides; they came with coats and without coats. Some of them had ropes around their waists to hold their trousers up. They were all eager, willing boys, looking for something to do, and most of them were hungry, so hungry they looked as if they hadn't had anything to eat for weeks. In no time, we had added to the tent camp already at March Field. The boys learned to pitch the tents themselves. Good hot Army coffee and stew, plenty of bread and butter, and apple pie did much for the morale of those youngsters that first night. It was not long before they were able to run their own messes. We taught them to cook and wait on tables, and soon the CCC camps were self-supporting.

It turned very cold that first night, though. We found we didn't have enough blankets for all the CCC boys who came in, so a detail went around quietly and removed a blanket from each of our sleeping Air Corps soldiers and gave them to the CCC youngsters.

The Air Corps learned a lot from handling those boys. Officers who had never before thought about anything very seriously, except flying an airplane, suddenly found themselves faced with administrative and human relations problems. As contingent after contingent streamed in, we had to find new camp sites for them, be sure the land was clear and healthy, and that good pure water was available. At the arrival of every new group there had to be enough food, blankets, tents, tent floorings, and so on trucked up to the proper camp. If a truckload of lumber was dumped off in the wrong place, or the truck rolled off down the mountain, that was an Air Corps officer's problem. The CCC outfits brought small numbers of Reserve Officers with them for administrative purposes—some good, and some of poor caliber—but most of them were about as bewildered as the boys when they arrived.

The CCC boys had many hours to spare, during which a small amount of military training would not have hurt them, and might have benefited the country. They asked for it; indeed, they begged for at least enough instruction to enable them to carry out basic formations. However, we were going through a period in our country when we could not do anything that might make us look militaristic. Even toy cannon or soldiers were frowned upon. So military training for the CCC was not permitted. I will confess that when a delegation of the boys came to me and asked if they might be allowed to hold voluntary formations at reveille and at retreat to raise the colors and lower them, I said they could, and they enjoyed it.

The CCC responsibility—soon I had over thirty of these camps—continued to grow, and also emphasized the remoteness of higher headquarters in any big field. I shall never forget how the two CCC Companies sent out to handle the Death Valley project were composed of boys from, of all places, Jersey City, Newark, and Elizabeth, New Jersey—boys who had no knowledge of desert lore whatever, and because they did not know how to take care of themselves, might have perished from heat or thirst. However, on that desert job we were fortunate to have the advice of Colonel John White, Superintendent of the Death Valley National Monument, who had served with me in World War I, and of his assistant, T. C. Goodwin, both practical outdoor men whose help was invaluable to me.

We made our preliminary reconnaissance of the Valley in August, the hottest month of the year, and found it impossible to drive an automobile through the intense heat on the floor of the Valley for more than one-quarter of a mile at a time. At Furnace Creek Ranch, I asked the ranch manager if he stayed there every summer. "Yes," he said, "unless it gets too hot." "How hot" I asked, "is 'too hot'?" "Well," he said, "it went up to 135 last year, and I went out." His bed was outside an adobe building, under a lean-to which had a pipe running along the eaves of the roof with a spray of water coming down. An electric fan rigged outside blew the spray of water across the bed. By the time the spray hit his bed the water had evaporated in the heat but the air was cooler.

Later, one of our officers, driving up the Valley, found the body of a man lying beside that same road, obviously dead of thirst. We hastened to report it. "What did you find on him?" the coroner and sheriff asked casually. We said we hadn't found anything. The man was a tramp who had tried to walk the twenty-five miles from Daylight Springs to Furnace Creek. "Well," they said, "dig a hole and put him in." We did, and marked the grave with a stone cross. There are quite a few of those roadside crosses in Death Valley.

In February, 1934, over a year after President Roosevelt entered the White House, the Air Corps had one of the toughest assignments in our peacetime history tossed in its lap. Postmaster James Farley was at loggerheads with the commercial airlines about the rates which were charged the Government for carrying air mail. He decided on a showdown. Assistant Postmaster Harlee Branch was charged with finding an alternative way of delivering the mail. The Air Corps was approached, and General Ben Foulois, then Chief of the Air Corps, said he could do it.

Foulois, who has always taken the responsibility for this decision, has been harshly criticized for it. In view of what I have already said about the Air Corps' willingness to accept any and all challenges, with or without previous experience, I think it is doubtful if any other air leader in his place would have answered differently.

Within two weeks we were forced to realize that although the "will to do" might get the job done, the price of our doing it was to equal the sacrifice of a wartime combat operation. Courage alone could not substitute for years of cross-country experience; for properly equipped planes; and for suitable blind flying instruments, such as the regular air-line mail pilots were using.

Brigadier General Oscar Westover was placed in charge of the project. Major B. Q. Jones, with headquarters in New York, was given command of the "Eastern Zone." Lieutenant Colonel Horace M. Hickam had responsibility from Chicago to Cheyenne. The "Western Zone" was under my direction, with my command post in a hotel at Salt Lake City, and covered the area from Cheyenne westward to the Pacific Coast.

We were given ten days in which to orient ourselves. That is, my boys had ten days in which to "familiarize" themselves with the topography and weather idiosyncrasies of the air-mail routes. My pilots were mostly Reserve officers, none of whom, owing to the War Department policy of turning over Reserve officers in a squadron at the rate of 25 or 30 per cent a year, had had two years' service. Very few of the "regular" civilian air-mail routes had been flown over by these officers. They had none of the special air-line instruments; they must fly in whatever planes we had, including trainers. There was not—especially in the case of the open-cockpit fighter types that had to be flown—even enough space for the mail bags. All sorts of places had to be found to hold them.

On the 19th of February we started. And as if some derisive gods were pulling strings, that week a foul mess of weather dropped over the whole United States. Freezing, blinding blizzards; sleet; ice storms; squalls; rain and heavy winds, from one end of the country to the other. Anyone old enough to read at that time will remember how bad it was in the East alone. In the West, where some of my bases were seven thousand feet above sea level and the air-mail routes passed over mountains twelve thousand feet high, or ran through solid ocean fogs, it was worse. The beacons along the route were not fully developed, and were still inaccurate. One of the first of my boys to take off, Lieutenant Jack Crosthwaite, trying to make Los Angeles from San Francisco, found "L.A." completely socked in, and had to fly back to Sacramento before he could land. Soon the crashes began. Within a few days there were complaints and questions throughout the country. Within a week, the crack-ups were pushing Hitler, the New Deal, and the Stavisky case in France, out of the headlines. As the third week passed, the bad weather showed no sign of letting up; and neither did our casualties. It was tragic and it was maddening.

Ten days after the Army started carrying the mail, the whole country was angry. At first the editorials and radio commentators, especially those who wished to see the President win his fight against the commercial air lines, blamed us. What was the *matter* with our Air Corps, anyway? If it couldn't carry out a job like this, how could it ever fight a war? Wouldn't the Air Corps be expected to meet any and all flying conditions in wartime? This was a good test!

Soon more thoughtful portions of the public began to realize that perhaps it wasn't such a good test at all. Politics was costing the lives of a lot of boys who, day after day, and night after night, were doing far more than anybody had a right to expect of them under the circumstances. It was pointed out that we were actually flying about the same percentage of scheduled flights as the commercial air lines had flown. Also, a number of our casualties occurred on "shuttle-runs," or ferrying trips, when no mail was being carried. There was another thought raised by the tragic happenings: if we had been given the planes, the personnel, and the funds for training for which we had battled all these years, we *would* have been able to carry out the air-mail assignment with far greater efficiency. In that light it *was* a good test. It gave us wonderful experience for combat flying, bad weather flying, night flying; but, best of all, it made it possible for us to get the latest navigational and night-flying instruments in our planes. Mixed with the tragedies, there were a few laughs. One of these occurred when there was a discussion about who was in command of the Air Depot at Chicago. Then it was that Horace Hickam sent his famous telegram to the War Department: "Who *is* commanding this thing anyway? Make up your minds. Love and kisses (signed) Horace."

No matter what happened, and something happened practically every day and night, the spirit of our pilots never let down. Often when the weather was bad I wouldn't go to bed at all, for I knew I would only be wakened in a little while to begin receiving the same kind of news.

We had to improvise in order to find space in which to carry the mail. The story is told that six months after the Army stopped carrying the mail, mechanics were overhauling a plane at one of our depots, pulled the turtleback off and found a bag of U.S. Mail still inside. I can't vouch for that one, but another incident shows the kind of men we had flying those planes. One of my young pilots, covering the route from Salt Lake City to Los Angeles, ran into a snow squall about eighty miles southwest of Salt Lake. Everything went dark. He couldn't see any beams or beacons and his training plane was not equipped for radio flying. Suddenly through the snow he saw a flash almost directly ahead, and knew it was an airport. In order to get in before the next snow squall hit him, he went in fast, and landed downwind.

Meanwhile, back at Headquarters, we wondered what had happened to him. He should have checked in hours before from one of our Sub-Stations. Finally the telephone rang and I heard his voice at the other end: "Sir, I am checking in from Tintic." "Are you all right?" "Yes, sir. I'm all right." "How about your plane?" I asked. "Well, sir, it's a bit damaged." "How much?" I asked. He hesitated. "Well, it has no landing gear." "Is that all?" I asked. "Well, the lower wing is off." "What else?" "Well, the tail surface is broken off, and the engine flew out of the fuselage, sir." As a matter of fact, next morning the mechanics found that airplane scattered all over the field, and the U.S. Mail scattered over an area of several acres!

By the time we were relieved of carrying the air mail—on May 16th—and the commercial lines again took over, public opinion was clamoring for an investigation, not only of the air-mail situation, but of half a dozen aviation matters. The President probably didn't feel like risking it with a Congressional Committee, so a Military Board was appointed, headed by Major General Hugh A. Drum, and with General Foulois a member. Presently a committee of noted civilians was added, under the chairmanship of former Secretary of War Newton D. Baker. Out of this "Baker Board" the next year, came the formation of the General Headquarters or G.H.Q. Air Force, the first real step ever taken toward an independent United States Air Force.

When I got back to March Field, after the air-mail assignment was over, Mrs. Arnold and I started off to Jackson Hole on a fishing trip. We had driven only as far as Salt Lake City when a barrage of telegrams and telephone calls summoned me back. I found a wire waiting, from General Foulois. I was to report at once at Wright Field to organize and take command of a bomber flight to Alaska.

Upon arriving at Dayton, I found the planes to be used were the new Martin B-10's. Until the B-17 came along, the B-10 was the air power wonder of its day. A low-wing monoplane, it was the first all-metal bomber, the first of the 200-mile-an-hour bombers. It had a range of approximately 900 miles, and was very clean in design. After conferring with General Westover and the others planning this flight, I realized its importance. Major Hugh Knerr, of Langley Field, in general charge of the development of bombardment in the Air Corps, was assigned as my Executive.

The course was to be from Dayton to Washington, D. C., thence via Minneapolis, Regina (Canada), Edmonton, Prince George, and White Horse, to Fairbanks. We were to fly over extensive Alaskan territory, taking aerial photographs in order to secure detailed information for use in mapping airways in and out of Alaska, and to various ports of entry to Alaska from Russia, or from across the Arctic Circle. We were then to return to Washington by way of Juneau and Seattle. The flight was composed of ten of these new B-10's, with a personnel of fourteen officers and six enlisted men.

After nearly a month of careful preparation, we took off for Washington on July 18th. Before we returned to March Field, we had carried out our mission, and covered a distance of 18,000 miles over some of the roughest flying country in North America, without incident except the sinking of one B-10 in Cooks Bay, Anchorage, whence we were able to raise it from forty feet of water and continue it in operation. That was quite a job that far from home bases. I must remember the outstanding performance of Technical Sergeant Henry Puzenski, my crew chief for the B-10. After that trip, he remained my crew chief until I retired as Commanding General of the Army Air Forces some thirteen years later.

The mission was without precedent, but, at the same time, not unusually tough. We averaged 820 miles a day, and, from Juneau to Seattle, since there was no landing field between, had to cover 990 miles nonstop through fog and rainstorms. Returning first to Washington, on August 22nd, we then continued on to our home station, March Field. We had been back only five or six days when we were called east again to take part in General MacArthur's maneuvers. The idea was to show how fast a formation of modern bombers could be moved from one coast to the other. We didn't do so well on that mission. Preliminary plans showed that we should have been able to make the flight within twenty-four hours. However, bad weather and engine trouble delayed us. Taking off at about 2:00 A.M., on September 3rd, from March Field, we reached Langley Field at 1:20 A.M., on the 4th.

Aside from the efficiency of the Alaskan trip, and the implications for bombardment, two special incidents stand out in my memory. One was a session of the House of Lords, some time later, where our flight was drawn into a debate concerning the age at which Royal Air Force officers should be retired. One of the Lords thought they were getting out too young. He cited a letter from a doctor friend in Regina, Saskatchewan. His friend had gone out to see the formation of American bombers when they landed at Regina, and had wondered what sort of officers would be leading them. To the doctor's surprise, when the American air commander climbed down, he turned out to be "a white haired old gentleman"! (That was "Hap" Arnold, aged forty-eight!)

The other thing was a visit I received from a stranger in my hotel at Fairbanks. It was one of those days when it was raining hard. We couldn't fly to make photographs and there was little to do but sit around. My telephone rang. A voice with an accent informed me I did not know its owner, but he would like to come up and speak to me.

When he appeared, it turned out that he was a German who had been a flyer in World War I. Since then he had drifted around the world in various jobs, studying aviation in Russia, England, and France, and more recently, in Germany. He was very interested in our B-10's which he had seen at the field, and seemed to be leading up to something. Finally he said, "You think you have a good bomber out there, don't you?"

"The best bomber in the world," I said, "bar none!"

He said: "What would you say if I told you the Germans have a far better bomber today than you have in that B-10 out there?"

I replied: "I couldn't say anything, except you're a damned liar!"

He said: "Well, they have."

When I protested that this was impossible; that Allied Inspection Officers were all through German industry; Allied Commissions were going around everywhere to insure that no instruments of war would be built, he smiled.

"Just have your Military Attaché go to the Junkers plant, the Heinkel plant, or the Dornier plant, and take a good look at the ships they are calling 'high altitude transport planes.' They are making pursuit planes, as well. The component factories are well dispersed from the parent assembly plants, but if your attaché is smart, he'll find them."

It took my breath away. I asked him: "What are you doing up here in Alaska?" He said he had come up to establish a freight and passenger airline running between Fairbanks and Livengood. "You don't have to be afraid of me," he said. "I've already taken out my first papers for American citizenship; but these are things that you should know." Then he left.

As soon as I got back to Washington I took this matter up with G-2, but War Department Intelligence had no information on the subject of the Germans building transports and fighters. I asked that our Military Attachés in Germany look into it, though I realized that the setup in Nazi Germany made it especially difficult for regular attachés to get such information. Within a few months, before I ever heard from our attaché at Berlin, Goering announced that he was re-creating the German Air Force, and, on March 16, 1935, boasted that the Luftwaffe would be the strongest air force in the world.

As a result of the findings of the Baker Board, an entirely new air setup was arranged. The "General Headquarters," or G.H.Q. Air Force, was created, composed of the "striking forces" of the Air Arm, under the command of Major General Frank Andrews. Though the Chief of the Air Corps continued in office, and though the Air Corps remained responsible for all procurement and supply, including that of the G.H.Q. Air Force, the latter did not come under the operational jurisdiction of the Air Corps, but existed beside it, reporting directly to the Chief of Staff of the Army.

Andrews set up his headquarters at Langley Field on March 9, 1935, with three Wings in his command. I was given command of the 1st Wing of the G.H.Q. Air Force, and promoted from Lieutenant Colonel to temporary Brigadier General. The geographical limits of my new outfit were roughly analogous to those of the "Western Zone" during the air-mail operation. My headquarters were still at March Field. The units involved were the same: three fighter outfits and three bomber groups at March, Rockwell, and Hamilton Fields, of which I already had command.

Jurisdictional troubles still existed with the Air Force crossing wires with the Ninth Corps Area Commander at San Francisco, who still, for example, had court-martial authority over us.

General Foulois was "Chief of the Air Corps," handling Air Corps administrative, procurement, and other functions. The Air Corps, it was said, had now only been split in two, the argument being whether the "independent air striking force" of the G.H.Q. Air Force should head up under the Chief of Air Corps, on whom it must depend for all technical air supplies and training of its personnel, or report directly to the Chief of Staff.

Regardless of these contentions, establishment of the G.H.Q. Force was an exciting "shot in the arm." Out on the coast where our new B-10's were already being succeeded by the improved Martin B-12 bombers, we felt it strongly. The classes at the Air Corps Tactical School, at Maxwell Field, Alabama, were just then beginning to develop strategic and tactical doctrines that would later guide our air campaigns in World War II.

As regards strategic bombardment, the doctrines were still Douhet's ideas modified by our own thinking in regard to pure defense. We felt, out in the 1st Wing, that we were doing much to furnish the practical tests for, and proofs of, the Maxwell Field theories. A different attitude from Douhet's toward bomber escort and a very different view of precision bombing resulted.

The fighter exercises against the B-10's and B-12's were at first deceptive, because the 200-mile-per-hour bombers were only some 20 miles per hour slower than the fastest fighter we had then (the P-26). Naturally, notions that unescorted bombers might be able to out-run defending fighters, temporarily existed. This idea was further encouraged by the information that the four-engine B-17 was planned to do 250 miles per hour and would be faster than any fighter yet seen, and heavily armed. Nevertheless, we became convinced—at least I certainly did—that long-range, heavy bombers must have not only increased fire power and mutual support, but also a fast maneuverable fighter escort which could go with the bombers to their targets.

Part of this conviction came from a constant development, as airplane types diversified and became more and more refined, of a thought the Wright brothers had started to hammer into me in the days when such terms as "fighters" and "bombers" were unknown even to them: "Large airplanes built with the same shape and relative dimensions as small ones, will not have the same relative performance."

Those who thought it was a miracle that long-range fighter escort for our bombers appeared over Germany at just the critical moment in the fall of 1943 apparently do not realize that, like the B-29, this was something we started developing before the war. I should have preferred never to send any unescorted bombers over Germany.

As fire power on airplanes increased, I was anxious to see the results when .50 cal. and .37 mm. shots were fired through the metal skins of our new B-10's and B-12's. When an interested group of congressmen from the House Military Affairs Committee came to pay us a visit, I decided this was a good time for the test. Naturally, we had some .30 and .50 caliber machine guns, but I had to borrow a .37 mm. cannon from the National Guard. First I fired .30 caliber shots into the metal fuselage of a plane; practically no damage was done. Then I poured some .50 calibers into it; larger holes, but nothing serious. Then we tried the .37 mm. cannon. This made big holes and where explosive bullets went through, whole sections of the metal were torn out. The congressmen were impressed with the demonstration. So was I. In accordance with the regulations, I at once forwarded a full report through Corps Area Headquarters to my Chief in Washington. It did not get past San Francisco. Back it came with a crisp indorsement on it: "By whose authority did you use .37 mm. ammunition?" I replied: "By my own authority." Back came the third indorsement. "Whose .37 mm. ammunition was used?; who signed for it?; who is accountable for it?; and who should be charged with it?" As I had already discussed the experiment with the Chief of Staff in Washington, and he had expressed keen interest in it, I did not answer this until I went to San Francisco when I explained it. The matter was dropped. However, the incident showed the general attitude in Supply Services when funds are scarce. To be able to account for ammunition was far more important to them than to determine the effectiveness of modern weapons on the metal fuselages of modern planes.

As I write this, I have before me an old chart from the 19th Bomb Group at Rockwell Field. It shows that, bombing steadily from an altitude of 15,000 feet, with the Norden bombsight, the 19th Group began on the first day by placing its eggs within 520 feet of the target, closing the gap to 480 feet at the end of seven days, to 300 feet at the end of twenty-seven days, and placing its bombs regularly within 164 feet of a target no bigger than a woodshed, at the end of forty-one days.

Over Germany, direct hits were made from nearly twice that altitude; but for 1935, a near bull's-eye from almost three miles up struck us as being pretty good. If airmen got to talking a little too confidently in those days about "tossing it right in the pickle barrel," or "hitting a dime from twenty-five thousand feet," our continued improvement in bombing with the Norden sight may explain why.

Because of all these things the 1st Wing was supposed to be a very cocky outfit, practically an "independent air force" in itself. This is undoubtedly said of all top-notch units. Anyway, the reputation didn't always win friends and influence people on the other side of the Rockies.

Looking at one of our maneuvers one day, a visiting staff officer said wryly: "It's wonderful, General, but I don't think it'll become S.O.P. (Standard Operating Procedure). Anything connected with 'Hap' Arnold has the 'kiss of death' on it back there."

We tried out all kinds of things, some of which, happily, were forgotten by everybody. I came on some clearly plotted pictures the other day which wouldn't have helped us a bit in the war, but might have been invaluable to the Germans. They show the results of some experiments with air-to-air bombing, a technique we had worked out with five-pound bombs. None of the clumsy attempts of the Germans at bombing our formations ever inflicted widespread damage; but no expert who has seen these pictures has failed to exclaim at what might have happened to one of our tightly stacked formations of B-17's if the Luftwaffe had hit on our "California" idea. The Germans had no such formations to bomb.

One reason for our outfit's tendency to independence was, I think, psychological. In World War I, comparatively few of these men had gone overseas. The pilot training program of that war had been highly successful, and thousands of men had received their wings; but since airplane production had not met the program until too late most of the pilots never flew in a combat plane. The majority of those who did get overseas never progressed further than school in France or England. Consequently it was natural that the western group, which included many outstanding airmen but few returned heroes, should draw together in solidarity.

Few ground force generals led as pleasant an existence as our lieutenants did in that Command, or worked harder. That—and necessarily the youth of our air unit commanders, whose huge responsibilities— often a young air colonel would have more men and equipment under his charge than a ground major general with two brigadier assistants— caused a lot of the grumbling about us. When I got to Washington it was a grumpy refrain. We damned airmen were "too cocky, too big for our boots, undisciplined, too damned free all round!" My answer to that is one which I feel more strongly today than I did then, and I shall refer to it again. Of all the Air Force's faults, its greatest has always been the fact that it has made its work seem too easy.

So, as I say, there were a few resentments in the distance, human ones in the trapped Washington atmosphere, resentments both walking and airborne. Alas, I was soon to know more about it!

Ben Foulois, Chief of the Air Corps until December, 1935, was an old friend. Frank Andrews, Commanding General of the G.H.Q. Air Force, was an old friend. On their staffs, as well as in the War Department building in general, were many officers with whom my own past service in Washington had given me the closest personal relationships. Even the successive Chiefs of Staff of the Army happened to be men I had known personally and pleasantly throughout my service. Summerall had been one of my instructors at West Point, and our friendship continued. Douglas MacArthur and I had served together in Washington between 1911–13, and the famous story of his vote against Billy Mitchell's sentence at the court-martial (an enterprising newspaper man from a Washington paper had searched the wastebasket for the ballots) had reached us through Billy himself. Malin Craig, the then incumbent Chief of Staff (he had been appointed in 1935) was an immediate personal associate who, as Commander of the Ninth Corps Area in San Francisco, made things far easier for me at March Field than they might otherwise have been.

Still, it seemed better for me to keep away from Washington. I knew what was going on there (or at least I thought I did). My allegiance in the "Air Corps vs. G.H.Q. Air Force" controversy was naturally to the latter, since our Wing was one of its three field components, and, also, because it was the nearest thing to an independent Air Force yet realized. True, the G.H.Q. Air Force represented only a minor fraction of the total Air establishment, small as that was altogether. True, the problems of air supply and air procurement; the fight with the War Department about control of "air support units"; and much of the political battle for air recognition, generally, were still in the hands of General Foulois' (soon to be General Westover's) Air Corps headquarters. Also, the independent (strategic) air function of the G.H.Q. Air Force had not been exactly determined. Still, the mere existence of the G.H.Q. Air Force was a big air step forward, and we figured that we on the Coast were carrying it further. With the contention of General Andrews that his G.H.Q. Air Force should not report to the Chief of the Air Corps at all, but should head up directly under the Chief of Staff, we enthusiastically agreed.

It was a rough blow, then, when General Craig, as Chief of Staff, in December, 1935, sent word for me to fly to Washington a few weeks after General Westover had become Chief of the Air Corps, succeeding General Foulois. General Westover had requested me as his Assistant Chief of the Air Corps—and General Craig thought it was a good idea!

I liked Oscar Westover very much indeed—personally—but I protested with all my heart that I would rather stay on the Coast with my silver leaves back; really, would rather be a lieutenant colonel running my present command than a staff general in Washington! No use. General Craig had already approved the change.

In January, 1936, the entire Arnold family said good-by, in tears, to March Field, and moved—back to that hectic town, Washington. I was a gloomy man. It had always seemed to me—and I knew the place pretty well—that the honking traffic jams, the waiting in anterooms, clerks colliding with their stacks of papers in the endless corridors, the sharp tongues at cocktail parties confiding what they seldom really knew, were not merely the Face of Washington, but much of its Inside Story. Friends or no friends, I thought, it was no place for me. Also, it was good-by to Command!

If I had realized then that I would stay in Washington for ten consecutive years, right up to my retirement, I would almost have dared to turn my overloaded car around and drive straight back to California. As it turned out, it would be my lot to have a Command again—one of the biggest commands in history. But even at the peak of that, I was still always to remain partially a staff officer. The Chief of the Air Corps was to be also Deputy Chief of Staff of the United States Army. The Commanding General of the Army Air Forces would still be a harassed member of such undreamed-of, high-powered Staffs as the Joint and the Combined Chiefs of Staff. There would be many thrills, but the pure exuberance of that command on the Coast was never to come back.

There was even a certain amount of embarrassment in my new post, since now I was ranged with the Air Corps Headquarters, across the fence from the G.H.Q. Air Force, whose side of the intramural arguments had been my own enthusiastic side in California. I was to learn more about this controversy almost immediately, and, going through it myself, to acquire a new kind of sympathy for the chiefs of the Air Corps and their deputies who had preceded Westover and me. The ramifications of the job spread far beyond any jurisdictional rivalry with the G.H.Q. Air Force. The War Department, Congress, appropriations, public opinion, the definition of our program when nobody—not even the G.H.Q. Air Force—had any real program at all; the headaches of "defending" our accident rate against the newspaper agitation begun at the time of the air-mail disasters back in 1934, all became my problems as Assistant Chief of the Air Corps. Often there were bitter battles on behalf of the independence of the "rival" G.H.Q. Air Force. One of our toughest fights was to see that the War Department did not use all our meager appropriations for the procurement of light planes for the support of ground troops.

And still, embarking on this new dull, thankless kind of duty, I was lucky again; luckier than I knew.

For, almost at the same moment I arrived in Washington, the first real American Air Power appeared. Not just brilliant prophecies, good coastal defense airplanes, or promising techniques; but, for the first time in history, Air Power that you could put your hand on. It didn't appear in the distant California I had just left, but close to Washington.

Early in the spring of 1936, the first two four-engine bombers landed at Langley Field, Virginia.

★ *9* ★

I have purposely postponed discussing the development of the four-engine bomber until now because it was such a turning point in the course of air power—of world power, as it worked out—that it is necessary to stop a moment and consider what the four-engine bomber was and what it really meant.

The Boeing Flying Fortress, the B-17, was the first of the four-engine bomber type. It had only one predecessor of equal importance in air history. That was the first "military aircraft" of the Wright brothers in which Lieutenant Tom Selfridge was killed in 1908. The patterns were sadly alike. On its first official flight at Dayton, Ohio, on October 30, 1935, the first B-17 crashed before the eyes of the high Air Corps officials who had come to decide upon it, and killed Major P. P. Hill, one of the finest test pilots in the Air Corps, killed the Boeing test pilot, injured four others of its crew, and looked like a flop. Maintenance people had failed to familiarize themselves sufficiently with new features; the horizontal tail surfaces were not properly unlocked, and almost as soon as it was airborne the great new bomber was in flames on the runway.

However, as with the first Wright plane, the specifications and the preliminary performance of the first B-17 had been too impressive for this tragic accident to wipe the Flying Fortress out. The 750 h.p. engines, demonstrated by Major Hill on earlier flights, and the size of the craft combined with its featherlike maneuverability, had astonished seasoned observers. The introduction of a co-pilot's seat—it was not thought of then primarily in terms of the eventual teamwork between two pilots, but had been installed because the implied range of this airplane suggested that a single pilot would not fly it all the time—showed a new conception of air power.

"With all those guns, it looks like a fort that can fly," somebody said, and the name stuck, though the early armament was nothing compared to the guns put on it later.

Despite the disaster, further trials were indicated. It wasn't altogether simple. Westover had to go to bat, and he did, standing up before the criticism and alerting the lower echelons of the Air Corps on what could be expected from that criticism with the same kind of letters a commander might send down in wartime. The upshot was that thirteen more B-17's were ordered, and as already told, the first two Flying Fortresses actually to be accepted by the Air Corps arrived at Langley Field almost at the same time I arrived in Washington.

From then on, the B-17 was the focus of our air planning, or rather of the Air Corps' fight to get *an* air plan—some kind of genuine air program—accepted by the Army. "Precision bombardment," of course, was not new. I've already told something of our pioneering with bombardment on the West Coast, where my 7th and 19th Bomb Groups had been entrusted with the first Martin B-10's, and the first Norden bombsights. The tough part of aircraft development and securing an air program is to make Congress, the War Department, and the public realize that it is impossible to get a program that means anything unless it covers a period of not less than five years. Any program covering a shorter period is of little value. Normally, it takes five years from the time the designer has an idea until the plane is delivered to the combatants. The funds must cover the entire period or there is no continuity of development or procurement. For years the Army—and the Army Air Forces while a part of it—was hamstrung in its procurement programs by that governmental shortsightedness.

Great strides had been made in the East in recent years by Major Hugh Knerr, despite the fact that neither the topography of the eastern states as regards bombing ranges, nor the equipment given him had been as good as ours. Knerr commanded the 2nd Bomb Group at Langley Field, and that unit received the first B-17's.

Our horizons had been strictly limited prior to the arrival of the four-engine bomber. Range, fire power, bombload—in all respects, our bombers before this had fallen short of the thing we all preached and hoped for, the "other" independent function of air power in which we had so long believed, which Billy Mitchell had described as if it were already there.

True, the "strategic" function of this new plane, as laid down by the over-all plans for national defense at that time, was still only a "tactical" employment. The B-17, too, was intended to sink enemy ships approaching our shores. It was some time later that General Frank M. Andrews still had to argue in the struggle for its procurement that the B-17 was "especially useful for coastal patrol." But even at that, the interception would be hundreds of miles farther at sea and formations of Flying Fortresses could cover in an hour more distance than a fast enemy ship could be expected to cover in a night. (Realizing this soon, the Navy raised hell like a country gentleman finding poachers on his property.)

The four-engine bomber was the first positive answer to the need arising from the United States' modification of the Douhet theories, which we had been teaching as an abstract science at the Air Corps Tactical School for several years. Ever since Versailles, Germany had been considered the next enemy by most strategists, including Billy Mitchell, whose notion, however, that Japan would come flying to attack us "some fine Sunday morning" was less heeded.

The large bomber was the center of the "bomber controversy." If one thinks of the state of the world in 1936, the year the Spanish Civil War began, the year after Mussolini invaded Ethiopia, the year immediately before Japan went into China proper, the year in which Hitler's remilitarization of the Rhineland took place, it would seem that the time was overdue for some kind of clear-cut thinking about American air power to have started in the War Department. It hadn't. And in that connection, this is a good place to note one or two facts that are sometimes oversimplified.

Despite popular legend, we could not have had any real air power much sooner than we got it. By that, I mean the genuine nucleus of air power, able to expand quickly enough to meet whatever demands were made upon it, that was foreshadowed technically by the appearance of the four-engine bomber, and which was to obtain its real Magna Carta in the office of President Roosevelt on September 28, 1938.

Unbelieving men in high places, battleship admirals, generals, and others who seized on Billy Mitchell's sins to eliminate him, didn't eliminate air power at all, nor retard it half so much as has been said. Actually, they didn't even eliminate Billy. They broke his heart, but from the day of his trial, public opinion was mostly on his side. The point is, that kind of public opinion couldn't help air power then in any conclusive degree, and no other kind of public opinion was ready.

There were three Billy Mitchells: there was the man they court-

martialed, not personally known to the public, who wouldn't rest until
he became a martyr; there was Mitchell the air prophet, not in the sense
of popular but of highly scientific forecasts. And then there was the
third Mitchell, who included the first two, but added something. This
was the Billy the public loved, and whom the Air Corps loved. Quite
aside from his fine war record and his leaping mind, this Mitchell was
the hero who had always had the American public on his side—the
dashing, colorful doer-of-deeds who cut red tape, defied the stuffy boss,
snapped his fingers in the face of authority, cried, "What, I can't sink
your ships?" and sent them to the bottom; exposed the evil interests,
paused in the midst of it all to marry the charming girl, and in short,
did everything Billy did. After he had gone too far, for a man in uniform,
and his superiors had crushed him, the public and the Air Corps still
loved him, and Billy, in cits, went right on fighting. But the point I want
to make is that a different outcome to the trial might not have had any
immediate effect. People have become so used to saying that Billy
Mitchell was years ahead of his time that they sometimes forget it is true.

Only once before the later 1930's, when the combination of technical
advances and the state of international relations also gave "air power"
a chance for mushroom growth, had air power on its own ever seemed
likely to appear. This was the period just before the armistice that ended
World War I.

The use of Allied (American, British, French) airmen under Mitchell,
despite the fact that the American contribution represented less than
40 per cent of the joint effort, and in British-designed planes at that,
had been a formidable factor in the outcome of the critical St. Mihiel
and Meuse battles of 1918. The massed air-striking power, including
about 1500 Allied planes in all, had been more of a "tactical" troop-
support performance than an independent one. But bombardment had
played a part in the coordinated attacks on both the flanks, and on the
supplies and communications behind the lines of the enemy. There was
talk of the further "strategic" work this independent Allied striking
force, the air on its own for the first time, would carry on—air raids
against Berlin itself, etc. Before such operations could be implemented,
it was November, 1918.

In the years that followed, the vision of permanent peace took hold
of all the nations of the world except the defeated Germany and Russia;
and Italy and Japan, who could be counted only technically among the
victors. The public enthusiasm that greeted Billy Mitchell's sinking of
the *Frankfurt* and the *Ostfriesland,* and later of the obsolete American

battleships in the 1920's was not for air power—it was for Billy. The corollary suggested—that one mode of making war was being made impossible by another—was not so generally felt as some boosters of air power wished and preached. Indeed, to the American people then, Billy and his antiquated bombers were not so much a new weapon as the death knell of weapons. To hell with all armament; to hell with everything to do with war! The Navy sensed this with a special shudder, since it was the very moment of the World Naval Disarmament meetings in Washington and London.

As far as the public was concerned, airplanes, aviation, were fascinating. Bombers in themselves, and in the only meaning to be drawn from them, were not. Look back on the first object of bitterness of the university students who organized, in about this same year of 1936, when I came to Washington, those derisive "veterans of future war" associations. (As an example of the way public opinion shifts with the wind, within six years many of those same boys were to be among our most eager pilots, and some couldn't even wait for that but rushed ahead to fight with the Eagle Squadron or the Flying Tigers.) Look back on the way in which, as World War II crept closer and closer, bombardment came to be classed in the public mind as akin to the criminal in warfare, an attitude enlarged by the indiscriminate attacks of German and Italian planes on Guernica, Barcelona, and Badajoz during the Spanish Civil War, and by Mussolini's bombing of native hut-villages in Ethiopia.

Where Hitler would strike first after the holocaust of Warsaw was uncertain, but whether it would be London, Paris, or Rotterdam, the American people were certain it would be from the air—with bombs. Long before this, a prejudice against bombardment, as perhaps less humanitarian than, say, an infantry attack, 16-inch artillery shells, or other presumably unbarbarous forms of warfare, had sprung up in the Anglo-Saxon countries. Indeed, in some quarters, it endured right through our war against Hitler's Germany. I remember with particular distaste a much-publicized telegram from a number of worthy citizens grouped together on behalf of the Federal Council of Churches of Christ in America, who at just the moment in 1944 when the losses of our Eighth Air Force were heaviest, protested manfully against our bombardment of "defenseless cities of Germany."

The foretold second war with Germany, the prophesied Sunday morning when the Japs would come, the technical discussions, the "three-pronged suspension" of national defense with strong air bases in Alaska, the St. Lawrence, and Natal, were not best-selling subjects. The economy —yes. But here Billy was a little misleading, since while it was obvious that a certain number of airplanes could be bought for the price of one vulnerable battleship, the total cost of even a minimum adequate peacetime air force would far exceed the whole national defense budget of those days. Naturally, the comparison, unit for unit, might stand; for to be adequate, the Army ground forces and the Navy also would require big increases. The point is, it didn't matter whether battleships, bombers, or the United States Infantry rifle, Model 1903, were under discussion—America wasn't buying any. If the public of the 1920's had really been given a breakdown on the amount of money, planning, and effort needed to establish an air force effective even for the middle 1930's (I am considering this now in the light of what had to be done only two years after I returned to Washington) they would indeed have been very leery of an adequate air program.

Look at Britain in the same years. Trenchard hadn't had our troubles, but the R.A.F. in 1935–36 was in no better shape than we were. The Royal Air Force had won its autonomy as a third and separate service in 1918, before World War I was over, but it was not until 1935, just as the first B-17 came out of the Boeing factory, that the first Manchester (from which the subsequent York Lancaster was born) and the first plans for the four-engined Stirling and Halifax were laid down. Trenchard, a great airman and a great organizer, had preached the meaning of strategic bombardment, of the "independent" air mission, to England from the time he commanded the British Army's Royal Flying Corps in France. He was given his independent R.A.F. promptly, despite the Royal Navy. For eighteen years prior to my arrival in Washington from March Field, the R.A.F. had had its own Ministry, its own uniform, its own auxiliary services, its own budget. But no air power.

As Hitler's Luftwaffe hurtled westward virtually unchecked, and his Panzer Divisions came barreling across France, the Royal Air Force still remained a negligible power except for its individual and collective courage, some of its plans, and the possession of a few—a very few— of those beautiful Spitfires and Hurricanes, waiting in England. Its "Advanced Striking Force" in France consisted, at the critical moment, of less than a hundred airplanes, two-thirds obsolescent bombers, the rest obsolete fighters. The bombers, only a handful a year after Warsaw, were not yet the ones dreamed of in those blueprints of 1935–36.

Elsewhere, around the world, the R.A.F. story was the same. Despite the fact that the demands of the British Empire have always involved a relatively active employment of regular forces in peacetime, and that the Royal Air Force as a coequal service now shared in this responsibility, the British air arm did not develop.

I do not say this in disparagement of the Royal Air Force, but to emphasize the true situation of our own prewar Army Air Corps as regards this question of "independence." It has been frequently misunderstood.

The R.A.F., in those years, slender purse and all, accepted as part of the price of autonomy, entire self-maintenance. In our "independent" United States Air Force today, attached Army forces, technical, administrative, housekeeping or what you will, still help to "Keep 'Em Flying." But look back on that skimpily supported R.A.F. of the 1920's and 1930's. It suddenly had to supply everything out of what was in its own pocket: the materiel, the training for every man whatever his job, not only the planes, the pilot and airmen, but cook, baker, military policemen, signal personnel, medics—all of it.

This kind of burden was what we meant when we consistently told the boards and committees before which we were always appearing that we didn't want an independent Air Force until we could sustain it properly.

As late as July of 1936, I was still saying at a committee hearing: "The G.H.Q. Air Force is as much of a revolutionary step as should be tried at this time . . . we can't at this stage stand on our own feet." I talked, it seems, about the big bomb loads that were coming ("two thousand pounds for five thousand miles"), and spoke of a "bomber range of eight thousand miles," not bullish prophecies at all in terms of the commonplace air thinking of today, and far too modest as to pay load, in terms of World War II.

Despite all the misinformed writing about our disagreements, I thought Frank Andrews, who had set this particular investigation off with his mistrust of the War Department's sincerity regarding air power, was right. I agreed with his testimony that "as a consequence" of the Army G-3 Section's fear that "the Air Corps, including the G.H.Q. Air Force might grow to over-shadow other elements of the War Department . . . concrete results had been inadequate." And that "the greatest ultimate advantage would accrue to the Army if, for the time being, the War Department did make its major effort to national defense in the maximum development of air power."

I also agreed with the Chief (General Westover) that "to set up another agency separately with its own formulation of war plans, if such have to be tied up with the Navy plans or the Army plans, would create a complicated situation, and it would be much simpler to adhere to our present two-headed organization.

"We are still," said Westover, "dependent upon ground facilities, upon the earth for our sustenance and maintenance. We have to have places in which to live, all of which can be provided through existing agencies of the Army and the Navy. I believe that the time has not yet come when the Air Corps can demonstrate its fitness to sustain itself and operate independently of other units."

This doesn't mean that any of its responsible officers accepted the view that the Air Corps was still, in 1936, nothing more than a branch of the Army, like the Cavalry, or the Signal Corps. We were confident that the B-17 would help the G.H.Q. Air Force demonstrate to the public the striking power of "the air" on its own, though just how much was a guess. The demonstration would require equipment, and the equipment would be forthcoming only as the result of proof.

Despite all the public writing and talking about air forces in those days, it was doubtful if any such proof would be available until the actual meeting with an enemy's air power took place. If it seems from this that the Air Corps was trying prematurely to get more than its reasonable share in the national defense setup, to have its cake and eat it too, consider that the administrative arrangement we desired was very like the one under which we did operate in World War II.

Some individuals, to be sure, pressed impatiently for the "independent" Air Force idea. That World War II establishment, headed by the Allied Combined Chiefs of Staff and commanded in each nation by Joint Chiefs of Staff for Army, Navy, and Air, involved, as some people still fail to understand, a practically autonomous American Air Force within the Army, but coequal with the total of the Army's ground forces, its commander serving as Deputy Chief of Staff of the Army, as well as sitting on both the Combined and Joint Staffs.

Throughout this book, I am trying to resist the temptation to quote individuals, sometimes very important individuals, who in one way or another were outstanding in their failure to grasp the meaning of air power. The purpose of this volume is not to make anyone feel foolish, and besides, there isn't space enough to do everybody justice. Even when one recollects, say, such an article as Senator Elbert Thomas of Utah (Chairman of the Senate Military Affairs Committee) wrote in the

April, 1946, issue of the *American Magazine, after* the defeat of Germany and Japan, asserting that precision bombardment was "a hoax," there never had been any such thing, etc., it doesn't seem worthwhile. Lord knows, no proofs of the meaning of any military operation on earth have ever been so clear as the conditions the Navy and the Army ground forces found when they finally entered Germany and Japan.

But for the sake of history, it ought to be understood what we were still up against in those last two years—1936–38—before the big turning point in the development of American air power came. And why I say it was fortunate we weren't "independent" before.

After Billy Mitchell's sinking of the battleships in 1921, the sneers of those who continued to claim that it couldn't be done were not the important thing, as so many pro-air journalists have written. What was important was the way in which the implications *were* grasped in terms of their own limited mediums by elements in both the Army and the Navy. The Navy, as usual, was more alert to its own interests. The Royal Navy's converted carrier *Argus* had already attracted our Navy's attention, and one of the most immediate results of Billy's sinkings off the Virginia Capes was the launching, a year later, of the first built aircraft carrier in the world—the U.S.S. *Langley.* In the next few years, the admirals and elderly naval captains who enrolled as flying cadets were indicative of an advancing frame of mind. Now, in 1936–38, the meaning of the B-17 struck home to the Navy with equal force.

In the Army, there were no responsible quarters, either, who still doubted that the airplane had become an indispensable military weapon. But that meant as direct troop support, aerial reconnaissance for the ground forces, communications, and transport. Bombardment on its own, to some extent—yes. But the twin-engined B-10's and B-12's seemed good enough for that. No powerful sympathy for the "independent air mission"—the kind of strategic air campaign which the B-17's and B-24's over Germany, and the B-29's over Japan were to carry out—existed in the War Department.

The best efforts of Malin Craig, when he was Chief of Staff, the ups and downs of Secretary Woodring's understanding, never changed the basic conviction of the Department that allocation of the skimpy funds it had for the purchase of airplanes should be put into medium bombers and other ground-support planes. Even when George Marshall first took over in 1937, he needed plenty of indoctrination about the air facts of life. The difference in George, who presently was to become one of the most potent forces behind the development of a real American air power, was his ability to digest what he saw and make it part of as strong a body of military genius as I have ever known.

The words of an official War Department spokesman at the July, 1936, hearing which I mentioned above, are a good example of the typical Service attitude toward air power at that time. Brigadier General Stanley B. Embick himself was not too much to blame, since he was voicing only the "party line" of the General Staff. In the course of a familiar speech, in which he assured the committee that neither the United States nor Japan "can be subjected to a hostile air invasion," he spoke, as they always did, of the "peculiar elements."

"With respect to the analogy between the land and sea forces, it should be said that the land and naval forces operate in elements which nowhere overlap. The line of demarcation is the coastline. But throughout its entire extent, the element of the air forces overlaps the element of either land or the naval forces.

"Each of the latter forces remains permanently in its peculiar element, and each can gain and maintain exclusive control of its own element.

"On the other hand, an air force can remain in its peculiar element for only a short time; it must rise from and return to the element of one of the other two forces, and it cannot control any element, even its own, except temporarily, throughout a limited area. So an air force cannot obtain a decision against troops on the ground, nor occupy territory nor exercise control of the sea."

This was some thirty-seven months before Hitler invaded Poland. On these occasions, nobody was ever rude enough to remind the official spokesman that all seaborne vessels, except the accursed *Flying Dutchman* (even stationary lightships), also have their bases ashore. This sort of thing, the division of responsibility at the shoreline, went on until the idea was blown up by Jap air power at Pearl Harbor.

In 1928, Mason Patrick, retiring as Chief of the Air Corps, had complained that "the Air Service, or rather the air effort of the United States since we entered the World War has probably been the most investigated activity ever carried on by the United States Government."

True, and though we couldn't see it then, it worked out to our benefit. The jurisdictional dispute—"Who the hell is going to run this thing anyway, and why?"—was the great bequest Billy Mitchell left us. More than anything, its continuance kept us alive and lively, because it was never settled. Despite the legislation of 1947, it isn't settled yet—witness the effort of both the Navy and the Air Force to control and build long-range bombers.

Looking at things as they were in 1936–38, how did our little Army Air Corps stand in relation to the air power of other countries as the war clouds took definite shape over Europe, Africa, and Asia?

Well, to be realistic, we were practically nonexistent. The Baker Board, which had given us the G.H.Q. Air Force and thus the all-important B-17's, had helped—and incidentally, had produced, in Jimmy Doolittle's minority recommendations for an independent Air Force, a historical document of lasting interest. But we didn't have all thirteen of the B-17's until the end of 1938—and even then we had to keep on fighting for them. Our officer strength then was 1650; our enlisted strength about 16,000. (All our pilots were commissioned.) The number of cadets at our Primary Flying School never exceeded 500 at one time, and at the Advanced Flying School seldom reached 270. We never had more than 1000 ground crewmen at our Mechanics Training School. In 1936 we had very few first-class airplanes—only a handful of P-26 fighters, and a small number of B-10 and B-12 bombers. The rest of our assorted equipment was obsolete.

Still, in spite of our smallness and the perpetual discouragements, it was not all bad. Progress in engineering, development, and research was fine. At my old stamping ground in Dayton, I found the Materiel Division doing an excellent job within the limits of its funds. Westover was calling on the National Research Council to help with problems too tough for our Air Corps engineers to handle. We were already doing business with such important members of the Council as Dr. R. A. Millikan, Vannevar Bush, C. F. Kettering, C. J. West, Frank Lilly, F. B. Jouett, Carl Compton, Lyman Briggs, Arthur Compton, J. B. Conant, and other outstanding scientists. Few high-ranking Army officers seemed aware of the close relationship developing between these specialists and the little Air Corps—a relationship that was to grow to such importance in World War II that civilian scientists would work side by side with staff officers in our overseas operational commands, frequently flying on combat missions to increase their data.

Once, after George Marshall became Chief of Staff, I asked him to come to lunch with a group of these men. He was amazed that I knew them. "What on earth are you doing with people like that!" he exclaimed.

"Using them," I replied. "Using their brains to help us develop gadgets and devices for our airplanes—gadgets and devices that are far too difficult for the Air Force engineers to develop themselves."

"Does the rest of the Army use this same organization?" George asked. I had to confess I didn't know.

One of my earlier and most unforgettable contacts with an academic scientist had been in 1934 during a visit to the California Institute of Technology, when Dr. Millikan introduced me to Dr. Irving Krick, in charge of meteorology, who was making a study of the Swedish system of air masses, cold fronts, warm fronts, tropical fronts, and polar masses. Down there in Cal. Tech's "weather" section, Dr. Krick told me one of the most impressive things I had heard in my twenty years of flying. He said quite calmly that, in the light of his researches, when the Navy airship *Akron* left its hangar on April 4, 1933, it was doomed. It had flown into a clear area where it was completely surrounded by extremely turbulent fronts. Its only hope was to continue flying within that clear area. As soon as it attempted to turn back to its hangar, it must run into one of these fronts. No matter which way it turned it was headed for destruction. Unfortunately, in 1933, such weather prognostication was little known in the United States.

Naturally, I watched Dr. Krick's work eagerly after that. Weather is the essence of successful air operations. In that terrible year of the air mail—1934—a time of tragedy still hounding us in the headlines whenever we lost a plane in 1936-38, it was a thrilling thought that with a little faith and study on our part weather might be licked. One day Dr. Krick told me that at last he could really predict weather—prognosticate it a month in advance. He showed me telegrams. He had advised a Christmas tree harvester in Nova Scotia about the best time to get his trees in, avoiding frost. It had worked to a T. He had a wire from a tugboat operator who didn't want to cross Lake Michigan in a storm. Dr. Krick had told him to stay in the Illinois River for a couple of days, had finally given him clearance, and then told him to go on through. The captain found the weather clear. Another communication was from a gold mine operator in Alaska, asking how much longer he would be able to work his diggings there before winter closed in. Dr. Krick told him when to stop work—and *that* clicked. From then on, we had an advanced Air Corps weather service. Later, Dr. Krick joined us directly, becoming a key member of our wartime meteorological service. Before that, the way all Hitler's operations moved or stood in marvelous relation to the weather indicated to me that there must be a Herr Doktor Krick in Germany too.

Our tools, as far as quality was concerned, advanced well. All the things that go into the making of an airplane—a complicated mass of equipment not dreamed of by the average American man in the street—kept improving. Bombsights, navigation instruments, the navigators' school at Hondo, gunnery and the special meaning of gunnery to the new B-17—these things were not only in good shape but growing in excellence.

I actually believe in retrospect that theoretically, in the sense of "air power thinking," our meager little Air Corps may already have been the best in quality, that is, the best rounded, best balanced air force in the world. Since we were still in the Army, the "strategic bombardment" lectures of Hal George and the others at the Air Corps Tactical School were not allowed to obscure the need for "tactical" ground-support operations. In the independent R.A.F. this happened, and was not corrected until real air-ground cooperation was reborn under Tedder, Coningham, and Montgomery in Libya in 1942.

By then, Brereton's composite strategic and Desert Air Force already found American planes and crews playing a solid part in the fighting, learning from the British combat and African experience, but not new to the idea.

In the worst of times, the Air Corps had maintained and trained a "tactical" force of one attack group, three bombardment groups, five pursuit groups, and fourteen observation squadrons. The smallness of the Air Corps had at least the beneficial result of producing a fine esprit, of making the concepts of air power mentioned above well understood. Out of this nucleus unit came the air leaders of the war, at the Air Force, the Command, and Air Division, Wing, and Group levels.

The War Department kept giving us the B-17's on paper, then they kept taking them away. When I came to Washington in January of 1936 ten changes in allocation of funds for the purchase of B-17's had already been made, but the order for thirteen of them on August 17, 1937, raised our hopes of finally getting a small number of Flying Fortresses. However, not only the pressure for troop support planes instead of bombers, but a preference for twin-engine bombers as supposedly cheaper (the superiority of one B-17 to two B-10's for instance, was a mystery to Secretary Woodring and his people) continued to postpone their advent in spite of the fact that we were getting runways ready for their arrival.

As late as May 13, 1938, the Adjutant General sent to the Assistant Secretary of War the following note:

"No military requirement exists for the procurement of experimental pressure cabin bombers in the fiscal year 1939 or the fiscal year 1940, of the size and type described. The Chief of the Air Corps has been informed that the experimentation and development for the fiscal years

1939–40 will be restricted to that class of aviation designed for the *close-in support of ground troops* and for the production of that type of aircraft such as *medium and light aircraft, pursuit and other light aircraft.*" (Italics supplied.)

The Chief of the Air Corps was informed that no military requirements existed for the type of military aircraft (four engine) referred to. We fought that. We kept doing everything on earth to make the situation understood—by special people and by the public.

Not publicly, but with remarkable vision, the Navy, with its eye closely on that same B-17, put out a classified pamphlet in 1937 which took better note of the strategic meaning of the Flying Fortress than the Army seemed able to do. "If the Army is to advance or even to continue to remain in position, it must be ready to suppress enemy operations *behind the front.*" And, "the front is formed by the limits of possible aircraft in flight, but within aircraft range. Nothing behind the enemy front is entirely secure from observation and attack."

And then we find this statement: "If the Philippines were to fall into the hands of the Japanese, aviation would gain an increased potential influence in the defense of Japan's control of the China Sea and the Western Pacific."

And finally: "It may be well to reiterate that a sustained *air offensive against an enemy's interior organization will usually be a test for aviation strategy* which will lie entirely outside the sphere of normal military and naval activities."

We realized, and apparently the Navy realized also, the requirements for long-range bombers, whether the Army did or did not. But did the Navy want the growth of the G.H.Q. Air Force, or did they want those B-17's themselves—for the things their real airmen knew the carriers could never do?

Westover worked harder than anybody. Too hard. He flew all over the country, always flying his own plane, landing here and talking to some group or other about air power while his sergeant got the ship ready for the next hop, then flying on to give another enthusiastic talk to people in another town. It was too much for any man his age whose flying reflexes were being sapped day after day the way Oscar's were at that nerve-racking task.

Looking back on it, I think one of the most wasteful weaknesses in our whole setup was our lack of a proper Air Intelligence Organization. It is silly, in the light of what we came to know, that I should still have been so impressed by the information given me in Alaska by that casual

German who called my hotel and told me about their "new bomber." I know now there were American journalists and ordinary travelers in Germany who knew more about the Luftwaffe's preparations than I, the Assistant Chief of the United States Army Air Corps.

From Spain, where our Army observers watched the actual air fighting, reports were not only weak but unimaginative. Nobody gave us much useful information about Hitler's air force until Lindbergh came home in 1939. Our target intelligence, the ultimate determinant, the compass on which all the priorities of our strategic bombardment campaign against Germany would depend, was set up only after we were actually at war. Part of this was our own fault; part was due to the lack of cooperation from the War Department General Staff's G-2; part to a change in the original conception of the B-17 as a defensive weapon to a conception of it as a weapon of offense against enemy industries.

In September, 1938, Oscar Westover was in California on one of his flying trips. I was filling in as Acting Chief of Air Corps. On the afternoon of the 21st, at about five o'clock, just as I had returned from the Munitions Building to my home in Chevy Chase, I heard the phone ringing. It was a long-distance call from Major K. B. Wolfe, our factory representative at the Lockheed plant in Burbank, California. "K. B." told me that General Westover and Sergeant Hyman, his mechanic, had just tried to land at the field and had crashed. He said that as he was talking to me the plane was still burning on the runway. Oscar and Sergeant Hyman were both dead.

I joined my wife and we went down to wait in the lobby of the Kennedy Warren, hoping to reach Mrs. Westover before she heard about it over the radio.

Eight days later, on the 29th, I was appointed to succeed Oscar as Chief of the Air Corps.

On the day after that, without firing a shot, dropping a bomb, or even starting an engine, Hitler's Luftwaffe and his armored forces won for him his first major victory of World War II.

Neville Chamberlain signed the appeasement pact at Munich.

☆ *10* ☆

It will be noted that eight days elapsed before my appointment was confirmed.

I presume that when any man gets his head up above the pack in public life, he must expect to be a target for public criticism, and even be ready for a smear campaign. When my name came before the President, he was informed that I was a drunkard; that when on duty in Honolulu I had frequently been seen drunk around public places. This suggestion was weakened by the fact that I had never been stationed in the Hawaiian Islands. Further, as my friends knew, I hadn't had a drink of hard liquor since 1920. My appointment was not held up long, but it was obvious that somebody—I never found out, nor care to find out who—disliked the idea of my being Chief of the Air Corps.

Nor did I ever discover who it was that was tapping my official telephone wire a few days after I took over—or was in some way causing a leak in my office. I first realized this when I made a call over a private line to the Materiel Division at Dayton, Ohio. Within less than three-quarters of an hour, the topic of my conversation was called to my attention by a member of Congress—who had nothing to do with my business. Investigation showed that nobody else had talked to Dayton or had time to check the call. I had the whole place searched, but could never locate a dictaphone. As far as I know, however, there was no repetition of this kind of thing. Air Marshal Bertie Harris, during his visit with the British Purchasing Commission prior to our entering the war, complained of a similar incident after he went directly from a highly secret meeting of British Air people in his hotel room to a trans-Atlantic phone, only to hear, through the accident of a crossed wire, all the confidential transactions being discussed in detail by persons unknown. In Washington you never know just who is trying to find out just what, or just how, or just why.

Presently, I was even more surprised to learn that there was supposed to be an Air Corps "gravy train," and that all kinds of people, in government, business, and everywhere, were getting ready to cut in on the projects which they were sure the President's now accelerated program for the National Defense situation would create. All at once, everybody seemed highly interested in getting a finger in what was called, to my perplexity, the Air Corps "pie." After a careful study, I presented to the Chief of Staff a diagram showing the forty-two different government agencies with which the Chief of Air Corps had to do business on strictly air matters. Later, when George Marshall became Chief of Staff, this chart helped us get the relatively autonomous status under which we fought the war when America came into it. But first, this desire of various people to get a piece of the Air Corps pie put me behind the eight ball. Indeed, it almost terminated my position with the United States Air Arm before I got fairly started. However, more of that later.

My first intimation of the interest of outside agencies in the Air Corps came when Aubrey Williams, head of the National Youth Administration, brought to the War Department a scheme for taking over all surplus and unused tools and ship equipment so that the NYA could train aircraft mechanics. As a general idea, this was a worthy project. Ever since my experience with the CCC on the Coast, I had hoped that some of the work of the national welfare bureaus which involved manpower might be shaped so as to aid our National Defense shortages. But I was not eager to see Air Corps machinery, or tools required for essential Air Corps maintenance as well as training, taken over by any outside agency. However well intentioned the outside agencies might be, the training of Air Force mechanics was one function that lay too close to the heart of things to be entrusted to any possible "hit or miss" project. No element in the airman's life, including his personal flying ability, plays a larger part than the skill, closeness, integrated understanding, and all-out, day-by-day, hour-by-hour familiarity with Air Force equipment that our mechanics must possess. Crew chiefs must be bred inside the Air Force family. Fortunately, after continuing for some time, the NYA conferences on this subject lost their impetus, and presently died out.

The next federal agency to make its appearance in the air world was the WPA. This was a different matter—the beginning of one of the most valuable associations that the Air Corps, or I, personally, ever had. The first contact was made by my old acquaintance, Colonel "Pinkie" Harrington, then of the Works Progress Administration. His boss was Harry Hopkins who was to become not only one of my best friends and a staunch supporter of the Air Corps through the next few critical years, but one of the three men outside the Air Corps who did most to help me with my job. The other two were George Marshall and Bob Lovett.

Hopkins was just back from the West Coast, where the President, his mind now full of Hitler's probable intentions with regard to this hemisphere as well as Europe, had sent him to get an over-all picture of our aircraft industry and its capacity for expansion. The ideas expressed by Hopkins and Harrington were good ones. Since it was plain, even at that early date, that a far greater airplane production capacity in the United States was an urgent necessity, they suggested that they use their WPA funds to help build more factories.

It was evident to me that the heads of existing aircraft companies would also have to change many of their ideas regarding techniques of production if we were to secure maximum results. Above all, the problem was to establish a definite requirement program—a program covering the air needs not only of the foreign nations we wished to aid, but also of the United States Army and Navy air forces in the immediate future. From the start of our association, I found Harry Hopkins to be a far-sighted, intelligent person with whom to do business. Once a good presentation of a problem had been made to him, it did not take him long either to accept it or to find out its weak points.

After reviewing his survey of the subject, I arranged a meeting of representatives of all the aircraft, engine, and large accessory plants in the country. With the British, French, and Swedes coming to America to make contracts for planes and engines, and with conditions in Europe shaping up as they were, I had a hunch that the time was short now before we, too, would be expected to build up our Air Force—and, as usual, be expected to do it overnight. I figured that if an energetic expansion of the aircraft industry for the purpose of supplying our European friends could be begun without delay, the plant power, floor space, machine tools, etc., which we needed would be more readily available when the time came for us to use them for ourselves.

But even before that meeting, the cramped nature of our habitual thinking was brought home to me by a session with my own staff. We had been fighting so hard and so long to get the few planes, the gasoline, the pilots, the mechanics, everything we had, that at first, even after Munich, it was difficult to get my staff to adjust their minds to a realistic plan. At this meeting the Air Staff sat around a long table, with an easel off to one side, and I explained that events in Europe made it necessary to be ready to submit to the President, the Secretary of War, the Chief of Staff, and to Congress an air program to meet the critical conditions.

How many planes did they recommend as essential? Let everyone use his imagination; nobody hold back! I went around the table asking each officer, in turn, writing his estimate on a piece of paper hanging on the easel. The estimates added up to a total of fifteen hundred—one thousand, five hundred combat airplanes to meet American requirements all over the world! (Eventually, the total number of factory acceptances for planes during the years 1940–45, including U.S.-financed Canadian production, was 229,230.)

I was shocked. I tried the question a different way. "What is the maximum number of airplanes you could use in the Philippines if YOU were Commander over there and had the defense of the Philippines in your hands?" An answer, and a number was written on the easel. "And what if you were Air Commander in Panama?" Another figure written down. "In Hawaii?" "In the United States? In charge of training? Trying to protect our shores? Defending the East Coast? The West Coast? Would want available for a strong striking force?" Put on this more personal basis, the estimates leaped up. But in the end, they totaled only 7500 planes. I left the figures on the easel, and in after months when one of my staff seemed to be thinking in small terms instead of looking at the big picture, all I had to do was to point at that piece of paper still hanging in the conference room.

The Administration's move in late 1938 toward expansion of the national air facilities was still rather sketchy as far as our own Air Corps was concerned. The President was still thinking largely of how American industrial power might help to supply the air needs of those obvious friends abroad who were now being squeezed to the point of desperation by Germany. As his first, or at least one of his first, technical advisers on air matters, however, he turned to me for guidance.

If it seemed to us in the United States Air Corps that we, ourselves, were not being directly included in the expansion, we could nevertheless count positive gains. At that time, we were still taking abuse for *not* "being able to standardize our aircraft types," but that juggling was actually to develop the B-9 into the B-17, and later into the B-29, each with its proper equipment and replacements at the proper time. In regard to this major factor of replacements, we didn't fall into the errors of the Luftwaffe, either—a failure which was probably one of the reasons Germany lost the war.

In 1938, however, as I have indicated, we still didn't understand half of what we should have known about the Luftwaffe. For example, a report from the war in Spain about the protective dispersal of aircraft on airdromes might have meant much if we had applied it in Hawaii before Pearl Harbor, as we finally did everywhere overseas after that. "The aircraft are spaced out at twenty-yard intervals, different units occupying different parts of the airdromes, but in general, there is never more than one squadron on any one airdrome." And again, from the Franco side: "I saw some Messerschmitt 109's on the airdrome, but these were obviously kept out of my way and therefore I am unable to say much about their use. Since returning to Paris (the Attaché continues) I have heard that they are not very successful in Spain on account of their very high speed and lack of maneuverability. (!) None of them are in the hands of the Spanish pilots, as yet." The Germans were not giving out any information then about the Me-109, that vital fighter and fighter bomber which our bomber crews and fighter pilots over Europe and our ground forces in Africa were to know so bitterly later. We should have been able to read more between the lines.

"The weight saved by the removal of radio apparatus from the fighters," says another report, "has been used to install an armor plate shield behind the pilot's seat, and these have proved of great value." Later, our fighter pilots had both, of much better quality, but at that time we knew relatively little about armor, and our potential Allies, the British and French, withheld such information as they had from us as carefully as did the future enemies.

From the Loyalist side came another observation for us to think about. "We detected in one of the heavy bombardment squadrons a note of anxiety about the increased number of German fighters." (Apparently there were far more of the Me-109's in Spain than we knew of.) Item which might have affected our own ideas about bombers in regard to fighter escort: "The escort of bomber formations proceeding to and from their objectives, by double, or more than double, their number of fighters, has been found on both sides to be a necessity, notwithstanding the ability of the bomber to shoot down fighters." Yet we in the United States were still debating the need for fighter escorts for bombers.

My first big meeting with the representatives of the aircraft industry in the Munitions Building that autumn was a lively affair. Even at that date, it was still not unusual for two or three of them to come to Washington to battle for a contract of, say six airplanes, or a half-dozen engines, and we couldn't promise them anything more. But they knew

what was going on abroad, and they were interested; they followed my
ideas alertly about the need for thinking in terms of thousands and tens
of thousands, instead of tens and dozens, as they had been doing in the
past. Some of them balked when I said that in the face of the gigantic
production problem we were about to meet, they would have to conceive
of one paramount change. The parent airplane factories must be subsequently little more than assembly plants. Small parts, various components, and subassemblies would have to be farmed out, with their
detailed drawings, to all kinds of industrial plants that could be recon-
verted. I must admit that most of them accepted the idea, but a cry went
up from some to the effect that "We can't have everybody do our work
because they don't understand how to work with aircraft metals!—They
don't understand our tolerances!—We have an entirely different technique than they have, etc.!" Still, a successful meeting broke up with
hopes of another in the near future.

Incidentally, along with the excellent British "Volunteer Reserve"
setup, this idea of farming component production out to subsidiary manufacturers was one of the few definite advantages the independent R.A.F.
had established well before we did. In the so-called "shadow factory
plan" of 1936, it was determined that, in the event of emergency, the
British automobile industry should at once be closely linked to aircraft
manufacture.

Regardless of jurisdictional troubles, continued headaches about appropriations, and the up-and-down battle for the B-17, the Air Corps
had come a long way by the year 1938. Far off were the old stick-and-
wire kite days in which I had learned to fly.

The year itself was full of triumphs. An authorized expansion of our
officer strength in April, to 2092! And in June, an enlisted growth to
21,500! Lieutenant H. L. Neely flew across the country in a Seversky
P-36 at an average speed of 287 m.p.h. The successful goodwill flight
of three B-17's to Bogotá, Colombia, occurred in August. That same
month the first B-15 was delivered to the 2nd Bomb Group, a bigger
bomber than the B-17 but already relegated to a lesser place in our thinking. It was presently abandoned, but remained an example of elastic
experiment. In 1938, the B-24 Liberator was designed.

Many technical advances had been made, including work with auto-
gyros. The Collier's Trophy had been awarded to the Army Air Corps
for development of the plane in which Lieutenant B. S. Kelsey reached
an average speed of 350 m.p.h. between Dayton and Buffalo, in October;
a B-18 bomber made the first transcontinental nonstop flight from Hamil-

ton Field, California, to Mitchel Field, New York; and the 1937 Mackay Trophy was awarded to Captains G. J. Crane and G. V. Holloman for their work with an automatic landing system.

Major Robert Olds in a B-17 flew from Virginia to California and back in January—thirteen hours going west, eleven hours coming home to Langley. This flight was followed by the famous mission of his 2nd Bomb Group's six B-17's to Buenos Aires in February, the longest distance performance of its kind on record. The names of some of the pilots are a partial roster of World War II's air leaders: Bob Olds, himself; A. Y. Pitts; Vincent Meloy; Robert B. Williams, who was to lose an eye as a bombardment observer in the London blitz, and two and a half years later to lead the 1st Bombardment Wing to Schweinfurt; Caleb V. Haynes, who commanded the Assam-Burma-China ferry, his first job being to have gasoline waiting for Doolittle's Tokyo raiders. Also, John A. "Sammy" Samford who was to be Fred Anderson's and later Doolittle's Chief of Staff in the Eighth Air Force; Cornelius W. Cousland, who took the first group of B-17's (the famous 97th) to England in July, 1942; Harold L. George, who was already the principal lecturer on the theory of strategic bombardment at the Air Corps Tactical School, and was to command our world-circling A.T.C. in the coming war; Curtis E. LeMay, who later became a great Group and Air Division commander over Germany and commanded the B-29's against Japan.

A bit later, in the spring, Olds ran off another practical test which first elated the Air Corps and then resulted in one of the most dampening orders the War Department ever issued. To see how good our navigators really were, the G.H.Q. Air Force had sent three B-17's far out to sea to "intercept" the Italian liner, Rex. Olds and his wingmen had "hit" the Rex right on the nose, 615 miles out from our coast, dropped a message on her deck, and come home with the idea they'd proved something. It immediately turned out that they had.

Somebody in the Navy apparently got in quick touch with somebody on the General Staff, and in less time than it takes to tell about it, the War Department had sent down an order limiting all activities of the Army Air Corps to within 100 miles from the shoreline of the United States. Incidentally, this was shortly before the President announced that it would be the duty of the Air Corps to prevent enemy landings not only on this continent, but in South America as well. Perhaps President Roosevelt hadn't heard about the War Department order.

There has always been a lot of mystery about that "hundred mile" order; how it was transmitted, who received it, etc. The fact is, it was issued verbally to the G.H.Q. Air Force. We were even more burned up by the fact that we never saw it on paper. I tried several times to obtain copies of it from the War Department files, but no copy was ever available. As far as I know, however, that directive has never been rescinded. A literal-minded judge advocate might be able to find that every B-17, B-24, or B-29 that bombed Germany or Japan did so in technical violation of a standing order.

The heavy part played by the Luftwaffe in the appeasement at Munich was not lost on the President, any more than on Harry Hopkins or George Marshall, and two days before the pact was actually signed, he called some of us to a meeting in his office. Secretary of War Woodring was there, Secretary of the Navy Edison, Secretary of the Treasury Morgenthau, and their assistants, Mr. Oliphant of the Treasury, Louis Johnson, our Assistant Secretary of War, General Craig and his deputy, George Marshall, and Admiral Stark, besides Colonel Burns, the Secretary of the General Staff, and myself. And, of course, Harry Hopkins.

To the surprise, I think, of practically everyone in the room except Harry and myself, and to my own delight, the President came straight out for air power. Airplanes—now—and lots of them! At that time, the War Department was handling the entire expansion for the ground *and* air forces, but F.D.R. was not satisfied with their submitted report. A new regiment of field artillery, or new barracks at an Army post in Wyoming, or new machine tools in an ordnance arsenal, he said sharply, would not scare Hitler one blankety-blank-blank bit! What he wanted was airplanes! Airplanes were the war implements that *would* have an influence on Hitler's activities!

Some of those present were obviously unprepared for the forceful way in which he had made up his mind (I know that part of this stemmed from the long conversations Harry Hopkins and I had had together). Everybody began to talk, counterproposals were put forward; if the Air Arm was to be suddenly expanded, the Navy and the War Department said they would like to have similar consideration.

It was plainly a bolt from the blue, but the President, with equal plainness, made it clear that he had assembled this meeting to discuss aircraft production and air power in general. He himself had some potent proposals which were obviously not made up on the spur of the moment. My notes indicate that his first suggestions centered about an amendment to the existing Procurement Bill, not to extend the manufacturers any gamble for large private profits, but to make a limited, reasonable percentage of profit a certainty, as an incentive. Under the existing emergency, wasteful competition must be eliminated. The law must be changed. Contracts must all be on a cost-plus–fixed-fee basis, allowing for an adequate return on the business investment, less depreciation.

The goal must be fewer alterations in aircraft types, a speedier production line—in short, a successful mass production of combat airplanes, for our friends abroad and for ourselves. The President reiterated our own responsibility for air protection of the entire hemisphere. He said he wanted an actual 10,000-a-year plane production in the United States, with an all-out capacity for production of 20,000 planes a year. He called on me for a breakdown of the air strength of other nations—600 serviceable military planes in France; in England between 1500 and 2200. On the other side, 6000 first-line combat planes in Germany, with about 2000 more in reserve; Italy then had about 2000 first-line and 1000 second-line aircraft. The President spoke shrewdly about these, and other American air problems, such as routes and areas covering the North and South Poles. He talked most about "mass production." Many of the President's ideas for increasing the production capacity of our aircraft plants sounded very familiar, and well they might. They had been talked over time and time again among Assistant Secretary of War Louis Johnson, Colonel Burns, his Executive, and myself, or had been the subjects of discussion between Harry Hopkins and myself on many occasions. In any case, there was no difference of opinion among us about the best way to reach more rapid aircraft production.

Noting in my own memorandum that I would immediately call a second meeting of U.S. airplane manufacturers, and would now suggest that there be no competition in bids, but a fixed fee of 8 to 10 per cent as a fair return on each investment, I also pointed out to the President that the idea of "mass production" must be qualified. A lot of airplanes by themselves (the fate of the Italian Air Force was soon to prove this) were not air power. "The strength of an Air Force cannot be measured in terms of airplanes only. Other things are essential—productive capacity of airplanes, of pilots, of mechanics, and bases from which to operate. A sound training program is essential to provide replacements." This meant the flow of men and equipment, in the air and on the ground, necessary to keep a combat group up to its full planned strength at all times— regardless of losses—including the extras that technical air improvements were bound to introduce. Planes became obsolescent as they were being built. It sometimes took five years to evolve a new combat airplane, and meanwhile a vacuum could not be afforded. Constant experiment had to be continued.

Training demands, especially in the face of our present air poverty, would be enormous, and procurement of training planes would have to be skillfully coordinated with the procurement of the combat planes the trainees would presently be ready to fly. A steady flow of replacements, in men and planes, was probably the most important thing of all. I could not give that whole lesson at the general meeting. I had to give it to Harry Hopkins, and through him, to the President. The President, though he was still primarily engrossed with the problem of sending planes and materiel to Britain and France, seemed to understand this.

We had been trying a long time to convince the War Department General Staff of the same thing. In any case, President Roosevelt said he envisaged an American Air Arm of 10,000 combat planes, for which provision was to be made in two budgets from the War Department— one for the 178 planes covered by the regular budget for 1940, and the other for an additional 10,000 aircraft. The total appropriation would be about $300,000,000. He wanted a plan drawn up along that line. It would be a good idea if the Government owned a sizable proportion of its plants, but the main thing was to build up that production capacity of 10,000 and then 20,000 planes a year. (The Air Corps was soon to show him how we could go one better by hitting at 20,000 for the first year, resulting in an output of 40,000 the next.)

After various estimates, President Roosevelt concurred with my request that we set up immediately an Army Air Corps of 7500 combat planes (3750 ready for combat, 3750 in reserve), with an additional 2500 available for training establishments throughout the country.

The first action Colonel Jimmy Burns and I took after that meeting was to drive the Chief of Staff, General Malin Craig, over to my office and give him a get-rich-quick course in the elements necessary to make an Air Force. He was a very apt pupil, and from then on until his tour was completed, fought for our program.

It will be seen why I left that meeting of the 28th of September, 1938, with the feeling that the Air Corps had finally "achieved its Magna Carta." It was the first time in history we had ever had a program—the first time we could shoot toward a definite goal of planes from the factories and men from the training fields. A battle was won in the White House that day which took its place with—or at least led to—the victories in combat later, for time is a most important factor in building an Air

Force. There is no substitute—five years to secure a plane after the designers get the idea, and one year to train personnel after they are inducted.

The outstanding thing was that the President had not only made permissible but had required the development of the long-range heavy bomber, "hundred mile order" or no.

George Marshall, becoming Deputy Chief of Staff at about that time, helped enormously. He understood, and he was already at work on the General Staff explaining why the B-18 or other medium bomber types were not the economical things they seemed to laymen—why it had to be the B-17. He called me in one day and told me that he could not get the data he needed from the War Department General Staff for a real air program. So the two of us worked out the details of an entire air plan for the War Department. Conditions changed, of course, but this, in general, was the program we used eventually in breaking down the requirements for fighters, observation planes, light bombers, medium bombers, heavy bombers, transports, and trainers.

Incidentally, I was amused after the war to read the "inside" report of a Washington columnist that *I,* of all people, resisted the President's wishes for a large number of aircraft at that famous meeting. It wasn't the columnist's error which interested me, but his source, for a circumstance I still remember with a fair amount of surprise is that I looked around and saw that no one but me was taking notes. So it is my notes against someone else's memory.

Understandably, the aircraft industry felt as if they had been given a shot-in-the-arm as they started to get to work on the new air deal, and we found a way to begin training the required flying personnel without delay. Existing training facilities, even for the main category—student pilots—were, of course, only a drop in the bucket. Our training command officers maintained that if Randolph Field and its counterparts couldn't handle the rush, we should build more Randolph Fields—there must be no substitute for quality. Randolph held the "know-how." I agreed there shouldn't be anything but the best of training, certainly no letdown in standards, but how long and how much time would it take to build the two, three, four, five, or what-have-you Randolph Fields that would be necessary? At the present time, if we were capable of keeping three full shifts going, Randolph itself might be built up to an output of 1500 pilots a year—but what was that?

Often, I've been asked if I frequently overruled my experts. The answer is, yes, whenever in my opinion it was justified. In fact, once I had the organization of the Air Staff's Plans Section checked over by the civilian efficiency expert firm of Clark Wallace.

I overruled the Air Staff this time. Against the advice of my own training people, I invited some of the best civilian flying school people in the country to my office. I made them a proposal. I told them I didn't have any money, but was sure I could get the support of Congress in the next appropriations bill. Would each of them be willing to go out and set up at his private school the facilities to house, feed, and train flying cadets for the Army Air Corps? (This meant primary training only, of course.) Right now, we needed to train 100,000 pilots and the most we were turning out were about 750 a year. The procedure would be about as follows:

They would send their instructors to Randolph Field for indoctrination in the Air Corps' method of pilot training. We would furnish them the planes and the small supervisory personnel necessary; they would be paid so much a head for graduated students and a smaller flat sum for each washout. I assured them I would give them West Point graduates to indoctrinate the ideas of discipline and establish an honor code following the pattern in effect at Randolph Field. My training experts thought I was slightly balmy.

At first, the civilian contractors were flabbergasted. Then, when they began to talk it over, I left the meeting. After a while, their representatives came to my office and said, "Well, we might be able to do the job but it would entail an initial expenditure of a couple of hundred thousand dollars for each school." I replied, "You can borrow the money, can't you, until I can get a congressional appropriation?" They thought they could. Late that afternoon, they came in to see me again, and told me there was no doubt about it—they could do it!

And they did! Indeed, they did! Oliver P. Parks, of the Parks Air College, Incorporated, East St. Louis; C. C. Moseley of the Curtiss-Wright Technical School at Glendale, California; Theopholis Lee, of the Boeing School of Aeronautics at Oakland; the heads of the Alabama Institute of Aeronautics, the Chicago School of Aeronautics, the Dallas Aviation School, the Lincoln Airplane and Flying School in Nebraska, the Ryan School of Aeronautics in San Diego, the Santa Maria Flying School at Santa Maria, California, the Spartan School of Aeronautics at Tulsa, Oklahoma—other teachers have helped shape the world, but nobody ever had more distinguished pupils than the young men these instructors and their associates turned out.

The factories also accepted the challenge, taking on 100 to 125 of our student mechanics at a time, boarding them, putting them up, and training them on the planes they were still building, as Tom Milling and I had been trained on the far simpler Wright flying machine in the factory at Dayton many years before. Once in a while some plant representative failed to understand and made trouble, but in the end we sold most of them the idea.

The next big job was to get the radio operators, gunners, navigators, and bombardiers. This required a general construction program of specialist schools at suitable locations all over the country. But it was working!

Only one thing was still wholly uncertain. In planning any military force, the amount of wartime attrition must remain a pure estimate until the particular weapons and techniques have been tested under specific combat conditions. No war is ever like the last, and in the case of the air power of World War II, there was no precedent at all. What losses in men, planes, and other equipment would we have to plan to replace? This was perhaps the most vital question of all, for unless losses were faithfully replaced, the strength of the original striking force was meaningless.

The Germans presently found this out. Their actual combat strength, like that of the British, decreased alarmingly after a few weeks of actual combat. Now that it can be told, Air Force veterans may be a little startled to learn that the losses that we guessed would be necessary and which we planned to sustain as we entered the war, were figured at a rate of 25 per cent of planes and combat personnel per month. Our replacement figures from schools and factories and operational training units were based on that figure. Fortunately, our losses reached that figure in but one or two months throughout the entire war.

We moved into the year 1939. Czechoslovakia was grabbed, like Austria, and the Luftwaffe pointed toward Poland. Nevertheless the strides made since the President's September meeting by no means represented the sum of American public opinion. In the spring of 1939, I was still having to defend the estimates for additional airplanes in Congress.

"Will you tell this Committee just what you mean by 'emergency'?" "What is 'a sudden emergency'?" "Who is this new country that we fear?"

I spoke of Munich, of the belated and desperate effort of Britain and France now to build up their own air power. I reminded the isolationist congressmen that, so far, this expansion of ours was mostly a matter of insurance. Every week, it seems in retrospect, the Secretary of War, the Chief of Staff, the Deputy Chief of Staff, were called to Capitol Hill to answer a similar challenge. In the summer of 1939, the same congressmen still indignantly asked the same question: "But I want to ask you—who are we going to fight?"

* *11* *

Before that summer passed, I became entangled in a more personal
"isolationist" problem. For a while in Washington it was I who was
isolated. By then I also understood what all that talk about "getting a
piece of the Air Corps pie" meant. Late in 1938, in addition to the forty-
two government agencies, all milling around the now cooking Air Corps
with eagerness, a forty-third finger was added. The Secretary of the
Treasury had apparently taken note of Lord Beaverbrook's authority
over aircraft procurement in Britain. Mr. Morgenthau, who had pleased
the President with his ruling that money which went into plant expansion
for the shipment of aircraft overseas would be tax exempt, since this
expansion would soon undoubtedly revert to our national use, felt a
special interest in Mr. Roosevelt's desire to supply our foreign friends
with airplanes. So did I, fully realizing what the ability of England and
France to hold on with their backs to the wall had meant to us in 1916,
and knowing that again we must depend upon them while we prepared.
At the same time, my obligations to my own country and my own Corps
were definite. Between "helping to arm our future Allies" and giving
everything away, a realistic line must be drawn, or there would never
be a United States Air Force except on paper.

With all the confusions and overlapping authorities, it probably could
have come from anywhere, but it was in Mr. Morgenthau's office that the
trouble originated which put me in coventry for some months of 1939.

At that time there was a security regulation which the President's new
orders had not revoked. The Joint Aircraft Board release policy of the
Army and Navy for aircraft and equipment was still in effect in 1938–39.
Considering that no reciprocal flow of information about weapons yet
existed between "the future Allies" and ourselves, and in accordance with

the President's approved policy, we continued to operate under the principle that no military combat aircraft would be released for export for at least six months after the delivery of the second "production article" (the aircraft's status "in being" in our own Air Corps). The order also provided that foreign representatives could not be given demonstration flights in aircraft coming within the scope of this policy.

Early in December, 1938, a French mission came to the United States and wanted to look at the new, and still highly classified, Douglas A-20 attack bomber. Instead of approaching the White House, the War Department, or the Navy Department, the only three agencies able to make an exception to our foreign sales policy, the Frenchmen went directly to the Secretary of the Treasury, perhaps because of Mr. Morgenthau's "over-all" procurement function regarding many of our governmental supplies and those going abroad.

The first I heard of the deal was when, following a visit from Mr. Morgenthau to the Secretary of War, I received an order to clear the French commission for "one hundred per cent cooperation" at the Douglas plant in Los Angeles. Mr. Woodring had been told by Mr. Morgenthau that a letter from the President covered the instructions. After at first objecting because it was contrary to our approved policy for handling releases to foreign nations, when the Secretary told me it was the desire of the President, I immediately sent an authorizing telegram to Major K. B. Wolfe, our representative at the Douglas plant.

On January 23, all hell broke loose. The Associated Press broadcast a story about an experimental model of America's most modern light bomber crashing in flames, killing its pilot and injuring its mechanic and a passenger at first known as "Mr. Schmidt," but now identified as Monsieur Chmidelin, a technical adviser to the French Air Ministry. Ten persons, including four women, were injured by flying pieces of wreckage; nine automobiles were demolished. This dispatch was called to my attention while I was on the witness stand before the Senate Military Affairs Committee, defending the estimates for the Air Force for the coming year.

At a meeting of the Senate Military Committee the next day, Senator Bennett Clark and the rest of the Committee (some of whom were outstanding isolationists) were understandably hostile to such apparently high-handed procedure and disregard of approved policies. I explained as best I could, but it wasn't good enough. "Does the Secretary of the Treasury run the Air Corps?" "Does he give orders about Air Corps procurement, etc., etc.?"

The next blast came when, having read the teletype of the Senate Committee's meeting, the Secretary of the Treasury hit the roof. "It was *Arnold* himself who signed the order!" he pointed out.

Curiously, despite all the public blame concerning the security break, the administrative confusion, etc., it was the semblance of trying to balk him, of questioning the wide-open access to our equipment by friendly European commissions that seemed to irk the Secretary most. He lost no time, apparently, in going to the White House with his story.

At the White House, soon thereafter, in spite of our pleasant relationship before, I felt that I was about to lose my job. In the presence of the key Military and Naval personnel from the two Secretaries down, the President, in unmistakable language, covered the necessity for cooperation and coordination concerning foreign sales for aircraft and latest equipment. Bringing out the desirability for everyone to be on his guard in answering questions before congressional committees, he expressed dissatisfaction with the manner in which questions had been answered in the past, particularly by War Department witnesses. And then, looking directly at me, he said there were places to which officers who did not "play ball" might be sent—such as Guam. He also intimated that if Bureau chiefs could not take care of themselves before a committee, it would be necessary to send the second or third in command up to represent the Bureau before such legislative bodies. To say that he accused me of "dragging my feet" was putting it mildly.

The responsibility for building up an Army Air Force was not that of the Secretary of the Treasury. He might give away, sell, or what-have-you, every plane produced, the latest planes which our engineers could develop, the most modern gadgets and devices out of our factories, and would lose nothing by it. It was someone else's responsibility. It was mine. To build up our Air Force was an obligation that I had to Congress, to the President, to the people of the United States. It was a job that was still ahead of me, for at that time we had no Air Force. The job could not be done without careful planning. There could be no planning with a hit-and-miss policy that permitted the Secretary of the Treasury to give away to the French and English whatever he desired.

Regardless of all those practical principles, the fact was that I was "taboo" at the White House for a long time. I was not wanted there during the conferences that determined foreign policies, the future of our Army, Navy, and, what to me was far more important, of the Air Force. I had a genuine worry because I had lost the President's confidence at probably the most critical period of my professional career.

Incidentally, I also had the uneasy feeling, ever constant, that my hours in Washington were numbered.

The Secretary of War, Harry Woodring, and the Assistant Secretary, Louis Johnson, could not help me a bit, for they were having one of their jurisdictional rows. However, I was most fortunate in having two friends who were wonderful—George Marshall and Harry Hopkins. They kept me in touch with the progress of events.

Looking back on those early White House conferences, it seemed strange that no records of events, no minutes were kept until after several meetings; then, George Marshall, seeing the necessity, gave instructions for a junior officer of the Army to attend the meetings, sit in an obscure place in the room, and make notes of all that happened. Those notes were a great help to me.

All this time we tried to stay abreast of the Luftwaffe's newest trends. The Nazi's own attitude toward "security," unparalleled except by the Russians, then as now, made it especially difficult for our regular attachés, even good ones like Truman Smith and Arthur Vanaman in Berlin, to collect information. I received a second-hand invitation from Goering to come to Germany myself, and would have given anything to go, but "top flight" in the War Department said such a visit at that particular time was contrary to policy and might be misunderstood. So I tried to get anyone and everyone I knew who had come back, and who had been able to visit German aviation installations or agencies, to tell or write down his impressions of their preparations.

Charles Lindbergh had been living in England in 1938, and it was about this time that his connections with the so-called "Cliveden set" hurt his popularity here at home. While on a special visit to Germany, he had been given by Goering and Ernst Udet a look at the Luftwaffe such as probably no other foreigner—certainly not our attachés—had ever had. As soon as he returned to England he had organized his mental notes into a carefully written report, which, as a Reserve Officer in the Air Corps, he turned over to Colonel Martin Scanlon, Air Attaché, and Colonel Raymond Lee, Military Attaché, in London. Receiving it through channels, Ambassador Kennedy was so impressed by its wealth of detailed information and its general critique that he forwarded it to the State Department.

As I knew later, the report made the German Air Force and the German war machine look very strong indeed, and it was understood publicly that Lindbergh's testimony before the British Cabinet had done much to influence Chamberlain's preference for appeasement. I never did see Lindbergh's memorandum myself, though I believe the State Department sent it on to G-2 of the General Staff. But having heard of his privileged inspection of the Luftwaffe from Vanaman in Berlin, who urged me to "get in touch with Lindbergh soon, because he knows more about this German Air Force than anybody," I started up an immediate correspondence with him in England and Normandy. His letters were full of striking information, and I wrote him that as soon as he returned to the States, I was most anxious to talk with him.

One day in May, 1939, just as my wife and I were about to drive to West Point to see our son Hank, Lindbergh radioed from his ship that he would dock in New York on a Friday night. I replied that I would spend the night at the Fountain Inn, in Doylestown, Pennsylvania and whenever he could spare the time, would hope to see him.

About midnight, the proprietor of the hotel ran up the stairs, greatly excited, woke me, and said that Lindbergh was on the telephone. I got up immediately, put on a dressing gown, ran downstairs, and asked Lindbergh where he would like to meet me. He said he had spent most of the time since the ship had docked dodging a hundred or more reporters—in fact, had just managed to get off the ship, and he didn't want to go through that again the following day. I thought of a well-guarded place.

"How about meeting my wife and me at West Point for lunch at the Thayer Hotel?" He agreed.

The next day, Lindbergh, Mrs. Arnold, and I had lunch alone in the main dining room of the Thayer. To help us hide Lindbergh from the curious, the manager had closed its doors to the public, diverting the rest of its clientele to the grill. After about three steady hours of talk, we realized from the fidgeting heads popping in that the waiters had to get the place ready for the evening, but we hadn't half finished listening. Where could we go to continue our confidential talk uninterrupted?

Over on the Plain, Army was playing a baseball game with Syracuse. We went to the ball field, stopping for a moment at the track meet where not a soul recognized the lanky figure. As we walked toward the grandstand, two or three cadets did spot the famous flyer and one asked permission to take his picture, but they were the only ones.

For the rest of the afternoon while he continued to tell us about Hitler's Air Force, we sat unnoticed in the grandstand, surrounded by rooting cadets, and right behind a row of reporters from the New York papers, which were trying desperately to locate him all over the East.

Lindbergh gave me the most accurate picture of the Luftwaffe, its equipment, leaders, apparent plans, training methods, and present defects that I had so far received. Chief of the German Air Force's shortcomings at that time seemed to be its lack of sufficient trained personnel to man the equipment already on hand, a fact which might make unlikely powerful sustained operations through 1940.

Goering's neglect of strategic bombardment and logistics was not yet apparent. On the contrary, German industrial preparations were enormous, and bombers with a range for strategic attacks almost anywhere in Europe made up a large part of his force, though these same DO-17's and He-111's could also be employed for direct support of ground troops. Lindbergh felt that Hitler held the destruction of any major city on the continent, or in Britain, in his hands.

I asked Lindbergh if he would be willing to serve on a board to determine what changes we should make in our own airplane development. He assented, and together with General Kilner, Colonels Spaatz and Naiden, and Major Lyon, set about on May 5, 1939, to revise the military characteristics of all types of military aircraft under consideration in our five-year program. The value of the findings of that Board was inestimable. I can still see poor stolid Lindbergh being trailed through the halls of the Munitions Building by excited clerks and predatory newspapermen as he did his job. He remained a valuable technical aid to the Air Corps throughout the war, though the President's public criticism of his speeches opposing our intervention in World War II led him, in April, 1941, to resign his Reserve Commission.

Three days after Pearl Harbor, he again volunteered his services to the Air Corps, but by then his activities as a member of the Board of the America First Committee had alienated him permanently from President Roosevelt's good will and the President would not change his mind about having him commissioned. It is to be noted that when Lindbergh tested P-38's for us in combat in the Pacific, and shot down two Jap Zero's, he was still a civilian.

One result of the Kilner-Lindbergh Board's work was the understanding with England and France that they could buy any planes from us if (1) they furnished us with their own latest combat airplane data; and (2) all our planes could be brought up to date with technical knowledge secured from them. The agreement had a healthy effect in our development of heavier armament, more and larger guns, leak-proof tanks, longer ranges for our fighter planes, and tail guns on all bombers.

Throughout the spring of 1939, progress and headaches both built up rapidly. Typical of the progress was the way in which the primary training of Army pilots in civilian flying schools was leaping ahead. The first target we had given those schools was an output of 2400 pilots a year. This we had soon boosted to 12,000 a year, and finally, before 1939 came to an end, to 30,000 a year. The civilian schools took the increased load without turning a hair.

On the headache side, there were naturally a thousand things as the war in Europe drew closer. One of the greatest was the failure of our own leaders in the War Department, despite our continued educational efforts, to understand that a mere budget for so-and-so many airplanes was not air power. Far too many high-ranking officers in the War Department were more interested in supplying "thousands" of aircraft to be sent abroad and to provide protection for the South American coasts than in getting the B-17's essential to our own Air Force. As these B-17's cost a great deal more than other types, they were passed over in favor of just "a lot of planes" that cost less. Despite exasperating War Department cancellations, we did get a few B-17's though not nearly a satisfactory nucleus for an American strategic bombardment force. We were also able to order B-24's that year. These Liberators were not delivered to us until 1941.

To keep the quality factor alive, in terms of the real air power of B-17's, I had to resort to a bit of "hands-faster-than-the-eyes" technique. I presented, for War Department approval, a list of aircraft that met the total number of planes called for, but in order to provide a reasonable number of B-17's and stay within the allotted budget, I had included a few "light aircraft"—in fact, quite a large number of those tiny, inexpensive Piper Cubs, etc., which Sunday afternoon pilots enjoy under the name of "puddle-jumpers." However, since the Army wanted them for liaison work, everybody was happy.

Fresh justification came after the first of our B-17's—the production model of that type of plane—was delivered in July, 1939. That one B-17 made and broke five international records for distance and weight-carrying in July and August. One record which stood for a long time was the flight from Burbank to New York on August 1, 1939, in nine hours, fourteen minutes, at an average speed of 260 miles an hour. Another great performance was the trip of seven B-17's to Rio de Janeiro and return with no troubles of any kind. Brigadier General Delos C. Emmons, who was later to succeed General Frank M. Andrews as head of the G.H.Q. Air Force, was in command of this flight.

On the 1st of September, George Marshall and I, in separate planes, were both headed for Denver as the first stop on our way to the Coast when my radio operator received the message that George had been made

Chief of Staff of the United States Army. It was a noteworthy coincidence that, as we later learned, Hitler had started into Poland at that very moment, and World War II had begun. Not exactly sure where George's plane was, I sent a congratulatory radiogram out into the blue, hoping it would reach him, and thus it was that he received the first of many congratulations on his new job.

On the way back East, after witnessing the first real practice amphibious operation in which both Army and Navy participated, George expressed a desire to send a radio message congratulating Admiral Stark, the Chief of Naval Operations, on the success of the maneuvers. We sent it out in a routine manner while over Arizona, but on our arrival at Washington, despite Admiral Stark's noted regard for protocol, there was no reply. Presently, however, there arrived a cordial but somewhat cautious acknowledgment from Admiral Byrd at the South Pole.

On investigation, it seemed that the message had left our plane all right as "From Marshall to Stark." At the first Army ground receiving station at El Paso, however, it had somehow got changed into "Marshall to Stork." From then on, as it was passed through the Army ground station at Leavenworth to the Navy station at Arlington, it was probably inevitable that the heading should end up "Marshall to Bird."

Back on the ground in Washington, the news from Poland hit us full force. As that short, historic week developed, it was plain, not only to American airmen but to everyone, that our worry about the German Luftwaffe had been well founded. Only some 40 per cent of Goering's front-line air strength—between 1500 and 2000 combat airplanes, including about 250 tri-engined JU-52 transports, with a few light liaison planes—were employed. But it was the Luftwaffe—the 700 twin-engined bombers, mostly DO-17's and He-111's, the 400 fighters, Me-109's, Me-110's, and Heinkel 51's—that made the advance of the Wehrmacht's ground forces a walk-in. Poland died on its airfields, from which the Luftwaffe never allowed the Polish planes to take off. As one Polish General commented bitterly: "The decisive factor in the German success was their overwhelming air superiority which enabled them to maintain close contact between their isolated mechanized columns and facilitated the early breaking up of Polish counterattacks." Another Polish officer said: "The Germans' decisive advantage lay first in their Air Corps, and second, in their armored vehicles and artillery."

The method the Germans followed was the same one by which we, on a far larger scale, would defeat Germany: first, by destroying the enemy's Air Force, and then those objectives which made it possible for the ground forces to move their reserves and supplies from one area to another. Meanwhile, they were hitting strategically far behind the enemy lines. The bombers that wrecked Warsaw and the other cities were not to be compared with those which we and the R.A.F. sent against Germany four years later. However, for that period, the Germans gave a perfect example of strategic air power. Their range was such that they did not have to be moved up from their original bases. This greatly facilitated the mobility of German troop support air units as they advanced to take over the Polish airfields.

German thinking showed a sound strategic concept here which, after that, for some reason, was lost. It never appeared in German air thinking again. I have often wished that before Goering committed suicide I could have asked him, among other things, why?

Naturally, the effect of the Polish blitz was immediate in Washington. On September 8, President Roosevelt declared a state of National Emergency.

I at once sent two of the best officers in the Air Corps, Lieutenant Colonel "Tooey" Spaatz and Major George C. Kenney, to Europe as combat observers. I didn't know how close they could get in touch with the actual war theater, but I knew those officers, and was sure they would get actual combat data. And indeed, their flow of accurate reports presently affected our preparations and plans through the fall of France and the Battle of Britain. By a coincidence, Spaatz was eventually to command our strategic air war against Germany, and Kenney, the strategic campaign over Japan.

Our efforts to overcome severe shortages, such as in special kinds of machine tools, were feverishly increased. There was a particular shortage of aluminum. Most of our bauxite was coming up from British Guiana at that time, and the German submarines were making that situation worse by sinking the ships crossing the Caribbean Sea. They were reaping a toll in the Atlantic as well.

While the Navy pressed for a first priority on battleships, destroyers, and aircraft carriers over heavy bombers, we battled for a green light to speed up a real—not paper—production of combat airplanes. Isolationist activities, technicalities involving the Comptroller General's office, the realistic elimination of competition between aircraft manufacturers still stood in our way. I felt that every factory must be given orders for maximum production, whether it had won a design or flight-test competition or not, whether it built planes of its own design or some other firm's. The channeling of our aircraft production down a single line could not be achieved with scores of people in different offices all trying to run the show on their own.

For example, a feature that I could not get used to was the manner of handling disagreements at Treasury Department conferences. A subject would come up for discussion—but not discussion of a kind Army people were used to. It had always been my belief that in civil or in military life, the senior authority not only welcomed but required the ideas of his technical experts and advisers before coming to any final decision. But with the Treasury Department, it was different. At the first hint of criticism on our part, we would be asked: "Then I am to tell the President that you will not comply with his directives?" The Secretary of the Treasury was personally close to the President; and, as I think I have made clear, at that time I was not.

Part of the constant effort was to get Mr. Morgenthau and others to understand that because—and not regardless—of events in Europe, we had to plant *now* the "seed corn" from which an American Air Force could grow. This, in the long run, would be our great contribution to our Allies.

I also had trouble convincing people of the time it took to get the "bugs" out of all airplanes. Between the time they were designed and the time they could be flown away from the factory stretched several years. For example, the B-25 was originally designed in 1938, but the first plane was delivered in 1941. The P-38 was designed in 1939, but not in use until 1941. The P-47, delivered the same year, had come off the drawing board in 1937. The B-17 was designed in 1934, but it was 1936 before the first service test article was delivered. The first production article was not received by the Air Corps until 1939. You can't build an Air Force overnight.

The grim events in Europe made us look anxiously in the other direction as well. Late in September, with my aide Major Beebe, I left San Francisco via Pan-American Clipper for an inspection of our air defenses in Hawaii. For nearly a month we made a complete survey of the territory, going from airfield to airfield and from one island to another.

On our return to Washington, I was quoted by the newspaper commentators as having said I would have liked nothing better than to have a chance to take a crack at Pearl Harbor from the air with all those ships lying at anchor. Whether I really said it or not, the target presented was an airman's dream—a concentration difficult to find. But worse, it seemed to me—though about this I could say nothing publicly—was the lack of unity of command in Hawaii. Here the dismal idea of "responsibility of the Army and the Navy being divided at the shoreline" was as sadly evident as I had ever seen it. Actually, nobody was in over-all command, and thus there was no over-all defense. I remembered back in 1926, at the time Billy Mitchell was presenting air policies to the country, reading a statement by Admiral Moffett, then Chief, Bureau of Aeronautics. Asked who would make the decisions, whether the Army or the Navy would control the joint operations of our forces in the Pacific in the event of attack on Hawaii, Moffett had replied: "If a dispute arose between them at that time, it might be very critical. It might have to be referred to the Secretary of the Navy and the Secretary of War, and they might have to call upon the President. Of course, the battle might be over by that time."

I found on my visit that "paramount interest" could never take the place of "unity of command" and I never forgot it.

Nine months had passed since that unhappy meeting in President Roosevelt's office at which "Guam" had been mentioned as a place for uncooperative Army and Navy officers to be sent. At last, I was invited to a small dinner at the White House. I was received genially by the President who was sitting beside a table upon which the fixings for cocktails were set out.

"Good evening, Hap," he said. "How about my mixing you an Old Fashioned?"

"Thanks, Mr. President," I replied. "I haven't had one for about twenty years, but I assure you I will enjoy this one with you, tremendously."

We then talked together for quite a while. We discussed British aid, aircraft production, the building of an Air Force, conditions in the Pacific, and when I arose from my chair, upon the entry of some higher ranking "brass," I realized I was out of the "dog house."

☆ *12* ☆

For the Air Corps, like the rest of the world, 1940 was a fateful year. One of the most important milestones we passed during those critical days, was on July 10, 1940, when Colonel Henry L. Stimson returned to the post of Secretary of War. His mature experience, advice, and recommendations had long demanded careful consideration in every government agency from the White House down. From the airman's point of view, Henry Stimson was an outstanding choice. The War Department team was finally complemented by Under-Secretary Judge Robert Patterson, sometimes considered by air procurement and production leaders to be a bit "set in his ways"; but he was an official with solid understanding, whose determination, unyielding personality and great legal experience were definite assets in the astronomical business deals on which he had to pass.

I had less to do, personally, with the new First Assistant Secretary of War, J. J. McCloy. He too was a highly efficient administrator and an important member of Mr. Stimson's official family. Of George C. Marshall, who completed the War Department team, for the moment, as Chief of Staff, I have already spoken. It is hard to think how there could have been any American Air Force in World War II without him. On November 7, 1940, however, another name was added to the top level in the War Department which was of towering importance to our Air Force. Robert A. Lovett came to Washington as Assistant Secretary of War for Air. I found in Bob Lovett a man who possessed the qualities in which I was weakest, a partner and teammate of tremendous sympathy, and of calm and hidden force. When I became impatient, intolerant, and would rant around, fully intending to tear the War and Navy Departments to pieces, Bob Lovett would know exactly how to handle me. He would say, with a quiet smile: "Hap, you're wonderful! How I wish I had your pep and vitality! Now . . . let's get down and be practical." And I would come back to earth with a bang. I can't imagine a finer team to work with than those men made during the tough years from 1940 to the end of 1945.

By the early Spring of 1940, I was convinced that neither the inter-service squabbles, troubles with isolationist congressmen, the sniping from various public quarters, nor the problem of trained manpower was one fraction as big a hurdle as the matter of aircraft production. We were still not building planes in accordance with our planned program, nor, despite all the talk, was there a production program in being which really seemed likely to meet the needs of the British, the French, the Russians, and the Chinese, as well as those of our own Army and Navy. It was not the fault of the aircraft companies. Until the government furnished them with a full-rounded production schedule which took into account the steady maintenance of our Air Force at a programmed strength—that is, a production schedule insuring not only a given number of aircraft at a certain date, but thereafter the unfaltering replacements for these planes—the aircraft factories could not make proper plans. Only on the basis of such a program could they plan their subsidiary components, put in orders for their machinery and raw materials, start training their mechanics, and figure out the output they would have available. These same principles applied to engines and other accessories.

I have always thought President Roosevelt believed he was accomplishing this when he designated Secretary of the Treasury Morgenthau to handle production matters. The President probably assumed that Mr. Morgenthau would follow the precedent established in England when Beaverbrook was placed in charge of military production. Beaverbrook had done a masterful job. Our problem was different from that of the British. They were not plagued with the "giving away" angle; they were building up the R.A.F., purely and simply. It was the rosy dream of some Americans that we could save the world and ourselves by sending all our weapons abroad for other men to fight with. If this priority thus deprived our own air power of even its foundation stones, certain people seemed to take the view that it was just too bad.

Let us note some of the things going on in 1940 as far as allocation of airplanes and engines was concerned:

January 11, 1940: The French asked for 25 P-40's; the Finns asked for 40 P-35's.

January 12, 1940: England negotiated for 20,000 planes.

March 19, 1940: It was decreed that no military developments should be divulged or released to any foreign purchaser, unless or until a superior plane was actually in the process of manufacture for the U.S. War Department. No delivery delays were to be tolerated in our operating requirements.

On May 16, 1940, I called a conference with the aircraft industry to determine ways and means of expediting production of Army airplanes, and to determine what additional facilities and machine tools or help from the government might be needed. On May 17th, the conference was called off, by order of the Secretary of War, at the request of the Secretary of the Treasury. On May 18th, the conference was "on" again, called, this time, by the Secretary of the Treasury, who wanted it held in his office; consequently, no further action was taken by the Chief of the Air Corps.

The conference was held—in the Office of the Secretary of the Treasury—but it was not a success, for none of the industrial people were able to find out the purpose of the meeting, or why they had been called to Washington. Afterwards, many of the factory representatives came to my office to ask what I could tell them about the "programs." Where were we headed? What were they to do? And I gave them the Army Air Corps picture.

June 5th: The Swedes made requests for P-36's which were badly needed by our Army Air Force.

June 18th: The Secretary of the Treasury was making arrangements about who would handle the Rolls-Royce drawings and blueprints. He finally decided to turn them over to the Army Air Forces Materiel Division.

July 9th: The British requested the Secretary of the Treasury to arrange delivery of 3350 engines.

August 9, 1940: The Secretary of the Treasury asked for release of 50 Allison engines to the British, although at that time they were needed by our Air Force. Consequently, we had to recommend disapproval, for just then we had airplanes without engines, and pilots waiting for airplanes to fly. That about ended the appearance of the Secretary of the Treasury in the picture.

August 15th: It developed in conference that the British had orders and options for 42,000 engines to be built in the United States, or 80 per cent of our total output, which would leave only 20 per cent to fill needs of the U.S. Army and Navy.

August 26th: The British put in a request for 68 B-17's, and one-half of all the B-24's produced.

The above items indicate the confusion that existed, primarily because action to implement requests was not channeled through one source or through proper agencies. Furthermore, the directives, in many cases, were contradictory.

By the time the big blitz started to sweep across France, we knew Britain was up against it, but the answer to the dilemma was not simple. Too many months had been wasted. The phrase "Arsenal of Democracy" was a handsome one, but none of the planes we were building then could be ready in time to help stave off the surely imminent assault against the British Isles. As it turned out, the R.A.F. did not save England with American-built aircraft, and the first weighty contribution from the "Arsenal of Democracy" was our share in replacing the armament the British had lost at Dunkirk.

In the summer of 1940 our plans had to envisage what the situation would be if Britain went down. It seemed to some of us that the time might be almost at hand when the "Arsenal of Democracy" would find itself with no usable weapons left at all except those in the United States Army and Navy, and the Army Air Corps. If Britain did survive, we were certain to be fighting beside her soon.

In view of this situation, it was no wonder that Army Air Corps officers were enthusiastic over the appointment of William S. Knudsen, on May 29, 1940, to take over the U.S. military production of arms, armament, and airplanes. He could not help what had gone before, but he could, after he got his teeth into the problem, lessen further confusion and start our production along a proper course. Bill Knudsen understood quantity production, machine tools and factory layouts, manufacturing technique and procedure, the skill and the spirit of both management and labor. With his arrival in Washington, the Air Corps production problems decreased as each day passed, and many of my headaches gradually disappeared. Bill Knudsen talked our language.

His appointment didn't come a moment too soon. On April 9, 1940, the Germans had invaded Norway and Denmark. June 15th saw the Maginot Line broken. By June 22nd, France was completely defeated; Petain signed the Armistice. On August 8th, the Luftwaffe began its air blitz of England. On September 27th, Germany, Italy, and Japan signed their ten-year "Axis" pact. Japan was still using China as a proving and training ground for her troops, as Germany, Italy, and Russia had used Spain before; the only difference being that Japan was playing for keeps

—she stayed and held what she conquered. War flames had broken out from the western coast of Europe to the eastern shores of Asia.

Of the war in Europe, on August 9, 1940, Secretary Stimson said: "Air power has decided the fate of nations; Germany, with her powerful air armadas, has vanquished one people after another. On the ground, large armies had been mobilized to resist her, but each time it was additional power in the air that decided the fate of each individual nation. The French Army, despite its 3,500,000 men, proved inadequate. French deficiency in air power, to a large extent, explained the subsequent disaster."

On the eve of the Battle of Britain, in August, 1940, the Luftwaffe still seemed to be the most efficient and effective air power in the world. However, figures are frequently deceptive. For example, against a strength of about 7000 front-line German combat planes, with a reserve of 3500 planes complete with crews, the total air strength the Allies seemed able to muster for fighting in Europe was about 6000. Later, we found out that the German strength was actual, while the Allied force was not. It included a French Air Force that never had anything more than a miscellaneous assortment of 2000 airplanes, with air and ground crews well trained, partially trained, and badly trained, but mostly for close support of the French Army. The R.A.F. had about 3000 combat planes, readied for immediate defense of the British Isles, but it never (fortunately, as it turned out) sent more than about 500 of these, equipped for close support work under the designation of the Air Advanced Striking Force, to France. The numbers of the "combined" Allied Force on the Continent meant nothing.

Unlike the hardboiled, business-like Luftwaffe, the Allied Air Force had no strategic plans, not even a regular tactical plan. No unity of command. While the German Air Force was attacking Allied airdromes and communications, destroying Allied airplanes, and making Allied air power ineffective, only isolated attacks were made by the Allied Air Force against German airdromes or the Germans anywhere.

Incidentally, the reports of Spaatz, Kenney, and the others indicated that while our own tactical school theories seemed to be generally in accord with German tactics, most of the American airplanes in Allied hands had already shown themselves to be obsolete. One thing stood out. As we had conjectured, even bombers with a good armament needed fighter cover, and no fighter in the world had long enough "legs" yet to give that protection over the distances that bombers could travel. Also, once an air superiority as complete as the Germans had won over the

Continent was attained, any old kind of airplane could be used. The Germans even used their puddle-jumper, the Fiesler Storch.

The successful coordination of the German air-ground team, the way their real unity of command worked out at this stage, was in line with the commonplace but sound maxims their leaders had published prior to the attack on Poland:

"In making preparation for possible commitment against a modern army on a modern battlefield, we must not be shackled by precedent or tradition.

"There must be no rivalry between branches; it must not exist.

"You must wage war with the entire manpower and material resources of the people; war must become a mode of national existence. With air mastery over a territory, you can advance more troops hundreds of miles faster than Napoleon ever dreamed of military movements. This is the 'blitzkrieg' idea of today."

That doctrine merely modernized one that Frederick the Great had pronounced: "Never give battle merely to beat the enemy; your aim should be to carry out plans which would be impossible without the victory. . . . Small minds want to defend everything. Intelligent men concentrate on the main issue; parry the heavy blows, and tolerate the small evils in order to avoid a great one. He who wants to save everything, saves nothing."

The great Frederick may have been wrong about that last. On the 8th of August, 1940, the R.A.F. Fighter Command took off to save everything, and between then and the end of September they saved it all.

In many ways, in all history there was never such a battle fought. It was not only the first all-air battle in the world, it was perhaps the most epic. Suddenly, the inept, the pursued, became the foxy killers; not merely the defenders, but the hunters. Air Marshal Dowding's long, mousy preparations, the great warning system, the movements of the fighters back from base to base as the South England dromes were bombed out, the air-ground control system, the tireless morale of the British pilots, their skill and courage, and the Spits and Hurricanes, paid off.

At the peak of its triumph, Goering's Luftwaffe was suddenly demoralized—not merely outfought, but out-thought. By the end of the battle, both air forces had scraped the bottom of the barrel; both British and German pilots and planes were nearly gone. But in the mutual exhaustion, the English victory was complete—not only on a ratio of two enemy planes shot down for every R.A.F. fighter lost—but because the Anglo-Saxon world still stood intact; it had weathered the most terrific storm that Teutonic might and power could bring against it, and from then on, the German sense of inferiority seemed to grow.

Goering's personal interference (by 1945 he was blaming the Fuehrer's personal interference), the miserable German fighter tactics, hugging the bombers too close to give them real support, the inadequate armament on the German bombers, the collapse of the Luftwaffe's replacements, the strife that sprang up between German bomber and German fighter men—none of this explains it all. Except briefly, in support of Rommel in Africa, and in support of the advance on Stalingrad, the Luftwaffe never took the offensive in a major sense again. Its strength at its peak was to be poured into a single-engine fighter defense against our own daylight bombers. That defense was also to fail.

After the Battle of Britain, we rushed more air officers to Britain to learn everything we could.

Far away at home, as October ended, we began to breathe more easily, for another quieter blow against the Luftwaffe was taking place, without physical action, which has never been publicized.

Earlier in this book, I mentioned the operations of the air line Scadta, under Captain Von Bauer, who started his German company in Colombia in 1919, with a group of ex-Army officers and pilots from the German and Austrian armies. Captain Von Bauer had come up to the United States in 1924 with the idea of organizing a group of American and European businessmen to operate an air line between Key West, Florida, and Colombia, via the Panama Canal. The American businessmen were to be on paper only. It has also been noted that when Von Bauer arrived in Washington, he could not get the air-mail contract, and (after our paper Pan American Airways had forestalled him), gave up the idea. But that did not stop the Germans from opening up a new air line into South America.

As a matter of fact, by 1940 the Germans and the Italians controlled and operated air lines in South America covering more than twenty thousand miles of scheduled routes. Their lines extended across the South Atlantic to Recife in Brazil, and from there, down to Buenos Aires, and across to Santiago, Chile. In addition, they had lines running to the north of Brazil, and across the Andes to Lima, on the Pacific Coast.

As early as 1934, the Lufthansa, which was the controlling interest over all the German companies operating in South America, opened up air-mail service between Central Europe and South America, via the

West Coast, with a regular weekly schedule. It was the first all-air, transoceanic airplane route in the world. In order to insure reliability, the planes had depot ships stationed in the Atlantic, and were catapulted off these depot ships on their take-offs. The air lines that the Germans and the Italians were operating used German and Italian personnel, most of whom had been, or still were, in the military service of their countries. These operations were a potential threat to the Panama Canal and to any operations which we might have started across the South Atlantic. The planes used were land and sea planes of the tri-motored Junker-52, and the Focke Wulf-200 four-engine type.

Off the northeast coast of Brazil, a distance of 300 miles, was the island of Fernando de Noronha. This was a control point and communications center for the Italian and German operations across the Atlantic. The Italian radio set installed there continued operations even after we were in the war, and stayed there, much to our annoyance. It probably caused us to lose a few of our trans-Atlantic planes, until the time came when we were able to eliminate the Nazi influence from Brazil.

We had considerable difficulty in evaluating the potential military possibilities of German operations in South America and it took careful and diplomatic manipulation to eliminate the Scadta Company from Colombia. But in 1940 the Pan American Airways bought sufficient stock from the Colombian Government to take the German air line over. In the meantime, the complexion of Brazil changed from pro-Nazi to pro-United States—or better, perhaps, to anti-Axis. That was most important to our Air Force, for we were trying to secure and equip air bases extending from the Windward Islands, along the north coast of South America, down as far as Natal, not only to facilitate our trans-Atlantic operations, but to give us another route to India, China, and the Far East.

Though isolationist resistance remained active, the fall of Paris brought at least enough change of heart in this country for Congressional Appropriations Committees to begin asking (instead of "Who are we going to fight?") "How much do you need?" "How much can you use?" Between January 1, 1940, and October 8, 1940, $2,380,408,570 was turned over to the Air Corps—enough funds for a total of 19,960 airplanes. New factories, schools, and barracks began to spring up all over the United States. However, money couldn't make up for the time already lost. A year to a year and a half was still required to build these factories, get tools, and lay out a production line; another six to nine months were needed to get the planes through the factories and start the flow of production, even after designs and production drawings were completed.

In evaluating the air preparations of 1940 and the early part of 1941, it must be borne in mind that our country was not yet at war; that the President, usually six months to a year ahead of the average man in the street was getting ready as well as he could for the inevitable.

By this time, realizing how critical the situation was, the Air Force hoped to have a million men by October 1, 1942, and 18,000 airplanes by 1942. This would involve a production of 36,000 planes a year for the Army Air Forces, and an over-all production of some 57,000 planes a year to include the necessary shipments to Britain, Russia, and China. This program provided for a total of about twenty-five combat groups by April 1, 1942, but, it must be noted (and this is important), that our production program of airplanes, equipment, and personnel was planned to enable us to maintain that strength, regardless of our losses and attrition. In short, our combat strength would increase—in spite of all losses—until our maximum strength was attained.

Bill Knudsen saw at once that it was impossible for us to furnish the British all the airplanes they wanted, and at the same time build up the Air Force we projected. It would require more airplanes than the industry could turn out. Hence, one of his first tasks was to insure that the new factories to be built doubled or quadrupled the existing aircraft production. He could see, after talking it over, that some 500,000 men would be needed in the immediate industry within a year, and they could not be secured in the localities where existing airplane factories were situated.

Consequently, it was not long before he had plans for expanding the industry by building factories in other parts of the country; a new Douglas plant at Oklahoma City; a new Consolidated plant at Fort Worth; a new North American plant at Dallas; new Curtiss plants at Columbus and Cincinnati; a Martin plant at Omaha; a Bell plant at Marietta, Georgia—all these factories to be modern, with the latest improvements in design, in order to insure the maximum efficiency and output and also the greatest comfort for the workmen.

The purely "Hemisphere Defense" plan mentioned earlier (it was not a plan for defeating Germany), called for about 250 airplanes in Hawaii, including one group of B-17's. At that particular moment, while accepting the probability of Japanese aggression in the Philippines, we could not see that we could make a very determined resistance with the troops and equipment available, so we didn't figure on sending many additional troops, airplanes, or equipment there. In the Caribbean, we planned for two groups of heavy bombers and two of fighters. The big Borinquen base was being built in Puerto Rico. We had gone so far as to make arrangements with the British whereby we would have a group of heavy bombers and a group of fighters on Trinidad.

Though to this day Alaska has never received the attention in our national defense planning that it deserves, in 1940 we figured on having at least three or four squadrons there. The other two points which had been part of American air thinking since Mitchell—Newfoundland and Natal—were also theoretically covered: a group of fighters, a group of medium bombers, and one of heavy bombers on Newfoundland, and the erection of large American bases at Natal, Recife, and Belém. The latter project succeeded only with difficulty, and owed much to the persuasive powers of George Marshall during a special tour to Brazil. The Brazilians didn't want us down there as an armed force. At first they said that only mechanics would be admitted—no weapon-carrying troops. Any arms that went down would have to be under cover—shipped as tools in tool chests; they could not be worn by soldiers. Finally, between George Marshall and the changed attitude of the Brazilian government as represented by a new President and a new Minister of War, we were given permission to occupy our bases without subterfuge.

Naturally, after the establishment of the Vichy government, the composition and condition of the French fleet at Martinique also had to be taken into consideration. We could get very little information on what was taking place there. The Vichy Frenchmen and our State Department warned that American planes would be fired upon if they flew over that island. I talked the matter over with Colonel Ira Eaker; and soon thereafter, as he was flying an amphibian plane southward past the Windward Islands, he happened to have sudden engine trouble. He was just able to make the harbor of Martinique. He paid his respects to the French commander and told him of his difficulties. The Commander gave him twenty-four hours to make repairs. That was time enough to convince Eaker that neither the ships nor the men were in any condition to help the Germans by making sorties against our commerce or engaging our naval vessels, and we breathed much easier.

Most of the airfields and installations that we set up in the good-neighbor countries had to be built under contract with Pan American Airlines. A direct and honest approach by the U.S. Army Air Forces would not have been according to protocol. We were not at war, and a polite fiction was insisted upon, though our armed convoys were already engaging German submarines at sea. Still less were we thinking in terms of fighting the potential enemy on his own soil.

Most of our critical air problems had to be solved by similar personal action. Take, for instance, the aluminum shortage. As the German submarines sank more and more of the ships carrying bauxite (precious aluminum ore) bound northward from South America, we hoped that American air protection, based in British Guiana, might be an eventual answer. Still, even if all those bauxite ships got through, our manufacturing capacity wasn't large enough to produce the aluminum ingots we needed for our 1940 aircraft production. Early in that year, apparently, there would be a shortage of some eighteen million pounds of aluminum. As in all large organizations, nobody wanted to believe the worst. My anxious requests brought forth the answer that I was a pessimist. There couldn't possibly be such a shortage. In desperation, I asked George Marshall if he would like to go goose shooting. He said he would. We drove up to Glenn Martin's factory at Black River, north of Baltimore, in the heart of very good goose country. Glenn Martin met us, and, since we had plenty of time before the flight of geese began, I suggested to George that we first go through the new Martin plant. Glenn met the situation beautifully. In row after row, new machines stood idle; not a workman anywhere around; nothing moving. Only a small part of the factory was in operation. The conditions here were quite similar to those in all our aircraft factories. However, Martin's was one of the worst. As we walked past the empty machines, I asked Martin why he wasn't using them. "How can I?" he replied. "What do you mean?" I asked. "No aluminum," he said. George Marshall looked at him sharply and said, "Now wait a minute. What do you mean, 'no aluminum'?" Whereupon he and Martin entered into a long discussion. The following morning, after we returned to Washington from goose shooting, George put in his own grim plea for more aluminum. It was more than an enthusiastic Air Force officer asking now—it was the Chief of Staff. Overnight, the attitude of the men in charge of aluminum production changed. New installations, greater production were planned and attained. The aluminum shortage problem was wiped off my list of troubles.

I was still having a hard time convincing the people in the upper brackets that our training program must expand evenly and be coordinated with our airplane strength. It was just as essential to have a balanced production of trained combat and maintenance crews as it was to have planes. At a meeting in the White House, on May 14, 1940, the

President agreed that I should get 106 million dollars for a training program, including building costs, gasoline, transportation, and training airplanes of the primary, basic and advanced types.

Once Congress had okayed this Executive Directive, we had in sight a setup which would permit the training of 6300 cadets simultaneously. It enabled the Air Corps to start training pilots at the immediate rate of 7000 a year, and promised me a 12,000-pilot production within a year. Under the new system, we would graduate about ten classes of 400 men each from the civilian flying schools, this number later advancing to 1000 per class. The method proved so successful that before the war was over, in 1945, we were graduating pilots at the rate of 105,000 a year. Our output of men with other specialties, such as mechanics (5000 now training at one time), navigators, bombardiers, radio operators, gunners, and some types of ground experts, kept pace with the growth of the flying schools.

On October 30, 1940, in addition to my duties as Chief of the Air Corps, I was made a Deputy Chief of Staff of the Army, to handle all Army Air matters. There were now three Deputies, the other two being General William Bryden, who handled all administrative affairs; and General R. C. Moore, who handled most construction, maintenance, and materiel problems. I wasn't eager to accept this appointment, since the now enormous business of being Chief of the Air Corps already took more time than I had. Still, the benefits to the Air Corps expansion program were obvious. Since I would have to be absent more frequently, I appointed Major General George Brett as Acting Chief of the Air Corps, with instructions that he keep in daily contact with me.

An incident occurred about that time that illustrates how much red tape we still had to lick. On one of my trips to Kansas City to see the Secretary of War, I was traveling in his personal plane. I was acting as copilot, and I flew along headed straight for some clouds. The pilot shook his head, and said, "We must by-pass them." I said, "Why not fly through on a straight course?" He pointed to a sign on the instrument panel which read: "This airplane will not be flown through rain or through moisture-laden clouds."

I couldn't believe my eyes! Airliners had been flying through heavy rainstorms as confidently as in normal weather for a long time. This was the Secretary of War's plane, and if the Army couldn't give him a plane as good as those in which civilians flew, we were in a mighty bad fix. The pilot could give me no further information, so I sent a radio to the Air Materiel Division, at Dayton, asking that all men responsible for the equipment in the Secretary of War's plane, and the restrictions on its flying, be assembled when we arrived.

Following our aircraft production conference with the Secretary of War at Kansas City, I stopped off at Dayton. There were the men, some 18 of them, waiting—engineers, draftsmen, equipment experts—but none would, or could, assume responsibility for the ignition harness that would not permit the plane to be flown in moisture-laden air. Nor could I find out who had directed that the placard be placed on the instrument panel.

The gist of the matter seemed to be that despite my efforts to get the best possible equipment, it was still the War Department policy, supported by the Controller General, that Air Force equipment must be bought by giving a contract to the lowest bidder—period. In the case in point—the Secretary of War's airplane—the lowest bidder, though he had met the over-all specifications for the aircraft itself, hadn't had an ignition harness that our experts considered good enough to warrant the plane's flying through rainstorms or moisture-laden clouds. I then told them to get a new ignition harness for the Secretary of War's airplane— but this request got me nowhere. There were too many regulation-conscious officers and civilians present.

Thereupon, I said: "O.K., forget it. I will get one myself," and flew back to Washington. When I arrived, I called up American Airlines and secured from them two sets of ignition harnesses of the type they were using. We put them on the Secretary of War's plane, and, thanks to the courtesy of a civil aviation company, the Secretary of War no longer had to detour around damp clouds.

From that time on, I found it much easier to get things done at the Materiel Division. Their position had been clarified. After that, it was obvious that if obeying the "letter of the law"—even of a flying safety program—meant risking the lives of crew and passengers, or restricting airplane performance because of inadequate equipment, the inflexible regulations must, and would, be broken.

☆ *13* ☆

Early in 1941, the over-all policy on war defenses in the Pacific was fundamentally changed. Before then, the War and Navy Department scheme had contemplated that troops in the Philippines would hold out only as long as they could do so on their own; no provision was made for sending them reinforcements. In February, 1941, the War Department General Staff had disapproved an Air Force request for routes for heavy bombers across the Pacific to the Far East. The War Department had no plans for such routes, nor, we were told, was there any necessity for movement of heavy bombers by air to that part of the world.

A little later, in 1941, a sharp change materially affected our whole Air Corps problem. The Philippines would be not only defended but reinforced. Hitherto, we had not planned to have any heavy bombardment planes in the Philippines. Now we must take them from outfits allotted to other places, in other theaters close to the European zone of conflict, and send them to the Philippine Islands.

There were other problems, too. For instance, if the big planes were sent to Manila in ships, completely disassembled, we would lose many man-hours before they were loaded, reassembled, and flown to their destination. It would be much simpler to open up an air route across the Pacific. Longer and more solid runways in the Philippines would also be necessary. More money must be sent to General MacArthur, who was building up the national defenses of the Philippine Commonwealth.

The route chosen as easiest was Hawaii, Midway, Wake, Rabaul, Darwin, and on to the Philippines. We had already flown B-17's to Hawaii and we knew, as far as distance was concerned, we could accomplish the rest of the flight without trouble. The 2400 miles from San Francisco to Hawaii was the longest hop on the entire route. Considerable

208

airport construction had to be completed at the other bases before we could start the B-17 movement to MacArthur. We fully realized that this route was wide open to Japanese attacks and it was not long before another less exposed airway, via Christmas, Canton Islands, Samoa, Fiji, New Caledonia, Townsville, Australia, up to Darwin, and then on to the Philippines, was planned. This latter route required much construction work and was not available until some months after the Japs had attacked Pearl Harbor.

Our B-17's started flying over the more direct, Midway-Wake-Rabaul airway in the summer of 1941. At first, until actual war turned the impossible into standard operating procedure, we thought that only the four-engine Forts and Liberators would be able to make the flight, and planned to send all two- and single-engine planes by boat. Flying two-engine planes across the Pacific was another case of debunking the "Can't-be-done" theory. It was impossible, we had been told, to train navigators in the short period of two or three months so that they could "hit" the small islands along the route. Navigation was veiled in mystery. Only sea-faring men understood it, and then only after long courses, covering many months. We were giving our navigators a mere three-month course. The skeptics kept warning us that such a meager background would not enable even exceptional navigators to find the small atolls in the Pacific. Transoceanic experience certainly indicated it was not practicable to make the flight in two-engine airplanes. What if one engine quit on one of the long hops? All this we heard many times. But, as before and after, the youngsters in our Air Force didn't know that the experts had said it couldn't be done, so they went ahead and did it. They began to fly these two-engine planes across the Pacific, and hit the little islands right on the nose time after time without a miss.

When I was made Deputy Chief of Staff, I also became a member of the Joint Board—*under certain conditions.* When air problems came up, I sat in as a member of the Board; at other times I could sit in as a "listener" but not as a member. Accordingly, I never had access to all the secret information available to most high-ranking officers in the War and Navy Departments relating to Japanese movements in the Pacific.

For instance, I never saw copies of the intercepts of the Japanese cables and radiograms, nor the breakdowns of their code messages, until after Pearl Harbor. So my knowledge of what the Japs were then doing was very sketchy, and I had to guide myself by what I could read between the lines in conferences on the Joint Board, or in conversations between Admiral Stark and General Marshall or between the Navy or

Army Planners. I did know the Japs were fortifying some of the mandated islands and putting air bases where they could. I surmised that they were getting ready for something—but exactly what?

Early in 1941, trying to get better information about the war in Europe, we sent officers abroad from all parts of the Air Force organization—combat units, staff, Training Center, and Materiel Command. Whether they could be spared or not made no difference. I followed the same procedure during the war because I thought it far more important to give these men a crack at combat operations than to keep them on duty in Washington. I always remembered my own frustrated attempts to get overseas in World War I. Thus, with full awareness of the difficulties it implied, the policy of "rotation" was adopted for the whole Air Corps, but—not uniformly followed. Far too many commanders in the States found reasons and excuses for keeping their most efficient officers.

Chiefs of Staff of the Air Forces, like Spaatz, Eaker, M. F. Harmon, Stratemeyer, Delos Emmons, and such advisers as George C. Kenney and the late Frank M. Andrews were sent overseas to big commands of their own. Acting Chiefs of the Air Corps and Deputy Chiefs were changed as often, no matter how good they were, but, unfortunately, many good men never had a chance to demonstrate their ability in combat.

In 1940, when it became apparent that a real, honest-to-God air ferry line, and perhaps an air transport line, must be built across the North Atlantic, several plans were prepared. The Royal Air Force and the Royal Canadian Air Force were doing their best to operate a ferry service, with one terminal at Gander in Newfoundland and another in England. They asked President Roosevelt for help. He, in turn, asked me what we could do to assist the British in ferrying the American-built planes to the United Kingdom, thus releasing the British and Canadian ferry pilots for combat duty. I suggested that it might be possible for some of our civilian agencies, preferably for one of the air lines, to tackle the job. The President agreed to this plan, which was the start of our overseas Transport Service.

As we went into the problem, it became apparent that the weather and the radio services the British were using were of doubtful value. As long as everything went along all right, their planes made the flight across the ocean in good shape. When mechanical troubles developed, bad weather was encountered, or the pilots got off the beam, almost anything was likely to happen, and did.

After President Roosevelt transferred the fifty destroyers to Great Britain, on September 3, 1940, the British, in exchange, permitted us to establish air bases at a number of key points in their possessions. Thus, we started our airfields in Newfoundland, in Bermuda, in Trinidad, and in British Guiana.

We soon realized that, unless we had intermediate fields between Newfoundland and England or Scotland, the North Atlantic ferry route could not operate successfully. These intermediate bases were essential for short-legged planes, in case of trouble or bad weather, and as sites for additional beams and beacons to aid all planes. The Free State of Ireland, for her own Irish political reasons, was forever out of the picture, though Northern Ireland later became one of our stepping stones. It was obvious that if airfields were built on Greenland and Iceland, with weather stations farther north in the Arctic, say in Baffin Land, our North Atlantic ferry route could be made a reality. Early in 1941, we secured permission to use Greenland and Iceland and started to explore their shorelines to locate suitable sites for landing fields. We studied our maps more closely to determine possible places for weather stations toward the North Pole. An obstacle was the fact that only a couple of dozen men had ever been in the Arctic long enough really to know anything about it. In the case of Baffin Land, no ship had entered its harbor since 1857. I saw that in fairness to the boys we were sending up into the frozen north, we must know considerably more than we did.

Alaska had always been, and no matter what happened in any theater of war, always remained, to me privately, a high priority. But we were never able to get the money or allocations for the Air Force that we really needed there to give us the kind of bases we required then—and need more than ever now. Much spade work, education, and discussion of Arctic strategy had been necessary to get a survey party consisting of Colonel John C. H. Lee, Major Dale Gaffney and Major Longfellow ordered to Alaska, early in 1938, to locate a site for a cold weather experimental station. By that summer, Fairbanks, Alaska, had been selected. The first construction personnel had been flown to Fairbanks in the fall of 1938, and once more, to the surprise of sourdoughs, experts, construction people, and the oldest living inhabitants, the impossible was done. Concrete work, as well as carpentry, was carried on throughout the Alaskan winter. By early summer of 1940, Major Gaffney, Commanding Officer at Fairbanks, had construction well in hand. In September, 1940, our first air troops arrived, and our first aerial Arctic outpost was established.

Accordingly, when we opened our route over the North Atlantic, we had some background on cold-weather flying. True, it wasn't the most practical background because we had not been at it long enough, but we had sufficient experience, for example, to know that steps must be taken to cope with the extreme changes in temperature incident to operating aircraft in this subzero climate. The Fairbanks cold-weather station was continued until 1943, when under the lend-lease arrangement, we turned the facilities over to the Russian pilots as the starting point for ferrying planes over the Siberian route to Russia.

Some years prior to this, my predecessor, General Westover, had engaged Dr. Vilhjalmur Stefansson to prepare a book on life in the Arctic, and how to live in that desolate country. But that exhaustive book was so voluminous that the average soldier would not be likely to read it. Hence, I had a summary made, and a manual prepared which was available to all Air Force officers and enlisted men who were sent to the Arctic. This handbook covered only the area around Alaska, but the salient principles held true for all Arctic regions.

More than any book, however, we needed men who had lived in the Arctic—one such man, if this were possible, at every station we established. We figured on at least two air stations on the west coast of Greenland, one in Baffin Land, one in Iceland, one in Labrador, and an additional one in Newfoundland.

One day a member of my staff came in and said he had a man outside who would just fit the Greenland job—if only I could get him commissioned. Greenland was a real trouble spot. Very few people had been on top of the ice cap. Few knew what was up there, or how to get there, or how to live if they did get there—and here was a man who had served for many years in Greenland.

"Well, why *don't* you get him commissioned?" I asked.

"Regulations," my staff officer replied, "he's blind. The Adjutant General says nothing doing."

"How blind is he?" I asked.

"I don't know if he can see at all," the officer said, "but he sure knows Greenland."

He told me the man was a Dane; that his name was Escanon; that he had worked and lived under the toughest conditions in Greenland for over seven years.

"Send him in," I said.

I liked the way the man looked and the way he talked. He was wearing glasses with thick lenses. I asked him: "Would you mind taking off your glasses?" and I held up three fingers. "What can you see?" I asked.

He said, "I can't see anything."

When he left, I went to Secretary of War Stimson's office. "Mr. Secretary," I said, "I would like you to commission a man in the Air Force for me."

"Well," the Secretary of War said, "why don't you go ahead and get him commissioned through regular channels?"

"Because the War Department won't do it," I replied.

"Why not?" asked the Secretary.

"He can't see," I replied.

"Can't see?" repeated the Secretary, "then why do you want him?" I told him the whole story. Red tape never stopped Stimson for a second if a thing ought to be done. Within a few weeks, Mr. Escanon, by then Captain Escanon in the Army of the United States, was doing exceptional service for us in Greenland.

Up to that time, with our meager knowledge, we knew only that the Greenland ice cap was about seven thousand feet above sea level; that it was covered with ice; that the wind blew violently there in gusts as high as 200 miles an hour. It was said there were high mountains rising some 14,000 feet above the smooth surface of the ice cap. But these were only rumors; facts were conspicuous by their absence.

The sons of famous people are always targets for criticism. When I commissioned Elliott Roosevelt as a Captain in the Air Corps I was severely taken to task and all kinds of stories were circulated. One evening as I sat down at my own dinner table, I saw that my son, David, aged fourteen, had a button in his lapel. It read, "Papa, I want to be a Captain too!"

In any event, Elliott Roosevelt was the first man to come to me with a plan for flying over the ice cap. He had selected a crew, had a plane picked out, and all he needed was my authority. Elliott Roosevelt took the first airplane across the Greenland ice cap. When he returned, he brought first-hand information. There were no big mountains, 14,000 feet high. There were a few hills, a few mountains, but they weren't especially tall. In general, he reported, the top of the Greenland ice cap was a big dome, made of solid ice. The wind blew and there was apparently one blizzard after another, but the weather wasn't impossible for flying by any means. In many places it would be possible to land airplanes successfully, Elliott thought, so we might even get airplanes in and out in case of emergency. That picture tore away the veil of mystery in which the Greenland ice cap had been shrouded for centuries. Later on, when we had forced landings on the ice cap, our young men lived up there for many days—even weeks—without many of the articles of equipment the Arctic explorers had said were essential to life. These youngsters used the emergency equipment in their airplanes, and did the best they could with it until we were able to locate them and parachute supplies down, and then get them out by dogsled or other means. In some cases we even landed ski-planes for rescue work.

After Elliott Roosevelt completed his pioneering in the North Atlantic, he asked for permission to make a photographic exploratory flight over Africa. I was most interested because at that time the French had in effect turned over their Government to the Germans but were themselves holding a line of airports from Dakar eastward almost to Khartoum. That string of bases paralleled the airway we were using from Accra, in the Gulf of Guinea, just south of the African Bulge, to Khartoum.

We used this route to carry supplies and personnel to MacArthur in Australia, to Wavell in India, and to Chiang Kai-shek in China. Occasionally our planes would get off their course and land at the Vichy French airdromes. The crews were interned and some of them, despite our sharp notes, didn't get back until our North African campaign was over.

When the Germans held the North African coast line, they sent motor caravans across the desert, and established bases. Then they dispatched air attacks against our airports between Accra and Khartoum, destroying our facilities, burning up our gasoline and supplies. Gasoline was then almost as precious as gold and as hard to get in the central part of Africa. At Fort Lamy, for instance, one of the bases the Germans knocked out, we had to deliver the gasoline by camel. It required something like twenty-four camels to bring in enough gasoline to fill one B-24.

It can be understood why I was glad to have a qualified observer go down into that section of Africa and photograph those French air bases. Elliott Roosevelt volunteered to do the job, and, as usual, got his pictures. From them we were able to determine just what was going on—what kind of installations the French had there.

We were really at war prior to December 7, 1941. Our convoys to England had already been attacked and the shooting war in the Atlantic had certainly been recognized by the Navy at least. In the midst of this peculiar beginning—(isolationist congressmen and senators were still bellowing manfully against the "warmongers")—there were problems more difficult to understand, and, in some cases, to solve, than production, procurement and the training of manpower.

One problem, not at all complicated, but annoying, was brought up by the R.A.F. Mission to Washington.

The suggestion was that if, and when, the United States entered the war, our airplanes, manned by our crews as individuals, should be incorporated into their own squadrons to help build up the depleted strength of the Royal Air Force. I still cannot believe that this proposal was made seriously. Certainly, anyone offering it could never have gone through 1917–18, and must never have heard the story of Pershing and our Allies, one of the most annotated and rehashed sagas in history.

It was interesting to reflect, at least, that the stepchild's share which had been the Air Service's lot in the 1917 controversy had now become the whole inheritance, since in the early days of World War II no Allied soldiers could even get near a battleground in Western Europe except the airmen. There was a warm feeling for England in America in that year after the Battle of Britain. We sent abroad everything we had and even tried to send her things we didn't have. Fortunately, the British idea of using the planes and crews of the American Air Force as replacements for the R.A.F. was not entertained, and nobody should be more grateful for that than the English themselves.

So many different problems were cropping up with the British that it became apparent I must make a trip to England. I wanted to get personally acquainted with Sir Charles Portal, Air Chief Marshal of the Royal Air Force, and talk many things over with him across the table where it could be done so much better than by cable or through even the best of emissaries.

On that trip to England, I hardly knew what to expect. I knew I would meet Air Chief Marshal Portal and his subordinates; I thought I would also be introduced to Lord Beaverbrook, who was in charge of production. Beyond that, I could not see why I should be received by any of the top-ranking British officers and had little hope of meeting any of them, for at that time in the United States I was definitely in the "minor league"; I had not reached the "major league" status in the military setup. I hoped to learn from Portal not only about his Air Force, its equipment and operations, but also about the war in general, and, from others, the activities of other arms of the service.

On my first night in London, I heard from British pilots stories of their unsuccessful attempts to do daylight bombing. One pilot who had been over Germany twenty-four times said it would be impossible for us to use our bombsight because of the heavy antiaircraft fire and the

German fighter attacks. Bombers over German cities had to use continuous evasive action and could not fly in a straight level flight long enough for accurate sighting. That was my introduction to a general campaign that later developed into an official deprecation of our daylight bombing and a constantly nagging effort to get us to go along with the R.A.F. in their night bombing.

I had dinner with Portal at the Dorchester Hotel where he lived and where I was also staying, and with Colonel Scanlon, our Air Attaché in London. After the first formalities, I told Portal that my mission in general terms was "to find a practical way in which the U.S. Army Air Corps could be of maximum aid to the British." Portal and I talked that problem over at length, but I was tired from my trip and soon excused myself, saying I would continue the talk the next day.

The next day, April 13th—Easter Sunday—we had a conference with Air Marshal Slessor, General M. F. Harmon, who was in England as an air observer, Colonel Scanlon, and Colonel Lee, our Military Attaché, about the best way to accomplish the mission I had set up. We had to know what the "musts" were, and what other things could be postponed until a later date.

I also discovered the British were just about as publicity crazy as we were in the United States, for there must have been twenty newspaper men and women, with photographers by the score, waiting for me that morning. I gave them a brief interview, had my picture taken, and then went on to my official business.

In spite of its being Easter, we started work at once, with a conference with Air Vice-Marshal Garrod, the R.A.F. Chief of Training. We discussed, (1) the plan for the British to use one-third of our training facilities and establishments in the United States; (2) our furnishing ferry pilots for all R.A.F. planes crossing the Atlantic; (3) our route across the Atlantic, via Greenland and Iceland; and (4) the prospect of having the British use our Navigation School at Miami.

I told them I had every reason to believe we would be able to get some sort of an agreement on these subjects before my departure. Incidentally, it turned out a bit later that at least one Air Vice-Marshal refused to believe that American flyers could even be taught navigation. He thought it was "a shame that your people don't know how to navigate—that you have to use beams and beacons and such gadgets on all your flights when you won't have them in combat." He had apparently received the wrong impression on his short hops across the United States. In any case, quite aside from the Eighth Air Force's problems with the elaborate R.A.F. navigational aids a few months later, our two-engine transport planes were picking out those lonely little atolls in the Pacific with uncanny accuracy. Certainly, we needed to apologize to no one for our navigators, their training, or their ability. The trans-Pacific flights spoke for themselves.

Later in the day I called on Portal's assistant, Air Vice-Marshal Freeman, where in the midst of our discussion about plane type priorities I made my first acquaintance with the English institution of Teatime. Thereafter, I realized that no matter where one was in England, or with whom one was talking, when Teatime came, tea was served, even if it temporarily broke up a conference. Like many another American in England, before and since, I was soon won over to the ritual myself.

On the way back to the Dorchester from Freeman's office, I went through a part of London that had been destroyed by the German bombing. The whole area had been leveled off. There were no air raids during my first and second nights in the city, and I admit I was a trifle disappointed. I wanted to see exactly what happened—how the German Air Force came in to bomb, what the actions and technique of the anti-aircraft artillery were, and what my reactions would be. However, I had to wait for that.

On the 14th, the next day, I had a very candid talk with Ambassador Winant. He agreed with me that there should be an air officer on all boards and committees so that our setup would balance—Army, Navy, and Air—with the British.

Later that morning, I went to Lord Beaverbrook's office. He was then in charge of all Army, Navy, and Air production. We talked about the production of airplanes, both in Britain and in the United States, as well as about methods of delivery. In general, he approved everything I proposed concerning the allocation of planes from our production and their equipment. I asked him if I could get two Spitfires, two Hurricanes, two Wellingtons and two night fighters for tests in the United States. He assured me I could. He then arranged a program for me to see the British planes and factories and told me I could see everything the British had. This came as most welcome news and indicated the British were willing to cooperate far beyond my highest expectations. It would give me, as a neutral observer, an opportunity to see firsthand the types of planes the R.A.F. were using, and such accessories as armor, guns, radio, etc. This information had never been sent back in all its detail to the United States. Beaverbrook struck me then—and I have never changed my opinion of him—as a most capable, far-seeing man, with tremendous executive powers.

That same day, I met W. Averell Harriman for the first time. He was in England as a special representative for lend-lease. I also met Air Marshal Courtney, and while the three of us were lunching together, I gave Harriman a complete picture of why I was over there and what I was trying to do. Harriman told me Churchill would like to see me on the following Saturday. That was the first intimation I had that I was going to get out of my own sphere, which was "Air," and take up matters of a more international character.

One of the things that astonished me more than anything else was the calm and peaceful manner in which everyone worked in Harriman's office. No hurry nor excitement anywhere. He knew the British, their peculiarities and their good qualities, and was able to organize his work and his efforts accordingly. They liked him and respected his ability.

As soon as one left an office building the situation changed—everything was different. There were sandbags, bomb holes, craters, revetments, and barbed wire entanglements. Everywhere one went passes were required; guards of all kinds checked people as they went in and out. Outside there was certainly an atmosphere of war, but inside the buildings, everything was calm and serene. Barrage balloons were all over the city and around every important industrial center, as if to attract the German bombers to these critical points. I was told by one of the balloon officers that so far during the war the balloons had brought down 114 British planes and 17 German planes. Right or wrong, that was the story he gave me!

After lunch with Harriman and Courtney I called on Harold Balfour, the Assistant Secretary for Air. There I talked with Freeman, Balfour, and Courtney. They gave me a pass that would admit me to all the various governmental buildings and made special arrangements whereby I wouldn't have to wait at the door while my pass was being inspected, guards notified, guides secured, etc. That saved me a lot of time.

On the way back to the hotel, I passed Buckingham Palace and noticed that bombs in the latest raid had fallen and exploded so close to the Palace that many windows had been broken; that there were bomb craters in the Palace grounds and across the street.

While I was talking with Beaverbrook, he told me that the Germans, by bombing the British airplane factories, had reduced the production in some months as much as 33.3 per cent, but not more than that. For instance, in the month of March the production should have been 1800 planes, but was cut down to 1200 planes. Next morning I found myself again in Beaverbrook's office talking over production of all kinds; discussing every possible way and means of expediting it, both in the United States and in England; discussing standardization of engines, accessories and equipment, and getting some of the R.A.F. experts over to Wright Field and some of the Wright Field experts over to England. Also, we talked about ferry service; the priorities for production; the new 12,000-plane program. It was clear that the British did not have any idea of what our production was; what our plans were; the type of Air Force we were building up; and that we were really ready to operate the ferry service and take that load off their hands. As far as I was able to tell from my talk with Beaverbrook and with his assistant, Dawson, they were in general agreement with the U.S. Air Force program that we had sold to the President, the Chief of Staff and Congress, although, of course, they still wanted all the airplanes they could get.

In the afternoon, I took Quesada with me and we went to see the Eagle Squadron which was made up of volunteer Americans. The British had had some trouble with them—too many prima donnas. As a matter of fact, other R.A.F., Colonial, and volunteer squadrons, organized and trained at a much later date, were now fighting in Africa, on Malta, or from operational bases in England while the Eagle Squadron was still waiting to move up for combat duty. Douglas had just made up his mind that the American outfit was going to start operating immediately, or else. I told him I thought it was a good thing—that it should either start fighting or be disbanded, and the men sent home. Douglas agreed with me.

After visiting the Eagle Squadron we went to the Air Defense Headquarters and saw the plotting boards; had a briefing on the methods the British used for operating their fighter groups; how they located the German squadrons; how they identified them; how they notified particular British squadrons when to take off, in what direction they should take off, and where they would fly to intercept the approaching Germans. While we were watching we saw on the board four Luftwaffe squadrons take off from their airdromes somewhere near Calais. Immediately, British squadrons were sent up to intercept them. For a moment it looked as if we were going to see, depicted on the board before our eyes, an aerial battle, but for some reason or other the Germans turned back. There was no fight that day. That afternoon gave me detailed, inside information about what air defense really meant—something we in the United States had been getting piecemeal.

From Douglas, I got this information which was extremely valuable upon my return to America: A day fighter should have maximum performance at both 23,000 and 37,000 feet. That might require two planes. The Douglas DB-7 (the one in which the Frenchman, Chmidelin, had made such a highly-criticized flight at the Douglas plant) was a mighty good two-engine night fighter and daytime attack bomber, but it needed certain modifications. The British believed in having a minimum of 33.3 per cent enlisted pilots.

Douglas also said there was no need for automatic pilots in fighter planes. At that time, the G.H.Q. Air Force in the United States was making a strong bid to get automatic pilots in all fighters. That clinched the matter for me. If the R.A.F., in combat, did not need the automatic pilot, certainly we did not need it in the United States. The British had gone 100 per cent for hard-surface runways. There was only one hangar on any of the new British fields. After that very interesting conference with Douglas, I returned to London.

That night I found out that whether I liked it or not, I had to be in the "big league." A dinner was given by Australian Premier Menzies at which none but "brass hats"—big "brass hats"—were present: Field Marshal Sir John Dill, Chief of the Imperial Staff; Admiral Sir Dudley Pound, First Sea Lord; several members of the Cabinet; Mr. Bevin, Minister of Labor; the Secretary of State for Air, Sir Archibald Sinclair, and his assistant, Balfour; Air Chief Marshal Portal and his assistant, Freeman; the Earl of Semple, a member of Parliament whom I had known back in 1917–18 when he came over to the United States with the Handley-Page project (he it was who had read the letter from Regina in the House of Lords about my being a "white-haired old gentleman," commanding a U.S. squadron en route to Alaska); Arthur Greenwood; and Ambassador Winant. During the dinner we talked about everything —war in all its phases. I found myself sitting between Menzies and Bevin. We talked about the situation in the United States—labor, strikes, the efficiency of the personnel in our factories and in British factories, what the United States' policy was with reference to Germany and Japan, and what it might be in case of some untoward incident—all kinds of things I probably had no business talking about, but subjects which they were obviously eager to discuss and have some kind of answer to. As a rookie in the "big league," I did the best I could.

After dinner I set out for the hotel. I had no more than reached the street when the sirens started wailing, searchlights combed through the sky, and the antiaircraft guns began to bark. London was about to be bombed again. The guns across the street, in Regent's Park, had not yet started firing, but soon I could hear the first bombs exploding. The sound of the bursts came closer and closer, and the sky grew red beyond the city—flats and warehouses were burning. The German airplanes seemed to be concentrating on the center of London. The antiaircraft guns in Regent's Park opened fire with ear-splitting cracks. The German planes were soon directly overhead.

The noise was deafening with the firing of the guns and the bombs dropping—and then, almost as quickly as the raid had started, the noise rapidly receded and all was silent again, leaving the sky bright from the fires. At twelve o'clock there was another raid. I watched both from the roof of the hotel. I must admit it was a big thrill, but it was not—according to my mind—in any way a display of Air Power.

☆ *14* ☆

Next day I met Sir Henry Tizard, Permanent Secretary of the Department of Scientific and Industrial Research, and later went to Bomber Command Headquarters at "Southdown," where Air Marshal Peirse was then commanding. The British, according to Peirse, had no place for the light bomber. There was nothing the light bombers could do that the medium or heavy bombers could not do better. That idea was far afield from the dictums of our General Staff who looked to the light and medium bombers as the answer to all problems.

Peirse's entire headquarters and plotting establishments were built underground. He had planned to send 200 airplanes to Berlin that night, but because of weather the plans were changed and the raid was made on Bremen.

The R.A.F. bombers, pilots, and crews were enthusiastic over the 4000-pound bomb that carried 3000 pounds of explosive. It was made of thin plate shell riveted together—a steamfitter, or sheet-metal job, rather than the forged or welded type we were using in the United States. In time of war comparatively few men are available who are technically qualified to make bombs according to our conventional design. The British bomb construction required no such technical "know-how"; it was therefore a valuable saving of manpower. The 4000-pounder—the "blockbuster"—like the one used by the Luftwaffe, exploding above the ground, got its results by blast rather than from fragments. A spoiler arrangement that checked its speed, was, in this respect, similar to the blockbuster bombs the Germans used. The German Air Force had dropped one at Hendon. Thirty-six houses had been completely destroyed; a hundred others made uninhabitable. Peirse was getting the same results with his. This was the type of bomb I wanted to talk with our experts about when I returned to the United States. We had nothing like it as yet.

That night when dark came I watched one unit of the R.A.F. heavies take off. The flight of the bomber squadrons was started with 140 planes for Bremen instead of 200. The R.A.F. was apparently having as much trouble with canceled missions in war as we were having in peace. The necessity for local reserves to maintain combat strength was apparent.

I went out to look at some of the bombers. Each plane was loaded with six cases of incendiaries and a 500-pound bomb. Only two planes out of the 140 going had the 4000-pound bomb aboard. The bombers took off at two-minute intervals. No strength through mutual support was necessary at night. Their target was the Bremen shipyards. I listened to the squadron commander briefing his crews. It was much the same as one of our own briefings, since a lot of our pre-mission technique was originally obtained from the R.A.F. I waited around the airdrome until the planes came back, in order to get the results of the raid and hear the reports of the crews to their station Intelligence officers, who seemed to me, at their interrogation tables, to use psychologists' methods in getting accurate answers from the crewmen. The trip had been a 400-mile flight each way, and all planes on this particular mission returned safely. All but one dropped bombs on the target, according to the crews. One had shot down a JU-88 which had come out of the clouds directly in the rear, and was knocked down immediately. It never had a chance to open fire on the bombers.

Very interesting to me was the British method of marking the airdromes so the returning planes could find them. Red lights were placed in the center of the field, with a small line of markers—all electrically lighted. Each plane fired an identification signal on approaching the field. Then a beacon on a nearby field guided the plane to the vicinity. As the plane circled, a tee was lighted and when the plane came in and had definitely committed itself to its glide the lights on the tee were turned off. They had glide lines along the runway with instruments that showed red when the pilot was coming in too steep, amber when he was coming in too shallow, and green when he had obtained the correct angle. Floodlights were turned on when the plane came over the edge of the field and were kept on until the wheels hit the ground; then they were turned off and a small truck with dim lights guided the plane to its parking place. They had to be careful of this, because on several occasions

German planes had followed the British bombers home and shot them down in the landing pattern.

The next day, once more, I found myself at the "top level" of British planning. I called on Field Marshal Dill, of the Imperial General Staff. He had with him General Venning and General Nye, his two assistants. We discussed Russia, Turkey, Spain, Portugal, the Balkans, England, and Greece; the English shoreline from the Wash to Lands End; how the British would be able to hold if the Germans made a determined effort to land on the beach. Sir John Dill hoped for a return of the 1918 conditions, when for no apparent reason the German morale had broken. It was at this point I stuck my neck out: this time, I said, the "no apparent reason" would be the bombing by the Air Forces, which would deprive the German Army of the things they needed to fight with. Sir John Dill, with his customary British conservatism, said, "Perhaps that will be it."

We discussed the merits of fighters, light bombers, and "puddle jumpers" (Piper Cubs, etc.) for use in cooperation with the ground forces. I learned the Artillery preferred the "puddle jumpers," but the British Staff favored the light bombers. They all agreed there was no place for "gyros" or balloons. Speed was necessary for accomplishing the mission, even though the observer could get few details; the slow plane could not survive. Before we got through, General Ismay, who later was to be Chief of Staff for Churchill, came in. He was more optimistic than any of the officers with whom I had talked in the Imperial General Staff's Office.

The general impression of the British Staff at that time seemed to be that mountains could stop the German Panzer Divisions, but nothing in the Greek-Yugoslavian campaign had borne out this opinion. The Panzer Division went through apparently because no way had as yet been found to stop armored cars when advancing in large numbers supported by aircraft. Some might fall into tank traps and ditches, but the others kept coming right along. The mass kept moving forward. The one means of defense heretofore found successful was to let the fighting wave go through and then stop the supply columns. No gasoline—no advancing fighting wave.

During these talks at British Headquarters I learned the British consistently estimated the German first-line aviation strength at about 2000 under our own Intelligence figures, which would put it at about 5000 total combat planes. Perhaps they were right. The British line of reasoning seemed to be that since by radio intercept it was possible actually to make a record of each airplane as it took off from the airdrome, from no matter what part of Germany, they knew where every squadron was located and its exact strength—often even the names and voices of its pilots. It was only a matter of adding up the radio intercepts to get a complete picture of the German Air Force.

The British had treated me everywhere as though I were a special emissary from the War Department, with top-flight credentials from the Secretary of War, the Chief of Staff, and probably the President. The Imperial General Staff took me to their war room—their "holy of holies"—where all the Army, Navy, and Air operations were coordinated. They showed me how they kept track of each Army and Air Force unit on a large map; how all maps were kept up to date at all times; the weaknesses in their defense system, and their strength; and they also gave me complete information on the German Battle Order, as far as they—the British Staff—knew it. My mind was so full of secret information I was afraid I would talk in my sleep.

Next day I took off for a flight to Cambridge. Bomb craters were everywhere—near airdromes and cities, out in the country, sometimes near large estates far removed from any city or military objective. It looked as if the Germans in their efforts to get rid of their bombs, dumped their loads wherever they saw a light. The real answer was that through radio control the British were able to bend the German radio beams and the German crews never knew exactly where they were. The Germans also did this to the R.A.F.

It was during that flight that the question again came up about daylight bombing. Once more I was told by an R.A.F. officer that daylight bombing was impossible. The R.A.F. reasoned that it would be necessary for planes to have at least a twenty-second straight run of approach to the target in order to use any bombsight properly. They were sure that a straight run could never be obtained because of the extreme accuracy of the German flak and the activity of the enemy aircraft. The only way it could be done was at top high altitude.

In a notation I made at the time, I find the following: "Either I am an optimist or just plain dumb, but I think the British still have much to learn about bombing. But who am I to question the experiences of the R.A.F. in two years of bombing in real war? We must make a study of the whole matter of day and night bombing as soon as I get back. The British are not using the Sperry sight that we sent over."

I mentioned earlier the German air raid over Hendon. On landing from this flight, I saw the devastation. One German 4000-pound, light-skinned bomb had damaged and made uninhabitable whole blocks of houses. It was terrific.

When we landed at Hendon, the veil of smoke was still over London from a raid the night before. The chauffeur said London had been hit hard—the worst raid yet—and as we drove from the airport we saw the results of the bombing everywhere, from Hendon to the Dorchester. People were salvaging what they could from the wrecked stores; glass covered the streets; buildings were flattened; fire departments were everywhere putting out fires and helping to bring order out of destruction. Where streets were impassable, traffic was being rerouted. Such a disturbance in one of our American cities would have caused almost impossible traffic jams—witness a large football game. Here in London, however, traffic moved in an orderly, precise manner, in spite of the wreckage and detours. There was a report (untrue, it proved) that Selfridge's store had been destroyed. Four bombs had been dropped within 150 feet of my hotel, wiping out two houses. The bombs had made craters that broke water and gas mains, but the British maintenance crews with specially prepared sections of pipe had quickly connected the broken terminals so that water and gas could continue to flow normally. Five hundred German planes had taken part in the bombing the night before. The raid had started at 10:00 P.M. and continued until five in the morning. Fires burned all day long.

Beaverbrook's house had been hit, and on his return home, while he was trying to retrieve a carved wooden lion that had been blown from one of his hallway newel posts into the street, "The Beaver" himself was surrounded by a crowd of angry Londoners who mistook him for a looter.

During a conference with the R.A.F., the Royal Navy, and the British Army that day, the following points came out: The R.A.F. was optimistic over the outcome of the war, figuring on successful air reconnaissance missions ranging from Iceland to Singapore, as well as on bombing targets in Germany from England, and, in addition, on aiding the Navy with its Coastal Command against submarines.

The Navy was not so optimistic. They had had some hard bumps and were spread from "Hell to breakfast" over the Seven Seas, trying to keep down the German submarine menace, take care of the German raiders that appeared from time to time, and keep the convoys moving. They were not sure that they would be able to provide the necessary support to get those convoys, with their munitions and supplies, from the

United States into England. As a matter of fact, the Navy verged on the pessimistic in their views of the outcome of the war.

The Army was decidedly gloomy. They had been awaiting reinforcements, with one corps here and another division there for a long time. Their view of the future was influenced by the withdrawals of the past. With continued inaction, because of lack of numbers and equipment, the British Army was far from cheerful in that April of 1941. It is interesting that these attitudes seemed to continue during the next few years in our Combined Chiefs of Staff meetings—the R.A.F. quite optimistic, the Royal Navy not so optimistic, and the Army definitely pessimistic with regard to future war operations.

Hundreds of people were killed and injured in the raid that night, but the papers gave each casualty only a small official notice—"Killed in action" the little notices simply said. No details; just that squib which attracted no attention. Occasionally there were bright flowers in window boxes right in the midst of ruins. The fire at Selfridge's big store was still burning, but steps were already being taken to open up for business on the ground floor. People were still groping in the wreckage of their homes for salvage. There were scars on the buildings from bomb fragments and as we progressed we found more and more bombed homes. Fires still burning in ruins; vacant spots where rows of houses used to stand. Six thousand bombs were dropped that night; 600 people killed; 4000 injured. The hospitals were filled. Some injured were being evacuated to the country and to small towns. The people maintained their calm and worked hard at cleaning up the city.

The thought occurred to me: this wreckage has been caused by not more than 500 German bombers. In the United States we are thinking in terms of not less than 500, and perhaps more than a thousand bombers. Suppose London had been hit by 800 or 1000 bombers last night. The greater part of London might have been wiped out. Air power means employment of airplanes in numbers large enough to secure complete destruction.

That day I went for lunch at the Savoy. A land mine had hit between the hotel and the river and there was a great hole in the underground railroad which ran close by. Both ends of the subway had been filled with debris and all the windows and doors in the front of the Savoy had been broken out. Sinclair, who was giving the lunch, first took me to the Air Raid Precaution Office where there was a map of the city showing the location of all the bombs that had been dropped. They were spread all over London, in most cases close to railroad stations.

switching points, power houses, transformers, bridges, docks, warehouses, and factories; but a lot were in the residential districts. Every bomb dropped was accurately plotted, for many did not explode and the demolition squads must locate them, dig down, remove the fuse, and then the bomb.

We had a delightful lunch at the Savoy, and talked about the aid the United States could give to Britain. It was an appropriate moment for such a discussion—the day after what turned out to be the last big air raid on London. It demonstrated clearly to me that air power to be effective must take the offensive and carry the war home to the other fellow by defeating his air force so that he could not carry the war home to you.

I found working with Britain's top-flight leaders a pleasure. Their method of doing business was different from ours but, because of my experiences in World War I, I was not entirely unprepared for that. I was glad to have the opportunity, for instance, to become well acquainted with Sir Charles Portal. In my opinion, he was one of the most brilliant of the British Chiefs of Staff. He had a remarkably agile and logical mind. He was far-sighted in his military planning, and on the many problems we had in common we worked extremely well together.

Sir John Dill, Chief of the Imperial General Staff, was a natural psychologist, who seemed to have an inherent ability to size up people and handle them. I took several trips over the United States with Sir John later, and he was never at a loss under any circumstances. He knew Americans and their way of doing things.

Sid Dudley Pound, the First Sea Lord, was one of the British war leaders I never expected to meet on my trip to London. I had no connection with the Navy and was delightfully surprised to meet him and have the opportunity of meeting his Staff and going through the Admiralty. Sir Dudley was an outstanding person, as well as a wonderful war leader. He was one of the "old salts" from way back, who had joined the Navy at the age of fourteen and had served in it all his life. He knew his Navy and the navies of all other countries. At that time he was aging rapidly, but his mind was alert and realistic.

General Ismay, who soon would be Chief of Staff for Churchill, completed the list of British conferees. Quick, and well-fitted for his job, he had a knack of getting along with everybody. He was able to size up complicated situations and make immediate decisions. In that respect, he had qualities similar to Harry Hopkins'. I met no British officer during

my travels whom I considered to be better qualified to carry out the job
of Chief of Staff for Churchill than "Pug" Ismay.

One of the things I expected least when I took off for London was a
chance to talk to the Prime Minister. When the invitation came for a
week end at Dytchley Castle with Churchill's official family, I found
myself in a somewhat awkward position. I had asked the British officers
in Washington prior to my departure whether or not I should take a
dinner coat and was assured that they were not worn in wartime England. Yet, when I asked the Military Attaché in London about what I
should take to Dytchley Castle, he said, "A dinner coat." Accordingly,
I had to run around and hunt one up. Colonel Mike Scanlon, our Air
Attaché at London, was about my size, so I finally borrowed his.

Dytchley Castle was owned by the Ronald Trees who bought the
Castle sometime before my visit. It was a tremendous place, dating back
to the 1600's, with extensive lawns, a lake, and big trees and woods
checkerboarding its landscape. Its gardens were contoured with shrubs
rather than flowers. In the Castle were trophies and heads of deer that
had been shot by various people, mostly royalty, back in the early days.
Under each deer head was a name plate commemorating the date on
which the deer had been shot, and the place where it had died. For
instance,

> 1608. August 26. Munday. King James made me run for life from
> dead man's ride. I ran to Goreil gate, where death for me was biding.

And another,

> 1608. August 26. Munday. King James made me run for life from
> dead man's ride. I ran to Goreil gate, where death for me was biding.

I had driven down to Dytchley Castle with Averell Harriman who
gave me a wonderful background of information to help bring me up
to date for my talk with Winston Churchill. I had talked with Ambassador Winant in London, but I hadn't been able to get the complete picture.
Among other things, Harriman told me that Churchill would talk long
into the night—but I didn't expect him to talk as long as he did.

At dinner, there were just a few of us—Mr. and Mrs. Churchill,
Harriman, Mrs. Tree, Brendan Bracken, myself, and Churchill's Commander of the Guard. After dinner the men adjourned to a small room
where we sat around and the talk started. The conversation that night
covered a wide field. We talked about the United States; what help
might be expected from us if we went into the war; what our first

offensive would be; airplanes and their crews from the United States as units; additional airplanes and equipment for the Royal Air Force.

I remember well asking Mr. Churchill about Russia. Russia was then an enigma; her future actions in Europe formed a big question mark in international discussions. While she was not yet at war with Germany, she had changed the color of her coat so many times that we all wondered just what the future might have in store for her. So I asked Churchill what he thought of Russia. I have never forgotten his reply: "Russia is like an amoral crocodile, lurking in the depths, waiting for whatever prey may come his way."

Churchill could not see how the British could make any appreciable gains in the war in 1941; said the German Army could roam at will over all continental Europe. He said, then, that the Battle of the North Atlantic could and must be won by American aid. Nineteen hundred and forty-two was indicated as the year for increasing the strength of our armies with which we were going to lick the Germans. He agreed with me there must be bases for our aircraft in Greenland; that we must furnish long-range bombers to the British as fast as we could get them over. He thought the British Army had more equipment than it had trained personnel to handle the equipment. And during the night, once again I heard that famous statement: "England may not always win battles, but always wins wars," made by the Prime Minister. As we talked, it became obvious Churchill's idea was that the Allies must plan for equipment, the raising of manpower and training for as far ahead as 1943.

At this point in our conference, Sir Charles Portal joined us. He emphasized that we must have pressure cabins, longer-range bombers and larger bombers. Churchill talked as if he were convinced that the submarine menace could be licked by the present convoy organization. At that time the German Focke Wulf 200 was going far out to sea and hitting convoys. They were a serious menace. The British leaders thought the Focke Wulf four-engine bombers must, in turn, be hit by pursuit planes operating from vessels in the convoy. The consensus of those present seemed to be that those pursuit planes must, after combat, land wherever the fuel they carried would permit them, and the pilots save themselves if they could.

I learned about skip bombing that night. The talk brought out the fact that while comparatively few British and Allied ships had been sunk during April, many German ships had been sunk by a new method which the British Coastal Command was using. Light bombers, flying low over the water, released their bombs just as the bomber approached the target; the bombs were in an almost horizontal position when they hit the water. When they struck the sea they bounced and if close to the ship penetrated at the water line. The British claimed to have had wonderful success with that method and to have made far more hits than with high-altitude bombing.

As soon as I returned to the United States, I had the skip bombing method tested at our training ground at Eglin Field, Florida, and later it was used successfully by General Kenney against the Japanese convoys coming south into the Coral Sea.

We talked all through that night, until about three o'clock the next morning. By that time my mind was full. I was sleepy and ready to go to bed.

The following day, the Prime Minister and I continued our conversation. We discussed the British plan for a base at Basra; an American air depot south of Cairo. We talked about what was going to happen in Norway; how we should, by all means, establish bases in the Azores; and then North Africa came up, and the question of the North African campaign. And we talked about Suez, Greenland, and Iceland.

Churchill brought up the necessity for publicity. According to him we were not using the right sort of publicity in America. There was a great need for the proper kind, so that the people would understand just what was happening and what the United States must do. Included in this publicity should be proper propaganda, handled by someone who understood the psychology of the American people; a distribution of information where it would do the most good. Brendan Bracken joined in this opinion. I hazarded the thought that President Roosevelt was doing exactly that, and that he was about six months to a year ahead of the people in international affairs. Churchill agreed, but still insisted that this propaganda must be carried on by others high in governmental circles.

At lunch the next—or, to be exact, the same—day, with Prime Minister and Mrs. Churchill, were President Beneš of Czechoslovakia, his Prime Minister, his Chief of Staff, and Averell Harriman. President Beneš wanted to know why the United States had failed to recognize his Government and to give him aid. I replied that I couldn't answer that question; I was sorry, but our State Department handled our foreign affairs in its own way, and to understand just what was going on, one had to be close to that Department.

President Beneš struck me as being kindly, clear-headed, and courageous—a man who was willing to fight for his country and for what he thought was right, to the bitter end. I was very favorably impressed with him. He was well informed on the affairs of the world and was endeavoring to let the people of other nations know of his problems so that they could help.

After lunch, Churchill, Beneš, Harriman, Bracken, and I drove thirty miles to the Czech Camp, where we reviewed President Beneš' Army. He said sadly, "Two thousand; all that is left of an Army of 1,500,000 men." Those veterans gave a wonderful demonstration when Churchill appeared. They were fine looking men, keen and alert, equipped with British arms and wearing British uniforms.

After the review, we rode through the countryside to various small towns, and continued our discussion. I found that Churchill had a wonderfully detailed knowledge of all phases of military operations, past and present. He had a remarkably retentive mind. This tour reminded me of one of Roosevelt's in that everywhere he was received with great enthusiasm and spontaneous ovations. I noticed Churchill was able to change his manner, his approach, depending entirely upon the particular situation confronting him, or the plight or circumstances of the people with whom he was talking. He could register pathos; he could be gracious and winning in his ways; he could register sorrow or great joy, or be enthusiastic, or sympathetic; he could be kind and tender, all depending upon whether it was the widow of a man lost at Dunkirk, or a small girl bringing him a bunch of flowers, or a leader of a delegation of citizens welcoming him to a community.

That night after dinner, Winston Churchill and Sir Charles Portal did most of the talking. Portal handled himself brilliantly and was able to hold his own in the conversation with the Prime Minister, in spite of the many quips the Prime Minister made, either seriously, or in a joking way, about the Air Force. During the talk around the dinner table, and after dinner, there was considerable discussion about who was the brains in Germany—whether it was Hitler or Himmler, or some of the various German generals who at that time seemed to be near the driver's seat. All the British agreed on Hitler as being the real brains behind all the major policies.

Later, both Churchill and Portal started working on me, saying that we, the United States, must come into the fight, and soon. Once more we stayed up, and by 2:00 A.M. I had all the messages I could remember to take back to the President, to the Secretary of War, and to General Marshall.

As time went on, the more I talked with the Prime Minister, the more I became impressed with his all-inclusive mind and tremendous personality. There seemed to be no limit to the subjects on which he could talk: it might be the Battle of Gettysburg, the Boer War, World War I, or World War II—or what was happening in the United States. He was the natural leader for Great Britain during those extremely perilous days.

The following morning (or, rather, later the same morning) I went to Churchill's bedroom and talked for twenty minutes with him, interrupting his habitual period of dictation in bed. He gave me many messages to the President, which all boiled down to this one simple sentence: "You tell the President for me that with you—the United States—in the war, we cannot help but win."

It was natural that British leaders in those talks should make what, to us, were exorbitant demands. They needed equipment badly; they were fighting and we were not; and they did not know whether we could really build an Air Force or whether it would be any good if we did build one.

Nevertheless, I was faced with a very delicate situation. I wanted to give the British all the equipment they could use, but not enough for a surplus. Visiting one R.A.F. station, I saw some of our B-24's just sitting, waiting for some future date when they would be put through a modification center. Had we been able to keep those planes, each one could have trained four or more combat crews.

As I went out the front door of Dytchley Castle, I found a Guard of Honor waiting for me; I received the honors, inspected the Guard, and rode off with Air Marshal Portal to Hertford, where we met Lord Beaverbrook. Here were assembled for display various types of the latest British airplanes. It was an impressive exhibition. The British were certainly showing me everything they had. In addition to the R.A.F.'s latest models of the new Typhoon and the new Mosquito planes, about which I had not seen or heard much, they had one of our Douglas DB-7's mounted with twelve guns, and another with four cannon. A multitude of senior officers were there at the exhibition, as anxious to see the show as I was.

There I met Forrestal for the first time. Harriman, Ambassador Winant, our own Military Attaché, Colonel Lee, were among those present. After the inspection, I climbed into Beaverbrook's auto and rode away. He and I talked all afternoon about ferry service; interchange of planes; the necessity of sending experts from our factories to England, and experts from England to the United States; British production; the effect of bombing on British production; the Sabre engine and the development program.

That night we had an interesting dinner at "The Beaver's" house in the country. The guests included the First Lord of the Admiralty, Alexander; Field Marshal Dill; General Pyle, Chief of the Anti-Aircraft Artillery, and two members of Parliament. From the subjects discussed the talk might well have been limited to officers of the British Staff, with no outsider present. Certainly I was getting an earful from the Most Secret Holy of Holies. The discussion might have been to impress me with the necessity of the United States' coming into the war, or it may have been straight from the shoulder—in any event, it sounded awfully pessimistic.

There was an undercurrent among all those present that suggested a fear of losing the war; at the same time, there seemed to be a calm determination to fight on to the last defense. To say the least, I was greatly surprised when Beaverbrook turned to me and said, "What would you do in the United States if Churchill were hanged and the rest of us were in hiding in Scotland, or being run down by the Germans—what would the people in the United States do then? That might happen to us now any day. We are up against the mightiest Army the world has ever seen!" Naturally, such a question coming out of a blue sky threw me back on my haunches, particularly when I was making my first appearance among the British leaders.

Almost everyone at the table agreed Germany could establish a bridgehead on England's shoreline any time she was willing to make the sacrifice. It was the general opinion that the attack might well be made in the vicinity of Dover. It could be done by establishing a line of mines at each end of the English Channel, protecting the mine field by smoke, and making the landing under cover of a determined bombing attack. It was not a question of whether the Germans could make the landing; the question was: could the British keep them from extending their bridgehead after a landing had been made?

That night, London was again bombed by the Germans. Waterloo Bridge was hit and closed. The Thames was reported to be blocked. Two railroad canals were closed up. Debris was strewn everywhere when we came back into the city the following morning.

That afternoon I had a talk with Jim Forrestal and Admiral Ghormley. I had talked with Admiral Ghormley before about the necessity of having an American Air officer, in addition to our Army and Navy officers, on the Military Planning Commission that was being set up in

London, because I thought it essential that our organization match the British Army-Navy Air setup. Wars of today being so dependent upon the air, it seemed to me imperative to have an Air man at military conferences, but there was no provision for such a U.S. Air representative. Admiral Ghormley would have none of it.

My discussions in England with Portal, Churchill, and the others left me with the impression that by air alone we might bring Germany so completely to her knees that it might be unnecessary for the ground forces to make a landing. Certainly, destruction by air power could make a landing of ground forces possible. The Navy could insure the existence of England, but air power and air power alone could carry the war home to Central Germany, break down her morale, and take away from her the things essential to combat. The British Air Force at that time was helping the Navy by knocking down the Focke Wulfs, which were doing so much damage to the convoys, and by destroying bases for submarines and surface raiders. All the people with whom I talked in England were convinced that the Air Arm, by bombing factories and military installations in interior Germany, might well destroy the Nazi "will to fight." Wishful thinking? Perhaps. They all agreed the land phases would not and could not come into the picture except in a minor role for some time. Modern war had completely changed the old concepts.

During the conversations in London I learned that two ports, Liverpool and Glasgow, were receiving 90 per cent of all supplies received in England.

One thing was apparent—either the British were actually in an awfully tight spot, and knew it, or they were deliberately trying to paint the picture as black as they could possibly make it so that I would take that picture back to the President of the United States. Now, with a perspective on the period, I am inclined to the former opinion. The British were desperate—so desperate that for once their cloak of conservatism was cast aside; their inbred policy of understatement thrown into the discard. They needed help, needed it badly, and were frank to admit it.

Sir Henry Tizard, head of Scientific Investigation, was worried about our airplane developments, and the quality of our airplanes. Admiral Osborne was concerned about our having only one source of supply for the turrets for our airplanes. Everyone had ideas or worries about our production.

I spent most of one day in the Admiralty with Admiral Pound, who explained how the escort for the convoys coming from the United States arranged to meet the ships and bring them in. He also showed me the general areas in which the submarines waited for convoys; the gradual increase in cruising radius of the subs; what happened when the convoys were unescorted in the submarine zone; and how the destroyer escorts were compelled to go out farther and farther to meet the convoys beyond the submarine zone. In the early war days, when the destroyers operated from Ireland, it was possible for them to reach the convoys before the submarines did. Then the submarines extended their rendezvous, first to the 17th meridian; then to the 22nd; the 30th; and finally to the 35th meridian. All of these extensions made it necessary for the destroyers to go farther and farther from England to meet the convoys and bring them in. At that particular time the destroyers had reached their limit. It was, therefore, important that the United States establish patrol bases at Greenland, Newfoundland, and Nova Scotia, so the whole sea lane would be covered all the way across the Atlantic. The British already were operating bases in Scotland and North Ireland, but Admiral Pound wished me to impress upon the President and Secretary Knox that the Royal Navy could cover only the eastern half of the Atlantic.

That night I had dinner with Sir John Dill and he told me *his* troubles in this war business. When the war broke out, his Army had had no rifles, no tanks, and very few supplies. He said he never realized what poor soldiers the Italians were until 5000 of his troops captured over 120,000 of them in Africa. Referring to the campaign in North Africa, he gave it as his opinion that the Germans ordered the Italians to attack because the Italian desert troops consumed too much water—a precious commodity which the German Afrika Korps did not like to see used up for nothing. Thus, the Italians were taken prisoners, and the Germans did not have to bother about their Ally's water ration any more.

Air raid sirens screeched off and on for hours that day and night in London, but no bombers came over the city.

I went again to the Air Ministry and talked with the Intelligence officers in the War Room. I learned there that the British were having abnormal losses with their night bombers. Out of twenty-eight Wellingtons, for instance, in one night's mission, six crashed, four of the planes being totally burned and their entire crews lost. Three other British airplanes did not return. We were to find out later that the percentage of losses for our daylight missions might be much higher or much lower, depending upon many things.

Next day I had the surprise of my life. Out of the blue, I was told the King would see me at twelve o'clock noon. At once I was bombarded with instructions on etiquette. Everyone, Britishers and experienced Americans alike, proceeded to tell me what to do, what to say, what not to do, how to act. I reached Buckingham Palace and was passed into a waiting room where an Equerry, a Major General, called for me and conducted me to the King's secretary. The secretary talked with me for a few minutes, and then a messenger came and said the King would see me. There was a long walk through the corridors of the Palace, seemingly endless in length and chilly from the drafts through the bombed-out windows. Pictures of Royalty and pictures of famous horses, the horses of former kings, all hung in proper sequence on the walls. The guide seemed to know why they were there and the story of each picture.

Then I entered a room, and there was the King.

We shook hands, sat down before an open fire, and talked. The chilliness disappeared. There were no embarrassing pauses—King George is a wonderful conversationalist. We talked of everything, from Hitler to Washington, from war to peace, from conditions in Europe now to conditions two years before; of our help to England, and of our Air Corps and the R.A.F., in which he had once served. I was greatly impressed with his charming personality. He was the kind of man I always imagined the British King would be.

After I had been with him for over forty-five minutes, it occurred to me he must be a busy man and I should get out. I suddenly realized I didn't know how. Everybody had told me how to go *in* to see the King, but no one had said a word about how I was to get out. What did you say? What did you do? Who starts the leaving business, the King or you? I went back in my mind to everything I had read about kings, but no answers came. Finally, in desperation, I just got up and said: "Sir, I know you are a very busy man and have a lot to do, so I will leave." He shook hands, with his affable smile, and though I thought it was rather strange that there was no escort to take me back through the long, chilly corridors, I didn't realize my crime until I arrived at the anteroom where I had left my hat. "My *God,* Arnold! *You* don't leave the *King!* Not ever! The King always leaves *you!*"

Well, no matter how seriously they took it, the King himself didn't seem unduly disturbed. And almost immediately he sent personal messages to Washington, thanking both the President and the Secretary of War for their cooperation, and for America's aid to Britain.

While waiting to find out when my plane would leave for the return trip to the United States, I called upon Anthony Eden and had a long talk with him. He spoke mainly of possible American aid to Morocco. He said it was essential that Americans get into that country and win confidence there before the Germans had really established themselves. The Germans were there right now, and doing a fine job of building up good feeling. The appearance of our ships in any of their ports would help a lot. Certainly, we should have ships going into Casablanca to find out what was going on. He also said we should know more about the Azores; we should have warships there to help dissuade the Germans from taking over the islands. He said Egypt needed help badly—tanks, bombers, antitank guns, and antiaircraft guns. He, as all others, was very interested in what was going on at Dakar. I promised him I would fly over Dakar on my way home and see what I could find out.

The next day being an off day, I took a trip through British aircraft factories. I noticed they had smoke pots located around their buildings just as we have them in our orange groves in California. The smoke from the pots completely obliterated the factories. Balloons floating above the factory areas, however, made it possible for an enemy plane to pin-point an important area from miles away. The hangars and other buildings of the factories were completely camouflaged by painted screens draped over the roofs and the walls. I saw screens that had been made from shavings of metal from the lathes and milling machines, put together so perfectly that it was impossible to see the factory from a distance of 100 feet. Most of the factories had air raid shelters built into the sides of hills.

I talked with test pilots who had taken planes up to 36,000 feet, repeatedly, according to their stories, without any ill effects. Later, I told our Flight Surgeon observers in London to get in touch with those test pilots to find out how it was that they could do it and we could not.

Next day I went to Bristol, and after inspecting the Bristol Aircraft and Engine Plant, I went through the city and saw the bomb damage. I was billeted for the night with F. O. Wills, one of the leading tobacco manufacturers in England. His house was about one mile from the center of Bristol. That night sirens sounded, and we went out to see the raid. The A.A. guns started firing and bombs dropped on the city. It continued for some time. After watching for a while, my host invited me to sleep in the bomb shelter, but I couldn't see my way clear to depriving any of his family of their beds in the shelter. I declined and went to the bedroom assigned me in the house and slept like a log. Next morning Mr. Wills told me the raid had been a bad one and another large section of Bristol had been destroyed. I could not help but feel that he was disgusted with me because I had slept through it.

Going from the Wills house to the airport from which we were to take off, we had a series of unscheduled incidents, much to the dismay of the R.A.F. officer whom Portal had sent to shepherd me. In the first place, the car we were to use was late in arriving; in the second place, the guide, who said he knew where the airport was, became lost and we had to stop and ask where we were. The R.A.F. pilot took the lead, and he became lost. Then our host, Mr. Wills, caught up with us in his car and said he would show us the route. We followed him, and once more were lost. After asking a few questions, we finally took off again, and this time found the airport—fortunately, still in plenty of time for take-off.

It was not surprising to me that so many people—even Englishmen— got lost in those days, because there were no signs on the roads. All the signposts had been taken down so that in case of a German invasion, the Germans would have just as difficult a time figuring out what road to take as we did. In any event, we arrived at the airport and took off as scheduled in a DC-3, again one of the curtained-in KLM planes, and landed in Lisbon at 5:20 P.M., after having traveled about 1000 miles. We stopped at the Hotel Avis. As Lisbon still housed a veritable nest of spies, we, as usual, locked our secret documents in the Embassy safe. I kept in my hand baggage some papers, the loss of which could do no one any harm. Among other things, I kept two photographs, one showing Hamburg Harbor before it was camouflaged by the Germans; the other after they had cleverly disguised it with rafts so that only expert photo interpreters could tell which was real harbor and which was phony. They had done an excellent job—even placing synthetic roads and houses on the rafts.

Next morning, bright and early, I took a walk through Lisbon. When I came back, sure enough, I found my baggage had been rifled. The two pictures of Hamburg Harbor were gone. Fortunately, I had duplicates in the locked pouch at the Embassy to show at home.

We took off in the afternoon from Lisbon for Bolama, 1830 miles away, with twenty-eight passengers aboard. I told the skipper I would like to fly over Dakar for many reasons. He said it was against rules and regulations; that if we did we would get into trouble with the State Department. I told him it was far more important for me to get the information I needed than it was to worry about getting into trouble.

We approached Dakar in the early morning. In the harbor were fourteen merchant ships riding at anchor; one ship which we first took for an airplane carrier but which later observation showed to be a French warship under repair, three other warships, two submarines, and three seaplanes. On the runways were fourteen two-engine bombers and two two-engine pursuit planes. The airport had two runways, each about 5000 feet long and at right angles to each other. It was obvious this airport could be used by any type of plane without difficulty. A few land defense guns could be seen on the ridges around the harbor. A good camera would have been a godsend but the Portuguese had inspected for cameras when the planes left Lisbon, sealed them, and would check them again at Bolama to see that the seals had not been broken.

We made stops at Bolama, Para (later Belém), and Trinidad, spent the second night in Bermuda, and finally landed at LaGuardia Field at 11:35 next morning. I went straight to Washington to make a report of my trip to the Chief of Staff and the Secretary of War, deliver my secret documents, and prepare my reports to the President.

☆ *15* ☆

Upon my return from England, I went to the White House for two
meetings with the President in quick succession. At both conferences
Harry Hopkins was present. Mr. Roosevelt was keenly interested in
hearing the story that the British leaders had given me, and asked many
questions about British military dispositions and the British estimates
of German strength and probable intentions.

We discussed in particular detail: (1) the inability of the British to
extend their destroyer and airplane convoy protection any farther to
the west; the ever-increasing range of the German submarines, and the
ability of the German submarine packs to hit convoys almost within
gunfire of the American shores; (2) the British solution to this problem,
which was for the United States to establish bases in Greenland, Labrador, Newfoundland, and Iceland for air ferrying, air patrol, and
destroyers; (3) the necessity for, and the possibility of our taking
over such patrols; (4) the probability of our assuming responsibility for
ferrying all airplanes across the North Atlantic along the then partially
created ferry route; (5) the need for us to get airplanes to the R.A.F.
as fast as possible; (6) the need to establish air and sea bases in the
South Atlantic for the protection of convoys making the South Atlantic
crossing. Discussed as potential bases were Bermuda; the West Indies
islands, including Trinidad; the Azores; British Guiana; Natal and
Ascension Island. I also told the President and the Chief of Staff that
our top military leaders should get acquainted with the British leaders
and suggested that the President get acquainted with Churchill. More
can always be accomplished across a table than by sending cables or letters.

I gained the impression this was the first time the President, as well
as his cabinet members, including the Secretary of State, the Secretary

of War, and the Secretary of the Navy, had received a complete report on military dispositions and conditions in Europe, from the point of view of the British High Command.

One of the most important pieces of information I was able to secure while in England concerned the first jet-propelled airplane the British had built—a plane such as I had never seen before. It was powered by a Whittle jet-propulsion engine of an entirely new design; as far as I knew, no such device had yet advanced beyond the drawing-board stage here in America. In England, I saw this propellerless plane taxiing around the air field and making short flights. I knew then and there I must get the plans and specifications of that jet plane back to the United States.

I talked the matter over with Lord Beaverbrook, who was in charge of all production; with Sir Henry Tizard, the scientific expert, and with Colonel Moore-Brabazon, Minister of Aircraft Production. They unanimously agreed that I could take all plans and specifications that were ready home to America. The rest would follow as soon as they were completed. The only restriction they made was that the entire project must be kept secret.

I had learned that Whittle had begun his experiments with the jet-propulsion engine about 1936. The engine was sufficiently developed to be installed in a Gloster plane in 1941, and I was fortunate enough to have been in England when it made its first taxiing and test flights.

As soon as I had wound up my top-level conferences on the British priorities, I called Mr. Larry Bell, of the Bell Aircraft Company, and Mr. D. R. Schoultz, of the General Electric Company, to a conference in my office. I explained just what the jet-propelled airplane was—its advantages and its disadvantages, and told them I should like very much to have General Electric go ahead with the engine, and Bell build the plane. Their engineers should be tied in close enough to work together as a team. I hoped this collaboration would weld the jet engine and the jet plane into one single project. As far as my office was concerned, reports on the project as a whole would be all that was required. In coordinating this with our Engineering Department at Dayton, I learned for the first time that General Electric engineers had been thinking along jet-propulsion lines for some years, but were not yet ready to deliver an engine.

Perhaps a general description of the first Whittle engine will not be amiss right here. It had ten combustion chambers which drove a turbine at a rate of 17,750 revolutions per minute. This, in itself, indicated there would be turbine vane problems and probably material failures such as we had with our superchargers when they turned over that rapidly. The engine weighed 650 pounds and gave more thrust power than the Rolls-Royce Merlin, which weighed 1650 pounds. The British experiments indicated the jet plane would have a speed of 300 miles per hour at 40,000 feet, and 400 miles per hour at 20,000 feet. This was far better performance than that of any of the orthodox-type airplanes. The number of moving parts in the jet-propelled plane was cut down to about one-fifth the number used in the orthodox combustion engine aircraft.

The greatest disadvantage of the jet engine was its tremendous consumption of fuel. It used about twice the amount required by an ordinary engine. On the other hand, it could burn any kind of fuel—alcohol, kerosene, or diesel oil, or, the R.A.F. swore, mild and bitter beer! I also knew the first jet plane might not be produced in this country for a couple of years, and, when it did come out, would probably not have long enough "legs" to participate in our combat missions. However, I was of the opinion that if the British had jets in production, the chances were good that the Germans did also. Actually, the first jet plane was tested by the Luftwaffe in 1941, about the same time the British tested theirs. Those Me262's built by Goering caused us great concern in our bombing of German industry in the latter part of the war.

One of my chief interests when I returned to the U.S. was the development of incendiary bombs. We had made little advance in this field, although the British and Germans, whose incendiaries were different from ours, had used them very effectively. With samples of the British and German bombs to guide us, I called a conference of the Ordnance Department, the Chemical Warfare Service, and Dr. Vannevar Bush.

It was during those discussions that Dr. Bush first told me about an incendiary jelly. When the container broke after one of these bombs hit its objective, the jelly was thrown in gobs in all directions. The gobs stuck to the wall and ignited, causing fires that were very difficult to put out. We went further and talked about incendiary bombs that could be used in any kind of container if they were in a semiliquid form.

These new bombs, which we later called "Napalm," burned with such intensity and with such explosive force that if dropped near the entrance to a cave or a building, they caused all the air to rush out; and anyone inside died from lack of oxygen. They could be used over water and on water, as well as against land targets.

That was the start of a new era in incendiary bomb construction for the AAF.

In the light of the situation that existed throughout the world, and the feeling in the United States toward Britain, as opposed to Germany and Japan, it was a foregone conclusion there must be additional conferences between us and the British staff officers. I was not surprised, therefore, when Harry Hopkins called me to the White House and told me he was going to England in July. We talked over many projects we had discussed before and that I had discussed with the British Chiefs of Staff in London, as well as the necessity for continuous staff conferences between the two military forces, the nature of such meetings, and the composition of the personnel. He took me into the President's bedroom, where, with the President still in bed, we continued the talk.

The next time I saw Harry Hopkins was when he arrived on the battleship *Prince of Wales* at Argentia, and came aboard the *Augusta*. But while he was in Washington, I hadn't the faintest idea there were to be inter-Allied conferences as soon as that, or where they would be held, or that when we had them they would mean so much.

During the weeks that followed, I received several cables from Harry in London, telling me what he proposed, or was going to propose, regarding aircraft, aircraft movements, aircraft allocations, ferrying planes across the Atlantic, and the training of British pilots. His messages indicated that we were forming a very close alliance with the British; much too close for the eagle-eyed congressional investigating committees and isolationist senators who were increasingly hostile to any action they interpreted as leading to war.

We had to build up our airports as rapidly as we could for ferrying airplanes across the North Atlantic, across the South Atlantic, and across the Pacific. We had to make provisions for units to man the bases that were to be established in Labrador, Greenland, Iceland, down in the West Indies, in Brazil, and across to the Azores.

President Roosevelt personally approved one move after the other and furnished the driving power which made it possible to complete the projects in much less time than would have been normally possible. For instance, on July 5, 1941, we had a pursuit squadron traveling on the aircraft carrier *Wasp* from which the fighter planes flew to their base on Iceland.

On the other side of the world, even at the time of the big Louisiana maneuvers, we were still attempting to get information about the Japanese in China. We dispatched General Claggett to confer with what Chinese officers he could and send us back information about their facilities, airports, etc., and how we might be able to help build up their strength.

In May, shortly after my return from England, President Roosevelt sent a memorandum to the War Department stating he believed we should build our heavy bomber program up to 500 a month. At that same time my Air Staff, after looking over the preliminary layout of the B-29 and talking with the Boeing Company's engineers, informed me that the superfortress would be able to reach all points in Germany from any place in the United Kingdom—if they were based there. Needless to say, we went ahead with that project.

The Russians were now in the war, and in trying to obtain aid from the United States, were already displaying their peculiar methods of doing business. In their endeavor to get the best we had, they immediately started voicing the opinion, loud and strong, that none of our airplanes were any good. They did not want any B-25's or B-26's; the only plane they wanted was the B-17. The total number of these available was far too limited to permit us to give away any to anybody, then, or for some time to come.

Early in July, 1941, the President asked the Secretary of War and the Secretary of the Navy to prepare an estimate for an over-all production that would enable us to defeat our enemies. The Air Force prepared its first all-out production program, predicated on an air strength, by 1944, of a total of 26,000 combat planes and 37,000 training planes; in addition to 17,000 aircraft for the R.A.F. The President tentatively approved this program, known as AWPD-1. By June of this same year, AWPD-1 had progressed to the point where we started taking transport planes away from commercial air lines because we foresaw the necessity of establishing air lines of our own to bring home the ferry pilots who were delivering planes to Britain.

The British program for training R.A.F. flying cadets in the United States was finally approved by the President on May 20, 1941, and the first of the 4000 English and Dominion boys began to arrive shortly thereafter.

Meanwhile, our national defense plans, because of their lateness, were encountering worse troubles—especially in aircraft production—than had arisen from the need to supply Britain, France, Russia, Norway, and China with planes while trying to build our own Air Force. In the factories there was one strike after another. The wisdom of Bill Knudsen helped, but even that was not enough. There were strikes in the main plants, strikes in the components' factories; eleven thousand men stopped work at North American for six days; strikes were called at Curtiss-Wright, at Ford, and in the lumber industry. A strike in Pittsburgh tying

up deliveries of steel and freight between the mills and the aircraft factories almost "fixed our clock." In all, during the first six months of 1941,
there were strikes in aircraft or aircraft accessory plants employing
204,000 men. It has been glibly argued in some quarters that these work
stoppages did not really result in a serious loss of production hours, compared to losses for other reasons. No such comparison is valid. With national
defense production barely beginning, these lost production days—whether
they were one, six, or ten at a time—were days gained by Hitler when
he was calculating his time advantage in terms of hours. The Germans
did not allow the problem to exist in their militarized state. If they had
not committed serious errors of other kinds, the effect of American
strikes on our time schedule throughout the war might have proved
disastrous. Should another global war ever come upon us, the experience
of World War II indicates, to me at least, that drafting our young
manpower to go out and fight for us is neither equitable nor enough, so
long as we are unwilling to draft industry in the same way—management as well as labor. By 1941, the hard-pressed British had found this
out and acted on it, not only men but women being required to participate
in the national effort.

British experience showed beyond any doubt that our bombers and
fighters must go through modification centers before they could be used
in combat against the Germans or the Japanese. At first, we fed the airplanes to our supply depots for the necessary changes, but later we
established regular modification centers to take care of the extra work
load. Also, my concern about return transportation for ferry pilots proved
well founded. On July 23, 1941, I received a cable from Harry Hopkins
in London, saying that at a meeting with the Prime Minister, Beaverbrook,
and representatives of the Air Ministry, a discussion had centered around
our supplying more personnel for ferrying airplanes to both the United
Kingdom and the Middle East. He asked me to make a further study of
the subject with a view to setting up operational training units in the
United States which would complete the training of crews from the
Canadian schools by qualifying them to fly any kind of plane to the
United Kingdom.

Just ten days later, while making an inspection of the training schools
in the southeastern States, I received a message from General Marshall:
"Return to Washington; arriving not later than ten P.M., Saturday, the
second. Marshall." When I arrived in Washington, General Marshall told
me we would leave on a trip on Sunday, August 3rd, at noon, from
Gravelly Point, Washington Airport. Heavy uniforms would be required,

he said, and I was to be prepared for an absence of about ten days. He did not tell me anything about where we were going, or what we were to do. I must admit my imagination did not measure up to the occasion; I could not even guess our destination.

I spent all Sunday morning getting together such details regarding the Air Corps, particularly production of equipment, as I thought I might need, regardless of where we went. At the airport I found that, besides General Marshall and myself, the party included General Burns and Colonel Bundy. General Burns had been in the Assistant Secretary of War's office, working on all kinds of production matters for several years. Colonel Bundy was in the War Plans Division of the U.S. Army General Staff.

At the 125th Street docks on the Hudson River, we were met by Commander Forrest Sherman of the Navy, an old friend of mine. There, too, Admiral Stark and Admiral Turner joined us. We went by barge to a destroyer leader out in the river, then down the Hudson through Hell Gate to College Point where the *Augusta,* Admiral King's flagship, and the *Tuscaloosa* were anchored. General Marshall and Admiral Stark went aboard the *Augusta;* I to the *Tuscaloosa.*

We cruised eastward along Long Island with four destroyers in advance, and spent the night at Smithtown Cove. Next morning, we were on our way again. Standing on the bridge of the *Tuscaloosa* with Forrest Sherman, I asked about the signal flags that appeared on the *Augusta.* He told me Admiral King was signaling commands to the various ships. At my request, he translated the flag code. Admiral King's bridge was the highest on board the *Augusta;* below his, was the Captain's bridge. Suddenly, from the *Augusta* appeared more flags than I have ever seen on a ship at any one time in my life—two or three halyards full of them. "Forrest," I exclaimed, "will you kindly tell me just what in hell all that business is?" Sherman hesitated and at last said reluctantly, "That's Admiral King asking the Captain of the *Tuscaloosa* just what the hell he thinks he's doing, anyway."

The maneuvers took us out beyond Montauk Point, outside Block Island. We anchored at Martha's Vineyard for the night. Living aboard the *Tuscaloosa* was most pleasant. The quarters were comfortable and the food was good. I thoroughly enjoyed the trip. While we were at anchor on Monday, August 4th, Admiral Turner, Burns, Bundy, and I went over and called on Admiral King. We had not followed protocol— we had not announced our coming, and Admiral King was annoyed. However, everything soon cleared up.

General Marshall and Admiral Stark came in and then we were told the purpose of the trip. The President would join us that night from the *Potomac,* and we would take off next morning and head for Placentia Bay, where there would be a meeting with Prime Minister Churchill. We were also told that Sumner Welles and Averell Harriman would meet us at Argentia, in Placentia Bay, and that Harry Hopkins would come with the Prime Minister on a British "Battle Wagon."

The *Potomac* joined us during the night and discharged its passengers aboard the *Augusta.* We were under way at 6:30 next morning, headed toward Nantucket Light.

All through the 4th and 5th we continued our course, zig-zagging up the coast.

If I could possibly do it, I was determined to have General Marshall, Admiral Stark, who was head of the General Army and Navy Board, and the President accept a program embodying the following principles: (1) Development of our Army, Navy, and Air Force to meet the present international situation; (2) As a policy, give to the British, the Chinese, and other foreign governments only such items as they could use effectively, after first meeting our own requirements under our adopted plan; (3) No commitments to be made until our experts had an opportunity to study the proposals and requests, with all their ramifications, made by the British.

These principles were accepted by General Marshall, Admiral Stark, and finally by the President, so I felt better. My trip to England had impressed me with the thoroughness with which the British prepare for such conferences. As far as I knew, we were going into this one cold.

I often wondered how I came to be included in that party going up to Argentia. Prior to that time, Air items on a higher level had been handled by the Chief of Staff and by the General Staff. At all conferences, even though an Air representative sat in, the General Staff or the Chief of Staff did the talking. Later I learned it was Harry Hopkins who had insisted that, in view of the British organization—Army, Navy, and Air—our organization must parallel their setup. So I was selected as the Air man for this conference. This was the forerunner of an organization that finally grew into the combined Chiefs of Staff.

We entered Placentia Bay and anchored off Argentia the morning of August 7th. At 10.00 A.M. the President called a conference. He had received a message from Washington relating to planes we might be able to give Russia, and he asked us to prepare a reply to that message. We agreed that Russia should receive about 70 fighter planes during

September, October, and November, and 5 B-25's a month during those three months. It was also confirmed that we would build up the Air Force in the Philippines to one complete group of P-40's and one group of B-17's at once. That was a distinct change in policy. It was the start of a thought to give General MacArthur weapons for offensive operations by air.

When I arrived on the *Augusta,* the President was fishing and had just caught one toadfish, one dogfish, and one halibut. He and I talked over the various proposals for helping the Russians, helping the British, strengthening the Philippines. He also asked me if I could have Elliott, his son, aboard the *Augusta* by the next day. Elliott at that time was stationed at the Gander Air Base. I told him I could. I also told him about the program I hoped to have adopted before we talked with the British. He approved that in principle. During the afternoon of August 7th there was another conference aboard the *Augusta.* At first, it was a meeting of only the Army and the Navy personnel. At that session it was brought out that: (1) We had a responsibility to the people of the United States for what we had been doing with the money they had appropriated for building up our Army and Air Force. We had had the money, and we had had the time, and they, the people, would demand results. (2) Such items as we could make available to the British, by all means should be sent to them, for they had to maintain their existence. They had to have all the supplies that could be used effectively and efficiently. (3) We, the United States, must be prepared to put a military force into the war, if and when we entered it, as the people of the United States would want action, not excuses, and we, the leaders, would be holding the sack. Time, then, would be just as important to us as it was to the British, now.

In the following assembled conferences, the President discussed the defense of convoys, the United States' responsibility for getting cargoes safely delivered. He said it was too late to start shooting after an attack had been made by submarines; the responsibility for safety applied to a whole convoy, and not just to any one part of it. He drew, on a map, a line of responsibility extending from the east of the Azores to the east of Iceland, and outlined the duties and responsibilities of the Navy up to that line. He mentioned the things the British would probably request from the Maritime Commission; the tanks they would need from the Army; the airplanes from the Air Corps. He said he wanted the marines on Iceland relieved by soldiers. Then he talked about sending airplanes to Russia; about augmenting the supplies and equipment that went to the Philippines, the necessity for B-17's, P-40's, tanks and antiaircraft guns there. He said he would turn a deaf ear if Japan went into Thailand, but not if they went into the Dutch East Indies.

The following day I had just about finished preparing for the next meeting of the staff, when General Harms and Captain Elliott Roosevelt arrived. Harms was then in command of all troops in the Newfoundland area, and he, as all field commanders, had a hatful of troubles.

Just about the time we were getting squared away with Harms, General Marshall came in and said, "Come on, we have an amphibian and the Commander-in-Chief has given us permission to fly to Gander Lake and St. John." So General Marshall, Captain Roosevelt, General Harms, and I took off and flew two and a half hours from Argentia to Gander Lake and St. John, then returned to our mooring. We noticed the Navy station at Argentia seemed to be building more rapidly than ours.

We found new ships in the harbor. There were several corvettes, some new destroyers, a couple of destroyer leaders, cruisers, a battleship, two tankers, an aircraft carrier, and about 18 PBY's and PBYM's. Quite a fleet was being assembled—a good target for a German submarine. Just as we were about to get up to the *Tuscaloosa,* in came a four-engine flying boat, and on it were Sumner Welles and Averell Harriman.

The next morning—Saturday, August 9th—we had a long conference with Elliott Roosevelt and General Harms about changing the route of the ferry service to Montreal, Holsteinsborg, Glasgow, with alternate fields at Baffin Land, Fort Chimo, and North West River, in order to by-pass the absolutely abominable weather that was normal in and around southern Greenland, Iceland, and northern Ireland. However, right in the middle of the conference, we heard a lot of noise, and an orderly came in to announce that the *Prince of Wales* was entering the harbor. We adjourned and went on deck to see her steaming in accompanied by two destroyers—flags flying, sailors parading on the deck, side boys up, bands playing, marines at Present Arms. It was an inspiring sight.

We, the staff aboard the *Tuscaloosa,* were ordered to be aboard the *Augusta* at 9:30 A.M. and were received on the deck by the President, Admiral Stark, General Marshall, Admiral King, General Watson, Elliott Roosevelt and Lieut. (j.g.) F. D. Roosevelt, Jr. First to appear on deck was Sumner Welles, then Averell Harriman. Soon a boat from the *Prince of Wales* pulled alongside and Harry Hopkins came aboard. He did not look well; certainly the reports concerning his poor health were not exaggerated. The band started playing "God Save the King," the side boys saluted, the sailors paraded, and Winston Churchill, wearing a Navy cap and a Navy uniform, came up the ladder and saluted the

President. He was followed by Admiral Pound, Sir John Dill, Air Vice-Marshal Freeman, and the others in the party. There were general introductions, and there was lots of talking.

Later, we had lunch aboard the *Augusta*. After lunch, General Marshall, Sir John Dill, General Burns, Averell Harriman, Air Vice-Marshal Freeman, Colonel Bundy, and the R.A.F. junior officers came to my suite on the *Tuscaloosa* where we had a conference on aid to Britain, which lasted all afternoon. There was one item that stunned me: the British were asking for 6000 more heavy bombers than we were then producing. That caused me much concern, some heavy, deep thinking, and many headaches.

At 4:30, we went aboard the *Prince of Wales* to make a boarding call and pay our respects. I had an opportunity to become acquainted with Captain John Leach, her commander, who had fought her against the *Bismarck* in the engagement in which the *Hood* was sunk.

We had sherry in the Captain's lounge. The Prime Minister came in and joined me and we talked about the changes that had taken place in the war situation since my visit with him in England. Then we went into the war room where complete records were maintained for the Prime Minister of all ships, convoys, bombings, sinkings, and other items of interest. We stayed aboard the *Prince of Wales* all afternoon and didn't get back to the *Tuscaloosa* until about five o'clock.

Just before dinner, a messenger came in to deliver a message for General Marshall. I said, "He is not here." Finally a message came which said, "If General Marshall is aboard, notify him he is expected aboard the *Augusta* at 18:45 for dinner." I sent a message—a signal, as they say in the Navy—saying, "General Marshall is aboard the *Augusta*." Twice that same message came, and twice I sent the same reply. At 6:45 when we were about halfway through dinner, an orderly came in with a message from the *Augusta*, which said, "Re my message, etc. The name Arnold should be substituted for Marshall."

That put me in one awful predicament. Right then, I was ten minutes late for dinner with the President, the Prime Minister, and an impressive bevy of four-star admirals, generals, and air chief marshals. I immediately excused myself from dinner, changed my clothes and took off in the captain's gig. I reached the *Augusta*, found the party at the dinner table, went in and apologized to the Prime Minister and to the President. I then passed Admiral King, the host, whom I had known for a long time, and said, "Ernie, I'm awfully sorry I'm late, but there was a mix-up." He replied, "Were you late? I hadn't noticed."

After dinner there were speeches by the President and by the Prime Minister. Churchill told us, in effect, that this was a mechanized war, not a war of 1917–18 where doughboys in the mud and trenches fought it out to a conclusion. This was a mobile war, in the air, on the land, and at sea. It was a scientific war where mechanized equipment was used to an extent never dreamed of before.

He said the British needed bombers to bring home to the Germans the horrors of war, just as the Germans had brought it home to the British. Britain, he said, could not give up her position in the Near East; she would lose too much prestige there after having invested so much. The United States must give Britain material aid in personnel, ships, tanks, and antiaircraft.

He pointed out that British policies from now on would be to attack the Germans at all points; that in the areas where the Germans had long-extended lines of communications the British would meet them on even terms. By constant hammering, it was possible to prevent the German army from spreading out any further, and the British attacks should ultimately aid in breaking Germany's morale.

It was necessary, he continued, for the United States Navy to give the British aid by taking over the convoys in the North Atlantic, thereby making it possible for Britain to transfer 50 corvettes and destroyers to other vital points. Churchill went on to explain that Germany always used submarines at points where she could do the most harm with the least possible loss. As the British extended the range of their destroyers and corvettes farther westward, he said, the German submarines also extended their combat zone, until now practically the entire route across the North Atlantic was covered by the Royal Navy, and the Germans had moved their submarine packs down to the South Atlantic, where they were doing considerable damage to shipping.

The United States, England, and Russia, he insisted, must send an ultimatum to Japan relating to the Far Eastern situation, this ultimatum to cover, in general, a statement that if Japan went south into the Malay Peninsula, or into the Dutch East Indies, the United States, Britain, and Russia would use such means as necessary to make her withdraw; that we would use force, if required.

He concluded by urging that when all this disturbed condition in Europe was over, we form some kind of League of Nations, or similar body, to maintain order throughout the world and to prevent a recurrence of any such terrible tragedies as we were now witnessing.

The Prime Minister's talk that night gave us a clear indication of the requests we might expect from the British at the staff conference to follow. The next day being Sunday, we had church services aboard the *Prince of Wales,* which the President, the Prime Minister, their respective staffs, and all the seamen attended.

After the church service was over, I had a conference with Freeman to find out exactly what the British were talking about when they asked for thousands of bombers. I wanted to get a copy of Freeman's British program for an air combat strength of 10,000 airplanes. The 4000 heavy bombers he asked for immediately worried me. The British production at that time was planned for 500 a month, but actually was only 250. Our production had not reached 500 a month. We couldn't meet the 4000 heavy bomber request for some time, and then, probably, only at the expense of our own Air Force.

Freeman made his position clear. The British had obtained some very optimistic figures from our production people and had unquestioningly used those figures 100 per cent instead of trying to analyze them and arrive at some realistic ones, based upon actual production. If we had given the British what those hastily arrived-at statistics called for, they would have received 100 per cent of all planes produced in the United States. Our Army, our Navy, the Dutch, the Chinese, and the Russians would have received none. I explained this to Freeman and he was greatly disappointed. He had thought we had those planes in production and that they would be available.

Lunch aboard the *Prince of Wales* with the President and the Prime Minister stopped further discussion. It was a good lunch—caviar, vodka, mock turtle soup, grouse, champagne, port, coffee, and brandy. Both the President and the Prime Minister spoke for a few minutes and then withdrew. Admiral Pound said he would call a meeting of the Chiefs of Staff at a later date.

We were all back on the *Augusta* by six o'clock—Marshall, Freeman, Dill, Burns, Watson and myself, with the President and the Prime Minister. There was a round-table discussion with talks about increasing production of tanks, of big bombers, the Liberian air fields, the air fields at Dakar, the Azores, what was going on at Cape Verde and the Canaries, priorities and their all around effects. Then we went aboard the *Prince of Wales,* through fog and heavy rain, the normal weather for Newfoundland. That night, Sir John Dill gave a dinner for some of us in the Admiral's cabin.

The next day, we were led to realize how difficult it was to negotiate definitely with the British, with our existing setup. The sole representative for air matters for Britain at this conference was Air Vice-Marshal Freeman. Speaking for the United States were Admiral Stark, General Marshall, Admiral Turner, General Burns, Commander Sherman, Colonel Bundy (and myself, of course), all giving our ideas and opinions on aircraft uses and allocations.

It was no wonder that Freeman said to me when he left that meeting on Monday, August 11th, "When Portal comes over, I am going to insist that he see just two people; one is the President of the United States, and the other is you." I told him I thought we would get more done if that arrangement were made.

We had another meeting that afternoon aboard the *Prince of Wales* with Admiral Pound presiding. During the Conference, someone asked where Lord Beaverbrook was. We found he had been grounded at Gander Lake and would be down the next day.

Next morning I asked Bundy if he would like to go over and talk with General Marshall for any last-minute instructions, for the following day everybody was going home, each in his own way. I was returning to Washington by airplane, because I wanted to see more of Newfoundland, especially the Navy base at Argentia. Marshall and Stark were going back with the President on board the *Augusta*. The *Prince of Wales,* of course, was taking the British war leaders back.

Incidentally, throughout the Argentia talks, Harry Hopkins was quite sick, so sick that he was having blood transfusions all during the conference. Sometimes he did not make an appearance at all; sometimes he would come in late.

During the conference, he told me how confident the Russians were of beating the Germans. The Russians claimed they were producing 25 combat planes a day, not counting the 15 training planes they were daily turning out. Two of their factories had been destroyed by bombing, but that had not slowed up their production. Stalin had told Hopkins the Russians had 24,000 tanks in service. The Russians also said that, because of Russian defensive tactics, the Germans had had to change the organization of their Panzer Divisions and the technique of their operation. The Russians seeped in among the advanced elements and attacked the Germans in the rear along their lines of communications. Accordingly, the Germans were forced to attach tanks and armored cars to all motorized elements. It was a new concept to me; the only information we had received concerning the Soviet campaigns indicated the Russians were having serious troubles.

I found Harry Hopkins very bitter about the attitude of the American public toward our all-out industrial production. He talked about the 600,000 automobiles produced. Automobiles for whom? All those automobiles rolling out for pleasure-seeking people when we needed airplanes and engines and tanks so badly. He said the automobile productive capacity might very well be transferred to aircraft production.

We finally took off from the *Augusta* at 10:30 to go over to the *Prince of Wales* and say good-by to the British. We met the Prime Minister and he invited me down to his cabin for a glass of port. We then went into the Admiral's cabin and I stopped for a moment with Hopkins, Harriman, and Beaverbrook. (Beaverbrook had just arrived from Gander Lake.) We had our final meeting of the two groups of Chiefs of Staff that afternoon. We even went so far during that meeting as to talk about reorganization of the missions in Washington; what the United States would do if we entered the war; also, we discussed the ABC (American-British-China) plan. We were planning for the war, even though we were not in it.

We left the *Prince of Wales* after lunch, and returned to the *Augusta* where Admiral Stark, General Marshall, Admiral King, Admiral Turner, General Burns, Colonel Bundy, Commander Sherman, and I formed a reception line in front of the ship's airplane hangar. Then Franklin Roosevelt, Jr., came along with the President. He took his position facing us. Admiral Pound, Sir John Dill, and Vice-Marshal Freeman followed in turn, said good-by to the President, and went down our line, saying good-by to us. Finally, the Prime Minister came by and did the same thing, and one after the other they went down the ship's ladder to their boat, the band playing "God Save the King." After the President retired, we said good-by to Admiral King and his ship's officers, and I took off for the battleship *Arizona* where I was to spend the night.

From the *Arizona* I could see the flags and pennants flying from the *Prince of Wales,* low-hanging clouds cutting off the view to shore, the fog forming in back of all the ships. The *Prince of Wales,* her decks lined with sailors, pulled up her anchor and the band played "The Star-Spangled Banner." We could see Winston Churchill, Admiral Sir Dudley Pound, Sir John Dill, and Air Vice-Marshal Freeman standing on the afterdeck as the *Prince of Wales* steamed out of the harbor.

As the mighty ship started moving, the band on the *Augusta* began to play "God Save the King." The sailors and marines on board the *Arizona* stood at attention and their band, too, played "God Save the King." The *Tuscaloosa* followed suit with its band, and the destroyer and escort picked up speed rapidly, following the *Prince of Wales,* signals being sent in all directions by lights and flags. We were never to see the *Prince of Wales* again, for shortly thereafter Jap planes sunk her off the Malay Peninsula.

Then the *Augusta* picked up speed. We saw General Marshall, Admiral Stark, Pa Watson, and, yes, the President up on the bridge. The *Augusta* was followed by the *Tuscaloosa*. Destroyers followed, all disappearing in the fog. The harbor was deserted except for a couple of destroyers, a tanker, and the *Arizona*.

The meeting had given the British staff officers and us a wonderful opportunity to meet and make a personal estimate of one another; it gave us a better understanding of the British problems and their urgent desire to do everything they could to save themselves from destruction. There was no doubt about it, the British Chiefs of Staff came over with a prepared statement. Maybe it was hastily prepared, but it was prepared, and they came with a common thought in mind on all the subjects under discussion. The United States Chiefs of Staff had not met together before. We did not have a prepared agenda, and we had to meet each question as it was brought up.

By the summer of 1941, the British had received 1985 aircraft from the United States. Most of the P-40's had to be modified, and were run through modification centers at the rate of about thirty a week. The Douglas DB-7's had likewise to be modified for use as night fighters. The R.A.F. had also received 23 B-24's and 20 B-17's.

Hopkins was told the British were using some 400 pilots for ferrying, and that they would like to have all of them replaced by American personnel. They wanted to send about 200 aircraft a month across the Atlantic during the coming winter. They talked about establishing an American depot in the Middle East where American mechanics could work on American planes. We agreed to do these things, and later the Douglas company set up a depot on the coast of the Red Sea where all American airplanes in the Middle East were repaired and overhauled by American mechanics.

Another point brought out was the need for additional transport aircraft in the Middle East to bring back ferry pilots on the Takoradi Route; to increase the mobility of the squadrons in the Middle East; and to allot to the Free French in Africa. This meant that we had to make contracts with commercial air lines, for at that time our transport production was not nearly large enough to meet the demands made upon it.

General Royce of our Air Force, on duty with the embassy in London, thought it might be possible for our Navy carriers to take our fighters across the Atlantic and let them fly off the carriers some 200 miles offshore from Lagos. The American pilots could then land at Lagos, refuel, and follow the airline through to Khartoum. This would expedite the delivery of fighters to the Near East. That suggestion seemed to be acceptable to the British, and was proposed to me by Hopkins. Later on, we used that method. Then we sent a fighter group to Cairo in time to join Montgomery and Alexander when the British were starting their campaign to drive Rommel back from Alamein.

☆ *16* ☆

During the next few weeks, following my return from Argentia, I came to appreciate Bill Knudsen as never before. He coped in his big Danish way with problems that required coordination with hundreds of different agencies throughout the United States. Planes for Britain, Russia, China, the Australians, the Canadians and the New Zealanders (all deliveries to be guaranteed with complete confidence six months in advance) were only one phase of his activities. In addition, he dealt with tanks, guns, cannon, and various war equipment; but his greatest headache was airplane production.

As time passed, my staff in Washington and the commanders in the field, acquired a better concept of the change in mission of our Air Force. Detailed plans for our expansion and aid programs were rapidly completed. New sites for bases, stations, and schools were selected. The Air Force was rapidly changing its status from one of peace to one of war, although the actual declaration of war had not yet arrived.

Meanwhile, I continued my travels around the country to press forward our training plans, organization of the ferry service, and Lord knows what. At such times, a strong personality like Horace Hickam's was sorely missed. Had he lived, he would surely have been one of the great commanders of World War II.

I missed some of the others, too, like Frank Andrews, who at that time was on duty in Panama. Soon afterwards, Andrews left to head the American missions in the European Theater, where early in 1943 he was to lose his life when his transport plane ran into the side of a mountain in Iceland. I have always felt that if General Andrews had not been killed, he might well have been the over-all Commander of the

American troops in Europe in World War II, for he had all the attributes for that job.

Our reservoir of skilled and experienced officers was so shallow that every time we lost one he was almost irreplaceable.

Everybody on the Air Staff was now working under forced pressure, day and night. In many ways we were already at war. Abroad, things were going badly for the Allied cause everywhere. In North Africa, Rommel was temporarily drawing back before a new British offensive launched on November 17th, but it looked as if things would get a lot worse before they got better, which indeed soon proved to be the case. By the time sufficient British air power appeared to turn the tide at Alamein the following year, American planes and crews were part of it. Moscow was in a state of siege, Stalingrad making a last ditch stand, the whole Russian Front in sharp danger of collapse. The sinkings by German submarines in the Atlantic were increasing at an alarming rate, the U-boats now even appearing boldly in the Gulf of Mexico. Japan had occupied southern Indo-China since July; and Kurusu and the other polite Japanese emissaries were in Washington carrying on the smiling negotiations that were still to be in "hopeful" progress on the morning of Sunday, December 7th.

On top of other headaches was the daily business of satisfying White House, congressional, civilian and War Department superiors who were constantly receiving phone calls, visits, and letters from people in all walks of life, official and unofficial, American, British, French, Dutch, Chinese, Siamese, Polish, Russian, refugee German, Italian, and what not, criticizing the Air Force's procedures, offering free advice and recommendations, or demanding a priority share of our equipment.

In the fall of 1941 I had to make a decision which few people know about to this day.

As already stated, our whole fight for an Air Force had come to center more and more around bombardment, precision bombardment by daylight, all the things summed up by the great word "B-17." I now had to decide whether the four-engine bomber, and the whole bombardment program we had worked toward for so many years, should take second place in favor of something else. This time the problem was not pressed on us from outside the Air Force. We faced it ourselves, deliberately. The reason for it was not any lack of faith in our development of precision bombardment. There was the possibility that we now had something still more useful in our air power arsenal, when and if we entered the war against Germany. The "something" was nothing less than a highly improved version of that same little pilotless Bug which we had devised in 1917–18, and had kept on developing as well as the strict attention to "Economy in Government" permitted.

Recently revived trials indicated that the Bug was now ready for operational use. Its flight-tested range, in December, 1941, was better than 200 miles, both this and its accuracy apparently being capable of rapid improvement. It might be necessary to change the original concept. It was now controlled by radio. We could employ one of the many other modern scientific devices that would insure it a direct-reckoning course to its objective. The pilotless Bug was, in any case, already a modern military weapon in being. It would cost, per unit, between $800 and $1000 as compared to $200,000 for a medium, or $400,000 for a single heavy bomber, and could be produced quickly in large numbers.

For the price of one B-17 with a bomb load of 6000 pounds, we could send 500 of these little Bugs over enemy territory, each carrying about 800 pounds of explosive. Much more important than any monetary factor was the possible saving in human life. It has been mentioned that some time before this we had come to the decision that the loss rate for which we must be prepared in an all-out air war would probably be around 25 per cent of our combat planes and combat personnel per month.

As it turned out, despite such grim days as the first Schweinfurt-Regensburg mission, the second Schweinfurt or the Oschersleben-Halberstadt-Brunswick attacks of January 11, 1944, the over-all rate was never that high. Nevertheless, the War Department's final statistics show that except for the infantry, always the hardest hit, no group in the Army, in the air, or on the ground, including paratroops and armored divisions, suffered as high a casualty rate as did our heavy bomber crews over Germany. As that was about the way we thought it would be if such a campaign ever had to be fought, it can be imagined that in December, 1941, the Bug seemed a very tempting proposition.

C. F. Kettering, of General Motors, the real father of the Bug, not only had an initimate knowledge of its development from the start, but in the intervening years had worked on devices to perfect it. Elmer Sperry, who had made the first controls for the full-size pilotless plane, was dead, but his Sperry Gyroscope Company was still in full stride. Orville Wright, and some of the men in the Aeolian Company who had pioneered with us in the earlier experiments, were still active. There was no doubt that the Bug could be put into large-scale production within a very short time.

I called a meeting at which only Kettering, Bill Knudsen and myself were present. We discussed the availability of bases; of targets; the cost; production; comparison of production between the Bugs and heavy bombers; raw materials needed for the two types of weapons. We finally came to the conclusion, unanimously, that even with the most improved type of Bug, the best we could do from England would be to hit Paris, or some of the other large cities in France, Belgium, or Holland. We could not get at the real heart of our enemy—interior Germany itself.

Had we been in the position the Germans then were, and had the Germans instead of the English inhabited the British Isles, the story would have been very different. We could, and we would have concentrated the flight of thousands upon thousands of these Bugs on practically all the interior of southern and middle England, including the key industrial areas. We could probably have had this assault in full swing by late 1942, or early 1943, and have used the Bug by the thousands and tens of thousands. The Germans could have done little to stop it. As it was, the first pilotless bomb did not buzz across the English Channel from a German launching site until the night of the 12th of June, 1944, a week after our ground forces had landed in Normandy, and two and a half years after Kettering, Knudsen, and I held this discussion in my office.

Early in 1941, the British had made requests upon us for B-17's. We finally gave them twenty, as I have described, which were delivered in the early part of the year. These Fortresses went through the British modification center to make them what the R.A.F. called "an effective bombing plane." British Bomber Command sent the first B-17 combat mission over the French coast in July, 1941.

Here the trouble began which was to hound us in our bombardment relations with the R.A.F. for a long time. As a matter of fact, it was not until I had Tooey Spaatz and Ira Eaker join forces with me at Casablanca, in January, 1943, that I was able to convince the President and the Prime Minister of the effectiveness of the B-17 when employed as we employed it. We were able to furnish the proofs entirely from the work of the U.S. Eighth Bomber Command on German targets in France at that time, and despite all British arguments our program of precision bombardment by daylight was able to continue as a first priority. However, in the R.A.F.'s hands in 1941, the long-awaited combat showing of the B-17's was a fiasco.

The British had been carefully warned to use these first twenty B-17's in combat with caution. These planes were not the Flying Fortresses with their big spiny tails and turning turrets, bristling with fourteen .50-

caliber guns, so familiar later to the English and to every small boy in America. The twenty Forts the R.A.F. got early in 1941 were B-17-C's. They had only four flexible (hand-held) guns for armament, no computing sights, nor even any tail guns (that famous "stinger"), only a gunner lying on his stomach and firing rearward from a slit in the "bathtub" where the ball-turret would be on later Forts.

The method of employment, which was the whole basis of the B-17's existence—a close mass of bombers flying under its own protection, bringing to bear on attacking fighters the mutual defensive fire power of all the .50 caliber guns in the tightly stacked formation—was ignored. The R.A.F. used no formation to speak of. The Flying Forts were dispatched in two's and three's and similar ineffective numbers, often to be shot down, or in any case to fail in their mission. Their bombing was poor. In the first four months during which the R.A.F. used these planes, 46 per cent of all missions assigned to the B-17's were abandoned. Only about 5 per cent of the trouble was traceable to mechanical difficulties; the remaining 41 per cent was chargeable to bad weather conditions or to other reasons. None of these B-17's ever reached a point anywhere near Germany.

If this description sounds at odds with the performance of R.A.F. Bomber Command crews later, it should be remembered that the delicate technical finesse they developed in their great night campaign under Harris after May, 1942, had not yet appeared. R.A.F. Fighter Command was still in a class by itself.

When British Bomber Command's blows against the German cities were in full swing, their operations involved an intricate system of pathfinders, radar, skillfully dropped flares to show the way in, and target markers. Master bombers circling over the targets at low altitudes directed the miles of Halifaxes and Lancasters to their aiming points, and so on.

The R.A.F. was able to teach our own Eighth Air Force a great deal, especially about radar, radio, and navigational aids. However, at the time, the first B-17's were so badly mishandled by R.A.F. Bomber Command's people that it was obvious it was their place to learn; and they didn't.

At first, just after the Battle of Britain, gunnery modifications on the twin-engine Blenheim had given the R.A.F. the hope that this relatively light bomber might be able to continue daylight bombing operations over Germany. Even Colonel Tooey Spaatz had written home that he and Colonel "Monk" Hunter thought it might. "A well-trained formation of

[British] bombers with adequate firepower built up of two sections of three planes each is able to cope with any type of attack so far delivered by the German Fighters," he wrote optimistically, and added, regarding the gunnery improvements on the Blenheim: "Pilots of the squadrons we visited were confident of their ability to operate on daylight raids with this armament." That confidence was soon knocked into a cocked hat, along with an alarming number of Blenheims.

In the face of the German flak and fighter opposition, the British turned away from long-range bombardment in the daytime in favor of night operations which, in those pre-radar days, offered a better chance of getting home, though other advantages were doubtful. The R.A.F. never gave the Flying Fortress a chance. On the other hand, we probably never gave the R.A.F. the right number of B-17's.

There was one encouraging thing in this experience. Repeatedly, the British-operated B-17's came home from the most savage battles with enemy fighters or badly shot up by German flak, but managed to land in controlled flight at their own bases under circumstances which no other planes in the war had been able to survive. Sometimes they were literally shot to pieces, but still they came back. Under fighter attack, it was the R.A.F. procedure to dive the Forts into evasive action. Naturally, the Me-109, which could dive faster than the B-17, soon caught up with it and threw terrific gunfire into the frame of the bomber.

For instance, in August, two of the Forts were sent alone to attack the *Scharnhorst* and the *Gneisenau* at Brest. Apparently, on this occasion, the battleships were fairly well bombed from the high altitude of 31,000 feet. The strong German fighter squadrons based in that area immediately appeared and engaged the bombers. One B-17 was hit many times by He-111's and Me-109's. Twenty millimeter cannon shells exploded all through it, six bursting in the fuselage. The airplane was a shambles. The bomb bay doors could not be closed; very little aileron control was left, one aileron having been shot away; the rudder was badly damaged; the tail wheel section was hit, the wheel itself hanging down so that it could neither be retracted nor lowered. In spite of all this, the crew finally landed their airplane back at their base.

Naturally, we were greatly pleased, as such reports bore out our conviction that the Flying Fortress could absorb terrific punishment. The R.A.F. combat operations confirmed the decision I had made before this to build our own Air Force around the B-17. From that time on I started the ball rolling to allocate, hereafter, B-24's to the British. They seemed to like that four-engine bomber much better than the Flying Fortress anyway, and used it very successfully for coastal patrol and for other missions of that type.

Our production program contemplated that by August, 1941, the R.A.F. should be getting twenty-five B-24's a month. We figured if we gave the British a maximum of four B-17's a month, that would take care of the losses among the original 20 they had procured, and would lull further demands from them for Flying Fortresses. Our Air Force officers were very well pleased with this decision.

At the time President Roosevelt decided he wanted the output of heavy bombers stepped up to 500 planes a month, the Navy was carrying on a very active campaign against giving big bombers the highest production priority—a priority that insured the B-17's and B-24's first call on critical items. Every time we had an Aircraft Board meeting, Admiral Towers would put up a fight for materials for battleships, destroyers, cruisers, and aircraft carriers, as against bombers. However, the Presidential memorandum of June 23, 1941, for the large bomber program had stopped further open objection on that score.

In August, 1941, I sent General George Brett to England with instructions to do what he could to iron out some of the difficulties we were having in carrying out the program agreed to in the various meetings with the British Air Chiefs. I cautioned him that, in addition to the requests made on us by the British, the Dutch and the Chinese were also making demands—and that we also had our own Air Force problems to look after. Hence, he must balance the world-wide demands against those of any one nation.

Later in the summer I wrote a paper for the Secretary of War which I hoped he would use as a guide in outlining any future policy in regard to giving away airplanes and air equipment. I stressed the following points:

1. A powerful air offensive must be carried on by the United States if Germany is to be invaded;

2. England probably cannot conduct such an air offensive, even if adequate material is furnished by the United States. She is having great difficulty at this moment in operating the small Air Force she now has, because of her shortage of personnel for fighter groups. However, the British Bomber Force can still be augmented considerably. There is no great shortage of bomber personnel in Britain;

3. The United States is capable of creating an adequate Air Force, and conducting a decisive air offensive in about two years if England survives to provide air bases;

4. The United States is not capable of creating the Air Force necessary to take decisive action if large quantities of long-range aircraft are exported and expended in a nondecisive effort;

5. England must have aid in the form of American airplanes if she is to survive and provide bases for decisive American offensives;

6. Medium bombers, light bombers, and pursuit planes are the most suitable types for export to England;

7. Our heavy bombers are suitable for a decisive air offensive against Germany;

8. An Axis victory would jeopardize the security of the United States. It is mandatory that the minimum force required for defense of the United States and its overseas possessions be established.

In conclusion, I stated that the United States must build, as quickly as possible, an Air Force capable of waging a decisive air offensive against the Axis powers in Europe, and this Air Force must consist predominantly of Heavy Bombers.

The Secretary of War accepted these principles, and in his memorandum to the President, made this statement: "I believe the moment has now come when we should give our primary attention to a prompt development of a well-armed, well-rounded and well-trained American Air Force, and I have, after a most careful study, reached the conclusion that it would be unwise to divert further production from our Air Force until such time as the main requirements for the Air Force are fully completed."

A short time later, Secretary Stimson sent a break-down for the production program to Mr. Knudsen. It covered a production rate of 36,000 combat airplanes a year, of which 17,400 would go to our Army, 4000 to our Navy and approximately 11,000 would be available for export. In that memorandum he made a very wise statement: "It is believed the breakdown for the 11,000 tactical planes referred to in the production schedule should be prepared by a joint British and United States Army committee."

That recommendation, together with the stand taken by Harry Hopkins and myself, made possible my meeting with Captain Balfour, the British Assistant Secretary for Air, in October. We sat down with our assistants and figured out the future production of airplanes in the United States, together with the best use that could be made of them. We then decided upon the allocation that would be made to Great Britain and to her dependencies. From that time on, it was always a question of a representative from the R.A.F. sitting down at the table with the Commanding

General, Army Air Forces, and discussing the number of airplanes that should be allocated to the British for the ensuing six months. Very seldom did higher authority have to make the decision. I think on only one occasion was it taken up to the President.

During all this period, Mr. Lovett, Assistant Secretary of War for Air, carried more than his share of the air expansion load. Early in the year, we had found there was a distinct shortage of machine tools and unequal distribution among the various industries engaged in war production. Bob Lovett took that case up and worked it out with the OPM so that everyone received at least some part of the output of machine tools and not all went to any one industry, regardless of whether it was making aircraft, battleships, or tanks. He had to deal with one such problem after another. The results made Bill Knudsen's task much easier and enabled us to carry out our plans with less interference.

A little later, we encountered a distinct shortage of propellers, engines, aluminum, and other accessories in the aircraft industry proper. The Curtiss-Wright Company, Martin, Boeing, Pratt & Whitney, and Douglas all cited lacks of highly important parts as the reason for their not producing airplanes as scheduled. Mr. Lovett took that problem up and worked it through the various agencies until a just solution was found. The difficulties Bob Lovett encountered in trying to correct these defects in programming and distribution may be imagined when one realizes that at least nine men had to be seen before an air production decision could be made. One of the first things Bob Lovett did was to straighten that situation out: he reduced the number to two.

Just prior to my trip to the West Coast in November, 1941, I sent him a series of typical memoranda on matters requiring his attention. They covered the status of reserve officers we planned to send to China to join up with the Flying Tigers; information relating to a carrier to deliver pursuit planes to England; and information regarding the possibility of completely breaking down the Japanese code, following the incident when the Japanese Attaché at Rome sent a message to Tokyo giving the entire station list of the U. S. Army Air Corps. Since it was an exact copy of our list, from it the Japanese code could be broken down very readily. (At that time I did not know the Navy had already broken the code, and I did not have the low-down on what was happening in the Pacific.) The memoranda also covered the possibility of our getting 65 heavy bombers to the Philippines by December 6th; the use of the TWA four-engine school to maximum capacity of twenty-four crews a month; Kindelberger's winterizing of B-25's; the log jam in the Pacific, where the Navy wanted to complete construction on Palmyra, while the Army Air Force needed an air base on Christmas Island—and needed it badly. (Christmas Island could be completed by January 30th, and God only knew when we could have finished Palmyra.)

All these things were hanging fire at the time of my short trip to the West Coast in November, 1941. With that data, I figured the Assistant Secretary of War for Air would have a complete file of the vital items that might come up and I felt free to take off for California to visit aircraft factories and bases, and perhaps get in a little hunting.

At the time of my departure for the West Coast trip in late November, 1941, the Air Force had 32½ combat groups of various kinds deployed in different parts of the world. The officer strength was 22,000; the enlisted strength, 270,000. Airplane strength in the United States was 9000; overseas 1100.

Of the 9000 AAF planes, only 3000 were combat types; and of those a mere 1100 were actually fit for war service. We had but 159 four-engine airplanes in the Air Corps and they were scattered pretty well throughout the United States (being used for training purposes), in Hawaii, and on the way to the Philippines. By the first of December, 1941, there were 26 B-17's in the Philippines, and an additional 13 B-17's were assembled on the West Coast, ready for the flight to Hawaii, en route to the Philippines.

I was still trying to get aerial photos of Jaluit and Truk. For that purpose we had specially modified and armed two of the B-24's, which were to take pictures while flying over the Jap-held islands on their way to the Philippines.

Early in October, General Lewis Brereton had been sent to the Philippines to become General MacArthur's Air Commander. Colonel Eugene L. Eubank had already arrived with the first echelon of the 19th Bombardment Group, which contained the first real combat B-17's, with gun turrets. Brigadier General Henry B. Claggett was Interceptor Commander; Colonel Lawrence Churchill commanded the Service outfit. They were the senior officers in the Philippines on December 1, 1941. In Hawaii, General Frederick Martin was in command of all Army Air units in the Hawaiian Islands. They operated, of course—at that time—under the direct orders of General Walter C. Short, over-all Army Commander for the territory.

Things were always touch-and-go concerning command duties and responsibilities between the Army and the Navy, not only in Hawaii, but also in the Philippines. It seemed almost impossible to get a clear-cut line of demarcation as to where the Navy's responsibility ended and the Army's began.

We had been building up our military strength in Hawaii under the general theory that we would hold Hawaii at all costs, but as mentioned before, it wasn't until mid-1941 that we changed our policy with regard to the Philippines and started reinforcing the units there. It is to be noted that on December 1st I issued a memorandum to my office force, and sent a copy to General Martin in Hawaii stating that all possible B-17's would be sent to the Philippines as soon as they could be made available.

In my opinion, a satisfactory or adequate defense plan can never be obtained by trying to secure cooperation between two people in command. And that was the situation, both in the Philippines and in Hawaii in 1941. In Hawaii the Navy operated off-shore and was to give timely warning of an attack. In addition, the Navy was responsible for defense until the time the enemy crossed the shore line, and then it became the duty of the Army to keep the enemy from flying over, or landing on, the shore of the island. Such a policy obviously could not lend itself to satisfactory and efficient operations. In the Philippines conditions had changed for the better because General MacArthur had insisted upon a workable agreement with the Naval Commander, Admiral Hart.

Landing at Hamilton Field, on December 6, 1941, I assembled the officers who were to fly the thirteen B-17's to Hawaii on the first leg of their flight to the Philippines, and told them they would probably run into trouble somewhere along the line. When I said that they might have to use their guns, however, I had in mind the trouble they might encounter when flying over the mandated islands in the vicinity of Truk. I had no reason to believe the Japanese fleet had left the east coast of Asia days before, had headed eastward through the mandated islands, and was now a short distance from the Hawaiian Islands. That bit of information—about the Japanese fleet being loose, known to many War and Navy Department officials—had never been given to me. Like most officers in the War Department, I was under the impression that, if a Japanese attack occurred, it would be made first against the Philippines and then would be carried down the east coast of Asia to Singapore, to the Islands of Borneo, Java, and Sumatra.

Accordingly, I was afraid our B-17's might reach critical points in the Southwest Pacific after the Japanese had declared war—this, in spite of the fact that the Japanese so-called "ambassadors of peace" were still in Washington talking with the Secretary of State.

There has been a lot of discussion about why the Army airplanes in

Hawaii were all huddled together in one large group, wing to wing, making it possible for the Japanese to wipe out practically all of them when they made their attack. To get a clear picture of that, one must understand the setup.

General Short was then in command of all troops. He had interpreted the War Department warning order as an order against sabotage. In his opinion the way to prevent sabotage of airplanes was to get them all together, thus requiring a minimum of guards to protect them. It must also be borne in mind that, at that time, Army Air Force troops were being used by the Hawaiian Command for all kinds of duties other than those for which they were organized and trained. In the emergency plans for Hawaii, many of our mechanics were to be used for general military police and patrol duties and would not be available to the Air Commander, General Martin. Several officers, Army and Navy, upon studying the conditions in Hawaii, had expressed the opinion that if there was an attack by the Japanese it would come from the direction, and at about the time it actually happened—on a Sunday morning, when, they said, it would be least expected. Why it would be least expected at that time, and from the northeast, I could never figure out—but they appear to have been right.

Many officers had also stated that under the existing command setup in the Hawaiian Islands, a Japanese air attack might be successful and prove disastrous before our Army and Navy commanders could get coordinated.

However, even with that background, when I gave my little talk to the crews of the B-17's at Hamilton Field on the night of December 6th, I did not expect them to run into trouble in the Hawaiian Islands. Had I known that the Japanese Fleet was running loose through the mandated islands, I might have had other ideas—maybe not.

After I saw the airplanes disappear into the west out over the Pacific Ocean, I took off in my own plane and flew to Bakersfield. There I met Donald Douglas, the aircraft manufacturer. The next morning, Sunday, December 7th, he and I went quail shooting. When we returned to the cabin that afternoon Mr. Douglas' father was sitting by the car listening to the radio.

As I came up he said, "The Japanese have struck Pearl Harbor!"

I couldn't believe it. Then he gave me the details that had come over the radio: how the Japanese had sunk our battleships, destroyed our airplanes; how they had made a mess of things in general in and around Pearl Harbor and Honolulu. The war was on.

Looking back on it, I doubt very much if there were many officers in the Army or the Navy who really expected the Japanese to start the war by attacking where they did. Despite the predictions quoted above about what conditions would be in Hawaii *if* the Japanese were to attack there, the general assumption seemed to have been that they would hit the Philippines first. Perhaps some of the officers who had been following the radio intercepts might have been able to come to a better conclusion. Certainly I could not.

Where would they strike next? Would they make a landing on the Hawaiian Islands? Or would they—now that our fleet was out of action —make a hit-and-run attack on our aircraft factories on the West Coast where they could cause disastrous damage with practically no loss to themselves? These speculations were going through my mind as I rode from the hunting cabin to the airport at Bakersfield.

Upon arriving at the airdrome I found everybody greatly excited— commotion, disorder, confusion everywhere. Washington wanted me to get in communication with them at once! Radio, telegraph, telephone, any way I could! Just get in touch with Washington! Army Head- quarters in San Francisco wanted me to get in touch with them im- mediately! Call March Field at once! The Chief of Staff wants you to call Washington! Your office in Washington wants to get hold of you at once! Ignoring all these messages, I climbed aboard my airplane and flew to March Field. After arriving there, I established a headquarters and radio; telegraph and telephones began to buzz with connections to Wash- ington and San Francisco. I had General Marshall on the phone shortly thereafter and told him I would be back in Washington the next morning. He told me he thought I should go to see General DeWitt, the Army commander at the San Francisco Presidio. I said I would. I did what I could to start the ball rolling at March Field, putting the personnel of my old stamping grounds there on a war status for a possible sneak attack in the Los Angeles area.

I then took off and flew to San Francisco. I found General DeWitt very much on the job, thoroughly alerted and much worried over the possibility of what the Japanese might do to the West Coast. Frankly I could not share all his apprehensions. With General DeWitt and General Fickel, our air commander, we decided upon the course of action to be followed. General DeWitt then gave me certain messages for General Marshall and I departed.

As I traveled from military post to military post, from headquarters to headquarters, more and more information came in about the attack on Pearl Harbor, so that by the time I reached Washington I had a fair idea of what had happened. The one point I could not understand was how the Japanese had been able to launch their blows from a point perhaps 200 miles off the Hawaiian Islands, and get away, when we had a Naval Task Force on maneuvers just to the north of Oahu, seemingly right in their path. It looked to me as if some kind of interception might have been made. At the same time, I am not a naval authority, and there is a lot about it that I shall probably never understand.

As was to be expected, immediately following the attack on Pearl Harbor, everybody began to ask for airplanes. Every commanding officer everywhere needed airplanes to stop the Japs from attacking his particular bailiwick. They all wanted heavy bombers and light bombers; they wanted patrol planes and fighters, and they wanted captive balloons to protect the installations in their areas. Alaska was about to be invaded, the West Coast was sure to be the next point of attack, the Hawaiian Islands could be captured without effort.

Incidentally, this last was pretty close to the truth, for the chaos and confusion that followed the attack by the Japs on Pearl Harbor were so great that a landing made anywhere on the Islands could probably have been carried out without much opposition from the defending Army, Navy, and Marine Corps. We had several hundred fewer airplanes on December 8th than we had had on December 6th, because of the good job the Japanese had done on Hickam Field; and within the next few days they did a good job of destroying the airplanes of General MacArthur in the Philippines.

It is one thing to sit on the sidelines and say what should or should not have been done in order to prevent this or that from happening—it is another when you have the responsibility for the task staring you right in the face.

As soon as I could make telephone connections, I talked with General Martin, our Air Commander in Honolulu, to find out exactly why his airplanes had been so concentrated that they were all destroyed or damaged at once, with no chance for any to get off the ground. I learned that actually there were isolated instances in which a few of our fighter pilots had gone up and had given a good account of themselves, shooting down two or three Japanese planes; but that in general there was no interception. The planes had been treated like artillery or tanks or any other war equipment; their value as a highly mobile striking weapon seemed to have been lost. We could forget about that phase of the war and try to prevent the same mistake from being made again.

Accordingly, I then talked on the telephone with General Brereton out in the Philippines to try to give him some idea of what had happened at Pearl Harbor, so that he would not be caught the same way and his entire air force destroyed. He explained to me what he was trying to do; but in spite of all the precautions taken, in spite of all the book-learning, in spite of all the experience we had accumulated during maneuvers, and in spite of all the technique that had been taught at the Tactical School, within a few hours we also lost most of our airplanes in the Philippines— practically all the B-17's and most of our fighters on the ground. I could not help thinking that there must have been some mistake made somewhere in my Air Force command, and I took it upon myself to tell Brereton so.

In reply, I got a cable from MacArthur—a wire that once again made me realize there is a great deal of difference between sitting at a desk in Washington planning perfect situations with the rule book beside you and being out at Clark Field or some other place in the Philippines with only one or two airdromes to take care of your few B-17's, and trying to meet the Japanese with the minimum of losses.

"Every possible precaution," said MacArthur's cable, "within the limited means and the time available was taken here with the Far East Air Force. Their losses were due entirely to the overwhelming superiority of the enemy force. They have been hopelessly outnumbered from the start, but no unit could have done better. Their gallantry has been conspicuous, their efficiency good. No item of loss can properly be attributed to neglect or lack of care. They fought from fields not yet developed and under improvised conditions of every sort which placed them under the severest handicap as compared to an enemy fully prepared in every way. You may take pride in their conduct. MacArthur."

Loyalty-down is as essential in any command as loyalty-up, and General MacArthur always had loyalty-down—to the lowest soldier in the ranks of his Army.

In any event, I never have been able to get the real story of what happened in the Philippines. Brereton's diary does not give a complete and accurate account. A story from General Sutherland, MacArthur's Chief of Staff, does not completely clear it up, by any means. The fact remains that, as a result of the Japanese attacks, practically all the planes of the Army Air Forces in Hawaii and in the Philippines were destroyed within the first few days of the war. It is true that we were surprised and outnumbered, but I had always believed that our airmen would fight it out in the air; they should never have been caught flat-footed on the ground. It was a very sad blow to me. Should the same thing happen everywhere, we would never be able to build up an Air Force, for to start with, we were outnumbered in every theatre.

☆ *17* ☆

On that historic day of December 8, 1941, when the United States declared war on Japan, the whole picture was changed.

The pre-Argentia staff meetings were, to a certain extent, "off the record," since we were not then at war or a "fighting" ally of Great Britain. At the same time, there had been certain prewar ideas that had to be discussed between the United States and the British military staffs. The Argentia conference had gone a little further. It considered actions that would be taken if and when the United States did go to war. So we were prepared for a permanent joint staff organization. Following the Japanese attack on Pearl Harbor, the "Combined Chiefs" became the permanent top staff.

On December 21, 1941, on a Sunday afternoon, the President assembled in his study Harry Hopkins, Admiral Stark, Admiral King, Secretary Stimson, Secretary Knox, General Marshall, and myself. From that time forward, there was no doubt about the Commanding General of the Army Air Forces being a member of the President's Staff, and accepted as a member of the Combined Chiefs of Staff under whatever name they might be called.

The following is from notes I took at the time.

At that meeting, the President told us that Mr. Churchill, accompanied by Air Chief Marshal Portal, Admiral Pound, Field Marshal Dill, and about eighty-two other officers, clerks, etc., would arrive in Washington the following day. The President said he would like very much to have a meeting of minds before the conference with Mr. Churchill and his party was held, and that he expected, on Tuesday at five o'clock, to have a conference with the British during which we would discuss the general strategic problems confronting our two countries. The President said that on Monday night he would talk with Churchill by himself.

When that preliminary meeting was opened, the President asked what we thought would be the best general plan of discussion for the forth-coming meetings with the British. General Marshall gave him the War Department outline of procedure and an estimate of the situation. The President discussed the air situation in the Far East and how we were going to get reinforcements to that region by air, across South Africa. He was concerned about actual air transportation to the Philippines. I went over details of the existing routes to the Philippines which had not been cut by the Japs, but which we expected to be severed very shortly, either at Wake or at Rabaul. Next, I told him about the new routes, through Christmas, Samoa, Fiji, and into Australia, and when I expected to be able to use them. Then I told him of the activities along our trans-South Atlantic-Equatorial Africa-South Asia route.

The President switched to the South Atlantic and the feasibility of our taking over the Azores. He talked about Dakar and the Cape Verde Islands. This provoked considerable discussion by everybody present. I held out for occupation of the Azores and Dakar, both of which I con-sidered essential from the air point of view because of the air routes across the Atlantic. Secretary Stimson agreed with me in this.

The President then talked about taking over Iceland—the Army to operate the bases there. He discussed the use of North Ireland; and the possibility of our aiding the British by air operations from England and North Africa. I assured him this matter was under study, and that as fast as we could build up the necessary units we would send them over to operate out of England or from North Africa.

Mr. Roosevelt asked me when I would be able to take over the North Atlantic ferry service. I told him I could take it over under present limiting conditions then, but it was impossible to fly regularly in the Arctic in the winter owing to weather conditions; however, we hoped to build up bases and facilities for full-time operations by the following spring.

Finally, he discussed the necessity for more and better airplane service on the Takoradi-Khartoum-Karachi-Far East run. I assured him this route was being developed constantly, and that additional transports were being provided and used as fast as they could be obtained. As a matter of fact, we were sending planes over that route then, for Europe and China, and for MacArthur via Australia.

Before we adjourned, the question was raised of where the Supreme War Council (meaning the joint U.S.-British military representatives, still not called "the Combined Chiefs") was to hold its meetings. It was decided it should meet in Washington. It was also determined that each member of the Supreme War Council should have a deputy, and that the deputy should be kept informed on all major items. As we adjourned, the President reminded us we would have a big meeting with the British Chiefs of Staff at five o'clock the following Tuesday afternoon.

Before the arrival of the British on Monday, General Marshall and I talked over several things, including what we considered the principal matters to be discussed in the meeting. Thus, the following evening when I talked with Sir Charles Portal and Air Marshal Harris about the air part of the picture, I was not entirely unprepared.

Portal's first interest was in the future employment of the U.S. Air Force and its units; where and how they would be used; what their relationship would be to the British. I assured him they would work wherever the Chiefs of Staff decided, and on an equal footing with the British.

Portal then told me the British were worried about Singapore; they could not afford to see Singapore captured by the Japanese. I replied that neither could we afford to see the Philippines captured by the Japanese, but we would probably have to take it—and not like it. I declared that we would build up the air strength in the Philippines, Australia, and the Dutch East Indies as fast as possible. An extensive Service of Supply was already being established in Australia to be commanded by General Brett, and we would cram into Australia as many airplanes as we could assemble.

Portal went on to say the Japanese had a total of only 3600 combat airplanes; that their productive capacity was only about 300 a month. He asked what we were going to do about attacking them. I gave him such meager information as we had on the proposed operations from eastern China, and said that preliminary negotiations indicated we would soon get permission to operate from bases near Vladivostok. He expressed doubt that we would ever get bases in the vicinity of Vladivostok. (It turned out that Portal knew the Russians and their way of doing business far better than I, for we never did get such bases.)

Portal said, in his opinion, attacking Japan was a Navy job, that the carriers, even at this early date, could sneak up to the vicinity of Japan and make the same kind of attack that the Japanese had made on Pearl Harbor. He claimed that the carriers would take no more risk than the British carriers had taken at Taranto, or the Japanese carriers at Hawaii. This strategy would also have some influence in causing the Japanese fleet to return to Japanese waters. I always thought that Portal mixed wishful thinking in with his reasoning concerning the Pacific aerial strategy. I thought he was afraid if our Air Force planned to use heavy bombers against Japan it would cut down the number he would receive.

Portal then outlined the general thought of the British Chiefs of Staff. in Britain. They believed it was necessary for the British to gain control of the whole North African shore of the Mediterranean. For British steamers to reach the North East, under conditions that then existed, they had to go 12,000 miles around the entire continent of Africa, whereas if they could reopen the Mediterranean, a vast amount of shipping could be sent over that route, some 3000 miles only.

He believed the French, if properly approached, would grant permission to use French Morocco, which would enable the United States and Great Britain to operate air bases along the entire north coast of Africa. Then he discussed possible operations against the Cape Verde Islands, Dakar, and the Azores, feeling as I did, that the Azores should be given first priority.

He said he looked forward to United States bombers being stationed in England to help with the R.A.F. bombing effort. The R.A.F. had passed its peak in the fighter line he said, because he did not have the fighter personnel that he had formerly. He had reached the saturation point as far as fighter aircraft in England was concerned. He said, however, that his Bomber Command had not yet reached its full strength and that he had more bomber pilots than bombing planes. United States planes and pilots must be provided for the fighter units in North Africa.

Portal then made a summary in which he estimated British production to be about 2500 planes a month, that of the United States about 3000, which with Russia's 1500 would give a total of about 7000 planes a month for use against the enemy. We need not have any fears about numerical air superiority, since the best the Germans and the Japs could do was Germany's 2500 planes, Italy's 300, Japan's 300, or a total of 3100 planes a month.

We both agreed that the mission of the "Allied Council's" conference (note the new name) should be: (1) to prepare a sound strategic plan; (2) to discuss the forces and equipment necessary to carry out that strategic plan; (3) to plan for the forces, equipment, and facilities available to carry out that program; (4) allocation of equipment.

Portal agreed, in general, to the plan the War Department had prepared and which General Marshall and I had discussed prior to that meeting. I talked with him, also, about British plans. It was agreed it would be in order to have a meeting between the President and the Prime

Minister, at which the Chiefs of Staff would all be given a briefing on the topics to be discussed.

As to the method in which business was conducted: First, the United States Chiefs of Staff met with their planners; then the United States Chiefs of Staff met with the President to outline the policies agreed upon; then the Staff met again to make any changes in the major plans the President's decision might make necessary.

In all these meetings, however, it is to be noted that once the President of the United States agreed upon the general principles, he relied upon his Chiefs of Staff to carry them out--to make plans for the consummation of these general ideas. If we made independent decisions, we would tell him about them later.

The British, on the other hand, seemed to be reluctant to commit themselves to plans independently conceived until they had a chance to check them over with their Prime Minister. That was the major difference in our methods of operation.

On Tuesday afternoon, December 23, 1941, we had our first official meeting of the Combined Chiefs of Staff. Present were the President of the United States, Prime Minister Churchill, Secretary Stimson, Secretary Knox, Lord Beaverbrook, Sir John Dill, General Marshall, Admiral Stark, Admiral King, General Watson, General Hollis, Captain Beardall, and myself. The President sat behind his desk; the Prime Minister sat at the President's left. The rest of us sat in a circle around the room in front of the President. In general, the British Chiefs of Staff sat near one another, as did the American Chiefs of Staff, in order to be able to talk things over when a disputed question arose.

This same arrangement was carried out regardless of whether we met with the President and the Prime Minister in Washington, in Quebec, in Cairo, or in Teheran. The following is from notes I made at the time.

The President opened the meeting by stating he and Churchill had concluded that there would be no peace without the concurrence of all until we had complete victory. He then said he and the Prime Minister had agreed we would start heavy bombardment operations from England as soon as possible. The number we would start with need not necessarily be large, but the morale value would be extremely high. Later on, he asked what the smallest unit was that we could send. I said we could not send less than one Group because the Group was our smallest self-sustained unit; that I could probably get the first Group of our bombers over to England by the following March. (In these discussions with the President and the Prime Minister, the same rules applied as in our sessions with the President. It was an open conference where anyone could voice his opinions or sentiments at any time.)

The President carried on, making, among others, the following points:

Iceland: There should be unity of command there, and the shipping problem would be less if United States troops instead of British were stationed there.

Greenland: Greenland would require a small number of troops, mainly weather, radio, and airfield maintenance men.

Central Atlantic: Naval support was needed in this area. The Azores, the West Coast of Africa, and the Cape Verde Islands were all discussed. The United States, the President said, thought the Verde Islands were of supreme importance in maintaining an air route over the South Atlantic. (It is to be noted the Verde Islands disappeared from the picture and were hardly ever discussed after this first series of conferences.)

Southwest Pacific: Both the President and the Prime Minister reiterated that we must hold Singapore and the Dutch East Indies even if we lost the Philippines; and we must provide for the safety of New Zealand and Australia.

China: We must keep the Chinese fighting. The President agreed with me that we must establish air bases in China for our bombers and transports, and that we must get more transports over there at once. He also realized that supplies for China would have to be taken in by air. This was the real start of the "Hump" operations.

Russia: The President said he had learned the Russians were taking troops from Eastern Sibera and sending them against the western front of the Germans; that no help could be expected from the Russians against Japan until March or April. (Actually, we never did get any help from the Russians against Japan.)

North Africa: We must get into western North Africa before the Germans. He did not believe the Germans were making any preparations for an attack on Spain, Portugal, Gibraltar, or Morocco, but he cited information, which was sometimes reliable and sometimes not, that the Germans were going to move into Portugal on December 27th. He said to take it or leave it; he didn't know whether to accept it or not.

Expeditionary Air Force: We must have an Expeditionary Air Force, ready to move out at once to any of these theaters as fast as we could build it up.

Transportation: Transportation should be used for whatever movement the Allied Council might consider most important, regardless of whose nationals were being accommodated or whose transports were being used.

Referring to the Navy plan for modifying the *West Point,* the *Manhattan,* and the *Washington* into aircraft carriers, he said this matter should be held in abeyance until it was determined what transports were actually needed. Air and sea communications across the Pacific should be built up at once.

Ireland: United States forces would take over all North Ireland. Both North and South Ireland were discussed as possible bases for PBY's and submarine patrol planes. The President said he believed we should put the whole 69th New York Regiment in South Ireland and then we could probably get the Irish to do some fighting and not so much talking. At present it looked bad to him, but he thought something might be done about getting them to swing into action with the rest of us.

Warships to the British: The President did not think much could be gained right now by such transfers because of a shortage of trained personnel in Britain. He finally decided Admiral Stark and Admiral Pound should work out one solution.

Objective 1944: The President reasoned that if we started production programs in 1941 or early 1942, it would be 1944 before we could get airplanes, tanks, or ammunition in sufficient quantities to attain our objectives.

When the President completed his remarks, the Prime Minister spoke. In general, he said, he was in accord with everything the President had outlined. He appreciated, more than he could tell, the air assistance that had come from the United States. He emphasized the necessity for sending three American armored divisions to North Ireland to replace the British divisions, thereby releasing the latter for use elsewhere.

Churchill dwelt at length on the attitude of the French, and on the Vichy problem which was coming to a head very soon. He said he believed when this happened the British would push right into Tripoli. He hoped by then the British forces would be operating against the Germans and Italians in Libya and could reach the gates of Tunis in about a month. This victory, coupled with the United States' entry into the war, would, besides having a deteriorating effect upon the Germans, boost the morale of the French and encourage them to put up a fight for their rights. (Actually, we did not get into Tripoli for many months after that.) The United States must be ready with a task force to enter Morocco in 1942 and must carry on the campaign on the northern coast of Africa.

The President gave his O.K. to the remarks made by Churchill. He then asked the Prime Minister if it might be possible for the French troops to operate against Dakar from the rear. This matter was not taken up any further.

Churchill emphasized that the American troops must get into the war as soon as possible, both against the Germans and against the Japanese, to bolster the morale of the other democratic nations in the world and brought up the possibility of our troops going into Norway. He also emphasized the necessity of sending U.S. bombers to England at the earliest possible moment to bomb German forces and industries, and French ports used by the German raiders.

Even at this early conference, efforts were made to determine definite dates on which we could carry out some of these operations. Actually, we did not have the troops; we did not have the equipment; we did not have the transports, so there was little point in trying to set dates.

Churchill then discussed the use of troops for the defense of our West Coast, Alaska, and Hawaii; also the possibility of dispersing our industries, rather than having them all in one spot as some of the most important were, for instance, in Los Angeles. In England, industries were dispersed to lessen interruptions due to bombings. Churchill suggested that Beaverbrook and Knudsen get together to see if they could find ways and means of doing the same thing here. (At this time there was hysteria all over the West Coast. Everybody expected the Japanese to appear suddenly from who-knows where with a large force and bomb our cities and factories. Actually, it was still a long way from Japan to the United States, and although most of our Navy had been destroyed at Pearl Harbor, the Japanese had not the equipment nor the "will-to-do" required for such an operation.)

Churchill went on to say we must keep open our supply line across the Pacific. He thought the British should take over the Eastern Atlantic and the United States should handle the Pacific. He also stated that in all probability Syria would be the next theater of operations; he expected a spring campaign to be carried on there. It was most important, he said, that the British hold the Nile Valley, and he was confident now they could, because of the Russians' success against the Germans and the British successes in North Africa. (A few months later, Rommel was knocking on the very doors of Cairo and looking right into the Nile Valley. He didn't reach it, but he certainly gave everybody in Cairo a scare—to say nothing of a few other people around the world.)

Churchill then went on to discuss our aviation program and the need for sending supplies to build up our bases and our schools in England. He finally took up the question of Malaya. The British policy, he said, was to retreat as long as they could, but when they got down to Singapore to hold until the last.

At this point, I asked if there was any policy in regard to keeping the Burma Road open. Churchill replied that they would fight to keep it open; that Indian troops would be used if necessary; that Wavell was being reinforced and they would do everything possible to keep that route open. (Note: It was not kept open and the only supplies going into China from India during the next two years were those which went in by air, over the Hump.)

This completes my notes on the first Chiefs of Staff conference.

These details are given to show the wide variety of subjects discussed at the "Big Two Conferences," and the tremendous amount of information that had to be obtained before it was possible to make the definite decisions that would enable us to destroy the fighting power of the Germans and the Japanese. After the major differences of opinion were settled in these conferences, the British Chiefs of Staff and the American Chiefs of Staff could decide which of the various problems had priority and which should be turned over to our respective working committees.

These committees usually consisted of representatives from each country's Army, Navy, and Air Force. Our own working committees would prepare plans to be submitted back to the American (Joint) Chiefs of Staff, who would in turn go over the plans and submit them to the President before the next meeting with the British. In the meantime, the British would have their reports from their working committees. The papers would be placed on the agenda and brought up at a joint staff meeting where they could be discussed, and decisions made.

The meetings of the Combined Chiefs of Staff (as this group was henceforth to be called) were quite formal. On one side of a long table, in the center, sat Sir Alan Brooke, Chief of the Imperial General Staff. On his right was Sir Dudley Pound, First Sea Lord. On Brooke's left sat Sir Charles Portal, Chief of Air Staff. On Portal's left usually sat Sir John Dill, and on his left, General Ismay, the military representative of the Prime Minister. Such planners or experts as were desired sat on the right and left of Pound and Ismay.

Opposite Brooke sat, at first, Admiral Stark, then Admiral Leahy, when Leahy became Chief of Staff to our President. On Leahy's right was General Marshall, then myself. On Leahy's left sat Admiral Ernest King. Our planners and experts sat along the sides of the table near the ends. There were variations from time to time, but this was the normal seating arrangement.

These conferences carried on until January 14th. During that period there was at least one meeting—often two—every day, whether of working committees, or the Chiefs of Staff themselves, or with the President and the Prime Minister.

Before we adjourned on January 14, 1942, the name "Joint Chiefs of Staff" for the American Chiefs of Staff had made its appearance, and the designation "Combined Chiefs of Staff" for the American and British Chiefs of Staff had been accepted for that body.

One of the most difficult problems to resolve during our staff meetings, whether it concerned the joint operations of the United States Army and Navy in the Pacific, or the combined operations of the Americans, British, and Dutch in Southeast Asia, was unity of command. We attained it in the ABDA (American-British-Dutch-Australian) Command with considerable difficulty when Wavell was made Chief, before the islands of Java and Sumatra fell. However, we never were able to secure it for the Pacific as a whole where the U.S. Army and Navy only were involved. We secured it in Europe, with Eisenhower in command, but still have not attained it in the postwar operations in Germany.

The Japanese always had that distinct advantage—one commander operating in a theater such as the Southwest Pacific, one commander operating down through Southeast Asia. Such a commander could throw his ground troops in any direction he wanted; he could use his air forces and Navy at any place and at any time he thought best. Against him we always had two or three commanders, representing the Army, the Air Force, or the Navy, with overlapping areas or operating ranges of equipment.

Some idea of the difficulties confronting the Chiefs of Staff when trying to secure unity of command can be appreciated when we take the ABDACOM area as an example. At one of our White House meetings with only the American Chiefs of Staff present, a few days after Christmas in 1941, the Secretary of War brought up the question of unity of command in that area. Mr. Stimson insisted it was a necessity and both General Marshall and I agreed. It was something that just had to be done. The President was with us.

We then discussed the man. The President asked me if it would be possible to get MacArthur out of the Philippines. I assured him it could be done if we did not wait too long. The President thought an American would be more satisfactory to the Australians and the Dutch than a Britisher, and he suggested MacArthur. He then asked who should be second in command.

As a matter of fact, the American Chiefs had already talked the matter over. I think the President was a bit surprised when all of us suggested we start the discussion with the British by proposing that Wavell be placed in command with an American as second, or as a deputy. After considerable talk, this was agreed upon, General Marshall emphasizing that lack of complete unity of command would be worse than none at all.

Later, when we met with the British, we found there was considerable opposition to the project. As a matter of fact, my impression was that, for a while at least, most of the British were dead set against unity of command, but I think the President caught them with both feet off base when he proposed General Wavell as commander for the ABDA area. Brett, our Chief of the Air Corps at that time, was designated as his deputy.

The President detained me after General Marshall and the others had left. He told me he had had a meeting with Lord Beaverbrook concerning aircraft production. Beaverbrook had said that in a nation of forty million people where all raw materials had to be imported, the production of aircraft was greater than that of a nation where the population was three times that, and where there were abundant natural resources. Of course, he was referring to England as compared with the United States.

The President asked me what I thought about it. I reminded him that we had not been at war as long as England, but that our production was going up all the time. As a matter of fact, the "will to do" had just made its appearance in some of our factories, and as soon as that feeling permeated all of our plants we would surpass the British production with a rush; without the will to do, we never would. I gave as an example the Boeing Company which had really gone to town. We had anticipated and programmed thirty-seven B-17's per month, but the Boeing Company had actually produced fifty in December, 1941, and expected to reach seventy-five in January.

Mr. Roosevelt asked me something else at that time. He said he thought we should build up bases in the Far East as soon as possible. From these, we should plan to work northward gradually, meeting the Japanese on even terms at every step, until sooner or later we drove them out of all their present conquests. I assured him that as far as airplanes were concerned the time was not far off when we could do that, and more. We would have superiority in the air in a very short time, in spite of the large number of planes we were sending to England and Russia. The President then said, "When will you be able to do this?" I replied, "Some time in the coming spring we should have enough planes to meet them on better than even terms." I missed that a bit, for it was not until the fall that our airmen were meeting the Japanese on better than even terms.

It was during these conferences that the first talk of landing in North Africa came up. Considered were such issues as the number of troops it would take; where we would get the ships; in what localities we could land; the kind of bases required; when it was thought such a landing might be made. As a matter of fact, the term GYMNAST—the first code name for the landing at Casablanca and on the North African coast— made its original appearance in the conferences we had with the British in the Combined Chiefs of Staff meetings prior to January 1, 1942.

At this first meeting of the Combined Chiefs of Staff, other matters on which decisions were reached were:

The employment of the *Queen Elizabeth* for taking United States troops to Australia.

The use of the *Aquitania* on the run from San Francisco to Hawaii

The use of the *Queen Mary* for taking troops from New York around the Cape to Australia.

Sailing dates for American troops going to North Ireland.

The extent to which shipping United States supplies to Russia would affect Operation GYMNAST.

The earliest possible date when a landing might be made in North Africa. (We fixed on May 25, 1942.)

The duties of the Combined Chiefs of Staff.

Definition of the term, "Combined Staff Planners"; description of their duties.

What was meant by the "Agenda for the Combined Chiefs of Staff"; the Combined Secretariat—what it was.

Who the Joint Staff Planners would be.

We agreed the Combined Chiefs of Staff should recommend the broad program of requirements based on strategic conceptions; submit general directives on the policy covering disposition of available weapons of war; settle broad issues of priority for overseas military movements.

It was decided this group should meet weekly, or more often if neces- sary, with an agenda circulated before each meeting to give each member an opportunity to obtain and study information and data concerning the particular subjects to be discussed; that Field Marshal Sir John Dill should remain in Washington as a senior representative of the British members of the Combined Chiefs of Staff; that the United States should plan for the security of Northeast Brazil; that 24,000 United States troops should be in Iceland by March; that 21,000 more should be sent to Australia.

When the Prime Minister heard the outline of the troop movements, he said he was afraid the plan was made up too hurriedly. Then followed a discussion of advantages and disadvantages, of loadings and unloadings, of disorders and delays of shipments to the Russians, who would probably yell like hell if ships were taken away from them. However, it was decided we would not cut down on the shipment of troops to Australia, and that with a little more study it would probably not be necessary to curtail shipments to Russia.

Harry Hopkins brought out the fact that the shortage of ships would only amount to about seven vessels, and thought that since the United States and Great Britain were using over 2400 ships, it should not be any great task to make up those seven.

It was finally agreed the President and the Prime Minister would take the responsibility of finding the seven ships and thus eliminate any delay in sending supplies to Russia. I said that those seven ships would also be needed to carry air supplies to the combat units we expected to have in the Far East, that the planes there would be no good without them. Beaverbrook said he would be very sorry to see the ships taken from the Atlantic. Whereupon, the Prime Minister asked if this whole question, as a matter of fact, was not caused by the air activities of General Arnold. I replied that it was, and explained that the delay of seven ships a month would stop air activities for perhaps sixty, perhaps ninety days.

Hopkins said he couldn't see that the seven ships we were talking about would make any difference when we were going to launch forty ships that very month.

The Prime Minister said if that was the consensus, we should accept it and find the seven ships, but if we didn't, the President would have to talk to the Russians.

The President replied, "How do you get that way? We'll both do it!"

Practically one entire meeting was taken up with the discussion of the facilities required for the new air route between Hawaii and Australia, running from Hawaii to Palmyra, Christmas, Canton, American Samoa, Fiji, and New Caledonia. It was agreed the United States should arrange for the local defense of Palmyra, Christmas, Canton, American Samoa, and Bora Bora (where a new air depot was planned). The Dominion of New Zealand would be responsible for the defense of Fiji, the United States to assist in that defense. New Caledonia should be principally an Australian responsibility, but the United States should, as a temporary measure furnish forces as soon as possible for the defense of the Island.

At meetings on January 4th, I met with Harry Hopkins, then the President, and finally the Prime Minister. Hopkins asked about the organization of the Air Force, and what, if anything, was interfering with or retarding its expansion. I assured him that the Chief of Staff was in full accord with the one million-man, one hundred and fifteen-group Air Force program which at that time was our objective, and that the only thing delaying it was the approval of the President. Given this approval, and the approval of Congress, we could reach the one hundred and fifteen groups by December 31, 1942, and would have 800 heavy bombers in England by December, 1943, and about six pursuit groups (432 airplanes) in the European Theater.

I told the President and Harry Hopkins that we expected to have two heavy bombardment groups or about 80 planes; four pursuit groups or 320 planes; and one dive bomber group of 52 planes in the Far East within the next couple of months, and we believed these forces, together with what the British were able to get together, would give us superiority over the Japanese in Southeast Asia.

Hopkins asked if I expected to run into obstacles in meeting this program. I told him that as far as training was concerned we were getting along beautifully, although we would have to bring in administrative civilians to replace the trained Army Air Corps officers who must go to tactical units. I further told him if there were any additional hurdles, I intended to ride them out.

The President talked over aircraft production and said, as Harry Hopkins had, that he wanted 48,000 planes produced during 1942 and 100,000 in 1943.

I assured him there had been a general awakening throughout the whole United States regarding the needs of our Armed Forces and that it looked as if we should get maximum production soon. I spoke again of the jump in output at Curtiss and Boeing. The President asked about the movement of air units overseas, and once more I gave him our program, saying I thought we could get along with his blessing on the one million-man, one hundred and fifteen-group program. His blessing on the program came immediately.

President Roosevelt discussed the Brazilian problem, the Natal bases, and went into detail about why President Vargas of Brazil could not leap into action and give us permission to put more troops on the Natal Peninsula. Vargas had to feel his way—be sure of his ground. I remarked to the President that Natal was essential to the success of our ferry service across the South Atlantic. He said he realized that.

Churchill was interested in how I was getting along with Portal; what planes we were going to give the British and what units we were going to send to England and to the Far East. I gave him the same information I had given to Hopkins and to the President. He seemed very pleased and asked when we could get the staffs over to England so they could become acquainted with British methods and problems.

I assured him they would be sent over shortly—it was a matter of weeks, not months. He expressed great pleasure and asked many questions about the British airmen who were being trained at our schools. Finally, he said that he would be out of town for about a week and that would give me a good chance to get better acquainted with Portal. I told him that was exactly the opportunity I was looking for, because I wanted to take Portal to Florida, and let him meet some of our American people and see a different part of our country.

As a matter of fact, Portal and I did go to Florida and we had a wonderful time fishing and loafing. Air Chief Marshal Portal did so well in getting acquainted with the local people, including the then Mayor of Tampa, that he just about set himself up as the Mayor's successor.

Shortly after the British left in January, the United States Chiefs of Staff had another meeting with the President at which a subject was introduced that was to plague me for the next two years—how to increase the supplies going to China. I told the President the only way I could see was by air transport, that we were working on an air transport line that would supplement the Chinese (CNAC) air line then running into China from India, and hoped to get it in operation soon.

The President asked, "How about getting heavy bombers out to General Wavell?" I told him we were flying them to him by way of India, to Sumatra, to Java, then on to Australia. The smaller aircraft (pursuit planes) had to go by ship. I said, however, one of our immediate problems was to repair the damage done by the Germans when they cut our air ferry line by bombing Fort Lamy, the last stop before Khartoum. The loss of gasoline there was a serious matter.

We talked about a line across Africa farther south; we also talked about Ascension Island. I said we would have Ascension fixed up very shortly, and would be flying our short-legged planes across the South Atlantic by stopping there.

Then the question came up of bombing Japan. How should we go about it? What problems of supply would it involve? At that time, the Doolittle project was under way, but all those present did not yet know about it and we didn't want it to be common knowledge, so I steered clear of it and talked about bombing Japan from China and Russia; about the difficulties we had in trying to get gasoline and other supplies into our bases in those areas. I said that from the viewpoint of both Japanese and American psychology, it was essential that Japan be bombed as soon as possible. We talked about establishing bases in northern China and in the Aleutians.

It was pointed out that Wavell had not as yet been put in command because the Prime Minister, now en route to Great Britain, had not approved his appointment. Also, the Dutch were in an angry frame of mind because they had not been consulted. Something had to be done to straighten matters out. As the Japanese moved farther and farther south, a great deal of face-saving was urgently necessary for the leaders of the small nations and dependencies. What could they tell their people?

The Australians wanted to have the same representation on the Combined Chiefs of Staff as the British. Had that been sanctioned, the Combined Chiefs ultimately would have become too unwieldy to do business. The stand had to be taken that the Combined Chiefs of Staff would continue as it was originally organized.

Obviously, the British Chiefs who had to return to England could not be present at the weekly meetings. Accordingly, substitutes were designated to sit in the Combined Chiefs of Staff meetings in the United States, but whenever the Big Two (the President and the Prime Minister) or the Big Three (the President, the Prime Minister, Stalin or Chiang Kai-shek) met in various parts of the world, the senior officers of the Army, Navy, and Air for both the British and the American services, were to be present to advise Mr. Roosevelt and Mr. Churchill.

For instance, after Admiral of the Fleet Sir Dudley Pound, and Air Chief Marshal Sir Charles Portal returned to England with the Prime Minister, they left Field Marshal Sir John Dill as the senior British representative on the Combined Chiefs of Staff in the United States; Admiral Sir Charles Little as Naval representative, and Air Marshal A. T. Harris as the Air representative.

At the time of Pearl Harbor, we had en route to the Philippines fifty-two dive bombers. The Japanese had moved to attack the Philippines within the next few days. This, obviously, made it impossible for the ship with the fifty-two planes to go into Manila, so it was directed to Australia.

At that time, I was supposed to know the location of every individual airplane in the United States Army Air Forces, and it was no uncommon thing for the President or the Secretary of War to call me up and ask, "Now, where are those two planes which are supposed to have left Hawaii—or Natal or Khartoum—yesterday?"

Fortunately, my memory was then fairly good, and since we did not have too many airplanes moving at that time, I could easily answer the questions. Those fifty-two airplanes, however, were a pain in the neck, because when they landed at Townsville, Australia, there were no trained mechanics available to uncrate and assemble them. The inexperienced men at Townsville did not know that the solenoids which controlled the firing of the guns on those airplanes were in boxes nailed to the inside of the crates, although the packing list on each crate gave the contents. When the planes were taken out of the crates, the crates were thrown on a trash pile and burned. Thus, with the assembly completed, there were no solenoids to be found, and the pilots couldn't fire the guns. Immediately, radios and cables started coming to the United States demanding solenoids, so that they could put the planes into action and help Mac-Arthur. And almost every day I was asked by the White House or by the Secretary of War for a report on what I was doing about those solenoids.

Actually, I had sent 104 of them by air across the Pacific—enough to take care of all the planes; to make sure, another 104 went by boat across the Pacific, and another 104 went by airplane across the Atlantic, Africa, and Asia, so that of the 312 solenoids shipped, some should ultimately get there.

However, people were impatient, and one day the Secretary of War called in Bob Lovett.

"Bob," demanded Mr. Stimson, "where are those things you need on those airplanes? Those things you need to make the airplanes shoot properly—oh, what's the name—hemorrhoids! Where are those hemorrhoids, anyway, Bob?"

Throughout the war, I tried to have the Air Force operate under certain fundamental principles:

1. The main job of the Air Force is bombardment; large formations of bombardment planes must hit the enemy before the enemy hits us. In short, the best defense is attack.

2. Our planes must be able to function under all climatic conditions from the North Pole to the South Pole.

3. Daylight operations, including daylight bombing, are essential to success, for it is the only way to get precision bombing. We must operate with a precision bombsight—and by daylight—realizing full well that we will have to come to a decisive combat with the enemy Air Force.

4. We must have highly developed, highly trained crews working together as a team—on the ground for maintenance and in the air for combat.

5. In order to bring the war home to Germany and Japan, and deprive them of the things that are essential for their war operations, we must carry our strategic precision bombing to key targets, deep in the enemy territory, such as airplane factories, oil refineries, steel mills, aluminum plants, submarine pens, Navy yards, etc.

6. In addition to our strategic bombing, we must carry out tactical operations in cooperation with ground troops. For that purpose we must have fighters, dive bombers, and light bombers for attacking enemy airfields, communication centers, motor convoys, and troops.

7. All types of bombing operations must be protected by fighter airplanes. This was proved to be essential in the Battle of Britain, and prior to that our own exercises with bombers and fighters indicated that bombers alone could not elude modern pursuit, no matter how fast the bombers traveled.

8. Our Air Force must be ready for combined operations with ground forces, and with the Navy.

9. We must maintain our research and development programs in order to have the latest equipment it was possible to get, as soon as it was possible to get it.

10. Air power is not made up of airplanes alone. Air power is a composite of airplanes, air crews, maintenance crews, air bases, air supply, and sufficient replacements in both planes and crews to maintain a constant fighting strength, regardless of what losses may be inflicted by the enemy. In addition to that, we must have the backing of a large aircraft industry in the United States to provide all kinds of equipment, and a large training establishment that can furnish the personnel when called upon.

Lieutenant General William Knudsen's genius continued to dominate the production picture. There are few countries (Britain was one of them) that could, as we did here in America, change a piano company into an outfit that would turn out airplane wings within a few months, or change a railroad car factory over to an airplane factory, a toy factory into an agency from which we were able to get all kinds of gadgets and accessories for our airplanes. A tire manufacturer, for instance, built fuselages and tail surfaces; a pickle plant turned out airplane skis and floats, and a manufacturer of girdles and corsets made parachutes. There are hundreds of other examples to show what makes American industry great; but without the proper leadership, it is exceedingly difficult to keep it geared to any emergency program. Bill Knudsen was such an industrial leader during the war.

The over-all program for the Army Air Forces required an overwhelming air superiority over our enemies in the shortest possible time. Our global field of operations required men from all walks of life. Each had a part to play, whether he was a hotel clerk, a railroad man, a shipping man, a barber, an auto mechanic, or a painter. We had need for all of them, each one fitting into his proper place—square pegs in square holes and round pegs in round holes. Our administrative officers had to be trained as rapidly as possible so as to release all flying officers who could possibly be replaced. An Officer Candidate School had to be built up at once.

During those early days, a great many Air Corps officers had the idea that everybody in the Air Force should be a pilot, regardless of whether he was running a hotel, a bus line, taking charge of motor transportation, or planning a hydroponics garden for the Pacific.

As in several other cases, so in this instance I immediately ran into old-fashioned opposition—indeed, a regular sit-down strike. Every time I asked when we could establish an Officer Candidate School I was told, "Well, it will take six or eight months to build the schools; then it will take another six or eight months to get the necessary instructors and books," and before I got through questioning, a year was accounted for and I didn't have plans for starting my school.

I stood this for some time, until February, 1942, when I called a conference of the training specialists at my headquarters in Washington. I reopened the question, "How long will it take to establish a ground officer school?" The reply was standard: "Well, it will take us three months to secure a site; three months more to set up the schools; three months more to get instructors, books, etc." I told them Hitler would not wait that long, and neither could I. While the officers were sitting and wondering what my next move would be, I called my secretary on the office phone and said, "Get me General Miff Harmon, down at Shreveport, Louisiana."

My secretary, Miss Adkins, a knowing soul, understood as usual. In a few minutes she sounded my buzzer.

I picked up the telephone and said, so that everybody could hear: "Is that you, Miff? O.K. How are you getting along? Finding things pretty busy? You need more officers? Well, that is not a circumstance to what you are going to need when you tackle *this* job. Well, don't be surprised. How long will it take you to get me L.S.U. (Louisiana State University)? You think you can get it for me in three or four days? Well, that's great. I'll tell you what I want. I want to get a place like that to establish an Officer Candidate School. Yes, an Officer Candidate School, and we may have as many as two or three thousand candidates—maybe more than that before we get through. But you think you can get it for me in three or four days? Well, that's wonderful, Miff. Thank you very much!"

I hung up the receiver and said, "Gentlemen, you see what you can do when you have the will to do?"

Whereupon, General Walter Weaver jumped up from his chair and said, "May I be excused? I want to leave right away and go down to Miami!"

I said, "By all means."

That afternoon he called up and said he had flown to Florida and could take over some 300 hotels at Miami Beach at once if I would approve the project. He would then be ready to open the school the following Monday. I told him to go ahead and get it working. It wasn't "Monday," but classes did commence the week after that.

During that long-distance telephone conversation with "General Miff Harmon," there had actually been nobody at the other end of the wire except Miss Adkins in the outer office.

In leasing these hotels and facilities, the cost was about $119.00 per man, and when we got through with the buildings and equipment, we could turn them back to their owners. We didn't have to pay for permanent construction, which normally amounted to $1000 per man. Still, we had trouble in convincing the high-ranking officers in the War and Navy Departments that this was a much simpler and cheaper way of doing business than the construction of temporary buildings. Before we got through with our training program, we had in the Air Forces alone over 500 hotels, with the necessary garages, theaters, and warehouses, in which we were giving various kinds of instruction. By this means we were able to start the Officer Candidate School, and other schools, almost at once.

The deal was actually a boon for the Miami Beach hotel owners, most of whom were going broke at the moment. But later on, when the war was about over, most of these same hotel men put in claims against the government for the business they said they "might have had" had the Army not taken over their establishments.

The attack on Pearl Harbor brought us renewed pleas from all parts of the world for personnel, airplanes, engines, parts, and supplies. Ships were too slow and were subject to attack by submarines. The war would be lost if we confined ourselves to such slow means of transportation. Airplanes, as weapons of war, must not be held on the ground to become a liability instead of an asset. We had to keep them in the air and keep them moving. This required supplies and replacements in a constant stream.

Early in the period when the Ferry Command was being created, General Bob Olds, in command at that time, came to me and said he was having trouble getting his planes and equipment into Accra, on the Gold Coast of Africa, because of submarines lying in the Gulf of Guinea off the Gold Coast. The result was, his bases at Lagos and Accra could not be built. I asked if he had taken the matter up with the Navy. He replied in the affirmative, but they had no destroyers available with which to drive the submarines out.

I said, "Well, Bob, did you ever consider making your own navy?" He asked, "What do you mean?"

I said, "Just that. Get some old hulk somewhere, put armor on it, put guns on it, and go out there with your own navy and drive the German subs out of the Gulf of Guinea."

Bob Olds was an ingenious soul. All he needed was an idea and he would carry it out if it were humanly possible.

He smiled and said, "Can I do that?" I replied, "Yes," and he ran out of the door.

I called, "Wait a minute. Before you actually do it, go and tell the Navy I said this Ferry Service is so important, not only to us but to our Allies, and to the Navy, that if they don't get those subs out of there I am going to give you permission to build your own navy to run them out so you can get your airfields started."

A short time after that, Bob came back and said, "We don't have to build our own navy. They have agreed to send destroyers there to get our transports through." I believe that Bob would have built his own navy if it had been necessary.

It was in July, 1942, that the name of the "Air Ferrying Command" was changed to "Air Transport Command." The units of that command were extended to all parts of the world. At that time, I called into the service Mr. C. R. Smith, then President of the American Airlines. I put General Harold Lee George in charge of Air Transport Command and made Smith his deputy. They made a wonderful pair. General Olds was given a combat command.

Once I had George and Smith running our military air lines, I did not have to worry about that problem any longer. No matter what mission I gave them, I could count on its being carried out 100 per cent. The two officers complemented each other in ability, experience, and judgment—they made a perfect team.

The growth of the Air Transport Command paralleled closely the expansion of the whole Air Force. It started out with two officers and one clerk in a small room and within two years totaled over 85,000 officers and men, and had lines extending to practically every corner of the world. In one day, for instance, the ATC carried 680,000 pounds of materiel and supplies by air to one theater of operations.

✻ *18* ✻

I remember the cocky and uneducated Press comparisons that were made in those bad months, disparaging our airplanes in favor of the enemy's. Not only were the P-38's, the P-39's, and the P-40's "terribly inferior" to the Jap Zero, but even our P-47's and P-51's would never stand a chance against the Luftwaffe's Messerschmitt 109 and the Focke-Wulf 190. Columnists returned from "get-rich-quick" trips abroad and gave interviews, or wrote articles, making it clear that when compared to the German aeronautical genius, our American aviation setup was in a pretty sad state. It was predicted that our boys would have to pay for it.

These stories came home to the fathers, mothers, wives, and friends of the boys who were fighting, or going to fight, in our Air Forces. I realized the impression being created must be corrected as soon as possible. I figured that if I could convert one or two of the worst offenders, say Geoffrey Parsons of the New York *Herald Tribune,* and Tex McCrary of the New York *Daily Mirror,* it would help to get some of the other critics back on the beam.

Accordingly, I had a large chart prepared. That chart was broken down to show the various categories of airplane performance, such as speed, climb, maneuverability, and firepower, of all the fighter airplanes in the world—Japanese, German, American, or British. Naturally, as some of the planes were equipped with superchargers to get maximum performance at 7000 feet; others to get it at 9000 feet; others at 10,000, 15,000, or 20,000 feet; and others at top altitude, no one airplane was best on the ground nor at any one altitude up to the extreme combat ceiling.

Different fighter types have different purposes. So, whereas one airplane, as indicated on the curves of performance would be better at 7000 feet, another would be better at 10,000 feet, and still another at 13,000 feet or at 20,000 feet. The curves on my chart were numbered and not named. All the casual observer could see when he examined the chart was a mass of intertwining curves, each one with a number on it, each one showing the performance of an unspecified airplane.

When this layout was completed, I invited Mr. Geoffrey Parsons to come down and see me, and requested him to help me select the best airplane for use by the United States Army Air Forces. He said he thought that was a little too much to ask of him. I replied, "Well, you have just been overseas, and you've been writing stories in your *Herald Tribune,* giving information concerning the best fighter planes in use today. That indicates you are an expert. You have about two million readers who all think you are an expert, so I don't think it is asking too much of you." I then explained to him what the chart was, and asked him to go ahead and select the best fighter plane, so I could produce it

He hesitated a long time, and finally said, "How about this one?"

"Well," I said, "as you see, this chart is a bit complicated, but that happens to be one of our own airplanes—the P-47."

Then he said, "Well, how about this one?"

"That happens to be our P-38," I told him.

"And how about this plane?" he asked.

I said, "That's our P-51."

Then he said, "I give up. You win. Why don't you tell this story to the people of the United States?"

I replied, "Mr. Parsons, I don't dare tell the public that. If I did, Mr. Hitler and Hirohito would know as much about our planes and about what we are doing, as you do, now."

Mr. Parsons, a very generous and far-sighted person, said that, in that case, the next best thing would be for me to come up to New York and have a talk with Mrs Ogden Reid and the *Herald Tribune's* editorial staff. "You will help us out a great deal by giving them the straight facts, just as you have given them to me," he said. I said I would be delighted. I went to New York, made the presentation, and from that time on, the New York *Herald Tribune* was one of the best friends the Air Force had.

I used the same technique in convincing Tex McCrary, of the New York *Daily Mirror.* When I got through, Tex just looked at me and said he wanted to join up with us. I commissioned him and sent him overseas for public relations duty with the Eighth Air Force.

There was another critic whom I never was quite able to convince. He was a good friend of many Air Corps officers, but for some reason or other he seemed to think that I, and I alone, was responsible for not buying all the planes he could build when, sometime prior to this, he was running his own factory. Despite all our tests at and recommendations from Wright Field, he still thought his own planes the best. His name was Alexander de Seversky. My officers came to me and said I was wrong about him; that he wasn't really as bad as I thought; that I should have a talk with him.

Major Seversky came to my office, and after the customary polite preliminaries, I said to him, "Now look, Alex, you're an expert, and all the people in the United States realize you are. I would just like to ask you two questions: first, what are the things I'm doing now that you wouldn't do if you were in my position; and, second, what are the things I must do in the future according to your ideas?"

Seversky looked at me visibly shocked, and said, "Well, obviously, I can't answer those questions sitting here right now. You are coming at me too fast."

I said, "O.K. How much time do you want?"

He said, "I couldn't do it inside of a week." I said, "Well, let's say ten days. Come back in ten days and we'll talk it over then." To the best of my knowledge, Seversky never returned. Constructive criticism was certainly hard to get in those days.

Immediately following Pearl Harbor, the President was insistent that we find ways and means of carrying home to Japan proper, in the form of a bombing raid, the real meaning of war. We thought that out for some weeks. I talked it over with some key members of my Air Staff and then with Mr. Roosevelt. Just who originated the idea that a raid on Japan should start from an aircraft carrier I do not know. In any event, early in 1942, Admiral King came to see me and asked if I thought it was feasible to use B-25's launched from the deck of a carrier. I assured him I thought it was, provided the carrier deck was large enough to accommodate the number of B-25's that should be sent out on such a mission. From that time on, the Doolittle Toyko Raid was an approved, and Top Secret, project. Very few officers in the Air Force, or in the Navy, knew it was to take place. President Roosevelt was kept constantly advised on the details.

Closest cooperation was maintained with the Navy to insure proper carrier technique. The Navy assigned Lieutenant Miller to help Doolittle

during the training period, in connection with carrier takeoffs and landings. He did a grand job.

On April 1, 1942, sixteen B-25's were hoisted aboard the *Hornet* at
Alameda, California. The next day, escorted by two cruisers, four
destroyers and a tanker, the Air Force officers and enlisted men assigned
to this mission, together with the B-25's, sailed out through the Golden
Gate. Vice Admiral William Halsey was in command of the expedition.
None of the crews were to know what they were to do until the time came
to take off from the carrier.

The selection of Doolittle to lead this nearly suicidal mission was a
natural one. As I have indicated earlier, he was fearless, technically
brilliant, a leader who not only could be counted upon to do a task
himself if it were humanly possible, but could impart his spirit to others.

As an illustration, when we first received the B-26 from the factory
early in 1942, most flyers considered it a very dangerous airplane. On
paper, actually, it was little different from the B-25. The test pilots who
flew it claimed it had about the same performance as the B-25. Yet, for
some reason or other, it received a bad name and when a plane gets a
bad name, it is mighty hard to change it.

Our new pilots were afraid of the B-26, and we had one accident after
another. Seemingly, all that was necessary was for one engine to go sour
on a B-26 while in flight, and it would crash.

At the time the B-26 trouble was at its height, I called Doolittle to
my office, told him I would like to have him go out, take a B-26, fly it
under any and all conditions, and then go down to the B-26 outfit, take
command, and show those boys that flying this ship was no different
from flying any other. Doolittle did this, and before he left the outfit he
had the boys flying the B-26 on one engine, making landings and taking
off with one engine, just as easily as they had formerly done with two.

The original plan of the Tokyo raid called for a dusk take-off from
the *Hornet,* and a night attack on the city. However, after the task force
had reached a point 650 miles from Tokyo and been sighted by patrol
vessels, there was the danger of an alarm all over Japan. Admiral Halsey
decided the B-25's should take off at eight o'clock in the morning. This
was eight hours in advance of the schedule which had been furnished
Generalissimo Chiang Kai-shek, who did not seem to like the project
anyway, and had tried to delay it.

These changes in plans did not disturb Doolittle nor his crews. They
threw in a couple more cans of gasoline which they planned to pour into

their tanks while they were in the air. Knowing they had some 650 miles to go before they would reach Tokyo, they took off.

The first plane to become airborne was Jimmy's own. He took off down a plunging deck. The sea was rough, and sending blue water over the flight deck as the carrier pitched and rolled. Never before had a take-off with a heavy plane been accomplished under such conditions. Yet each of Doolittle's B-25's took the air without a hitch. It required one hour for all the planes to clear the deck and start toward Japan. The Naval task force then turned and headed toward home without interference.

The bombers flew along unopposed, and went right into Tokyo before meeting any Jap planes. They reached the city just as an air raid drill was being carried out. Doolittle's lead plane made its attack about noon, then the other planes came in, one after another, at intervals of a few minutes.

The actual damage done, as we learned later, really was comparatively light, but the effect on Japanese morale was terrific. The bombs hit oil farms, factories, depots; one of them hit a carrier in drydock. Some of the bombs fell in thickly settled districts. Fifteen of the sixteen planes reached their objectives. They then headed toward their temporary "home" fields in China, on a continent they had never seen. But fate was against them. In the darkness they encountered rain and clouds. The bomber crews could not see, and with no navigational aids on the ground, they could not find the landing fields. They were forced either to crash-land or to bail out. One B-25 flew north and landed near Vladivostok where its crew was interned. Two planes landed in enemy-held territory. Two of the men who landed there were executed by the Japanese. One died in a prison camp. Fourteen crews came through alive. All sixteen planes were lost.

After landing, Doolittle assembled such men as he could, and notified the Chinese authorities who aided in assembling others. All who could be collected were taken into Chungking, where they were decorated by Madame Chiang Kai-shek, and were later returned to the United States. Almost as soon as he got back on American soil, Doolittle was called to the White House by the President and given the Medal of Honor. Jimmy's wife was flown in to Washington and hadn't the faintest idea what was going on until the ceremony started.

Meanwhile, the German submarine menace in the Atlantic grew worse, so much worse that people walking on our southern beaches were sighting U-boats temporarily stranded on sandbars with small boats out, or cruising about at will in shallow water. Excited telephone calls did no good. I became more and more interested in the eager work of the Volunteer Civil Aeronautics Patrol. My old friend, that shrewd air expert, civilian aviation authority, and World War I army pilot, Gill Robb Wilson, had approached me with this idea way back in 1938, just after the Munich Pact. Ably aided by Tom Beck of *Collier's,* and Guy Gannett, the newspaper publisher and air enthusiast, the C.A.P. idea was built up into a sort of aerial "Lexington and Concord" as the title of its semi-official history indicates—"Flying Minute Men."

There was a distinct shortage of Navy and Army planes at that time; few were available for such duty. We had to look to other sources for the patrol planes and personnel—for the moment, at least. The civilian pilots of the C.A.P. in their private planes mostly little puddle-jumpers, undertook to spot Hitler's arrogant sea invaders and help to change the picture. In the end, the C.A.P. had about 80,000 people at work on various jobs. Very few of them had ever flown across large bodies of water with their little low-speed, short-range Piper Cubs and what-not; but now they were doing it, both men and women, with marked success. And they had been growing not only more expert but continually more enthusiastic, though they never received more than a per diem of eight dollars to take care of all their expenses (a few state budgets, as in Gill's own New Jersey, helped wonderfully).

One time, a C.A.P. pilot saw a submarine cruising inside the shallow water area, but the sub paid no attention to the harmless little plane overhead. The pilot said he flew low enough to throw a rock or a wrench and hit the submarine, yet the U-boat in shallow water went moving along just like a cabin cruiser. When it was ready, the sub went out through a gap in the shoals and sank a ship.

I asked Gill Wilson if he thought the C.A.P. pilots, dressed in civilian clothes and having no military status, would object to carrying bombs on their puddle-jumpers. As usual, Wilson was enthusiastic and asked, "Where do we get them?"

Accordingly, I had special bomb racks built at one of our depots— bomb racks that could be attached to these small planes in a very short time. We also built a cheap bombsight, and thereafter most of the C.A.P. planes carried bombs—fifty pounders the pilots could drop on the submarines, knowing full well that if they were taken prisoner in civilian clothes, they would not be considered part of our armed forces, but guerillas.

Before the C.A.P. had finished their task in the war, they had flown more than twenty-four million miles, mostly in single-engine, small land planes, well out over the ocean. They also performed other tasks. They flew courier service; they towed targets for antiaircraft batteries; they tracked for searchlight crews; and they flew sentry duty along the Mexican border looking for spies. They spotted forest fires and helped put them out; they were used in time of emergency when there were floods or other disasters; they located one lost plane after another in mountainous and wooded terrain. In addition to all this, they furnished a reservoir of cadets and enlisted men for the Army Air Forces. They did a magnificent job all through the war, and they did sink some submarines.

In the late spring of 1942, our strategic planning began to crystallize. The President designated the Pacific Theater for "holding" operations— to contain the Japanese in the area they then occupied, if this were possible. Defense was the primary objective. We were also to make attacks upon the Japanese line of communications and bomb Japan proper as soon as feasible. The Navy was to destroy as many Japanese ships as it could.

In the India-Burma Theater, the main task was to open up an air route to keep China in the war and to put supplies across the Hump, using all available air transports for that purpose. Meantime, if the British and our forces could do it, we hoped to carry on an offensive operation that would reopen the Burma Road.

The President reiterated time and time again, that Russian armies were killing more Germans and destroying more materiel than all the other twenty-four United Nations together. Therefore, to help the Soviet Union was a primary consideration, and we must maintain a flow of goods into Russia. But above all, we must also organize a second front. In order to make any ground operation in western Europe possible, we first had to gain control of the air over at least the Netherlands, Belgium, and France. Repeatedly, the President stated that we must establish a front somewhere in western Europe, where "we can actually fight the German ground forces face to face as soon as possible!"—this not only to pull some of the German juggernaut off the hard-pressed Russians, but to insure that the Russian stand would not be wasted in the Allied world-strategy picture by reason of our own delay. If Hitler got another chance to turn on one enemy at a time, he might still win.

The Atlantic Theater, covering all Europe, was given first priority by the President as an offensive hemisphere. The President was worried about the opinion of some of the military men that no operations would be possible in Europe before 1943. He forcibly stated that, if possible, we must get operations of some kind started in the European Theater, or in North Africa, right away, as early as it could be done. He even went so far as to say that such a move in 1942 by Britain and the United States might be called an "operation of desperation."

That strategic concept immediately became the guide for all planning by the Army and the Air Forces. However, it also became a pain in the neck, for while lip-service was always given to priorities for the offensive operations in Europe, the continued requests for planes from the Pacific had no direct relation to the immediate importance of the two theaters in the over-all strategy. "Theater-itis" remained one of my chief plagues throughout the war.

During those early war days when we did not have combat units, personnel, or equipment, we were all in a quandary about what dispositions to make of our meager forces. Everyone wanted them! It was easy enough to visualize a campaign that hit on the edges of the German or Japanese area of occupation, but much more difficult to peer into the future and plan for the final, killing operation that would end the war. Most of the early conferences wound up with discussions of minor operations.

I have a distinct recollection of sticking my neck out at the Allied Staff Conference with the President and the Prime Minister at the White House in December, 1941, when everyone was having his say about how the war should be won.

"I think," I said, "the way to win the war is to hit Germany where it hurts the most, where she is strongest—right across the Channel from England, using the shortest and most direct road to Berlin. We will have the air power to destroy her factories, communications, facilities, concentrations of supplies, and to defeat her Air Force. We can also isolate, by bombing, any part of the coastline in the area we desire to use for landing troops. We will be able to secure command of the air and remove that threat from the troops making the landings."

Secretary Stimson joined in my recommendation, but there was considerable opposition from the British. Now wasn't the time. A great deal of preparation was necessary; other campaigns should be considered first. The War Department planners were of the same opinion I was.

At the beginning of 1942, it certainly looked as if the Allies were losing the war, and we had to fight with what we had. The United States Chiefs of Staff were afraid that unless we pressed hard for a cross-

Channel invasion as soon as possible, we would never get it at all. I have said that the first mention of operation GYMNAST (later called TORCH), the North African invasion, came during that visit of Churchill's to Washington, just after Pearl Harbor. His talk then about North Africa was by no means casual, but an energetic British counter-measure to the zeal with which we of the American Chiefs of Staff urged a cross-Channel invasion.

Still remembering Dunkirk, Churchill spoke of "a Channel full of the bodies of British soldiers." He talked convincingly, and would have argued the President out of it in favor of the "soft underbelly" had he been able to at that time. The British never did like the idea of striking straight across the Channel until after it was successfully accomplished.

On the other hand, the Russians wanted an assault on the Normandy beaches to take place almost before we were equipped.

I now feel, with the benefit of hindsight, that the Air Force available in 1942–43 might not have been able to maintain the "local" air suprem-acy necessary to establish an invasion bridgehead on the Continent and then cover the Allied advance: nor could our strategic bombardment of Germany have begun to achieve its results much sooner than it did—late in 1943. Nevertheless, in early 1942 the situation seemed to offer a golden opportunity for such a bold stroke.

In any case, my notes indicate that either because of Churchill's influence on the President, or for other reasons, the assembled Staffs were not quite ready for anything as definite as that cross-Channel operation so early in the war. As I have said, Secretary Stimson favored it, but with a few British arguments against it there was no further dis-cussion on a cross-Channel offensive at that time.

However, by April 1, 1942, the War Department General Staff and the Army Air Forces Staff had again worked up a general plan for such an operation (BOLERO, ROUNDUP, and finally, OVERLORD). On April 1st, Harry Hopkins invited me to lunch at the White House and a talk with the President. Before seeing the President, Harry and I dis-cussed the major operations that might be possible against Germany, and I told him of the War Department's plans for an all-out offensive from England, directed toward the heart of Germany, preceded by a maximum air offensive and ending with the ground troops' invading France and meeting the German army where it was strongest. I also told Hopkins I thought he would be well pleased with the plan as drawn up.

Hopkins talked openly of the obstacles that would be thrown in our path by some of the higher ranking officers in our own Navy, and by the British. I did not think any Navy opposition would be serious, since Admiral King would be present when the President received the plan and discussed it. We both agreed the situation was different with the British. It would be necessary for someone to go to London to sell the idea to Churchill and to the British Staff. Harry suggested that I should be the one. I insisted it should be General Marshall, who had much more prestige among the British top-flight personnel than I. Hopkins finally agreed with me.

Harry also talked over the proper approach to Churchill, knowing that the Prime Minister was already considering several other plans for the invasion of Germany, in addition to the one across the Channel. Harry finally said the approach, as he saw it, must be the direct one, and that Churchill would have to go along, as the temper of our people was for an all-out offensive with the least possible delay.

After lunch, Hopkins and I went to see the President, with whom we had a short talk. Later, Secretary Stimson, Secretary Knox, Admiral Stark, Admiral King, General Marshall, General Watson, and I assembled with the President and Hopkins. It was one of those meetings where everyone came in the back door and went out the same way to avoid attracting the attention of the White House correspondents.

At the meeting, the President brought up the all-out offensive against Germany. General Marshall presented the Army plan for ROUNDUP in 1943. The President read it, paragraph by paragraph, asking questions about the various phases as he went along. He finally accepted the plan and gave instructions that we were to go ahead and make the necessary preparations for carrying it out. He put special emphasis on the movement to England of the air units as outlined.

Harry Hopkins then made this remark: "I want to be sure that everybody is in accord with this program. Admiral King, do you see any reason why this cannot be carried out?" Admiral King replied, "No, I do not."

Hopkins asked, "Assuming that commitments in the Far East and the Pacific stand as they are, without any further reinforcements, will this program interfere with your operations, and will you have sufficient airplanes?"

Admiral King replied, "I will not have as many as I should like, but I am willing to make the sacrifice in numbers because I think I can get along."

The next subject brought up was the matter of equipment for the operation. I stated that as far as equipment was concerned, the Air Forces were treated like a sort of stepchild. After all other nations were given the airplanes they asked for, the United States Air Forces received what was left. I pointed out we could not fight a war along those lines. Both the President and Secretary Stimson said that such procedure must stop; that hereafter the United States Air Forces were to receive their share of airplanes, based upon the tasks we had to perform.

After General Marshall covered the details of troop movements and supply ships available, the open discussion stopped. The President said General Marshall and I would have to decide between ourselves who was to go to England. I told him that in my mind there was no question but that General Marshall should go; that he was far better qualified to make the presentation of the whole subject. The President decided that General Marshall should accompany Hopkins, and that they should leave at the earliest moment; also, that the entire trip should not take much over a week.

The approved plan for ROUNDUP, in which I was most interested, provided for air units to leave as soon as possible and start operating at once. These units should reach a maximum by April, 1943. By that date, we should have about 1500 fighter planes and 1000 bombers in England. I was sure we could reach that figure if we had no further diversions to other theaters and if we could continue to have priorities. About 400,000 ground troops should also be in England by April 1, 1943.

This conference was of particular importance to me because I was being besieged by military and naval commanders in all theaters of the world for more and more planes. Naturally, every theater commander thought his command the most important, and the most deserving of top air priority.

The President's approval of the strategic plan for winning the war gave the Air Force the impetus so badly needed to start our bombers and fighters moving to Europe as fast as our combat units completed their training.

General Marshall and Harry Hopkins left for England on the morning of April 4th and did a wonderful job selling the idea for the trans-Channel operation—apparently against much opposition. They came back with British approval for preparations for a landing on the northwest coast of France in the summer of 1943, or as soon thereafter as possible. This did not mean that the possibility of a North African invasion in late 1942 was canceled.

About two weeks later, the President sent for me and talked for a

The official United States Air Force photographic portrait of H. H. Arnold as a four-star general. (Photograph is from the General H. H. Arnold Collection of the Library of Congress.)

Lieutenant Arnold in flight training at the Wright Brothers Flying School, Sims Field, Dayton, Ohio, 1911. (Photograph is from the General H. H. Arnold Collection of the Library of Congress.)

Brigadier General Arnold at March Field, California, in October 1937 after a Martin B-10 bomber flight. (U.S. Air Force photograph)

General Arnold meets with automobile industrialist Henry Ford (on General Arnold's left) at Wright Field in Dayton, Ohio, in May 1941 to plan increased production of aircraft engines. (U.S. Air Force photograph)

The Allied Combined Chiefs of Staff pose after meeting with President Franklin D. Roosevelt (left, seated) and Prime Minister Winston S. Churchill of Great Britain (right, seated) at the Casablanca Conference in January 1943. General Arnold is standing in the first row at the left. (U.S. Air Force photograph)

General George C. Marshall (left, foreground) and General Arnold meet with the Allied Combined Chiefs of Staff at the Casablanca Conference in January 1943. (U.S. Air Force photograph)

General Arnold attended the Cairo Conference in 1943. Seated, left to right, are Generalissimo Chiang Kai-shek of Nationalist China, President Franklin D. Roosevelt, Prime Minister Winston S. Churchill of Great Britain, and Madame Chiang Kai-shek. Standing, left to right, are the Chinese aide to the Generalissimo, Lieutenant General Brehon B. Somervell, Lieutenant General Joseph Stillwell, General Arnold, Field Marshal Sir John Dill, and Lord Louis Mountbatten. (U.S. Air Force photograph)

General Arnold discusses air tactics with General Dwight D. Eisenhower at Castelvetrano Airfield, Sicily, in December 1943. (U.S. Air Force photograph)

General Mark W. Clark and General George S. Patton meet with General Arnold at Castelvetrano Airfield, Sicily, in December 1943. General Clark is seated at the left. (U.S. Air Force photograph)

General Arnold with his son, Bruce, on Okinawa. (U.S. Air Force photograph)

General Arnold and his wife, Eleanor, attend his retirement party in March 1946. (U.S. Air Force photograph)

General Arnold in retirement at his ranch in Sonoma, California, in 1949. He died at the ranch in January 1950 and was buried at Arlington National Cemetery. (National Air and Space Museum photograph)

long time about the route into China. He told me he wanted combat planes used for combat purposes, and that cargo planes only would be used to ferry supplies into China. We would use the DC-3 type as long as it was possible. Efforts would be made to base American air units, operating against Germany, in Russia (shuttle-bombing), so we would not have that long haul back to England after hitting targets in eastern Germany. Insofar as raids against Tokyo and Japan proper were concerned, except for repetition of raids of the Doolittle type, they were for the moment impossible, since we had neither the bases nor the required types of planes.

I assured the President that I should like nothing better than shuttle-bombing between England and Italy to Russia, hitting targets in eastern Germany en route. I told him I would start the ball rolling at once. However, as in all cases where cooperation with the Russians was desired, much time was lost in endless discussions and delays before we could actually start operations.

As a result of the President's various decisions about the strategic lines to be followed in defeating the Germans and the Japanese, and about the allocation of supplies and equipment produced in the United States, it was obvious that the number of airplanes the British were receiving must be reduced. The same applied to Russia. Mr. Roosevelt agreed.

On May 19, 1942, the President wrote a letter to his friend, the "Former Naval Person" in Britain, in which he expressed the thought that a reallocation of airplanes should be made—more airplanes should go to the United States Air Force, and the number of airplanes scheduled to go to the British Air Force should be cut down. He advanced the principles that the maximum number of planes should be maintained in combat, and the minimum number consistent with security be held in reserve and in operational training units; that American pilots and crews should be assigned to American-made planes in far greater numbers than they were at present on the combat fronts.

After a discussion with Hopkins and me, the President proposed that Admiral Towers, head of Naval aviation, and I go to London at once to meet with Air Chief Marshal Portal to discuss this very important matter, and if necessary, have Portal return to Washington with Towers and me after the discussions in London were completed.

On May 20th, just before our departure, at a meeting attended by General Marshal, Admiral King, Admiral Towers, Mr. Hopkins, and myself, the President repeated the points he had made to Churchill, and said that in general they would apply in all theaters. There might be certain isolated exceptions, such as Russia. There, because of geographical, logistic, and national problems, American planes would generally be flown and maintained by the Russians, though it might be possible at a later date to use American personnel. Left for later decision was the question whether to make an exception of the Transport and Coastal Command planes for British units. After considerable talk, we also decided that in North Africa for the time being, at least, the British would operate such American-type planes as we could supply, and that we must supply them with enough to maintain their existing strength. This would necessitate our building, maintaining, and operating depots for the repair of our American equipment. Provisions were made covering American air units, and maintenance and equipment in Australia, West Africa, India, and Syria.

The United States would have to supply replacements to all groups overseas, United States or Allied, that were using American aircraft, regardless of what the monthly losses might be. In 1942, we figured the saturation point of the United States would be an Air Force of about 270 groups, but early in that year we had less than 50. We could never get the additional 220 American groups on the fighting fronts or on our training fields at home if we continued to allocate so many planes to foreign countries.

There was a notable group of high-ranking officers on the C-54 that took off from Bolling Field on May 23, 1942: Major General Mark Clark, at that time Chief of Staff to General McNair, head of the Ground Forces; Major General Dwight Eisenhower, then Chief of the War Department's Operations Division; Air Marshal Evill, Admiral Towers, Colonel Hoyt S. Vandenberg, and myself, besides our respective aides and secretaries. Our course was from Bolling Field to Montreal, to Goose Bay on Newfoundland, and from Goose direct to Prestwick in Scotland.

There was no question of bickering with the British over the allocation of supplies, including aircraft, which we well realized they needed from us and which we would have liked to give them. The question was whether we could continue our present commitments to build up the R.A.F. without curtailing the United States Air Force to such a degree that we could not employ to the maximum the splendid young men we had available in this country. There was no doubt in my mind that our own personnel and equipment could be welded into combat units that had no equal in the world.

The difference between the R.A.F.'s night area-bombardment plans and the American determination to go ahead with precision bombardment by daylight threw monkey wrenches in the machinery and made procurement difficult. Our program was still untested in combat, but we were certain that we were right and so must not lose production priority.

In their extensive Coastal Command operations, the British were employing American bomber types like the B-24's and the few B-17's they still had, valuably, to be sure, against submarines and surface ships; but they were not using them effectively in the bombardment of Germany.

R.A.F. Bomber Command, too, was still expanding. Would it, and would its operational needs, expand beyond the ability of the British aircraft industry and of British manpower to supply it? I thought it would. It was necessary to reach a whole new understanding about air matters between our two countries, and especially a better coordinated view of aircraft allocation. Those were the main reasons for this trip, as far as I was concerned.

The weather was bad when we landed at Prestwick, and we talked over how we were going to proceed to London. Liberators and other American planes were parked around the airport. Turrets were being fitted; extra gas tanks were being installed, but a lot of airplanes were not being worked on at all. The changes made on Liberators, for instance, took about two weeks. About eight thousand men were modifying these airplanes, but from my point of view, too many of the planes were just standing there when they were badly needed elsewhere.

We checked the weather later in the day and it wasn't too good, so Admiral Towers, General Eisenhower, General Clark, and Air Marshal Evill decided to go to London by train. Vandenberg, Beebe, my aide, and I decided to go the next morning by plane. However, just about the time the decision was made, a message was received from the Prime Minister, saying he was having a conference the next morning and wanted us all to come down together by train that night. So we drove to Glasgow, boarded the "Scottish Chief," and headed for London. Our party had a special car on the train.

Next morning, prior to a conference in Air Chief Marshal Portal's office, I had the opportunity to talk with Air Marshal Freeman, General Chaney, Ambassador Winant, General Eaker, and Colonel McClelland. Mr. Winant said he had just talked to Molotov, who had left for the United States for his first conference with the President as we were leaving Prestwick. Molotov and the Russians wanted a treaty with the

United States guaranteeing the integrity of certain key countries in Europe.(!)

We talked at length about American pursuit planes. General Chaney doubted the efficiency of both the P-38 and the P-39. He thought we would be making a mistake if we used either of them. I told Ambassador Winant and Chaney we should at least give them a trial in combat before we said they were no good, because their performance, certainly in peacetime tests, justified their production.

After I had a promising talk with Portal at ten o'clock, we met at eleven with the Prime Minister and held a general discussion. Present were the Prime Minister, representatives from the R.A.F., and the party from the United States. The Prime Minister said he could not understand why, with a 60,000-plane production in the United States, we raised an issue over allocating a mere 5000 planes to the British. He wanted to make sure that the effective fighter strength in any one theater, or all theaters, was not decreased.

In general, he was in favor of American pilots flying American planes, but he reiterated the necessity for maximum impact against the enemy. We must have the maximum number in action at all times and the greatest possible number of bombs must be dropped. It was a question of maintaining strength *for the next few months*—not a year from now. He closed by saying he wanted us to talk openly and freely and then he asked for any remarks I cared to make.

I told the Prime Minister we had exceptional young men in the United States available for the Air Force. They were the "cream of the crop" in the nation, and they could fly the United States planes better than the youngsters of any other country. I told him about the lend-lease and defense-aid hearings before Congress; how the Secretary of War, the Chief of Staff, the Chief of the Air Force, and Congress had always agreed that by furnishing planes to other nations we would be building up production capacity in the United States for the time when we ourselves needed it. I told him the people of the United States knew that; that they wanted a United States Air Force now; they wanted action in Europe.

Our production couldn't meet the present allocation of planes to Australia, the R.A.F., the West Coast, the Russians, the Navy, the Chinese, if at the same time we were to build up a United States Air Force. We wanted, above all things, to retain the present air strength in our defensive areas and to build it up in Europe. We had no intention of allowing any theater to have a smaller number of airplanes in combat than it now had, and by using our plan, we would greatly increase the number. I outlined the many calls made upon us for airplanes, and totaled them, showing what a tremendous number must come out of that 60,000 a year we were producing.

The Prime Minister outlined the situation in the various theaters, calling attention to the critical condition in India, the Middle East, and China and to the BOLERO-ROUNDUP project (landing in France by the Allied forces) in particular.

When he finished he called on Admiral Towers for anything he wanted to say. Towers said his problem was simple and could be ironed out without difficulty. The British Navy needed only torpedo planes, dive bombers, and fighters for carriers and coastal patrol work. That was all.

The meeting adjourned when the Prime Minister gave instructions for a detailed discussion in the afternoon. He then took me into the gardens in the rear of No. 10 Downing Street, where we sat, walked, and talked for almost an hour about airplane production and allocation. After I left him I came to the conclusion, that we would be able to sell our airplane allocation policy to him. The rest of that day was spent in conferences—conferences between lower and upper echelons; visits from one place to another and talking and more talking.

Among other people with whom I talked was Miss Jackie Cochran, who was in Britain trying to establish a women's ferry command for the R.A.F. It was then we first talked over the idea of creating an organization of women pilots in the United States Air Force ("WASPS").

I found London very different from my last visit. People were not so listless; the city had been cleaned up and bomb marks were rapidly disappearing. However, one curious phenomenon was the appearance of the fire flower in the ruins of buildings. It had not been seen since the great Fire of London in 1666.

The following morning I went out to Bomber Command, where Air Marshal Harris was in charge, and looked over the pictures of the destructive raids they had made on Rostock, Augsburg, and other industrial cities. He showed me pictures of the Heinkel works where fuselages had been pulled out of the destroyed buildings and were lined up in the yard for assembly in the open. He told me that Bomber Command at that time had a total of 640 airplanes, of which 450 were in commission; but that he had pilots and crews for only 380 planes. I could see that R.A.F. Bomber Command was doing a magnificent job. Their operations gave us something to shoot at.

The following day, I had a conference about the needs of the Coastal Command and learned they wanted nine squadrons, or 144 planes. They figured attrition during seven months to be about one hundred, so they asked for a total of 244 B-17's for the Coastal Command between May 31 and December 31, 1942. They required a range of 1400 miles for their work. I looked in the record and saw they were receiving a total of 150 Catalina's between May and August. I told them the number of planes they asked for looked excessive, but that this would have to be settled upon one issue only: which was more important—using heavy bombers to carry bombs into Germany, or using them to hunt for submarines in the Atlantic? That was something for the higher command to decide.

The next day I visited the budding headquarters of Eaker's Eighth Bomber Command at Wycombe Abbey. Until the airplanes came, and he could get them into action, Eaker was keeping his staff in trim by turning them out for compulsory athletics every afternoon. Among the officers playing touch football on the lawn of the stately girls' school, beside a lake of peaceful swans, was a young man I had known since he was born. He was Major Frederick C. Castle, Ira's A-4, who had been our (1907's) "Class Baby." Eighteen months later, on Christmas Eve, 1944, Freddy, a Brigadier General then, was killed in action, leading his combat wing, and received posthumously the Medal of Honor.

Admitting the desire of our various bureaus and departments to help the British, I did notice this: When the Prime Minister or Air Chief Marshal Portal would ask what, if any, assistance could be expected from the United States Navy—if it could send any units over to help out on the Coastal Command—the answer was always, "We have too many activities at home." When asked what solution they might have for getting greater production and making more planes available to the British, or for securing more air transports, the answer of the Navy representatives was, "Stop manufacturing B-17's at the Long Beach Plant, and build cargo planes." (Someone else's production.) When Freeman asked what the Navy was able to give up to help, if the Army Air Forces stopped manufacturing B-17's, our Naval officers said, "Nothing—there is nothing the Navy could give that would help any." It looked to me, at that time, as if we were traveling a one-way street. The Army Air Forces was expected to give everything to everybody, and nobody was going to help the Army Air Forces. Naturally, from then on, I had to take a much more hard-boiled attitude.

With the R.A.F., we went over a map, and discussed in detail the airdromes the United States Air Force would use in England. Agreeing to eliminate all nonessentials and come down to the bare necessities of life, we talked about our reception centers; how our pursuit squadrons would work—first with the British, until our units became seasoned and could be formed into American sectors and commands; what sectors would be held by the bombers and what by the fighters; how we could pool our resources in the building of airdromes, which would be given us as fast as they were completed, all of them to be finished by December. There would never be enough airdromes for everybody, but by doubling up we could accommodate all the bombers and fighters we planned for.

Portal and I finally settled that I should take back with me, for approval by the President, the following points of agreement:

1. In general, the air strength in all theaters would be maintained or increased.

2. All American crews available would be supplied with American planes.

3. The United States would furnish to Operation BOLERO about 300 heavy bombers, complete with crews.

4. Except for a possible number of heavy bombers for Coastal Command, the British would be given no heavy bombers. In view of the duties performed, Coastal Command should get as many PBY's as they could from the Navy.

5. The R.A.F. counted on using four Coastal Command groups with as many Catalinas as they could get, 144 Flying Fortresses, or substitutes, with attrition of 100—this to be reached by December 31, 1942. (I assured Portal at that point I could not agree with him about the Flying Fortresses and suggested they take instead as many Liberators as they could get and forget about the B-17's.)

6. The British would take no medium bombers, except 108 B-26's for North Africa, to be manned and operated by American personnel in United States units.

7. The British could take all Martin "Baltimore's" they needed; furthermore, we would give them the "Hudson" production, which was a Lockheed plane, and we would furnish them with DB-7's (A-20's), the Douglas light bomber which they called the "Boston," with certain definite squadrons set to work with ground troops.

8. The British said 1440 pursuit planes were more than could possibly be used in England. They said they could use 1000, but could not furnish airdromes for any more.

9. In the Near East, the British needed 100 heavy bombers. If we couldn't operate them in that area, they must. Hence, we must increase what we called "the Halverson outfit" to one complete group, and Brereton's outfit by two groups, or, as an alternative, furnish 100 heavy bombers or replacements to the British.

Colonel Harry A. Halverson, at that time, had been designated as commander of a group of Liberators—slated to bomb Japan from China. However, en route to their Chinese bases through the Middle East, they had been held over in North Africa for training for a special bombing mission against Ploesti, the German oil production center in Rumania. General Brereton had been moved from the Far East and was in charge of all American aviation under Montgomery's command, helping the R.A.F. and the Desert Rats drive Rommel back from Egypt.

10. The British needed, and could not secure from any other source, 480 pursuit planes. They counted on American fighters being furnished.

11. Portal thought he must come to the United States with the Prime Minister to receive final decision in this case.

I told him I would take this agreement back to Washington with me, think it over, talk it over with the President, and get a final answer for him.

That night, I had another talk with Sir Henry Tizard, the Scientific and Research Chief, and was told the R.A.F. now had three jet-propulsion planes—one ready to fly; one with the engine on the test stand; one ready for installation in a long-range plane. They were very pleased with the results obtained so far, and had confidence in the future of jet propulsion. They had surging trouble, but thought they had it about licked. I outlined where we stood as a result of our jet experiments and operations to date.

A conference with Chaney indicated he was fearful that I personally was committing the Air Forces, when such commitments should clearly be decided by Spaatz and Hunter. Spaatz was to come over to take command of all Air Forces in England, and Hunter was to head the fighter units. Chaney was afraid that I was fixing too many things too firmly, such as the method of training pursuit units and individuals, and the specific airdromes to be used for fighters.

I assured him my only interest was to make certain that our fighter units got to England as soon as possible, and had airdromes and facilities ready for them when they arrived; that arrangements were made to acquaint them with the R.A.F. techniques of operation, communications technique, procedure and language; and that all such general subjects were fixed just as quickly as possible. How the units performed after arrival was not my job, but that everything be ready for them was my responsibility indeed. I also assured him I would fix things up so that except for fundamental principles, anything I agreed upon could be changed after Spaatz and Hunter came to take over. The main thing was to secure the maximum effectiveness so that as soon after their arrival as possible our Air Forces could get into action.

Later that night, I had a talk with Air Marshal Sholto Douglas, who was in charge of British fighter outfits, and told him what I had told Chaney about our fighters, their preliminary training, the airdromes, and the tie-in with Spaatz and Hunter. Hunter would command the United States Pursuit, but Douglas would direct all operations until they were able to stand on their own feet.

At night, at the hotel, Clark, Eisenhower, and I talked over conditions in England and the need for a theater commander who could meet the British senior officers on even terms. We agreed it must be a man who had the experience and knowledge of our ways of doing things, and was fully acquainted with our War Department plans. He must have the confidence of General Marshall and the Secretary of War. We also agreed that the man selected should get to London as soon as possible.

Eisenhower left, and Clark and I talked further about who the man should be. The two of us came to the conclusion that it should be Ike. Clark thought that since I knew Marshall better than he, I should present Eisenhower's name after the three of us told the Chief of Staff of our conclusion that a change should be made at once. That settled that matter for the moment—until we reached Washington.

The following morning I learned that Air Chief Marshal Portal was ready to sign the agreement about the allocation of airplanes to the R.A.F. It followed with few changes the ideas I had when I left Washington. That afternoon, I packed my bag and took off for "Chequers" for a visit with the Prime Minister. Admiral Towers accompanied me, and we arrived about 5:30 in the afternoon.

Present as guests that night were Ambassador Winant, Portal, General "Pug" Ismay, the Prime Minister's Military Aide, Harriman, Towers, and myself.

I have remarked before that often, during the forty years in which I watched air power grow up, I happened, with uncanny luck, to be present at the turning points.

This night, the 30th of May, in some ways topped them all, and for me personally provided luck that was rather mixed. As we sat down to

dinner I knew beforehand—even without the Prime Minister's jubilation
—that the R.A.F. was taking off for the greatest bombardment operation
ever launched. It was not merely, as Mr. Churchill had told Harry
Hopkins on the phone to the White House a few hours earlier, that the
R.A.F. was sending out twice as many bombers as had ever hit Germany
at once. It was not, for those of us who knew the R.A.F.'s actual heavy
bomber strength, a matter of literal belief in the powerful phrase "Thousand Raid." Of the 1047 "bombers" that took off from all over Middle
and North England for Cologne that night—including even little Oxford
trainers that could scarcely hope to reach the target—715 were twin-
engine Wellingtons, old Whitleys and so on, by the R.A.F.'s own
standards soon to be rated as medium bombers.

That didn't matter. The fact that Bomber Command had already carried out those impressive attacks on Rostock and Luebeck did not count.
Nor did the fact that 400 actual heavy bombers of the R.A.F. would
presently be causing more damage to city after German city than the
first "Thousand Raid" did to Cologne. This was the real beginning, in
the world's eyes and in Germany's eyes, of the campaign we later came
to term officially "Air Offensive Europe"—the "round the clock" destruction of Germany from the air. That night all of England was a
bomber base.

As an airman who had preached bombardment for so many years,
I was as thrilled as the Prime Minister himself. But—and here is what
I mean by "mixed luck"—as Commanding General of the U.S. Army
Air Forces, I happened to be on the spot at an ironic time. Of all the
moments in history when I might have tried to sell Mr. Churchill and
his R.A.F. advisers on the future of American precision bombardment
by daylight, I had picked the night when they were selling their own
kind of bombardment to the world.

It was not merely the difference between night and day operations.
It was a whole new conception of target values, the big beginning of
"night area bombing," as opposed to an attack on a precise industrial
or military objective. Although "aiming points" in Cologne were given
at the briefings, the crews soon understood that their high explosives
and incendiaries were really to be sown between these points, blasting
and gutting the whole city. As if higher headquarters were nervous
about their reaction to this new kind of task, the crews were briefed to
the effect that dead workmen and civil employees or workers demoralized
by the loss of homes and families were as much a blow to the German
war machine as smashed factories.

The target was as much public opinion as Cologne, with a special eye on opinion in America. Actually, the slim, newsprint-rationed papers in London next morning, and the BBC, could carry only a fraction of the enthusiasm that burst into print and excited broadcasts all over America in the next few days. Mr. Churchill and the R.A.F. knew it would be that way. One of the two American intelligence officers stationed at Marham that night has told me with amusement of the way in which Air Vice-Marshal Baldwin warned the crews that the whole world would be watching this performance, especially, he added with a wink, "our friends overseas" who needed a bit of jogging up. The American officer tells me there was a moment of embarrassment as the crews started to look his way, but the Air Vice-Marshal turned it into laughter by shouting jovially: "You see! They have their spies everywhere!"

Harris and Eaker came in for dinner to tell us how it was going. While we were eating, the Prime Minister, full of the subject of air power, asked certain technical questions about some of our airplanes which I couldn't answer. I said, "My pilot is a short distance away; could I bring him over?" Churchill said, "By all means." So I telephoned and Colonel Beebe came over, sat next to the Prime Minister at the table, and answered the technical questions about the capabilities and performance of some of our airplanes.

When it came time to go to bed after the long "sit up" hours the Prime Minister always enjoys, even when Thousand Raids are not in progress, Beebe was faced with the question of whether he should go home or whether he should stay at Chequers. Churchill solved it by saying, "You stay here and spend the night." Beebe answered, "But I didn't bring my pajamas." So the Prime Minister, who is about six inches shorter than Beebe, suggested lending him his. They scarcely covered him, but Gene Beebe slept in the Prime Minister's pajamas that night.

After dinner, Churchill and I went over the memorandum I had made during my conference with Portal. The Prime Minister gave me the impression that he was almost ready to accept the agreement in full, but I was to get his final answer the following morning. It was plain that now there would be renewed pressure from the British to get our four-engine bombers for the R.A.F.

The next morning, I did not awaken until about nine o'clock. A bell cord was within reach which was supposed to be used to call the valet. I pulled and pulled and pulled until 9:30, but nobody came. I couldn't find my clothes. Finally, when I was almost desperate, the valet appeared and gave them to me. Hot water was brought in and I shaved. Then I ordered a bath. The valet told me my bath was ready. I went down the hall, found an open bathroom, climbed into the tub and started scrubbing.

I had been in there hardly a moment when the door opened, the valet stuck his head in and said, "I beg your pardon, sir, but this bath is for Lady So-and-So. Your bath is down the corridor." But it was too late then.

When I finally went downstairs, no one was about but "Pug" Ismay. The Prime Minister was dictating in bed, and Portal had returned to his job in London. Ismay, Towers, and I had breakfast together and talked about the Raid. Apparently the German radio was screaming bloody murder. Cologne was still burning fiercely. Bomber Command had lost only 39 planes. After breakfast, Admiral Towers and I both had to go to the "johnny." The door was one of those cumbersome affairs with locks dating back to Elizabethan times. I had no trouble, but Admiral Towers couldn't get out. He called to me in great consternation to come and help him. Thirty-odd years before, he had contributed to the invention of aviation's first safety belt, but it couldn't aid him now.

I called the valet. He called the plumbers, the carpenters, and the chambermaids. It was Sunday, and they were all down at the pub in the village.

A bit later, with Mrs. Churchill, I was walking in the garden when to our surprise, we saw first the feet, then the blue uniform trousers, and finally the full uniform of an American admiral climbing out of a window on the first floor of Chequers Castle. Mrs. Churchill said, "My, what an extraordinary way to leave the house!"

From 11:15 until 1:15, the Prime Minister and I sat in the garden and talked about the new program for reallocation of airplanes. Finally, he agreed to the proposal I had made to Portal. I was ready to return to Washington.

That night I had my farewell talk with Portal and we went over each other's figures again. Next morning I said good-by to him, to Freeman and Sinclair; then to Winant and General Chaney. Winant sent this final message to the President: "England is the place to win the war. Get planes and troops over here as soon as possible."

I signed the various agreements with Portal, left copies with him, and brought other copies back to the United States with me.

After a stormy Atlantic crossing, our party, including Lord Mountbatten, Air Marshal Slessor, and Mr. Harriman, landed at Goose Bay at midnight where an incredibly bad cold meal was waiting for us. The

American mess sergeant said we were having trouble with the Canadians because of our superior rations. They wouldn't let us run our own mess. "In fact, General," said the mess sergeant, "they actually take our good food out and bury it in the woods." I made up my mind to do something about the setup at Goose the minute I got back to Washington.

After V-J Day, General Marshall wrote of the summer of 1942:

It was a very black hour.

In July, Admiral King and I went to London for further meetings with the British Chiefs of Staff to determine if there was not something that could be done immediately to lessen the pressure on the Soviets, whose armies were facing a crisis. Poverty of equipment, especially in landing craft, and the short period remaining when the weather would permit cross-Channel movement of small craft, ruled out the diversionary operation SLEDGEHAMMER for 1942.

After prolonged discussions, it became evident that the only operation that could be undertaken with a fair prospect of success that year was TORCH, the assault on North Africa. Landings there would be a long way from Germany, but should serve to divert at least some pressure from the Red Army, and would materially improve the critical situation in the Middle East. It was therefore decided, with the approval of the President and the Prime Minister, to mount the North African assault at the earliest possible moment, accepting the fact that this would mean not only the abandonment of the possibility for any operation in Western Europe that year, but that the necessary build-up for the cross-Channel assault could not be completed in 1943. TORCH would bleed most of our resources in the Atlantic, and would confine us in the Pacific to the holding of the Hawaii-Midway line and the preservation of communications to Australia.

General Eisenhower, who was then established with his headquarters in London, directing the planning and assembling of American resources, was, with the generous acceptance of the British Government, appointed Commander-in-Chief of the British and American Forces which were to carry out the landings in North Africa. . . . The target date was fixed for early November.

Things had moved fast after my return from England in June. The

320

document which I had signed jointly with Portal had helped us to jump a big hurdle in our race to build a U.S. Air Force at the same time we supplied our Allies. The President and General Marshall had listened with interest to my report on Churchill's and Portal's understanding in the matter of the delivery of planes. The Prime Minister's comprehension of our own problems, I pointed out, did not diminish one of his greatest fears: that we would not get planes to England in time, whether heavy bombers or troop-support types. He realized the necessity for a U.S. Air Force. He wished to see the biggest one we could get. But he wanted it over there—at once—fighting alongside the R.A.F. He feared that reasons, and good ones, would be advanced for delaying the movement.

I told the President that we were already doing everything possible to assure that our airplanes were sent to Britain on schedule in the numbers planned by Portal and myself; that we had settled that one way to keep all adjustments up to the minute was to get together personally once every six months. The President agreed with me in everything I reported, and told me if I ran into trouble at any time to let him know.

Of course, these conversations, taking place in June, preceded by several weeks the decision to make the North African invasion the all-out priority for 1942. At the Joint Chiefs' level, the U.S. Army, the Navy, and Air Forces were equally disturbed. For the moment, at least, my own top priority was knocked on the head. Our plan for the rapid build-up of an American heavy bomber force in Britain, striking at Germany itself with a thousand Flying Fortresses and Liberators by April, must wait.

I would shortly have to tell Tooey Spaatz, in London, and Ira Eaker, whose eager little nucleus of a Bomber Command was just then welcoming the arrival of its first combat group, that not only must the original schedule be abandoned, but this very bomb group with which they were about to begin, the 97th, would soon be taken away from them and sent to Africa. So would two of the next three heavy groups that followed the 97th to England. Of the eight fighter groups that Brigadier General Monk Hunter was to have assembled in England for a few weeks that late summer, only one, the 4th, made up of pilots who had flown in the R.A.F.'s American Eagle Squadron, would remain in the Eighth Air Force. The rest were all earmarked for North Africa. At the same time, I privately resolved that wherever the exigencies of the new priority permitted, I would somehow keep our Eighth Air Force building at the most rapid pace still possible.

The direct strategic bombing of Germany by the R.A.F. and ourselves remained, as I continued to state, the central road to Germany's defeat. Apart from the over-all effect of this air assault on Hitler's war factories, cities, fuel, and communications, and on the morale of the German people, it would produce rapid benefits for both the Russians and the two British-American fronts in Africa. This was subsequently proved by the way in which our Britain-based bombers began to pull the Luftwaffe back from those theaters to the defense of France and the Reich itself. Within ten months, the daylight attacks of our still small VIII Bomber Command had completely changed the disposition of the German Fighter Arm. In January, 1943, 42 per cent of the German fighter strength was concentrated in Western Europe, 33 per cent of it in Russia, and 25 per cent in the Mediterranean area. In October of that year, the line-up was 19 per cent on the Russian Front, 12 per cent in the Mediterranean, and in Western Europe 60 per cent. How much faster the relief for the Russian and Mediterranean fronts might have been effected had my original plan of a thousand heavy bombers in Britain by April not been interrupted, is indicated by the conventional estimate that TORCH set our bomber offensive back by four months. That air offensive over Europe, as planned and as later carried out jointly with the R.A.F. night bombers, was itself, of course, a Second Front.

Marshall wrote Eisenhower that the projected invasion of North Africa had, in the opinion of top advisers in Washington, only a fifty per cent chance of success, though he qualified this pessimism by saying it was "immediate and artificial" in his own view.

As we tried to build up the enormous preparations for TORCH without letting anybody know we were doing it, the uninformed pressures became tremendous. American popular opinion looked toward the Pacific. A separate intramural war, which, as we shall see, required a personal trip on my part to try to temper things down enough to get the necessary air power for TORCH, flared up at this same time. The Navy's carrier-based air victory at Midway did not settle, but vindicated in the Press the immediate need for more planes in the Pacific. To come from where? From us! From the Army Air Forces!

The cries naturally included a plea for heavy bombers. The Press, and the American people, didn't know about TORCH. All the smaller Air Forces I was just then setting up—and which were to grow, each one vitally important in its strategic spot, as any vein in the body is important —could not answer the public demand, the international demand, for a Second Front.

Butler, in Alaska, Brereton's Ninth Air Force arriving in the Middle East, Willis Hale's Seventh Air Force in Hawaii, such far-flung and unsung U.S. air efforts as our Persian Gulf Command or the outfit in Iceland, were doing critically important work. But they were not a Second Front. Still, everything taken away from each one of these hurt the balanced air war effort, as planned up to that moment, in some degree.

For replacements in planes and crews that hard winter, VIII Bomber Command used the people and the B-17's of the 92nd Bomb Group, part of its planned operational strength but now necessarily broken up. Most of the original combat personnel of the 92nd were lost in action, mourned doubly by their own old outfit because they went down as losses of the 91st, the 303rd, the 305th, or the 306th.

My own view of TORCH was based on a larger strategic aspect than that of air power alone. It seemed to me, and I was not alone in this idea, that we were dispersing our military power, even before we really had it. The "accepted" strategy against Germany was the massing of our full strength—air, ground, and sea—at the most direct point, and an all-out assault from England as soon as possible. But, despite the President's directive, not only did the Navy and other dissident points of view continue to argue, especially as the Pacific crisis grew; it was the President himself, with the Prime Minister, who decided to make this gigantic diversion, TORCH, our first priority. And having done so, it was presently Mr. Roosevelt who unwittingly gave ammunition to the Navy in its opposition to his own established plans by insisting that Guadalcanal be held "at all costs." This is not to imply that Guadalcanal should not have been held, or that the heroism of the Marines there was in any sense wasted. I simply mean to emphasize that the interservice and intertheater wars for priority continued as steadily as any effort against the foreign enemy, with no holds barred.

A natural word of encouragement from the President was at once seized upon as proof that he had changed his mind. As far as I know, the President, no matter what he said, never actually altered his original view that Germany must be defeated first. However, it is true that, as Mr. Stimson puts it, "the Mediterranean Basin fascinated him" more than it did the American Joint Chiefs of Staff.

A year before, in the summer of 1941, Hitler had given military students one of the most horrible examples in history of what the wasteful dispersion of forces can do. In the opinion of such members of the German High Command as Keitel, Jodl, Heusinger, and others at the end, it was just there that he lost the war, when he had only to follow through to win it.

Following the Battle of Britain, the German war machine still held Europe. Blunders and all, Germany was still in control of everything between the North Sea and the north shore of the Mediterranean, between the Channel and the Russian border. Where the Wehrmacht wasn't actually in control, it could acquire domination at will, merely by moving in, as in the Balkans. Despite the bravest resistance of the Royal Navy, Crete fell. Within three days, 25,000 German paratroopers, and other airborne troops, descended on Crete's three airfields, and captured that vital air-sea base. Wavell's fate seemed sealed. All that massed German air power, all that airborne power that had grabbed Crete, was now everywhere around him, and behind him, waiting to drop on his rear. As for Malta, even after the war the R.A.F. never estimated that even the most heroic air defense could withstand a concentrated assault by 400 bombers of the type the Germans now had within easy reach. The whole Mediterranean, Egypt, Suez, Syria, the oil fields of Iraq, the life line through to India was apparently gone.

Hitler solved it for the Allies. He suddenly pulled most of that assembled air strength back from the Mediterranean to the eastern border of the Reich to refit, and three weeks after the fall of Crete, invaded Russia.

The next year, in the spring of 1942, in the same gambler's spirit, Hitler and Goering suddenly withdrew a heavy part of their air strength from the Russian Front and again concentrated it in the Mediterranean. But now it was too late. The time Hitler had given us had enabled us to get American P-40's ("Kitty-bombers" they called the P-40's modified into fighter-bombers), A-20's ("Bostons"), and other American planes to Tedder's Middle East Command and to Coningham's Western Desert Command. The Desert War was no longer solely one of tank against tank, although it was still that too. It was no longer just British ground forces against outnumbering air superiority. It had become primarily what Tedder called: "A battle for airfields. Lose them, and you retreat. Hold them, and you advance." Tobruk had fallen at last because Rommel had captured the air bases ringing it in the Cyrenaican plains, putting Tobruk beyond the defensive range of the British fighters and attack bombers. But those R.A.F. planes were still intact, retreating with relatively small losses of their ground equipment in a masterful manner.

The numerical air superiority of the Axis notwithstanding (achieved on paper by adding in the Italian Air Force), the truth was that in the past year the R.A.F. had built up so tremendously that its air power in the Western Desert and in the Middle East strategic operations (bombing of shipping, ports, etc.) was at least equal to, if not greater than, the Luftwaffe's. The German air strength in the Desert had not built up at all, though the introduction of a certain number of Me-109's had provided marked improvement in quality. By the time the plans for TORCH were being completed, just before Alamein, Brereton's fighters, fighter-bombers, and B-25's had joined the British in the battle. His few B-17's and B-24's, operating singly and in pairs, usually at night, were already affecting the delicate balance of logistics.

That balance remained so tricky in this corner of the war that the loss of a single ship could spell either temporary victory (as Lewie Brereton wrote happily when one of his bomber units wiped out a good part of Rommel's immediate oil supply by sinking a 10,000 ton tanker), or could mean disaster (as when Lewie wrote me gloomily that the sinking of one British ship had cost him all the long-awaited equipment for a new depot at Gura in Eritrea, setting that project back several months). The cooperation of the Ninth Air Force tactical planes with Coningham's Western Desert Command, provided an invaluable experience for our American crews, flying the same type of aircraft. Brereton's few strategic bombers flew under Tedder's administrative jurisdiction but under Lewie's operational command. His force, at the time of Alamein, comprised only 164 of the 1281 British-American planes engaged, but they carried a weight out of proportion to their numbers. The Axis Air strength was about 2000, but well over half of these planes were Italian.

Meanwhile, General Geissler's Sicily-based Luftwaffe fleet gave Hitler more or less complete air superiority in the western half of the Mediterranean. It was a main cause of gloom to the TORCH planners, who decided, after unusually detailed deliberation by the Joint and Combined Chiefs of Staff, that since Algiers was already within the Luftwaffe's range, it might be suicidal to try to push any part of the landings farther east than say, Philippeville and Bone, the main idea being to land as close to Tunisia, the real goal, as possible.

After the invasion, when we had got so close but were still so far away, it was argued that we should have taken the risk. Admiral Sir Andrew Browne Cunningham, R.N., Ike's Naval Commander for TORCH, was emphatic about it, and said, in effect, that we had missed the boat by not landing closer to Tunis. But at the same time he was saying it, he had to express himself as "disinclined" to send any more shipping east of Bougie, because of what Geissler had already started to do from the air.

On the eve of TORCH there was no philosophic satisfaction among American air leaders—twenty-one years after Billy Mitchell had sunk the *Ostfriesland*—that from the military point of view, Mare Nostrum had become mostly an air problem. There was air power on both sides of the problem now, and in Northwest Africa the Allies held the short end. From the American point of view, TORCH offered about as poor an air deal as could have been dreamed up. Practically every one of our own principles for the use of air power in amphibious landing operations on a hostile mainland had to be violated.

The factor of surprise, the political machinations, fancied solutions, uncertain notions about whether the French would fight or not, ruled out any softening-up operations with our bombers. Anyway, even if there had been any strategic bases other than the jammed-up way station of Gibraltar, with the guns of Hitler's friend Franco pointing down on it through the barbed wire a few yards away, with that vulnerable gasoline cached all over the Rock, making Governor-General Mason-MacFarland and Eisenhower look for an all-out German air attack right up to the night of the invasion, there were no strategic targets in French Northwest Africa.

There were no industries to speak of, from the military point of view; no depots, oil stores, railroad yards, supply dumps other than a few installations we hoped to find intact for our own use if we got ashore. Certainly nobody wanted to harm that single narrow road along the coast from Casablanca through Algiers to Tunis, over which Patton's Western Task Force must hurry as fast as it could get itself and its air support together. The few precious airfields were not targets for our bombs but immediate objectives on the ground. Until they were secured, our planes would not be able to operate.

There could be no land-based air support for the men hitting the beaches through the mountainous Moroccan surf. Naval carrier-based aircraft, our own over the Moroccan coast, and U.S. Navy and Royal Fleet Air Arm planes at Oran and Algiers, would be their sole protection from the air until the French fields were seized and our ground people were able to service our arriving P-40's, and Air Marshal Welch's Spits at Algiers. We knew that we could count on the high quality of the Navy airmen at all points, but it was still a poor setup, and their ability to knock down the faster Dewoitines and French P-36's (remnants of Pierre Côt's pathetic attempt to buy a French Air Force after Munich) would be more a matter of their personal skill and courage than of the right conditions.

The first P-40's of General Joe Cannon's Western Air Task Force would have to fly ashore from a carrier or carriers, hoping to find their air service people at Mehdia airfield when they got there, instead of hostile Frenchmen. The air service people must land with the first wave. In any case, our P-40's would be out of gas.

We knew they could make it off the carriers all right, as we had landed 68 P-40's, reinforcements for India, China and Brereton, off the *Ranger* not long before. Despite the fact that none of the pilots had ever made such a take-off, all had got into the landing field at Accra, 125 miles away, without mishap, to start their journey across Central Africa to the Middle East, South Asia, and China. Also, our carrier, *Wasp*, had twice flown R.A.F. Spits off to the relief of Malta earlier in the year.

The planes accompanying more than supporting the landings at Oran and Algiers must first accomplish the long hazardous flight down from England to Gibraltar. All ended their flights nesting under Franco's guns when they made it.

The only other land in sight, as they waited for TORCH's D-Day, was Spanish Morocco, just across the Straits. From there, Ike and his staff, worrying about Hitler and Franco, could remember that the Luftwaffe's Ju-52's, in July, 1936, had flown the Moorish mercenaries to Northern Spain to put the Spanish dictator in business. The TORCH planes assembling at Gibraltar—until at last there were over six hundred of them on the narrow little field—would have to take off for Oran and Algiers long before the landings occurred. Arriving at Tafaraoui, Maison Blanche, and Blida airfields out of gas, they must hope that things had gone well. If not, they would be written off.

If things had gone well, then they could gas up and get quickly back into the air to meet the Luftwaffe counterattack that was sure to come. A long paratroop mission, coming all the way from England, was part of the plan, which eventually was carried out with all the high courage and all the high confusion I had expected. Worst of all the North African rainy season was at hand. Whichever side won the race for Tunisia would be sitting on the only air bases with adequately hard runways and dispersal points in that part of the world.

Because of the weird air aspects of the intended assault, I sat in on the detailed planning for TORCH to a far greater extent than I did on the tactical preparations for other landings. In time, however, I saw that, as usual, I must start working in some other part of the world, if the materiel for this particular operation was to be available.

I left Spaatz, who would be Eisenhower's over-all air commander, to carry out the movements from Britain to North Africa in general, and Brigadier General Jimmy Doolittle, whom I had put in command of the newly formed Twelfth Air Force, to work out the tactical details with Ike's staff in London.

Logistics were my biggest headache now. Where was the air power for TORCH to be assembled from? Like Marshall for the Army, and Ernie King for the Navy, for the Air Forces I was the end of the line in this respect. When, after long travail, sweating, and brilliant argument, the plans were at last settled upon in any given theater, its commander would turn to the Joint Chiefs and say: "Well, here it is. This is the minimum. This is what we need." Then what?

We had to get it for them. The Joint and the Combined Chiefs of Staff were entirely responsible to the President and the Prime Minister, naturally, but though the Big Two might disapprove some plan we had agreed upon and submitted—the priority of TORCH itself was a reflection of this—when they said Yes, it simply meant we had their approval to go ahead on our own. Having finally reached an agreement among ourselves, with all the international and interservice differences at stake, the Combined Chiefs were free, indeed ordered, to go out and get it. That probably meant taking it away from some other theater, from some of your own people, whether you were Air, Army, or Navy.

While all these preparations were going on in quiet chaos, and attempts from the Pacific to make that theater the top one were still strenuous, TORCH or no, the following things happened.

We carried out our first heavy bombardment mission against German-held Europe.

This was the mission by thirteen B-24's led by Colonel Harry A. Halverson, from Fayid, Egypt, on June 12, 1942, to attack the most important target in the war—the oil refineries at Ploesti. The target was not much damaged. The very improbability of this two thousand-mile round trip was its best protection, and enemy opposition was not heavy.

Though the ships had to land all over the Middle East on their return journey, four being interned in Turkey, only one was lost, in a crash landing at Habbaniya. The Russians felt this American bombardment mission on their Front with impressed surprise. The R.A.F., Tedder and his people, who had told Halverson my orders could not possibly be carried out, also felt it. The handwriting for the epic Ploesti mission of August 1, 1943, for the later attacks of the Fifteenth Air Force from Italy for the whole long-range American air offense, was on the wall. Had the headlines not been so full of the battle of Midway in the Pacific

that week, this extraordinary mission—virtually into the unknown—
would have been better appreciated at the time.

On July 4th, six American light bomber crews in R.A.F. Bostons
signalized the date by flying from the English base at Swanton Morley,
together with six R.A.F. crews, in a low-level attack on coastal airdromes
in Holland. Two of our crews and one R.A.F. crew were lost. Captain
Kegleman turned on the flak tower that had knocked out one of his two
engines, bounced a wing off the ground, destroyed the flak tower with
his guns, and came on home on a single prop. That night in London,
Eisenhower, reading this report of the first official American encounter
with the enemy in his Theater, wrote an immediate recommendation for
the D.S.C. across it.

On August 17th, commanded by Brigadier General Ira C. Eaker, the
first dozen B-17's of the Eighth Air Force made their famous beginning
against Rouen. Next day found twenty-four helping in the Commando
landings at Dieppe; two days later twelve again being used against the
little Le Trait shipyards. But our heavy bomber missions were started,
even if their communiqués, self-conscious about the R.A.F.'s tons, announced the number of "pounds" they had dropped.

Their fourth mission was the smallest yet, but made the most history
so far. On the morning of the 21st, after a couple of aborts for mechanical failures, a formation of only nine Forts, on its way to bomb the
docks at Rotterdam, was nearing the Dutch coast when it was recalled,
ordered by radio to abandon the mission and return. As the Forts turned
along the coast, out of the clouds suddenly appeared twenty to twenty-
five of the toughest fighters in the world—all FW-190's and Me-109's.
In a running battle, the unescorted Forts beat them off. In the B-17 of
Lieutenant Starks, his copilot, Lieutenant Walter, was killed, first Fortress crewman of the Eighth Air Force to die in action. Starks' own
hands were badly burned. Up into the cockpit climbed Lieutenant
Sconiers, the bombardier—a washed-out flying cadet, as I remember—
and took over at the controls. And they came on home behind the others,
straggling on two engines, crash landing at an R.A.F. base, but home!
The first of thousands!

What a pattern this became! In Washington our hearts soared. Starks
and his crew were the first of that long gallant company who were to
capture and then hold on to the daytime air over Europe for a year and
a half until the long-range fighter escort came.

I had seven air forces overseas by then, as well as the four big ones
at home, and a letter from Butler in Alaska summed up the mail from
all of them: "I need everything!"

The only place where everything was going fine was on the North Atlantic Ferry Route.

That bad meal I had had at Goose had done history a good turn. As soon as I reached home I had hit on the very man. I had my old friend of two wars, Major A. D. Smith (later promoted to Brigadier General) fly up from Albuquerque, told him what I wanted up at Goose, and without even giving him a chance to change out of his summer sun-tans, shot him off to Labrador. We never had any serious trouble up in that vital spot after that. The Canadians liked A. D. Smith, and he liked them.

Different climatic conditions, whether in the Arctic or the South Pacific, were now constantly bringing out freakish facts about our radios and other equipment. Sometimes, at certain temperatures, the best equipment wouldn't work at all. All this emphasized the troubles global warfare would bring to us.

For example, the shipping shortage being what it was, we were overjoyed at the capture of all the gasoline in the Dutch East Indies. Manna from heaven! Our planes out there would have their fuel right at hand, without worrying about long-range transportation. But things didn't work out quite that easily.

At that time we were installing leak-proof tanks in all our airplanes. During the tests in the States, and by the British overseas, these tanks worked fine. However, they had no sooner reached Australia and been fueled with the Dutch East Indies gasoline, than the self-sealing compound within the metal shell started to decompose. This left us with a mass of jelly inside our tanks that not only eliminated completely the self-sealing features, but also clogged fuel lines. Immediately, we had to find some kind of composition for treating the self-sealing tanks that had to use gasoline with such high aromatic content.

Sometimes we had to guard against the wrong mixture of human "chemicals." When ABDA (American-British-Dutch-Australian) Command was formed, in the winter of 1941–42, General Wavell was put in command, with General Brett as Deputy. It was thought Wavell might be able to assemble enough ground troops, equipment, Air Force, and Navy to stop the Japanese before they occupied Sumatra, Java, and New Guinea. However, Java capitulated early in March; Sumatra, late in March. This completely destroyed ABDACOM, so Wavell, out of a job, returned to India. Brett, an excellent administrative and supply man, went to Australia, where he was to build up a Supply Service and take command of all our troops in Australia, pending General MacArthur's arrival.

General MacArthur arrived on March 17, 1942, and, from the first, it became evident that he and General Brett could not get along. Brett should have done the "getting along," as he was the junior. When I heard of the situation, I talked it over with General Marshall. He agreed with me a change had to be made.

Looking over my officers, I thought of George Kenney, an officer who had served in World War I, and who had performed very successfully various and sundry jobs in the Air Corps since then. He had served with the G.H.Q. Air Force; done duty at the Infantry School; been in command of one of our Air Forces in the United States; had worked at the Materiel Division, and he had a general over-all picture of conditions in the United States. His name was sent to MacArthur, accepted, and within a very short time Kenney was on his way to Australia as Commander of General MacArthur's Air Force.

Always present was the question: To whom should we allocate our airplanes? It wasn't always a problem of "Theater-itis." One of our greatest troubles was in determining just how many transport planes should be left with the commercial airlines here at home. On this point an interesting document was sent to me which originated with the President. It was dated May 5, 1942, and was titled, "A Memorandum for the Secretary of War and the Chief of Staff." It read:

> I fully appreciate the needs set forth in the Chief of Staff's memorandum of April 27th in regard to Transport planes for Russia, and the need for Transport planes in Panama and in Alaska and in later operations in several other places.
>
> But it does not make much sense to me, in view of these great needs, not only in the future, but at the present, merely to carry out the mechanical allocation of these Transport planes of the U.S. commercial airlines by earmarking them for Army use.
>
> Please let me know just how many U.S. commercial airline planes carrying passengers and carrying U.S. mail there are in the United States, together with their age, carrying capacity and radius.
>
> The old expression, "pigs is pigs," should be translated into the modern term, "planes is planes."
>
> No matter what planes are in civilian hands at the present time, they are available for Army and Navy use, and the Army and Navy say they are short of planes.
>
> *Signed:* F.D.R.

In reply, I sent to the Chief of Staff a memorandum for submission to the President, answering his questions and covering the following principles for approval:

a. *Domestic Air Carriers:* Only personnel engaged directly in prosecution of our war program would travel by commercially operated airplanes, and no cargo or mail would be carried, except that required by our military services, or in the production of supplies destined for military service.

b. *American Air Carriers Operating Outside the U.S.*. The transportation of personnel, cargo, and mail would be limited to the requirements of our international policies.

This the President approved.

On May 6, 1942, I received another memorandum from the President, dated May 5, 1942, marked "Secret," which read:

MY DEAR GENERAL ARNOLD:
I gather that the air ferry route to China is seriously in danger. The only way we can get certain supplies into China is by air.

I wish you and Mr. Lovett would confer immediately with Dr. Soong and General Shen on alternative air routes. I want you to explore every possibility, both as to airplanes and routes. It is essential that our route be kept open, no matter how difficult.

Very sincerely yours,
FRANKLIN D. ROOSEVELT

Attached to that note was another from Harry Hopkins:

DEAR HAP:
The President is very anxious that you see Soong today sometime, if you can.

H.L.H.

I saw Dr. Soong that same day, and went over with him the plans we had for building up the Air Transport Command for carrying supplies into China. Soong seemed to be well satisfied, and assured me he would convey to the Generalissimo the message I gave him about the airlines.

Constantly claiming attention were new ideas about how the war would be won; what we should do with reference to certain areas. There follows a memorandum from the President:

WHITE HOUSE
Washington

Very Confidential

MEMORANDUM FOR GENERAL ARNOLD:
T. V. Soong tells me that:
a. A very large amount of Japanese equipment is being made at Shanghai.
b. This equipment is dependent upon power from the Shanghai Power Plant, which is the only source of power.

c. If this power plant were destroyed, it would slow up Japanese production for six months.

He therefore suggests that, at the earliest possible moment, we bomb the Shanghai Power Plant, and try to put it out of business. His thought is that our planes should take off from India, thus constituting a complete surprise. The planes, after putting the Power Plant out of business, to land at the Chengtu Field near Chungking.

Will you speak to me about this at your leisure?

F.D.R.

My reply was sent the following day, in which I stated that Dr. Soong's proposal for bombing the Shanghai Power Plant was being studied very carefully, and that the preliminary report indicated it might be possible to bomb the plant from India, stopping either en route to or returning from the target at some point in China to refuel.

I was always trying to keep our bombing programs headed toward a definite objective. We couldn't just bomb anything that happened to catch the bombardier's eye, or the eagerness of well-meaning laymen at home. A scientific selection of the right targets around the world was as important as the ability to hit them. A formulation of these objectives into a whole bombardment philosophy, a related system of targets whose destruction would most probably reduce the enemy's war potential, was as precise and tricky a part of our global air war as the dropping of our bombs. In the deliberations of the Combined and the Joint Chiefs of Staff, the question of target priorities for our bombers, especially over the heavily dispersed areas of industrialized Germany, remained high on the agenda, though when Portal and Spaatz were appointed as the Combined Chiefs' deputies for strategic bombing operations, they operated with fairly free hands.

At that time, July–August, 1942, Lieutenant Colonel Richard D. Hughes and Major Henry Berliner, who, with General Hansell, Colonel (presently General) Cabell, and others, had helped start the nucleus of my Air Intelligence setup in Washington, were already wrestling with this problem in England. The so-called "Joint Target Committee," or "Jockey Committee," or whatever its final designation may have been, ultimately resulted in a remarkable body of operational intelligence. By the end of 1943, the information available to us when we considered attacking any target in Germany reflected a combined knowledge about that specific place which included everything known about it at that minute. The details ranged from the most abstract evaluations of civilian scientists through the best British-American photo interpretation; the latest reports of our own and the R.A.F.'s combat crews; the reports of

General Donovan's OSS operatives behind the German lines; the careful estimates of British Ministry of Economic Warfare experts, of our own Bureau of Economic Warfare, and what not.

Often, in the case of critical targets, engineers who had built or worked in the plant under discussion and knew every foot of it, sat with our planners. Our target data, with very few exceptions, became so accurate that a young Air Division bombardier could brief his commander and his staff on the most vulnerable aiming points within a given factory area as precisely as if he had been walking through the German plant himself that afternoon.

A file of the critical targets in Japan and Asia was also being started in Washington.

Accordingly, when we got a message such as the one concerning the power plant at Shanghai, that installation was thrown into the general list of targets, and evaluated with a view to determining what effect its destruction would have on the enemy's operations, as compared with all the other aiming points under consideration.

Early in the summer, the various commanders in the Southwest Pacific began yelling their heads off for airplanes. Nine heavy groups were supposed to go to the Middle East; eleven to the projected North African operations, and nine more were to go to the Southwest Pacific area. Out of a total of fifty-four groups originally slated for the air offensive based in England, this left only twenty-five. I could not see any logic in sending the nine groups to the Southwest Pacific at that time.

> The Air Forces of the United Nations (I wrote the Chief of Staff on July 29th) are the only weapons at our command with which we can, at this time, exert direct pressure against Germany. The operations of these air forces are now, and must remain for many months, our only hope of a second front. Further, air action is the only direct offensive operation against the Germans which is not completely contingent upon the status of the Russian Front.
>
> Successful air operations depend upon the continual application of massed air power against critical objectives. Germany remains our primary objective, and I feel strongly that the Air Force operating directly against her, which is permitted only from Bases in the United Kingdom, must be maintained in sufficient strength to permit strict adherence to this principle.
>
> Under the terms of our latest plan, Western Europe becomes virtually an air theatre. Our air strength in this theatre, however, has become reduced to less than half the strength available under the combined Air-Ground Plan. Comparison with the original concept of this as an air theatre shows a great discrepancy.

In the Southwest Pacific Area, the initiative still rests with the enemy, and suitable objectives may not be available for effective full-scale operations. It should also be noted this theatre cannot, at this time, safely and properly sustain operations of an Air Force augmented over nine additional Groups because of the dangerous concentration which would result from limited Base areas and Base facilities.

In order to employ most effectively Army Air Force units, and direct action against vital enemy objectives, I strongly urge:

a. The maximum number of Air Force units be committed to direct action against Germany from United Kingdom bases, as early as possible.

b. The reinforcement of the Southwest Pacific Theatre by nine Groups not be initiated until the modified BOLERO and TORCH Plans have first been completely implemented.

c. Under no circumstances should any Air Force units be held in mobile reserve in the United States.

Signed: H. H. ARNOLD.

I find among my notes, dated August 7, 1942, the following:

"Lunch at the White House—the President; Mrs. Roosevelt; Queen Wilhelmina; her Lady-in-Waiting, also her Chief of Staff; Admiral King; General Arnold and Admiral Leahy."

After lunch we were asked up to the President's study to help outline to Queen Wilhelmina our progress in the war. The Queen, the President, and I got into the White House elevator and started up—and the damned thing got stuck between floors!

On August 24th, the President asked General Marshall to:

Have General Arnold submit his judgment of the number of combat aircraft, by types, which should be produced for the Army and our Allies in 1943, in order to have complete air ascendancy over the enemy.

This report should be prepared without consideration of any existing schedules, or production possibilities, or any other competing military requirements. I am asking for this because I would like to know what the theoretical requirements are, to get complete control and domination of the air.

I realize fully, however, there are limiting factors to the creation of air power, such as the availability of pilots, high-octane gasoline, transportation, competition of other essential critical munitions of war.

Also, I would like you and Admiral King to submit a second schedule, based on these realities, and the proper relationship of air power to the Navy and our ground forces.

Four days later I submitted a plan to the Chief of Staff which went to the President, for a total of 134,934 operating planes in the U.S. Services, of which the U.S. Army Air Forces would have a total of 60,670 combat planes, 32,647 training planes—a grand total of about 99,000. In general, the projected strength list for the various operating agencies ran about as follows:

Army Air Forces	60,000
Navy	2,500
Great Britain	14,300
Australia	3,100
New Zealand	792
Canada	2,464
Netherlands	155
Russia	12,000
China	2,540
Brazil	577
Mexico	149
Other Latin American countries	158
Total combat planes	98,735

As a matter of fact, the figures for the Army Air Forces came out very close to that by the end of the war. Instead of having 60,000 combat planes, we actually had 57,000.

As the war in the Pacific developed, and the request for additional airplanes grew more and more frequent, it became increasingly evident to me that sooner or later I must make a trip to the South Pacific to determine exactly what the situation was, and to what extent, if any, our Air Force plans, the type of equipment or the number of planes being used, would have to be changed. According to the best estimate I could get, the United States, in all the Central and South and Southwest Pacific areas—in other words, including MacArthur's, Ghormley's, and Nimitz' commands—had a total of 1314 airplanes available for use, with 302 more en route, making a grand total of 1616. The best figures we could get for the Japanese indicated they had a total strength of 554.

The advantage on the Japanese side, however, lay in unity of command. They had one commander who could move troops, ships, airplanes from one section of the theater to another to get superiority whenever and wherever desired. He was not hampered by having to coordinate all his actions with several other commands.

Furthermore, by operating on interior lines, and being able to move their forces around as desired—for instance, from MacArthur's Front to Nimitz' Front—the Japs had a further distinct advantage over the United States' forces. We had established artificial boundaries between Ghormley's (later Halsey's) Command and MacArthur's Command, between MacArthur and Nimitz.

There were constant disagreements about the limitations and capabilities of the P-39's we had in combat in the Southwest Pacific. We weren't helped very much by the reports we received from our U.S. Army Commander in the Southwest Pacific, General M. F. Harmon (AAF) who stated the P-39 was of no use in operations in his theater, except in an extreme emergency. The Navy F-4-F was of much greater value. Harmon wanted fighters of the P-38 type.

It was naturally difficult for us in Washington to understand this, for the score of P-39's against Japanese Zeros up to that time was four to one in favor of the P-39's. During the last week in August, or about a month prior to the time about which I am writing, the score was two to one. Also, back in the United States our test pilots showed the P-39 had performance at least equal to, and in some cases superior to the Navy F-4-F. It was supposed to have better fire power, better armor, tank protection, and more speed at certain altitudes, but was not so maneuverable, and could not climb so fast.

Meanwhile, we had no P-38's available. We were having production difficulties with the Lockheed Plant, and only a very few P-38's were being produced. We told General Harmon he could improve the P-39's by taking out about 1500 pounds of equipment; that we had asked General MacArthur if he could spare any P-38's, but MacArthur had said No. As soon as General Harmon began yelling about the poor performance of the P-39's, Admirals Ghormley and Nimitz took up Harmon's battle cry and shouted to high heaven, until every brass hat in Washington heard the echoes.

As stated before, I was somewhat at a loss to know what to do next. The Southwest Pacific was the secondary war theater. The best information we had indicated that the Japanese had only about 535 planes spread from the Celebes eastward to the Solomon Islands, inclusive, and of that number, 150 were on two carriers. The United States had, in Australia, in the Southwest Pacific islands, and in Hawaii, a total of 900 Army Air Force planes, with 280 more en route. Furthermore, at that particular moment, there were only two bases from which land-based planes could operate against the Japanese in the Solomons. Yet, the Navy commands were asking for more and more planes. We did not have them to spare, without taking them away from the European Theater.

We recognized the fact that the Navy was hard-pressed at Guadalcanal. They did need a "shot in the arm"—and needed it badly; but I was not sure that the way to give it to them was by sending airplanes that might better be used against the Germans from England.

So I was not surprised when General Marshall said he thought it was a good time for me to go to the Southwest Pacific and have a look around. I said, "O.K. Perhaps it will help me to change my ideas on the disposition and employment of aircraft." The most immediate way I could help TORCH and the Eighth Air Force was to turn my back on both and go to the Pacific.

That same day, there was quite a flare-up at the Joint Chiefs of Staff meeting, when Admiral King asked for more planes for the South Pacific. I said planes were not what they needed: landing fields were the determining factor; not planes. All they could do with the planes, in excess of 80 or 100, was to let them sit on the few landing fields they then had. With no training, the pilots would get stale, while in England they could be used against the Germans every day.

King said, "There should be a reconsideration of allocation every time there is a new critical situation; the Navy is in a bad way at this particular moment." That particular moment was September 16, 1942. I told King that General Marshall and I had agreed to divert fifteen P-38's to the Southwest Pacific, and to send one squadron of heavy bombers to that area from Hawaii. He replied we must keep the Southwest Pacific saturated. I asked, "What is the saturation point? Certainly, not several hundred planes sitting on airdromes so far in the rear that they cannot be used. They will not do us any good, and may do us some harm." Then I told him I was getting down there to see what, if anything, should be done, and requested that further action be withheld until my return.

General M. F. Harmon was in command of the Southwest Pacific Area for the Army. He had under him, General Alexander (Sandy) Patch, Ground Force Commander, and General Nathan Twining, Air Force Commander. I had known "Miff" Harmon since he was a cadet at West Point and I was at Governors Island, and I had served with him in practically every grade from second lieutenant up to the time I made him my Chief of Staff, prior to his going to the Southwest Pacific. I had great confidence in his ability. He had been in the Air Force for over seventeen years, and knew airplanes and how to operate them. So I was eager to go down and talk with him about actual conditions.

Before leaving for the Southwest Pacific, on September 18, 1942, I saw General Marshall and asked him for some hints about what I should or should not do. He gave me some very good suggestions which I appreciated and tried to follow. Here they are:

1. Listen to the other fellow's story.

2. Don't get mad.

3. Let the other fellow tell his story first.

On the 20th, with General St. Clair Streett, Colonel C. P. Cabell, and Colonel Emmett McCabe, all on my staff in Washington, I flew from Hamilton Field to Hawaii, and from there continued on, via Christmas Island, Fiji, to New Caledonia. We were met at Honolulu by General Delos Emmons and General Willis Hale. General Emmons, before taking command of the Hawaiian Air activities, had been in command of the G.H.Q. Air Force in the United States. He had just returned from the South Pacific where he had spent considerable time with General Harmon, Admiral Ghormley, and General MacArthur. I was somewhat depressed after hearing Emmons' report on MacArthur's estimate of the situation. MacArthur, at the time, he thought, seemed not to be in too good health; and blamed our Air Force commanders for failure of the Air in the Philippine Islands.

In my talk with Admiral Nimitz and his Staff, I found Nimitz to be far more optimistic than General Emmons. Emmons was convinced that Guadalcanal could not be held; Nimitz was just as sure it could be. Nimitz' idea was that the Japanese shipping losses were so great they could not keep up such operations indefinitely. The Japanese were getting worried. Nimitz' estimate was:

1. The Japanese would probably hold the north shore of New Guinea, try to take Port Moresby, and move southeast against Guadalcanal.

2. They had only half as many men down there as we had.

3. We could meet their move and defeat it.

4. The Guadalcanal Airport would be ready for use within a few days.

5. The Japanese would move down through Ellice Island.

6. The Japanese losses in planes last month had been terrific—the total from Midway through Guadalcanal to New Guinea being 650 planes.

7. All planes on two Japanese carriers had been lost.

8. The Japanese planes and pilots were both of inferior quality, and the *war could be won in the Pacific.*

9. The bombardment of Germany was of no use.

10. The target of first priority for our aviation in Australia was shipping.

11. There was no need for more aircraft in Alaska.

12. The Japanese had no idea of moving eastward through Alaska.

13. The Japanese would not reinforce Kiska with either planes or ships.

14. The Japanese were moving everything to the southeast—planes,

troops, and ships—from Sumatra, the Philippine Islands, Borneo, and the Celebes.

Nimitz admitted his losses of ships had been very heavy. Before I left Admiral Nimitz, I told him I would see him on my return.

No one I had met so far had a very good idea of the location of the Japanese main body. Everyone was certain it was somewhere north of New Guinea, northwest of Guadalcanal, and perhaps south of the Island of Truk.

We took off for the Southwest Pacific and, after stops at Christmas Island, Vite Levu (the headquarters of the western Air Force), and Tonga Tabu, landed on New Caledonia. "Nate" Twining was waiting for us and after we landed we took a B-17 and flew the 120 miles to another airport, 30 miles from the city, which had two short runways.

For the first time on this trip, we experienced landing on pierced-steel plank runways—a development that General Gene Reybold, Chief of the Army Engineers, and I had gone into quite extensively early in the war. Now it was being used all over the world, enabling heavy airplanes to land and take off as smoothly as at La Guardia, in places where previously it was not safe for a man to walk.

General Patch was waiting for us when we landed at Nouméa, and we drove to the city. General Harmon was at Guadalcanal at the time. We stayed at Patch's quarters where we changed our clothes and then went out to Admiral Ghormley's headquarters ship.

It was obvious to me that the Naval officers in this area were under a terrific strain. It was also obvious that they had chips on their shoulders. Admiral Ghormley said he had been so busy he had not been able to leave his headquarters office on the ship for about a month. I assured him that probably was the cause of some of his troubles, because no man —I don't care who he is—can sit continuously in a small office, fighting a war, with all the complicated problems that come up, without suffering mentally, physically, and nervously. A change of scenery is required for anyone doing a wearing job under constant strain.

I had been told when I was in London that I carried with me the "Arnold Guillotine"—meaning that I always cut down on the requirements and the allocations of airplanes and personnel so that no one ever got what he asked for. Just what the Navy command at Nouméa thought of me, and why, I do not know. Obviously, there was something about my arrival I did not understand. Admiral Ghormley lost no time in telling me that this was *his* theater and that no one could tell him how to command it. I assured him all I wanted was information; I was not trying to tell him in any way how to run his command. Things smoothed down after that, but it was clear that Ghormley and the other Naval officers in that area—Admiral John ("Slew") McCain and Admiral Daniel Callaghan—were very worried about the situation there.

Admiral Ghormley was particularly concerned about the logistics of his operations. He had eighty ships in the harbor which he could not unload. Gasoline and supplies at Guadalcanal were very short. Ships were hard to get into Guadalcanal. He feared another big movement by the Japanese to the southeast; and the Marines were holding on only by a shoestring.

The first thing that amazed me was those eighty ships in the harbor at Nouméa that couldn't be unloaded. One reason Ghormley's people gave was that they didn't know what was on the ships; consequently, they explained, the transports had to be sent down to New Zealand to be completely unloaded, and new manifests made out. This, when there was a distinct shortage of shipping in all other theaters of the world! At that moment the planners of TORCH were going nearly crazy in their search for ships.

Admiral McCain was Admiral Ghormley's air strategist. He had been working with our air men, particularly with Colonel "Blondy" Saunders, who was up at Espiritu Santo. Admiral McCain knew how our pilots operated. He also knew the technique of our heavy bomber operations. He never hesitated to say so, either, when he wanted to clinch his remarks.

It was obvious the Navy could not hold Guadalcanal if they could not get supplies in, and they could not get supplies in if the Japanese bombers continued to come down and bomb the ships unloading supplies.

Admiral McCain was perfectly frank in his statements. They must have B-17's to send out on reconnaissance and they must have fighters to stop the Japanese bombers. This was also amazing to me, in view of the propaganda we had heard prior to the war, that the big PBY's, the Navy flying boats, were the airplanes the Navy was going to use for reconnaissance and on long-range patrols. Here they were asking for our long-range bombers to do their work for them.

After we left Admiral Ghormley, General Patch was very insistent that the Navy had no plan of logistics; that the Marines and the Navy would both have been in one hell of a fix had he not dug into his reserve stock and furnished them with supplies. General Patch said the Army had to give the Navy and Marines 20,000 pairs of shoes and tons of other items in order to make the Navy's operations on shore effective. Further, the Navy had not given importance to either airports or gasoline. Accordingly, for some time after landing on Guadalcanal the planes had no reserve of gasoline at all, very little for actual operations, and but one airport.

When I tried to find out about the relative merits of the P-39's and the other airplanes, General Twining said his pilots had found the P-39's very satisfactory. Admiral McCain quoted his pilots as saying they reluctantly accepted the possibility that the P-39 might be O.K., but wanted nothing but P-38's.

After leaving Admiral Ghormley's office, I went back to General Patch's headquarters and there met Admiral D'Argenlieu, French Military Commander of New Caledonia, who was saying good-by and heading back for Fiji, Tahiti, and Dakar. He did not say it, but everyone assumed he was moving in accordance with orders from General de Gaulle.

My estimate, upon leaving Admiral Ghormley's headquarters, was this: So far, the Navy had taken one hell of a beating and at that time was hanging on by a shoestring. They did not have a logistic setup efficient enough to insure success. The Marines were very tired and would grab at anything as a possible aid—something to restore their confidence; at that moment everyone just happened to be thinking of B-17's and P-38's.

Talk among the Navy staff officers indicated that conditions in New Guinea were very, very bad. One heard the Australians would not fight. They would give up without firing a shot. Port Moresby would probably be taken. The Japanese would take over all of New Guinea soon. It looked to me as if everybody on that South Pacific Front had a bad case of jitters.

The next day I went back to see Admiral Ghormley and his staff. Admiral McCain came to me and said, "Your bombers are doing no good over in England; your fighters are being wasted in Europe. Here is where they can be of use; here is the only place where they can get results. MacArthur may need them, but we need them more than he does."

So the whole question revolved around: "Where is this war to be won? What is our plan for winning the war—if we have a plan? Is this a local affair, and should it be treated as such?" Quite obviously, I thought, everyone in the Navy Department and in the South Pacific should be indoctrinated with the idea there was a United States plan— an Allied plan—for winning the war, and all must conform to it.

Everything I had seen up to that time indicated the necessity of having one leader—one command extending from Honolulu to Australia; one commander who could dictate an operational policy against one foe; one man who could move his air, sea, and ground forces on his own initiative to the place or places where they would do the most good. The Japanese, in that respect had, as I say, a distinct advantage over us.

When I went into the question of using P-38's out of Nouméa, I was confronted with the fact that they had no way to get them from the ships on which they arrived to flying fields. They were too big to get over the roads, and there were no docks near the airfields. It looked as if we might have to float them to a point up the beach where an airport could be improvised.

After talking with General Harmon, I was convinced he had reversed his position on the P-39's; he now thought it was a very good plane; probably not as good as he would like to have, but good enough for fighting the Japanese.

Another problem was immediately brought to my attention. There was a general campaign in the Navy against high-altitude bombing, and it apparently went from top to bottom, although our high-altitude B-17's had made plenty of hits and had, on occasions, turned back Japanese movements headed toward Guadacanal and toward New Guinea. On most of their missions, our heavy bombers were operating at their extreme range. This was the worst possible condition for securing bombing accuracy, yet it was a daily affair.

One thing I thought was very unfortunate: General Patch had two divisions on New Caledonia which were not being used at Guadalcanal. He was ready and eager to use either one or both of them, but he was never given the opportunity by the Naval commander. In spite of that, the Marines used to march past his house and chant, "Why doesn't the Army fight? Why doesn't the Army come up to Guadalcanal? What is the Army down here for?"

The Marine transport planes, like their other units, were doing an excellent job. A grand job! They made the 800-mile trip into Guadalcanal, carried enough gas for the return trip, and still lugged 3000 pounds of cargo. And they carried out as many of the wounded as their planes would hold.

On September 25th I left Nouméa and headed for Brisbane, some 850 miles away. We arrived there at noon and found General Kenney waiting for us. We took off in a Lockheed for an airport closer to Brisbane, where General MacArthur and General Dick Sutherland met us. Almost as soon as he saw me, General MacArthur started talking about the Japanese and the right plan for winning the war.

MacArthur said:

1. The Japanese were better fighters than the Germans.

2. The pick of the Japanese was in the South Pacific.

3. He did not have the troops to hold the Japanese back.

4. The Air Force had increased in efficiency materially after the arrival of General Kenney. General Walker and General Whitehead were outstanding and he would not exchange his Air Force units for any others.

5. He was afraid the Japanese could take New Guinea at will; they could take the Fiji's and could control the Pacific Ocean.

6. The Japanese general strategy was to move into the Aleutians and be ready for a general move into Alaska.

7. He needed 500 more airplanes to hold the Japanese. Our planes were fine, excellent! Give him any kind of combat planes!

8. England could only be considered as a "besieged citadel."

9. It would be very difficult to establish a Second Front from England.

10. Movements into North Africa would be a waste of effort.

11. A sufficient number of air bases could never be established in England to provide air cover for a Second Front.

12. The Japanese had better coordinated teams than the Germans.

13. Our present "cordon defense system" across the Pacific was as old and out of date as the horse and buggy.

14. Our plan should be to give more aid to Russia; put troops in there and work from interior lines against Germany and Japan.

15. We should stop building up an Army that we couldn't use; building tanks and autos we couldn't send overseas.

16. We should build up Australia as a reservoir of supplies, troops, and planes, and use them in any direction against the Japanese.

My impression, after talking with General MacArthur, was that he was very battle-weary; he had not, as yet, had a chance to recover nor to get the whole world picture. He did not know the details of what was going on in the other theaters. I was convinced of this, for I have always had the most profound respect for his judgment, his knowledge, his intuition, and his method of doing business. I have always classed him as one of our top-notch military leaders. I was sure the statements he made to me as he walked up and down in his office were not ones he would make six months hence. Therefore, most of them should be ignored.

One thing was certain—and that was the main thing I had wanted to find out from General MacArthur: he had implicit confidence in General Kenney, in General Walker, and in General Whitehead. He liked the airplanes and equipment he had and he believed that with more airplanes he could hold the Japanese, and with more troops, drive them back.

In the afternoon I had a talk with General Kenney who told me among other things how he had carried an entire brigade of ground troops by air from Australia over to Port Moresby in time to stop the Japanese. When it looked impossible, he had cut the chassis frames of trucks in half with acetylene torches so as to get them into airplanes, and after they landed in New Guinea, had used the same acetylene torches to weld the frames together again for the battle.

Kenney had certainly developed into a real leader and he had one of the finest groups of pilots and combat crews I have ever seen. Many of those who were nervous and worn out, and who had wanted to go home when he first got there, had withdrawn their requests and now wanted to stay.

General Kenney and I went on to Townsville and Port Moresby, where we were met by General Blamey and General Rowell, of the Australian Army, and General Walker of the Army Air Force.

As we breakfasted, we talked over the future of the 19th Group. This was the same 19th that had been one of my old outfits at March Field. It had gone over to the Philippines with the first of the B-17's, had been badly shot up, and by the time it reached Australia had very few of its original planes or personnel left. The crews were war-weary. They needed a refresher course; they needed to get away, to recover their sense of proportion. Both Whitehead and Walker thought the whole Group should be moved back to the United States.

I had a long talk with General Eichelberger. He already had his plans for going from the defensive to the offensive. Without such an objective, the Americans at Port Moresby would be driven into the sea. The Air Force was accepted by all as an absolutely necessary part of the team.

While at Moresby I heard this story—apocryphal or not—from one of General Kenney's staff officers, about the time Kenney, Eichelberger, and Blamey had got together to fly the brigade of Australian troops to stop the Japs threatening the Port.

After the daring air delivery of the troops and their equipment had successfully begun, General Kenney thought he would tell General Mac-Arthur what was going on. He went in to see MacArthur and said, "General, I just did something you should know about."

"What is it, George?" the General asked.

"Well," said Kenney, "I am starting to take one of our brigades across to Port Moresby by air. I expect to have the whole brigade over by night."

General MacArthur is reported to have said, "What? You don't tell me! I think that's grand! I think that's wonderful!"

And then General Kenney said, "Well, General, I think you should know some more. I propose to take another brigade over there as soon as General Eichelberger, General Blamey, and I can get it ready."

MacArthur said, "That's fine! That's wonderful! But, George, does my Staff know anything about this?"

"No, Sir." George Kenney is supposed to have said. "They don't know anything about it."

"Don't tell them, for God's sake," MacArthur replied, "or you will scare them to death!"

After inspecting the ground troops, the Air Force units, and the airdromes, and after talking with Generals Blamey, Eichelberger, Kenney, Whitehead, and Walker, I wrote down these impressions of the situation in New Guinea:

1. If we don't take the offensive soon, the Japanese will drive us out.

2. We have enough troops to do it, since there are only about 4000 Japanese in that particular part of New Guinea.

3. By taking the offensive, we can secure bases at Buna, Lae, Salamaua, and operate strongly against Rabaul.

4. If we don't take the offensive, we will lose Port Moresby, the south side of New Guinea, and open up the north shore of Australia to attack and possible occupation by the Japs.

Later, at Espiritu Santo, I had a long talk with Colonel "Blondy" Saunders and Admiral Fitch. Fitch was a solid citizen and he wasn't too demanding of the Air Force so far as the needs of the Navy were concerned. He wanted more airplanes, yes, but not to the extent of ruining operations in other theaters. He was very reasonable.

As I was flying back to Nouméa the thought occurred to me: the youngsters who were actually doing the fighting, actually meeting the Japanese in combat, were not the people who were jittery. They had no doubts about their ability to lick the Japanese and they were positive of the action that could and must be taken. For instance, Admiral Fitch was not worried about Guadacanal; Saunders was not worried about operating against the Japanese and defeating them. Kenney, Walker, and Eichelberger were all confident they could lick the Japanese.

Other points that became clear to me, after talking with our operating personnel throughout the Pacific area, were:

1. High-altitude bombing was effective.

2. High-altitude bombing permitted continuous day-after-day efforts.

3. Our losses had not been excessive, and permitted continuous bombing. The figures given to me relating to Navy dive bombing indicated their losses were very comparable to ours.

4. Low ceilings did not permit dive bombing. Low ceilings also prevented high-altitude precision bombing without instruments for seeing through the overcast.

5. When the interceptions were made by Japanese planes the dive bombers, in many instances, did not get home. The B-17's, normally, did get home.

6. We had averaged, so far in our combat, ten Zeros for every B-17 lost. The average in all of the South Pacific operations, according to Saunders, was 320 bomb drops; 34 hits on ships.

After landing at Nouméa, I sent informative cables to General Marshall and General Stratemeyer, my Chief of Staff, and then went to Patch's headquarters and had a long talk with him.

At 4:30 I went aboard Admiral Ghormley's ship and attended a conference with Admirals Nimitz, Ghormley, Callaghan, and Turner; General Sutherland, MacArthur's Chief of Staff; Generals Harmon, Kenney, and Streett, and Colonel Ritchie. Admiral Nimitz gave an outline of the reason for the meeting. Admiral Ghormley told of the progress of operations, the probable Japanese movements, and the future Navy plans. General Sutherland gave MacArthur's ideas. Admiral Turner talked about the Navy's strategy. I talked on the world conditions and general plans for campaigns in the various theaters, stressing demands that were being made for airplanes, tanks, and ships.

As a result of this conference I was more convinced than ever that there must be unity of command in our Pacific operations if we were to get economy and maximum effectiveness. There was no doubt in my mind that the axis of advance of Ghormley's force would intersect the axis of MacArthur's advance somewhere near Rabaul. Accordingly, long before that time both sides would be using their long-range bombers against the same objective, without coordinated effort. Similarly, the time was coming when Nimitz' axis of advance would intersect MacArthur's axis of advance, and then again we would have two commanders operating over the same area with their airplanes, and probably with their ships. In time their troops must meet at some point.

Sometime fairly soon I hoped to have our long-range B-29's operating, and they would function in areas beyond Nimitz' and MacArthur's advance. They would operate directly against the Japanese homeland, which influenced the movements of both MacArthur and Nimitz. Yet, with operating areas set up as they were, I could do nothing but retain command of the B-29's myself—something I did not want to do. I could not give them to MacArthur because then they would operate ahead of Nimitz' command; I could not give them to Nimitz since in that case they would operate in front of MacArthur's advance. So, in the end, while everybody wondered why I kept personal command of the Twentieth Air Force—the B-29's—there was nothing else I could do, with no unity of command in the Pacific. I could find no one out there who wanted unity of command, seemingly, unless he himself was made Supreme Commander.

After the conference on Admiral Ghormley's flagship, we made plans for returning to the States. I had to wait for the return of Colonel Cabell, who had gone up to Guadalcanal to get information on what was happening there. Cabell arrived in the late morning with his report. According to him, the Marines on Guadalcanal wanted to know when the Army was going to relieve them. The Marines had understood they were to be there for a few days only, and then were to be relieved. Where was the Army?

Naturally, as this whole area was a Navy command, that was their business, not ours.

As I traveled through the Southwest Pacific, it was impossible not to get the impression that the Navy was determined to carry on the campaign in that theater, and determined to do it with as little help from the Army as possible. It was their fight, the Navy's fight; it was their war against the Japanese; and they were going to clean it up if they could.

During my various stops on the Pacific trip, I interviewed a number of combat crews who had "ditched" in the Pacific and had been rescued after having floated around in their rubber boats. In no case could I find that rubber dinghies were available or used as originally planned when the equipment was put into the bombers. There were always one or two rubber rafts short. I also learned that the water in the containers was not changed often enough. The rations were usually spoiled or the crews, after ditching, didn't get the rations into the boats at all.

I was told by one of our fighting units that the Japanese and the U.S. Air Force used the same wave length and occasionally it was possible to hear Japanese talking in English. In one case, one of our fighter groups was flying over Buna, New Guinea, when they saw twelve Zeros about to take off. The leader of our formation called down to them, "Come on up, you yellow-bellied S.O.B.'s! We can't get a medal for knocking you down on the ground!" And as each of the Jap Zeros took off, one of our boys attacked and shot the plane down, until a total of ten planes had been destroyed. Two other pilots cut their motors, jumped from their planes and ran. Our pilots got both the Zeros on the ground, with no losses to our P-39's. Naturally such reports as these did not help to justify the criticism that the P-39's were no good.

When we got back to Hawaii, General Emmons was waiting for me. Emmons and Nimitz were getting along very well. Emmons thought Nimitz was one of the most brilliant Naval officers he had ever met. It was a fine setup for both Army and Navy to have such a feeling, but, to say the least, not the usual one.

There were numerous things throughout the Pacific the Army did not like. One was the apparent fact that the Navy would do anything to keep control. They used higher-ranking officers than we had, and so normally retained command. While Naval officers could command an Army outfit, it was very seldom an Army officer ever commanded a Navy unit. A general impression existed that the Navy did not understand the technique of ground operations, nor the technique of our air operations. They did not plan logistics in supplying troops in accordance with the Army system. Their plan of putting air units into operations and the way they had them distributed in depth, instead of using the mass of air units to destroy the Japanese Air Force, seemed poor to me—a waste of planes and trained airmen when we were so short of them. Our own doctrine was to use the mass of planes available to break the back of the enemy's Air Force as soon as possible.

We took off from Hawaii on October 1st, headed for San Francisco, some 2400 miles away. As we came into San Francisco at night, searchlights played on us from all points of the compass. Thinking of the hills and mountains around San Francisco, I could not see how the pilot was able to fly through such brilliant lights and keep his course without running into trouble somewhere. But I was getting accustomed now to seeing these boys do anything.

We did not stay long at Hamilton Field. We had landed at 9:50 P.M., and took off at 11:15 that same evening. As we took off, the supercharger on No. 4 engine caught fire and it looked for a while as if that would be the end of our trip—and us. We were about twenty feet in the air when a blast of flame came out of the supercharger, surging about twenty feet to the rear. We thought for a while it would burn off the whole wing from the airplane, for with the hot flame came a roar that accompanies fire only under heavy pressure. At the same time, the odor of gasoline all through the cabin of the fuselage was overpowering. Even if the wing wasn't burned off, if a spark came into the fuselage it would be good-by for everybody.

However, after the No. 4 engine was shut off the fire subsided and went out and we climbed on three engines. I talked it over with the crew. They thought they could turn on Engine No. 4 and get something out of it and we could then either go back to Hamilton Field or keep on going to Washington. We had a heavy load of gas for a nonstop flight across the Continent. I told them to keep going.

We finally reached Washington at four o'clock the next afternoon. Our trip, which had started September 20th, was completed on October 2nd—a total of 12 days. During those 12 days we had covered 21,143 miles. The crew was tired, my Staff was tired, and I was tired. But it was a worthwhile journey. We had all learned a lot.

As soon as possible after my return, I went over my notes in great detail with General Marshall. He, in turn, told me I should give the information to the Secretary of War and to Admiral King. I gave the same report to the Secretary of War and he thought I should give it to the President—which I did. Mr. Stimson also thought I should give it to the Secretary of the Navy and to Admiral King. Admiral King had several of his staff officers present when I went over my notes. They all seemed very interested in my observations. Mr. Forrestal, Under Secretary of the Navy, was there and asked many questions. He appeared to be trying to get all the facts he could.

Later, however, my reception by Secretary Knox was not so hot. He sent for me and I reported, glad to talk about the trip if it would help. I started to tell him of the problems—the lack of unity of command; the concentration of ships in the harbors when there was such a shortage of ships on the other side of the world; the stacking up of airplanes, with the planes and crews in reserve, unused, when everybody was yelling for airplanes; that all this was contrary to the principles of the Army Air Force. I had just gotten to that point in my notes when Secretary Knox told me he did not care to have me criticize the Navy! I replied I was giving him the facts as I found them on my trip and that I had not asked for the interview with him; if he did not care to hear what I had to say it was all right with me. That ended our interview.

☆ *20* ☆

Mrs. Marshall, in her charming book, has told how she, my wife, and I heard that the TORCH landings had taken place. She had tickets for a night football game, which George abruptly, for reasons Mrs. Marshall could not yet know, was unable to attend. I knew why, but was as thrilled as the ladies were at the silence of that crowd as the game was suddenly stopped, and the loudspeaker blared, "The President of the United States announces the successful landing on the African Coast of an American Expeditionary Force. This is our second front."

"Like the waves of the ocean," Mrs. Marshall remembers (as everyone who was there does, I guess) "the cheers of the people rose and fell, then rose again in a long-sustained emotional cry. The football players turned somersaults and handsprings down the center of the field; the crowd simply went wild, for this was the heartening news that America, agonized by one defeat after another, had been waiting to hear. We had struck back."

As previously suggested, the conditions of that landing from the air point of view were not the most desirable. But our people performed magnificently, including those who had to operate as ground soldiers for the moment. Some of our officers found themselves commanding certain sections of the landing areas, and our air service troops, heading the grab for those vital airfields, were among the first to hit the beaches. Such stories as the way in which Colonel Demas T. ("Nick") Craw and Colonel Pierpont M. Hamilton won the Congressional Medal of Honor, Nick dying on the ground from French bullets after all his hairbreadth escapes in the air (as well as in a number of Axis-held countries as one of our "observers," a category Nick never quite accepted for himself)

351

have become famous tales of the invasion. Joe Cannon's P-40's, flying ashore off the *Chenango,* landing on bomb-pocked Mehdia airfield, with smashed landing gear, but getting in, just as their mechanics and other ground people got in on the ground, were splendid. So were the C-47 pilots trying to get the paratroopers to Oran from England, the fighter pilots making the split-second arrivals at Oran just as it was taken, and up again in combat as soon as their gas was rushed to them from the landing places. The details of TORCH, British and American, from Algiers and Oran to Casablanca, have been too well told for me to repeat them here.

After the airfields were secured, Doolittle, our Air Commander under Patton at Casablanca, had his most difficult task on his hands.

In a letter dated November 19th, eleven days after they got into Africa, he wrote as follows:

The American carrier-borne Navy aviation at Casablanca, and the British Fleet Arm at Oran, did the larger part of the air fighting. By the time the airports were secured, they had destroyed, either in the air or on the ground, the majority of the French aviation.

Joe Cannon, at Casablanca, has done an outstanding job. The 33rd Fighter Group gave air support and the necessary reconnaissance to General Patton's forces. Joe unloaded some 72 aircraft from the *Chenango* at Port Lyautey. The principal runway had been bombed, and was not usable. The field was soft and 70 aircraft sustained minor damage on landing. Part of these aircraft were later moved to the Casablanca airport, and some 35 more were shot off the *Archer.* [The *Archer* was a carrier.]

Joe now has, in addition to these, a half-dozen B-25's from the 310th Group, and more are coming in steadily. He also has such transports as required, of the 62nd Group.

In addition to Port Lyautey, there are good fields at Sole, Rabat and Casablanca. The field at Casablanca is large but has no prepared runways, and there are spots that will not hold a B-17. I proved this the other day by landing there and bogging down. Apparently, the small footprint and the high unit loading was more than the sod could stand. It required four tanks to pull the B-17 out so it could take off again. Joe and George Patton have the western situation well in hand and are getting along together beautifully.

The first airport was secured at Oran at noon on D-Day. Twenty-four Spitfires of the 31st Group, with Hawkins in command, hopped over from Gibraltar. Four aircraft, which the boys took to be Hurricanes, were doing lazy eights high overhead. As the squadron was landing, they peeled off and attacked. One of the Spitfires which had lowered its landing gear and flaps, was shot down, and the pilot, Lt. Byrd, was killed. Three ships which had not landed immediately attacked the four ships, which turned out to be Dewoitine 520's, and shot down three. The fourth got away. The Dewoitine 520's, apparently, were no match for our modern Fighters.

I cannot speak too highly of the work done by these Groups. They twice stopped mechanized columns who were attacking the airport at Tafaraoui from the south. The ground units had moved forward to take Lasenia airport, which is closer to Oran proper. Had it not been for the prompt and efficient action of the Spitfires, Tafaraoui and our air units would have been lost, and the war at Oran lengthened and made more bloody. One column taken out and routed was the French Foreign Legion, moving in from its headquarters at Sidi-bel-Abbes. Our Fighters destroyed five tanks of this outfit, burned the supplies coming forward, and routed the foot soldiers.

Lasenia was secured, lost, and secured again. During the process, it was bombed by our people and shelled by the French. We have finally moved to Lasenia, in addition to Tafaraoui, and are rehabilitating it.

The necessity for marrying ground and air forces on the field of battle precluded the training and study in organizations necessary to secure perfect collaboration. In spite of this, the cooperation was of the highest order, and in only two instances were mistakes made. On one occasion, we were directed to attack an enemy column east of La Macta, on Arzeu Bay. By the time the message got to us, it read *west* of La Macta. The airplanes flew over the column to the west, which was actually ours. The ground forces, being light on the trigger, cut down on the airplanes. The planes, feeling, in spite of the American appearance, they must be French troops, started to strafe them. Fortunately, our tanks were not as vulnerable as the French, and no damage was done to our ground troops; but two of our planes were shot down by our own people.

As a matter of fact, an operation of this kind promptly separates the sheep from the goats, and I am happy to report that all of our people showed up well, and most of them were superior.

Two of my principal worries were the concentration of aircraft on Gibraltar, and the long flight down from the United Kingdom in the season of bad weather. Gibraltar is now pretty well cleaned out, and to date, far less difficulty than I anticipated is experienced in flying the aircraft down.

When I was last at Casablanca, there were about 4000 air people ashore; yesterday, at Oran, we had 14,000 men and about 1000 officers. These are stationed at Tafaraoui and Lasenia.

The fight has moved to the eastward. In order to get the Hun out of Tunisia and occupy this area before he can, we will have made available to the Royal Air Force, to General Anderson's army, as many of our units as they can use. This arrangement, under which these airplanes are made available, is for the British to assign the missions, but we operate the airplanes.

We must keep the Straits of Gibraltar open and provide Fighter cover, and later submarine protection for our convoys along the north and west coast of Africa.

Now things at home, not only to keep the North African campaign going but to keep everything going, were intensified.

For example, on the eve of TORCH, one thing that still rankled in my mind was the talks I had during my recent trip to the Southwest Pacific with combat boys who had had to "ditch" in those inadequate rubber boats. I had found, that it was the "usual" condition for a minimum of six, and in some cases for as many as eight men to end up in one four-man dinghy, with most of the emergency equipment lost overboard.

As soon as I returned to Washington, I sent for the people at Dayton who were responsible for designing and procuring the rubber escape boats. When they were assembled, I asked them to inflate the four-man boat. This they did. Then I said to the first eight men, "Climb in!" "But," they replied, "it is only a four-man boat!" I said, "I don't care if it's a four-man boat or what it is; climb in!"

They climbed in, and as was to be expected, their feet were pyramided in the center to such an extent it was obviously very uncomfortable. Then I asked, "How many of you have ever been in one of these boats in the water?" Strange to say, as I remember it now, not one said he had. "O.K. Now, this afternoon, go down to the Potomac River. I want you to put eight men in a four-man boat. I want eight men to climb into the raft from the water, with one man standing or kneeling on the side of the boat, the same as he would have to at sea, putting all of his weight there, and see what happens. If you haven't bathing suits, get them, because this is going to be a practical test and when you get through, I want to talk with you some more."

When I had finished with those instructions, I asked, "Who is responsible for the fishing tackle in these boats?" One young officer said he was. I asked, "Where did you get your advice as to the kind of tackle you should use in these boats?" He replied, "From a sporting goods store in Dayton." I asked, "What experience with deep-sea fishing had the salesman from whom you bought it?" The salesman, it appeared, had never been fishing in a body of water larger than Indian Lake, which is north of Dayton. I told him they would have to redesign the type of fishing equipment and the method of securing the rations to the boat, so that even if it went under when it was thrown from the door of the plane, the rations and equipment would not be lost.

The following morning, the men returned to my office and said they had made the experiments in the Potomac River. I asked them how they liked eight men in a four-man boat. They said they didn't. I said, "Well, until we have larger boats or more small boats, you must accept that condition as normal. Any airplane in combat must expect at least one of its boats to have enough machine-gun bullet holes to make it unserviceable. From now on, we will have two five-man boats and one four-man boat in every one of our heavy bombers." Furthermore, we had men experienced in deep-sea fishing, design and assemble our fishing tackle. Also, we had experienced men teach us how to get fresh water from sea water.

It was a rather difficult task to plan operations two or three years in advance when every theater commander was working constantly on higher headquarters for all the airplanes he could get, regardless of real needs and allocations already agreed upon. Had we listened to all of these demands, we never could have met our Number One project: A United States Bomber Command in England. We should never have been able to build up our training units in the United States. Nor would we have been able to organize our operational training commands to turn out the combat groups as rapidly as we could equip them.

For instance, on October 24, 1942, I received a copy of a memoradum from the President, directed to Admiral Leahy, Admiral King, General Marshall, and myself, as follows:

My anxiety about the Southwest Pacific is to make sure that every possible weapon gets into the area to hold Guadalcanal, and that, having held in this crisis, munitions, planes, and crews are on the way to take advantage of our success. We will soon find ourselves engaged on two active fronts, and we must have adequate air support in both places, even though it means delay in our commitments, particularly, to England. Our long-range plans could be set back for months if we failed to throw our full strength into our immediate and impending conflicts.

I wish, therefore, you would canvass, over the week-end, every possible temporary diversion of munitions which you will require for your active fronts, and let me know what they are. Please, also, review the number and use of all combat planes now in the Continental United States.

Signed: ROOSEVELT

It is important to note some of the expressions used in that memorandum: "We will soon find ourselves engaged on two active fronts," and ". . . in both places, even though it means delay in our commitments, particularly, to England." Those two quotations in themselves might have changed completely our strategic planning for operations against Germany, for if aid to the Pacific meant delay in our commitments to

England, it could not help but delay our operations against the Germans. Take another item in that memorandum: "Please, also, review the number and use of all combat planes now in the Continental United States." Time and time again I thought I had demonstrated the need for a definite number of combat planes in the United States in which to train combat personnel prior to going overseas. In every one of our operational training units, we tried to use the older type of equipment, planes that would give our combat personnel the know-how without holding the latest types at home.

We had to modernize our ideas continuously, and plan new figures. This we did in two ways: First, we increased the number of airplanes in each group. For example, the heavy bomber units originally had 35 planes per group. We built that up to 55, built up the mediums from 57 to 69, the fighters from 80 to 105, and so on. Secondly, we increased the number of squadrons in a group from three to four. Third, we increased the number of groups. There wasn't any distinct shortage of personnel in the Air Force, because it was a popular branch.

In the fall of 1941, we had a 45-group program. In January of 1942 we had a 115-group program. By July of the same year we were trying to get a 224-group program. And in September of 1942, we finally had received approval of the 273-group program, which remained our guide approximately until the end of the war.

All that was required to meet these various schedules was the assurance that we had the equipment coming through the production lines, and the personnel coming through our schools. Neither of these was a super-colossal job. It was always necessary to keep the President informed and get his blessing, but usually he would go along with almost any large aircraft program we projected. With Harry Hopkins' aid, I had no trouble at all in getting the large aircraft production projects started through the White House, nor in maintaining our gigantic training programs.

My office organization in Washington contained an Advisory Council, a group of young men, the brightest I could get, who sat in an office close to mine, and whose instructions were: "Don't get mixed up with any routine business. What I want you to do is sit down and think. Think of the problems confronting us. Think of the solutions to those problems. Bring in new ideas. If you bring in one new idea every two or three days I will be satisfied. But don't get mixed up with the routine operations of this office. Think! Think of the future of the Air Force!"

That Advisory Council, made up changeably of anywhere from three to five officers, was invaluable to me. They brought me new ideas; kept me up-to-date, and best of all, made certain that I was very seldom caught off base by higher authority with any new problem before I had been able to give some thought to it.

The large organization I headed in Washington changed from time to time. It altered with the conditions under which we were operating. A bureau, a section, independent today, might be combined with another one tomorrow. As soon as any agency was able to stand on its own feet and no longer required my personal attention, when I felt sure that a general directive would be carried out without my going into the horrible details, I turned its people loose on their own, and forgot about them. A typical example of that was the Flying Training Command. It started out as a half-dozen different things—the technical training, the flying training, the ground training, the ground officers' training, and so on. But after each one got on the beam, headed for the right objective, it was combined with another, until I finally ended up with one grand Training Command under a Lieutenant General, a West Point classmate, Barton K. Yount. He did a grand job. From then on, I did not have to worry about the Flying Training Command. I knew it would function in accordance with the general directive it had received.

The same thing applied to the Air Transport Command. Once it had established its bases around the world, and General George and General C. R. Smith were operating it, I was able to forget about it, and all I had to do was change the directive from time to time, as conditions throughout the world, and the war, demanded such changes.

In this way, in spite of the fact that the Air Force was growing with tremendous rapidity, the chain of command actually became simpler as we progressed. The number of people with whom I had to do business decreased with each reorganization.

My own staff was composed of the Chief of Air Staff, and three Deputy Chiefs of Staff. I had Assistant Chiefs of Staff for Personnel, for Intelligence, for Training, for Materiel and Distribution, for Operations, and for Plans.

The number of different activities in which we found ourselves engaged by the end of the war is unbelievable. For instance: Hydroponics, a name that meant nothing to me until, on one of my inspections at Miami, I found at the hospital there a hydroponics garden—a "garden" that grew three or four times the normal number of vegetables grown on a single vine. The principle was a tank filled with ordinary gravel.

Into the gravel was poured, from time to time, the liquid chemicals needed by the various plants to insure the maximum amount of growth and the maximum production of vegetables.

In certain parts of the world, where the natives were not particular about the kind of fertilizers used, or in areas where the soil was poor, such gardens would be invaluable. Accordingly, in 1943 the Air Force started a Hydroponics School at the hospital in Miami, and we trained personnel in the techniques and vegetable selection best suited for such gardening operations. Before the year was out, we had hydroponic gardens at British Guiana, at Ascension Island, and at places in the Pacific. Had the war continued, hydroponics would undoubtedly have played a much more important role than it did.

Women pilots were first used by the Ferrying Division of the Air Transport Command in September, 1942. At the same time, a training program was started for training women pilots at a school at Sweetwater, Texas. The Women's Air Force Service Pilots, the initials of which more or less spelled WASP, were so known during the remainder of the war. This organization increased in size until we had over 1500 women pilots on active duty with the Army Air Force. In addition to ferrying airplanes to any point in the United States and Canada, the WASPS made weather flights; flew administrative missions; as cargo plane pilots, flew equipment from one point to another where it was urgently needed; ferried air transport planes; and towed targets for antiaircraft fire. Still we could never get authority to put them on an equal status with the WACS.

The WASPS did a magnificent job for the Army Air Forces in every way. It was common for commanding officers to say they would rather have WASPS ferry airplanes across the United States than male pilots, because the WASP normally reached her destination a day or two ahead of the time required by a male pilot to do the same job. When pressed for reasons, the answer usually given was that the WASP didn't carry an address book with her.

As time passed, it became apparent that greater and greater political hostility was being built up against the WASPS. In my own mind, it was because the airline pilots were a bit jealous of the women flyers, and were perhaps apprehensive about what might happen after the war. In any event, a move was started in Congress, obviously backed by male pilot organizations, to put an end to the WASPS. This was after the shortage of manpower was over—when the war was nearly finished. It started when I asked for appropriations for the WASPS for the year 1945.

A bitter fight was carried on in the Civil Service Committee in the House of Representatives over whether the WASPS should be allowed to continue as a government organization. Everyone admitted they had done a wonderful job. Yet when the matter was taken up with Congress the answer was, "Thumbs down! No more money for WASPS! Discharge your women and send them home."

A lot has been said about waste in government contracts; the uneconomical method employed in doing business. Scandals in procurement are often hinted at, but few people see the other side. For instance, as early as 1942, I realized our supply depots were not organized for maximum efficiency or economy. In order to get the best advice I could on the question of supply and storage depots, I asked General R. E. Wood, President of Sears-Roebuck Company, if he would come down and help me. This he agreed to do, and for the next three years he spent his time going around from one depot to another, from one supply center to another, with a view to simplifying our methods of operation, of cutting down our overhead, of eliminating unnecessary items. By June of 1942, as a result of his efforts, we had canceled contracts for 355 million dollars' worth of unnecessary supplies!

However, it is to be noted that Bob Wood, prior to World War II, had allied himself with certain individuals in Chicago who had incurred the hostility of President Roosevelt, and try as I would, I was never able to get him commissioned. His entire service, like Lindbergh's for the same reason, was performed as a civilian.

The training task we had undertaken was terrific. By the end of 1942 we had graduated 266,000 mechanics. By the end of 1944 we had graduated 997,000 mechanics. Our pilot training schools were built up in a manner almost beyond comprehension. Whereas we had only about 9000 pilots under instruction in 1941, by the end of 1943 we had 25,000 men learning to fly. By the end of 1944 we had graduated 226,000 pilots. As a matter of fact, we had so many pilots by then that even though peace was not yet in sight, we knew we had more than we could use. So although at that time we were graduating pilots at the rate of 105,000 a year, we cut down our rate of training until by March of 1945 we were back to a rate of about 30,000 a year.

Similarly, the production of heavy bombers had been built up from about 100 in 1941 to 2500 in 1942, and in 1943 to 8600. Other plane production increased in direct proportion, until during the year 1943, the Air Force received over 12,000 fighter airplanes.

Whereas in 1942 we told the President of the United States we wanted a total of approximately 60,000 planes in the Air Force, in 1944 we actually had 72,700.

By the end of 1943 we had close to a million enlisted men overseas. At the present time we are talking about a 70-group program for a post-war Air Force. Perhaps a better idea of the growth of our wartime Air Force may be obtained by considering it in terms of groups. In 1941 we had 18 groups overseas; in 1944 214 groups outside the country.

Sometimes I think General Marshall must have been a little disturbed by my memoranda, but if he was he never showed it. In a memorandum I wrote to him on August 21, 1942, I called his attention to the fact that our plans for the landing on the North African coast called for a total of about 675 U.S. Air Force planes, 150 British planes and about 80 to 100 Navy type, or a grand total of approximately 925 airplanes. Against this we estimated the Germans could bring about 495 bombers the first day, and after the first day, a total of about 623 bombers, and a considerable number of fighters.

I went on to show how we were dispersing our Air Force by following a policy that contemplated building up aerial superiority in Alaska, Hawaii, the Southwest Pacific, Australia, India, the Near East, and North Africa, all at the same time, meanwhile maintaining a fairly large force in the Caribbean area. I showed that, in the Aleutian Islands, for instance, the Japs had probably less than 100 planes; closer to 50, perhaps. Against those 50 airplanes, we had some 215 airplanes. In the Southwest Pacific, from the Celebes to the Solomons, the Japs had somewhere in the neighborhood of 300 airplanes. In that same theater we had approximately 500 airplanes in Australia, 130 in the Pacific Island, and 250 in Hawaii, all of which could be concentrated at a critical point within a period of 36 hours.

I said, further, if decisive results were ever to be obtained in this war, offensive operations against the center of the Axis strength—industrial Germany—must be continued relentlessly from every possible base. I further added that the major bombing offensive must come from the British Isles, but the action in North Africa was complementary to that major offensive.

I ended by stating I considered the matter very grave; that instead of dispersing by sending airplanes to the Pacific, we should concentrate our forces and move airplanes from the Pacific to the North African and the European theaters.

Naturally, my recommendations along these lines could not, and did not, make a hit with either the high ranking officers of the Navy, or, probably, with General MacArthur.

I have always had the utmost respect for great industrialists and notably for Mr. Henry Kaiser's extraordinary ability to build up one wartime industry after another, invariably meeting his production schedules. That is, of course, in everything except airplanes. I figured that after some thirty years' experience with what they were and where they came from, I probably knew more about airplanes and their production than Henry Kaiser.

Accordingly, when he arrived in Washington with his ideas on how to build airplanes, I could not go with him one hundred per cent, particularly when he wanted to build a large, unproven type of transport plane to take the place of standard transport models. I was one of the first who recommended he get in touch with the aircraft manufacturers, such as Glenn Martin, Donald Douglas, and people who had experience in building transport planes, and talk over with them the difficulties he would certainly encounter.

However, there are always "Yes" men and "Me, too" men around who work on the Big Man's ego until the Big Man allows himself to be carried away against his better judgment. In my opinion, that is what happened to Mr. Kaiser and his project for building big cargo-carrying planes to beat the submarine menace, in 1942.

I think he was given wrong information on two counts: First, on the practicability of the plane he had under consideration; Secondly, on the time it would take to build the airplanes after the project was started. I remember quite well a conference at the Army and Navy Club in Washington, with Mr. Kaiser; General Somervell, our Army Services of Supply Commander; General McNair, Commander of our Ground Forces; Mr. Eberstadt, Chairman of the Army and Navy Munitions Board, and one or two others. Nearly everyone there tried, in a polite way, to show Mr. Kaiser the obstacles which would be met with in trying to put across that large, cargo-carrying plane program. General Somervell was always outspoken, and when Kaiser talked of the things he could or could not do, and compared himself with Henry Ford, it immediately brought fire into Somervell's eyes. He suggested that probably Kaiser thought he was a better man than Ford. That started repartee back and forth between the two. As a matter of fact, the conversation did not become too heated, and there were no fisticuffs, newspaper accounts to the contrary, nor any thought of fisticuffs (I hope!). The conversation was brought under control without any difficulty by the host, who happened to be me. General Somervell and Mr. Kaiser left the luncheon good friends.

As to the main point at issue, everybody now knows that the large transport plane Henry Kaiser had in mind was never completed during the war. As late as July, 1948, it is still an untried, unproven article.

Another battle that was carried on mostly in Washington was the fight over antisubmarine operations. At first, when the Japs attacked Pearl Harbor, neither the Army nor the Army Air Force had had the necessary airplanes with which to carry out antisubmarine operations. As early as December 8th, the day after the sneak attack, the Commanding General of the First Bomber Command ordered over-water reconnaissance flights to locate possible enemy forces. This was done in cooperation with the Navy Eastern Sea Frontier Command, which assumed operational control on March 26, 1942. Ship escort operations began in April, and the formal convoy system in the following month of May. During the summer of 1942, Army Air Force units and the Civil Air Patrol covered the Eastern and Gulf Frontier, which embraced an area of about a million square miles. The antisubmarine patrol began experimentally in the Cuba and Trinidad area in August, 1942. In October of that year a definite program was activated, combining Army, Navy, and Civil Air Patrol airplanes. During the year—January, 1942, to March, 1943—the Air Force patrol sighted 241 enemy submarines and attacked 147 of them. As a result, the number of submarines making their appearance declined, and the heavy sinkings along the Atlantic Coast diminished. The U-boats were driven eastward beyond the range of our air patrols. By the end of 1943, the Army Air Force had 25 land-based squadrons, or about 254 airplanes on antisubmarine duty, operating from bases from Newfoundland to Cuba and Trinidad, and from England to South Africa.

As the Navy secured more airplanes, they took over the work from the Army Antisubmarine Command. In July, 1943, a memorandum came out which stated the Army was prepared to withdraw from antisubmarine operations at such time as the Navy was ready to take over those duties completely, but that the Army antisubmarine airplanes would continue in that service as long as the Navy needed them. Furthermore, the Army Air Force would transfer to the Navy such equipment as the Navy required, until it could get its own equipment. This policy

MISSION ———————————————————————————— 363

applied to our antisubmarine work in the European Theater as well as in the American Theater.

However, we ran into one thing over there that we did not encounter on this side of the water. That was the desire of the British to keep the RAF-AAF antisubmarine work a going concern. As soon as we (the Army and the Navy) had agreed to turn the entire operation over to the Navy, Winston Churchill sent a letter, dated July 22, 1943, to the Secretary of War. "We earnestly hope," wrote the Prime Minister, "that the American Navy will take over sole responsibility in all other theaters before doing so on the Eastern Atlantic, and that, meanwhile, not only the two Army squadrons now operating with the Coastal Command will be allowed to continue in that task, but the four other Army squadrons will operate until the Navy squadrons are fully trained and available to relieve them."

That letter further complicated our program. The Army Air Force, from the start, never did really want to continue the antisubmarine patrol work. The job was forced on us because of the shortage of airplanes and equipment. We tried to keep it for a while, for the mere reason that no bureau ever wants to give up anything. But it was a drain on our equipment and personnel. We really wanted to turn it over to the Navy and let them do their own work.

I don't think the American public ever understood the tremendous success the airplanes of the United States Army and the Royal Air Force operating out of England had in locating and destroying the submarines. In the first place, five out of six of the U-boats operating in the millions of square miles between Cape Farewell, the Horn, and the Cape of Good Hope, passed to their repair bases through the Bay of Biscay, where they could be found and attacked by aircraft from southern England. Second, in the month of May, 1943, 82 per cent of the U-boats crossing the Bay were sighted by aircraft. In the month of June, 71 per cent were sighted. Third, the long range B-24's operating in the Bay sighted one submarine per seven sorties. All other planes operating in the Bay during the same months sighted at the ratio of one U-boat for sixteen sorties. Fourth, it required about eight months to bring a pilot to the experience level for successful U-boat operations, and four or five months specially to train their navigators and radio operators. It can be readily understood why Winston Churchill had no desire to see the Army Air Force squadrons taken away at that critical period. In the end after protracted controversy he won his point, in that the two Army Air Force squadrons remained in England.

One reason we were ahead of the Navy in antisubmarine work, though by no means wholly prepared ourselves, was that the Army Air Force put the necessary radar gadgets, the micro-wave gear in their B-18's, and had them working, before the Navy procured this equipment. We had even started a radar school for antisubmarine instruction. The hard part from my point of view was this: At the time we were doing this work with our long range bombers the Navy still carried on its campaign to get first priority for production for everything else *but* long-range bombers!

Another matter that greatly concerned me from the very beginning of the war was the health of our men in the Air Force. From the start of aviation it had always been apparent that the task confronting the flight surgeon was different from that of the ordinary doctor in the Army. Aside from the special psychiatric problems of flight under the most nerve-racking combat conditions, of battles fought on oxygen five miles above the earth, there was, say, the problem of fingers and toes freezing at high altitudes, and the selection of suitable clothing to prevent such freezing.

Then there was always the problem of "combat fatigue," of whether the members of a crew were really war-weary, were actually worn out, had had too much combat flying, or were just "gold-bricking." A flight surgeon had to be able to determine these things from his personal knowledge of the airmen, of their characteristics, and their individual ways of doing things.

Our Air Force was fighting over all the globe, and the air personnel were subject to hazards ranging from the extreme cold in the polar regions to the tropical diseases around the equator. The airplane went from one extreme to the other in a matter of hours, instead of weeks and months, as in the case of ground soldiers.

Then came the question of hospitals to take care of the airmen who came home hurt or unwell. It is a pretty well-known fact that as soon as a man goes into the average hospital, he loses his identity and becomes a number. His particular disease or disablement, or the extent of his recovery make no difference; he must follow a routine. The result is that in the average Army hospital many men are carried along for extended periods who might far better be back with their units, or on leave at home with their folks. I personally never approved of our existing methods of handling the convalescents, especially after an experience of my own in one Army hospital, even though, at that time, I happened to be a four-star convalescent.

I determined, with my senior surgeon, General Grant, that we in the Air Force must have our own hospitals, that our men needed special treatment.

The next problem we had was that of getting the airmen who were wounded or sick back to the Air convalescent hospitals in the United States with the least delay. This meant air transportation. In order that the men might be handled properly en route, there must be nurses who knew the particular problems presented by flying. Accordingly, we started an Air Nurses' Corps, and a special school in the United States to provide these nurses. People asked, "Why do you have to have a school for Air nurses?" The answer was simple: There was no other way to get them.

Our flying doctors became expert in their tasks. We developed a hospital service that moved with the Air Force. For instance, six days after an Army hospital at Nome, Alaska, had burned down, a new and complete 25-bed hospital had been flown in over a distance of some 3400 miles. When General Kenney moved his Air Force across the Owen-Stanley Range of mountains in New Guinea, two field hospitals accompanied it. A 50-bed hospital was moved 44 miles by air over the Mediterranean from North Africa to Sicily, was set up and had patients in the receiving ward two and one-half hours after it was originally dismantled!

Flying fatigue was one of our worst problems. We established rest camps in our theaters of operation throughout the world, and Flight Surgeons kept a constant eye on our personnel to discover what men needed rest in order to prolong their lives as combat flyers, or should be taken off combat altogether.

To deal with the problem of rehabilitation after the war we set up special centers in the United States where every known facility was available to help disabled airmen regain for themselves a place in civilian life. I have in mind a visit I made to our Rehabilitation Center at Pawling, New York, part of the tireless program of Dr. Howard Rusk, where I saw two men, tumbling and jumping on a canvas mat supported by springs. I was told, "One of those men has a leg off—has an artificial limb. Which man is it?" When I saw the two men jumping, tumbling, falling, first on one leg then on the other, landing on their shoulders and on their backs, and springing up to their feet, it was difficult for me to say which man it was who had only one leg. Finally, one of the men jumped off the canvas mat, and the other continued with his athletic exhibition. "Which leg is the artificial limb?" I was asked. And for the life of me, I found it difficult to say!

In war, a commander of any unit, no matter how large or how small, at times meets situations in which he cannot stand upon his dignity. He has to be human. I found that a commander can learn a lot by asking questions, such as, "How long have you been peeling potatoes?" "How long have you been driving a car?" "What station did you come from?" "Which of our schools did you attend?" "What training have you had?" And I have suddenly discovered on occasion that I was talking to a man who had been trained as an airplane or engine mechanic, and yet here he was, peeling potatoes, and had been peeling potatoes for more than three or four months, at a time when we badly needed airplane and engine mechanics in all our units. In any large command, there is always a fight to get people to put "square pegs in square holes, and round pegs in round holes."

In addition—as well as by way of relief from—these varied problems, there were the constant trips of inspection, of Air Force installations, bases, training schools, hospitals, factories, depots, landing fields. Occasionally on such trips, I managed to work in a little hunting and fishing. Once, I recall, after I had completed an inspection of an Air Force installation in Kansas, where our B-29's were being groomed for their flight across the Pacific and our crews instructed in how to handle and maintain them, I accepted an invitation from some North Dakota friends for a bit of pheasant hunting. When we reached Bismarck, we borrowed a car and started for the area in which we hoped to get some pheasants and grouse. We had a good day. The birds were plentiful, all of us shot our limit, and we were on our way back to Bismarck, some seventy miles out, when we had a puncture.

Naturally, we had to unload the birds and all the other equipment in the car to see if we could find any tools with which to change that tire. There was an extra wheel, also an extra tire—but no tools. We stopped every car that came along but none of the tools offered us seemed to fit. I remember that among the cars that came along was a big old converted truck—a dead animal truck—driven by two Indians. They were willing to do anything, but the tools they had didn't fit, and they drove on. Finally, it became almost dark. We were about to give up and were trying to figure a different approach when we saw the lights of a car coming toward us from Bismarck. When the car reached us, we saw it was a Ford. In it were an old rancher and his son. They had spent the day in Bismarck, and they had spent it well, for they knew no pain! When we asked them if we could borrow their tire tools, jack, and what-have-you, they were tickled to death. They would have given us the tools, their car, and their ranch if we had asked for them!

While the tire was being changed, some of my boys got to talking with the old rancher and became better acquainted with him. Just about the time everything was completed, and we had given the rancher a couple of pheasants, one of my officers came to me and said he would like to introduce me to the old man. I said, "Well, O.K. by me, but he won't know me from Adam's off-ox."

I was in shooting togs and probably looked like any one else who goes out to shoot pheasants in North Dakota, so when this youngster brought up the rancher and said, "Mr. Powell, I want you to meet General Arnold," the old man grabbed my hand and said, "I'm pleased t'meetcha." The youngster saw he wasn't getting anywhere so he said, "But, Mr. Powell, you don't understand. General Arnold is the man who is in charge of all these airplanes. He runs all these airplanes you see going back and forth across the United States. He is in charge of all our airplanes, all over the world, fighting Germany and fighting Japan!"

The old rancher looked me squarely in the eye and said, "That doesn't make a blankety-blank bit of difference to me; I'm still pleased t'meetcha!"

I recall very vividly a later hunting trip I went on with General Marshall in the same section of the country; I say vividly, because during it the Commanding General of the Air Force came very near being put out of commission.

The method of hunting pheasants in that country is to form groups of about six hunters. Three or four stand at one end of a corn field. The others move down between the rows of corn, driving the pheasants before them. A few of the pheasants get up during their movement through the corn, but the greater number run ahead of the hunters until they see the men stationed at the far end. Then the pheasants break to the right or left and try to get out of the corn field, either by running or flying.

Accordingly, it is the custom to put a couple of "flankers" out ahead of the main moving body. In this case I was a "flanker," a little bit ahead of the other hunters who were moving along between the corn rows. As we approached the men stationed at the far end, we could see there were literally hundreds of pheasants in that field. I was watching very carefully, for I knew we were getting close—too close, in fact—to the guns ahead, and someone might get hit. Suddenly, a pheasant broke from the corn. I saw one of the men at the far end of the field bring his shotgun up on the pheasant, which was headed in my direction. I knew I was in direct line of his fire, so I ducked my head.

It was fortunate that I wore heavy dark glasses, for the center of impact of that charge struck me square on the head and face. Some of the Number 6 shot went through several thicknesses of cloth in my cap and broke the skin on my forehead and on top of my head. My glasses were hit by about half-a-dozen shots; my face by five or six. My hunting coat was literally riddled, but luckily I had heavy shirts underneath, and the shots did not penetrate. One shot hit my thumb. I was so close, that the blast threw me over backward.

When I sat up and felt around, I discovered my face was covered with blood. I didn't know how badly I was wounded. As a matter of fact, there was so much blood I thought I might have lost half my face. I took my handkerchief out and started mopping up. It was all right. Only about five or six of the shots had gone into me deep enough to make the blood flow. After I had been given some first aid, we continued to shoot. That night, with my face covered with band-aid patches, I went to a local doctor in Bismarck and asked him if it wouldn't be a good idea to pull the shot out while the holes were still fresh. He assured me that that wasn't the way to treat shotgun wounds; the way was to leave the shot in. So today I am still carrying them around. Thus, the only wounds of my long military career were received not in battle but in a pheasant shoot.

☆ *21* ☆

From the day the Japanese hit us at Pearl Harbor, it was apparent we would lose the Philippines, in spite of the grand fight being made by Mac-Arthur's ground and air troops. There was no way to get reinforcements and supplies to the besieged troops in time. Because of lack of ships, lack of Naval strength, lack of air power, lack of an Army, we could put no obstacle in the path of the Japanese until they had completed the conquests of Indo-China, Malaya, Burma, the Dutch East Indies, and then swarmed across New Guinea, threatened New Caledonia and Australia, and approached the Ellice Islands.

I have always been of the opinion that, if the Japanese had had a well-prepared plan; if they had had the troops and the ships, they could have continued their attack upon Hawaii with a landing operation, and taken over those islands.

The only real limitations on the Japanese during those early war days were time, space, and shipping. Our ABDA Command, in the Dutch East Indies area, did little more than slow up the southward movement of Japanese troops. The British troops in Malaya and Burma were no match for the Japanese, who in their first forward movement toward New Caledonia and the Ellice Islands were hampered only by logistics. They could not supply themselves. The same was true in the North Pacific, in the Aleutians. There again, the Japanese were delayed only by the limited troops and supplies they had available, and by the inadequate number of ships for holding open their line of communication.

The questions naturally arise, then: Did the Japanese and the Germans have a definite, well-worked-out plan for a meeting of their forces in South Asia? Was Rommel supposed to continue eastward, until they met? Had there been such a plan, could they have been stopped? Frankly,

I do not know; but I am doubtful, now, whether either the Germans or the Japanese ever had such a strategy worked out. At one time I was sure they did.

Looking back, it seems to me now that after they had occupied their perimeter of outposts extending from the Aleutians to Wake, to the Gilberts, to the Solomons, to New Guinea, to Java, Sumatra, Singapore, and to Burma, the Japanese never had a plan for anything but defense. From that time on, they seemed only to be trying to hold what they had, and at the most to take advantage of what opportunities were presented. They lost further offensive power. Either they did not have the supplies, or they lacked the imagination to foresee that holding such a large area defensively was sure to spell their doom. History, time and time again, has shown that no war can be won by a strictly defensive operation. The battle of Midway was not the result of a general Japanese offensive; it was only a limited advance with a view to capturing the island of Midway.

I have always wondered why the Japanese did not move that last twelve miles into Port Moresby, New Guinea. From there, without much difficulty, they could have taken over the northern part of Australia, and perhaps even more. It certainly was not the small number of Allied troops in and around Port Moresby, nor the Army Air Forces on the various airdromes radiating out from Moresby, that stopped them. If there ever was an operation that was worth the gamble, it was a Japanese movement into Port Moresby, and then onto Darwin and Townsville.

Our air problem on December 7, 1941, was to build up enough combat units to send to the various theaters throughout the world, and at the same time to create in the United States the capacity to produce planes, pilots, bombardiers, skilled mechanics, and so on, in numbers that would insure a growing combat strength in all those theaters, *regardless of losses*.

One of the fundamental mistakes of the German Air Force was in this matter of replacements. The German air leaders did not make provision for replacement of planes or crews, or see the necessity for a replacement rate, as high as 25 per cent per month if necessary, to maintain a constant combat air strength. Neither did the R.A.F. Accordingly, when the Luftwaffe finally crossed swords with the Royal Air Force, neither side was one hundred per cent prepared for that duel to death. Both air forces lost men and planes in such large numbers that the available replacements became only a drop in the bucket. At the end of the Battle of Britain, both the German Air Force and the R.A.F. were, for the time being, mere shells of their former power. For a moment the war in the air stopped.

Nor did the Japanese Air Force have the wherewithal to maintain its strength in proportion to the losses which were incurred. As the war in the Pacific progressed, the Japanese found they were losing their most experienced leaders, their air staffs, their planners and best mechanics, in a strange way. Their key people were being marooned and by-passed as we advanced across the Pacific. The loss of such specialists helped to break the strength of the Japanese Air Force. No air force can lose hundreds, perhaps thousands, of its trained personnel—especially in the experienced technical and staff categories—and maintain the same standard of effectiveness. The Japanese had no other sources from which to pick up experience in the air. They did not have it in China, or in Japan.

One of the big things, in my opinion, that made our Air Force great, was that, regardless of losses, our missions sent into Germany as the war progressed were always of relatively the same, or greater, size and strength. After the first bad period, no matter how many of our planes the Germans might knock down on a given day, the Eighth Air Force could come back with the same number, or perhaps in greater numbers than the day before. By late 1944 the opposition became negligible, and we could go when and where we wished, with little or no interference.

Likewise, in the air war with the Japanese, our strength constantly increased; theirs steadily diminished. When we first started our B-29 raids over Japan, we had to operate at somewhat high altitudes (about 17,000 feet) or at night, and our losses were fairly large. As we approached V-J Day, we bombed Japan actually at will, at altitudes of our own choosing (as low as 8000 and even 5000 feet) with practically no losses. In the last phase, before Hiroshima, we used B-29's without armor, and with almost no guns. When it came time to drop the atomic bomb, we were so sure that any B-29 would reach its objective without opposition that we sent the second of these preciously laden planes without escort.

We were able to do these things in spite of the fact that at the end of the war there were thousands more airplanes theoretically available to the Germans than they had had at the beginning. The Japanese still had as many combat planes on V-J Day as at the start of the war. But they no longer had trained combat crews, mechanics, gasoline, or oil. Our bombers had attended to that.

But in 1942 both the long-range fighter escort over Germany and the B-29 were still a long way off. After several months of observation of operations in Guadalcanal and against the Japanese in New Guinea, the Joint Chiefs of Staff were convinced our technique for advancing across the Pacific must be changed. The President once said at one of our Joint Chiefs of Staff meetings with him, that were we to continue our present method of crossing the Pacific, it would require us about 2000 years to reach the mainland of Japan. We talked about various methods, and finally the "leapfrog" technique was suggested, I believe by General Marshall, and was adopted in both the South and the Southwest Pacific. Islands and areas known to be strongly defended by the Japanese were by-passed, and the Japanese supply lines, stretched so thinly, could give the marooned garrisons no reinforcements or supplies. The by-passed garrisons could turn native; they could try to cut through jungles to tie up with other Japanese garrisons; or they could succumb to disease or hunger and "die on the vine"; and such localities were used as alternative targets by our raiding bomber crews, or to break in newly arrived bombardment units from the United States.

However, as I say, in January of 1942 this was still all very much in the future, and the period between January and the late summer of 1942 was one of confusion, uncertainty, and considerable vacillation in the United States. During this time the Japanese and the Germans both pushed forward in many areas. The British received more setbacks as Rommel advanced toward Egypt. The pocket battleships *Scharnhorst* and *Gneisenau* escaped from Brest to Germany. The British and the American people demanded action—and it didn't seem to make any difference what action.

As the Japanese drove down into the Malay Peninsula and captured Singapore, sinking the *Repulse* and the *Prince of Wales* from the air almost as a by-product of their passage—as they finally captured all of Burma, the British cry was: "More aid to the Royal Air Force in the Far East! More aid for the ground forces in Burma!" The British seemed to think more in terms of retaining what was left—or not quite left—of the British Empire, than in terms of carrying the war to a successful conclusion in one major theater.

This attitude was not confined to the British. We had people in the United States who demanded reinforcements for MacArthur; reinforcements for the Philippines; reinforcements for our troops on islands in the Pacific; build-up of strength in Alaska; help for the Chinese. Some even protested against sending troops to Europe!

The trip of General Marshall and Harry Hopkins to London to nail down a plan for strategic operations in 1942 brought the tacit approval of all British and American top-flight leaders concerned for an invasion of Western Europe sometime in 1942 or in 1943. The exact date set for the invasion varied from time to time with the aspect of the war in Europe; whether the Russians were doing well or badly; whether the British troops in North Africa were holding Rommel, or whether Rommel was driving on toward Egypt.

So it was we talked of GYMNAST (the landings in northwest Africa), MAGNET (getting troops into North Ireland), BOLERO (preparations for the expeditionary force going into northwest Europe), ROUNDUP (the invasion of Europe in 1943), SLEDGEHAMMER (an air commando invasion of Europe as conditions warranted) or TORCH (a revised GYMNAST, or northwest African project). For a matter of weeks, it was impossible to say just which, if any, of these projects we would carry out, or when. It seemed to be a case of "off ag'in, on ag'in, gone ag'in, Finnegan." By the summer of 1942, it was generally accepted that the strategy would be TORCH and ROUNDUP, and a continued hammering of interior Germany by our heavy bomber concentrations. The British always by-passed SLEDGEHAMMER, so this project was finally thrown out the window.

The Army Air Forces proceeded with their plans for concentrating as many bombers as they could in England, and destroying the targets that would do the most harm to the German war effort.

In the opinion of the Air Staff—an opinion in which I concurred heartily—every time we changed a strategic concept of how to win the war, or the sequence of operations in the various theaters; every time we moved heavy bombers from England to North Africa or to the South Pacific, we were delaying the end of the German war to that extent. From this point of view, the constant agitation for two or three additional groups of heavy bombers to the Southwest Pacific or to MacArthur, or to Burma or to China seemed wasteful.

For instance, early in the spring of 1942 it was decided the 97th Bombardment Group would fly its B-17's, the 1st Pursuit Group its P-38's, and the 31st Pursuit Group its P-39's to England, via Presque Isle, Maine, Goose Bay, in Labrador, then to Ireland and on to England. It was also decided General Frank O'D. Hunter would have charge of the air movement. The B-17's were to lead the flights of fighter planes across the Atlantic, in order to provide a regular navigational team in charge of each particular element of the flight. The three groups moved up to Maine, and were getting their final training in that area when the Japanese Fleet steamed toward Midway.

Orders went out from Washington suspending the movement of all planes and directing the 97th Bomb Group and the 1st Pursuit Group to go to the West Coast for assignment to the Western Defense Command until it was definitely ascertained what was going to happen out in the Solomons. In the meantime, the P-39 Group (the 31st), not having any B-17's to lead them over the Atlantic, were sent across to England by boat. When they arrived in England, they were equipped with British Spitfires.

The 97th left the concentration area in New England on June 2nd, and reached our fields on the West Coast the next day. While they were there, the Staff decided that the critical conditions in the Pacific were over, so by the 18th of June, the group was back at its station in preparation for the flight across the Atlantic. The 1st Fighter Group which had never gone any farther than Morris Field, North Carolina, was returned to its concentration area from there.

On June 23rd the B-17's of the 97th Bombardment Group, the P-38's of the 1st Fighter Group, started their movement across the North Atlantic. They were followed closely by the 92nd and 301st Bomb Groups, the 14th Fighter Group, and the 64th Troop Carrier Group. At the end of August, 164 P-38's, 119 of our B-17's, and 103 of our C-47's had flown the Atlantic to England.

We had anticipated a loss of about 10 per cent in this mass movement, but actually our casualties were about 4 per cent, 862 of the assorted planes that had started the hazardous trans-Atlantic trek arriving at their destination in perfect shape.

All U.S. planes in Europe were already under the command of General Spaatz, who had arrived in England at about the same time as Eisenhower. VIII Bomber Command, the carrier of our real hopes against Germany, was under Brigadier General Ira C. Eaker, who had arrived with the first small nucleus of his staff on February 20th. He had no airplanes until rather late that summer with which to answer the arguments of "Bomber" Harris and the other R.A.F. zealots for night bombing. In fact, on the 4th of July, when he received his first lone B-17, his entire airplane strength otherwise was one squadron of A-20's, attached to him temporarily on its way to North Africa, and one AT-6 trainer.

This was a rough time to have to hold the fort for American precision bombardment by daylight without any airplanes to prove your point. Since the first "Thousand Raid" on May 30th, the powerful prospect of bombing the life out of Germany had mushroomed up with still more

full-scale assaults on Germany by the R.A.F. But though public opinion
—in Germany too, judging from the screams in Goebbel's controlled
press—now was alerted to heavy bombardment as the Big Thing,
that meant the R.A.F.'s kind of bombardment—night bombardment of
the German cities. And having sold the idea, Bertie Harris and R.A.F.
Bomber Command were still only beginning, themselves, just as we arrived. They still had to get the real tools, the Lancasters and Halifaxes
that had been submitted as blueprints as early as 1936.

As the vanguard of the Eighth Air Force arrived in England, Bertie
Harris was still selling, as he had to do. And our vast reservoir of equipment was tempting. If our B-17's and B-24's were not adaptable to night
operations with the R.A.F., as we insisted, well then, argued numerous
Britishers in high places, what about switching a reasonable portion of
that great American production machinery over to the building of Lancasters? And so on. After all, the R.A.F. had proved this thing about day
and night bombing now! It was all friendly, but it was diabolically persistent. We had a tough time in Washington, and so did "Tooey" Spaatz,
Ira Eaker, George Kenney, and all the other Air Force commanders, and
we knew it.

As it had done all his life, Ira Eaker's natural gift for diplomacy
played a leading part in getting the Army Air Forces over this hump.
One time, in the very early days, at a dinner in a room in High Wycombe
where Disraeli had once spoken, Eaker was called on by the eager English guests for a speech. He rose, and did as well, I think, as Victoria's
Prime Minister could have done. "We won't do much talking," he said
quietly, "until we've done more fighting. When we leave, I hope you'll
be glad we came. Thank you."—and sat down.

In the end, as told elsewhere, when his pioneer planes and crews had
given him his first real ammunition, he helped me at Casablanca with
his intimate knowledge of daylight bombing. Backed by Spaatz, Andrews
and Eaker, I was able to convince the President, the Prime Minister and
the Combined Chiefs of Staff of the efficacy of daylight bombing, and
to tip the scales in its favor, for good.

We didn't know quite how we were going to make that offensive work
at first; we got conflicting advice from our Allies from every side. All
we knew was that we *would* make it work, it *could* work, and that *when*
it started to work, Germany would suffer in a way that R.A.F. Bomber
Command's heavy night assaults by themselves could not insure.

We faced the fact that weather in that theater, especially in the daytime, would remain as constant an enemy as the Germans. At first we

could count on an average of only seven operating days a month. For we had to *see* the target. At the beginning, the navigator had to find it through the foggy clouds to hit it; the bombardier had to see it with his eyes through the bombsight. The wonderful instruments, like H2X, H2S, Gee-H, Mickey, and Oboe, that were to allow us eventually to operate on any kind of day, had not made their appearance. These instruments, developed jointly by the British and ourselves, were to increase the precision of the R.A.F.'s night bombing until it compared favorably with ours. They were jointly shared, like our target intelligence.

As explained, we always knew that we would have to have long-range fighter escort to carry out the campaign to a conclusion; but we also knew we couldn't wait for it. It was a race. The technical innovations, the underground installations found in Germany at the end, even after the two-year round-the-clock pounding, proved that. Our long-range P-47 was not able to go 340 miles with the bombers until July, 1943. By constant driving and effort, this was raised to 425 miles, in February, 1944. The P-38's could go 585 miles by that month, and the escort fighter that marked the climax, the P-51 Mustang, had "legs" on it then that enabled it to dart ahead of the B-17's and B-24's, clearing the skies for them, for 825 miles, all the way across Germany.

But February, 1944, was quite a long time after August 17, 1942, the date of the Eighth Air Force's first little mission to Rouen. It will be understood why we were so excited when that first air battle over the Channel on the 21st of August—9 B-17's against 25 Focke Wulf 190's—proved that the Fortresses were going to be able to keep going on their own as no other unescorted bombers had ever before. Even in the bad month of October, 1943, deep in Germany, when the second Schweinfurt mission wiped out 28 per cent of the day's attacking force, the total loss rate for the month was 7 per cent. By October, 1944, the average had dropped to 2 per cent, and by March, 1945, it was down to 1.4 per cent. By then, not fighters but flak had come to be the worst casualty maker, especially at the distant, fiercely defended oil targets at Merseburg, Poelitz, and Brüx.

It may be said that we could have had the long-range P-51 in Europe rather sooner than we did. That we did not have it sooner was the Air Force's own fault. I have debated with myself how much of that story I should tell here. For seven years aviation people, in and out of the service, have been muttering about it. It seems to me, however, that one of the great "miracles" of the war was the fact that the full long-range fighter escort did appear over Germany at just the saving moment, in the very nick of time to keep our bomber offensive going without a break; and some of the people who achieved this were the same ones who made the initial mistake.

Briefly, in 1940, "Dutch" Kindelberger, of North American, was asked to build P-40's for the British. "Dutch" could not see his way to building P-40's, so he had his engineers dig down in their files, pull out a concept of a fighter, and modernize it. The drawings of this—the P-51—were completed by May, 1940, and submitted to the British as a substitute for the P-40. Our Materiel Division was not particularly interested, but they did say that if North American built these for the British, we were to get two P-51's for nothing.

The first airplane was completed toward the latter part of 1940. Production was not started until the middle part of 1941 (Jane's *All the World's Aircraft* states December, 1941). When I went overseas in the spring of 1941, Tommy Hitchcock and Mr. Winant talked to me about the P-51, although they didn't know much about it at that time. Spaatz and I went out to the North American plant in January or February— anyway, early in 1942—and it was then that we saw and inspected it and decided that we must have the P-51 for our own Air Force, in spite of the Materiel Division's turning it down.

We made plenty of other mistakes during the war. The case of the Mosquito is one. It was obvious from the start that we would have to have a very fast airplane, capable of flying at extremely high altitudes, to take aerial photographs. With height and speed, a photo reconnaissance plane could evade German fighter attacks. In the United States, our P-38 was the only plane that approximated these requirements. We tried our best to use it as a high-altitude photo-reconnaissance plane but with only fair luck. The only such airplane the Royal Air Force had was the twin-engine Mosquito, built of plywood, the most effective photo-recon plane yet seen in the war. The obvious thing to do was to get Mosquitoes from the British.

I thought it would be simple. We were giving the British, under lend-lease, and in other ways, thousands of airplanes, and it should have been an easy matter for them to turn a few hundred Mosquitoes over to us, thereby enabling us to get a high-altitude photo plane without going to all the trouble and expense of designing and building one of our own.

At first, we were told the British were going to build Mosquitoes in Canada; that we could get them from Canada. Later, we found out that plan was not going through. Then we were told we could have the drawings and build them ourselves. After our experience with the

British Merlin engine (trying to change their metric drawings into our standard measurements) that was out of the question. When we tried to buy some Mosquitoes from the British, we were told they didn't have enough for their own use and therefore couldn't spare any. We did ultimately receive a few, but not many, for use in the Mediterranean Theater and in England. Consequently, I looked around in the United States to find an airplane with comparable characteristics. The only one which seemed to fill the bill was Howard Hughes' famous F-11. Our experts looked over this plane and its drawings to determine whether it would actually meet all our requirements, and reported it would. However, when the matter was turned over to our Materiel Command people, they all recommended against procurement of the F-11, their main reason being, I think, the fact that they did not believe we would get the planes in time to fight the war. I rather doubted it myself, but I also knew if we did not *try* to get some, we most certainly wouldn't get any. At that point it was the Hughes plane or nothing. So, much against my better judgment and against the advice of my staff I gave instructions to buy the famous F-11 airplane. My guess was wrong. The F-11 was never delivered during the war. The first one was turned over to the Air Force about a year and a half after the war was over. This was the airplane that was the subject of considerable investigation by the Ferguson Committee in Congress.

But, all over the world during those years, we learned many things the hard way. Take for example, the lesson of the battle of Midway. Intercepted Japanese messages, decoded, gave us information that a Japanese Fleet was moving toward Midway, or perhaps Hawaii. Accordingly, from Hawaii west, all naval carriers and surface ships were ordered out to meet and destroy the enemy.

On June 3, 1943, part of the Japanese Naval Force was sighted from a flying boat some 400 miles to the westward of Midway. Next day, another part of the force, with heavy carrier concentration, was located 180 miles to the north of Midway. It was the largest concentration of Japanese naval strength yet assembled in the Pacific, and, apparently, it was heading toward Midway with the capture of that island as its objective.

In the two-day battle of Midway our B-17's, with Marine land-based aircraft, were used intensively. The pilots of the Forts and their green crews were firm in their conviction that they had not only hit some of the larger Japanese ships, but had sunk them. But it was really the carrier-borne Navy planes, on this occasion, that arrived in time to turn the Japanese expedition back. It taught me a lesson.

The battle of Midway was the reality which the Army Air Force had simulated for years. Yet, when the opportunity came, we did not measure up to the high standard we had set for ourselves.

Whatever the reasons, the battle of Midway was to be a thorn in my side for many months, as we were criticized from all around the compass for not getting more hits by our high-altitude precision bombing, and were called upon, time and time again, to make a restudy to be sure we were on the right track. Should we continue our high-altitude precision bombing, when we might have been making dive-bombing, or low-altitude attacks? It took a long time to prove we were right.

Air participation in the North African campaign was still a rather difficult arrangement to work out. In the first place, we had considerable trouble in understanding exactly what General Spaatz' relationship was with General Eisenhower with regard to the air arm in Great Britain. The Air Arm, of course, our first year and a half there, was the only force carrying on offensive operations against Germany. The ground troops were simply building up until they could attain sufficient strength to make a cross-Channel assault. In the North African invasion, Eisenhower was in supreme command; Spaatz was his air adviser; but Doolittle was in command of the Twelfth Air Force.

Doolittle's problems were complicated, as we have seen. So were Brereton's, who was with Tedder, Coningham, Alexander and Montgomery.

The strategic mission of Brereton's handful of heavy bombers was to destroy sea communications, harbors, and the Italian fleet. Up until the time Montgomery was able to break through the El Alamein line, the little Ninth Air Force, working with the R.A.F., hammered continuously at the Ports of Benghazi and Tobruk. As reports indicated, they reduced the capacity of the Tobruk harbor from 2000 tons a day to 200 tons a day. At Benghazi an ammunition ship was blown up, the destruction of which reduced the port facilities about 50 per cent.

The Ninth's fighter and medium bomber outfits were organized into the Desert Air Task Force, which cooperated directly with the British Eighth Army, with the primary objective of destroying enemy aircraft, tanks, motor transport and landing field facilities. Brereton had for this, first, one fighter group (P-40's) and one medium bomber group (B-25's), and later, an additional fighter group. These three mobile groups and their bases, with the rest of Coningham's Western Desert

Air Force, followed closely upon the heels of the Eighth Army in order to get the maximum troop support range. The small American part of that combined Desert Air Force, which was moving westward to join up later with Doolittle's Twelfth Air Force, was very proud of its accomplishments, and rightly so. It had a record, during the drive to Tunisia, of 42 enemy planes destroyed to every 1 of its own which was lost or missing.

In another corner of the world the Tenth Air Force had been organized in China—starting with the American Volunteer Group (AVG), the Flying Tigers, which later became our 23rd Fighter Group. It started operations on July 24, 1942, operating from the general area of Chungking, in Yunnan Province. In general, its mission was to destroy enemy airports, enemy airplanes; to attack with dive bombing technique gunboats, junks, barges. A little later in the summer the 11th Bombardment Squadron, with B-25's, joined up with the Tenth Air Force.

The B-25's hit shipping, docks, enemy airdromes, enemy supply depots, troop concentrations, and other targets which were known to be vital to the war effort. The tremendous distances in China made it essential that these B-25's have longer "legs" than those normally employed in other theaters and some extra morale. The legs they obtained by putting on extra tanks; the morale they supplied themselves.

Their operations were more in the nature of aerial guerilla warfare than of the stereotyped form of aerial warfare conducted, for instance, in the European theater. General Chennault, by his long years of experience with the Chinese, and his uncanny sense of anticipating what the Japs would probably do, was able to adopt formations and techniques for his Tenth Air Force which could not be used in any other theater.

General C. V. Haynes was actually in command of the Tenth Air Force; General Chennault was the air adviser to Generalissimo Chiang Kai-shek, in addition to being commander of all air units in China.

In the meantime, General Kenney, by his initiative and his new techniques, was able to overcome such major difficulties in the South Pacific as long distances over water; flights over jungles, over high mountains; the bad weather normal to his theater.

When the Owen-Stanley mountain range confronted the troops who landed in and around Port Moresby, and it was essential that bases be established on the other side of the mountains, Kenney didn't hesitate to use what undercover personnel and facilities were available, to locate level strips upon which light planes like Piper Cubs could be landed. The puddle jumpers would land, loaded with such hand tools and men as they could carry, and, discharging their personnel and "cargo," return across the Owen-Stanley range. The men who had been landed would make contact with the natives, and soon an air strip would be started. It would not be long before a large transport could come in with bigger tools, and the air strip would be further expanded, until finally it was possible to land earth-moving and road-building tools and equipment for expanding the air strip to accommodate the medium and heavy bombers. Shortly thereafter, fighter planes would go in. Infantry and other ground soldiers would be landed, and thus a stronghold would be established in the rear of the Japanese lines. Gasoline and oil would be made available to the fighters, which would give them, or the medium bombers, longer legs, so that they could operate farther and farther behind the Japanese lines. The Army Engineers who worked with General Kenney on this project, joined in the game with the same zest as their commander.

Kenney's letter, giving a general estimate of the situation, as of January 1, 1943, is of interest:

A few more days, and the action will be confined to keeping the Nip away from this area where I am flying the engineers, machinery, steel mat and bitumen over to make a 2-squadron Fighter layout as fast as possible. We will then enlarge the show for the light Bombers and provide for topping off the Mediums and Heavies to increase their range on other targets.

I am convinced that America, including the War Department, has no conception of the problem confronting them in this theatre. The Jap is still being under-rated. There is no question of our being able to defeat him, but the time, effort, blood and money required to do the job may run to proportions beyond all conception, particularly, if the devil is allowed to develop the resources he is now holding.

Let us look at Buna. There are hundreds of Bunas ahead of us. The Jap there has been in a hopeless position for two months. He has been outnumbered heavily throughout the show. His garrison has been whittled down to a handful by bombing and strafing. He has had no air support, and his own Navy has not been able to get past our air blockade to help him. He has seen lots of Japs sunk off shore a few miles away. He has been short on rations and has had to conserve his ammunition, as his replenishment from submarines and small boats working down from Lae at night, and, once, by parachute from airplanes, has been precarious, to say the least. The Emperor told them to hold, and, believe me, they have held! As to their morale—they still yell out to our troops, "What's the matter, Yanks? Are you yellow? Why don't you come in and fight?" A few snipers, asked to surrender after being surrounded, called back, "If you bastards think you are good enough, come and get us!"

The Jap asks no quarter, and expects none. His psychology is to win or perish, and I believe that is the national psychology. He is undoubtedly a low order of humanity, but he has sense enough to use the weapons of war, and does a good job of it! He is far better off in the army, where he is comparatively well-fed and clothed, than as a half-starved coolie at home. At home, he can't indulge in his Mongol liking for looting, arson, massacre and rape. In the army, he can look forward to all four. His future life is assured if he dies in the service of his god—the Emperor.

After eight years of constant warfare, which has not been all victory, he is about as war-weary as a hungry Bengal tiger who has just seen a fat lamb ahead of him on the trail. He can live off the country anywhere in this theatre.

Regardless of how soon Germany collapses, the Jap show is independent of Germany's. The Nip is taking advantage of our preoccupation elsewhere, but the collapse of Germany will not stop Japan from continuing her program, which, I believe, is to dominate Asia, and at least the western half of the Pacific—or perish.

The Jap weakness, and our real hope for victory, is in the air. His fleet and his army can hold their own in any league, but he simply cannot train airmen to compare with ours in a hurry. His original highly trained crews were superb, but they are dead. His new crews cannot fly in bad weather, his night efforts are piddling, and his combat skill is low. Our hurriedly trained youngsters are outflying and outshooting him at every encounter. All he has left is sheer guts. We wipe out a huge percentage of his raiding squadrons, but he keeps coming.

As in this Papuan campaign, we will keep on—first, gaining local air control, then, flying troops in and seizing some ground outside his position, bombing and strafing to kill him off and prevent his getting supplies and reinforcements. This part goes through quite rapidly. Eventually, however, the troops get in close contact in an area so restricted that if we bomb, we kill both our own troops and the Japs. This final, hand-to-hand, cut-throat, no-quarter, battle-to-extinction of the Jap, who is a master craftsman at organizing a piece of ground for a last-ditch defense, is what takes time. Our troops are not trained for it. Our school books haven't been teaching this game. This is a war of the highly-trained squad, the section and the platoon, whose actions must be coordinated by smart company and battalion commanders. We have got to get back to the days when we learned how to fight the Indians in the woods and eventually beat them at their own game. In this theatre we need lots of aircraft, lots of engineers to build and maintain airdromes, and a lot of comparatively small, highly-trained combat units of jungle fighters who can go over the trails, or be transported by air, or use native canoes, or barges, to work along the coast. They must, above all, be trained in night fighting. They must know how to live off the country, supplemented with iron rations on their backs, for a couple of weeks at a time. They have got to learn how to keep from getting sick. We have evacuated around 6000 from the north coast to Moresby by air this month, and three-fourths of them are sick. Some of it can't be helped, but lots of it can, with better education and discipline of the soldiers.

The above is not a plea for anything. You know what I want, and I know you are giving me all you can. All I am doing in writing this story is giving the picture as I see it. The picture is getting more vivid all the time. I'm afraid that a lot of people who think this Jap is a "pushover" as soon as Germany falls, are due for a rude awakening. We will have to call on all our patriotism, stamina, guts, and maybe some crusading spirit or religious fervor thrown in, to beat him. No amateur team will take this boy out. We have got to turn professional. Another thing: there are no quiet sectors in which troops get started off gradually, as in the last war. There are no breathers on this schedule. You take on Notre Dame every time you play!

Sincerely,
GEORGE C. KENNEY

In January, 1942, the strength of Kenney's Air Force was 13 heavy bombers and 101 fighters. By December, 1942, he had been built up to 81 heavy bombers, 83 medium bombers, and 238 fighters. Kenney's Fifth Air Force went along on that strength until the middle of 1943. By the first part of 1944 it was about doubled. There was no further increase during all his operations in the Pacific until the U.S. forces landed in the Philippines.

The conditions attending the operations of the Thirteenth Air Force, commanded by Brigadier General Saunders, were different again.

To start with, they were part of the Hawaiian Air Force; but at five o'clock one afternoon they received an order which directed them to move out the next day. One boatload of their ground personnel was loaded that same afternoon. It was the 24th of August when they took off for Samoa and Efate. Almost at once they were ordered to go out and hit the Japs.

The field at Espiritu Santo was supposed to be ready for use on the 31st of August. From that time on, Saunders' group started operating against Guadalcanal and Tulagi. They had no ground defense for the airdrome, which was cut out from the midst of a cocoanut grove; and the logistics were terrible. They had no maintenance personnel for weeks, except the men they had carried with them in their airplanes.

As a matter of fact, when they tried to get their ground personnel from Efate up to Espiritu Santo, no boats were available. However, a staff officer who was quite a "fixer," knew the captain of a copra boat. For two quarts of Scotch, the captain of the boat said, "If you will get all the squadron loaded tonight, we will take you up while waiting for the load of copra." (The distance was 180 miles.) And that was the way that squadron went up to Espiritu Santo.

There were no docks, no roads; no facilities at all. The Army and the Navy construction units had to build them. To perform longer missions, our airmen used the landing field at Guadalcanal, when it was available. That was after the U.S. forces had so cleared out the Japs that they weren't constantly fired upon, and the construction units had had time to give it a top surface to permit B-17's to land and take off.

In order to get gasoline on to Espiritu Santo, they had to dump it off the decks of the ships and "swim" the drums in to the beach. About 20,000 gallons of gasoline had to be landed on the beach in this manner every day, then loaded into trucks and stored in improvised dumps. Saunders modestly said, "The operations were difficult here." And then, later on, talking about his crews and the way they lived, Saunders said, "Our living conditions are very poor out here. When I left, after six months they hadn't gotten our combat crews off the ground. No lumber; no screening; not enough transportation. Every theater, I imagine, has its own troubles. We certainly didn't have conveniences. It was hard for the morale of the crews, having to come back from long missions, to a muddy tent. There was no place for recreation or rest down there. We did start sending some crews down to Auckland, New Zealand, the last of October—eight crews at a time, for a week—to afford them a little rest."

Saunders, while not complaining, said it was rather hard to adhere to the bombardment principles he had learned back in the States. The airdrome facilities did not permit his boys to take off in force to effect a good bombing pattern. They had many airplanes on the airdrome, but no circulating taxiways, and no traffic control. It took them three months to set up a traffic-control tower, which had to be built up above the cocoanut trees to give them the necessary visibility.

Most of their missions were search operations; hunting for the enemy fleet; any kind of hostile ships that might attack our own. But there were others. Saunders told of one occasion when a Marine colonel, a regimental commander, looked him up, and said, "I don't know whether you remember the incident, but I would like to shake hands with the pilot of a certain B-17." "What was the occasion?" asked Saunders. The Marine colonel said, "Well, three destroyers came in right after we landed at Guadalcanal, and started shelling our beaches. They were giving us hell. Then, one B-17, carrying four bombs, came back from its search, took a run on one of the destroyers, and knocked the stern off it; the others all took off." Saunders said that squadron leader was a wonderful bombardier; he never missed. The Marine colonel said, "All those 10,000 Marines on Guadalcanal were watching. Of course, they couldn't do a hell of a lot of watching from their trenches, but after that bombing they jumped up and all 10,000 of them cheered to beat hell! That was the most uplifting incident that ever happened at Guadalcanal!"

Saunders also said, "You are not going to hit a destroyer very often, because they can turn on a dime, and you have to go down to a very low altitude. We tried. The destroyers can get away from your pattern." Incidentally, he spoke more feelingly of the enemy's 16-inch shells on Guadalcanal than of his own bombs.

General Saunders said, "I can't stress too much here, the type of work our B-17 pilots have turned in on reconnaissance search missions. I think they develop contact much better than Navy PBY's. I say that, naturally, because they have better defensive equipment, and can stay around a little bit longer. Admiral Fitch was very commendatory in his comments about our search planes. It takes an experienced crew to hang around and develop contacts where carriers are involved."

The Thirteenth had to learn an entirely different method of navigating, as most of their flying was out over the water, and their return trips to the flying fields were made at night. Most of their targets were targets of opportunity: targets that appeared suddenly, and had to be attacked just as suddenly, or they would disappear.

The Eleventh Air Force, in Alaska, first under Butler and then under General Davenport Johnson, had problems still different from any of the others. Up there, the temperature goes down to 60° or 70° below zero for days at a time. At Fairbanks there is perpetual frost, perpetual ice, three feet below the surface of the ground. After an airplane was brought out of a hangar in this extremely cold weather, although it might have been well heated inside, the oil would congeal before the engines could be started.

Out on the Aleutians, the weather changed from snowstorms to rainstorms to hailstorms to fog—one following right after another. The "flyable" days, as we called them in the United States, were very few. The number of possible airport sites was closely limited, because the islands, themselves, seemed to be mountain peaks sticking out from the surface of the ocean. The only way we could make airports was to put dikes around the coastal plain, or saw off the top or the side of a mountain, in order to secure a sufficiently large level area.

When our airmen first went up to Alaska and had missions out of the Aleutians, they were appalled by the weather conditions. It was "blind" flying practically all the time: "blind" on take-off, until they penetrated above the clouds; "blind" on coming in for a landing, with always the threat of running into a mountain when trying to find their landing field.

On their search missions, the weather normally was so thick that, traveling at the speeds they flew—200 to 250 miles an hour—they would pass a Japanese ship, see it momentarily—in a flash—and lose it. Before they could turn to relocate it, it would be gone.

In spite of the apprehensions of all our various commanders, there wasn't any real threat in Alaska until June of 1942, and by that time we had a respectable Air Force there. It wasn't very large, but we didn't need a large Air Force up there, because of the small number of Japanese planes against which we operated. However, by June, 1942, we had a big air base at Anchorage; one at Fairbanks, and at Sitka; and one at Kodiak, for the Navy. In addition to that, we had smaller air bases out along the Aleutian Islands.

On June 4th there was an enemy bomber attack on our base at Dutch Harbor. Our Army and Navy flyers had located an enemy fleet, consisting of two carriers, two cruisers and eight destroyers, some 150 or more miles to the southwest. The weather, as usual, was lousy: fog, rain, and snow. In spite of this, our aircraft sank one of the enemy cruisers, damaged another, and forced the enemy to withdraw. Ten days later, however, it was learned by aerial reconnaissance that the Japanese had landed on Kiska island, then on Attu island, and then on Agattu. From that time on, everybody who had anything to do with the Alaskan Theater was on my neck to get more and more airplanes to the Eleventh Air Force in order to drive the Japanese out of the Aleutians.

Actually, the taking of the Aleutians by the Japanese was not a real threat to the security of the United States. It was only a thorn in our side, giving the local columnists and the commentators a subject to talk about. It was a fine theme to show how well the Japanese were doing— and how poorly we were doing.

As a matter of fact, our forces in Alaska, few though they were, drove the Japanese out—but didn't know they had done it until the aerial photographs we received in the United States indicated that the enemy bases in the Aleutians had been abandoned.

We had hardly solved the Japanese situation in Alaska, when we had the Russian situation thrust upon us. It was decided we would turn over our airplanes to the Russians at our Fairbanks station. The attitude of the Russians was not calculated to create good relationships with our people. They wanted to take over the whole Fairbanks base; they wanted to take over the best houses; they wanted to have everything given to them. By the 30th of October, I had felt impelled to write to the Chief of Staff: "Their attitude toward our aircraft is one of tolerant acceptance. At no time have they shown any enthusiasm regarding performance or other characteristics. They are definitely critical of the armament and mechanical deficiencies." In other words, they were not really so anxious to get the airplanes as the senior officers of the Russian Government would have our President and our Secretary of War to believe.

★ 22 ★

With the landing of our troops in North Africa, it had become obvious to the members of the Joint and the Combined Chiefs of Staff that there must be a meeting with the President and the Prime Minister to determine "where do we go from here." Not until the invasion was actually accomplished had we been ready, positively, to plan for what, where, and when our next action should be. Accordingly, arrangements were completed for a meeting of the "Big Two" and the Combined Chiefs of Staff at Casablanca, in January, 1943.

On January 9th, two C-54's were standing by at Gravelly Point, ready to take the Joint Chiefs of Staff and their advisers to the meeting place at Casablanca. The route to be followed was: Washington to Borinquen, Puerto Rico; to Belém, Brazil; to Natal, Brazil; to Bathurst, West Africa; to Marrakech, French Morocco, and then into Casablanca.

At 7:45 A.M., with everybody present and baggage aboard, the C-54's were ready to go. The secret papers were stored in steel locked boxes with detonators attached, so they could be destroyed in case of an emergency. The first plane carried General Marshall, Sir John Dill, myself, General Dykes (British Secretary of Staff), General Deane (Secretary of our Joint Chiefs of Staff), Colonel McCarthy, and Otis Bryan, captain of the aircraft. In the second plane were Admiral King, General Somervell, General Wedemeyer, Commander Libby, and Commander Cook.

We took off at 8:30 A.M., climbing through the overcast and flying in and out of clouds until the shores of Puerto Rico came into sight. We landed at Borinquen Field at 4:55 P.M. Here protocol took over unexpectedly and there wasn't much that could be done about it. General Marshall and Sir John Dill were the ranking officers in the first plane and it had been decided they would land first. However, either Admiral King's pilot flew a more direct course, or his plane was a little faster. It arrived first and had to circle around for forty minutes, waiting for the senior plane to arrive. A delay in landing, such as that, especially in hot weather in the tropics, always causes a bit of ill humor, but once we were down and had been assigned to comfortable quarters at the Borinquen base, everybody was happy again.

The night at Borinquen was most pleasant—cool, with a nice breeze blowing, so all slept well. The following morning all hands were up for breakfast at 5:00 o'clock; in our planes, and off at 6:15. We had the same kind of weather as on the preceding day—broken clouds with rough air in and around them, but no storms.

During such flights I always took my turn in the pilot's seat at the control and flew the plane for a regular two-hour stretch. This enabled me to keep up my flying experience and gave me an opportunity to get acquainted with the latest gadgets on the newer type of planes. It also permitted the regular crew to have more time off and longer rest periods.

The plane passed Cape San Vincente and from then on no land was sighted until we hit Dutch Guiana, Paramaribo, about 12:30. The coast line was covered—as was normal—with broken clouds. About 500 miles farther on we thought we were going to have trouble, when one of our engines kicked up. The trouble continued for about 500 miles—a condition that did not make me feel too happy in view of my passenger list and the unsettled jungle beneath us. However, the engine finally settled down and ran smoothly to Belém. We landed at 4:20 and were met by General Bob Walsh, the Army officer in charge of United States relations with Brazil, and Admiral Jonas Ingram, in charge of Navy affairs in South America.

I had a long talk with Admiral Ingram about conditions in South America and told him I would stop at Ascension Island on my return to get a better idea of operations there. The next morning we took off at eight o'clock for Natal.

During the trip I discussed with General Marshall and Sir John Dill the use of C-54's to replace ships in carrying our Air Force troops to Europe, putting fifty to seventy-five men on each plane. One hundred four-engine planes per month could take care of all our Air Force shipments. The idea sounded all right, but we reached no decision. At that time we were very short of ships and it was a question whether we would be able to get all our Air Force mechanics and other ground personnel across in time to service the airplanes we were ferrying overseas.

We flew over Fontenjaleos, a small town of about 5000 and were surprised to note it had two airports: one with no runways, and the other with a long "blacktop" runway. Obviously, the one without the runway was a standard Brazilian airport; the one with the "blacktop" was the airport that had been prepared by the Pan American Air Lines for the Army Air Force. Our plane flew along smoothly. Soon the country changed. We passed a bay that looked almost like Carmel Bay in California, with its backdrop of sand dunes. Natal came up above the horizon in direct contrast with the blue ocean on its east side. We had a composite picture of tile roofs; the airport—no trees nor grass nor vegetation; long, low buildings; airplanes of all types dispersed around the airdromes; long, "blacktop" runways; miles of open country. We landed at 1:45 and had lunch at the Officers' Club, inspected the Port and took off again at 4:55 P.M.

We crossed the equator at 8:05. I took my turn at the controls that night from 9:00 to 12:00 o'clock. It was on this leg of the flight across the South Atlantic that we had lost several Liberators during the preceding few months. Apparently nothing unusual happened along the route. We would receive the regular routine messages from the planes, giving their locations, the details of their flight, and then would come absolute silence. We assumed the losses were due either to German submarines operating in the South Atlantic, or to German raiders which carried fighter planes aboard. The Germans probably learned of the departure of our B-24's from agents at Belém, would hear the planes' radio messages, and send up rockets. Then, when the Liberators came down to a low altitude to see if the flares were being fired by a ship in distress or from a raft from one of our lost planes, the German antiaircraft or fighter planes would shoot them down. It would happen so quickly that the B-24's could send no distress message. This was all surmise on our part; we had no means of determining exactly what had happened to the lost planes.

Just before leaving Natal, I was told by one of the pilots who had come through from Africa that the concentration of the Combined Chiefs of Staff party, which was supposed to be a deep, dark secret, was known over all Africa and was being talked about at the various airports along the route. In that case, the Germans, too, must know that the U.S. Joint Chiefs of Staff were on their way across the Atlantic to meet somewhere in Africa.

At 12:05 GMT, I was alone in the cockpit, flying the plane. It was a beautiful night. The moon was shining above the clouds and we were just topping those large masses when all of a sudden, at 3 degrees North Latitude and 28 degrees West Longitude, I saw some rockets hurtling from the water about thirty miles away. Submarines hoping to lure us down? A raider waiting until we came within range of the anti-aircraft to take a pot shot at us? An Allied ship in distress? Did the rockets come from rafts from one of our lost planes? I remembered that a short time before, one of our planes had been hit by antiaircraft and had come back to the United States with six holes in it—3″x6″ holes in its tail surface—after just such an experience.

In the rear of my plane were General Marshall, Sir John Dill, and other high-ranking officers. I could not afford to take any chances. I rang the buzzer for the captain of the plane, pointed out the flares to him and said I was going to change our course. He said, "O.K." So we went into the clouds, made a detour, and circled the flares at a distance of thirty or more miles. (Incidentally, both General Marshall and Sir John Dill took me to task for the bump that almost threw them from their bunks when we hit the clouds.) We landed at Bathurst, found it dark and cold, and sent a message back to our Navy at Natal reporting our observation.

At Bathurst, General C. R. Smith, of the Transport Command, Generals Tom Hardin and Creighton, of the Pan American Air Lines, met me and reported on the possibilities of establishing an air base at Dakar. I was pleased to learn that General Smith, in spite of "run-in's" with the State Department officials, and with the Naval commander, had been able to make arrangements with the French whereby we would be able to use the Dakar airports in about three months.

Smith said at breakfast that three reporters had told him they were going to board the *Memphis* and visit the President when he landed in Africa; so apparently there were leaks all through government circles. I hadn't told anyone outside my own office that I was going on from Casablanca to China to see Chiang Kai-shek; yet General Smith told me exactly where I was going and when. He had picked up the information on the Air Transport lines across Africa!

From Bathurst, where more pierced metal runways had been laid over the treacherous sands, we flew over miles of yellow and brown sand dunes; dry water holes; volcanic mountains; not a single tree in sight from horizon to horizon, nothing but broken hills, salt sinks, dry stream beds and dust storms! We did see four camel caravans crossing a dry river. No other sign of life for hundreds of miles. Then, out of nowhere, the town of Adrar appeared right below us, a small French outpost with adobe buildings.

We had a 35-mile wind right on our nose, so it was longer before we saw the snow-covered mountains, 14,000 feet high, appear out of the north. The territory we had covered was quite similar to our own Southwest except there were no roads or railroads; only trails and very few of them. Five hundred miles of country with no signs of habitation; and then the wonderfully fertile valley in which Marrakech is located came into view.

Marrakech is a city of about 150,000 inhabitants. Around it are orange orchards, with irrigation ditches coming down from the snow-covered mountains. It is a typical subtropical town, with varicolored adobe houses, no two of them seemingly the same shade. The airport, whose four hangars were ruined by our Navy bombers when the French wouldn't surrender farther north, was otherwise in excellent condition. Various models of American and French airplanes now stood on the airport. We landed at 4:00 P.M. and were met by General Hyde and the American Vice-Consul.

The mixture of American and French planes here again reminded me of General C. R. Smith's troubles at Dakar. Seemingly, our diplomatic service was not geared to meet the wartime conditions confronting it. Though we had to have almost countless airdromes in a hurry to get our planes across to the combat areas, the American diplomats at Dakar seemed to go out of their way to find obstacles. Instead of helping General Smith, they explained why things could *not* be done. Yet, when Smith took matters into his own hands, he received authority from the French and we were able to get the airdromes completed in three months.

Driving in to Marrakech we were taken to the home of Mrs. Moses Taylor. In its beautifully kept gardens were palms, dates, olives, navel oranges, and tangerines—large sweet oranges, the like of which California has never seen. Beautiful, subtropical flowers were everywhere in profusion.

We took off at 8:30 the next morning for Casablanca. At 9:30 we were met at the airport by General Clark and General Gruenther. The British and the American Chiefs of Staff were to live at the Anfa Hotel. The President and the Prime Minister had villas close by, enclosed by wire fences.

I was happily surprised to find my son, Hank, on duty in the office at the hotel. I had expected him to be somewhere up in the front line. The last I had heard of him was from Kasserine, barely getting out as Rommel made that last dash of his through the Pass.

The British party landed at Casablanca at about 10:00 o'clock. It included the Prime Minister, Air Chief Marshal Portal, Field Marshal Brooke, General Ismay, Admiral Pound, Lord Mountbatten, and Air Marshal Slessor. After lunch that day, Admiral King, General Marshall, and I had a meeting to anticipate as much as we could the questions we thought might come up, and to discuss what seemed to us the wisest American stand on those issues.

I knew the question on which I would have the hardest, toughest fight: Would the U.S. Army Air Force be permitted to carry out its plans for daylight bombing? I knew the British had taken the matter up with the Prime Minister, and were determined that the Americans should not do daylight bombing, but should join their own night bombardment effort. I also knew the Prime Minister had already taken the matter up with the President; that the President, in turn, would take the matter up with Secretary Stimson and General Marshall, and all would start bearing down on me. I therefore sent for General Eaker, commanding our Eighth Air Force in England, to come down to North Africa armed with additional information to help me out. I thought that with the aid I could get from Spaatz and Andrews, who were already at Casablanca, and from Eaker, I could stop further controversy on the subject.

General Marshall, General Clark, Air Chief Marshal Portal, Sir Alan Brooke, and I had dinner together that night. After dinner we had a little time to ourselves, so I spent some of it with Hank and gave him some of the things I had brought with me from the States.

The next morning, January 14th, I had a very interesting talk with Portal and Brooke, who told me about Rommel and his attempted breakthrough into Egypt. They had just been talking with Rommel's deputy, a prisoner, who told them Rommel had said, "If Germany cannot win in the winter of 1943–44, Germany is licked."

On the 15th we had our Joint Chiefs of Staff meeting at 8:30, at which we discussed the many problems presented by the British. This was followed by a meeting of the Combined Chiefs of Staff, which started at 10:00 o'clock and adjourned for lunch at 12:45. We reopened at 2:30 and adjourned at 5:00. That was the normal daily schedule for our meetings during the session at Casablanca. During those meetings we discussed the war in all theaters and decided to have the planners work on the following: Assuming that Germany is the principal enemy, what dispositions and troops can be made in the Pacific to maintain pressure against the Japanese?

We heard, while at lunch, that the President had arrived at Bathurst on the *Memphis,* had been taken off by plane at 9:00 o'clock in the morning, and should arrive at Casablanca between 7:00 and 8:00 o'clock that night. Because of security, no military people would be at the field to meet him.

I find this note written in my diary: "Meeting today not bad. Everything seems to be smoothing out." And then I wrote—"I hope!" "However, the British and the United States have not, as yet, put all their cards on the table. . . . Perhaps things will get worse then; or perhaps, better."

After the Combined Chiefs of Staff meeting, Hank and I took an automobile drive to look over the city and the docks. Beautiful villas could be seen all along the coast. The land was very fertile; the city clean. Throughout the town were large, conspicuously painted buildings. At the docks lay the French Battleship *Jean Bart* with gaping holes in bow and stern, made, ironically, by 1100-pound bombs from the planes of our Naval Air Service while the battleship fired at our fleet. The bay was full of wrecks. One steamer was on her side; more hulks lay at various angles all over the harbor. French sailors on the ships at the docks did nothing, while American soldiers unloaded one of our ships after another.

I arrived back at the hotel to find the President had invited me for dinner that night at his villa. Other guests present were the Prime Minister, Admiral Pound, Sir Alan Brooke, Air Chief Marshal Portal, General Marshall, Admiral King, Lord Louis Mountbatten, Mr. Harriman, Mr. Hopkins, and Colonel Elliott Roosevelt. Many things were discussed, but our immediate concern was that both the Prime Minister and the President seemed determined to take a trip up to the front lines where the fighting was still going on. The members of the Combined Chiefs were equally determined that they should not expose themselves to such danger unnecessarily. The President and the Prime Minister could see no real danger. However, we felt there was a risk that was not warranted; one which the Americans present knew for a certainty the people of the United States would not approve. The President finally said, "You, Sir Charles Portal, Hap Arnold, and Bunny (meaning Elliott)—you make up the plan, but Bunny, you have no say in fixing the places where we go; you are merely Secretary." As we arranged it, the President did go to see some front-line fighting troops, but not in the actual fighting area.

"Who would govern France after the war?" This we discussed at dinner. Everyone agreed there should be a de facto government until the end of the war. De Gaulle and Giraud were both mentioned as possibilities, but as temporary possibilities only. Somehow they must be brought together and made to see the reason for France's having one chief, one head. Following on the heels of this question, everyone wanted to know, "Where is Lebrun?" No one seemed to know what had become of him. So the major problems confronting the Allied Nations were talked over, one after another until, before the dinner was over, Churchill made this statement: "This is the most important meeting so far. We must not relinquish initiative, now that we have it. You are the men who have the facts; you will make the plans for the future."

The series of conferences continued the next day. We had our regular Joint Chiefs of Staff meeting at 9:15; at 10:00 o'clock a session with the President telling him what we had done. At this conference General Marshall, Admiral King, Mr. Hopkins, Mr. Harriman, and I were present. Then I had luncheon with Generals Eisenhower and Marshall, and Admiral King, during which Eisenhower talked of his campaign.

Another Combined Chiefs of Staff meeting followed at 2:30, at which General Eisenhower presented the North African campaign officially from his point of view. At 4:00 o'clock the President and the Prime Minister joined us and we remained in session until 7:30 that night.

It was obvious from talking with Averell Harriman and Harry Hopkins that I had a rough time ahead of me with regard to daylight bombing. They agreed that the Prime Minister was set to make a good case against it. While taking a walk I met Mr. Churchill and talked with him for over an hour on the subject.

That afternoon General Alexander and Air Marshal Tedder had arrived from the North African Front. For two days we discussed the operations in the Mediterranean; the over-all concept of our war strategy and what steps we should take to carry it out; and the air command of the European theater, which had many serious phases.

I find a paragraph in my notes, dated Sunday, January 17, 1943: "No different from any other day." In other words, conferences on Sunday as well as on Monday, Tuesday, Wednesday, Thursday, Friday, and Saturday. This Sunday the Joint Chiefs of Staff met at 9:00 o'clock. At 10:00 o'clock the Combined Chiefs of Staff had their meeting and as the planners had not finished their work we adjourned until the next day, Monday. On Sunday, General Giraud and General Mast arrived for the conference with the President and the Prime Minister.

On Sunday, also, I talked with a group of pilots who had just arrived from England in P-39's. Ten out of 28 in one of our groups had not completed their flight. They had landed in Portugal. That was far too many to lose. Almost at the same time we had lost four B-17's trying to fly from Marrakech to Biskra. Instead of flying into Biskra, our base, they flew on into the area beyond the German lines. Hence, the Germans had four of our latest B-17's—and we were trying to keep them from learning the secrets of these planes. We were able to attack the captured Fortresses from the air with machine guns and bombs, while they were still in their original landing positions, and hoped we had destroyed or damaged them sufficiently to keep the Germans from getting much technical information about them. The ten P-39's which landed in Portugal were lost for good as far as the war was concerned.

I find this note for the following day: "Meeting of the Joint Chiefs of Staff. Not much agreed on. . . . Meeting of the Combined Chiefs of Staff started out with no accord and adjourned at noon. . . . Meeting of the Combined Chiefs of Staff after lunch. Adjourned to meet at the villa with the President and the Prime Minister." At this meeting we received an outline of a general war policy that was intended to get us back on the track again.

On January 19th, I had lunch with the Prime Minister. Again I outlined to him why we were so sure we could carry out daylight precision bombing and why we figured the Germans could not stop us. I told him of the various experiments we had made and how we figured our formations of B-17's and B-24's, subsequently with long-legged fighters, could protect themselves against German aircraft. I also told him I had at Casablanca, General Frank Andrews, General Spaatz, and General Eaker; that I would like to have him talk with each of them, in turn, so they could give him additional data and information. I talked long and hard!

The Prime Minister seemed willing to let the matter drop. It was quite evident to me he had been harassed by some of his own people about our daylight bombing program and had to put up a fight on the subject. Whether they were fearful we would use our airplanes ineffectively in the daylight missions; whether they were afraid we would waste airplanes; or whether they feared we would do something they could not and had not been able to do, I do not know. In any event, after Spaatz, Eaker, and Andrews had talked with the Prime Minister that same day, the Prime Minister told me he was willing for us to give it a trial; that he would say nothing more about it. That was a great relief to me and to my command. We had won a major victory, for we would bomb in accordance with American principles, using the methods for which our planes were designed.

After that I had a talk with the President and with General Marshall on the same subject and, as far as they were concerned, the matter was settled. Everyone said, "Go ahead with your daylight precision bombing!"

While we were at Casablanca, the Allied Forces had progressed so far to the eastward that it was apparent our African campaign was going to be successful. There was nothing the Germans could do to stop us. They had poured huge numbers of men and quantities of material into a campaign they could ill afford to lose. Yet in the end they lost all and had few, if any, replacements, while their main Army and Air Force in Europe had been weakened by just that much.

The most important problem of the Combined Chiefs of Staff now was to figure out the next movement to follow the Tunisian campaign. The British talked about a movement through southern France, but the American Chiefs of Staff still thought the main offensive should come across the English Channel into northern France. Naturally, had the men, materiel, equipment, and air superiority all been available at that time, we could have carried on with that campaign against the main German Army at once, but we were still short in many things.

Even though General Montgomery's army had driven Rommel's army from the gates of Cairo back to Tunisia; and even though we were driving now toward the tip of Tunisia from the other side, we did not control the Mediterranean. We had not opened it as a route of communications to the Far East. As long as the Germans held Sicily, Italy, and Greece there would be great difficulty in getting ships through that inland sea. Accordingly, the U.S. Chiefs of Staff agreed with the British Chiefs of Staff at the Casablanca Conference that, pending the time we could complete the mobilization of our Army and our Air Forces and until our Eighth Air Force operating from England could gain control of the air over the Continent, some other operation must be carried out so that the troops and equipment we did have would not stand idly by and give Germany an opportunity to rebuild its strength.

It was then the name HUSKY appeared in the picture: HUSKY— an assault on Sicily that was to be followed by a movement through Italy; a movement north through the Italian Peninsula, so as to open up that portion of the Mediterranean and remove the German threat to

Allied shipping. I also hoped this move would get us bases for our heavy bombers in Italy, which would enable us to strike Germany from two sides.

On January 23, 1943, General Eisenhower received the directive. The Combined Chiefs of Staff had resolved that an attack against Sicily would be launched in 1943, with target date in the period of the favorable July moon.

From the Air point of view, this was a most important decision, involving the first of the American airborne operations in Europe. Parachute troops and airborne infantry would be first to land in southern Sicily. This would necessitate special training, not only for our Troop Carrier Transports, but also for our Glider pilots.

There was nothing new about an airborne army. The idea wasn't conceived at Casablanca. Billy Mitchell received approval for such an operation during World War I. The Germans had used airborne troops successfully in Holland and overwhelmingly against the Island of Crete in 1941. It had been talked about in our Staff planning, off and on, ever since the Combined Chiefs of Staff had come into existence. It had been discussed in conferences at the Pentagon. It was simply a question of providing the necessary troops with the right leaders, and of building up in the staffs of our outfits throughout the world the will to use them.

Casablanca made little change in the strategic concept for employment of Allied troops in the other theaters of the world. We did agree that everything possible should be done to build up the offensive of the British troops in India; then, if possible, we would use Chinese troops with the British against the Japanese in Burma.

It was agreed that I should take a message to Chiang Kai-shek, giving him an outline in most general terms of our plan for employment of troops and Air Forces all over the world. Our hope was to obtain a better understanding with the Generalissimo and thus get more Chinese troops into the Burma area; but no change was made in our Pacific policy.

During the days that followed, I talked with General Andrews; with Tedder. We had talks by Giraud and by De Gaulle who when he first arrived was not sure whether he wished to see the President or not. In fact he did what few men could do—held over his appointment with the President until the following day. Always in the background was the big problem the Prime Minister and the President had to solve: Could they bring De Gaulle and Giraud together? Could they start them pulling as a team? Could France really become a help in the war?

When we had our picture taken with the President and the Prime Minister on January 22nd, we were all fairly sure the Conference was about to break up. We had been having our usual meetings with Mr. Roosevelt and Mr. Churchill; the Chiefs of Staff had been meeting by themselves; but when the photographers appeared, the end was usually in sight.

I had a long talk with Portal that day. He told me about his R.A.F. organization and his proposed program for future operations, supplies, and training. He was shooting for 537 squadrons, or 9870 airplanes by December, 1944. Then he would have about 1,200,000 men, which meant about 130 men per airplane. His 537 squadrons would, in our organization, be about 135 groups. We were shooting for a total of about 243 groups by December, 1944, with a total strength of 2,359,000 officers and men, and a total of about 52,000 combat-type airplanes to go with those 243 groups.

After talking with Portal and finding out exactly what his program was, I didn't feel so badly when I thought of how I had reduced the number of airplanes going to England. Our combat strength was almost six times as large as his. We were and would be fighting major wars in many theaters throughout the world. His Air Force was not, and, by nature of things, could not be so large as ours: he didn't have the materiel; he didn't have the personnel; and he didn't have the many requirements to meet.

We finished our work at Casablanca on the 23rd, and planned to leave for Algiers on Sunday, the 24th. The President and the Prime Minister expected to leave on Sunday, by automobile, for Marrakech and start for home the next day. Both the President and the Prime Minister, after conferences on the subject, gave me messages to be delivered to Wavell at New Delhi and to Chiang Kai-shek at Chungking. In addition, the President gave me a letter to the Generalissimo.

The last day at Casablanca was hectic. We had a Joint Chiefs of Staff meeting at 9:00 o'clock; a Combined Chiefs of Staff meeting at 10:00. We adjourned at 11:30, thinking we would see the President and the Prime Minister at lunch, but we did not. General Marshall, General Patton, and I took a trip to Fedala and inspected several of the troop camps along the road. We had a full description of the landing on the beach from Patton, and inspected the battle scars left in the various towns and on the French shores and were shown where the Moroccan troops had been stationed.

We returned to Casablanca to learn the meeting between the Prime

Minister and the President had been postponed until 5:30, so we continued our trip in the auto. General Marshall and I got lost and finally got back just in time to sit down at the meeting.

That night we met again from 9:30 until 11:30 and adjourned.

Next morning I said good-by to my son, Hank, and told General Marshall if I didn't see him at Algiers I would see him back in Washington. General Marshall and I, in our two planes, then took off, headed east, his ultimate destination the U.S.A., mine Chungking.

At Algiers we were met by General Spaatz and General Doolittle, and rode out to General Spaatz' mansion. It must have had about twenty-five bedrooms. Most of his Staff and all his senior officers lived there, and "visiting firemen" stopped there as they passed through.

During and following a large lunch, we had an informal Staff conference with Portal, Tedder, General Spaatz, and General Doolittle to bring everybody up to date. Afterward, I called on General Eisenhower and Admiral Cunningham, and in the evening had a conference with General Jean Mendigal, Chief of the French Aviation. He asked for a large consignment of equipment for the French. I made no promises and did not commit myself except about things we had already decided we would give to the French.

At breakfast next morning, Jimmy Doolittle came in and told me a story of two of our airmen who, returning from a bombing mission in Italy in a B-25, had their plane so badly disabled they had to ditch in their rubber boat, from which they were taken aboard an Italian submarine. They had no sooner been put below, and the hatches been closed as the submarine submerged, than one of our planes came along, bombed the sub, and broke it in half. The U.S. airmen were two of the few who came to the surface. They bobbed up in "Mae Wests" and were floating around when they were picked up by a British destroyer and later landed at Malta.

I asked that the story be put in memorandum form and sent to the President.

One of the objects of my trip between Casablanca and Cairo was to visit as many of our groups as I could. I wanted to talk to the group commanders, the squadron commanders, the pilots, the mess sergeants, the privates to find out what their gripes were, if any, and what I might do, if anything, to make things easier for them. My trip took me from Algiers to Telergma and from there to Biskra and then on to Cairo. There were some other stations I wanted to see, but I couldn't do them all.

As I visited the various camps, I realized our supply system was bogging down. There were too many bottlenecks along the ferry route. We had to speed up. For instance, we had three P-38 groups which should have had 240 planes; instead, they had only 90. I made arrangements to have another load of P-40's come over and be flown off the *Ranger* (Admiral King agreed to that) with the P-38's to come along as deck load. I also arranged for 90 additional P-38's to be flown down from England, and more P-38's to be flown across, via Ascension Island.

Talking to the group and squadron commanders, their first question was always: "When do we get our airplanes?" In all units I found the men liked the planes they were flying but had definite recommendations about making them better.

The day we hit Telergma, the P-38 pilots had had a field day. They had found the road south of Gabès filled with retreating Germans, and the P-38 pilots had gone down and attacked tanks, motorcycles, railroad engines—anything that was moving along the road. They must have destroyed literally thousands of German vehicles and men.

At the Biskra Airport, I was met by General Ham Atkinson, who had served under me at Fort Riley. His 97th Group, the first that had bombed Western Europe from Britain, had since flown many missions over Italy and Tunisia, including the key port of Bizerte; its losses were few, but its victories were many. That night I met with the aviators in the hotel we had taken over and listened to them tell of their experiences.

The Germans had raided the airdromes at Biskra many times, so all lights on cars at night were forbidden; everybody drove in darkness. I was riding in a car with General Jimmy Doolittle. His lights were on the bum, so instead of traveling with them dimmed, he had to travel with them full on. The sentry who stopped us didn't ask Jimmy what his name was, but told him he had been ordered by the Captain up in the control tower, "to come down and find out who that dummy was running around with his lights full on, against orders!"

The sentry said, "I want a copy of your orders."

Doolittle said he had no orders.

The sentry took down Doolittle's name, which the General gave as just "Doolittle." The sentry told him to report to somebody or other.

When we finally found our plane (entirely without lights now) the crew was there and we took off—at 10:00 o'clock at night. I awoke the next morning with the sun shining on my face, and climbed up to find Cairo directly beneath us. The airport; troops at drill; tanks being tested;

going through all kinds of paces and over all kinds of obstacles; Egyptian troops; British troops.

We landed before anyone realized we were there. Very soon, however, cars were out, and we started for town where General Andrews and General Crawford met us. We walked to headquarters with them, and then went to General Andrews' house to get cleaned up. On our way there we went through Cairo. I hadn't been there since 1909—thirty-four years before—but many things were still unchanged that I remembered having seen when I was returning from the Philippines as a young lieutenant.

That day we talked over with General Andrews, Air Marshal Douglas, Air Marshal Tedder, and General Brereton and his staff the employment of air in this and other theaters. General Brereton wanted definite information regarding his future status when the Ninth Air Force merged with the Twelfth under General Eisenhower. All I could say to him was that time would tell.

The following day we took off in a C-47 and flew 380 miles to Tobruk, where we inspected three fields. The 93rd (B-24) Group from England was there. It had been sent down with no ground crews, and after two months, still with no ground crews, was operating with such makeshift teams as it could get together.

We inspected B-24's and B-25's. The personnel were well pleased with their operations and quite satisfied with their equipment; but— the inevitable question wherever we stopped—when would replacements arrive?

As we flew over the desert we came on what, to me, was one of the strangest sights of the whole trip. From Tobruk to El Alamein we could see the marks in the desert where the Germans and British had moved their armored units and tanks into battle. Wrecks indicated where battles had been fought. By following the tracks of advances and withdrawals we could see the tactics of the whole three-year desert war re-enacted in the sand.

That night, after returning to Cairo, I had dinner at the home of the American Minister, Mr. Kirk, with General Somervell, Sir John Dill, and about twenty others. Sir John was to accompany me from Cairo to Chungking. Learning that the Prime Minister was in town and wanted to see me, I made arrangements to meet him the next day. Somervell was to leave for India, via Iran, the following day; Sir John would not be ready to leave until Friday. We would meet Somervell in Delhi after we had accomplished our various missions.

On the morning of January 28th, having no official commitments, we went out to see the Caves. The Caves, perhaps the source of the lime and sandstone with which the Pyramids themselves were built, were now used by the R.A.F. as "shops" in which to repair and rebuild salvaged engines, propellers, instruments, and radio sets. Eighteen hundred men were working in the Caves, turning out Allison engines, Cyclones, Packard Merlins, British Merlins, Bristols, Pegasus' and Hercules'. It was there that they straightened out propellers. When the tips were too badly damaged, they cut the "props" down, smoothed them out, rebalanced them, and sent them back into service. "Props" drilled with cannon-ball holes, came in for repair along with others. The mechanics would smooth them down, fill them up, or rebalance them, and send them back—with the holes still in them! Mile after mile of these Caves. And out of the Caves came 7 engines a day, with 14 engines a day as the program for the following week. One R.A.F. man for every two or three Egyptians.

That night we had a conference with Tedder, Drummond, Pirie, and Spaatz, and then went to dinner with the Prime Minister, at which the British Ambassador, our Minister, Mr. Kirk, and others were present.

Afterward I had a long talk with Mr. Churchill and found he had a new subject for discussion with me: the possibility of Turkey's entrance into the war; its value and effect upon the whole picture; and what, if anything, we might be able to do to encourage the Turks to come in. What could we promise them in the way of aviation—not in small numbers but in terms of real air strength? That, I learned, was the reason for the Prime Minister's visit: he was trying to find out what we must do to bring Turkey into the war.

I stressed the importance of timing; of singleness of objective. I said it was my opinion we should make no promises that would affect the other major war operations we had planned. Churchill said that with 82,000 planes being produced in the United States, there would be no interference, even if we gave a large number of planes to Turkey. But 82,000 planes by the coming December (eleven months away), I pointed out, was far different from 82,000 planes now. He said all he was asking for was 28 squadrons to be put into Turkey by June. He assured me, however, he would take no action that would interfere with operations already planned.

Churchill also told me he would like eight more C-87's for the Fifth Column work in Jugoslavia, and said he thought Sir John Dill and I should both return to the States via England when we came back from

China. I couldn't promise these things without more thought; but I told him I would look into them.

How often I wished it were possible to give everybody all the airplanes they wanted for their various missions and operations in the far corners of the earth! Certainly, we needed C-87's for Fifth Column work in Jugoslavia; but it was a question of whether we needed them more for the Fifth Column possibilities than we did for pressing ferry work around the world, or for carrying life-giving supplies over the Hump into China.

On January 29th, I picked up Sir John Dill as a passenger, and we took off about 7:30 in the morning.

The whole Air Force had been watching General Frank M. Andrews in his various jobs—first as Commanding General of the G.H.Q. Air Force; then, in command of the Caribbean Theater; and now in the Near East, with headquarters at Cairo. All Air Corps officers saw in him the leader among the Air Force generals who might become one of the outstanding combat commanders in the war. We were all immensely pleased when General Eisenhower, on January 17, 1943, recommended that he command American troops in England. Perhaps he might end in being Commanding General of all American troops in the European Theater. However, Fate willed otherwise; for, on May 10, 1943, as he was flying from England to Iceland, his plane crashed against a mountain in Iceland and General Andrews and those accompanying him were killed.

One of the missions given me by the President was to see what could be done to expedite the movement of U.S. planes through Basra to the Russians. The reports which had come to the President from Moscow indicated that planes were not moving through Basra as fast as they should because our people were not making the necessary modifications rapidly enough.

We landed at Basra and met Colonel Porter, the Commanding Officer. We were favorably impressed with the work he was doing, but we learned from him that the Russians were hard taskmasters; difficult to please. They demanded that everything be done to make the planes 100 per cent acceptable to them; but our standards were not considered, in spite of the fact that the planes were built for our own use.

Up to that time Basra had received a total of 86 P-39's, 31 P-40's, and 689 A-20's. We had delivered to the Russians 33 P-39's, 10 P-40's, and 634 A-20's. We had waiting for the Russians to move off the field 36 P-39's and 49 A-20's. Being assembled were 17 P-39's and 21 P-40's, as well as 6 additional A-20's. So, as far as I could see, any delay there might be was on the side of the Russians, not on ours. At that moment there were 85 airplanes ready for delivery, which the Russians had not seen fit to accept and fly away.

I found the Russians very comfortably fixed at Basra. They had their own barracks, their own halls, their own amusement places. They were much better off, as a matter of fact, than the American soldiers. Their buiidings and facilities were better than ours. I also learned they had brought down, as was the Russian custom, a considerable number of women whom they kept in one of the barracks. The Russians liked to talk to our boys; they liked to take a few drinks; but they would not talk about things happening in Russia.

When the Russians got drunk, they wanted to dance, and they liked to dance with our boys. Our men didn't think much of this, but the Russians were insistent. So there was great dancing until the U.S. soldiers were just about crazy. When they would get so exhausted they couldn't dance any more, the Russians, just as likely as not, would kiss them on both cheeks. At first that was just too much for an American boy, and many fights resulted. Soon the Russians learned it was not the thing to do. But when it came to our men talking with the Russian women—that was a different story; that was taboo! Our boys couldn't meet, talk with, nor dance with the Russian women. They couldn't cut in on that fun at all!

We had a conference with Colonel Petrov, the Russian Commanding Officer. He was a great big fellow, and undoubtedly would have made a hit in our movies, having the features and stature of a Clark Gable. I tried to get him to admit the work we were doing on the airplanes was satisfactory, but it was like pulling teeth. At first we did all our talking through his interpreter; but I could see we were getting nowhere. Lots of words; no action.

Then I called for our interpreter and told Colonel Petrov I wanted to tell him a story—a story about a Chinese witness on a stand in court in the United States. The question was asked the witness: "Were you, or were you not, on the corner of Sixth and Main Streets at 10:00 o'clock on Thursday?" The Chinese interpreter talked with the Chinese witness for fully forty-five minutes, and finally, the attorney becoming impatient, asked, "What did he say?" The interpreter said, "He said, 'Yes.'" I said, "Colonel Petrov, you remind me of that Chinese. We have talked and talked and talked now, for forty-five minutes, only you haven't said Yes or No; you just keep on talking. The Chinese did say 'Yes.'"

Eventually, Petrov did admit that the planes we delivered to the

Russians were in excellent shape; that unsatisfactory conditions were always corrected before we turned them over, and that we were not holding up deliveries. Sir John Dill thought the whole official conference quite strange—but distinctly American.

At Basra there were about 1500 Douglas employees and probably 800 enlisted men assembling and checking airplanes. That cold night after dinner, Sir John Dill and I both gave a talk to the Douglas employees and to the enlisted men, following which we went to bed early, to be ready for our long trip the next day.

We took off for Karachi at 7:05 in the morning. The country between Basra, Abadan, and Karachi was desolate. It reminded one of the country in and around Death Valley. I learned, before leaving Karachi, that General Somervell had tried to get into Teheran, but because of bad weather and high mountains had been forced to return to Habbaniya, and would be a day late in arriving at Delhi.

Flying along over the Persian Gulf became quite monotonous. I was in the radio cockpit, after having taken my turn at the controls up front. I started to fool around, and saw the top rear 50-caliber gun stowed away in its retracted position. Thinking it was about time we tried it out, I opened up the doors to the other sections of the fuselage, took off the top cover, and brought it down through the hatch and put it on the floor. I then took the gun out of its stowed position, adjusted it, and fired some shots out into the Persian Gulf. This was 50 miles out of Karachi. I put the gun back in its position on top of the fuselage O.K., but as I attempted to replace the fuselage cover, the draft coming through the hole caught the top cover (something like the hood of a car) as though it were a kite, and carried it up toward the outlet as if it were a piece of paper. Worst of all, I was being taken with it. I was reluctant to turn the cover loose, for I was fearful it might hit the rudder and wreck our plane. On the other hand, I didn't see my way clear to accompanying it out of the hole.

In just about the time it takes to make a critical decision, Sir John Dill grabbed hold of both my ankles and pulled. I released the top cover, which sailed off into space, missing the rudder by about six inches. It finally landed in the Persian Gulf; I landed on the radio compartment floor.

The net result was: gun tested and found satisfactory—but a very windy, drafty ride into Karachi. Fortunately, in Karachi, they had a "spare roof," as Sir John called it, and we traveled on from there without being blown by the air currents through the compartment.

At Karachi I was met by General Brady, General Wheeler, and Colonel Mason, and we had a delicious lunch. Colonel Brady had been in the Philippines with General Brereton, under General MacArthur. General Wheeler was in charge of all construction in India and Burma, so our conversation was interestingly varied and gave Sir John and me some background for what to expect in the Far East.

We took off late in the afternoon, headed for New Delhi, and flew through the darkness over India. For a long time we couldn't even see lights of any kind, only stars overhead, and our own exhaust flames. After some 600 miles of that blackness, punctuated only occasionally by the dotted lights of villages, we came to the glare of the busy smoke pots of a city. It was New Delhi.

We landed at about 10:00 P.M. and rolled up to the hangar where we were met by General Wavell, General Bissell, Commander of our troops in India and China at that time, and other staff officers. Sir John Dill was to stay with General Wavell; I had a suite in the hotel.

The next morning I met General Bissell for breakfast, and we talked over his air problems to get more background before I talked with General Wavell.

I met Wavell and Sir John Dill at 10:00 o'clock in the morning, and we agreed to have a series of conferences, with an agenda drawn up, and secretariats—similar to our Combined Chiefs of Staff meetings. The other U.S. members would be: General Stilwell, General Somervell, and General Bissell. The British members would be: Sir John Dill, General Wavell, General Auchinleck, and part of General Wavell's staff. We had lunch with General Wavell and his family. He struck me as being a very brilliant man, but apparently more of a student, a planner, than a leader in the field. He seemed to be tired and worn out with his combat experiences. It was not out of line at all.

General Wavell's Chief of Staff had given Sir John and me copies of what they called a "plan" for driving the Japanese out of Western Burma and securing a foothold from which the British could launch a new offensive to take over all Burma. Their latest effort had ended disastrously. After reading the paper, I met Sir John Dill after breakfast the next day and we had a long talk. He agreed with me that the paper as submitted was not a plan, but merely several pages of well-written paragraphs telling why the mission could not be accomplished.

So, when we met with the British at 11:00 o'clock, I repeated what Sir John and I had said of the paper. I told them, without mincing any words, how the paper impressed me, and I quoted the report of the

Combined Chiefs to the President and the Prime Minister to prove my point. The Combined Chiefs of Staff had agreed there must be a definite project or plan for an offensive into Burma, with a view to driving the Japanese out, and that it must be started as soon as possible. After my talk, General Wavell agreed the paper submitted was not final and said he would give additional instructions to have it revised.

At lunch I had a meeting with the American members who were present and we talked of what our next step should be. A study of the maps of Burma showed the location of the Japanese troops, their possible movements, and how their interior line of communication made it possible for them to take up positions where they could concentrate larger forces than the British and the Chinese were able to with their exterior lines.

Unity of command in the area was a necessity. This was one of the things the Joint Chiefs of Staff and the Combined Chiefs of Staff were trying to achieve—unity of command in the Burma area, not only for the British Army but also for American and Chinese troops which might be used for a joint campaign against the Japanese; whether an offensive from the western side of Burma, or a drive from the east or north. In any event, the operations must be synchronized.

There were other difficulties, also. There was the jungle; the types of uniform the British soldiers wore—short sleeves and shorts—which exposed them to mosquitoes, so that the malaria rate among them was extremely high. To illustrate: In one instance, an Australian regiment and a British regiment were stationed in the same locality. The Australian regiment had a malaria rate of about 20 per cent while the British unit had a malaria rate well up above 80 per cent.

Another obstacle was the terrain; the lack of roads; the difficulty in moving supplies. The Japanese soldier could carry his equipment, and rations for several days on his person. His rations consisted, usually, of a bit of rice and some dried fish. The British and the American soldiers normally could not get along on such meager combat fare.

I waited all day, February 1st, for the arrival of General Stilwell and General Somervell. Stilwell finally arrived about 10:30 that same night; Somervell got in about 9:00 P.M. I had a meeting with them early in the morning, on February 2nd, and talked over the existing conditions. Then we met with Wavell and his staff at 10:30.

Things went along much better at that meeting. It looked as if we might come to an understanding. We had lunch, and then talked things over again, and the whole atmosphere changed very rapidly. But, somehow or other, I could not get the impression out of my head that the British had been using India as a place to which to send officers who had more or less outlived their usefulness in other theaters.

We finally decided we would adjourn on the 3rd of February, and I would move on to Dinjan, with Sir John Dill; from there, on to Chungking, returning to Calcutta for a final session sometime about February 9th.

That night, the Viceroy, Lord Linlithgow, gave a very fine dinner for all the rank, but it didn't last too long.

The Viceroy's palace was as big as the Pentagon Building in Washington; there was more formality than in any place I had ever seen. The standing rule seemed to be that you talked with one person for three minutes, and then with someone else for three minutes. They had a couple of aides around to see that you didn't stop for more than the proper three minutes with any one person.

The next day we were out at the airport at 7:30 A.M. General Bissell and I took off in our B-17, headed for Assam. Sir John Dill was to go with General Stilwell. We reached Dinjan on time, landing in midafternoon. Taxiing to a dispersal point, we were informed we were to spend the night with one of the tea-growers in the area, and we looked forward eagerly to a bit of rest.

We inspected the A.A. unit, the gun positions, and the fighter squadron. They had dispersed positions under the bamboo clumps. It was very well prepared, for we could come within twenty yards of a plane without seeing it. The officers and men lived in small nipa shacks around the airdrome. I went to Group Headquarters where I met General Edward Alexander, one of the officers who had been with me at March Field. While I was there, an undercover man who had spent several months in the interior of Burma entered and reported. I enjoyed my conversation with him very much. How an American could run around loose in Burma for such a long period and get away with it, I don't know; but that American did.

As we were making the inspections and talking, I learned that Sir John Dill and General Stilwell had gone on to Kunming. The weather was fine; and the weather changes so rapidly and so violently over this southern end of the Himalayas that I said we too would start for Kunming immediately after dinner.

☆ 23 ☆

The flight from Dinjan to Kunming was about the same distance as from New York to Chicago. The route from Dinjan to Kunming, however, was over mountains some 18,000 feet high, and across terrain where the weather was most uncertain. At times the winds built up to a velocity of 100 to 150 miles an hour, without warning. An airman never knew what kind of weather he would hit when flying over the Himalayas between Assam and China.

I wanted to get an early start, and sent my crew to the flight office for their briefing while we were finishing dinner. The airdromes in and around Assam had been attacked by the Japanese a few days before we arrived. The wrecks of many of our transports burned by Japanese bombing were still lying in their parking places.

When the crew arrived at the plane I asked them about the briefing and received a rather sketchy reply. I made a serious mistake in accepting it. I had been flying long enough to know that one never can take anything for granted in the air, and certainly not in the presence of the enemy, over one of the worst flying routes in the world.

The route direct to Kunming is over ridges about 14,000 to 16,000 feet high. Farther north, the mountains rise higher—19,000 to 20,000 feet. At intervals, the ground was held by the Japanese and in between by guerillas who were in Japanese service. The town of Kunming and the country for a hundred miles to the west was in the hands of the Chinese.

I learned later, rather incidentally, from the local operations officer, that we could expect a tail wind of fifty miles an hour or more. After taking off in the dark, we climbed to 19,000 feet, and during the first two hours of flying we saw practically nothing in the darkness—not even a

410

light on the ground. In about two hours I noted a red glare to the south, and then asked the navigator at what time we were due to reach Kunming. After considerable delay, the answer came back, "In about twenty minutes, sir." I was talking with General Bissell, and wasn't thinking too much about the trip, and another hour passed before I checked again. Then I asked where we were, and when we would land at Kunming. I found there was considerable consternation and ignorance among the crew about both our position and when we would reach our destination. I had not known that the crew had not put on their oxygen masks, although we were traveling at 19,000 feet. I talked with the radioman and told him to put on a mask right away and then start using the radio to see if he could get a check with any of the various stations in North Burma, India, or China.

In the meantime, I asked the navigator whether he was taking oxygen. He told me he wasn't. I told him to start using it right away, then get on the job and find out where we were. I called the pilot back to the seats where General Bissell and I were and started talking with him. While he was standing there, he crumpled to the floor. No oxygen. I gave him my mask and soon got him back in shape. Lack of oxygen had certainly fixed up my crew.

In spite of the enemy, our unknown position, and a country where there were few fields in which we could land, all members of the crew had taken the flight as calmly as if they were flying from New York to Washington. After a while the navigator asked that we be allowed to continue our present course for another twenty or thirty minutes, pending the time he was able to get a "fix."

Considering that four-engine planes were then rare over China, there was no doubt in my mind that the Japanese were trying to discover the purpose of this flight. It was possible that they might send up planes to intercept us. They had radar and certainly were plotting the course of our aircraft very accurately. They must have known where we were, even if we didn't. Neither was there any doubt in my mind that we were well past Kunming, and were probably destined to have breakfast with General "Nogi" in Hanoi. At that stage of the war I didn't particularly care to breakfast with General "Nogi."

I directed the pilot to reverse his course and head back 180 degrees. I knew we had a strong tail wind—probably a hundred miles an hour— and guessed the red glare we had passed some hours before must have been Kunming. Then the question came to my mind: "O.K., but will we have gas enough to get back to Kunming, or will we miss it and end up in the Himalayas? If so, when and where? If we run out of gas will we have to jump?" The clothing I was wearing would not help me much if I had to walk through the jungle (low shoes and light trousers). Interesting for everybody if the Commanding General of the United States Army Air Forces, the Commanding General of the Tenth Air Force, and all the staff members with me, were taken prisoners.

The radio operator told me the only stations he could pick up were using foreign languages; he couldn't understand what they were saying. They were probably Chinese or Japanese stations. He couldn't pick up American or British stations anywhere. I learned afterward the Kunming station was off the air, and there was no way we could possibly have picked it up.

It was some time before the navigator gave us a fix. He said we were about 300 miles east of Kunming. Obviously, the strong tail wind coming from Assam had taken us well into Japanese-controlled territory.

Some time later the navigator secured a good fix—about fifty miles west of the first one. Up to then, we had been at 19,000 feet for over five hours. Some time after that the radioman picked up one English-speaking station and then another. Soon the navigator obtained a third fix, and we clinched our position.

We landed at Kunming about 2:00 o'clock in the morning. We had been due there at 9:30 the evening before. Everybody at the station was apprehensive and, even at that awful hour, General Stilwell, General Chennault, and Sir John Dill were at the airport to meet us. They told me the Kunming radios were out, but why, I never learned. A "ham" operator, with a radio of his own, however, had heard our messages. At breakfast we were taken for a ride about our midnight jaunt. However, it was much better than coffee with General "Nogi."

That morning I had long talks with Chennault, Stilwell, Wedemeyer, Bissell, and Sir John, and among us we fixed up a policy for operations in China to present to the Generalissimo. Then we made a tour of the post.

The old "Flying Tigers," now taken into our outfit as the Fourteenth Air Force, were ingenious people. For instance, they could not get belly tanks for additional gasoline for their P-40's from the United States, so they made the tanks themselves. The Chinese fashioned a skeleton of bamboo, covering the inside of it with cloth and then with mud. Building adobe around the bamboo skeleton and the cloth, they built up the tank until it was the proper shape. The cloth was then painted with a Chinese varnish to hold more cloth over the outside. A coating of aluminum paint gave a finish to a gasoline tank that it was almost impossible to tell from one of our regular aluminum tanks, and which worked just as well.

We were scheduled to take off without any delay for Chunking to see the Generalissimo, but I wanted the local picture first. General Chennault had given me a clear picture of the air situation in China, but to my astonishment, in spite of his Air Corps and Tactical School training, he was not realistic about the logistics of his operations. That we had to iron out later. General Stilwell had presented a graphic idea of the ground situation; so Sir John Dill and I felt we were pretty well prepared to go into our conference with the Generalissimo and his Staff. It was decided that since we couldn't get into the Chungking airport with our B-17, we would use one of the CNAC DC-3 airplanes.

As I went out to board the plane, I saw a pile of paper lying on the ground. "What is all that?" I asked one of the crew.

"That," he said, "is Chinese money, General."

I asked, "How much?"

"Why, I don't know. Maybe two, three, four million Chinese dollars," he replied.

"What are you going to do with it?" I asked.

He said, "We are taking it in our airplane to Chungking."

"Isn't anyone responsible for it?" I asked.

"Yes, we are responsible for taking it in there," he replied.

Then I asked, "Does anyone have to sign up for it?"

"No sir."

"Don't you ever count it?"

"No sir."

Remarkable! Had it been a pack of cigarettes or a jeep, it would have disappeared hours before.

Just before the plane took off, they threw the money aboard the airplane and it was delivered to Chungking without anyone's checking it in there—money that had been printed in the United States.

Upon landing at Chungking, I found the Chinese Minister of War, his Chiefs of Staff and Chief of Aviation waiting for us. I didn't know whether the review of troops they had lined up was for Sir John or for me. I told Sir John it was for him, and he said it was for me. So I said, "All right, let's take it together."

We were then taken to the stairway leading to the town from the airport and the river. (The airport was located in the river bottom, on a piece of flat ground.) Three hundred and forty-seven stairs led from the river up to the city of Chungking, on top of the plateau. Sir John and I climbed into sedan chairs carried by coolies. The Chinese dignataries accompanied us in other chairs. I had two men in front and one in back. The one in back seemed to have the "heaves" and I was sure that he could never make it to the top. I weighed close to 200 pounds and I had visions of his caving in and dropping. I would then spill over the back of the chair, down 347 steps, taking with me the Chinese coolies, Dr. T. V. Soong, General Stilwell, and all the other dignitaries in back of me. However, in spite of his physical ailment, the old fellow landed me safely at the top.

I was told, when I reached my quarters in Chungking, that the Generalissimo would see me the next day. That night General Stilwell gave a buffet supper for the visiting firemen, our Ambassador, Clarence Gauss, and the Chinese higher officers. It was a pleasant and interesting affair and gave me an opportunity to talk with some of the people with whom I would have to do business during the next few days.

Chungking is situated in the "V" of two rivers. The airport is on the island in the valley; the city is on top of a rocky plateau some 600 feet above the river, and had been bombed and re-bombed by the Japanese. The Chinese had dug caves in the side of the hill for refuge. Literally thousands of them had been killed. At the time of our arrival, the Japanese hadn't bombed Chungking for several months and it didn't look as if they would get back to it again for some time, in view of what Chennault had told me his Air Force was doing to keep the Japanese otherwise occupied.

Before leaving Kunming, I had asked what the weather would be like at Chungking. It would be nice and warm, I was told. I asked if I would need heavy clothes. No, I wouldn't need heavy clothes. The next day at Chungking, when we started for the Generalissimo's palace, I knew I had made a mistake. It had snowed the night before and was cold—very cold. Even the Chinese were shivering and there was little heat in any of the houses.

At Chungking I was again carried up stone steps to Chiang Kai-shek's palace, at the top of a wintry hill. I did not have to wait long for the Generalissimo, but I did have a chance to look around the room. There was a very small fireplace with a grate about the size of an ordinary dust pan. It was covered with charcoal and the charcoal was giving off its usual slow heat—the only heat in the room. I knew I was not going to get warm there. Within a few minutes the Generalissimo entered and I gave him the letter, which read:

THE WHITE HOUSE
Washington

Casablanca
January 25, 1943

MY DEAR GENERALISSIMO:

This note will be given to you by Lieutenant General Henry H. Arnold, U.S. Army, Commander of our Air Forces. I am sending him to you because I am determined to increase General Chennault's Air Force in order that you may carry the offensive to the Japanese at once. General Arnold will work out the ways and means with you and General Chennault.

General Arnold will also tell you about the plans to intensify our efforts to drive the Japanese out of the Southwest Pacific. As I wired you, I have been meeting with the Prime Minister and our respective Chiefs of Staff to plan our offensive strategy against Japan and Germany during 1943. I want Arnold to talk all this over with you in the greatest detail because I think it would be best that I do not put it on the cables.

Mrs. Roosevelt has seen Madame Chiang Kai-shek several times and we are all hoping that she can come to see us very soon. Her health is improving rapidly.

I have hopes for the war in 1943, and, like you, I want to bring it home on the Japanese with great vigor. I want to convey, not only my warm regards for you, personally, but my everlasting appreciation of the service that your armies are giving to our common cause.

Cordially yours,
FRANKLIN D. ROOSEVELT.

Chiang gave the letter to Dr. Soong for translation, and I thought: "How much English does the Generalissimo understand?"

I never was able to make up my mind.

The conference that followed between Chiang, T. V. Soong, Colonel "Louie" Parker (my aide) and myself, lasted for almost three hours. It covered many things: the world military situation; the Chiefs of Staff conference; the Burma campaign; an independent command for Chennault; the Chinese Air Force; and miscellaneous items.

The house remained cold. Hot tea was served about every five minutes. That helped considerably. When lunch was served it was excellent: delicious beef broth, fish, potatoes, roast duck, carrots, Chinese spinach, hot biscuits, lemon meringue pie, and more hot tea. Every once in a while, however, I found an excuse to get up and walk around the room and to edge over to that small fireplace with its slow-burning charcoal.

One of the main points at issue was Chennault's status. That colorful General's operations had been such that Chiang Kai-shek's confidence in his abilities was unbounded. He could see no reason why Chennault should not be given complete and absolute charge of the entire American Air Force operating in China and India. All during lunch the talk centered about that point: should he have autonomy, or should he stay under Bissell, whom we had sent out to the Far East to command all Air Forces in India and in China? Obviously, the man who commanded the India Air Force must command the Chinese Air Force, because the two were so interrelated that they could not operate independently of each other.

The operations over the Hump—carrying supplies into China—made that more essential than ever. Naturally, the Generalissimo's unlimited confidence in General Chennault complicated the problem terrifically. He believed Chennault to be the greatest air commander the world had ever produced and he wanted Chennault to head up everything. I knew the independent command idea for Chennault would not be acceptable in Washington, nor would it please Stilwell, who hadn't much use for him. I surmised there was a bit of jealousy there. Whether Stilwell's lack of respect for the Generalissimo automatically included Chiang's friend, Chennault, or whether he mistrusted Chennault's abilities, I did not know.

As a matter of fact, Chennault's record with the Flying Tigers and later with our own Air Force in China proved beyond any doubt that he had an uncanny talent for handling airplanes against the Japanese and for understanding the Chinese and instilling in them the techniques of aerial combat.

The meeting that Dr. Soong and I had with the Generalissimo at that lunch on February 6, included Colonel Louie Parker. Colonel Parker was an enthusiastic individual and I noticed that when the Generalissimo talked to Soong in Chinese, before Soong translated it into English, Parker would nod his head—"Yes, Yes, Yes, Yes." And when Dr. Soong, after hearing our reply in English, translated it into Chinese, Parker would still nod his head—"Yes, Yes, Yes, Yes." Finally, after observing this for some time, the Generalissimo said something to Soong in Chinese.

Dr. Soong then asked me if Colonel Parker could speak Chinese. I assured him Colonel Parker could not. Then there was more conversation between the Generalissimo and T. V. Soong, and Soong asked me if Parker could understand Chinese. I assured him that Parker could not understand a word. But that didn't stop Louie Parker. He kept on with the same technique. Then the Generalissimo said something else to Soong and Soong asked me once again, "Can Colonel Parker understand Chinese?" Again I assured him Colonel Parker could not.

The next time I had a conference with the Generalissimo—a secret conference—Colonel Parker's name was not among those who were asked to be present. I had to go alone, without an aide. Apparently, the Generalissimo thought Colonel Parker too good a linguist.

The question of aviation in China was a most difficult one, particularly for the Air Transport Command. In the first place, airlift carried more supplies over the Hump than could be transported to Assam by the existing facilities on the Brahmaputra River or on the narrow gauge railroad which paralleled it. As I remember it now, there were three different gauges on that railroad, so the supplies being sent by that route had to be trans-shipped twice to different railroad cars. Furthermore, the amount of gasoline used by the airplanes in China was tremendous. Even if we increased the airplanes in China to the strength desired by the Generalissimo and Chennault, we would not be able to get enough gasoline over the Hump to operate them, and continue to carry other kinds of supplies as well. As a matter of fact, before we finished our job of carrying supplies over the Hump we had to build special tank airplanes—modified B-24's—just to carry gasoline. We stripped them of everything except the barest operating essentials and, installing gas tanks, loaded them to their maximum capacity with gasoline.

As our discussions at the table progressed, the following points became clear—from the Generalissimo's point of view:

1. The Chinese lacked confidence in the present organization.

2. Additional planes put into China would be ineffective without a coordinated organization.

3. Chennault was the only one who could handle operations, because of the many complications.

4. Chennault was the only one who had the confidence of the Chinese.

5. There must be a complete understanding and accord between the Chinese and the U.S. Air Forces.

6. Chiang Kai-shek had reorganized the Chinese Air Force and wanted to place it under American control. Chennault was the only one whom he would consent to have handle it.

7. The Chinese had had no cooperation from the United States since the A.V.G. (American Volunteer Group) had been terminated.

8. Chennault was the one outstanding air tactician and strategist in the Far East at that time.

9. It would be very easy to get someone to handle the administrative end of things for Chennault. Hence, no administrative reason why he should not have the command.

I went over these things one by one with Chiang and promised that when I got back to Washington I would report the conference in full to the President and that Chiang Kai-shek would get from the President a statement on the decision.

The Generalissimo then said he had told me things he was saving for the President and was being entirely frank. I told him I appreciated his frankness and assured him I would not divulge what he had said, except to the President. However, a summary of the conversation that night left me with the following impressions:

1. The Generalissimo was not particularly interested in the Casablanca Conference nor in the Combined Chiefs of Staff, except where Burma or China were concerned.

2. He wanted a firm commitment for 500 additional U.S. planes at a time he designated.

3. He would not listen to logic or reason when it came to logistics realities; that is, supplies coming in over the Hump.

4. He wanted to build up the Chinese Air Force in numbers, regardless of whether or not there was gasoline for the planes to use.

5. Regardless of his brilliancy as a military leader when he so completely defeated his opponents in 1925, he did not display the same genius or logic in thought now.

There was no doubt in my mind that the area at Assam around the airports could be expanded to take care of a far larger number of transport airplanes than we were now using. At that time the road network was under construction and it would be completed shortly. That would aid our airlift materially. The airfields were being developed and their development would enable us to operate more transports to carry more supplies into China and also continue to transport, with their equipment, those Chinese Army soldiers—some thirty or forty thousand of them— who were being trained in India.

However, the whole logistical system of movement of supplies and personnel into China from Assam depended upon:

1. The capacity of river steamboats on the Brahmaputra River.

2. The railroad running from Calcutta up to Assam. It was being used to capacity at that time, but we expected to get additional rolling stock soon by putting pressure on and helping out the British.

3. The gasoline situation in India determined the volume of air cargo

that could be transported across the Hump and the air operations in China. All 100-octane gasoline used at Assam or in the Hump flights or in China had to be freighted, either up the river, or up the railroad. Eighty-octane gasoline came in through a pipeline which paralleled the river. Then all gasoline must be carried by air into China. In a regular transport plane, when a flight into Kunming was completed and gasoline for the return flight to India put into the plane's tanks, there was not much left for Chinese aerial operations.

Another serious consideration pertinent to the whole question of aerial operations in China was the lack of suitable airdromes in China itself. Additional airdromes must be built before there could be any substantial increase, either in cargo-carrying capacity into China or in combat airplanes operating from Chinese bases. The Generalissimo and Chennault glossed over these things with a wave of their hands. They could not, or would not, be bothered with logistics.

As I was responsible for General Bissell's being in command over Chennault, I was very interested in getting the Generalissimo's reactions and those of his Chief of Air in regard to Bissell. Bissell did not have the "We'll-get-it-done-in-spite-of-hell-or-high-water" attitude that Chennault had. The Chinese all had to admit he was a fine, efficient staff officer who properly planned every operation or maneuver in detail before carrying it out; but they regarded him as too careful; so careful that in one instance I heard the words "old woman" put down as a qualifying expression when they were talking about him. He was a "detail" man. Everyone agreed, however, he was getting results, though they would not concede, the logistics situation being what it was, that his detail work had made their operations under Chennault very effective so far. For example, Chennault had requested many more medium bombers. Well, had we given him medium bombers when he asked for them, there still would have been no possible way to get the gasoline into China for flying them unless we had stopped all shipments of everything else over the Hump. As the availability of gasoline in China increased so could we increase the airplanes available to Chennault.

What the situation added up to was this: Bissell was an excellent staff officer who carefully worked out every operation before he undertook it, or said he could not do it. Chennault had the originality, initiative, and drive the Chinese liked; also, a knack of doing things in China that was possessed by very few other American officers. He stood in well with the Generalissimo and Madame Chiang. On the other hand, General Bissell was not particularly liked by the Generalissimo. Chiang had made up his mind: Bissell must go; Chennault must be put in command. What was I to do?

While waiting for the meeting with the Generalissimo and his Chief of Staff that afternoon, I talked with Colonel Vincent and Colonel Holloway, both on duty in China. Both had flown P-40's in combat against the Japanese Zeros; both had flown the Japanese Zeros in test flights against the P-40's. It must be borne in mind that although the P-40's were on their way out as first-line U.S. planes, and would soon be declared obsolete, they were the same airplanes the news commentators in the United States had said were so inferior to the Zero that we should never use them against it.

Here is what Vincent and Holloway said about the Japanese Zero:

"It is a nice 'Sunday afternoon' plane."

"I feel sorry for the Jap aviators who have to fly them."

"It is so flimsily constructed that I could have bent the rudder bar with the pressure of my feet. I understand now why they fly to pieces when hit by a .50 caliber."

At 4:00 o'clock, Sir John Dill and I went up to the Generalissimo's cottage, through three inches of snow. Present were the Generalissimo, his Chief of Staff, his Air people, and many of the Chiefs of his Divisions, General Stilwell, General Chennault, Sir John Dill, and myself. After the Generalissimo had called the meeting to order, Sir John gave a very well-prepared talk on the situation in Burma. The Chinese asked many questions and I thought Sir John answered them in an exceptionally able manner.

Then the Chinese Chief of Operations gave his estimate of the Japanese strength: 77 combat divisions; 3000 combat airplanes.

General Stilwell told of the part the Combined Chiefs of Staff, the Prime Minister, and the President expected the Chinese to play in the operations against the Japanese in Burma. Chiang Kai-shek agreed to send a letter to the President and to the Prime Minister stating that he would join in the operations. We adjourned after that, until dinner.

The Generalissimo gave a beautifully arranged dinner for about twenty-four, including Ambassador Gauss, the military personnel who were in conference, and his own staff. After dinner, the Generalissimo, Stilwell, Chennault, the Chinese Chief of Staff, the Chief of Aviation, Dr. Soong, and I assembled to talk over air matters.

We had hardly started before the question of transport bogged us down, and we were unable to get any further that night. At that time our objective was about 4000 tons a month to be taken into China over the Hump. I tried my best to show it was impossible to stretch it to 5000 tons immediately, but I assured them I was shooting for 10,000 tons a month and hoped to reach that figure within a few months. The Generalissimo was not satisfied. He simply could not understand why the increase in tonnage could not be made overnight. Actually, the extra transport planes for the Hump run were not available to the Army Air Forces. He wanted my assurance that the 5000 tons a month would be reached at once. That assurance I could not give him. So the conference snagged on that one point and the meeting was adjourned. We walked back to our apartment. It was still cold and snowing; there was no heat in the villa; everyone went to bed to keep warm.

The following morning I arose in a cold room. A boy had brought in a brass brazier about 24 inches across, placed it in the center of the room, and lighted the charcoal, which was burning slowly. That charcoal was supposed to heat the room, which was about 12 × 15 feet, with a 10-foot ceiling, and it had been so cold that night that water left in the basins was frozen solid.

Right after breakfast I had another conference with Chiang and T. V. Soong. All the talking had to be done through Dr. Soong. The day before I had tried to find out just how much English the Generalissimo understood. Soong had been called from the room for a moment, so rather than sit at the luncheon table with Colonel Parker and the Generalissimo and say nothing, I had tried to figure out how I could do a little pantomiming. I recalled how it had been done by Harpo Marx in a show, and looked around for something I could say. In the center of the table was a bunch of flowers, and I looked at the Generalissimo. He looked at me and smiled. In my best pantomime I tried to ask, with appropriate gestures, "Were those flowers in the center of the table grown in a greenhouse, or were they grown out in the open?" I thought my pantomiming must have been pretty good, for the Generalissimo said, "Yes, Yes!" When T. V. Soong returned I asked him what the Generalissimo thought I had asked. After much talking back and forth in Chinese, Soong said, "The Generalissimo thought you had asked him whether the Chinese made tea out of flowers." From then on I knew I had to rely upon an interpreter.

The Generalissimo said to me, "I am going to be very frank with you; more so than I usually am. The conference we have had has, so far, been a failure and I want you to tell the President so for me. It has accomplished nothing.

"Our Army has been carrying on at war now for six years. We have gotten no supplies from anyone. Our movements have been made by our own legs; we have had no trucks; we have carried our artillery on our backs; our men have starved.

"If, as the Chiefs of Staff say, this is an important theater for operations against Japan, why are we not treated fairly? Why do we not receive supplies?

"Russia has been fighting, and fighting hard. She has killed many Germans. But so have we killed many Japanese. Russia gets convoys— even though they get sunk. You give them battleships and cruisers to protect them. I want you to tell the President that we are entitled to at least a regular flow of supplies; 10 per cent, maybe, of what the Russians get.

"This conference has been a failure. I have asked for things and the only answer I get from Bissell is an explanation as to why we can't get more tonnage; cannot operate more planes. He cites the railroad to Assam, the river traffic, and states that the airports will not be able to handle any more planes. Excuses, excuses.

"Tell your President that, unless I can get these three things, I cannot fight this war and he cannot count on me to have our Army participate in the campaigns:

"1. Independent Air Force in China under Chennault, who will be directly under me. Without this, we have no air force. Bissell has prevented our planes from operating. Without this independent air force I cannot go on. I want to put my air force under Chennault. The others are out. My men—soldiers and officers—have confidence in Chennault; but they will not serve under Bissell.

"2. Ten thousand tons a month over the air transport route into China. That must be done, not now, but at a stated time. Excuses do not go. I must have tonnage. When you suggested the four-engine cargo planes, Bissell gave many reasons why it could not be. He cannot handle this matter.

"3. Five hundred airplanes to China, operated by U.S.A. or China, by November. It is all right to say there is no gasoline, but there are ways and means of doing things and they must be done.

"I am speaking to you frankly because I want you to tell your President nothing has come, so far, out of this conference, and I want him to know it.

"I am sorry you are leaving. I had hoped you might be my guest for several days more, but since you must go, I hope you will tell your President what I have said."

Frankly, that threw me back on my haunches for a few minutes, so I had to collect myself before replying. My reply to the Generalissimo was:

"I want you to know that the people in the United States, from the President down through the War Department, the Secretary of War, the Chief of Staff, through the ranks, express nothing but the highest praise for the splendid courage and heroism of the Chinese soldiers. Their bravery and endurance of hardships are outstanding.

"I must tell you I am sincerely disappointed in your message to the President, for it is not in any way in accordance with my understanding of what has occurred. Upon my arrival here, I found there were but 62 transport planes on the India-China run. Within twenty-four hours, I had issued orders to raise that number to 137. The tonnage carried in December was 1700 tons. I have arranged to bring it up to 4000 tons by the month of April. It will be further raised as more planes and airdromes become available.

"I was told by the officer in whom you have the greatest confidence— General Chennault—that heavy bombers could not be operated out of China. He wanted medium bombers. Upon investigation it was demonstrated that the medium bomber could not operate as well as the heavy bombers could. Thirty-five heavy bombers have already been ordered to China for operations against the Jap air bases, coastal shipping, and other vital targets because they can carry their own gasoline into China from India and the medium bomber cannot.

"I have outlined to you a plan for creating one Chinese fighter squadron, then another, and if conditions warrant, building it up to a group. All that it needs is your approval.

"I also outlined plans for creating four bomber squadrons in the same manner. With your approval, we can start that at once. These plans may bring 500 planes to China, but not by November. As yet, I have not received your O.K. Five hundred planes in themselves mean nothing; but when they have gasoline, bombs, fields from which to operate, and American and Chinese combat and maintenance crews—that is something else.

"So we have accomplished quite a lot, if you will give us your aid.

"You told me you would give us aid and assistance in building new air fields, extending runways, and moving freight. For that we are grateful, for such action will be necessary to enable us to carry out the plans I have outlined.

"You must see now, why, when I take your message to the President,

I must also give him the plans I have outlined to you, which you have not accepted.

"As to the independent air force for Chennault, I am not in a position to approve such an organization, but I assure you I will repeat the remarks as given to me, to the President.

"As a matter of fact, in so far as tonnage over the Hump is concerned, we are not far apart. I have agreed to build up a tonnage of 4000 tons a month as soon as it can be done.

"I have given instructions to build it up beyond that, as soon as facilities are available; build it up as rapidly as we find ways and means to do so; but I cannot say it will reach 10,000 tons by November, 1943. I certainly hope it will." (As a matter of fact, we actually carried 6491 tons over the Hump in December, 1943, and from that time on it built up until it reached a total of about 32,000 tons the following December. By July, 1945, we had reached our peak—71,000 tons a month.)

"As I have said, we are practically in accord, in so far as the 500 planes are concerned. It may not be 500. It may be 600. It all depends upon the facilities available.

"So we are not far apart. You have great confidence in Chennault. I suggest you bring in Chennault, Sir John Dill, your two aviation heads, your Minister of War, General Stilwell, and any others you desire, and permit me to tell them my proposals and ask for their comments—particularly those of Chennault.

"The most important item is—are you going to enter into the Burma campaign with us? That you must answer. We need your help and will give you such supplies, aid, and staff help as we can."

All through the discussion, T. V. Soong acted as interpreter. Of course, I don't know exactly what he said to the Generalissimo regarding the last proposal I made, nor what the Generalissimo said in reply, but shortly thereafter, the visiting officers and Chiang's staff were brought into the room.

Chiang asked Sir John Dill a few questions about Burma. Sir John "smoked him out" about China's possible participation.

I insisted that the Generalissimo allow me to ask a few questions of Chennault about our transport; but that did not get very far as Chennault professed profound ignorance on the subject.

The Chinese Minister of War had his say. Then Chiang Kai-shek gave his summary of the conference. First, however, he asked Sir John Dill to give his impression of the meeting. Sir John replied that the conference had been very beneficial. He said, "It has brought out the difficulties which must be met in carrying out the plan for operations against the Japanese. Logistics and supply are still the determining factors." I said that upon my arrival in Calcutta I would take up the question of river tonnage. I asked Sir John to suggest to the British the possibility of increased tonnage on the railroad, and on the river into Assam. Sir John replied, "Most certainly we will take that up. You may be assured we will give it the most careful consideration and do everything possible to increase the tonnage."

I told Chiang I was glad China would participate in support of the Burma campaign, and that I would tell the President.

I asked Dill again, "Are you leaving with the firm understanding you can tell General Wavell the Chinese Army will give the campaign all-out support?"

He replied, "That is my impression."

Then I asked the Generalissimo, "Is that not correct?"

General Chiang Kai-shek replied that he was quite ready to play his part; but he repeated he needed increased tonnage: that 4000 tons over the Hump was not enough for his Army.

General Stilwell commented, "Of course, 4000 tons is not enough; it is a drop in the bucket. The Army needs more, much more. The question is, can we get it? Have we the facilities? We will do everything in our power to build it up. We will use every expedient we can. We will try every idea that comes to mind."

Then the Generalissimo made his summary, as follows:

1. The President and the Prime Minister had sent Sir John Dill and General Arnold to Chungking for a conference. We had had a most important conference among the United Nations.

2. He was gratified to learn there would be adequate Naval forces for the operations in Burma.

3. The military forces of nine Indian and British divisions and the Chinese Yunnan division were adequate to force the Japanese out of Burma.

4. Even the estimate of 10,000 tons a month from India to China, over the Hump, was a weak spot in the campaign, for his armies needed supplies urgently—and needed them now.

5. The United States' request for additional runways and new air bases in China would be met. He would give us all that we required.

6. Unless the air cargo capacity of 10,000 tons a month could be met

by the end of November; unless the air forces in China—the United States and Chinese—could have 500 planes for operation by November, he could not give any assurance of the success of the campaign.

7. If everyone would use all possible expedients, with the "will to do," the goals could be met. His demands were realistic; not impossible.

8. No battles could be won without having carefully planned timing and necessary quantities of supplies. They were essential to success.

9. He desired that the increase be made by November. If that was done he knew Japan could be defeated.

10. The three countries—China, the United States, and Britain—had met to find ways and means of defeating Japan. The President and the Prime Minister and the Combined Chiefs of Staff had stated China's participation was most important in organizing effective operations against Japan. The Generalissimo's requests were essential and must be met. Otherwise, it would be misleading to tell the President and the Prime Minister we could defeat Japan.

Then General Stilwell asked, "Does that mean the Chinese Army will not participate? That it will not fight?"

The Generalissimo replied: "China has been fighting for six years. It will continue to fight. China is ready to carry out its part. But supplies and equipment are necessary to give a smashing blow." And he continued, "You know we must use the troops in Yunnan in these campaigns, for you know you do not have enough. If our troops are not completely equipped they will march without shoes; they will have no motor transportation; they will suffer. It is your duty and your responsibility to give the troops the wherewithal to fight. That is the United Nations' job."

Then I commented, "As we have stated before, we will try in every possible way to build up the air transport line, to increase its cargo capacity to a maximum. We will continue to send in supplies for your ground troops. We hope to open up the Burma Road and get trucks in to you. We are highly gratified and greatly pleased to know China will play its part and will participate in the Burma campaign."

Sir John then said, "It is indeed a great satisfaction to know the Chinese will play their part in the campaign, but it must not be forgotten how much has to be done in training and in preparing to overcome the logistical questions which will arise when this campaign begins. There is time, but not too much."

With that, the meeting adjourned.

We left the Generalissimo's lodge and drove through the snow back to Chungking, where we took off through the overcast, returning to Kunming at 6:10 P.M.

The question of money was ever present. I have this note in my diary:

I airdrome costs $190,000,000.00 Chinese (without the equipment) ;
I package of cigarettes costs $120.00 ;
I suit of clothes costs $6,000.00 ;
3 mules, used six days, cost $5,000.00 ;
I tangerine costs $20.00 ;
I cup of coffee costs $14.00 ;
I gallon of gasoline costs $180.00.
(Note: All figures are Chinese monetary values.)

On our way back to Kunming I talked with Sir John. I thought the Generalissimo was not realistic. He brushed too many important things aside. He cast aside logistics and factual matters as mere trifles. Apparently, he believed in man's "will to do"; that will power could force the impossible. While on my job, I had forced the impossible many times, but I still realized one could not completely ignore logistics. Furthermore, the Generalissimo apparently did not have a global outlook. His only thought was: "Aid to China!; Aid to China!" Sometimes he gave evidence of quick thinking; but only at times. He had an orderly mind, capable of arranging details, and he asked very pertinent questions. However, the effort died out after the first few questions. There was no doubt that he had the power of life and death in his hands, as far as the Chinese nation was concerned, for as long as he wanted it; and he expected his subjects to remember that. Accordingly, he did not have to think his way through. It made no difference to him, so long as he had his way.

Dill agreed with me in my estimate of Chiang, but he suggested that perhaps the absence of Madame Chiang Kai-shek had had an effect; perhaps her influence on the Generalissimo would have made a difference.

That night when we were eating in the General's Mess at Kunming, all the American "experts" were airing their knowledge of the Chinese language. It was one way, apparently, of putting ignorant visitors in their places. One of them called the Chinese waiter and carefully asked in great detail, in Chinese, for a cup of tea. After a long wait, the Chinese boy returned with a plate of dinner—meat, potatoes, corn, and gravy. Everyone laughed except the "expert linguist." Then Stilwell asked the boy, in Chinese, to bring him a cup of tea; that was all he wanted; he did not want dinner. The boy brought Stilwell his cup of tea, and said in perfectly good English, "Here is your cup of tea, sir."

Next morning, as our B-17 had blown a tire, General Stilwell, Bissell, and I took off in two C-87's, carrying the Chinese Minister of War, the Chief of Staff, the Air Chief, and other Staff officers with us. There were no seats in the plane so we had to sit wherever we could.

We were met at Calcutta by General Caleb V. Haynes and several of the local people, and went to the Hotel Great Eastern for lunch. There I again met our General Alexander, commanding the Air Transport operations out of India, and told him the immediate plans we had made with the Generalissimo for the transport line running into China. I inspected Haynes' outfit, and we returned just in time for dinner with the governor of the Province at Government House; a delightful affair, with all senior officers present.

Next day we had a conference on the Burma situation with Wavell, all those attending who had been at New Delhi, and in addition, the Chinese Minister of War, General Ho. The air problem popped up time and time again. When the Chinese said 500 Japanese airplanes might be assembled in the theater to operate against them, I replied I couldn't see it. The Chinese had agreed the total air strength of the Japanese was between 2500 and 3000 combat planes. If all the Japanese planes used in the outlying areas were added together, they totaled about 2300, which left a total of 700 for Japan proper, Formosa, the Naval Air, and for Burma. Therefore, it would be impossible for the Japanese to assemble 500 airplanes in Burma.

The Chinese then indicated their decision to make an all-out effort to tie in with the British and the Americans, so it looked as if our work in Chungking had done some good after all. In the afternoon, the Chinese approved and signed the minutes of the meeting, as did everyone else, thus committing themselves to a Burma campaign in which British, Chinese, and Americans would participate.

I had a long talk with General Haynes at dinner that night. He told me that upon his arrival the Japanese had broadcast over the radio, in English, that, "The Japanese people need have no fear of Haynes—he was an old, worn-out transport pilot." Haynes had some paper slips printed in Japanese and Chinese (the Chinese did it for him), reading: "Presented by your 'old, worn-out transport flyer,' Caleb Haynes." Every time Haynes' outfit went on a raid they dropped several thousand of these little papers with their bombs.

I said good-by to General Stilwell, who was going back to his command in China. He gave me a note to give to General Marshall. Soong gave me a letter to give the President, in which no changes had been made in the demands of the Generalissimo.

With a brief stop at Panda, where I decorated some of the men who had been doing such a wonderful job against the Japanese out there, we arrived at Karachi that night in time for dinner. At Karachi we heard of an incident that illustrates the sense of humor of the American soldier. After the Hindu camel trains unloaded their supplies at Karachi and the men sold their wares, they climbed back on the camels and headed out in the dark, starting toward the interior while it was cool. The American airport was some fourteen miles from the city, and usually the camel trains reached the airport at the time the American soldiers were coming to work in the morning. The Hindus riding the camels, on this particular morning, were fast asleep. The American soldiers took the lead camel, turned it around without stopping it, and headed it back to Karachi. Naturally, it was followed by the whole train. Some three or four hours later, the Hindus awakened to find themselves back in Karachi, exactly where they had started.

That night Sir John Dill and I talked over the advisability of returning to the United States by way of England, as the Prime Minister had requested. We finally decided that actually we would get more done and get it done more quickly if we returned direct to the United States, notifying the Prime Minister by cable of the various discussions that had taken place.

I gave to Sir John another American word to think of—a word used very extensively during the war. The word was "theateritis." Sir John admitted that he had never heard of it before. I told him it was a disease that theater commanders contracted, usually after they had been with their new commands for a short time.

Sir John asked more about it: was it incurable?; what were its symptoms?; did every commander get it? I assured him that the symptoms were always the same, that it was not incurable, but in many cases almost so.

The symptoms; continued requests and demands for additional personnel and equipment of the latest type, regardless of the importance of the command in relation to others, regardless of the schedules worked out by the Joint or Combined Chiefs of Staff, regardless of production, and regardless of the effect upon other theaters. In addition, commanders with theateritis always suffered from the delusion that some mystic wave of the hand would bring about the impossible and secure thousands of airplanes overnight.

But in reality, despite the headaches, and the reams of unnecessary messages it made us send, theateritis was not such a bad disease. It showed that the commander was on the job and was willing to fight for his men and the equipment he believed necessary to do his job, even if the disease irritated most of the staff officers in Washington almost to distraction. I told Sir John that I would not have any other kind of commander running one of our Air Forces, but that in the China Theater, General Chennault and the Generalissimo certainly had a more acute case of the disease than anybody in any other theater. Most of our troubles in Chungking stemmed from that fact, and would continue to do so until the China Theater became a first priority for winning the war, if it ever assumed that importance.

The following morning we reached Salala, behind the barren Arabian Coast, and found Lieutenant Pike, USAAF, in command of an airport in the midst of the desert. It reminded me of our field at Muroc Lake, California. Tents and improvised mess halls and servicing facilities were all crude but in efficient working order. Lieutenant Pike, who had formerly been with Pan American Airways, had three sergeants and two privates in his command. Nothing seemed to daunt him: neither sand nor heat nor dust.

From Salala our course was due west. The map itself gave us a forbidding impression of what was ahead of us. It was marked *Unexplored,* but that wasn't the half of it. There wasn't a mark of any kind on the map nor on the ground for 500 miles.

As we approached the Red Sea, we came to the mountains. We were flying at 9500 feet and the mountains were about 4000 feet below us. Every now and then we would see a broad valley with green fields and the strange handiwork of men. High buildings nestling close together, forming towns—all made of stone; from a distance the same kind of skyscrapers seen in New York City.

Fifty miles to the north as we flew along, the mountains towered a thousand feet above us. High plateaus flattened out near the peaks. The land was cultivated. We saw dykes and water; streams and irrigated fields. The people in those villages lived happily at altitudes where we would have needed oxygen. Trails led from one village to another, but none of the trails seemed to lead to the outside world. I asked everyone on the plane if they had ever heard of this civilized area. None—not even Sir John Dill—had. Shelmire took photos from the plane.

Dropping down at last to the plains of the Red Sea, we flew some distance and landed amidst great consternation on the field at an airport twenty-two miles from Khartoum. We learned that the Governor was waiting for us at another airport three miles out of town. Sir John Dill, Colonel Shelmire, Colonel Petersen, and I were driven to Government

House; the others went to the Grand Hotel. We stayed at Government House on the steps of which Chinese Gordon had been killed by the spears of the Sudanese.

Governor Huddleson and his Lady were our hosts. That morning the Governor sent Sir John and me out in a car to Omdurman, the place where Kitchener completely destroyed the power of the Arabs who had followed the fanatic Mahdi.

On the 13th, after a beautiful sunset drive up the Blue Nile with Lady Huddleson, we took off about midnight, for Maiduguri. We wanted to fly over darkest Africa—the jungle, the desert, the uninhabited portion—at night so we wouldn't be bothered with its daytime dust and heat.

The first place we recognized in the morning was Fort Lamy, the point where, much to our disgust, the Germans had bombed out our gasoline supply. Soon we came to Maiduguri, in Nigeria, in Central Africa. The blacks were the blackest, tallest natives we had seen anywhere, mostly ragged or naked, but some reveling in the uniforms of the British African Corps. Even these wore no shoes, but strutted unconcernedly in bare feet over the sharp stones, their knives, canteens, and ammunition rattling impressively.

Our airfield there, operated jointly with the Royal Air Force, was well built, and was administered by a first lieutenant. There were more diseased natives at Maiduguri than I had seen anywhere outside of Dakar. I asked about the frequency of inspections made by the doctors and what attempts were made to keep our soldiers away from the sick people. Apparently the situation was being well handled, for our sick rate was normal. Most of the officers we had at these stations had served with Pan American Airways. They knew little about Army administration, but they certainly knew how to get along with the natives and how to run an airport in darkest Africa.

We took off from Maiduguri about noon and headed for Accra. Arriving in the evening, we had time to look around the place and saw it was a well-kept post. We changed airplanes and took off in a C-54, headed for Ascension Island, arriving there at 7:25 A.M.—Sir John Dill, General Somervell, Colonel Smart, Colonel Shelmire, and myself. We went through several thunderstorms as we crossed the equator; otherwise, we had an excellent trip. During the storms the plane jumped and bucked; lightning flashed and the clouds were black; but when we broke into the clear there was the Southern Cross, just over the bow. I happened to be taking my turn at the wheel just at that time.

At daybreak, we arrived at Ascension Island, a small volcanic island in the middle of the Atlantic, its runways, about six or seven thousand feet long, dug out between the hills. Though even water was a respected commodity in this remote place—they could get it only from rain clouds —some 2000 planes had passed through Ascension during the past year: transport planes, B-17's, B-24's, A-20's, and fighters. Of that total 2000, we had lost the crews of only four planes.

At Natal the heat was intense. The doors of the plane were kept closed while the medicos came through with a spray to disinfect the plane and us (required procedure). For several minutes we had to breathe the obnoxious fumes from the spray while we roasted in that hot plane; we weren't in a very good humor when we climbed out. General Bob Walsh was waiting for us and he suggested we go to Recife for the night, as the Minister of Air, Salgado Fihlio, and General Gomez were waiting for me there.

We climbed into a DC-3, took off, and arrived at Recife within an hour to find an escort of honor and a band. The Minister of Air and Gomez insisted that I take the review. The Brazilian Air Troops put on an excellent ceremony. It was nice and cool out on the beach. That night we had dinner with the Minister of Air and Gomez in town. We found the Brazilians wanted more training facilities for mechanics. This I arranged for at once with General Walsh. They wanted us to train more pilots for them—some 300 that year—and they wanted materials for their aircraft factory. I asked for a list of what they needed and said I would see what I could do.

Our B-17 came in and caught up with us, but my pilot, Colonel Petersen, went to the hospital. I told Colonel Shelmire to hold Pete there until he got well; that I would keep on traveling in the C-87.

At Natal we had a nice surprise—a message from General Marshall, which read: "Delighted to welcome you back to Western Hemisphere. All your families well."

We went through a very narrow weather front north of Belém and from that time on, we had the finest weather of the whole trip, to Borinquen. When we arrived at Borinquen, we found my old aide and pilot, Colonel Beebe, with his group, on the ground waiting for me. His planes were ready for the trip to Burma for operation with the Tenth Air Force in China under General Bissell.

I have a note here which says that, on February 17th, I dropped my watch on the concrete floor and it bounced. It also stopped running. On that day we reached Washington.

⭐ 24 ⭐

It can be seen that the personal clashes among the key leaders in China
made it rather difficult for me to give the President a clean-cut report.
Logistics, air and general military progress were one thing. Matters
like Chiang's attitude toward Bissell, his unlimited confidence in Chennault, Chennault's own oversimplification, along Chinese lines, of various
problems, and above all the personal position of Stilwell, who called
Chiang Kai-shek "Peanut Head" practically within the Generalissimo's
hearing—these were complications a bit beyond the Book. Despite the
keen assistance of such advisers as General Somervell, General Wedemeyer of the War Plans Division of the War Department, and Colonel
Smart of my own Plans Division, there was more behind the situation
to be solved than in any ordinary command decision.

If Stilwell, our theater commander in Burma, and theoretically
Chiang's American right hand, was part of the difficulty, he was also one
of the most forthright sources of information. One important document
I brought back to the President, the Secretary of War, and General
Marshall was the memorandum he had prepared for me expressing in
detail his cryptic and pessimistic opinion of the senior officers in the
Chinese Army—"God awful," he said.

That tale of corruption and inefficiency, in which the Hump, our
operations for getting supplies from Assam into China, the projected
reopening of the Burma Road, etc., would all have to be rooted—for of
course we counted on the full cooperation of the Chinese—was disturbing,
if not altogether new. The pipeline we planned across the jungle area of
Burma, so that we wouldn't have to carry all our own gas in by air, was
entirely dependent on Chinese assistance.

Stilwell's memorandum made such an idea seem farfetched. Naming names and units, he told of the losses on the Ichang front in the past four years—through sickness, not fighting. He described the "Coffin Racket" in the 13th Division.

"The Division Commander gets $15.00 per coffin. He keeps $7.00 and turns over $8.00 to the Hospital Superintendent. The latter keeps $4.00 and gives $4.00 to the assistant. The assistant keeps $2.00; the village carpenter gets $2.00 and a ration to procure the wood and make the coffin.

"On the Indo-China frontier at Lookay, if a Chinese soldier fires across the river and kills anyone on the enemy side, he himself gets shot. That is common talk. I have no evidence, but it indicates how anxious the Chinese are not to interrupt business.

"The second son of the Governor of Yunnan is reliably reported to be the head of a smuggling ring in Calcutta.

"During the Burma campaign, Yei Fei Ping, Chief of the SOS, on one day reported he had no gas with which to run his trucks. On the next day he reported he had no trucks to get the gas out. At that time he had 650 trucks and at least 20,000 gallons of gasoline. This same Yei Fei Ping was ordered by the Generalissimo, after appeal by radio from me, to deliver 150 trucks for troop movements. He started 39, of which 22 reached me.

"The Commanding General of the Fifth Army received six annas per man, per day, in lieu of fresh vegetables. Not one cent got to the Division. He drew this money on his certificate for 45,000 men, but he actually had about 25,000. He was putting about $6000 United States gold in his pocket every day."

So it went.

"No one dares to tell the Peanut (meaning the Generalissimo) the truth, if it is unpleasant. . . .

"The big obstructions are the General Staff. They are due to jealousy, inertia, laziness, pride, and crass stupidity. They continue because the Peanut is too dumb to realize what is being done.

"Anything that is done in China will be done in spite of, and not because of, the Peanut and his military clique."

Finally, I made my report to my superiors as I saw the problem, supporting my conclusions and inferences with specific details.

Then I returned to a pile of accumulated papers on my desk—and I mean pile.

Here are a few at random:

Memorandum (prepared by the Commanding General, Army Air Forces) for General Marshall to send to Mr. Hopkins re delay in deliveries of light bombers, stating that unless deliveries were expedited, commitments to Russia and England would have to be reduced, rather than have the United States run short.

Memorandum, Mr. Hopkins to General Arnold, quoting cablegram from Harriman relating to the Siberian Airplane Ferry Service, stating that the Russians should operate the planes, but that if we desired to learn the route, our officers might accompany the Russians. (Note: Even though we went into this, the Russians would never permit our officers to accompany them on their trips, so we never did learn the route, although the Russians, apparently, learned everything they wanted to know about Alaska.)

Memorandum: Plan for delivering ten transports to the Russians to be turned over to them at Fairbanks; to be operated by the Russians for the return of crews on the Siberian Ferry Service Route.

Memorandum to Mr. Hopkins, stating that due to shortages of C-54's, it would be impossible at this time to furnish one for the Generalissimo for his personal use.

Memorandum to Mr. Hopkins, outlining bombing of three railways connecting the Po Valley with Central Italy.

Memorandum to Mr. Hopkins, outlining the advantages of high-altitude bombing, and its effectiveness, with report of damage done by MacArthur's command to Japanese airplanes and surface craft.

Memorandum to Mr. Hopkins, suggesting the United States lead the way in using air power and getting an offensive started before Germany developed an air fortress-destroyer type of plane; that this plan be not interfered with by diversions to other theaters.

(Note: The preceding two memoranda were apparently written after the Navy, the British, the Chinese, and, perhaps, the Prime Minister had all tried their best to get us to divert our heavy bombers to other theaters.)

Memorandum to Mr. Hopkins, recommending we adopt a more aggressive attitude, and concentrate on the plans for bombing Germany, so we could make the trans-Channel landings on the French coast possible.

Memorandum to Mr. Hopkins, proposing that a United States air line be established across the Pacific which would not be dependent upon the French, the British, the Dutch, nor anyone else for maintenance.

Memorandum to Mr. Hopkins stating that production in fighters had been materially changed, the P-40 having been cut down in production in favor of the C-46, which we planned to use for over-the-Hump operations into China. No heavy bombers could be allocated to Russia until after June, 1944.

Memorandum to Mr. Lovett, stating that the Truman subcommittee had visited Patterson Field, and had made a report on the excessive costs of furnishing the Executive Office, and on recording devices used during the conference; also on the hoarding of civilian personnel, paving of parking areas, roads, etc.

Memorandum to Harry Hopkins, giving plan for round-the-clock bombing of Japan.

Memorandum to General Stratemeyer, stating that if 30 additional planes from our production, or from the Army stock, were made available to the commercial air lines without tying in with other demands, the Air Transport Command would find itself in a very embarrassing situation.

Memorandum to all Air Force commanders and Air Force task commanders throughout the world, stating that the tactical doctrines learned at our schools were being followed too closely in bombing, and not enough initiative was being displayed to cope with combat conditions as they actually existed.

Memorandum to my deputy relating to travel priority on Army airplanes: "By no stretch of the imagination will I accept the fact that these French diplomatic couriers have precedence and priority over our soldiers."

Memorandum to all Air Force commanders: "Young officers must learn to drink in such a manner that they will always have possession of their faculties. If not, they should stop drinking."

Memorandum to Staff, directing that we stop our "wishie-washie," indecisive program for cooperative training with ground troops.

Memorandum to A-2: "We must be as accurate as we can in coming to conclusions relating to German Air Force strength. We must not kid ourselves by accepting figures giving more planes destroyed than actually occurred. On the other hand, we do not want to underestimate our own ability."

Memorandum directing investigation of low flying over the White House.

Memorandum to General Marshall, stating we must keep flying under control, regardless of whether or not the offenders are returned combat flyers with high and efficient records. (A returned hero had just "flown tight formation" with a commercial air liner.)

Memorandum to Secretariat of Joint Chiefs of Staff: "In order to establish and maintain our control over the South and Southwest Pacific, we must build up, with the least possible delay, facilities for direct line air routes to our destinations. To maintain this control after peace is declared, we must have all-American air routes across the Pacific."

Memorandum to General Echols, re modification centers: "I strongly urge that the entire modification program be taken away from the people now handling it, and every effort be made to secure a group of civilians who have nothing to do but carry out modifications. It is obvious the present organization can't handle it."

Wire to Darryl F. Zanuck, telling him that "Purple Heart" is a misnomer for the picture, with reply from Zanuck telling General Arnold it was too late to change the name, but agreeing the criticism of the title was justified.

Memorandum to Dr. Vannevar Bush: "It is believed it is about time to stop fooling around with magnesium bombs as a sole source for incendiaries, and change our incendiary requirements to 50 per cent magnesium and 50 per cent gasoline."

Memorandum to General George, head of the Air Transport Command, telling him to get at a study on future air transport possibilities, and arrange for a committee or board to make a continuing study of ATC's existing and projected facilities, routes, methods of operation, and relationship of existing American and foreign air lines; determining and recommending to me the policy that should be adopted and action that should be taken, in order that we might have proper air bases for military operations in the future, after the war was over.

Memorandum, received, stating that American persons who had violated security were General Arnold, the Under Secretary of War, and Mr. Justice Byrnes, but it was very doubtful if any useful purpose would be served by disciplinary action in these cases. (I never did know just when, where, and how I violated "security.")

Memorandum to Training: "Replacement crews are going overseas who haven't fired a gun at altitudes over 16,000 feet. This is a hell of a way to send these boys overseas, and I will have to explain why they are sent. You might just as well start writing telegrams now for me to sign when I get back, and see that no more men are sent until they have had proper training at high altitudes."

Memorandum to Executive, regarding flying time of airplanes; directing that more hours be flown—a minimum of four hours per day for every fighter airplane; order to stop setting aside airplanes for "brass hats."

Memorandum to General George: "Speed up transportation to India and China. The ones that were to go next week, send this week; the ones that are to go week after next, send next week."

Letter from Mountbatten, thanking General Arnold for C-47, stating he has christened the new plane "Hapgift."

Letter to General Spaatz: "Just a short note to straighten out certain matters that have been brought to my attention—the character of instruction being given at the Operational Training Units in the United States and at Casablanca, and the type of instructors. One of my difficulties is to get training at altitudes above 20,000 feet. On this side of the world I find it rather difficult to have my instructions carried out, and I presume you have the same difficulties over there."

Memorandum from Harry Hopkins asking for an airplane to take Prince Bernhard of the Netherlands, the Dutch Ambassador, and the Prince's aide back to England.

Letter from General Eisenhower to me: "I tried to get an appointment to see young Hank. My instructions miscarried and I didn't get to talk with him on the phone. I am impressed by the fine qualities of your youngster. I am of the firm conviction that if our Air Force could operate at 100 per cent every day, we could finish this fellow off quickly (meaning the Germans). You do not need to sell me any bill of goods on the Air Force."

Letter to General Spaatz: "Just how many gliders do you want? Shall I turn on the spigot? How many can you really use? Are the troops in Europe being given proper training? Just what is your candid opinion of the whole situation?"

Memorandum to General Marshall, re landing in Sicily: "There is every indication that 42 transport planes, some towing gliders filled with troops, and the transports filled with troops, were shot down by the Royal Navy, the United States Navy, and our own ground troops."

Memorandum to my Deputy: "Butler, in Alaska, complains because he has received no replacement airplanes, no replacement crews, spares, or transport planes. He needs, also, experienced officers. As far as I can see, he needs everything."

Memorandum to my Chief of Staff re difficulty in trying to transfer airplanes to the Russians: "Their attitude toward our airplanes is one of tolerant acceptance, and at no time have they shown any enthusiasm regarding performance or characteristics. They are definitely critical of the armament and any mechanical deficiencies."

Memorandum to General Somervell: "What are you doing about getting supplies to troops in isolated places? The troops on Ascension Island had Spam for Christmas dinner."

Letter to General Kenney, stating that the 90th Group was being sent to replace the 19th: "I am convinced that the solution to the whole problem out there lies in the rapid advance from Australia to New Guinea to New Britain, rather than through the Solomons. I am also more convinced than ever that the ultimate solution must be a single commander for everything operating in the Pacific—a commander with a staff made up of officers of all arms."

Memorandum to the President: "In connection with courier service and other official air travel through the Azores, you are informed the field there will not be ready for operations until 19 November 1943."

Memorandum to the Secretary of State: I am disturbed over the lack of progress achieved in negotiations for construction, use, and control of a major U.S. air base on the island of Santa Maria, Azores. Every effort should be put forth at once to bring Santa Maria negotiations to a prompt and satisfactory conclusion."

The first thing we had run into on this was that by agreement, Pan American Air Lines was the only agency that had any right to open the question of new airports in the Azores. Secondly, the British had the Azores "sewed up" with their diplomatic agreements, and it was thus "diplomatically" impossible for us to enter into negotiations with Premier Salazar in Lisbon. These conditions held for some time. Despite our most strenuous efforts, it wasn't until June, 1944, that we could go ahead with bases in the Azores as we had planned. Then a cable from Europe indicated that the construction of the second airdrome was questioned by the British Ambassador in Lisbon. The American Ambassador, however, stuck to his guns and told him the second airdrome was a United States-Portuguese proposition, and had no connection at all with any British interests. So we finally got it through—for the war period only!

Copy of a letter from the President to General Marshall, asking him to explore the merit and possibility of putting an American Air Force on the Caucasian Front to fight with the Russian army.

Memorandum to L. S. Smith, who was in charge of Chinese cadets learning to fly. (They were wrecking too many airplanes.) "Isn't there any way you can instill in the minds of these Chinese students the idea they can use all of the runway, starting at one end, and continuing through to the other end?"

Letter to Portal, expressing belief there must be a plan for an earlier air offensive that would destroy Germany's air supremacy over Europe.

Letter to Portal, saying that the time was right for the establishment of formal machinery to coordinate and integrate our two bombing efforts; and suggesting a permanent coordinating body on the policy level.

Memorandum directing that program for creation of bombardment and pursuit groups be completely revised, since it was entirely unsatisfactory.

Letter from Spaatz, expressing opinion that in order to get proper flow of fighter airplanes, more chances must be taken with weather than we had been willing to accept in the the first movement. Fighter planes would be able to climb above overcasts and fly through bad weather and reach their destinations.

Memorandum criticizing the Eighth Air Force for holding too many bombers idle on the ground. We had made only two or three raids over Germany in February, 1943, while the British flyers had made seventeen that month.

Memorandum to General Somervell: "Too many Air Corps units are arriving in theaters without organizational equipment. Isn't there some way to see they get it?"

Memorandum to General Eisenhower, confirming the employment of long-range fighters in connection with our bombardment operations. (There has been much speculation about when and where the idea started that we give longer legs to fighters so they could accompany our bombers. It started with the plan for bombing interior Germany.)

Memorandum to Spaatz, asking him not to be impatient with me. "I have been impatient all my life, and probably will be until the end of my days; but that's my make-up—and that's that."

Memorandum to Air Vice Marshal Slessor, relating to over-all employment of air after the war was over: "I foresee a very widespread scrap after the war to keep air power in its proper place and I am afraid this war may end before it is proved, beyond doubt, that carriers are not a part of air power. Heavy taxation is necessary to maintain fleets of carriers, which I believe are already obsolete, except as transport auxiliaries to air power."

Memorandum to Commanding General, Air Force in England, stating that the Eighth Air Force was apparently going through a routine repetition of performance and finding alibis for not sending more airplanes out on missions. Suggestion made that perhaps more aggressive leaders were needed—perhaps bomb group, and wing commanders had been there too long.

Memorandum to Eaker, in England, assuring him of my faith in his ability, and that if there were anything detrimental to be said, I, Arnold, would say it directly to Eaker and not to any third party.

Letter to Devers, telling him Brereton was being sent to command the Tactical Air Forces, giving him Brereton's background, and saying Brereton was an excellent man for the job.

Memorandum to Eaker, expressing satisfaction that the bombing effort had picked up.

Memorandum, relating to the Navy's report on the Battle of Italy: "Admiral King's statement that 'concept of a mobile Air Force is not acceptable for the Mid-Pacific area' is wholly not acceptable to the Air Force. It is only by a mobile Air Force that the Pacific air war will be won."

Memorandum from General Stratemeyer to Mr. Lovett: Read newspaper article, "Replacement of General Arnold," in New York *Times; Herald-Tribune* stated General Brett was to replace General Arnold, who was to go to England. Mr. Stimson announced at a press conference there was not a word of truth in the report.

Memoranda—and letters—about the possibility of "cat and dog" fight with the Signal Corps relating to Air Force movies; decision for or against the film based on Doolittle's Tokyo raid; should we or should we not have a comparison between our accident rate and the Naval Air Service accident rate; should we or should we not have a comparison between R.A.F. and A.A.F. losses?

And so they went: 50 calibers in the nose of the B-24's; compass buttons, experimental, to be manufactured for the uniforms of all combat crewmen, for use if and when they were forced down in enemy territory and were able to get away from their planes; flak suits for airmen, to reduce wounds by fragments from antiaircraft guns; quick-release parachutes; tests for 4000-pound bombs; 20-mm. cannon versus 37-mm. gun; characteristics of the two-engine airplane versus the four-engine airplane; La Guardia's protest that the American airplanes were not as good as they should be and were not equal to the German airplanes; British antagonism to the B-17's; Mr. McCloy's memorandum (McCloy was Assistant Secretary of War) saying, "How about putting armor on the bottom of airplanes? The Russians are way ahead of you on that. What have you got to say about it?" (Note: I wonder if Mr. McCloy would like to exchange the Air Force we had at the end of the war for the Russian Air Force.) Hostile criticism of the Flying Fortress and the Liberator by Peter Masefield, top British aviation writer (one combat mission in a

B-17 made him an enthusiastic convert) ; memorandum to Mr. Lovett covering my dissatisfaction with the explanation for the failure of engines in the A-20's and the B-25's.

I was not present at the TRIDENT Conference in May. A bit of trouble with my "ticker" had me in Walter Reed Hospital, Washington, at the time. However, I was very pleased that General Wavell, Air Chief Marshal Portal, Averell Harriman, and others were able to get to the hospital to see me and talk over the proceedings.

At TRIDENT, it was decided to coordinate the land and air forces of Britain and the United States in Southeast Asia under one commander (at that time they were three separate commands) ; to increase the amount of supplies going over the Hump into China to 10,000 tons a month by giving the Air Transport Command top priority ; and to launch the campaign in Burma in the fall at the end of the 1943 monsoon season.

All these decisions were in accord with the discussions I had had with General Wavell and the Generalissimo during my trip to China and with the President in my subsequent talks with him.

In August at the QUADRANT Conference in Quebec, I met Brigadier Orde Wingate who had worked so successfully with a large number of men behind the Japanese lines in Burma. After having talked with the Prime Minister, Wingate appeared before the Combined Chiefs of Staff in Quebec with a more elaborate plan which involved the employment of a much bigger force for his next Burma operation. It was approved. I liked his initiative and imagination, his resourcefulness and his courage.

To give him as much assistance as possible, I reviewed the qualifications and personal characteristics of the available Air Force officers to decide who could best work with him behind the Japanese lines in Burma. I finally selected Colonels Phil Cochran and John Allison, and directed them to report to Wingate. These two officers were naturals for the job. They immediately organized Number 1 Air Commando outfit. Its equipment included everything from helicopters to puddle-jumpers to light and medium bombers, to fighters, gliders, and transports and all the latest gadgets and means then known for snatching gliders off the ground. This Commando organization played a most important part in making Wingate's mission a success and in making interior Burma too hot for the Japanese

It was also at the Quebec Conference that Lord Louis Mountbatten was appointed Commander of the Southeast Asia Theater. I offered him the services of my former aide, Brigadier General Eugene Beebe, as American Air Representative, an offer Mountbatten accepted. Major General A. C. Wedemeyer became his Chief Strategic Planner and his Deputy Chief of Staff. Commander Rogers became representative for the U.S. Navy. General Stilwell, then commanding the United States-China Burma Theater, was to be Lord Mountbatten's deputy. Operations in the Chinese Theater of war would still come under Generalissimo Chiang Kai-shek. General George Stratemeyer, who had already been sent into the Indian Theater to take over from Bissell, was to command our Far Eastern Air Force under Mountbatten. All the resources, equipment, and materiel we had in the China-Burma-India Theater were to be turned over to Mountbatten.

The QUADRANT Conference decided several other matters of great importance: There would be an offensive in northern Burma in the winter of 1943–44; the new road then under construction by American engineers, together with the pipeline, would be extended from Assam to the Burma Road to Kunming; a pipeline would be built from Calcutta to Assam (these lines would greatly increase the flow of gasoline into China); the capacity of over-the-hump supplies would be built up to 20,000 tons a month; everything possible would be done to expedite the operation of B-29's out of China.

The Quebec Conference also discussed changes in our plans with regard to our movements northward through Italy and plans for an Allied landing in southern France that would move up the Valley of the Rhone concurrently with the landing of Eisenhower's forces, though these matters were not quite ready yet to be considered in detail.

One of the most important subjects discussed was the "short-legged-ness" of British fighters. These Spitfires, Hurricanes, etc., excellent planes in other respects, wouldn't be able to stay in the air long enough after taking off from England to give real support to British troops landing on the northwest coast of France. That was indeed a problem. To solve it, someone had sold Churchill the idea of building floating bases out of a combination of sawdust and sea water. The notion was to force ammonia through pipes surrounded by sea water and sawdust (as is done in a regular ice plant) thereby forming large cakes of ice in the ocean or in the English Channel. With enough cakes of ice, it might be possible, by hitching them together, to create "landing fields" where the fighter planes could refuel. The plan was called, biblically, "HABAKKUK." At Quebec, the idea was outlined to the Combined Chiefs of Staff by Lord Louis Mountbatten. But it was a deep, dark secret; only the top-level planners were supposed to know anything about it.

At those meetings in Quebec behind closed doors, there were some very rough, tough sessions. Angry words were sometimes thrown back and forth. The Americans and the British did not always have the same ideas about what our future plans should be. The Americans were eager to get going and get the thing over with by making a landing in France as soon as the supplies, troops, and equipment could be gotten together. The British had a tendency to hold back until everything was carefully prepared. Many times the sessions were so hot that even the Planning Staff was not allowed to be present.

One day while we were out to lunch, Lord Mountbatten brought in a sample of his ice airdrome. When we returned and had reassembled behind closed doors, he talked about it and showed how it was constructed; explained its characteristics. To show how sturdy it was, how much punishment it would take, he stood off and fired a pistol into it—several pistol shots.

The HABAKKUK piece was then put back on a wheeled litter, covered with a white sheet, and rolled out of the door. It was several feet long. As it passed the planners, who all morning long had heard loud voices raised in argument, Air Marshal Walsh said, "My God! They're shooting one another! I wonder whom they've shot!"

Flying the plane back from the Quebec Conference, I had a few bad moments when I temporarily missed the "unauthorized" notes I had taken at the meeting. For a while I was sweating, remembering the young British officer in London who had gone to jail for several years for leaving a briefcase of merely "Restricted" material in a taxi. His Majesty's Government was not so lenient toward even local security violations as ours. However, when I called back on the intercom and asked my sergeant, with what I hoped was convincing calm, to bring my other blouse up to the cockpit, I found the papers.

For some time I had been receiving reports, letters, and telegrams from overseas, and verbal accounts from returning officers, that made it apparent I was getting out of touch with the Eighth Air Force in England. I therefore decided to make a personal inspection of its operations, to find out for myself what they needed in the way of equipment and personnel. With that in mind, I took off on August 31st, accompanied by quite a staff: my Chief Flight Surgeon, General Dave Grant, General H. S. Hansell, one of my planners, General Waite, Captain Hutchins, Captain Thackeray of the Navy, Lieutenant Humphries of the Navy, and others.

It was an average flight from Gravelly Point to Gander. From Gander, our C-54 took off in rain, mist, and fog, arriving next morning in Ireland at 7:30.

The weather was bad—low clouds and showers. As we approached the field at Prestwick, our destination in Britain, about 50 B-17's and B-24's from America were also coming in to land. Their pilots were new and inexperienced, and we didn't want to interfere with them in the bad weather, so we cruised around in circles out of the B-17 and B-24 area. Finally, Control tried to send us up to an airport that no one had ever heard of and which couldn't be found on a map. He couldn't tell us where we were or where we were to go; he didn't know where the airport was; so we landed at Prestwick about 9:30 A.M.—about twelve hours after our take-off from Gander.

I was not satisfied with the way incoming planes were being handled. We lost two bombers and two complete crews out of those planes waiting to land at Prestwick. They had all taken off from Newfoundland ahead of us. In fact, we had purposely waited an hour to give them a head start so they would be sure to get into Prestwick first. As we flew behind them over the North Atlantic, we had set our radio on their frequency. Approaching fog-bound Prestwick, we could hear them, one after the other, talking to the ground crew: "Number 26, 180 gallons of gas left." "Number 29, 140 gallons of gas left." "Number 32, only about 60 gallons left." And the ground control tower telling each one in turn at what altitude to fly, where to go, and what circles to make, so that those who had the least amount of gasoline left could land first.

Then, coming out of the clouds, a voice over the radio, "This is Number 62. You won't have to worry about me any more. I'm plumb out of gas. So long." And then silence.

We didn't know for a long time where that airplane came down, but we learned later that the pilot of Number 62 had brought his plane in safely through the "soup." It seems, during an instant's clearing in the dense fog, he had seen a beach ahead of him, and had slid in on his belly with his wheels up, onto the beach, up into a meadow three miles out of Prestwick, his entire crew safe. "This is Number 62. You won't have to worry about me any more. . . ." period!

Obviously a change in flying control technique was essential.

We went on to London and I noticed as we landed there that most of the ground defense precautions had been discontinued in and around Hendon.

We were met by General Devers in his car and went in to Claridges. That night, we had dinner with Eaker, Devers, and Edwards, and they told me just what was going on and what I could do to help.

The following morning I spent at General Eaker's Headquarters, going over his method of operations; the number of airplanes he had available, the type of formations he was using in order to minimize his losses, and so on. Then I went through General Miller's VIII Air Service Command Headquarters where I was given a complete picture of the system he was using to keep the maximum number of airplanes in commission at all times. In the afternoon, at a conference of all the officers of Eaker's staff, we discussed the employment of the Eighth Air Force; its present status and its ultimate objectives.

The following morning I visited some of the wings and groups that had been doing our bombing, among them the Fourth Wing (later, the 3rd Air Division) which had carried out the Regensburg "Shuttle" mission, led by Colonel Curtis E. LeMay, its rugged commander. It was the first time I had met him as a commander, but I was to see him in command of much larger and far more important units later. I also had a chance to get a first-hand account of the Ploesti raid from Colonel White and to talk to Brigadier General Bob Williams, who had served with me at Rockwell Field, later had lost an eye as an observer in London during the blitz, and had just been awarded the Distinguished Service Cross after leading his 1st Bomb Wing to Schweinfurt.

On this trip, I saw proof after proof of the sturdiness of the B-17. At Hethel, a badly shot up B-17 was being repaired. One tail flipper was gone; in the right wing was a hole as big as a bushel basket; there were holes in the fuselage from stem to stern; control rods to the right aileron had been shot off, and one engine had been blown from the wing. But that airplane had flown back to its home station with only two men out of a crew of ten wounded!

I made it a point to attend a briefing of the crews and was well satisfied with what I saw and heard. The careful preparation which the combat crews received before they took off on their missions obviously had much to do with their success.

During a call on Portal, I learned that Goering had given orders to his fighters (this was overheard by R.A.F. Radio Intercept) that "the Fortresses must be destroyed, regardless of everything else." German pilots were to close in and attack B-17 formations and stop attacking stragglers. Attacking stragglers, the Goering directive said, did not destroy the formations, and did not prevent the bombardment planes from reaching their objectives and carrying out their missions. Any German pilot who violated this order was to be court-martialed.

As a matter of fact, the maximum number of heavy bombers we had in the European Theater at any time during September, 1943, was 599. But those bombers, flying in formation to their targets throughout Germany in broad daylight were indicating to Hitler, the German Army leaders, and the German people, that American bombers would soon fly anywhere they wanted to, at any time, and that the German Air Force could not stop them! It is interesting to note that Goering's order did not help him solve his problem. Our Fortresses kept going into Germany in ever-increasing numbers.

The R.A.F.'s Air Sea Rescue Service was saving a good many ditched crews from the Channel. At one of the bomber stations I heard a very good story about that. It was our policy at that time, based on the recommendations of the flight surgeons, that bomber crewmen who had completed their twenty-fifth mission should be relieved temporarily from further operations over Germany and allowed to return home. A certain crew had arrived at this point. Before they took off on their twenty-fifth mission, the tail gunner drew a pint of brandy from his coverall pocket, and showed it to his fellow crew members. He told them they were all going to drink from that bottle on the way home after the mission. Then he put the brandy in the pocket of his flying clothes, and off they went. On the way back, they got pretty badly shot up by German aircraft and antiaircraft, and their airplane had to ditch in the English Channel. The tail gunner found himself alone in a rubber boat. He was cold and chilled. The rest of the crew were nowhere in sight, so he took his brandy out, and bit by bit, drank it all. He had hardly finished the last swallow, when he was picked up by Air Sea Rescue. Climbing onto the deck of their plunging launch, cold and shivering, he tried his best to appear sober in spite of the pint of brandy in him. The British commanding officer looked at him and said, "Lad, you are cold! Better get below and get warm. Don't stay up here in *that* condition!" The American flyer, a man of small stature, rose up in all his dignity. "Sir," he said, saluting, "I am not one who stays where he is not wanted," and so saying, he jumped back into the Channel. Needless to say, he was again rescued and returned safely to his base.

Many interesting things came up for discussion while I was in England this time; radio-controlled bombs, for example. The British experts and our own told me they had already used 24 of these bombs and had sunk four ships with them. We talked of rocket propulsion; rockets on fighters, and the radius of destruction of fighter-borne rockets; and about the launching sites in France—those mysterious installations of concrete—and how we were going to destroy them.

The next day at Duxford, we saw the new equipment the fighter outfits were getting: The new "Sabre Typhoon" engine; the new P-47 with a paper belly tank that seemed to work out very satisfactorily; the new P-51 with the latest cockpit cover, permitting better visibility; the "Spitfire" with eight rockets; the B-24 with carriers for rockets. We saw the method and gadgets for reloading rockets in flight—an operation that readied a new set of four rockets for firing within about three minutes. We talked over the performance of the P-47 as compared with the Me-109 and the FW-190, and found the crews perfectly satisfied with the P-47's. They wouldn't trade the P-47's for Me-109's or the FW-190's if they could get them. All they asked for was more belly tanks! More tanks, and still more tanks to give more miles so they could go deep into Germany with the bombers, stay with them to the end of the mission, and knock those FW's and Me-109's out of the sky. I told them the tanks with additional capacity were in production. It was only how great a load the fighter could carry that would determine its legs. General Kepner, Commanding General of the VIII Fighter Command and General Ed Anderson, commanding the 67th Fighter Wing, were doing a magnificent job with the fighters.

Following my visit to Duxford, I went to a medium bomber station at Earls Colne, under the command of Colonel Maitland. Theirs was an entirely different problem from that of the heavy bombers. The medium bombers had to go in low, and consequently encountered much small caliber antiaircraft fire that the heavies never experienced.

That afternoon, General Eaker and I called on Air Marshal Harris, A.O.C., R.A.F. Bomber Command, and went through his organization. The visit was very instructive, giving me a much clearer picture of how our two bombing outfits were working together—our Eighth Air Force by day, and the British Bomber Command by night.

That night I talked with Harris in generalities about the possibility of a single command for our British-American strategic bombers. I reasoned that with one person directing all operations, night and day, regardless of who the man was, we would get better results. We would be able to throw more planes into an emergency bombing situation than we could under the organization as it then existed. Air Marshal Harris was against it. His chief objection was that the Royal Air Force would probably not be put in command. (In that he was right, for we were building up rapidly in strength, and numbers alone should give the United States Air Force the command.) They therefore would lose control of their night bombing. Bomber Command now had virtual autonomy in its operations, with little interference from higher levels of the R.A.F., an arrangement that permitted Harris to go directly to the Prime Minister and give him full details. If they did not have control, the R.A.F. would lose prestige with the British people.

To me, it didn't make that much difference. It was a means to an end— a way to get the maximum destruction in Germany in the minimum time. But, now that the war is over, I am convinced it was not such a good suggestion after all. It would have caused many needless complications.

I learned that the Royal Air Force's average losses at night were proportionately as heavy as ours. Later, their operations were not so costly, until the unhappy spring of 1944 came (unhappy for the R.A.F., that is).

The following day, September 6th, I went to Burtonwood, our Air Service Depot near Liverpool, whence thousands of disabled planes and engines were returned to combat. Burtonwood was also the modification center for all combat planes arriving from America. Most of the mechanics were now American. The British, who had at first maintained the shops, had set as their goal the repair of 60 engines a month, and later, 80. We, with our methods of quantity production, line production, were able to turn out 570 engines a month. We had some 10,000 Americans in that one plant. Disabled engines were brought all the way from North Africa for Burtonwood to fix.

At the Admiralty the next day Admiral Neville Syfret, Admiral Pound's assistant, told me the U-boats were now hugging the Spanish coast as far as a point some 200 miles past Cape Finisterre; that the British had destroyed twenty-one U-boats the month preceding my visit. He said he was expecting the U-boats to come out with some new device very soon, for they couldn't stand such losses.

That night, General Eaker gave a wonderful dinner at which Marshal of the R.A.F. Trenchard, Winant, Portal, Harris, Slessor, Admiral Stark, and others were present. During it, I learned that in our raid the day before, we had "bombed Stuttgart and had lost over thirty planes." Ten crews were still missing, so our losses might be as high as forty. In spite of these heavy losses, the bombing results on Stuttgart "had been excellent." That Stuttgart mission of September 6, 1943, is a good example not only of what the Eighth Air Force was up against over Germany that fall, before the long-range fighter escort came and before radar instruments had licked the north European weather, but also of why I found it profitable to take personal trips to the various theaters from time to time.

Certain features of the operation never did find their way into the reports sent up through channels. The fact is, despite all the optimistic talk at the dinner table that night, the mission had been a complete failure. Of the 338 B-17's dispatched to hit the VKF ball-bearings plant at Stuttgart, not one saw its assigned target. Arriving over the city under fierce attack from more than a hundred enemy fighters—the same FW-190's, Me-109's, and rocket-firing night-fighters that defended Schweinfurt—the three Task Forces found it socked in by a solid overcast. Flak was moderate to intense, and accurate. Catching a glimpse of Stuttgart through a break in the clouds, 46 of the first crews in let their bombs go at "the center of the city." Most of the rest attacked Targets of Opportunity on the way back—Karlsruhe, Baden-Baden, Chartres, Wasselone, a number of unidentified targets, and some airfields and marshalling yards in France.

Although the 3rd Bomb Division, which was leading, bore the brunt of the enemy fighter attacks, 27 of the 45 B-17's reported missing were lost by the 1st Division. Units of this Task Force made a specially determined effort to hit their target, holding their bombs when the first run-up proved abortive and turning again for a second and then a third attempt. These extra maneuvers consumed precious fuel. By the time they had made the long haul back to the Channel many of the B-17's were entirely out of gas. Fortress after Fortress had to come down and ditch in the rough seaway. That night Air Sea Rescue, including the newly formed U.S. rescue service, picked up 118 American airmen in the English Channel.

The following morning, I talked with General Frederick E. Morgan about air operations in France, Italy, and Russia, strategic and tactical; about the airborne operations, and the operations leading to the defeat of Japan. Air Marshal Leigh-Mallory, who was to command the Allied Expeditionary Air Force in the invasion, joined us, and we went into detail about his projected operations.

The next morning, following a talk with Wavell, who had been made Viceroy of India, I had a conference with Sir Charles Portal. Our discussion covered a lot of territory. We talked about large staffs and the necessity for them; "empire building"; the scope of responsibilities of the various commanders; the status of the Royal Air Force, of the Eighth Air Force, of the United States Army and Air Force in North Africa; the feeling of the Americans in North Africa; the integration of United

States and British troops; Tedder's position; Spaatz' position; Eisenhower's position down in North Africa.

That afternoon, General Devers and General Eaker rode with me to Bovingdon, where I took off at two o'clock for Prestwick. We arrived at 4:00 o'clock and left for Iceland at 5:10. En route, Colonel Hull, Eaker's A-2, and General Strong and I discussed our losses and the grand job our bombers were doing in the European Theater, despite days like yesterday. Our losses looked very large to me, not that replacements were impossible, but I was thinking of the effect on morale. They assured me, however, that so far large losses had not affected the morale of the Eighth Air Force in the slightest. It was remarkable the way the youngsters were able to take their losses in their stride. Also, it was significant to note how they became aged, matured, experienced men in a very short time. I was told that the scale of operational accidents compared very favorably with the scale in the United States. There were very few, all things considered. The pilots and copilots were always on the ball. They had done the "impossible" in landing airplanes without rudders; with one flipper; with ailerons shot away; with holes in the wings, and holes in the fuselages large enough to shove a wheelbarrow through.

More surprising than anything I had heard, was the report on the war performance of the B-26's in Maitland's outfit. Maitland's pilots were bringing those once mistrusted B-26's back without ailerons; with one engine—something they could not possibly have done a few months previous and that nobody would have done two years before.

I was also told how the fighter pilots, once having mastered the P-47, flew rings around the German Focke Wulf 190 and the Messerschmitt 109. The belly tanks on our P-47's made it possible to get range the Spitfire couldn't even approximate. These P-47 fighters now went with the bombers to the Ruhr; the Spits had to return soon after they crossed the coast.

At Iceland we were met by Colonel Bernt Balchen and General Mickelson. At dinner I learned their problems were getting more and more remote as the war moved farther and farther away from Iceland. I did, however, send a wire from Iceland to Washington, asking that Balchen be ordered to Washington for one week to give a report on the Iceland air situation, so we could know what to do with the units we had there. I told him I thought we should send a whole new flock of pilots to Iceland and send the veteran pilots in his fighter outfit to England.

We landed at Goose early the next morning, and had breakfast there— a much better meal than the last time! Under A. D. Smith, everything had greatly improved. We took off at 6:00 A.M. in clear weather—the first clear day they had had for a long, long time; but soon we ran into the "customary" weather, and flew on instruments until we finally came out at Hartford, Connecticut. When we landed in Washington, we found we had flown from London in twenty-seven hours elapsed time.

☆ 25 ☆

At the Casablanca conference we had talked over plans for various operations in the future, the main one being the landing in Sicily, and subsequently, operations through Italy, and the ultimate landing in northern France. Later, we found it difficult in our Combined Chiefs of Staff meetings to see how we could get the maximum benefits from these operations unless they were tied in with the operations of the Russians. The Russians were driving the Germans to the west. At some stage, their activities on that front would coincide with our landings on the northern shore of France, and probably on the south coast of France, as well. Without coordination between the Russian advance and the Allied offensives in France and Italy, it might be possible for the Germans, operating on the interior lines, to move their Air Force and their divisions from one front to another, taking advantage of our lack of synchronized effort.

We were, therefore, all very pleased that we were to have a conference at Cairo and Teheran, known as SEXTANT, at which we would have an opportunity to talk to Chiang Kai-shek and Stalin and their staffs. We hoped to come to a far better understanding of what our common problems were, and of how best to solve them.

By that time, we had advanced sufficiently in our strategic bombing of Germany and with the build-up of our air strength to be in a position to say, "This is the plan we will follow: we will continue to carry our operations into the heart of Germany, completely defeat the Luftwaffe, and deprive all Hitler's fighting forces of the things they need most."

November 11, 1943, was a cold, cloudy, rainy day in Washington. We (twenty-two admirals, generals, colonels, and naval captains) arrived at Admiral King's flagship, the *Dauntless* at about 7:45 A.M. We shoved

453

off fifteen minutes behind schedule because one high-ranking officer was late. Down the Potomac we steamed, and at about 4:00 P.M. reached the *Iowa*. Going aboard with me from the *Dauntless* were Admiral King, General Marshall, General Somervell, Admiral Cook, General Handy, Admiral Bieri, General Kuter, General Hansell, Admiral Badger, General O'Donnell, General Roberts, Admiral Doyle, and others. At dinner that night, with the *Iowa* riding at anchor, General Marshall told a story concerning his final meeting with Churchill at Algiers. They had had a long, heated discussion about whether or not we should attack the "underbelly" of Europe or carry out the plans for landing on the northern shore of France. Before parting, Marshall said to the Prime Minister, "Well, you certainly fixed my clock!" Some time later, one of Churchill's staff officers met General Marshall and asked, "Did the Prime Minister really repair one of your clocks so it would run?"

Next morning we had an opportunity to look around the *Iowa* before the President arrived. It was a monster, 800 feet long, with more than 120,000 horsepower, and overflowing with antiaircraft guns. The main deck was tremendous. Sailors, more sailors, and more and more sailors, all over the decks! I never saw so much saluting in my life, not even at West Point!

At 9:00 o'clock, the President's yacht, the *Potomac,* came alongside with the President, Admiral Leahy, Harry Hopkins, and General "Pa" Watson. Their baggage and supplies were hoisted aboard, and at 10:00 A.M. we upped anchor and steamed down the bay. When we reached the submarine net at Hampton Roads, we stopped. A tanker came alongside, and we took on oil. That night, dinner and a movie with the President.

At the end of the movie, Harry Hopkins bet "Pa" Watson five dollars he could catch a fish from the deck of this Goliath, the *Iowa.* "Pa" Watson took him up. It wasn't long before Harry Hopkins came in with four fish. A Marine and a mess boy both swore Harry had caught the fish. "Pa" Watson said, "Ice box!" "Pa" probably was right at that, but the fish cost him five bucks.

We left Hampton Roads about midnight and were in the Gulf Stream by 10:00 o'clock next morning, with the weather clear and cold, but getting warmer. There wasn't much to do in the daytime but ramble around looking at the various gadgets, at the guns, at the gun control, and at the different radar, radio, and signal stations. The ship made about twenty-five knots. Zigzagging cut the speed to about twenty-three knots. Destroyers all around us seemed to be having a rough time in the heavy seas. Four destroyer escorts on each side of us furnished protection from submarines. The heavy seas continued all day until sundown. An occasional Navy plane flying overhead was part of our escort. That night, we attended another movie with the President called *The Phantom of the Opera.*

The following day the Navy decided to put on a show for us, so at 2:30 in the afternoon, gunnery practice started, with 150 antiaircraft guns firing at balloons. Commands seemed to come from all over the ship, but the firing was completely under control. Then, right in the midst of that imposing volume of fire, somebody shouted, "This is not a practice. Look! A torpedo wake coming directly at us!"

An alarm whipped from one of the destroyers. The whole character of the maneuvers changed instantly. We began to zigzag. All ships started to zigzag. More commands from everywhere. Whistles, flags, code signals. The din aboard the ship was terrific. The wake of the torpedo became quite clear. A depth charge went off, and another, and many more. Guns started shooting, but nothing hit the torpedo.

Before we left the United States, we had known a pack of German submarines was operating to the south and east of the Azores, but we figured we would miss it by 100 to 150 miles. With that torpedo coming toward the *Iowa,* it looked as if we hadn't.

What should be done with the President? Should he stay on deck? Should we take him to his cabin and put him in a safe place, protected by armor?

The torpedo missed the stern of the *Iowa* by a scant twenty yards.

A thousand sighs of relief went up. In everyone's mind was the question, "Suppose the torpedo had hit, and it had become necessary to take the President and all the high rank off the *Iowa* in those heavy seas?" Where had it come from? Were there any more?

Later, it was determined that a torpedo-tube man on one of our own destroyers had pulled his trigger by mistake. His tube, at that particular moment, was so aimed that the torpedo traveled on a straight line toward the *Iowa.* Some say the "trigger-happy" torpedo man was called on the carpet for his actions. Of that I know nothing. Harry Hopkins remarked, "It must have been some damned Republican!"

The following morning, at quite a long meeting of the Joint Chiefs of Staff, we discussed the possibility of having the joint R.A.F. and A.A.F. bombardment campaign commanded by one man; of securing unity of command for the Mediterranean area, and for the entire European theater. This last, we thought, would be quite difficult to get. There was one man we all believed should have the job. He was General Marshall.

However, we recognized the disadvantages of losing him from the Combined and Joint Chiefs of Staff and as a military adviser to the Secretary of War and to the President, so with the field wide open, we discussed Montgomery, Alexander, Eisenhower, and all other possibilities.

The next day, the Joint Chiefs of Staff had another meeting, which the President attended and at which we discussed, among other matters, the future of the French colonies—whether they should be completely under French control or under the French for civil administration only. We agreed that the French should not be armed too hastily, but should be given only such arms and equipment as were required by the units Eisenhower could use. Before we broke up, we discussed an agenda to cover our combined operations with the Chinese Generalissimo, and with "Red Joe."

The next day was an off day. I find an entry in my record which reads: "Gin rummy with Harry Hopkins. Harry Hopkins, 0; Hap Arnold, $3.00." And under it, "But look out for the deluge! I have never seen anybody take $3.00 away from Harry Hopkins without his getting it back." (A November 16th entry reads: "Harry Hopkins won all his money back at gin rummy—and some more.")

I also find this remark, made by someone at a Joint Chiefs of Staff meeting: "You can use the brilliant but lazy man as a strategist; a brilliant but energetic man as a Chief of Staff, but God help you with a dumb but energetic man!"

Despite all the supposed secrecy, on December 17th a report came from Cairo, released by the censor, stating that a meeting of the Prime Minister and the President, and their Chiefs of Staff, was to be held there within the next few days.

Naturally, the President was very much concerned, as was everyone else. We discussed changing the locale of the conference, thereby double-crossing anyone who had any idea of interfering with the proceedings at Cairo. The President called me in and talked with "Pa" Watson and me about it. He asked how much of a task it would be to assemble airplanes to move the conference to some other place—for instance, to Khartoum. After we had talked for quite a while, the President called in General Marshall, Admiral King, and Admiral Leahy, and discussed the subject further. A message was sent to General Eisenhower asking him in view of the breach of security what he thought of Khartoum as a site rather than Cairo. In the end, when all facts had been assembled, it was obvious that the many weeks of preparation for the conference at Cairo could not be duplicated within a few hours, so the site remained unchanged.

November 19th there were heavy seas, with green water coming over the bridge and crashing against the cabins on the third deck. Another Joint Chiefs of Staff meeting was held during which we talked over the agenda we were to take up with the British. Later in the morning, we were picked up by the *Brooklyn,* two more American destroyers, and two British destroyers. Just about that time, the sea and the wind abated. We were off Casablanca at 11:00 A.M. and entered the Straits of Gibraltar about 2:00 P.M.

At 7:00 A.M. on the 20th, with the *Brooklyn* leading the way, we turned toward the harbor lights of Oran, picked up a pilot and entered the submarine net. Twisting back and forth in the harbor to miss wrecks and avoid shallow water, we finally made a ninety-degree turn and reached our anchorage.

In the harbor was a British cruiser with a four-star flag (Admiral Cunningham's flagship). It didn't know, of course, that the President and all the senior officers of the Army and Navy were aboard the *Iowa.* Great consternation among our Navy officers! What should they do? How could they salute? Who would salute who and when? Navy courtesy required the junior to salute first. Finally, everybody swallowing his pride, our ship sounded the bugles, lined up its sailors, and did all the other things well-disciplined ships do when passing a foreign man-of-war.

Then the President went out on deck. His hat, his coat, his profile, the angle of his cigarette holder—all were a dead give-away to anyone who had ever seen one of our papers or magazines. Everybody on the dozens of French ships in the harbor took a look-see to determine who was aboard. So our "secret" was made still more public.

At Oran, we found everything very well organized. Each of us was given a slip of paper telling us in which car we would ride to our destination, and the number of the plane in which we would depart, what car we should get into when we reached our destination, and what we would do there.

As we left the docks, the cavalcade started: First, the motorcycles, then the President in his car followed by the Secret Service, then General Marshall and three cars, a detachment of more motorcycles, then Admiral King and myself and our cavalcade. Soldiers were posted along all the streets, at all intersections and curves, some facing out, some facing in, and acted as traffic cops. As we proceeded, crowds gathered here and there in back of the soldiers—Arabs, Frenchmen, and American G.I.'s, all attracted by the "parade," and trying to see who was in the cars.

We went through the American and French camps to the airport, and then directly to our planes. A large sign was in front of each plane. General Eisenhower took off with the President in Plane Number 1; Plane Number 2 took off with General Marshall and Secret Service men; Plane Number 3 with Admiral King and myself, and several staff officers.

At Tunis—the ancient city of Carthage—we were met by Eisenhower, Spaatz, Elliott and Franklin D. Roosevelt, Jr. We went to Ike's house, for a light lunch, then Spaatz and I left and went to his villa—a very large affair of twenty or more rooms, where he put up members of his staff.

President Roosevelt wanted to see the photo reconnaissance outfit commanded by Elliott. He and I took the review and drove around, inspecting the men, planes, and trailers. Then I left the President and went back to Tedder's headquarters where I had a few minutes with Portal. Later I returned to Spaatz' headquarters where I met with Spaatz, Doolittle, Norstad, and O'Donnell, and learned what was going on, in order to be the better informed when the Combined Chiefs of Staff meetings were held in a couple of days.

While we were having dinner at the villa, my aide and pilot, Colonel Petersen, showed up after having been held up at Natal for two days while they put a new engine in his plane. He brought with him a couple of stems of bananas. Knowing there had been no shipments of bananas to the British for many months, I called Portal, turned them over to him, and told him I thought he might like to send them back to England.

Next morning, after a tour of the city, Admiral King and I took off in Plane Number 3 at 7:40. General Marshall followed. The President took off at 9:30.

What had impressed me about Carthage was the way ruin was piled upon ruin. The desolation of World War II—ships sunk in the harbors on their sides and on their bottoms, with their masts and funnels showing, bomb craters everywhere—superimposed upon the wreckage and destruction of wars from 550 B.C. to 1943 A.D. The contributions that could have been made to our times by the civilization that existed when Carthage was in its prime had all been lost to us, sacrificed to the fury and relentlessness of one devastating war after another.

Now, as I flew from Tunis to Cairo, I looked for the marks of recent desert battles. The tracks of the vehicles were gradually disappearing, and where a few months before when I had flown across this section of the desert, every battle maneuver could be clearly traced in the sand, now it took a little imagination to figure out the track marks. One could still see the German orthodox trench system and the British fox holes, but the barbed wire was by this time partially or completely covered with sand. The tracks of armored cars and tanks fanning out in all directions also were slowly filling up. Here and there were wrecked trucks and tanks, some black from burning, others covered with camouflage paint, many partially covered with sand, others intentionally dug in to be held as strong points and then disabled by a shell or a bomb—still there as grim reminders of the desert struggle when Rommel almost captured Cairo and the Suez Canal.

Airdromes, too, stood out that had been occupied, in turn, by the R.A.F., the Luftwafte, and the American Army Air Force. Around the airdromes were wrecks of planes, most of them German, sprawled out flat on the ground, like animals whose legs had given way and could no longer support their bodies.

We came to Benghazi, Tobruk, and Sollum, where the American Air Force and the Royal Air Force, had they been given the word, might have blasted the road, filled the gap, and stopped Rommel's retreat, but had been prevented from doing so because the British High Command had wanted that road kept in shape for use by its armored force. We passed over El Alamein, where the scars of war were multiplied by thousands.

And then suddenly the Nile Valley—green, with running water, dotted with small villages and cities, and the sun setting over the desert, with the Pyramids and the Sphinx standing out in relief.

At the airport where we arrived at 6:15 Cairo time, we were met by Averell Harriman, Ambassador Winant, General Deane, General Stratemeyer, General Royce, General Chennault, Sir John Dill, and many others. The villa to which we were assigned was owned by an absent Greek. It had rooms enough for eight people, but only two baths. In the villa with me were General Marshall and his aide, General Somervell and his aide, Handy and Deane—eight of us altogether. The first night we were there, November 21st, we had as our guests Pat Hurley, Ambassador Winant, General Royce, General Stratemeyer, General Chennault, and General Stilwell. General Royce, by that time, had taken over our Middle East Command from General Andrews. General Stratemeyer was there as commander of the Tenth Air Force in India and China.

During dinner, Pat Hurley told us of a new oil field they had recently discovered in Arabia, that extended over 1000 miles right down to the seaport. It was greater than the oil fields of California and Texas combined, an oil field we all expected we might hear much about in the future—as I think we have.

Our talks after dinner usually ranged over a wide field. One night, I remember General Bill Somervell brought up the question of how the countries of Europe should be organized to prevent war in the future. No one there had much confidence in an organization like the League of Nations, or in its ability to enforce its decisions if it had no armed forces available.

Certain of the arguments presented, of the principles developed, were obvious. In the first place, everyone agreed that were it possible to establish a United States of Europe, most of our troubles would be over. To do that, the military barriers between countries would have to be broken down; also customs barriers must be eliminated in order to open up markets for greater production. All agreed that the present boundaries between nations in Europe were in most cases without rhyme or reason. Military leaders, diplomats, and peace treaties had changed the boundaries so often that there was today a great intermingling of races, languages, and religions.

A United States of Europe was generally accepted as probably the only solution. Certainly, all kinds of alliances, accords, and ententes had been tried and had resulted only in armament races and world wars. However, everyone recognized the practical difficulties which must be faced. The aims, ambitions, and objectives of the various countries, the national pride of the people themselves, the historic glories of the past, the world-famous war heroes—all these made the problem more difficult.

That first night in Cairo, we ran into something that is quite unusual in the military service: a super-secret plan that is really kept supersecret. Under the utmost secrecy, the Generalissimo and Madame Chiang Kai-shek and their advance party arrived at the airport. Protocol was shot to pieces. The plane with the advance party landed after the Generalissimo's plane. Their identity was so well concealed that there was no reception committee of any kind to meet either the Generalissimo or his advance party as they came in. Fortunately, General Chennault had had a hunch they were coming, so he went out and did the honors.

I always considered it very lucky that our military leaders could discuss with us their individual problems before we went to the Joint Chiefs of Staff and the Combined Chiefs of Staff meetings at places like Cairo—

men like Eisenhower, Stilwell, Chennault, Wedemeyer, Stratemeyer, and others from various theaters throughout the world. It gave us a much broader view of the conditions that actually existed in the various war theaters—a factual basis for our discussions.

At a Joint Chiefs of Staff meeting that morning Ambassador Winant, General Deane, General Stilwell, General Wedemeyer, and General Wheeler were with us. All outlined their problems—in England, in Russia, in China, in India. General Wheeler was the engineer in charge of increasing the tonnage going up the Brahmaputra River and over the railroad from Calcutta to Assam. In addition to his other construction, he was putting in the Ledo Road, with a pipeline running parallel to it, as well as a pipeline running parallel to the Brahmaputra River, which would enable us to get gasoline into Assam and across into China much more easily.

We had meetings all day, ending with a meeting of the Combined Chiefs of Staff, with the Generalissimo, General Stilwell, and General Chennault at 9:00 o'clock that night. There was none of the close fellowship between the Generalissimo and General Stilwell that there was between top leaders and their Chiefs of Staff in other theaters. Sometimes I wondered why we were saving China, for the dissensions among their war lords gave us few clues.

The next morning, after our usual staff assembly, we had a meeting with the President at 11:00. Present were the Prime Minister, the Generalissimo and Madame Chiang Kai-shek, all members of the Combined Chiefs of Staff, Lord Louis Mountbatten, General Stilwell, General Stratemeyer, Sir John Dill, and four Chinese generals. The discussion centered around air operations for the campaign against the Japanese from China and India into Burma—what the Allies could do to build up their forces, how we could get the campaign started more quickly. Before we finished, it became quite an open talk, with everybody throwing his cards on the table, face up.

Once more the whole problem revolved around ships: Would we have enough ships to take an expedition down to Rangoon? Would we have ships to land troops near Akyab? Would aircraft be available to attack Rangoon? Would naval support be forthcoming for either of these two campaigns, and so on.

After lunch we met with the Chinese once more, but we found that with the Generalissimo absent from the meeting, the Chinese generals would say little. Apparently, the Generalissimo made up their minds for them.

Following that rather prolonged session, we went to dinner with the Prime Minister and the British Chiefs of Staff. They were stopping at a house that had formerly belonged to an Egyptian Princess—quite racy in its choice of paintings and other decorations. However, I wouldn't have swapped the extra hot water we had in our villa for all the pictures and fixtures and fittings in their house, for while they had three baths, they had no hot water.

We had an excellent dinner—good food, good wine, splendid service, and good conversation. Genghis Khan, Kublai Khan, Knights Templars of Malta, Carthaginians, the Turkish conquest of the Mediterranean—we touched on all of these before we returned to our villa at 10:30.

As the days passed, the meetings continued—with the President, with the Prime Minister, with the Chiefs of Staff, and with Mr. Harriman. We discussed Russia, we discussed China, we had another meeting with the Generalissimo, and the Chinese generals, who told us why our plans to lick the Japanese would not work. When Mountbatten came in and discussed his India set-up, he told us why the Chinese plans would not work. So, back and forth, selecting charts, doing our best to work out the wisest plans for operations against the Japanese, and to make them acceptable to everybody concerned. We found it very difficult to reconcile the conflicting racial and national aspirations, ambitions, and prejudices: Chinese, Russian, British, American. All had so many different ideas about what to do and how to do it, and its effect upon the future not only of the conquered countries but of their own countries, that it was most difficult to come to any logical conclusion.

Through it all, it was clear to me that General Marshall was increasing in stature, in comparison with his fellows, as the days went by. He had more mature judgment, could see further into the future. What he said was said in a way that carried conviction. I am sure the President and the Prime Minister both felt the same, because each one called on him for advice and counsel at all hours of the day or night.

I find a note: "I went with the President to see the Sphinx today." While out there, we talked over the war command situation and the necessity for having a single commander in the European Theater. I stated my preference for General Marshall, but said I should dislike very much to see him go, because of his outstanding ability in the Combined Chiefs of Staff meetings, and because he was a superior adviser to the President himself. The President agreed with me.

Then we talked over the air problem and what I could give the Generalissimo. I told the President I couldn't satisfy the Generalissimo. Each time I said I could increase the tonnage over the Hump to 8000 tons, he would reply, "I am not satisfied. I must have 10,000 tons." If I said, "Well, I will build the lift up to 10,000," the Generalissimo would say, "Not enough, I want 12,000." I advised the President not to take the demands of the Generalissimo too seriously because regardless of the tonnage Chiang said he wanted I was going to exceed it within the next few months. I also assured the President that the time was coming when I would be able to get more tonnage into China by air than the Chinese would be able to haul away from the airdromes on the roads available in and around Kunming.

Still thinking of ways and means of increasing the air strike against Japan, of aiding the Generalissimo, of aiding Mountbatten, I must have stopped talking, because after a short while the President turned to me and said, "Hap, here we are, three of the world's most silent people: the Sphinx, you, and I." That was the first time in my life anybody had ever accused me of being silent.

The next day was Thanksgiving Day, November 25th. Eisenhower arrived with his staff, and we had a Combined Chiefs of Staff meeting, at which Eisenhower outlined his Mediterranean operations: November, 1943, found the Allies in Italy, advancing northward, but still well south of Rome; we had landed at Salerno and had captured Naples, and were moving forward slowly. Cassino and the Anzio beachhead were still before us.

The Combined Chiefs of Staff had a merry party Thanksgiving Day. We had had hard sledding over many fundamentals and weren't getting along very fast, so postponing any further action or meetings of our Plans Committee until the following day, we decided to have a Thanksgiving dinner. During the dinner, Air Marshal Tedder made the remark that: "We should decorate Kesselring for destroying the German Air Force, and we should decorate Rommel for teaching the British Army how to fight." After dinner, the Combined Chiefs of Staff went to an impressive service in the cathedral at Cairo, given by the British for the Americans.

After the activities of the day, I had a long discussion with Handy and Somervell regarding the command status of Mountbatten, the relationship between Stilwell and Stratemeyer, and the Tenth Air Force. Handy, at that time, was in the War Plans Division and Somervell was running the Services of Supply for the Army. We finally decided that to employ our equipment with greatest effectiveness there must be some closely knit organization. That called for one commander. We agreed everything should be under Mountbatten.

Next day the Generalissimo sent for me and took up the subject the President and I had discussed the preceding day: the tonnage over the Hump. I knew the President had been needled into taking that up with me. Chiang wanted to divorce Mountbatten completely from the China operations. He didn't seem to realize that without Burma, without India, and without Mountbatten to stir up the Indian communications people along the railroad into Assam up the Brahamaputra River, without forcing the Japanese out of Burma, there wouldn't be any Hump traffic. The Generalissimo could see nothing but his own requirements. After a long, hard argument, he accepted the fact that I was doing all I could to increase his tonnage, but he would not admit any connection between the Hump operations and Mountbatten's Burma campaign.

That afternoon we had another meeting of the Combined Chiefs of Staff, trying to come to agreement about how, when and where we would open the campaign in France against the Germans. That meeting almost resulted in a brawl because the Americans were insistent that something be done as quickly as possible, and the British were almost equally as insistent that we should wait, that we should further extend our operations in the Mediterranean and come to some definite conclusions about the Burma campaign before we decided upon the European program. Time and again, we almost reached agreement, and then some little point would pop up to postpone it. For instance, several times the amphibian operations of Mountbatten almost threw the train off the track, and we had to start all over again.

After the meeting, General Marshall and I walked back to the villa, about four miles, to get some exercise, and were almost run down by the scores of British Army, R.A.F., Egyptian, or U.S. Army trucks rolling along the road.

A report had been drawn up of the session I had with the Generalissimo, and just about the time I was getting into bed, word came that General Chen had changed the records of the meeting. We had agreed that no change could be made except by everyone who was to sign it. I put on my robe, went downstairs, and there met Somervell and Chen. The change was not too serious, but it was enough to make me want to have the agreement restored to its original form. One of the Generalissimo's discussion statements had been taken from the first part of the conference notes and put in the last paragraph as a conclusion. After some little argument we agreed to restore the original wording. I asked Chen to take it back for the Generalissimo's approval. He said he would.

The following morning we were up at 5:30, and around 8:00 o'clock took off for Teheran, over the Suez Canal and the shores of the Mediterranean, making a slight detour to pass over Bethlehem, Jerusalem, the Dead Sea, and the Syrian Desert. No trees, no green vegetation, no green grass—nothing but desert for miles and miles. Then the Euphrates, the Tigris, and finally, we landed at Teheran. There we found Russian soldiers scattered over the field. The President arrived shortly after we did. "Red Joe" had arrived the day before, the Prime Minister that morning.

Teheran is in a large valley surrounded by mountains from 17,000 to 19,000 feet high. It is a city of about 600,000, made up of many small compounds, with high walls, mostly adobe. The people of Iran were much better dressed, looked healthier and happier than those we had seen in the cities in North Africa.

The Russians, the British, and the Americans had taken over Persia. Beyond the mountains north of Teheran, to the Caspian Sea, the entire country of Iran was controlled by the Russians.

We drove through Teheran to the American camp where 2500 United States soldiers were quartered, and where we were assigned rooms in the Bachelor Officers' Quarters. The following morning we had our usual meeting of the Joint Chiefs of Staff, and then our meeting with the President at 11:00. On our visit to the President's "White House" we found the streets well guarded by Russian soldiers.

After our meeting with the President, George Marshall and I asked whether or not there was any possibility of a meeting that afternoon. The President said not, so after a late lunch, Marshall and I took off in an automobile for a trip through the mountains to the north, to see if we could find out what was going on, and to see how far north we would get before we ran into the Russian Zone of Occupation. As we were returning from our trip we were met by a messenger who informed us that a conference had been called with Stalin, the Prime Minister, and the President at 4:00. Since it was then 4:15 and we were about sixty miles out of Teheran, General Marshall and I decided they would have to hold the meeting without us. Admiral King would have to represent the United States Chiefs of Staff alone.

We finally reached our rooms, where Ernie King met us and told us the details of the meeting. Apparently Uncle Joe had talked straight from the shoulder about how to carry on the war against Germany, and his ideas, it seemed, were much more in accord with the American ideas than were those of the British.

During that meeting, King told us, when they were talking about what was going to happen to the Germans after the war, Stalin had said out of a clear sky: "I know 60,000 German officers I am going to shoot!" Thereupon Churchill arose, cigar in hand, and paced back and forth across the room saying such a thing could not be; it was not Christian; we were civilized people; it was against the laws of civilized warfare to shoot 60,000 officers! Back and forth walked Churchill, while Stalin sat at the table, not saying a word. Finally, Churchill returned to his place, and after everything had quieted down, Stalin once more, through his interpreter, said, "I know 60,000 German officers I am going to shoot after the war is over!"

Apparently Stalin understood some English, although he would not admit it. Whether he could speak English I did not know, nor was I ever able to find out.

The following afternoon we had a conference with the President, and from 4:00 until 7:00 met with all the "Big Three." Seated around the table, in order, were: The Prime Minister, next to him Anthony Eden, then Sir John Dill, Air Chief Marshal Portal, then the Russian Voroshilov, then Stalin, then Molotov, then myself, then Admiral King, General Marshall, the President, then an interpreter, Admiral Leahy, Admiral Cunningham, then Sir Alan Brooke, and another interpreter.

Not having met Stalin the day before, I turned to Mr. Molotov and said, "I should like to meet Marshal Stalin." Whether Molotov understood English or not, I don't know, but he turned to the interpreter, and I repeated, "I should like to meet Marshal Stalin."

There was considerable discussion—several long minutes. I don't know whether, in my expression, I had used the wrong words, or whether in being interpreted it had acquired another meaning. Perhaps, translated, it meant I was challenging Stalin to a duel. Anyway, I saw I wasn't getting anywhere, so I turned to Molotov and said, "Listen! All I want to do is to say, 'How do you do' to Marshal Stalin, to meet him, that's all." Apparently, Molotov and the interpreter understood, because they then introduced me to Stalin, and everything was O.K.

I talked with Stalin quite a bit after that about our airplanes; about our methods of operations; our heavy bombers; about the ability of the Russians to fly our airplanes, and how, before they could fly our heavy bombers, they would have to receive special instruction about all the gadgets in the cockpit.

Stalin surprised me with his knowledge of our planes. He knew details of their performance, their characteristics, their armament, and their armor much better than many of the senior officers in our own Air Force. I told him of my experience at Basra, explained how we were fixing the aircraft there, and that they weren't being moved fast enough by his pilots. He assured me that by this time they were moving on schedule. They were getting them out of there as rapidly as the planes were ready.

He asked me for improved airplanes and he asked me for heavy bombers. I told him if he wanted heavy bombers he would have to send his engineers and maintenance and combat crews to the United States to go through our schools, or we could send the necessary personnel to instruct his men in Russia. He thought over these two suggestions for a while and finally agreed that something like that must be arranged.

I told him if he would let us use bases in Russia for shuttle bombing, I would give him some 300 or 400 of our B-24's, which the Russians could use against the Germans from the Russian front to carry their campaign of destruction farther to the west. That offer of 300 B-24's to Russia was never followed up, and I have often wondered why. I think now Stalin may have felt that had he accepted my proposal, he would have been admitting the Russians did not know as much about bombing as we did. Their crews must come to the United States to be taught how to fly and operate the airplanes, and to learn the technique of bombing; they would then return and tell their own people that the Americans probably knew more than the Russians.

It was quite noticeable to all of us who attended the various meetings at Teheran when the Russians were present, that it wasn't the United States Secret Service who had the balance of power; it was the Russian guards. The Russian Secret Service controlled everything. Even when Stalin visited the President of the United States or the Prime Minister, there were Russian guards within the building when and where Stalin was present. This was very interesting to us who had been accustomed to thinking of our own Secret Service as the last word in protection for our President, or for other important personages.

During the Teheran conference, just after lunch one day, the Prime Minister announced he was going to confer an honor on Stalin. In the name of the King, he was to present to Stalin the Sword of Stalingrad. For that purpose a large reception room was cleared out, the Combined Chiefs of Staff and all the notables attending the conference were assembled. And then, from nowhere, in marched a detachment of Russian troops. They were all big and husky, none of them over 25 or 26 years of age, and all of them dressed as immaculately as the poor character of the Russian uniform would permit, all with the same kind of boots, the same cut of trousers, the same shade of uniform. Each had in front of him a tommy gun which he carried across his chest. The tommy gun was loaded and the finger of each man was on the trigger.

George Marshall and I happened to be sitting nearby, and I asked George how tall he thought they were, because they were the tallest group of soldiers I had ever seen together in any one place—fine looking, well built individuals. Marshall and I talked about it for some time, and finally I said, "I'll tell you what. I'll go and stand next to the shortest man there. I am 5′ 11″, and you can tell from that how tall that fellow is." So I stood behind the shortest man in the ranks, and when I came back and sat down beside Marshall, he said the man was at least four inches taller than I.

The sword was presented by the Prime Minister to General Stalin, and after the guards had marched out, we resumed our conference.

November 30th came, and with it a remarkable party—the President and Premier Stalin celebrating the Prime Minister's sixty-ninth birthday with us. There were toasts and more toasts, everyone toasting his opposite in rank and position in the armed forces of the other countries. The Prime Minister did very well at that birthday party. One speech followed another. Churchill extolled the President, glorified Stalin, then the United States, our armies, our air forces, our navies, and the Red army. In turn, everyone had to get up and make his little toast. The President seemed more reserved. He listened, talking when he thought it was necessary, but he never opened up to the extent the Prime Minister did.

Stalin was the "man of steel"; apparently fearless, brilliant of mind, quick of thought and repartee, ruthless, a great leader, and having the courage of his convictions. How much English he understood, as I say, I don't know, but his answer came so closely after any remark from Churchill or the President that it appeared he knew more English than he was given credit for. When he talked about the British, the Prime Minister, and the Chief of the Imperial General Staff, Brooke, he was half humorous, half scathing.

Stalin was dressed in a light brown uniform with red trimmings, two red stripes on the trousers, large gold epaulets on the shoulders, with a very large gold star, the coat of arms of Russia, and the insignia of the Marshal of the Russian Army. He wore but one medal, a red ribbon with a gold border and a gold star suspended below. He was not tall, about 5′ 9″, but handsome; a fine looking soldier. He was not only interested in aviation, but recognized the true value of tactical aviation in warfare, although he was just beginning to learn something about strategic bombing. He asked innumerable and very intelligent questions about our old and our new planes, and about our long-range bombers.

That dinner gave Roosevelt, Churchill, and Stalin a good chance to study one another, to figure out how to break through to the man behind the diplomatic mask. Each one, naturally, wanted to know the others' points of view on winning the war, their aspirations for the postwar period. I am not so sure we were as successful in discovering what the Russians wanted as they were in finding out what our objectives were.

As the toasts were made, Stalin went around the table and clicked glasses with all the military men. He drank his liquor out of his own bottle—it was rumored there was nothing but water in it—the rest of us had champagne poured for us by the servants who were standing behind our chairs.

Stalin made a couple of remarks that night which bear comment. Once, while congratulating the United States on its ability to produce war materials in large quantities, he made the out and out statement that the United States' production of planes was 8000 per month, which was more than the combined production of Russia, Japan, and England. He then said the production of Russia was 2500 a month, and that he hoped to build it up to 3000.

The Prime Minister turned to Portal and said, "What is our production of airplanes?" And, almost before the words were spoken, Stalin turned to his interpreter and came back with, "I'll tell you what your production is. It is 2500 a month, and you can't increase it very much!" The Prime Minister said, "Yes—but they are all combat types." And that ended that phase of the discussion.

During one of his speeches, the Prime Minister remarked that although the Russians had a Red government, the British government was becoming a little "pink" itself. Quickly Stalin flashed back, "Well, you haven't found it very unhealthy, have you?"

I think about a hundred toasts and speeches must have been given that night. Everyone was in a grand mood; it was Prime Minister Churchill's sixty-ninth birthday; everyone wanted to do honor to him. The best speech of the evening was made by Harry Hopkins, who was in true form and whose remarks were not only witty but carried a lot of weight. The party broke up when the Prime Minister gave the last toast at 11:00.

That evening I was struck by the difficulties of interpretation—of getting our ideas across to the Russians. For instance, in one of Churchill's many speeches, he talked of the allegorical "rainbow"—the "rainbow in the sky" that Americans hear so much about every day. In spite of the fact that we had the best interpreters from Washington, from Moscow, and from London available, it took five minutes to translate the word "rainbow" into Russian.

From my experience at the formal meetings, I learned there was very little the Russian generals would accept as firmly fixed without first going to Marshal Stalin himself. They would have "to think it over" or "talk it over" and "let us know the next day." That was the attitude we met when we took up the ultimate disposition of the B-29's that might land in eastern Siberia. The establishment of bases in eastern Siberia was a vital matter. It would allow us to operate from points much closer to Japan than any others we had under consideration. The Russians would have none of it. They would not consider anything that might mean endangering their peaceful relationship with Japan before an armistice had been signed with Germany. They did agree, however (with many qualifications), to our going ahead with our plans for these bases, to be used when Russia did declare war on Japan.

We also talked about shuttle bombing across Germany, with landings in western Russia. They agreed that we should go ahead and make actual plans for that; but as everybody knows, after we really started the shuttle bombing missions from England and Italy across Germany to Russia, things bogged down. For a while, the Russians were glad to have us. They permitted their people to come around and talk with our soldiers and officers, see what we were doing, and how we were doing it. It created a cordial relationship. But when our radios and our magazines—*Life, Time,* the *Saturday Evening Post, Collier's, Look, P.M.,* and such periodicals—started coming in to our various squad rooms, dayrooms, and clubs, and their people had an opportunity to see the kind of life we lived in the United States, apparently the Russian leaders didn't like it. Orders were given that there would be no more fraternization between the Russians and the Americans at the shuttle bombing bases. Almost as quickly as it had started, all contact with the Americans stopped.

My own experience with the Russians indicates that the only thing they respect is something that is stronger than they are. In my dealings with them, the only time I could get any kind of cooperation at all was when I took a forceful attitude and refused to budge from my stand.

At Fairbanks, Alaska, we leaned over backwards to help the Russians. We gave them everything it was possible to give them, even turning over to them the houses of our own officers and enlisted men and their families. We worked overtime to get the airplanes in first-class condition so that all the Russians had to do was fly them from Fairbanks to Russia. They never gave us any thanks; they never showed in any way that they were grateful for what we had done to make their stay in Fairbanks happy and pleasant, or regretted the inconvenience to our people. After the war was over, we practically had to use dynamite to get them out so that we could have our own station back.

The contrast between our hospitality to them and the way they treated our people in the Soviet Union is terrific. We did manage to send one mission into Russia. General Follett Bradley flew across Siberia when the war first started, with a view to establishing an airline across Alaska to Moscow, and was well received. It looked for a while as if we might get cooperation, as if we might be able to send our people into Russia to become better acquainted. But we were mistaken. I know the Russians do not understand our ways of doing business, and I am not sure we shall ever understand theirs.

In our meeting with the Russians at the Teheran conference we had great difficulty in pinning them down about when they would be able to make their offensive against the Germans. We wanted to know the exact time, so we could synchronize our landing on the Normandy beaches with their offensive against the Germans on the Eastern Front, and for the first time in the war, have really coordinated military action among all the Allies. But the Russians apparently could not say when they would make that attack, when they would reopen their front against Warsaw, or when they would start their campaign to move on toward Berlin.

I often wondered why they were that way. And then, as I got to know them better, as I saw the Russian armies move into Germany, and the Russian divisions moving around Berlin, I think I reached at least a partial answer. Their system of logistics was terrible. They used everything from railroad trains, trucks, horse-drawn vehicles, push carts, to baby buggies and people carrying stuff on their backs. With such transportation, in my opinion it would be practically impossible for the Russian army ever to decide very far in advance upon a definite opening date for a campaign.

They did a remarkable job with the materiel and equipment and the personnel they had. I think their ability to become familiar with our war equipment in such a short space of time was truly exceptional. But as for their over-all staff planning—after that I must put a big question mark.

The next day we took off from Teheran at about 8:00 in the morning and headed for Jerusalem, where, for a day, the British Chiefs of Staff entertained the American Chiefs of Staff, most of whom had never been to Jerusalem before. Under their guidance, we made a thorough tour of the city, one which I greatly enjoyed.

Rather an odd incident occurred while we were at the Church of the Holy Sepulchre. After some of us had visited the small recess (it was so small that only two or three could go in at a time) and were standing outside, I heard a voice say, "Hello, Hap."

I looked around and there were some Franciscan padres standing in line. All I could see was their brown cassocks and their hoods, and beneath the hoods, their bushy eyebrows, their dark eyes, and their beards. I couldn't make out who was speaking to me so I waited. Again the voice said, "Hello, Hap." I replied, "Hello," and walked over toward them. Again I said, "Hello." One of the friars said, "How are you, Hap? I'm glad to see you." I talked with him for quite a while, waiting for him to give me a hint about who he might be and where he was from. But I received no clues. At last I said, "Will you kindly tell me where we have met before?" (I thought perhaps it might be a boyhood friend, someone with whom I had gone to grammar school or high school.) He replied, "I saw your picture on the cover of *Time* magazine."

After talking for a while, he asked, "Who else is here?" I looked around and saw General Somervell standing on the other side, and I said, "That's General 'Bill' Somervell." "General Somervell?" he repeated. "Yes," I said. Then the monk said, "Hello, Bill." Somervell came up, as surprised and uncertain as I had been.

The next day we took off for the field at 11:30. I decided to return to Cairo with Portal in his converted Lancaster plane, a "York," for I wanted to see how their transport planes compared with ours. It had many good features and its appointments were generally much better than ours, but it had some disadvantages—for instance, it was so noisy that conversation was almost out of the question. It had a good view, better than ours, because it was a high-wing monoplane.

At Cairo that night I had a talk with my staff—Kuter, Vandenberg, and Hansell—and told them I was not satisfied with the number of bombers being used in England out of the available total, or with the number of bombs being dropped on targets, since the objectives themselves apparently were not being destroyed.

The following day we had a Joint Chiefs of Staff meeting, where General Sutherland, Chief of Staff to General MacArthur, told us of MacArthur's South Pacific plan; that he proposed to move up through the island of New Guinea and then into the Philippines. In the Combined Chiefs of Staff meeting that afternoon, the American Chiefs locked horns with the British Chiefs over the question of the island of Rhodes, the Dodecanese, the Dardanelles, and the Eastern Mediterranean.

Next day, December 4th, we had a long discussion with the President, the Prime Minister, and the Combined Chiefs of Staff about the war in general; how and when to invade France; how the Burma Campaign would be conducted; the Andamans and the Aegean Sea problems; and the problems of supply as applied to all our strategy.

That day, December 4th, the President decided General Marshall was not to take command of the Allied Forces in Europe. Eisenhower would go up from the command in the Mediterranean and would take over in England.

Incidentally, that was the day I received word from home that we, the Arnolds, owned a ranch!

On December 5th, we had meetings all day long, with the Joint Chiefs of Staff and the Combined Chiefs of Staff, trying to come to a decision about the Andamans, the Mediterranean, and what we could do to insure a united front on a plan to lick Germany.

The following day the Combined Chiefs of Staff arrived at a workable decision, and then talked with the President and the Prime Minister until 8:10 in the evening. They approved our final report on the program for winning the war in Europe and for carrying on the war in Asia. Everyone agreed the Turks didn't want to fight, but did want to get on the gravy train before the peace.

That night at dinner, General Marshall took a poll on when the various officers present thought we would have peace in Germany. (This was December 6, 1943.) Sir John Dill said February, 1945; Sir Alan Brooke, March or April, 1945; Admiral Cunningham, September, 1945; Portal, May-June, 1945; King, October, 1945; Arnold, March-April, 1945; Ismay, October, 1945; General Marshall, February, 1945.

Next day was another of those days when we had one knotty and controversial problem after another. I met Field Marshal "Jumbo"

Wilson for the first time, and had a long talk with him about Near East conditions. Then we had dinner with the Prime Minister. It was the second anniversary of Pearl Harbor. Also present at the dinner were Anthony Eden, Sir John Dill, Sir Alan Brooke, Air Chief Marshal Portal, Admiral Cunningham, General Marshall, Admiral King, Lord Leathers, and Field Marshal Smuts.

The Prime Minister was in fine form. He talked of history, history in the making, of our conference, the Russians, the European situation, the air, the navies, and peace. And he told a story that went back many years, to a time when Field Marshal Smuts, then a lieutenant in the Boer War, had captured young Winston Churchill, a war correspondent. Churchill had tried to talk himself out of being a prisoner, but Lieutenant Smuts wouldn't release him. Later, Churchill escaped and got back to the British lines. Now, here was Churchill, Prime Minister of England, and Smuts, long Prime Minister of his own country, the Union of South Africa.

We had another peace poll at that table, and the consensus was that if Germany did not crack at the end of the winter 1943–44, she would not break until the following fall.

Churchill came out with a sincere statement. In spite of everything that had gone on during our conferences with Stalin, he said he still feared the Russians, and warned us of the period twenty years hence. He said they bred like flies; that we, the United States and Britain, were far too conservative in handling the Russians on an even basis. He said that now the white population of the United States and Britain together was about equal to that of Russia, but in twenty years it would not be.

The talk then changed to peace with Germany, and General Smuts said, "We must not sugar coat the term 'unconditional surrender.'" Churchill gave his own interpretation of the phrase. To him it meant unconditional surrender in every sense of the word: taking away from the enemy all possibility of fighting, but insuring to individuals the rights of free people.

The next morning, December 8th, we took off from Cairo and returned to Tunis. The President and his party had just left for Malta.

In Sicily, where we arrived at 12:30, I had a chance to talk with General Clark and General Patton. Patton was down in the mouth. He had been relieved of his command because of the famous "slapping" episode. I tried to cheer him up, for I knew his strength as a war leader, but it would have taken a message from the President or from General Marshall to do the trick.

Soon the President arrived in his plane with Harry Hopkins, Admiral Leahy, and "Pa" Watson. I talked with General "Beedle" Smith and with Eisenhower about who would be the best general to head the Air Force under Eisenhower's command in England, and both agreed Spaatz was the man.

When I met the President, he asked me where General Marshall was, and I told him he was returning by way of Australia. The President seemed surprised, and wanted to know when that had been decided. I said I was sure I could not answer that question, but I thought General Marshall must have received approval either from him (the President) or from Admiral Leahy before he went on the trip.

We took off from Sicily and flew to Foggia. Hank met me, and we drove through the ruins of the bombed city to General Spaatz' house. Next morning we landed at Bari about 10:15. The harbor there was filled with sunken ships. The British Navy had anchored ships in the outer harbor side to side, with ammunition ships in the center. German aircraft had selected the ammunition ships as their aiming point. There was no air warning service in operation, so while United States planes and British Beaufighters stood on the ground with crews in place, British control personnel, although trying frantically to get them into the air to meet the oncoming German planes, had not been able to make contact. The German bombers had hit their targets. The ammunition ships were completely destroyed. The terrific explosion sank many other ships in the harbor, knocked down wharfs and docks, and even destroyed buildings in the city half a mile away.

At Naples, the next morning, we found the buildings around the airport wrecked and hundreds of smashed airplanes on the ground, the result of our bombing. The railroad cars in the yards and on sidings were a shambles. Some cars had been blown a hundred feet or more from the tracks. The city itself was not damaged much; here and there near the railroad yards one saw a wrecked building or a home that had been hit by a stray bomb.

Naples harbor was another scene of ruin. Ships on their sides and on their backs, with only funnels and parts of their masts showing; trucks destroyed; railroad tracks and trains torn apart, the wrecks towed or pushed away, so that when we saw it, 20,000 tons of shipping were being unloaded each day.

We went to our billet at the Caserta—a great palace built by the King of Naples over a century ago—and learned that its landscaped architecture had taken thirty-six years to complete. (It took us only eighteen months to erect the Pentagon Building!)

The day I left Naples it was raining. I talked with newspaper men for a while, said good-by to Hank, who had been serving as my aide, and found my airplane sunk in mud up to its axles. It couldn't be moved, so I took Spaatz' B-17 for Tunis, where I had two hours with Eisenhower and Tedder. We discussed the organization and command of Spaatz' Strategic Air Force, and Ike's American Air Force Commander. Eaker was to go to the Mediterranean to replace Tedder as Commander of the Allied Air Force; Doolittle was to take the Eighth Air Force; Cannon, the Twelfth, and Twining, the Fifteenth.

After lunch Colonel Petersen showed up with my plane. He had gotten it out of the mud with a bulldozer, and was ready to start for Marrakech and home. We had wanted to return by way of the Azores, but the weather was against it, so from Marrakech we went on to Dakar. Dakar was still showing signs of fear of invasion: barbed wire, trenches and pill boxes, all set up to keep the British and the Americans out.

The airfield was crammed with planes from Natal, with more en route —100 at Natal, 20 on their way across the Atlantic, 50 at Dakar, 50 at Marrakech, all with crews. The "pipeline" was full. Hundreds of young American combat crews awaited clearances to the Mediterranean, to Britain, where a year before, there had been almost none.

That night we took off at nine o'clock. There were 2400 miles to go, from Dakar to Belém. We landed at Belém at 4:00 A.M. where Bob Walsh met us. This time the post at Belém looked much better. After a bath, a shave, and breakfast, we took off for Borinquen Field at 8:30, arriving there in the afternoon with no untoward incidents en route. On the 15th of December I was back in Washington, having covered some 22,000 miles in the airplane quite handily.

As far as the Army Air Force was concerned, the thing we wanted most of all had been gained at the SEXTANT Conference. We had received confirmation of our present plans for bombing the interior of Germany to a pulp, and for bringing the B-29's into action against Japan as soon as we could get them there. In fact, the first B-29 operations were scheduled for about June, 1944.

As early as 1941, it had been apparent that the B-29—the Super-fortress—would not be in full production much before that time. It had also been evident that in order to use it against Japan, we must at first operate from bases either in the Marianas or in China. We did not consider Germany as a possible target for the B-29's because we figured that by the time they were ready, the intensive bombardment schedule we were planning with our B-17's and B-24's would have destroyed most of the industrial facilities, the communications systems, and other military objectives within Germany and German-controlled Europe. On the other hand, we figured Japan would be free from aerial bombardment until we could get the B-29's into the picture.

With this in mind, our Plans Division had drawn up possible methods of operation against Japan. Naturally, the idea that first came to mind was to operate out of China. But the Japanese, advancing up rivers and along railroads and roads, had deprived the Chinese of any suitable airports closer than Chengtu or Chungking. There still remained some smaller airports closer to the coast, which could be enlarged, if necessary, but since we were never sure the Chinese would hold them uninterruptedly, we could count on using them only for refueling, en route to or returning from the targets in Japan. Operations from the Aleutian Islands would be not only restricted, but definitely hampered by lack of airports of suitable size. Almost continuous bad weather was another serious objection—one which probably would have made our loss in bombers very high on both legs of the flight.

Accordingly, our Planners took a look at the islands in the Pacific Ocean, to determine which ones should be captured, having in mind suitable bases from which to operate up to 1000 Superfortresses. The Marianas, specifically Guam, Saipan, and Tinian, came closer to filling the bill than any others. The fly in the ointment was that we were still a long way from the Marianas. It would be some time, first, before we captured them, and secondly, before we could build adequate B-29 bases there. Accordingly, we had decided that we would send our first contingent of Superfortresses to China, via the South Atlantic–Trans-Africa air route, and operate from bases in the vicinity of Chengtu. Gasoline would be taken in by whatever planes were available, but we were relying mainly on the B-29's themselves to transport their own.

The distance from Chengtu to Tokyo was about 2000 miles. This made a refueling stop essential, either on the outgoing or on the return trip, which in turn meant supplemental bases somewhere in advance of the Chengtu area. Otherwise the B-29's would have to carry a reduced bomb load. As the distance from the Marianas to Tokyo was only about 1400 or 1500 miles, depending upon which of the islands were used for air bases, we were eagerly awaiting their capture.

Now, a bit about the B-29 itself. Conceived in 1939, the first production model was flown in July, 1943. It was an airplane that weighed about twice as much as the B-17. With its gross load, bomb bays full, and gasoline tanks filled to capacity, it weighed 120,000 pounds, as against the B-17's 67,000 pounds under a similar load. It had about twice as much horsepower as the B-17.

A pressure cabin on the B-29 made it possible to fly at extremely high altitudes. The plane had central control of gunfire. It was so large and complicated that it required about ten thousand drawings before it was possible to put it into production. A thousand engineers worked on that airplane. The drawings themselves cost us three million dollars.

The trouble we had with building the B-17 was repeated with the B-29. We had one grief after another with the engines and other minor parts; mostly with the engines. Months of engine trouble; trouble with fires; trouble with cooling. Several times the planes caught fire in the air, and in one instance, the fire was tragically serious. It occurred when the first model was being tested at the Boeing Plant on February 18, 1942. The pioneer B-29 caught fire in the air, and in spite of everything that could be done, crashed on landing, killing the entire crew. Eddie Allen, Boeing's chief test pilot, and one of the greatest the country ever knew, was flying the plane.

However, we could not and must not be stopped in our production. I immediately put General K. B. Wolfe of our Materiel Command in charge of what we designated a special B-29 project, and gave him particular instructions to expedite production in every way possible. By making this a special project, it was possible to assign to it personnel from any part of the Air Force, wherever they might be, and no matter how important the jobs they were filling. By the following June, 1943, we had built up Operational Training Units at fields in Central Kansas where we were flying the B-29's, getting our crews acquainted with them, and educating the staffs and commanders in the proper methods of operation. The B-29 unit was later to be called the Twentieth Air Force. (At that particular time, it was the 58th Bombardment Wing; then XX Bomber Command.)

In the meantime, we had been training mechanics at a school organized by the Boeing Company at Wichita—flight engineers for the combat crew, and ground crews to maintain the B-29's at their bases.*

As I have said, at the SEXTANT Conference the B-29 project was approved by the Joint Chiefs of Staff, the Combined Chiefs of Staff, and by the President, the President promising Generalissimo Chiang Kai-

---

* For a fuller account of the B-29 program see Colonel Harold B. Hinton's excellent *Air Victory*.

shek that the B-29's would be in combat some time around June, 1944. Chiang, in turn, promised the runways would be built at bases in China, ready for the arrival of the Superfortresses by April 15, 1944.

The sad part about all this promising was that the Chinese had no idea of time. They thought nothing of promising dates and then finishing the job when they got around to it. Accordingly, I sent General Wolfe to China in December, 1943, shortly after I returned from Teheran, and from then on he and his staff had to take charge personally of building the runways. These runways were built with Chinese labor, and, literally, by hand. Stones were placed by hand in their proper positions, with smaller stones on top. All stone used was delivered in baskets carried on the shoulders of thousands of coolies. Water to wet down the stones was carried in buckets by other thousands of coolies, and then the runway was rolled by a great roller, pulled by several hundred Chinese. It was a long, tedious process, but the airports were finally completed.

On March 8, 1944, I took a trip to Kansas to see how the B-29 units were progressing in so far as training, organization, and equipment were concerned. I was appalled at what I found. There were shortages in all kinds and classes of equipment. The engines were not fitted with the latest gadgets; the planes were not ready to go. It would be impossible for them to be anywhere near China by the 15th of April unless some drastic measures were taken.

Whatever may have been said about General Bennett E. Meyers since the war, he was a "go-getter," a pusher, a driver; he got things done. When he was given a task, he did it. In this particular instance, I told Meyers he had to get those airplanes out on time, and the crews must be ready to go with them. He must take every plane in turn, make a list of shortages, then get in touch with every factory in the United States that was involved, and insure that the parts were sent to the base by airplane. He was to send special airplanes for the parts, if necessary, so they could be installed on the B-29's with the least possible delay. Meyers had less than two or three weeks in which to finish the job if the planes were to get to China on the 15th of the following month.

Everybody pitched in and the first of the B-29's headed for China landed in India on April 2nd. The second airplane, as a matter of security, and also as a matter of fooling the Germans with a cover plan, took off from Miami and landed in England, quite in the open so that everybody could have a chance to see it; and as many people as possible were encouraged to take pictures of it. We hoped to give the Germans the idea the B-29's were going to be used to supplement the B-17's and B-24's in our offensive against them, and thus to keep the Japanese from anticipating our real plans for sending the B-29's to India.

The operations from China against Japan were not simple. After hauling their own gasoline and bombs from India, the B-29's would have to go back to India and refuel, taking on as much gasoline as they could, and return to China, where they would bomb up and take off for Japan. The distance from the Assam region to the Chengtu area was about 1200 miles; from China to the nearest point of bombing in Japan, about 1600 miles. So, when the airplanes finally got back to their bases in India, they had covered a distance of about 5600 miles, and had carried some 3500 gallons of gasoline into China. Their first actual bombing raid was on June 5, 1944, when they bombed Bangkok. On the 18th of June, they bombed Yawata, where they hit steel mills which were furnishing Japan with a considerable amount of steel for her war effort. From that time forward, it was just one target after another for the XX Bomber Command: Sasebo, Anshan, Palembang, Nagasaki, Yawata, and Anshan again; repeat raids on Formosa and on many other localities of principal military value to the Japanese.

But what the Japanese saw of the B-29's operating out of China was not a circumstance compared with what they would see when we started operating out of the Marianas.

✭ 26 ✭

Looking back on the Teheran Conference, I think everyone who had carefully thought out our over-all strategy for beating the Germans must have been in accord with Stalin's idea of how to win the war. In simple words, as taken from my notes, this was: "Hit Germany hard. Synchronize the operations of Allied troops on the two fronts, east and west. Then hit the Germans from both sides where it hurts most. Hit her where the distance to Berlin is shortest. Don't waste time, men or equipment on secondary fronts."

The prescription matched the planning of the Joint Chiefs of Staff in the United States, wherein we adopted the principle set by the President, of beating Germany first and then turning to Japan. However, I could scarcely agree with Stalin's view of the air war, since neither he nor his generals seemed able to comprehend the necessity for strategic bombing. They appeared to believe the air war might well stop within the battle areas, or the areas immediately adjacent, and apparently were entirely satisfied with that kind of aerial operations on their own front.

Regarding Japan, my impression was that Stalin had made up his mind and was not going to change it. Under no circumstances would he be drawn into a two-front war. Accordingly, as far as the Japanese were concerned, Russia was a neutral country. However, he permitted us to talk with his staff and make plans for occupying air bases in eastern Siberia, even going so far as to designate special areas in which we could operate, and outlining routes of ship and air communications in and out, not only across the seas (to reduce interception by Japanese submarines) but within Siberia itself. True, those operations never developed beyond the planning stage, but for a few weeks we thought we had the Russians convinced of their importance.

I was never quite able to understand the Russian attitude toward those of our bomber crews who were forced to make emergency landings in Siberia after raids over Japan. At first the men were treated almost like captured enemies, certainly not as Allies. Even at the last, after Germany had capitulated, the usual Russian conduct was so unfriendly that when our crews came down in trouble, they felt constrained to leave the scene of the landing at once, if possible, moving at night and concealing themselves by day, more like prisoners escaping than like comrades-in-arms.

The action of the Russians in confiscating our B-29's was, in my opinion, inexcusable. From their point of view, it probably was a practical way to secure the world's latest superbombers at no cost to themselves. For our own part, I never thought our Government tried too hard to get those planes back. As in 1938–40, "Don't do anything; it might make somebody mad at us!"

I think the story of the "General Arnold Special" might be of interest here, because it illustrates several things. On January 11, 1944, I was going through the Boeing Aircraft plant at Wichita, looking over the B-29's. When they told me how many they planned to get out that month, I picked out a bomber, just a little beyond that goal, and writing my name across the fuselage, said, "This is the plane I want this month."

That Superfortress, thereafter, became known as the "General Arnold Special." It was later accepted for the Government by General Knudsen at an impressive ceremony. The combat crew who came there to fly it away became known to everybody in the plant, and when the plane reached the Pacific, the factory employees followed each mission as closely as they could.

On November 11, 1944, the "General Arnold Special," with Captain Weston H. Price, of West View, Washington, as pilot, and Lieutenant John E. Flanagan, of New York City, as copilot, took off for a target at Omura, Japan. Running out of fuel on the return trip, they faced the limited choice of crashing in enemy-held China, or landing at Vladivostok. They headed for Russia and twelve hours and forty-five minutes after taking off from their home base, brought the "General Arnold Special" down safely at the Vladivostok Naval Air Station. They were well "escorted" for the last leg of their flight by ten Russian fighter planes. When they stepped out of their plane, they were immediately taken to Russian Naval Headquarters. That was the last time they ever saw their B-29. That was on November 11, 1944, and it wasn't until February 2, 1945, that the crew members of that airplane reached the Allied lines in Iran, and were returned to the United States.

The "General Arnold Special" was just one of the several B-29's that landed in Russian territory, and were kept permanently by the Russians without any explanation whatsoever.

But in the late summer of 1943 the B-29, though already flying confidently over Wichita and Seattle, was still quite a long way from Tokyo. We heard instead, with eagerness—when we could finally get a straight report—what the skip bombing of Kenney's Fifth Air Force had done to a heavily guarded convoy coming south through the Bismarck Sea from Rabaul to reinforce the Japanese posts at Lae, in New Guinea. For a loss of only 4 U.S. planes, 7 military transports and 3 of the 8 escorting destroyers had been sunk, with 5600 Japanese troops drowned, 500 captured, and 59 of 100 enemy planes "protecting" the Japanese convoy definitely shot down.

It was a welcome report after the "yes-we-hit 'em, no-we-didn't" accounts received from the Midway fight. To this day, I haven't the faintest idea whether the B-17's we had in the battle of Midway ever hit any Japanese ships or not.

In the European Theater this was what Generalleutnant Adolf Heusinger, Chief of the Operations Division of the German Army General Staff (OKH), later called "The Fateful Year." After Germany's surrender, Heusinger wrote out a gloomy document for us, tracing the "Strategic Turning Points."

1. A Triple Turning Point: Dunkirk.
2. A Greek Gift: Italy's Entry into the War.
3. The Fear of Decision: Abandonment of the Invasion of England.
4. The Mediterranean: Military Theater of Half Measures.
5. Return to a Two-Front War: The attack upon Russia.
6. The Time Factor Becomes Decisive: Declaration of War on the United States.
7. The Fateful Year—1943
   a. Loss of the Initiative: Stalingrad and U-Boat War.
   b. The Army Bleeds to death: Operational Principles, 1943–45.
   c. The Collapse in Three Dimensions: Turning Point in the Air War.

Everything that happened after that is reviewed under the single word: "Conclusion." Heusinger was right about 1943 being the turning point in the air war. It was increasingly apparent that our daylight precision bombardment campaign was not only beginning to hurt the industrial heart of the Reich, but was also accomplishing its other big job: the job of making the German Air Force come up and fight with ever-increasing losses. The R.A.F. could not do this at night.

The success of our missions was becoming apparent to the Prime Minister. "I shall be obliged," he wired, following the great attacks on Marienburg, Anklam, and Gdynia on October 9, 1943:

> . . . if you will convey to General Eaker and his Command, the thanks of the British War Cabinet for the magnificent achievements of the Eighth Air Force in the Battle of Germany in recent days, culminating in the remarkable success of last week. In broad daylight, the crews of your Bombers have fought their way through the strongest defenses which the enemy could bring against them, and have ranged over the length and breadth of Germany, striking with deadly accuracy many of the most important hostile and industrial installations and ports.
>
> Your Bombers, and the Fighters which support them in these fierce engagements, have inflicted serious losses on the German Air Force, and by forcing the enemy to weaken other fronts, have contributed notably to the success of the Allied arms everywhere.
>
> The War Cabinet extends our congratulations, also, to your ground crews of the Eighth Air Force without whose technical skill and faithful labor this feat of arms would not be possible.
>
> I am confident that, with the ever-growing power of the Eighth Air Force striking alternate blows with the Royal Air Force Bomber Command, we shall, together, inexorably beat the life out of industrial Germany and thus hasten the day of final victory.
>
> W. C.

Though it has become a familiar thing to read that "the first task facing the Eighth Air Force was the destruction of the Luftwaffe," and so on, this has often been misinterpreted as a reference only to our bombing campaign against the German aircraft factories. During that campaign itself, from April, 1943, to the spring of 1944, the fact that we had to return to the same targets and hit them again within a few months, had caused our bombing claims to be challenged.

It was not understood that the more valuable the factories were, the faster they were rebuilt, either in the same places or somewhere else. We not only had to knock them down, but keep knocking them down. As our ground forces finally entered Germany and found more airplanes parked around than Goering had ever had in 1943, and as captured production figures showed the monthly output of single-engine fighters to have been far higher *after* our campaign than before, there was another tendency to doubt. The Air Force, said certain ground officers and correspondents, had deceived itself—and the public! This bomber ballyhoo was all nonsense! Look there for yourselves! The Luftwaffe had not been destroyed at all!

Well, then, what did become of it?

The fact is, the bombing of the aircraft factories, while magnificently done, was only part of the picture. When I say that the Eighth Air Force's other big function was to make the German Air Force come up and fight, I mean just that. There was no analogy between this very grim attitude and that of a cocky champion calling on all comers to appear and be taken on. Our view was coldly scientific.

In our strategy for Germany's defeat, the first major step, conditioning all the others, was the elimination of the Luftwaffe; to eliminate the Luftwaffe we had to come to grips with it, not defensively, as the R.A.F. had done in the Battle of Britain, but on our own initiative. The German Air Force had to be attacked, and no airplanes existed at that phase of the war with the range, the fire-power, and the philosophy to attack it, except our daylight bombers. The decision was a grave one for the commanders. We knew what the consequences would be, the price that would have to be paid, until we could get our long-range fighter escort into action. We took our course deliberately, and in fact, however bad it was, it actually wasn't as bad as we expected.

At first the crews themselves didn't realize that their collisions with the FW-190's and Me-109's were more than the outcome of a calculated risk. The view of any combat crewman is necessarily more personal than strategic.

It has been written rather frequently that despite the twelve feet of concrete over the sub pens at Lorient, St. Nazaire, and La Pallice, we were heartened by the way the bombardiers still pin-pointed the targets. It was more than that. We knew before they left the saltflats of Lake Muroc that they could bomb precisely. But in this phase, without fighter escort, against the worst aerial opposition ever seen until that time, they proved much more about the future.

To the combat airmen of those days, to the little Eighth Air Force holding on in Britain, already beginning to force the Luftwaffe back before the first reinforcements came in April, 1943, the country owes a considerable debt. The fighter escort didn't arrive until the end of that year.

Their chiefs—Spaatz, Eaker, Fred Anderson, and Doolittle—such Air Division Commanders as Bob Williams, Curt LeMay, and Bill Kepner, who had already turned the VIII Fighter Command into a going concern before he produced the same change in our Britain-based Liberators, deserve a rather special kind of credit, too.

At first, in the early shallow penetrations over France, Galland's

FW-190 and Me-109 pilots had merely studied this new daytime weapon, the Flying Fortress. They watched warily, and on certain days, as if to give our bomber crews a taste of things to come, they put aside their waiting policy, and over Lille or Antwerp, or the Renault factory in Paris, did swarm up to engage our little formations. This was especially apt to happen if the Allied fighter escort missed connections. When these encounters occurred, even in the early days, they were savage and bloody on both sides.

In the fall of 1942 the B-17's were already returning to their bases with noses and tails shot off—in one famous case with the plane shot literally in half, the fuselage held together only by a bit of metal at the bottom, with dead and wounded men inside—but they came home.

The shape of things to come was being prophesied not only for themselves, but for the Luftwaffe. Galland told, after V-E Day, of the dismay with which his fighter pilots made their first acquaintance with the Fortress's armament, especially with the "stinger" in the tail. They changed their tactics quickly. With that typical German military inge- nuity which they never lacked except at the top levels of command, they found within a few weeks the place where a formation of Flying Fortresses was vulnerable. Fly your fighter units, said the *Tactical Regulations* presently issued by Kommodore Galland (the actual tech- nique was devised by one Major Egon Meyer, of Jagdgeschwader 2) "on a course parallel to and on one side of the bombers until about 5 Km. ahead of them, then turn in by *Schwarme* (elements of four) and attack head on. On this last stretch, fly level with the bombers for the last 1500 yards, open fire at about 900 yards, and get away by flying flat over the bomber formation." (Naturally, at a relative speed which would be the speeds of fighter and bomber combined.)

The first "head-on" attack occurred as early as the mission against the Avion-Potez aircraft factory at Meaulte, France, on September 6, 1942, only twenty days after the first little mission against Rouen. It was VIII Bomber Command's tenth operation. This day, the first 2 of the 4721 planes the Eighth Air Force was to lose went down. The "head-on" or "nose" attack did it.

Thereafter, at home, we went to work at once to develop nose arma- ment for the B-17 to take the place of the two .30-caliber guns for the navigator and bombardier which (when they could get to them) had been the sole weapons forward of the top-turret. The result, months later, was the familiar chin turret on the B-17G, operated from above by the bombardier. But long before that, indeed two days after Meaulte, the combat men in England themselves devised gun mounts for .50 calibers in the nose.

By January, 1943, German fighters came up savagely every time. These bombs on the German aircraft factories, the German fighters shot down by our gunners in the air battles, were the beginning of the end for the Luftwaffe. The number of enemy fighters claimed as destroyed, we soon discovered, was too high, the natural result of attempting to attribute to an individual gunner the destruction of an enemy fighter that had half the formation shooting at it. There was no corroboration like the fighter-pilot's gun-camera, but only the hasty eye-witness testimony of other combat crewmen in the battle. Yet, we do know that well before we could get legs on our fighters that would enable the "Little Friends" to escort the B-17's and B-24's to any target in Europe and back, the bombers, with nothing to protect them but their own guns, had so upset the whole German air strategy that the very composition of the Luftwaffe had been changed.

In 1941, when Milch, with an eye on increased American-British aircraft production, had suggested a minimum German fighter production of 1000 a month, General Jeschonneck, then Chief of the German Air Staff, remarked that he wouldn't know what to do with a monthly production of more than 360 fighters. By October, 1943—let it be repeated, well before our long-range fighter escort appeared over Germany —Milch's desperate April plan for 2230 single-engine fighters by December, 1943, had been boosted to a goal of 4150 single-engine fighters and 1750 twin-engine fighters by December, 1944.

Long before then, the Luftwaffe had pulled every available fighter plane back from the Mediterranean and the Russian front for the defense of the homeland. A majority of the twin-engine night fighters defending Germany against the R.A.F. had been converted into rocket platforms to send up against our formations in the daytime. Standing outside the range of our .50 calibers they would lob their rockets into the columns of bombers with sometimes terrible effect, while the Me-109's and FW-190's dived through the formation.

Although the over-all loss rate of the Eighth Air Force and of the Fifteenth Air Force against Germany was less than 3 per cent, it will be readily understood that on some of these deep penetrations without fighter escort in 1943 the losses were bitterly high.

From the strategic, though not the human, point of view, we could regularly replace our losses; the Germans, who also suffered heavily in these major air battles, could do so only sporadically.

When, at the end of 1943 and the beginning of 1944, I was able to get the long-range fighters to the Eighth Air Force, the long-legged P-47's, P-38's, and most notably, the P-51's, the Luftwaffe was finished. For the rest of that year there were rough battles, but after the great week of February 20th (Operation ARGUMENT), in which both sides figure the back of the German Air Force was broken, the outcome was never in doubt.

We took one of the waist-guns out of the B-17, cutting its crew to nine.

Though the Me-109's and FW-190's continued to attack for some time, for the most part they were destroyed far out of sight of our bomber crews. With the enormous weight of our bombardment force now equipped with the latest radar instruments even when the weather failed, and no mobile mass of enemy fighters sure to pounce upon them on every mission, our bombers now ranged across Europe almost at will, sometimes more than a thousand at a time.

It was not necessary to bother with the aircraft factories themselves much any longer. When it was necessary, either to keep an eye on the new production of the Me-262 jets or to see that a wholly rebuilt trouble spot like the big Focke Wulf plant at Marienburg was knocked down again, as on April 9, 1944, this was done.

Otherwise, in the spring of 1944 we turned our strategic bombers to the campaign against Hitler's last hope: the synthetic oil factories which the frantic efforts of Speer and Geilenberg had begun to develop with amazing possibilities, once it was plain that the Russian advance and the bombs of our Fifteenth Air Force were putting the natural Ploesti refineries out of their plans forever.

We interrupted this only to concentrate for a few weeks on those "interdiction" preparations for D-Day in Normandy which have become a classic in all war histories; that isolation of the battlefield which the Ninth Air Force mediums and fighter bombers carried out to the limits of their range, the Seine and Marne, while the heavies of the Eighth Air Force and the R.A.F. knocked out the choke points and bridges of the Oise and Loire beyond. It took one panzer division that ordinarily should have made it into Normandy in a few hours, fifteen days to arrive at the front.

Only once after February, 1944, did the Luftwaffe make a real resurgence. It is ironic how that happened. It did not happen against our Eighth, Ninth, or Fifteenth Air Force. It happened against the

R.A.F. at night, and for a while, for the first time in the war in the dark, or what had been the dark, it kept the R.A.F. Bomber Command from going into Germany, at least with any effectiveness. The Germans, who never lacked for ideas even when their strength was gone, found a last way to fling the Luftwaffe against us. Since the mass of single-engine fighters and rocket-carrying twin-engine fighters could no longer work against the U.S. Air Force in the daytime, how about hitting the R.A.F. with it at night?

Relatively, the R.A.F. had no defenses against concentrated fighter attacks at all. They hadn't needed any, and they were flying in and out of Germany with an extremely low loss rate these days, with losses due to navigational hazards and flak both lowered by improved instruments and experience.

By an ingenious combination of flares and radar devices, the Germans hit upon a way of "lighting up" the night sky. For a couple of months that spring it was catastrophic. On a single mission to Nuremberg, on the night of March 29th, the R.A.F. lost 96 four-engine bombers. The bombers were so badly scattered that leading citizens of Nuremberg, who kept minute track of all the attacks, said after the war they hadn't realized their city was the target on that night. On other spring nights, the losses were up in the eighties.

To the losses on missions like these, as on our own over, say, Schweinfurt or Oschersleben, another 10 per cent or so can be added, from crashes at base or ditchings in the Channel. Security aside, the world never heard much about this sad reverse for the R.A.F., since it happened to coincide with the period during which the heavy bombers of both Air Forces were frequently pulled back from Germany to help soften up France for the invasion. The fact that the R.A.F. Bomber Command carried out the majority of its operations over France for a while, did not, therefore, attract as much attention as it might have done at another time.

Presently the British, being even more ingenious than the Germans when it came to radar, found a way to fix things. With the help of a German plane that landed accidentally in England, improvements were made in the radar "eyes" of their own night fighters, and they were able accurately to locate the German attackers before they could get near the bombers, and then, as far as the Luftwaffe was concerned, it was over.

When our invasion forces finally landed on June 6th, not only was there no Luftwaffe left to meet them, but all the way across France, and in battered Germany itself, the Luftwaffe, except for token resistance, had been taken out of their way. However bitter those beaches may have been for the men in the boats, the German Air Force was not there.

As the experience of air commanders and flight surgeons all around the world had taught us to determine the actual number of combat missions we might expect the average pilot or crew-member in each theater to make without a break, we could now also judge the life expectancy of even the luckiest airplane. The average heavy bomber in the Eighth Air Force, for example—counting its original sixteen days' modification in England, and the days it would spend grounded in hangar or at air depot being repaired—could be counted on to give us a performance of 161 combat days. The battle damage some of those planes suffered would have caused them, in peacetime, to be junked. Instead, they were patched up and sent back to fight. A few even fought after they were finished. In 1944 we tried some interesting experiments with worn-out B-17's that were loaded with TNT, taken off by pilots who bailed out over England, and then, guided by radio control from a mother plane, sent against German installations as big flying bombs. We called them "Weary Willies."

Another kind of statistics concerned Bob Lovett and me at this time. As soon as it was possible to get it, we needed an accurate, unbiased analysis of the effects of our bombing on the enemy's economy, on his military operations, and on the termination of hostilities. We both knew that following World War I everybody claimed to have won it. Finally, to stop further arguments, people used to say the Great War had been won by the chaplains. What Lovett and I wanted to do was create an impartial agency which would have at its disposal all the data necessary for a frank report to the President. Was strategic bombing as good as we thought it was? Or were we carried away by our own bomber-mindedness? Of what real value was tactical bombing?

It was difficult to select the right man to head such an organization, but finally, late in 1944, we chose Franklin d'Olier, President of the Prudential Life Insurance Company, whose eminent business career provided exactly the objective judgment we were seeking. In order to make his committee's findings on the bombing results of the R.A.F., of our own Eighth and Fifteenth Air Forces, and of the Germans acceptable beyond question, we decided that the Secretary of War should ask the President for a White House directive, instructing the d'Olier Board to make a world-wide survey of strategic bombing.

Mr. Stimson accepted the proposal immediately, as did the President.

The special board of civilians was appointed—famous now as the United States Strategic Bombing Survey—and did an excellent job working right along with the troops as they moved forward, getting a true picture of what Allied air power had actually meant in bringing the war to a conclusion. Human morale under the bombs was as much a factor in their investigation as broken buildings. The Franklin d'Olier (USSBS) Report was not completed until September 30, 1945.

Although we had been doing business with key members in the American Academy of Science since the 1930's, there was no regular organized group in the Government setup to take care of the development of new scientific devices for the armed services. It wasn't until about June, 1940, that Dr. Vannevar Bush of the Carnegie Institute had put up a proposition to Harry Hopkins, later accepted by the President, whereby he would head a scientific research organization for the Government. Included in the directive was an examination into the "fissure of the atom, and development of atomic energy and the atomic bomb."

From time to time I had heard rumors and whisperings of what was going on in connection with atomic development, and occasionally one of my scientific friends would give me a little insight into what the problem really was. Then, one of the men actually in the "know" opened up and told me enough of the story to fill in a few vacant places in the mosaic I had been making. But I was given to understand that under no circumstances was I to tell anybody about this development—not a soul! This I adhered to religiously. From a distance, I followed the experiments as they went along. In May, 1943, we received information from Zurich that Professor Max Planck, at the Kaiser Wilhelm Institute, in collaboration with Dr. Otto Hahn, was working on the splitting of the uranium atom. Also, that other German scientists were on the threshold of solving this great and dangerous secret.

The Germans were supposed to have perfected an electric machine which would make it possible to complete the development of the atomic bomb. I was then asked to have our bombers in England make special missions against the various branches of the Kaiser Wilhelm Institute in Berlin. Prior to that, the British had destroyed a plant at Norway where the Germans had been experimenting with other phases of this project. So, piece by piece, little by little, the whole story was unfolding, but as I say, I was not allowed to tell a soul anything about it.

My scientific friends and I discussed how this device would be used and carried. Always the answer was: the airplane. (There were other possibilities, of course.) We talked about the size of the packet, the weight of the packet, and the gadgets that might have to go with the packet. There was only one plane that had sufficient range to carry the bomb to the objective we were after—Japan.

I could not see how the bomb could possibly be used against Germany, because judging from the information I received from the scientists, it would not be ready before a German surrender; but we could use it against Japan. We had already decided which Japanese cities would be targets for our normal bombing operations. To test the bomb's real destructiveness, three or four cities must be saved intact from the B-29's regular operations as unspoiled targets for the new weapon. Which cities should be spared was a problem. I talked the matter over with Secretary Stimson, and gave him a list of the target cities we planned to attack with the B-29's in any case.

Mr. Stimson struck off my list the city of Kyoto. Kyoto had a population of 753,000, and was an important manufacturing center. In my opinion it should have been destroyed. But the Secretary said it was one of the holy cities of the world, and of outstanding religious significance. So Kyoto was removed from the regular B-29 target file, and also eliminated as a possible target for the atomic bomb.

We selected four other cities for atomic attack, because of their size and manufacturing or industrial significance. Hiroshima, with a population of 218,000; Niigata, 119,000; Nagasaki, 197,000; and Kokura, a smaller city of approximately 51,600. These four were all industrial centers and were of great importance to the Japanese production effort. Kokura was at the south end of a tunnel connecting the island of Honshu with the island of Kyushu. I was anxious to see what effect the atomic bomb would have on the tunnel; whether it would fill it up with water; how badly it would spring a leak; or whether any of the effects of the bomb would be carried through the tunnel to the northern entrance.

In the War Department letter of instructions to General Spaatz dated July 25, 1945, these four cities were given to him as possible targets. Spaatz at the time was commanding the Strategic Air Forces in the Pacific. It was left up to him, depending on weather, tactical situations, and any other factors that might influence his operations, which ones he should attack, that is, once it was determined that the atomic bomb was actually to be dropped at all. That decision would not be made by me, or by any authority less than the President of the United States.

By hook or by crook, I managed to rearrange our bombing missions in Japan without revealing why.

Then the time approached when it looked as if the bomb might be nearing completion. Here was I, the only man in the Air Forces, theoretically (and I think I was, actually) who knew anything about it. I couldn't know what modifications in the fuselage of the B-29 would be necessary to accommodate the bomb without actually going into details with aviation engineers. For a few weeks I had visions, in order to keep this development a deep dark secret, of endeavoring to make the changes in the B-29 myself. This I obviously could not do. So I had to take somebody into my confidence.

Finally, I had a long talk with General Marshall, and we worked out a plan whereby I would tell just a few of our people. They, in turn, must be able to make the adjustments in the B-29 in such a manner that nobody would suspect the reason.

From that time on I was always kept fairly well informed as to the progress with the bomb, and finally, while we were at the Potsdam Conference, of the test made at Alamogordo.

In the meantime, we sent guarded information to General Eaker in England. He was thus able to direct the bombing of those portions of the Kaiser Wilhelm Institute that were most essential to the German atomic bomb project.

Also, in August, 1943, a movement was started by Churchill and Stalin for a combined British and American Strategic Air Force to carry out bombing operations with the Russians in the Caucasus. It was approved by the President about the same time. Our Chiefs of Staff heard of it in the fall, when it came out into the open. On October 4th, the President wrote to Churchill, telling him it was a solid commitment; that we would start operations in the Caucasus with heavy bombers as soon as possible.

The idea was to send in a token force, to let the Russians get some estimate of our air strength and to impress the Germans with the fact that we were helping the Russians. Stalingrad, at that time, was in a bad way. It looked as though the Germans were going to overrun all that portion of Russia, and that Stalingrad would fall by the wayside. The Russian Air Force was outnumbered three to one. On October 7th, Mr. Roosevelt notified Stalin that the movement would be pushed as rapidly as possible.

Conditions changed. Stalingrad did not fall. The Russians defeated the Germans. The Germans lost several hundred thousand men and had to retreat from that area, back toward the west side of the Black Sea. After that, Stalin apparently preferred not to have any Allied Air Force

—or other Allied observers—in Russia at all. The combined British-American bombing force never did operate from the Caucasus.

On August 1, 1943, at the very moment Mr. Churchill was discussing the project of bases in the Caucasus with President Roosevelt and Premier Stalin, the eyes of the world were attracted to the Balkan area by the daring attack of Brereton's Ninth Air Force Liberators (rein-forced by two groups of the Eighth) on Ploesti. No mission in the war was more carefully planned, with full knowledge of the odds against it, nor carried out despite mishaps in identifying the target, with more amazing courage. The damage done to the sprawling miles of Europe's Number One oil field was great—60 per cent of the total production capacity temporarily knocked out—but the cost was heavy. Fifty-four of the 177 B-24's dispatched on the 2400-mile flight failed to return. Some little glimpse of the determination of the men who carried out the Ploesti mission is obtained from the report of their long, quiet approach to Rumania and their target. As one of their key formation leaders suddenly spiraled down unexplainably into the Mediterranean, not a voice broke radio silence. The deputy leader, a young lieutenant, moved up to take his place, and the formation flew on. As for the bombing itself, the planes that came back had tree branches stuck to their bomb-bay doors. Some went in so low, undetected by the enemy's radar, that they were blown to pieces by the blast of their own bombs. For the first time in history five Congressional Medals of Honor were awarded for the valor of a single military operation. Colonel (now Major General) Leon Johnson and Colonel "Killer" Kane received theirs personally. The decorations of Lieutenant Colonel Addison E. Baker, Major John L. Jersted, and Lieutenant Lloyd H. Hughes were awarded posthumously.

Twelve days later, on August 13th, heavies of the Ninth Air Force hit the Messerschmitt factory at Wiener-Neustadt, outside Vienna (Operation JUGGLER)—the beginning of the two-way bombing of Germany. On the 17th—the same day Sicily fell, the same date on which the R.A.F., between the end of its "Battle of the Ruhr" and its next concentration on Berlin, bombed Peenemunde, only a few hours before Kenney's B-25's swept in at treetop height over Wewak on the other side of the world and destroyed 200 Jap planes in eight minutes— the Eighth Air Force attacked the ball-bearing industry at Schweinfurt and the Messerschmitt factory at Regensburg.

These weeks—Schweinfurt, the shuttle through Regensburg to Africa; Frankfurt, Stuttgart, Anklam, Gdynia, Marienburg, and so on—extend-ing to the second Schweinfurt mission on October 14th, were the high-water mark of our daylight bombardment without fighter escort. That attack, which cost us sixty-four engine bombers, is the one most remembered, but the fact is, August 17th was just as bad. The losses of the 1st and 3rd Bomb Divisions over Schweinfurt and Regensburg that day were 59, one plane less than in October when they hit Schweinfurt together. No such savage air battles had been seen since the war began. Our losses were rising to an all-time high, but so were those of the Luftwaffe, and our bombers were not being turned back from their targets. Could we keep it up? The London papers asked the question editorially. To this day, I don't know for certain if we could have. No one does. We had the planes and replacement crews by then to maintain the loss-rate of 25 per cent which I had originally determined must be faced; but obviously there were other factors. To obscure the argument forever, in mid-October the weather shut down foggily on southeast Germany for most of the remainder of the year. Until January, 1944, the only missions we were able to send into Germany were within range all the way of our longer-legged P-47's and P-38's. (Two exceptions, uneventful as far as enemy fighter interception was concerned, were long hauls in November to special targets in Norway.) By the time the weather let us get back to deep central and southeast Germany it was January and we had the P-51's. Though there was plenty of trouble over Oschersleben-Halberstadt-Brunswick on January 11, there was planned fighter escort all the way. The 863 bombers hitting Frankfurt on the 29th were similarly escorted. At first the Germans couldn't believe it. At about the time of the Battle of the Bulge, young General Adolf Galland himself flew out of a cloud front over the Ardennes and was promptly jumped by four P-51's which chased him all the way back to Berlin. He told his American interrogators in 1945 that this "convinced me."

That final conquest of range for our fighters reminds me of our attempts to get the British to put extra legs on the Spitfires. It looked for a while as if the short-legged Spits, with only enough gas to fly for fifteen or twenty minutes after crossing the French coast, might cause us to postpone our Normandy landings. I took the matter up with Air Chief Marshal Portal. Portal told me he did not have tactical control over the Spitfires and Hurricanes, he was not in a position to put those extra legs on his fighters. The R.A.F. must work through its Materiel setup, its production and its engineering outfits. The Ministry of Aircraft Production was not under Portal's command. So I said: "I'll tell you what. You give me the airplanes, and I'll put some tanks on them. It won't take very long. I'll show you how easy it is to do it." Accordingly, Portal shipped me three Spitfires by boat from England. Within two months the extra tanks put on them by our Materiel Command had raised their range to about 1300 miles. Best of all, the Spits *flew* back to England. I couldn't help sending Portal a message: "The Spitfires you sent me by ship have landed at London after crossing the Atlantic under their own steam."

The bases at Foggia in Italy now gave the heavies of our new Fifteenth Air Force a solid platform from which to operate. The campaign which was to end in the spring with the phenomenal fighter-bomber operations of XII Tac's P-47's over North Italy (Operation STRANGLE) was well along. With the collapse of Italy, the Italian Air Force had disappeared. Except for some of the operations of its Savoia torpedo bombers against Allied shipping, and the rare successes of the Macchi 200's and 202's in the Western Desert, its chief function had been to make the Axis air strength look greater on paper than it really was. The Germans didn't seem to miss Mussolini's "Eagles" much. "Good flyers, lousy fighters," our own boys reported.

At the conferences TRIDENT and QUADRANT, attempts had been made to fix approximate dates for the Normandy landings. The time set was May 1, 1944. It was the 6th of June, of course, before the landings were made. The reader should not get the impression that the Combined Chiefs of Staff, the President, or the Prime Minister could set any definite time or date as to when various maneuvers, operations, or landings would actually be carried out. The commander in the field was the one who had to make that final decision, based on weather, tide, moon, and other immediate conditions. Whether it was the D-Day for an invasion or a plan like the Ploesti mission, which was decided upon during our QUADRANT Conference, the Joint or the Combined Chiefs of Staff might suggest dates and exact strength, but the local commanding general made the final dispositions.

The hectic military leadership of the Nazi chiefs—or rather Hitler's persistent interference with his professional military leaders—was quite evident by late 1943. It was favorable to us, but not more. On the Russian Front and in the Mediterranean the initiative was wholly ours; but except for the heavy bombers of the R.A.F. and the U.S. Eighth Air Force, Germany was still far out of reach. What was happening there? What *could* happen from there that might abruptly change the whole tide?

We knew, from all sorts of sources, that the Germans had a number of "secret weapons" in preparation. We had reason to hope that our round-the-clock bombing offensive, plus the failure to follow through which had characterized all German military strategy since the jump from the Mediterranean to Russia in 1941, might prevent the planned use of these weapons.

On the other hand, it had to remain conceivable that if certain of these very plausible gadgets were completed, if enough of them could be used in the right way at the right time—especially before the Allies landed in Northwest Europe—they might have very disagreeable results. The whole main platform, not only for our combined bomber offensive but for the invasion—England itself—might be blasted.

Fortunately, judging from the mere 1100 that finally fell on England, chiefly London, the long-range V-2 rockets did not get into production until January, 1944. The planned output of 900 a month was not achieved, 50 to 300 being the number produced monthly until August. Between September, 1944, and March, 1945, the production rate was 700 a month. The first of these fourteen-ton missiles, which traveled at four or five times the speed of sound, were not launched against England from their bases in Holland and western Germany until September, 1944, at which time technical difficulties were still encountered. A large bombproof launching site was under construction in France as early as May, 1943, however, and another in August, at about the same time the V-1 launching sites were begun. The V-10 (A-10), a very large rocket intended especially for New York, was being built.

In the late summer of 1943 it was not the V-2's nor the jet planes that called for our special attention. We still knew little about the V-2's and we automatically dislocated production of the jets when we bombed the regular aircraft factories. (In 1944 we did go back to some of these complexes solely on the jets' account.) The secret German weapon that caused us to start intensive countermeasures in August, 1943, was the V-1. This was a gadget which a remarkably accurate R.A.F. Intelligence estimate sized up as a thin-shelled flying bomb, weighing probably around 2000 pounds (1000 Kg.), jet-propelled, using a fuel that involved dilute hydrogen peroxide, with a speed of about two hundred miles an hour, and certainly capable of being launched against Britain from across the Channel. Incidentally, this intelligence was not gained through the underground but from the air. It came from a detailed study of aerial photos by P.I. experts at Medmenham, including a young WAAF officer named Constance Babington-Smith, at this writing a member of the staff of *Life* magazine in New York. Once the specialists in hydrogenation plants had studied the high-altitude pictures of the buildings at Peenemunde, the experimental center where the Germans developed their V-weapons, they could even identify the type of fuel the robot probably used.

As we knew later, the V-1 was a close cousin to the Bug which we had been developing intermittently in our own Air Force since 1917. The curious constructions now suddenly appearing along the coast of France, some so shaped that they were called "ski sites," others mushrooming up in massive concrete blocks that left a problem, were obviously connected with the launching of this new weapon. The range from the Pas de Calais area of France was just what we would have desired if we were planning to send our Bugs down in thousands, and tens of thousands, on a concentrated target area. Apparently the Germans were getting ready to do just that to England.

The first retaliatory step was against Peenemunde itself. On the night of August 17th about 600 R.A.F. bombers, the crews only aware that they were attacking an important point of German "radar" development, did a fine job on the target. Though they didn't "wipe out most of the key scientists" as subsequently reported, they did cause the surviving gentlemen to move south to Kochl in the Bavarian Alps, where the last of them were nabbed by one of our Air Technical Intelligence teams, moving along with the 10th Armored Division, in April, 1945. Thus the three heavy attacks our Eighth Air Force made on Peenemunde in 1944 were superfluous, despite their perfection—especially as the experimental phase of the V-1 was then over.

In 1943, back home, we built scale concrete models of the structures revealed by our photo intelligence, and tried by every means—high altitude, low altitude, and skip bombing—to find a formula for destroying them.

That summer, as the German threat lined up for actual operations, it was plain that attacks on supply points, possibly determined assembly centers, etc., would not be fast enough. They, too, were carried out, and the United States Strategic Bombing Survey indicated that the over-all bombing of Germany, transportation, oil, etc., had something to do with the slowing down of the V-1 program. In the main, however, the launching sites themselves had to be attacked. These little pin-point targets, often safe under ten feet of concrete even if they were hit, were within the range of the "Oboe" instruments the R.A.F. was then starting to use. Neither Oboe nor the R.A.F.'s bombing, however, were yet up to the required accuracy. It was a precision bombardment job, and the Eighth Air Force was thus asked to take over the major part.

The Eighth Air Force did so, in addition to its other missions, and from August, 1943, until the summer of 1944, dropped approximately 100,000 tons of bombs on the mysterious little targets. At first, though the bombing itself was always tough, enemy opposition was nil. Then, as the bombs began to take effect, the flak concentrated in the target areas became severe. Crews who had survived Schweinfurt were lost over the Pas de Calais. As the world knows, the V-1's were finally launched. But apart from other failures to stop them, the USSBS estimates that these bombings by the Eighth, the R.A.F., and subsequently by both American and R.A.F. mediums, cost the German V-weapon program a loss of three to four months. The damage done to the sites once they started firing was not great. They had eventually to be captured by the infantry. But then it was too late, no matter what they did.

The bombs the Eighth Air Force sent down on the "No Ball" and "Cross Bow" targets between August, 1943, and the summer of 1944 amounted to 9 per cent of the bombs they dropped against Germany in that period. Apart from the human desolation when the reduced robot bomb program was finally launched—2752 civilians dead, 8000 injured, Churchill announced, after only thirty-five days of the robots on London —it can be fairly claimed that the diversion of so many bombers to such a defensive purpose proves the V-1 to have been much more than a nuisance weapon. I agree—if they had been used rightly, and in time. The USSBS states, by the way, that "It is to be noted, however, that these (our) attacks were usually made on occasions when weather prevented the dispatch of missions against other targets."

Anyway, I'm as glad as any Londoner that we did bomb those launching sites when we did. I happened to be there when the first V-1's came down on England, and regardless of larger strategic considerations there seemed to me to be quite enough of them.

In the Italian Campaign, we learned definitely as we moved from the south to the north that there were certain things air power could not do in Italy, and certain other things it could do. The Air Force could not completely dry up the flow of essential supplies to the Germans in Italy. They lived off the country, regardless of the attitude of the inhabitants. The German's frugality and will power—like the Japanese emerging stolidly from island caves, with their thin bags of rice or dried fish "field rations," after Napalm flames had been poured for weeks into their hideouts—made it possible for him to maintain himself in apparently impossible circumstances. While we isolated the battlefield, in so far as supplies and reinforcements were concerned, we did not always force the Germans to surrender.

What the Air Force did accomplish in Italy was this: It made it impossible for one of the best organized, best disciplined armies in the world to offer prolonged resistance to determined offensive on the ground—even in country as naturally suited for defense as German-held Italy was. On occasions, air power virtually eliminated an entire German army as an effective fighting force. By dominating the air and the battlefield in the enemy's rear, the U.S. Air Force made it possible for our Army to make its own disposition in supply and administrative arrangements in the most convenient manner. We had harbors and railroads working to capacity, and airfields packed with airplanes, all without any serious opposition, because we dominated the air.

To be sure, there were occasions when the German Air Force was still a nuisance; when it would sink an occasional ship with important cargo; when casualties were caused by a sneak raid. But once we had secured a lodgement for our planes, the Germans did not operate an Air Force in Italy. When we were operating against the eight German divisions still south of Rome at the end, we cut practically every railroad and road south of the Pisa-Rimini line. We even attacked important railroad centers north of the Apennines. We were destroying motor transports on the road at the rate of twenty to thirty a day, which represented a monthly loss of 50 per cent of all the motor transportation available to the Germans in Italy. Yet, somehow or other, those eight divisions held out and fought—fought well—for a remarkably long time.

There came a time, in 1942–43, when quite a commotion was raised about the rank of General Marshall, Admiral King, Admiral Leahy, and myself. It was based primarily and ostensibly upon the fact that, here we were—I, a Lieutenant General, General Marshall a four-star General, King a four-star Admiral, Leahy a four-star Admiral, doing business with our opposites on the British Staff who were either First Lords of the Admiralty, Field Marshals, or Air Chief Marshals, each with a five-star rank.

In my own case, rank never meant an awful lot to me. As Assistant Chief of the Air Corps during World War I, I was a Colonel when we had a strength of some 157,000 officers and men. Later on, I was senior air officer in southern California where I was pretty nearly always doing business with Admirals—and I was a Major. Sometime later, I was commanding what amounted to a Wing of the Air Force, operating in an area which covered everything between the Rocky Mountains and the Pacific Coast, and, in addition, was responsible for thirty C.C.C. camps— and I was a Lieutenant Colonel. When I went to England, as Chief of the Air Corps, I had two stars, but I found myself doing business with Air Chief Marshals, Field Marshals, and Fleet Admirals—men who had five stars and whose chests were bedecked with medals from one side to the other. I had two medals on my chest and two stars on my shoulders. As I said before, rank didn't mean much to me, but I did see the necessity for increased rank for Admiral Leahy and General Marshall. Marshall was in charge of an army of about eight million men. Usually, he was spokesman at our conferences. He was adviser to the President on military matters. He was also adviser to the Prime Minister, and at times gave advice to Stalin and to Chiang Kai-shek. Under those circumstances, he was entitled to increased rank; Admiral Leahy, as Chairman of our conferences, was also entitled to it. By the same token, the vast responsibilities of General MacArthur, Admiral Nimitz and Admiral Halsey in the Pacific, and of Eisenhower, who was leading an army in Europe much larger than that commanded by General Pershing, gave them a similar claim to top rank.

I know for a fact that General Marshall never agitated for the five-star rank for himself or for any of the other members of the Combined Chiefs of Staff. His attitude was one of, "I will accept it if the country gives it to me, but I will not go out and make an issue of it." I took the same attitude. As the campaign for higher rank progressed, however, in 1943, additional people entered the fight. Sketches were even drawn up indicating the kind of insignia that five-star generals and admirals should wear. These sketches, when they came over to the War Department, received very little attention from General Marshall. It wasn't until Congress finally acted upon the recommendation of the Secretary of War and the Secretary of the Navy for the five-star rank, that General Marshall paid any attention to the shape and form of the five-star insignia. Then he decided that a circular group of five small stars was a very fitting insignia for a five-star general or admiral. Later on, several of us talked to him about a small insignia of some kind to balance the stars. We pointed out that the Field Marshals all had, in addition to the crossed baton and sword, some other insignia, like a crown, pip, or something above it for balance.

After quite a session in his office, it was decided that perhaps the coat of arms of the United States above the five stars would look very nice and be appropriate. So the combination of the stars and the coat of arms was adopted as the insignia for the five-star rank.

In early 1944, war in Europe, in so far as the Western Front was concerned, had slowed down. In Italy, after the capture of the line along the Garigliano River to Pescara, there was not much forward motion for a period of about six months—not until the time of our landing in Normandy.

Eisenhower had been relieved of the Mediterranean Command by Sir Henry Maitland Wilson, whose deputy was Lieutenant General Devers, of the U.S. Army. Spaatz had been reassigned to London as Commanding General of the new setup to be called USSTAF (United States Strategic Air Forces) with operational control of the heavy bombers of the Fifteenth Air Force in Italy, as well as the Eighth's in Britain. Major General Fred L. Anderson was designated his Deputy Commander for Operations. Jimmy Doolittle had taken over the Eighth Air Force, succeeding Eaker, who had been moved down to command the Mediterranean Air Force, under General Wilson. General Twining, who had been operating in the Pacific, was brought to Italy and given command of the Fifteenth Strategic Air Force, and General Cannon was continued in command of the Twelfth Air Force.

In the meantime, in Sicily, Sardinia, and Pantelleria—which island had been the first to surrender to air attack alone—military operations had all been completed. A new arrangement of supplies, equipment, and materiel was being built up in order to take care of Operation OVERLORD, the main cross-Channel assault, and of ANVIL. Operation ANVIL, the code name for the landing in southern France in the vicinity of the Toulon-Marseilles area, was not to take place until sometime after OVERLORD had been launched.

☆ 27 ☆

At dawn on the 6th of June, 1944, the people in the inland villages of France, many of whom had risked their lives to hide our shot-down flyers, knew it was D-Day. Just before the landings six B-17's of Major Earle E. Aber's veteran 422nd Squadron flew unescorted over the Invasion Coast, fanned out singly and swept over towns and villages, dropping pamphlets to warn the French people to seek safety in the open fields and remain away from the highways. The long-awaited day of liberation had come at last!

Following it breathlessly, at home, minute by minute, the thoughts of America were too much with the men going through the Normandy surf for a remarkable thing to get much notice. The final bombs that paved the way for them, dropping only a few yards ahead of the first men to hit the beaches, went down through a solid overcast of clouds, without, as Larry Kuter wrote, "so much as scratching the paint on a single rowboat in that packed armada below." Long ago our scientists had taken from Hitler even the comfort of bad weather.

Realizing full well the implications that might follow Eisenhower's successful landing in Normandy, a Combined Chiefs of Staff meeting had been scheduled for London in June, 1944.

General Marshall and I took off in a C-54, headed for London. About a hundred miles out from Stevensville, Newfoundland, and for about fifty miles on, we passed over icebergs, some so big that they had their own lakes within their surfaces. We went through, above, and under overcast and undercast, with blue sky and full moon, bumpy clouds, smooth riding and rough, and finally, we went to bed at 3:00 A.M.

When we awakened we were told we would land in thirty-five minutes. Through occasional breaks in the clouds, we could see Ireland, but we were held over Prestwick above the clouds for an hour and thirty minutes before we could get down. Three planes below us were waiting to come in. The ceiling was so low that one of them made a pass at the field and couldn't make it.

So we were sent to a base on the northwest tip of Wales, 150 miles from Prestwick, Valley Station, an Air Transport Command base through which war-weary personnel returned to the United States.

Wales was rainy and cloudy. From Valley Station we went to London on the "Irish Mail," on which we had a private car. When we landed at London, we found blue skies and sunshine—Sir Alan Brooke, Sir Charles Portal, Admiral of the Fleet Sir Andrew Cunningham, General Handy, General Ismay, General Spaatz, and many others waiting for us on the platform. General Kuter and Colonel McCarthy had also flown down from Prestwick to meet us. I drove to my billet with General Spaatz, so tired that I actually went to sleep in the car while talking with him. Two and a half hours' sleep out of twenty-four did not go with me any more. We were put up in a beautifully furnished house at Staines, southwest of London, belonging to a Mr. Gibson, a wealthy engineer who had built many of the big dams on the Nile.

That night at dinner, conversation with General Bedell Smith and General Bull brought us up to date on the status of affairs in France. Next morning, at his headquarters, we talked over the war with General Eisenhower and his staff, and found them all very optimistic about our progress on the beachheads.

We also learned that the German Air Force had been conspicuous by its absence. The airmen cited an instance, during the landings, where 19 JU-88's had met up with 12 Spitfires. All the JU-88's had been shot down—no Spitfires lost. In another case, 39 German torpedo bombers, headed from South France for the beachhead, had run into their own flak. Four were shot down and 10 more turned back. The remaining 5 continued for a spell; then they apparently got tired, and turned back. This, at the moment our troops were landing on the invasion beaches.

The big question was: "What had happened to the German Air Force?" We knew we had defeated the Luftwaffe, but even half an Air Force would at least have tried to bomb those ports in southern England crowded with landing craft of all kinds, piled up high with supplies. Instead of that, no attacks had been made on the installations prior to D-Day, nor on the boats going across the Channel during the assault, nor on the beachheads after the invasion. Had our daylight bombing been effective? Had our plans for "round-the-clock" bombing of Germany borne fruit? We needed no further proof.

We had a Combined Chiefs of Staff meeting in London the day after our arrival, with the regular personnel present, to discuss the progress of the war in France, Italy, Burma, the Southwest Pacific, the Pacific, China, and in Russia. One of the subjects brought up was the traffic over the Hump into China. I was glad to be able to report that the Air Transport Command had carried over 11,000 tons during the preceding month. It looked as though we might reach 16,000 tons for July.

We discussed future operations in North Burma; also, cargo-plane requirements for the British troops near Imphal. All these problems were much easier to solve than they would have been six months or a year before, because we were getting real airplane production now; in fact, most of the theaters were becoming saturated, and the demands for airplanes were being met everywhere. We considered the possibilities of the next meeting, including an agenda, and the trip of the Prime Minister, with General Marshall, Admiral King, and myself, to the beachhead.

One of the points at issue was, "What reserve of gasoline should be carried in the different theaters?" I knew that in the Pacific Theater they had to get along on less than two months' reserve of gasoline; that in the Mediterranean they maintained less than six weeks' supply; but I also knew the British demanded that they have a six months' store of our gasoline in England at all times. This I could not understand, for whereas it required several weeks to get the gasoline from the United States to the Mediterranean, or to the South Pacific, it took only ten days to get it to England. So, in spite of British arguments, we planned to cut down their extra stock of gasoline to a three months' reserve. Spaatz and Knerr agreed there was no objection to this reduction.

Next morning, June 11th, Admiral King and I decided to go to SHAEF, General Eisenhower's headquarters, to bring ourselves up to date on the war picture. It had been suggested that the information would be six hours later if we went to Air Marshal Leigh-Mallory's headquarters than if we went to Eisenhower's. We started, after assuring ourselves that the aide and the chauffeur knew the route. It was supposed to be only twenty minutes from the Gibson house. After forty-five minutes we had not yet arrived, and we asked airmen, soldiers, "bobbies," and civilians, all to no avail. We finally returned to the Gibson's house without ever reaching our destination, and with no new war information. Admiral King was somewhat irked.

When we got back, we found that General Marshall had not yet returned from Chequers, where he had gone to visit the Prime Minister. At 1:30 we had lunch with the Combined Chiefs of Staff, and then another Combined Chiefs of Staff meeting where we made preparations for the trip across the Channel to the beachhead the following day.

At eight o'clock that night we were to depart on the Prime Minister's train, but the train was late, and for forty minutes we sat in the station— General Marshall, General Kuter, Admiral King, and I. Ultimately the train arrived and we had dinner on it. In the dining car were Mr. Churchill, his aide, Field Marshall Smuts, and Mr. Martin, secretary to the Prime Minister, awaiting our party. Everybody was in a jovial mood at dinner. At 11:00 P.M., the Prime Minister said that since we had to get up early we had better go to bed. All were up next morning at 5:30. Before separating, we discussed how we would return to London. Marshall and King wanted to come back on a destroyer and on the Prime Minister's train—four hours on the destroyer, and seven hours on the train. I wanted to spend more time on the beachhead and return by plane —one hour and thirty minutes.

At Portsmouth, General Eisenhower met our train. We found Portsmouth Harbor jammed with ships. We boarded a destroyer, the U.S.S. *Thompson,* and left the harbor, traveling at 30 knots. Hundreds of ships of all kinds, escorted and proceeding singly, moving en masse. I had never seen such a jam of ships before; but they all moved on, unimpeded, headed toward the French beachhead—and without a sign of a German airplane overhead! It certainly was a tribute to the work the British and the American Air Forces had done in preparing for this landing.

If there ever was a bomber's paradise, it was the harbor of Portsmouth and other harbors along the English coast, and this unprecedented mass of ships, moving from England across the Channel and concentrated along the coast of France. Literally hundreds of ships were anchored offshore. What a field day it would have been for the German Air Force, had there been one. One plane coming in couldn't miss, even by skip bombing. It could have hit one ship with every bomb. Every once in a while, there was an explosion; but it wasn't from enemy bombs. It was the sound of German mines being detonated by the clean-up squads.

We left the destroyer and went aboard a sub-chaser, Admiral Kirk and Admiral Hall joined us. We saw the first of the harbors formed by a breakwater improvised with a long line of floating tanks. This line of steel tanks was backed by sixteen ships sunk, bow to stern, headed by the British battleship *Centurion* and the cruiser *Phoenix.*

Closer in to shore, a dock had been made with tremendous blocks of hollow concrete sixty feet high. Each block had been towed across the Channel and sunk in line to form the harbor and the pier. Inside that breakwater, and tied up to the pier, were ships of all kinds. There were our old friends, the cruisers *Augusta* and *Tuscaloosa;* American battleships; British and American destroyers; Liberty ships; tankers; LST's and LC ships; "Ducks" and "Crocodiles," going and coming, pushing up to the beach to unload; a few broken in half by mines; some wrecked on the beach.

We could see trucks on the beach, being driven from the LST's up a road to a cliff beyond. There was the ever-present sound of explosions as the bomb-disposal squads of the Engineers continued to set off German mines.

After a tour of the harbor, a Duck came alongside and we started toward the beach. The tide was low, and we hit the top of an obstruction. Fortunately, no mines were attached to it, so we slid off and continued through more obstacles to the beach, passing wrecks and ships unloading. When we climbed out on the beach, we were met by Generals Bradley, Quesada, Royce, and Corlett, and many other old friends.

We piled into jeeps and cars and went up to the landing strip. Then General Marshall, Admiral King, Ike, and I went aboard a C-53, filled with wounded—17 of them. We said "Hello" to those who could speak, and we talked with the nurses. The way those nurses went about their business, taking care of the men almost within speaking distance of the front line, was inspiring.

We went on to General Bradley's headquarters by way of the Field Hospital. A German Battery of 155's was still in position—one piece destroyed by a thermite bomb; others O.K. The Germans had left in such a hurry that they hadn't had a chance to take the cattle or chickens belonging to the French farmers with them; the livestock and fowl were still on the farms. The crops were untouched. The telephone and telegraph lines were not destroyed. The roads and bridges were still in place. Relatively few mines had been planted.

After lunch with Generals Eisenhower, Bradley, Courtney, Hodges, Collins, and Gerow, I left with Larry Kuter and Pete Quesada to visit the Air Force Headquarters and some of its components. We soon would have four landing strips. One was being used now; one more would be available that night; two more would be ready in forty-eight hours. There were hundreds of U.S. planes around, but not a single

Luftwaffe plane yet! Four thousand U.S. and R.A.F. planes were in the air that day, hunting for the German Air Force!

We returned to the airport on the beach late in the evening and flew toward England over the ship concentrations. It was a wonderful but terrifying sight. To think what a few German bombers could have done!

Next morning, we went to General Eisenhower's headquarters and had a long conversation with Eisenhower and General "Beedle" Smith, after which we went to London for a meeting of the Combined Chiefs of Staff. We had lunch with the British Chiefs of Staff at 1:30. That afternoon, we went over the messages covering the operations, which the Combined Chiefs of Staff were to send to General Wilson and General Eisenhower. Apparently the messages to Wilson and Eisenhower had been changed by the Prime Minister, and the British Chiefs of Staff didn't want to change them back to the original form until they had received Mr. Churchill's blessing. However, this was finally agreed to, and the messages were sent off.

General Marshall and I took off in the afternoon with General Fred Anderson, since January Spaatz' deputy commander for operations, in a Lockheed, to visit some of our combat units. First we saw the 91st Heavy Group—B-17's; then the 325th Fighter Group—P-51's; then the 355th Medium Bombardment Group—B-26's. Doolittle went around with us. When we left Fighter Command, we picked up General Kepner, and he too accompanied us.

On this trip I had one of those encounters that make you feel your age. At Bassingbourne I shook hands with Colonel Ross Milton, a boy whom I had known when he was growing up with my own boys at Fort Riley. Now Ross was a Lieutenant Colonel and Group Executive of a heavy bombardment outfit. Eight months before he had led the 91st on the second Schweinfurt mission, when 60 B-17's were lost. There was still a German Air Force that day!

As I went through from group to group, I couldn't find anything these boys wanted that they didn't have. They seemed to have all the planes, all the crews, and all the parts they needed.

The following morning, I had a conference with Spaatz, Brereton, Doolittle, Knerr, Anderson, and Vandenberg to find out what, if anything, we could do to improve our operations. I received some good ideas, and then I had to rush to meet the King. I was with him from 12:15 until 1:07 P.M., and this time, I knew better how to go in to see His Majesty, and how to take my leave of him, than on my first visit.

Next afternoon we had a Combined Chiefs of Staff meeting, which lasted until five o'clock. We got back to the Gibson house at 5:30, and at 8:15, went to No. 10 Downing Street where we had dinner with the King and the Prime Minister. Also present were: Field Marshal Smuts; Air Chief Marshal Portal; General "Pug" Ismay; Sir Alan Brooke; Admiral King; Admiral Cunningham; Deputy Prime Minister Atlee; and Mr. Menzies, Aide to the King.

The dinner was quite an affair. Both the King and the Prime Minister were in good form. One of the subjects brought up by the Prime Minister was—and I couldn't make out whether he was really serious or whether he was throwing out a "feeler"—that constituents of either democracy, England or America, should be able to go to the other country and become citizens under local law. We had toasts, more toasts, and discussions, until 1:00 A.M., when the King, who was sitting next to me, turned to me and said, "Doesn't anyone ever go to bed around here? How long do we sit up and wait?"

I said, "Well, your Majesty, you are the one to set the pace."

The King turned to the Prime Minister and repeated his question. Said the Prime Minister, "It is early yet; we still have a lot to talk about." So we kept on talking!

Three years before, when I had been at Buckingham Palace after a German bombardment, the windows of the Palace had been blown out and the draft in the halls had made it a cheerless place. The King had talked with me anxiously about how long it would be before we would be able to get air and other assistance to England to change the character of the war, to swing the tide in favor of the Allies. In 1944, the tide had now swung, and the King's attitude was different. And not only his. Over all the people in England had come a transformation, for now there was no German threat from the land, the sea, or the air.

Or so it had seemed until two nights ago. On the night of the 12th, at 11:45, there had been an air raid alarm, but we couldn't figure out its meaning. At 5:30 in the morning, there was a long series of explosions following one another in quick succession, most of them several miles from the Gibson house, but a few very close by. The charges were quite heavy and we couldn't figure out what they were. Bombs? Rockets? Something with delayed fuses? What were they? I ran out of the house to see. A pilotless plane was flying through the air, circling right above the Gibson house. It just missed the house. It came down out of the clouds in a dive, leveled off, made a low turn, then crashed into the ground and exploded about a mile and a half away! The force of the explosion lifted most of the Staff out of their beds. About seven of these missiles hit within five miles of our house. It looked, as a matter of fact, as if the Germans might have heard that the American Chiefs of Staff were living in the Gibson house and had selected that locality as the center of impact for their first V-1 attack.

After that, the V-1's came over with regular frequency throughout the day—one about every five minutes. I drove over to see the destruction caused by one of them. It had landed in an orchard, about 100 yards from a small village. The explosion had knocked out all the window panes and crushed in the roofs; blown down a few trees, and made a crater about six feet across and four or five feet deep; but had done no other damage. As nearly as I could judge, the gadget (V-1) weighed not more than two thousand pounds, carried probably not more than 500 pounds of explosive. It was obviously made of pressed steel, had a 26-foot wing spread, was jet propelled, and had an autogiro pilot.

This particular "drone" had come down through the clouds in a dive with a dead engine, then leveled off and made a semicircular course before it hit the ground. Around the crater were the steel cylinder. a fuselage still bolted together, steel sheet wings; jet tubing from the engine; hundreds of feet of flexible cable; insulating tubing; hundreds of small, finger-sized dry batteries; actuating valves; bell cranks for controls; many small pieces of metal, $1\frac{1}{2}''$ square; synthetic rubber gaskets; very sturdy pieces of metal, probably from the main cylinder; pieces of wing, one part of which looked as if it had been perforated by antiaircraft fire; and many pieces of what might have been smaller cylinders.

Later, the Prime Minister asked for my reaction to the V-1 attacks. I replied, "If the Germans were as efficient as we were in our fabrication, they could produce these V-1's with about 2000 man-hours and at a cost of about $600. They could launch them from tracks at the rate of about one every two minutes, per track. They could turn them out, headed toward England at the rate of 14,000 in twenty-four hours, which would cause great consternation, and finally, might even break down normal life in Britain." I might have added that, if concentrated on central spots, they could even dislocate the war effort. No one could predict where they would hit. You could only hear and see them coming with a noise like an outboard motorboat. They were difficult to dodge. Later, one went over General Eisenhower's headquarters while we were there. I wondered if the Germans had followed this thing through, or if, in their desperation, they had started using the V-1's before they had enough to send over at regular intervals in large numbers. We knew that during the past nine months we had knocked out many of the launching sites themselves. That may have explained the delay in launching their attack until after we had made our landing. In any event, we had not been able to destroy enough of their launching platforms. The air raid alarms and the explosions continued, and there were about 200 casualties from V-1's that day.

The morning after the dinner with the King, June 15th, we finally landed at Leigh-Mallory's headquarters. I met Air Marshal Harris, Air Marshal Douglas, Air Marshal Roderick Hill, and all the American Air Staff, and heard their presentations. I had to leave before the meeting was over, for I was due at Portal's office at noon. Changing problems would face the two Air Forces as the Allied armies reached their objectives; the imminent movement of certain parts of our Air Forces into Germany; changes in targets.

After lunch at the Dorchester with Portal and his wife, Portal and I returned to the Air Ministry at 2:30 where we had a conference with Air Marshal Courtney, Chief of R.A.F. Supply. Then, at 3:30, followed a Combined Chiefs of Staff meeting, where we talked over the Pacific and Southeast Asia situations. This time we had an excellent meeting without dissensions. Everybody agreed with our plans for licking the Japanese. We adjourned at 5:30, after one of the best conferences the Combined Chiefs of Staff ever had; no acrimonious discussions, no discord, no scrapping—and nobody rolled out on a stretcher under a sheet!

General Marshall, Admiral King, and I went to Eisenhower's headquarters, where we talked over the V-1's, the war, and the problem caused by de Gaulle, and sent a message to the President.

During lunch with Ike, I talked over with him and with Beedle Smith the current air organization. Both agreed to a reorganization which would provide for American control over a fast-growing, very efficient, more effective Army Air Force. They did not see the need for so many R.A.F. officers divided between Brereton and Ike. We had a strong Air Force and had demonstrated we knew as much about operations now as the R.A.F. Therefore, we should control our own operations.

At this lunch, too, I learned more about these things then called the "drones." They had a speed of about 340 miles per hour; they were picked up by British radio and plotted on their take-off. Most of them came from the Calais area. R.A.F. planes had shot down twelve; four in the night and eight during the day. All exploded in the air when hit. These were their general characteristics: they had a long nose and

rectangular wings; weighed about two tons; had a spread of about
16 feet, a length of about 25 feet; their range was about 200 miles; they
could go up to about 5000 feet. They were mid-wing, steel-structure
monoplanes, simple to design and easy to assemble. Their rudder and
elevator were operated by a pneumatic servo unit, coupled to an automatic
pilot, monitored by a magnetic compass. Their range was governed by
a clock which shut off the gasoline. The warhead was comparable to the
1000-kg. German regulation bomb, equipped with a sensitive impact
fuse. We knew later that between the 12th of June and the 13th of July
they had launched some 3450 of them, but 30 per cent of them failed to
cross the Channel. We knew of fifty sites in France from which they had
launched from 150 to 170 per day.

That afternoon we said our good-bys at the Gibson's house. Admiral
King left at noon for Plymouth on his way to Iran. General Marshall
and I started for Chequers and arrived there at 7:30 for a visit with the
Prime Minister and Mrs. Churchill. We had a fine dinner and a very
pleasant talk. I told Mrs. Churchill about the ride in an ox cart my wife
and I had had from the dock at Guam to the little town of Agana when
we landed there on our honeymoon. She said, "Tell Mrs. Arnold when
Winnie and I were on our honeymoon we visited Venice. I wanted to
ride in a gondola; he insisted on a motor launch—said it was far more
healthy; the fumes killed the germs, and so on. So we rode in a gasoline
launch! There is not much romance in Winnie." I told her the ride in
the ox cart had been a very, very pleasant one.

We said good-by to the Prime Minister and Mrs. Churchill, and took
off from Chequers, arriving at Bovingdon to take our airplane. With
good flying we landed at the Naples airport at 6:10 P.M. the next day,
where General Eaker, General Devers, and Field Marshal Wilson met
us officially. My son, Hank, was there to meet me, personally. At Wilson's
headquarters we had a conference on the war, and on the part the air
would play in landing in southern France.

The main problem was in determining the size of the Air Force and
the source from which we would get the planes. At that time, while the
British and Americans had over 1400 Allied planes in Italy, there were
less than 200 German airplanes in the Italian Theater. Obviously, there
should be no difficulty in getting enough airplanes from the Allied Command in Italy to cover the next invasion.

Next day, General Marshall, General Barr, General Devers, General
Handy, Colonel McCarthy, Hank, and I flew over the Salerno beaches
and up to Anzio.

Hank had been on the Anzio beachhead and I was anxious to have him take me around and show me what he had done; where he had landed, and so forth. We landed on the beachhead airstrip and saw the wounded being taken off by the hundreds in C-47's. We saw the foxholes and tunnels the men had lived in; as many shell holes as there were square yards on the beach. It made one wonder how anybody had remained alive. The saving grace seemed to be that there was no shortage of supplies.

Marshall went to the cemetery to pay his respects at the grave of his stepson who had been killed during the landing operations. Handy, Hank, and I went down to the port. It was a wreck. But by tearing down houses to make a water front, and using LCT's and LST's and bringing them up to the sea wall, it was possible to unload 1000 tons a day normally, and up to 3000 tons a day in a pinch. Four ships, at that time, were lying offshore, heavy seas preventing unloading.

We saw thousands and thousands of tons of supplies the German Air Force could have destroyed if they had had an Air Force. Everywhere were ships and supplies, and no one paying much attention to any protection from air attack. We returned to the airstrip and talked with the officers and men of the Photo Squadron who were doing a grand job in their P-38's. Then, with Marshall, who had rejoined us, I walked across the field to pay a visit to the sick and the wounded in the twenty ambulances waiting to unload patients on planes. We visited every ambulance in turn, and spoke to the men. Finally we came to one man who wasn't the least bit bashful; he was eager and waiting for us to ask him where he was from. "Texas!" he cried. "By God, I am from Dallas!"

Then we took off from Rome, and flew over the marshaling yard and the river Tiber (about as wide as Constitution Avenue in Washington). After we landed at the airport, Marshall departed with Generals Clark, Handy, Barr and Colonel McCarthy. Generals Eaker, Cannon, Johnson, Saville, and I took off in another direction. That night, I heard Clark, Truscutt, Wilson, and Alexander all say that without our air operations, success of the Italian Campaign would not have been possible.

Next afternoon we drove to Rome and picked up an Italian colonel who acted as a guide for us through the city. He said he had been a patriot partisan, doing undercover work during the German occupation. He took us through the Forum, the different arches, St. Peter's the amphitheaters, and finally, to the marshaling yard.

One of the hottest potatoes I had had to handle during the war was the mission of our bombers in support of the Allied troops moving up through Italy. We had finally come to the conclusion that if our bombers could cut the railroads running north and south in Italy, all supplies to Kesselring's army would be stopped. Then had arisen the question of bombing the marshaling yard in Rome. Through the President and the Secretary of War, influences from all sides were brought to bear to prevent me from bombing Rome. I told them I was confident we could hit the railroad yard, destroy it, and thus cut that last link between north and south Italy without badly damaging a single church. If we destroyed that yard it would be impossible for Kesselring's army to receive any supplies except by road, and I was convinced that our light bombers and fighters could take care of the road traffic. Finally, very reluctantly, we were given the necessary authority. Now I saw that we had destroyed the marshaling yard and made it look as if it had been shaken by a gigantic earthquake, without extending the damage to the city outside. With the exception of a few buildings close to the railroad tracks which had been hit by fragments, there was no evidence in the vicinity of any bombing. Miraculously, we hit but one church, and that only slightly. We had cut the last railroad link between north and south Italy.

Later in the day we drove to Viterbo. It was a terrible sight! Scattered all along the way, on both sides of the road, were thousands of tanks and vehicles, from the big "Tiger" with its 88-mm. gun to the baby size; trucks, large and small; half-tracks; passenger cars; lorries; buses; rolling kitchens; gasoline drums; trucks loaded with everything—typewriters, food, some burned, some half consumed. In most cases, the rubber tires were off the wheels of vehicles.

Here and there bridges were blown out by bombs, roads made impassable, as at Viterbo itself, where a tunnel was blocked by our bombing, completely cutting off the railroad. Towns held by Germans as strong points were turned into piles of rubble and débris. Our fighters and bombers had changed those German divisions from crack combat units into panic-stricken men rushing northward to escape capture. What a comparison with the German Air Force in the heyday of its power!

Returning to Rome, we took a plane to Naples and flew over Cassino and the Abbey; two more monuments to destruction. Here and there it was foggy. "Sunny Italy" was not as sunny as the prewar tourist agencies had led us to believe, or as we had hoped to find it when we moved our heavy bombers there. We heard later that this was supposed to have been the worst winter in forty-seven years. (One might have thought he was in California!)

That afternoon I went to Eaker's office, and heard his excellent presentation in his War Room. I saw Generals Marriner, Twining, and

Born and other commanders of the Fifteenth Air Force and had lunch with them. Following a conference attended by all Eaker's senior officers and commanders, at which I gave them an outline of our world-wide air problems and an estimate of troubles brewing in the future, I went back for a meeting with General Marshall, Admiral King, Field Marshal Wilson, Air Marshal Coningham, Air Marshal Slessor, General Devers, General Brooke, General Kuter, and General Eaker. We went into plans for future operations of Wilson's forces and their effect upon Eisenhower's operations; and the movement up through southern France.

That night there was a dinner which lasted until late. Present were Ambassadors Kirk and Murphy, General Marshall, Field Marshal Wilson, General Alexander, General Devers, General Eaker, General Twining, General Cannon, General Kuter, Air Marshal Slessor, General Barr, and myself. I had a long talk with General Alexander about de Gaulle and his place in French affairs, and about the fighting efficiency of the German Army. I was apprehensive that the German Army might collapse suddenly before we were ready to take advantage of the break, as the German Air Force had. Alexander thought that while the complete disintegration had not yet started, the German Army had begun to topple. It was not fighting with the same vim. It lacked leadership; particularly leadership in the noncommissioned officer grade. It was short of supplies.

As to de Gaulle, Alexander agreed with our ideas. De Gaulle, in his opinion, was a selfish, egotistical man who was interfering with our operations without considering whether his actions were hampering the Allied commanders or not. He gave two instances: (1) de Gaulle branded the franc which the Allied Army was using in France as counterfeit, and circulated that idea among the French. Yet those francs had the backing of the U.S. and the British Government. France had neither francs nor a government; (2) de Gaulle refused to permit the trained French liaison officers to accompany the Allied forces into France. There were some 200 of these, but none of them went into France. De Gaulle was a fine patriot, I am sure, but was no help to Alexander, and not much help to Eisenhower during the final phases of "The Liberation."

Next morning, after saying good-by to Eaker, Devers, Barr, and Edwards, General Marshall and I took off for Casablanca at 3:30 A.M. On board the plane was a stack of newspapers, all dated June 16th, carrying, as the main news item, the B-29 operations over Japan.

The general impression among the higher officers of the Allied Command was that the high command of the German Air Force had made one blunder after another—not only in the technique of employment but also in their command strategy. However, our people did not hold the German Air Force Command and staff completely responsible. They thought "our secret weapon" was Hitler. Hence, "do not bomb his castle; do not let him get hurt; we want him to continue making mistakes."

Our Ground Force officers were beginning to form a similar opinion of the Fuehrer's decisions affecting the German Army. He was making the same mistakes with regard to ground dispositions, mistakes that redounded invariably to our advantage.

The weather was perfect as we flew along until we came to a point about 100 miles west of Algiers, when we found ourselves above an overcast. We came down through and started to land at Casablanca, but as we were coming in for a normal landing, out of a clear sky came a P-39 so close to us I thought it was going to hit our C-54!

General Marshall was very much disturbed. I was more than disturbed. How anybody who could fly a P-39 would have the ignorance to approach that close to a large airplane like the C-54, I couldn't understand. So, naturally, when I landed on the airdrome at Casablanca, I was boiling! I called for Malloy, the commanding officer, and asked, and wanted to know, who that man was; where he was! I was told he was a Frenchman. General Marshall listened to everything I had to say. He didn't say a word; just listened. He knew I was boiling mad, though.

Finally I said, "You get hold of the French commander and tell him he doesn't get a single airplane from the Americans from now on until his men learn how to fly, and he teaches them to conform to airdrome regulations. When they do learn to fly and conform to airdrome regulations, we will continue to give them airplanes, and not until then!" General Marshall nodded assent.

We stayed there just long enough for lunch and then took off for Lagens, in the Azores, one of our new fields. There we were met by General A. D. Smith. He drove General Marshall, General Handy, and me over all the island of Terceira, ending up at his quarters for a drink. We then went to the mess hall where we met the R.A.F. commander and had dinner together.

About 35 to 40 planes were passing through the Azores every day on the new runways that had been constructed. The airport had several runways so there were no tie-ups any more, because of cross-winds. Establishment of this new airport on the island of Terceira was one of the best moves we had made, and General Smith deserved a lot of credit for his share in getting it operating.

We took off at 9:15 for Stevensville where next morning we break-fasted at the commanding officer's house, found "yesterday's" Washington newspapers, and several friends en route to England.

We took off for Washington that afternoon in a light rainstorm. The area of bad weather extended all the way from Newfoundland to New York, one cold front after another. As we landed at Washington at 8:30 I was still thinking of what our officers had said in Naples yesterday morning: "Hitler—secret weapon of the Allies."

★ 28 ★

For ninety days prior to the actual landing on the beaches of Normandy, our heavy bombers had pounded the network of rail centers that were vital to the movement of German troops from the Calais coast to Normandy. We created a line of interdiction by cutting the bridges across the Seine River. This was followed by cutting the bridges over the Albert Canal and the Meuse, thus denying the Germans free access to the area between those two rivers. Air attacks were made to give the impression our landing might be made to the northeast of Paris, on the coastline between the mouth of the Seine and Antwerp.

More important still, this aerial bombardment cut the bridges and roads in the whole region and prevented a large part of the German Army from moving to Normandy, except on foot. On D-Day, the beachhead was established, the enemy ground forces forging a ring around the perimeter we had created.

The Air Arm next interdicted the line along the Loire River, completely sealing off the battle area and blocking German attempts to supply and to move reinforcements from the South. Every time the Germans made an attempt by truck or by foot to move troops into that area, they were attacked from the air. As a result, the Allied offensive built up much more rapidly than could the German defense.

On July 25th, some 3000 aircraft—heavies of the Eighth Air Force and the R.A.F., Ninth Air Force mediums, light bombers, and fighters— hit the enemy defenses in a narrow sector along the Periers–St. Lo Road. The break-through thus made possible started the infantry and armor moving swiftly to the south and east. George Patton was on his way.

We can take the work of General O. P. Weyland's "XIX TAC"

with General Patton's Army as typical of all tactical Air Force operations. Once General Patton's Third Army was on the move, there was a continuous protective escort of fighter bombers over each armored division. Every hour a fresh group of planes relieved the preceding flight. Theirs was the duty of preventing attack by enemy Air and of knocking out anything that might hold up the armored columns. Working closely with the tanks through radio communications, the planes destroyed concealed flak guns, marshaling yards, bombed important road and rail junctions, railroad and road traffic, and gave any other support for which they were called upon that would enable the column to keep moving.

General Patton knew, by the time he reached the Loire River, that the Germans had a minimum of about 30,000 troops south of that river, and to General Weyland he turned over the task of taking care of his south flank, completely and entirely—certain proof of the confidence Patton had in his air support. This was about eleven days after the break-through from the Normandy beachhead. Weyland's fighter bombers were able to dissuade that enemy force from moving further north, either to attack Patton's Army or to try to join the other German Armies, with which it was intended to make contact. As Patton moved farther eastward, the enemy air activity became severer, and Weyland found it necessary to divert some of his planes from ground targets to air-to-air fighting, as well as to increase the bombing of the Luftwaffe's remaining airdromes.

But the Eighth Air Force had not left much Luftwaffe to interfere with Opie Weyland's continuous wrecking of rail and road traffic. Flak was now the worst enemy for his crews.

On a single day, as Patton swept on toward the Rhine, Weyland's airmen destroyed 29 locomotives, 137 freight cars, 195 motor vehicles, 10 fuel and ammunition vehicles, 16 horse-drawn wagons, 17 tanks, 11 flak positions, and 5 fuel dumps.

Another phase of the aerial effort was to cooperate with the ground troops in every way in annihilating those sections of the German Army which were cut off in "pockets," like the big one at Falaise. When the First Army joined with the Third Army, near Argentan and pocketed some 57,000 Germans, Weyland's Air Force came in to help force their surrender. In one day, he destroyed 400 to 500 enemy vehicles, burning and blowing them up. One German officer, in surrendering, said: "You have bombed and strafed all the roads, causing complete congestion and heavy traffic jams; you have also destroyed most of our petrol and oil dumps, so there is no future in continuing to fight."

By August 25th, the German Fighter Force in France was practically a thing of the past. On that day the IX and XIX Tactical Air Commands destroyed a total of 127 planes—77 in the air and 50 on the ground. General Patton commended the XIX Tactical Air Command in the following words:

The superior efficiency and cooperation afforded this Army by the forces under your command are the best examples of the combined use of air and ground troops I have ever witnessed.

Due to the tireless efforts of your flyers, large movements of hostile vehicles and troop concentrations ahead of our advancing columns have been harassed or obliterated. The information passed directly to the heads of the columns from the air has saved time and lives.

I am voicing the opinion of all the officers and men in this Army when I express to you our admiration and appreciation of your magnificent efforts.

At our London conference, Project ANVIL—the landing in southern France—had been scheduled for about the 15th of August. All landing craft were assembled; all supplies were in place and most of the ships were partially loaded, when early in August the Prime Minister wanted to divert the operations from the landing in southern France to a landing in Brittany. At that time, the ships were in position in the Mediterranean. Everything was ready to start landing operations.

We had made no plans for a landing in Brittany, and we did not know how long it would take to put the ports in Brittany in usable condition after capture; we had not studied the operation. But Churchill sent a message to his Chiefs of Staff in Washington, asking for the change. The British Chiefs of Staff backed the Prime Minister, but the President backed the American Chiefs of Staff. In the end, Churchill graciously accepted the decision we had made, and in a message to the President, said: "I pray to God that you may be right. We shall, of course, do everything in our power to help you achieve success."

So on the 15th of August, the Seventh Army, under Lieutenant General Alexander M. Patch, made its landings in southern France, in the vicinity of Toulon and Cannes. The air offensive conducted by the Strategic Air Forces prepared the way for the invasion and supported the Army in its landings and in its movements from the coast to the north.

The Allied Airborne Army, under General Brereton, also took part in the invasion of Normandy and southern France, as it had earlier in Sicily and Italy. Its employment, however, was not altogether in accord with the Air Force's concept of airborne operations. We accepted the parachute and glider landings as carried out in Sicily, in Italy, and in southern France. We also accepted, after considerable protest, the inclusion of two parachute divisions in the components for the invasion of Normandy, but we did not agree with the strategic concept for their use.

It was obvious that General Eisenhower's staff had no intention of using airborne troops except for tactical missions directly in rear of the enemy lines. The Air Force wanted to use these troops strategically, i.e., take a mass—four or five divisions—drop them down in a specially selected transportation center, for example—an area where there were several aviation fields, a locality that would be astride the German lines of communication, a position, the holding of which would make it impossible for the German troops to advance reinforcements and supplies, but definitely an area some distance behind the actual battlefield and beyond the area in which reserves were normally located.

For instance, the spot we had selected in connection with the Battle of Normandy was an area somewhere around Paris, where we believed the dropping of four, five, or six airborne divisions would make it impossible for the Germans to hold out for any length of time against our troops which were then on the beachheads. And the site we had tentatively selected for strategic paratroop operations when our troops reached a position approximately along the Rhine was an area far to the rear of the German lines, about halfway between the Rhine and Berlin— a zone far removed from any German reserves, which contained air-dromes that we could use for supply, reinforcements, and such operations as were deemed necessary.

We presented these ideas to General Marshall, and he in turn asked us to send our planning team to Europe to sell the proposal to General Eisenhower and his staff. We sent them, but we didn't sell the idea to the SHAEF Staff. We felt one of the advantages of these operations would be that the troops would drop in localities where there was no assembly of enemy reserves. We knew that every time we dropped airborne troops directly in the rear of the German lines, the paratroopers came down right in the midst of the reserve German divisions, and the landings of our airborne and glider troops following them in had to be made under the most difficult conditions. The Germans, anticipating this close-in drop, usually set up stakes and wires in the open fields.

Until the end of the war we hoped the time would come when we would be able to try at least one strategic drop—one landing of airborne troops that would have a decisive effect upon German operations, rather than the limited effect of a tactical drop immediately behind the German lines. Kenney had done it once, in the rear of the Japanese lines in a small valley some 100 miles west of Lae (Markam Valley) with amazing success, and we had hoped his example might be a guide for future operations. We were never able to put the idea across.

With the big invasion finally under way, along about the middle of the summer, 1944, I was ready for a change and a rest. Service in Washington, from the start of the war, had been a long, hard grind, during which we—General Marshall and I, and particularly Marshall—had to deal with all kinds of intricate and complicated problems. Consequently I suggested to him that we take off for a fishing trip in the High Sierras, and he agreed. Before we left Washington, Communications experts made a "dry run" of the whole trip to demonstrate beyond any shadow of a doubt that we could be in constant touch with our headquarters in Washington by radio. A radio set, with an excellent operator, and a Signal Corps officer were to be with us during the entire trip. We landed at Bishop, California, by plane early one morning, and then, accompanied by the local foresters, rode by auto and horseback up into the Sierras. Thereafter, for ten days, the Chief of Staff and the Chief of the Air Forces operated from the High Sierras, directing the war in all parts of the world by radio.

Each morning we rode to a new camp site. About noon, an Army plane, attracted by the colored smoke from a flare at our camp site, would fly in and drop pouches, securely locked. General Marshall and I would go through their contents and then would send out by radio such messages as were necessary. But on one occasion, a young WASP who was flying the courier plane became over-anxious and dropped the pouch into a clump of woods in the mountains, some two miles distant from our signal flare and the little valley where our camp was located. To say there was confusion, apprehension, and concern is putting it mildly, for here were many secrets of the war, lost somewhere up in the High Sierras. We established markers toward the spot where the bag was last seen disappearing behind the mountains, drew lines to the point, made intersecting lines, and people started out by horseback.

One of our party became overly enthusiastic and said he would go to the spot on foot. He thought he would be able to see us up the mountain, though we wouldn't see him, and asked that we keep him on the line to the pouch by directions with flags when he fired a Very pistol. His plan was all right in principle, but it didn't work out in practice. We couldn't see him and he couldn't see us, and every time he fired the Very pistol he started a small forest fire. Before we knew it, we had a half dozen forest fires between us and the place where the pouch was dropped. Each fire had to be extinguished, and there was no way we could get word to him to stop firing that pistol. In time, however, he ran out of ammunition; the horseback riders made their way up over the crest of the mountain, some 7000 feet, and down into the valley beyond, and there, lying next to a creek, was the missing pouch.

After having been out for a period of about ten days, we rode back to Bishop, climbed aboard our airplanes, and returned to Washington. Very few people, even in the War Department or in Washington, knew that the war, as far as we were concerned, had been run from a Command Post 2400 miles from Washington, at altitudes above 10,000 feet, in the middle of an excellent fishing ground. And I am sure the people in the Pentagon got along just as well as if we had been there.

On September 11, about a month after the Allied landing in southern France the Combined Chiefs of Staff again met with the President and the Prime Minister at Quebec, to consider the present situation and make plans for the future. By that time, the Allies had advanced up the Italian Peninsula beyond Rome to the Pisa-Florence Line. In that theater, the German Air Force was practically at its lowest ebb. A total of not more than 200 German airplanes were operating there, and only occasionally at that. In France, Eisenhower's Army had broken through and had started to move toward the German border. The British Army had reached the Albert Canal. Patton's Army had reached the Rhine, in the vicinity of Metz, and the main American Army had reached Luxemburg. General Patch's Army had landed between Toulon and Cannes, had defeated the Germans, and with air support had moved up the Rhone River, reaching a point beyond Lyons. On the 15th of September, the U.S. and French Armies in southern France were combined under the command of General Devers. The Russians were moving toward the west and had reached a point beyond the Warsaw-Budapest Line.

The air-supplied Burma campaign was progressing favorably. In the South Pacific, the Navy force had moved forward; MacArthur had pushed past Finchhafen on New Guinea, and New Britain the year before; in the spring he had reached Biak, and by September, was on the

Island of Morotai, to the west of New Guinea. In the Central Pacific, the Navy had captured Tinian and Saipan in June, 1944, and Guam in July. The Palau Islands fell in September, 1944.

The Twentieth Air Force was being organized very rapidly. We were bringing home experienced commanders and staff officers, squadron leaders, pilots, and mechanics, and putting them in the new B-29 units in order to get the most experienced personnel for the attack into Japan proper from our bases in China and in the Marianas. In spite of the long run from the Chengtu area to Japan, the XX Bomber Command was to increase the tonnage of bombs dropped on Japanese targets from about 200 tons a month, in the middle of 1944, to a maximum of about 2000 tons a month by January-February, 1945. In March, 1945, the XX Bomber Command would leave China and join up with the XXI Bomber Command, forming the Twentieth Air Force in the Mariana Islands.

On the 30th of June, 1944, we had started building our B-29 installations on Saipan. Thirty days later, the field at Saipan was handling Army, Navy, and Marine air traffic for the Central Pacific. Then the Seabees and the Army engineers put the finishing touches on these airdromes to take care of planes as heavy as the B-29's. In November, 1944, we would make our first bombing raid from the Saipan fields.

This, then, was the general situation when the Combined Chiefs of Staff arrived at Quebec for the OCTAGON Conference. Prior to the meeting of the main body, Air Chief Marshal Portal and I had a session in which he asked for more C-54's—two per month—to put on a run between Ceylon and Australia. He wanted the command of the Strategic Air Forces changed to provide for a Committee of the R.A.F. and A.A.F., operating under Portal and Arnold for the Combined Chiefs of Staff; he also wanted a British commanding officer for the American forces under Mountbatten; and he wanted Lancasters to operate against Japan. He said the new Lancasters had had additional tanks put on them which would give them a much longer range and would make the missions possible. Since most of these items would influence, or interfere with, our global operations, I could not agree to any of them at that time, but said I would talk them over with my fellow Joint Chiefs of Staff members.

That night, at a dinner with the Governor General, the question of aid to Poland came up. Several messages arrived from the Russians and from Harriman relating to Polish patriots in Warsaw. General Marshall and I talked this over at length. For some time it had been apparent that if some help was not given to the Polish patriots in Warsaw they would be exterminated. The last time the R.A.F. had sent supplies to them by air they had lost some 48 planes, or about 35 per cent of the total number involved. Furthermore, refugee Germans, not Polish people, had gathered and collected most of the supplies the R.A.F. had dropped by parachute. Now the British were trying to force the Russians to assist in this enterprise.

To us it looked as if the Russians would just as soon have all the Warsaw Poles exterminated; as if they were interested in the Ukrainian Poles only. As far as I could figure out, the Russians simply stood by and watched this Warsaw debacle, when they might well have expedited their offensive, captured Warsaw, driven the Germans out and put an end to it.

However, when aroused public attention focused on the lack of help being given the Poles in Warsaw, the Russians came back with: "Who started this unfortunate uprising in Warsaw? Why weren't we notified of it? How can you get our help if you don't let us know? That is our war theater and you must not interfere. We will do the job.

"If you now feel that you want to help the Poles, give us your plan. Tell us what you are trying to do. Let us look it over, and then we will tell you what we can do!"

It gave the Combined Chiefs of Staff, Mr. Churchill, and the President something serious to think about. Could we help the Poles in Warsaw, even though we wanted to? That rather large problem was never completely solved. We did our best to drop supplies to them from the air, and to help them in every other way, but the help we were able to give was never enough.

In the meantime, I cabled General Spaatz to arrange with General Deane, heading our Military Mission in Moscow, about supplying the Warsaw patriots. I sent another cable to General Deane to coordinate this action with the Russians. That was as far as we were able to go.

At dinner that evening were the President, Mackenzie King, the Prime Minister, the Combined Chiefs of Staff, and ladies. It was one of the first of these high-powered dinners at which Mrs. Roosevelt was present. Heretofore, they had extended far into the night, but on this particular occasion, promptly at eleven, Mrs. Roosevelt said, "Frank, it is almost eleven o'clock!"—and the party broke up. (Incidentally, this was, I believe, the first conference outside of Washington at which "Falla," the President's Scotty, was present.)

During that dinner the Prime Minister came out with new ideas about winning the war. At that particular moment he thought it a matter of vital British interest that we (including the R.A.F.) get more planes, ships, and soldiers into the final battle of Japan as soon as we could. I told him the question of putting planes in there wasn't quite that simple. There were not enough land masses in the Pacific Ocean to use the heavy bombers we would have available from Europe when that phase of the war was over. As a matter of fact, if we could use 1500 out of the 3500 we had in the E.T.O., we would be very, very lucky. Certainly, we would much rather have the B-29's, with their longer range and their heavier bomb load than we would the B-17, the B-24, the Lancaster, or the Halifax. Where would we use the R.A.F. heavies? We realized that both their four-engine bombers and our own had done an excellent job over Germany where the distances were comparatively short, and the land masses great. But when we started operating against Japan, unless the Russians broke down and gave us permission to use bases in Manchuria, we had no place where we could use either the R.A.F. bombers, or our own B-17's or B-24's, to any extent. There is no doubt about it, the Prime Minister had been "needled" into his proposals by his own R.A.F. And rightly so. The R.A.F. had done a grand job. It wanted to be in at the kill of Japan, as well as at the death of Germany.

The next day, during our talks at the Combined Chiefs of Staff meeting, most of our discussion concerned British participation in the Pacific against the Japanese. Other important questions came up, also, such as: (1) What would happen in Italy when the final collapse came, and what would be done with our troops—ground, Air, and Navy—there? (2) Could we help the Russians in their operations in the Balkans? That led to a discussion of Russia's desire to have a group of small German states, and Britain's desire for a small number of larger states as a buffer between Russia and the "White Cliffs of Dover."

As the days passed, it became more and more apparent that the Prime Minister desired, for political reasons, to see Britain in on the final conquest of Japan. He wanted to be there with his main fleet; he wanted to be there with some 500 to 1000 heavy bombers; and there was no doubt that the President would like very much to have it arranged along that line. The Prime Minister said the British would not be able to hold up their heads if they were denied this opportunity to cooperate. Then he turned to me and said, "With all your wealth of airdromes, you would not deny me the mere pittance of a few for my heavy bombers, would you?"

I assured him that was something for the Combined Chiefs of Staff to figure out; as far as I was concerned, the B-29's were moving in—they had started their operations, and we planned to use all the airdromes available at Guam, Saipan, Tinian, and Iwo Jima. If the Combined Chiefs of Staff decided to replace B-29's with Lancasters, it was all right with me.

One morning we had a meeting of the Combined Chiefs of Staff at which everything went along normally and without excitement until the British again brought up the question of participation in the Pacific. Then all hell broke loose! Admiral King could not agree that there was a place for the British Navy in the Pacific, except for a very small force. The American Navy had carried the war all the way from Honolulu to the west and it would carry it on to Japan! In time, the tempest subsided, but the problem was still unsolved.

That question of a British share in the now certain V-J Day was continued at lunch and at cocktails. And I note we had a meeting about it at which the Royal Canadian Air Force commander, Robert Leckie, Sir John Dill, his aide, General Marshall, and I were present. We talked over a possible phase for the R.C.A.F. in the Pacific war. They wanted to put in 47 squadrons! Just where we were to base them, I did not know.

These questions were never finally or firmly decided. Time settled them, rather than the meetings of the Combined Chiefs of Staff; for the Japanese surrender came so quickly on the heels of the German collapse that there was really no chance to get the British heavy bombers out to the fields on the islands in the Pacific. Neither was there sufficient time for the British to get their components out to join our Navy before the Japanese surrendered.

September 14, 1944, is a very important date in relation to our operations, and in the meetings of the Joint Chiefs of Staff. That night while we were at dinner, something happened—a culmination of the preparations for our Pacific operations—that called for an immediate decision. Two or three days before, Admiral Nimitz had offered to place the Third Amphibious Force, which included the 19th Army Corps then loading in Hawaii, at General MacArthur's disposal for the attack on Leyte. General MacArthur's advice had been requested; he had been asked what changes it would require. He advised the Chief of Staff he was prepared to shift his plans and land on Leyte on the 20th of October instead of the 20th of December, as he had previously intended. The message came while we were having dinner.

Admiral Leahy, General Marshall, Admiral King, and I excused ourselves, read the message, and had a staff officer prepare an answer which naturally was in the affirmative. The message, after preparation, was rushed back to us and we had a conference then and there. So less than two hours after we, in Quebec, got the wire from MacArthur, he and Admiral Nimitz both received their instructions to execute the Leyte operations on October 20th instead of December 20th. This necessitated the abandonment of three intermediate landing points. General MacArthur's acknowledgment of our orders was received by General Marshall inside of a few minutes, something of a miracle considering the distance.

One afternoon during the Conference, Admiral King announced that he had a guide and wanted to take the Combined Chiefs of Staff over the battlefield on the Plains of Abraham, down on the river, to show where the British troops and the Colonists had landed to make the attack under Wolfe. Everybody was eager to go. When we arrived at the river below the Plains of Abraham, we found the lecturer was only a regular tourist guide who really knew little more about the movements of the various troops than General Marshall and I did. Marshall and I had visited the spot earlier, and had obtained our information mostly from reading up on the Battle of Quebec and from the monuments placed around the area. So, after listening to the guide for a while, George and I left the main body and walked off to see a new marker. There we met a Catholic priest who, we discovered, spoke only French, but he knew more about the Battle of Quebec than anyone we had met, and he gave the two of us a very interesting lecture. Then the others began to drift over. Presently this Catholic priest, with no idea of the identity of his audience, was giving the Combined Chiefs of Staff—Sir Alan Brooke, Admiral Cunningham, Sir Charles Portal, General Marshall, Admiral King, and myself—a very absorbing critique of the Battle of Quebec—in French.

During the Quebec Conference, the Prime Minister and the President talked at considerable length about what would happen after the war. The Prime Minister said that when Germany was overcome there would have to be a redistribution of effort in both his country and ours, and he hoped the President would agree that during the war with Japan Britain would continue to get food and supplies from the United States to cover her reasonable needs. The President concurred in that.

The Prime Minister also said he hoped the President would agree that it would be proper for lend-lease and munitions to continue on a national basis, even though this would enable the British to set up free labor for rebuilding, exports, etc. If the British munitions production were cut to three-fifths, United States assistance should also fall to three-fifths. Mr. Morgenthau, who was there, suggested it would be far better to have definite figures. He said he understood the munitions assistance required had been calculated by the British to be three and a half billion dollars for the first year, on the basis of the strategy envisioned by the OCTAGON Conference. The exact needs would have to be recalculated in the light of decisions on military needs reached during the meetings. The nonmunitions requirements had been put at three billion gross. The President agreed it was better to work with figures like these than on a proportionate basis.

The Prime Minister emphasized that all these supplies should be lend-lease. The President assented. The Prime Minister also was worried about how the United Kingdom was to pay its way when its export trade had shrunk so. Somehow it must be re-established. No articles on the lend-lease should be exported, or sold for profit; but it was essential that the United States should not attach any conditions to these supplies which would jeopardize the recovery of Britain's export trade. To this the President also agreed. It was then decided that a special committee should be set up with Mr. Morgenthau as chairman, to see how that could be worked out; and until the committee made its recommendations, no decisions affecting lend-lease would be made without its approval.

On September 16th, at the final meeting with the President and the Prime Minister, we went over the report of the Combined Chiefs of Staff. I didn't think the President was up to par. He didn't seem to have the same pep or power of concentration; he didn't make his usual wisecracks, but always seemed to be thinking of something else. Also, he closed his eyes and rested more than usual. He and the Prime Minister received our report with only a few minor changes.

Taking it all in all, Octagon was one of our better conferences. We had fewer disagreements than heretofore about the way to bring the war to a conclusion. Yet plans could always fluctuate. Even Stalin didn't hold firm to the general plan for winning the war. As late as October, 1944, he told Ambassador Harriman he thought it was a mistake to try to break the German lines in Italy and the Siegfried Line; that as many Allied divisions as we could get should be sent through Austria to outflank the Germans and assist the Red Army's advance through Hungary into Austria. This, after his inflexible pressure for a drive from the West. Stalin's attitude about Switzerland was characteristic of the Russians. He said, at one of the conferences with Churchill and Harriman, that Switzerland should be forced to allow the transit of Allied troops through her territory to outflank the German strong position. When

Churchill protested, Stalin said Switzerland had played a false role in the war and should be made to cooperate. Such incidents indicate how very, very difficult it was, even as late as 1944, to arrive at and maintain a firm plan for carrying the war home conclusively to Germany.

Early in the Fall of 1944, it had become apparent that our output of pilots, gunners, bombardiers, navigators, mechanics, and all other qualified personnel had reached a point where our production was far in excess of our demands. In fact, we were replacing losses in our overseas combat units faster than they occurred. The same condition held true with regard to most types of airplanes, except for very heavy bombardment planes (the B-29's) which were just beginning to roll off the production line.

Our plans for meeting estimated losses up to 25 per cent per month had worked out very satisfactorily. There were few months when we actually needed such replacements, but when we started rolling, the 25 per cent margin came in handy as a reserve for many unforeseen situations, and enabled us to build up our programmed strength much more quickly than we could otherwise have done. December 31, 1944, found the Army Air Forces with 41,600 airplanes in the United States and 31,100 overseas. Of this number, 407 were B-29's operating out of China, or getting ready for service, either in China or in the Pacific.

As to personnel, the end of 1944 found us with 1,100,000 officers and men overseas, out of a total strength of 2,359,000.

Taking all this into consideration, Bob Lovett and I decided that although the end of the war was not yet in sight, there were certain things we could do to cut down the size of our establishments and save the taxpayers' money. We realized there was always a possibility that something unforeseen might happen that would throw our calculations off and put us in a jam, but we thought that was highly improbable, and it was a risk we were willing to take. The "pipe lines" were full of airplanes and combat crews and trained personnel of all types; and still equipment and personnel were coming out of our factories and our schools. Accordingly, in the fall of 1944, when we were training pilots at the rate of 105,000 a year, we decided to start cutting down. First we cut the pilot output rate down to 60,000 a year; then to 40,000, and by February, 1945, we had lowered it to 30,000. Similarly, in February, 1945, some four months before V-E Day, we slowed our production of airplanes and canceled orders to the amount of seven billion dollars, even though we had not, as yet, completely beaten the Germans nor defeated the Japs.

During the year 1944 the U.S. Army Air Forces dropped over a million tons of bombs on the enemy, fired over 225,000 rounds of ammunition, destroyed over 18,200 enemy aircraft, and sank over 950,000 tons of shipping in the Pacific alone.

This was accomplished by ten separate Air Forces in combat, plus two B-29 commands operating from the Twentieth Air Force. Flying hours meant little, for in the continental United States we flew over thirty-seven million hours and used over five billion gallons of gasoline. At its peak, our training program called for about 50,000 airplanes.

The Air Transport Command had developed into the largest outfit of its kind the world had ever seen or would see again for a long time. During 1944, we carried 1,200,000 passengers and 400,000 tons of cargo and freight. A.T.C. was operating approximately 3000 airplanes when it attained that record. In just one month of 1944, in returning evacuees to the United States, more than twenty-four million air-patient miles were flown.

November, 1944, found our air units roving at will over all Germany, and the Luftwaffe's air and ground defenses helpless to do anything about it. On one auspicious day, General Doolittle's Eighth Air Force sent P-51's and P-47's on a strafing and bombing mission over the heart of Germany that covered a round-trip flight from England of over 1100 miles. On this mission our airmen destroyed 27 German aircraft, including one German jet-propelled Me-262, in the air, and destroyed 64 planes, among which were 30 jet-propelled planes, on the various airfields over which they passed. Every time they saw an engine, a train, an oil car, a marshaling yard, they dove down to smash it. That day's report showed the destruction of 131 locomotives, 24 railroad cars, 42 oil cars, none of which would ever run again. On their way home, the fighters wiped out factories, warehouses, and airplane hangars. As a result of the day's work, in which 400 of our fighters participated, we lost eight airplanes.

By November 30, 1944, the Army Air Forces casualty list totaled 104,818 men. They were wonderful young men. I have always felt deeply Alma Dean's "Letter to Saint Peter."

> Let them in, Peter; they are very tired;
> Give them the couches where the angels sleep.
> Let them wake whole again to new dawns fired
> With sun, not war; and may their peace be deep.
> Remember where the broken bodies lie;
> And give them things they like. Let them make noise.
> God knows how young they were to have to die! . . .

Cutting down on our air training program and our production sched-ules gave the Army Air Forces opportunity to stop and consolidate, to do some constructive thinking and planning for the future. For now, regardless of what the Germans did in the air, or what the Japanese did, the strength of our air power would be constant. All we had to do now was to figure out how properly to employ that strength to play our part along with the Royal Air Force, the ground forces, and the Navy in bringing the war to a close in the shortest time. This breathing spell was most welcome to all of us.

Of course, we still had two main jobs ahead of us: To complete the bombing of Germany, which was by this time more or less routine, and to deploy our B-29 outfits after completion of their training for the destruction of the Japanese mainland. The latter included, also, the steps that must be taken by the Air Force with regard to the atomic bomb, which we had every reason to believe would be completed within the coming year.

As Chief of the Army Air Forces, I had yet another job. That was to project myself into the future; to get the best brains available, have them use as a background the latest scientific developments in the air arms of the Germans and the Japanese, the R.A.F., and determine what steps the United States should take to have the best Air Force in the world twenty years hence. There was no doubt in my mind but that a different pattern must be followed in so far as radar, atomics, sonics, electronics, jet planes, and rockets were concerned. This applied not only to airplanes, to the rockets used from ships and from airplanes, but also to such types of projectiles as the big German V-2 rocket. When we added all such developments together, what did it mean for the future? What kind of Air Force must we have? What kind of equipment ought we to plan for twenty years, or thirty years hence?

To get the best thought on the subject, I went to my friend Dr. Robert Millikan at California Tech, and asked him who was the best man to head a committee of scientists—practical scientists—and engineers who were experienced in sonics, electronics, radar, aerodynamics, and any other phases of science that might influence in any way the development of aircraft in the future. We talked over the problem for a long time. He finally decided our man was Dr. Theodor von Kármán, a member of his staff at Cal Tech. He said he hated to let Dr. von Kármán go, but that my job was more important than his, so he would let me have him.

Accordingly, it was not long before von Kármán arrived in Wash-ington and shortly after, one by one, scientists—men who understood the advanced theories of these new developments—began to appear. I told these scientists that I wanted them to think ahead twenty years. They were to forget the past; regard the equipment now available only as the basis for their boldest predictions. I wanted them to think about supersonic speed airplanes, airplanes that would move and operate without crews; improvements in bombs, so that we could use smaller bombs to get greater effect; defenses against modern and future aircraft; communication systems between airplanes and the ground, and between the airplanes themselves in the air; television, weather, medical research; atomic energy, and any other phase of aviation which might affect the development and employment of the air power to come.

I assured Dr. von Kármán I wasn't interested in when he submitted his report. He was to go ahead, wherever he wanted and whenever he wanted; to pay no attention to tomorrow's airplane, or the day-after-tomorrow's airplane, but to look into the future twenty years and determine what we would have to have then, and make a report that would be a guide to the commanders of the Air Force who would follow me. I gave him and his associates free rein—to go to England, Germany, Japan, Italy—even to Russia if they could get in.

We were never sure just how much the Germans knew about our equipment, nor whether we knew all we should know about theirs. However, the first week in November, 1944, we received detailed information of a German lecture on the development of jet fighters in England and the United States, which was accurate. I noted in one place that they said our jet development was started from information brought to the United States by General Arnold in 1941, which was, of course, the fact. Hence, we know they were acquainted with the beginning of our jet development, if nothing else.

The German scientist went on to say that the British furnished the United States a jet engine in 1942; that the first jet airplane flew in the United States at the end of 1942, about three months after the first flight of the German twin-engined jet, Me-262. He might well have gone on to say that on our side the jet engine, in the development stage it had reached at that time, would have been of no value in our operations, for it did not have long enough "legs"—it couldn't stay in the air long enough to reach any worthwhile targets. It could have had a nuisance value, and that was all.

In the early days, the Air Corps did not have a real Intelligence Section; it had what was called an "Information Division," whose responsibilities were considerably limited, mainly because the G-2 section of the

War Department had feared a duplication of information and activity.

Naturally, we had not known in what areas of the world we would operate, though we were fairly certain one of our main enemies would be Germany and another Japan. We believed it was essential to start what we called "Target Folders"—information relating to probable and possible targets, in probable and possible enemy countries, at the earliest possible moment. However, the G-2 section of the War Department maintained they had all the information we needed, or, if they didn't have it, they could get it. It was not necessary, they said, for us to duplicate their efforts.

Now, what did our actual war experience reveal? When we moved into Baffin Island, for example, the steamship which took our detachment there was the first one to enter the harbor since 1856. And no later information about Baffin Island had been available! Similarly, when we were talking in the Joint and Combined Chiefs of Staff meetings about possible landings on the island of Hokkaido, in Japan, the only information I could get from the G-2 section of the Army or the ONI Section of the Navy was a book dated 1858!

When it came to establishing the Target Folders that would give us the size, location, general characteristics, special distinguishing marks, the type of construction, and other details necessary for bombing operations against a target like the complexes of the I. G. Farben Company, or the Krupp Works—such data did not exist in the United States. Accordingly, the Air Force had no recourse but to go to other sources for its information.

Earlier, I have mentioned the target committees. In developing our own technical agencies for analysis, Mr. Lovett suggested that the easiest way to secure the information would be to get it from engineers, bankers, or construction people who had actually done construction in foreign countries; men who had loaned money, and, in loaning money, had secured descriptions of various plants. To build our target section, we secured the services of Elihu Root of New York. He, in turn, used men who had actually been in Germany and in Japan, who gave us information to help the Target Folders. When it came to such islands as Hokkaido, however, we were told by various agencies that no information was available. Other Japanese targets were similarly shrouded in the unknown. I found, then, that there was one man who never told me that such and such was not available. He was incapable of a defeatist intelligence answer. This was General "Wild Bill" Donovan, who was running the O.S.S. He would say, "What do you want? When do you want it?

I'll get it for you." To out-of-the-way places he would send details, or scouts, spies, or small detachments, to secure the information we needed, and would always give us the data in time.

This is the point: The old Army and the old Navy were not ready, in so far as their G-2 sections were concerned, for the new kind of war that was being forced upon them; the G-2 men could not see over the hill to the necessity of establishing an agency for securing the new kinds of information needed for an air war. No operations of any part of a modern war machine can be static. The techniques and lessons cannot remain unchanged from one war to another. Information, classified and filed in the Intelligence offices of the armed services, must be of a character to meet the requirements of land, sea, and air forces in future wars regardless of the kind of equipment those services may use hereafter.

☆ 29 ☆

It had seemed to me as the war progressed that the Air Force's part in the Pacific was ignored by the press—not in so far as the actual raids themselves were concerned, but in the build-up for the future. Before we got the Marianas, the columnists, commentators, and newspaper reporters had all talked about the *Naval* capture of the Islands. The *Navy* would take the Islands and use them as a base. No one had mentioned using them as bases for the B-29's, yet it was the B-29's and the B-29's only that could put tons and tons of bombs on Japan. The fleet couldn't do it; the Naval Air couldn't do it; the Army couldn't do it. The B-29's could. Even after Tinian, Guam, and Saipan were safely ours, this attitude persisted. Finally, I decided it was essential that this phase of the Pacific campaign be brought to the attention of the American people.

Just about that time I was taken sick. I did not know how ill I was, but I knew I was a very sick man. I find this memorandum which I wrote to General Giles:

> I have noted several editorials and columnist's articles re Japanese Mandated Islands, always giving credit to the Navy, stating we must hold on to them for the Navy.
>
> It should be made clear in a press conference, that the Army Air Force is far more interested, right now, than anyone else in the United States, in holding not only the Japanese Mandated Islands, but all other bases essential to the proper functioning of our Air Power in its operations for the conquest of Japan—and any other mission assigned to them.
>
> It should be brought out it was the Army Air Forces that first thought of a practical operating need for these Island bases, and made the strongest bid in efforts to get them, to prosecute the war.
>
> H.H.A.

And then I passed out of the picture with a heart attack, and went to the hospital at Miami. The sudden realization that a man isn't as good physically as he had thought himself to be comes as a distinct shock.

The worst part of my predicament, as I saw it then, was that the Yalta-Malta Conference was coming up within a few days and I had expected to be present. I knew it would be an important meeting. Subjects would be discussed that would materially affect our future operations, and perhaps influence the peacetime setup of commercial aviation. I wanted to be present to exercise my influence when the Russians, the British, and the Americans talked about these matters, but I had to send a substitute. General Kuter went in my place and, incidentally, did a wonderful job.

As the days and weeks passed, I had time to think of many things that had happened during the war, things that were still happening, and things that had yet to happen before we completed our victory.

My experience during the war indicated that it is very easy to see the mistakes the other fellow makes, but far more difficult to give him credit for the good things he does, and see his side of the picture. For instance, there is no doubt in my mind that during the first part of the war, taking it all in all, our U.S. Navy was not particularly glad to see our Army Air Forces building up to its great strength. They did not want us to get the priorities in materials and machine tools to build our heavy bombers. They would have preferred that we did not have B-17's and B-24's—that they have the heavy bombers. Then, too, we found fault with the Navy—the manner in which they operated and in which they employed our combat units.

When we were talking about unity of command, unification of the services, Admiral King said to me, "Trouble with all this rearrangement and reorganization is your Air Force, Hap. If you would take your Air Force and bring it over to the Navy, then the Navy would have an Army in the form of Marines, and with your Air Force, real air power. With our battleships, cruisers, carriers, destroyers, and submarines, the Navy would be the largest and most powerful force in the world."

I agreed with Admiral King that, looking at it from a straight Navy viewpoint, he had something on his side. They would indeed have a unified service under the Navy Department, and by building up the Marine Corps, they might have a real amphibious Army. With our Strategic Air Force they would have the heavy bombardment, which we were using over Germany and Japan. The idea of concentrating all of that power in the Navy Department did not appeal to me. So I could not go along with Admiral King, and had to say, "No, Ernie. That isn't the solution. It looks all right from the Navy point of view, but it is not all right from the Army, the Air Force, or the national point of view. Furthermore, I am not ready to change my olive drab for a slate gray uniform."

Some time later, Admiral Leahy made the same kind of remark: "Hap, if you take your heavy bombardment and turn it over to the Navy we won't have any of these troubles about unification, because the Navy will have heavy bombardment, a Strategic Air Force; it will have its close-in air for tactical support; it will have its carrier-based Air Force; it will have its Army in the shape of Marines, and it will have its Navy." And I said, "Yes, Bill, I think that is correct. But that still isn't the way to attack the problem. We must find a solution that will be satisfactory to all the various services and to the country at large."

Lying there in the hospital, I never questioned the wonderful work the Navy had done in the Pacific. In spite of all the obstacles, in spite of many mistakes, their movement across the Pacific was really a magnificent operation.

Likewise, their operations during our landings on the beachheads at Casablanca and at other ports in North Africa, at Sicily, Salerno, Anzio, and Normandy were carried out exceptionally well, and made the task of the Army very much easier. But on the other side of the ledger, the activities of the fleet up and down the coast of Japan, dropping bombs from carrier planes, firing their big guns at indefinite shore targets, did not do anywhere near the effective damage that our B-29's accomplished with their precision bombing.

Yes, the Navy had done a grand job, but a lot of its techniques were relics of the past. The United States should review all the operations of all the armed forces to determine which are essential in modern and in future warfare, and which can be thrown into the ash can along with the Mississippi gunboats and covered wagons and Gatling guns. That applies not only to the Army and the Navy, but also to the Air Force.

Then I thought of the War Department. The War Department, as a whole, did not support the build-up of the Air Force as a strategic weapon for many, many years; and the Air Force, we might say, came into its maximum power and efficiency in spite of the average War Department officer, rather than because of him. Frankly, it wasn't until George Marshall appeared in the office as Deputy Chief of Staff that we were able to get a real program for air development approved by the War Department. Prior to that, it was the Baker Board, the

Howell Report, and one committee after another, and then the findings would be buried somewhere, with no action taken.

I also thought how much easier Secretary Stimson had made my task. I could go to him and tell him my problems and the solutions I proposed. All he asked was a complete and thorough understanding, and generally he approved. As a matter of fact, I can remember very few cases when he disapproved any of our Air Force projects. Bob Lovett did a grand job in every way. He was a trouble shooter de luxe.

Through it all, however, there was still that feeling in some parts of the Army that the Air Force was an overrated unit which had yet to prove itself.

I thought about the R.A.F. and the wonderful job it had done in holding back the German Air Force during the Battle of Britain and its night bombardment campaign; how much we were indebted to them for giving us their ideas about the techniques of operation, the characteristics of the equipment itself, the changes we must make in our own airplanes and equipment to make them effective against Germany.

When I thought about the Chinese situation, my memories went back two or three years to the time when the Generalissimo, General Marshall, then the President, all asked for more tons over the Hump. It occurred to me that in November, 1944, we put 34,000 tons over the Hump—more than the Generalissimo had ever thought of asking for; more than Stilwell had ever hoped for! Thirteen thousand tons more than ever started over the Burma Road!

The Burma situation had changed materially since I had been out there a couple of years before. In 1944 the Japanese had received their first decisive defeat in Burma when the troops of Lord Mountbatten on the Plains of Imphal had inflicted losses on the Japanese of some 30,000 men. It was the start of rolling back the Japanese from the west— Stilwell had begun moving in from the north. The Allied troops had captured Chittagong, and, a big change, there was now always Allied air support available.

Then came the question of Stilwell himself. It was generally accepted that he was trying to handle too large a job. In addition to being on the Generalissimo's staff, he had three headquarters, separated by a thousand miles, which he had to visit regularly. When he was relieved, late in 1944, three lieutenant generals were appointed to take his place: Sultan was put in command of the China-Burma troops, Wheeler in charge of Supply and Logistics, and Wedemeyer made Chief of Staff to Lord Mountbatten.

In the meantime, Chennault was building up his Air Force—building it up too rapidly, in fact, because he was getting airplanes faster than he could put them to work in his combat groups.

In September it had been necessary for me to write to Harry Hopkins and call his attention to the fact that the existing plan for re-equipping the Chinese Air Force with modern fighting gear must be changed because they could not absorb the airplanes as fast as we were sending them. This information had come to me from General Stratemeyer, whom I had sent out as commander of the China-Burma Air Forces.

I had proposed to Hopkins that unless there were serious diplomatic reasons to the contrary, I would recommend to the Combined Chiefs of Staff that action be taken, and the Generalissimo advised that the allocation of aircraft for the Chinese Air Force would be cut approximately in half from now on, pending the time they could immediately employ the airplanes we had sent to them.

However, Chennault was doing a good job in China with his Air Force. He was meeting the Japanese on all fronts. He was sinking their ships, and destroying their bases and their installations. In order to make him more efficient in his operations, Mountbatten proposed (1) To secure an area near Myitkyina for new bases and fields so that the Air Transport Command could get more supplies into China; (2) To provide additional bases for air transport in India; (3) To divert bomber groups from the Tenth Air Force to the Air Transport Command if existing planes were not sufficient to carry supplies over the Hump to meet the plans as outlined. This I did not agree to. Combat planes should be used to carry supplies only in case of extreme emergency.

All this time, I knew Japan was getting a terrific plastering from our bombers. The Twentieth Air Force had been building up in the Marianas ever since the Islands had been captured by the Navy—ever since we had built the runway for the B-29's. One hundred B-29's left Saipan on November 24, 1944, and Tokyo was hit for the first time since Doolittle's raid in 1942. By the 18th of December, the B-29's had hit Toyko three more times, and then they hit the Mitsubishi Aircraft Plant at Nogoya, practically demolishing it. By the end of December, 1944, the Twentieth Air Force in the Marianas had 345 B-29's at its disposal at Guam, Tinian, and Saipan. That number was to be built up until it reached a total of about 1000 planes before V-J Day. By the end of December, 1944, there were 46,000 men and 5800 officers available for duty with the Twentieth Air Force in the Marianas. They had destroyed 254 enemy aircraft, and had dropped 9000 tons of bombs.

The average military man accepts certain principles of war as fundamental. Yet, these principles were violated, or would have been violated, time and time again, had we of the Air Force not fought against dispersion—against scattering our airplanes all over the world. It required constant attention and vigilance to assure that such diversions were not made. To end the war as quickly as possible, it was essential that we use such power as was available to carry out our major objective, which was to mass the maximum number of heavy bombers possible for the destruction of interior Germany, and in due course mass the maximum number of Superfortresses for the destruction of Japan. MacArthur yelled for the B-29's; Nimitz wanted the B-29's; Stilwell and Mountbatten wanted the B-29's—all for tactical purposes.

Even the French Navy asked us for planes. Admiral Fenard came to Washington and made a plea for land-based aircraft. We received information that his mission was strictly French politics; that the existing French Air Force in North Africa could sustain the French Air Force program, and the introduction of a French Naval Air Force element would reduce the fighting value of the existing French Air Force squadrons and create units of very doubtful value. Accordingly, I was advised we should not listen to Admiral Fenard's pleas.

Almost simultaneously, I received a telephone message from Mr. McCloy, the Assistant Secretary of War, stating that Admiral Fenard had impressed him with the righteousness of the French Navy's claim for aircraft, and that in his opinion I should get busy and give the French Navy the airplanes they wanted.

Just why these requests for aircraft for the French Navy were made to the Army Air Force and not to our own Navy I cannot see, but that seems to have been the way the war was run. The Army Air Force did most of the giving away of aircraft. Even as late as January, 1944, we still had to resist a pressure that would have weakened our bomber operations in the Pacific, destroying the genuine air power that comes only from mass formations of bombers. We were operating out of China then, from our Chengtu bases, but we were constantly hearing innuendoes and rumors that the Japanese might very well seize those bases soon, and we would therefore have to use our B-29's somewhere else.

Someone even brought the matter up to the Chief of Staff. Marshall talked with me at some length about the desirability of our having bases elsewhere to which we could move if the B-29 units in China and India were driven out. I explained to him that we were operating successfully from both places. We did have the gasoline. We did have the services.

And it was only a question of time before we would be able to move our B-29's to the Marianas and hit Japan from those Islands.

Every time this kind of "boring from within" began to endanger one of our existing and approved programs, it would presently develop that the forces behind it were trying to get the airplanes shifted to their own bailiwick. In this case, we had found that the longing looks at the B-29's were being cast from the South Pacific. But fortunately we were able to build up the Twentieth Air Force and keep it operating, as such.

Looking back, it seemed to me that one of the most difficult problems in building up the Air Force had been to synchronize the various components; to get replacement crews and planes to the various units at the fronts all over the world before they were actually needed, so the squadrons would always go out at full strength. We had to anticipate, for instance, the necessity of having fighters to accompany our bombers, for as I have said earlier, there was a school of thought in the Army Air Forces in our early days that bombers could take care of themselves, and needed no fighter cover. This notion continued for some time after the war started, and yet it was quite obvious to me, as a result of aerial operations in Spain, that bombers could not survive without fighter protection.

By January, 1944, with two 108-gallon wing tanks, the P-51 developed the then phenomenal escort range of 850 miles. The P-38 and the P-47 were excellent airplanes, there is no argument about that, but the P-51, with its Merlin engine, was the airplane for that job.

March 15, 1945, I was ready to leave the hospital and went back to work for a short time. Although during the latter part of my stay at the hospital I had been briefed almost daily on the progress of the war, it was a few days before I was back in the chain of thought of the higher command. I also talked with General Kuter about the Yalta-Malta Conference, and the plans for Eisenhower's final efforts against the Germans, and then, on March 31st, I left Washington, headed for Europe again.

It was my first visit to Paris in a long time, and we saw comparatively little evidence of bombings. On the outskirts, factories, railroad yards, airfields, and many buildings were knocked flat, but very few houses. The Eiffel Tower, as usual, stood out like a sore thumb. Paris, as a whole, looked very good.

As we landed at the French airport, we could see the French refugees streaming back from all directions. At the airport to meet me were General Spaatz, General Fred Anderson, Colonel Hoag, and Colonel

"Hank" Pool, my brother-in-law. We went to the Ritz and talked until dinner.

That night, when I was having dinner with Tooey Spaatz, he told me about the frame of mind Patton was in when he was making his famous march to the eastward, after the break-through from the beachhead. Tooey had asked Patton, "Don't you worry about getting out so far? Don't you worry about your flanks?" Patton: "No worries. The Air Force takes care of my flanks." Tooey: "But how about your supplies, your logistics—don't you worry about them?" Patton: "Not a bit. I have a G-4. He worries about my logistics. I'll tell you, though, he fainted three times on one day." That was during the big push to the Rhine, when the Third Army moved ahead so fast.

At the Ritz I was quartered in the suite that had been used by Goering. It had a tremendous bathtub, much larger than any I had ever seen, and some time or other he must have sat down in it rather hard for there was a crack across the middle of the tub.

Next day, accompanied by my doctor, by General Spaatz, and Hank Pool, we went to Rheims. It was a sorry looking city. Most of the stores were closed, there were scars from the street battles everywhere, factories bombed out, fragment holes in the walls of practically all buildings. The people were not badly dressed, and looked fairly well fed, but they were obviously trying to make a lot out of a little. DeGaulle was having a hard fight trying to make a victorious nation out of a country whose Army and whose Air Force had not won a battle. He was calling upon the whole world for representation at the peace table when, after we had given him vast quantities of equipment and supplies, only one French division had crossed the Rhine. That was the Moroccan Division.

There was no apparent food shortage anywhere. There were cattle and horses which looked plump and in good condition. The fields looked well tilled and there should have been a bumper crop. The Germans had not destroyed the fruit trees or the farm houses.

I had lunch at Rheims with Eisenhower, Tooey Spaatz, and Ike's aide. After lunch, Ike, Tooey, and I had a long talk. I sounded Ike out on the postwar situation, what he thought about future national defense, the organization for national security, and so on, and wrote down his views.

1. A Department of National Defense with three equal parts: ground, sea, and air. Common supplies for articles used by all three. We must have it to cut down expenses.

2. Air, ground, and naval forces of a size required to do the job; not a size based upon money.

3. Universal Military Service for one year.

4. Where we have island bases it would be far better to let the British take ownership, to prevent our altruistic Americans from giving the people who live on the islands their freedom and having them return to some totalitarian government, such as Japan or Germany.

5. Support aviation must be part of the ground forces.

6. Naval air should be limited to carrier and seaborne types.

Eisenhower seemed certain that the end of the war was in sight right then. The only fly in the ointment was the slow advance of the Russians. Ike was very enthusiastic about what the air had done in the war in Europe, and the support it had given to his Armies.

Our troops were moving forward so rapidly that we had gone into the supply business in Europe in the same big way as over the Hump in China. For instance, on one day the C-47's of the IX Troop Carrier Command delivered 250,000 gallons of gasoline to troops in advance positions. Next day, they carried 500,000 gallons to the various motor transport and armored units as they were moving up toward the Rhine.

I left Ike and Tooey at their headquarters at Rheims and returned to Paris. I had to keep short hours, so I went to bed early and saw no Paris night life.

While I was there in my suite at the Ritz, a German prisoner who was tired of the war and had flown an Me-262 out of Germany was brought in. I wanted to talk with him, for the twin-engine Me-262 was the first jet plane effective in combat. We later took the Me-262 and sent it to Dayton, for test. This German prisoner, a lieutenant in the Luftwaffe, said that in the interior of Germany the railroads were gone, the factories destroyed, there was no oil, the best of their pilots had been killed, bomber pilots were flying jet planes without sufficient training, and the war couldn't continue for more than two or three weeks. All organized resistance would then be gone. As a matter of fact, he did not miss it by much.

On one trip we took off for Frankfurt by way of Aachen, Bonn, Cologne, and Coblenz. Aachen had been practically leveled by bombing. Duren was a mass of wreckage. Cologne looked terrible but the cathedral appeared to have come through unscathed. As we flew along, we could see abandoned trucks and tanks and trenches used by the Germans, and newly constructed by-passes where bridges had been destroyed.

When we came to the Rhine, we saw bridges down all along the line; innumerable barges and tugs were sunk. Yet, a few hundred feet away from the Rhine, all seemed peaceful and quiet, with no signs of war. As we approached, Coblenz did not seem to be so badly hit, but once we reached the city proper we could see it was heavily damaged.

We went over Frankfurt and found a large city with railroad yards and airports a shambles, runways pockmarked and unusable, the balance of the airport filled with bomb craters. At that time, our people had 2000 to 4000 German prisoners with trucks and bulldozers working on the field to put it back in shape. We couldn't land on that airport, so we picked another, southeast of town, where there was a good runway with several of our C-46's, C-47's, and a B-17 on it, but by radio we were told to keep going to an airport 66 miles south. Our flight had taken us over the front where our ground troops were slugging it out to capture the encircled German troops, south to Coblenz, and yet there was not a single German plane in the air. Finally, we came to our airport and landed. It had a runway marked with flags. Fifteen or more transports were lined up, nose to tail. They had delivered their supplies and were taking on wounded, loading almost as many German wounded as our own.

The airport was fifteen miles from the front line, but our transports came in and out completely unmolested by the Luftwaffe. There just wasn't any German Air Force any more.

We climbed into a car and started traveling down the Auto Bahn, passing German Air Force barracks, cars, and machine shops damaged or destroyed by our bombings. In the woods, miles away from the airport, were airplanes, more airplanes, and still more airplanes, all in good, serviceable condition; bombs, gasoline tanks, and repair hangars, concealed from above by the trees, but all accessible to the airport via the Auto Bahn.

We continued down the Auto Bahn until we reached General Patch's headquarters. General Patch told me of the advance of his Seventh Army up the Rhone River from Marseilles. My son Hank, a battalion commander of the 45th Division, was at Army Headquarters waiting for me. Eisenhower, Spaatz, and Webster came in and we had lunch together at Darmstadt as guests of General Barcus.

I asked Hank if he needed some whiskey or brandy, which I could send over from the States. He said not to worry; his outfit had just captured an enemy warehouse in which they found case after case of Scotch, French Brandy, Benedictine, and Cointreau.

After we had our lunch, Eisenhower and Spaatz took off for Rheims. With Hank Arnold, my medico, Colonel Marquardt, and my aide, Major Tom Sheffield, I went to battered Frankfurt to see General Patton.

Patton was much changed from when I had seen him in Sicily. Victory after victory had put him on the crest of the wave, and he was riding high, wide, and handsome. He was cocky and sure of himself, sure of where he was going and what he was going to do, and that it would be absolutely 100 per cent right. His headquarters was in an old German barracks. He said there were no German troops in front of him now, and he would keep going until he joined up with the Russians, but higher headquarters was holding him up in his present position until the First Army on his left, and the Seventh Army on his right, caught up with him.

He told me that while standing in front of his headquarters the day before, a German sniper had shot at him from a window across the grass plot—and had just missed him. They killed the German.

Periodically, there appear among our Army type of nonconformists wonderful war leaders who have originality and are respected by their men, but who seemingly cannot get along in the regulation-controlled, unexciting peacetime Army. Yet in war they stand out among their fellows.

During the Civil War, there were two such officers, men with outstanding war records who found it hard to settle down after the excitement of war. Major General George Custer was such a type. He was an individualist. He had long flowing hair, and his uniform was always different—a buckskin jacket with fringe. He always wanted action—he couldn't wait for normal developments. His impatience finally caused his death at Little Big Horn.

Major General George Crook was another of the same kind. After the Civil War, he found an outlet for his pent-up pressure in campaigns and dealings with the Indians but he was always a problem child for the War Department.

Another generation brought us General Billy Mitchell. Billy's youthful record in the Spanish War was beyond criticism. His World War I record was superb. As a leader, an air strategist, in employment of aircraft, he was unsurpassed. But—along with his fruitfully unorthodox imagination—his uniform was always a bit different from that of other officers; he couldn't wait for the normal routing of War Department procedures to get results, and he became a thorn in the side of not only the War Department, but of the Navy Department as well.

I have always thought that General George S. Patton was another of this Army breed. I knew him as a cadet and through the various grades, then as a four-star general. He was a natural leader. His men respected him as a combat commander.

Even after the face-slapping episode in Europe, when it was decreed that he should appear before his command and publicly apologize, he stepped out on the platform in front of the men and said, "Men, I just want you to see what kind of a sonofabitch your commander is." The cheers that followed were spontaneous, thundering, and sincere.

Yet he was a man of self-determination—he had to be different—a crusader. His two pearl-handled pistols were evidence of it. While other generals were satisfied with one set of four stars on each shoulder, I think that George Patton wore a set on his helmet, two sets on his battle jacket, and another two sets on his shirt. He liked the effect it made.

I often thought that he would have great difficulty in adjusting himself to the restraints and restrictions of postwar service in Europe.

The next day we flew to Luxembourg, where Spaatz, Vandenberg, Weyland, Quesada, and Stearley, all Air Force generals, were waiting for us. After lunch with General Omar Bradley, we took a ride through the city, and when we came back to the hotel, there were some 4000 people waiting at the street door. Apparently, as some of the officers said, the Luxembourgers liked the Americans and were glad when we came. They certainly turned out an enthusiastic ovation for me.

That night I had a fine talk with General Bradley. He was convinced there was no organized resistance in front of his Army. He had encircled several pockets in which there were a large number of enemy troops. These he wanted to destroy, and then move forward. He thought all resistance everywhere would be over in not more than six weeks or two months. Next morning, I went to Bradley's headquarters and had a war room presentation by his staff. Bradley's staff figured the enemy pockets—holding between 120,000 and 150,000 Germans—would be broken up within about ten days. Like Eisenhower and Patton, Bradley was very appreciative of the part the Air had played.

Next morning, back in Paris, I conferred with members of my party who had returned from touring other parts of the front. The report was the same everywhere—no organized resistance—the German Army evidently had ceased to exist as a fighting force. Peace must come within a short time.

That day I received a message from General Marshall: "I read of your presence and statements with various active commands. Where is that Bermuda rest? The lazy days at Cannes? The period of retirement

at Capri? You are riding for a fall, doctor or no doctor. (*Signed*)
GEORGE MARSHALL."

He was right and wrong. He didn't realize I was in bed for an hour
and a half every day after lunch, in bed at nine o'clock at the latest every
night, and didn't get up until about eight o'clock each day. However, I
was glad he was solicitous of my well-being.

On April 10th, I headed for the Riviera, where I planned for real
rest and relaxation. After about three hours flying, we landed at Cannes
with its olive trees, palms, oranges, wistaria, the bright sunshine and
blue water. But along the waterfront we saw the efforts the Germans
had made to prevent our landing on the southern coast of France. Using
the Italian soldiers and the French citizens, the Germans had constructed
real defenses. They had lined the main roads with concrete blocks about
five feet high and four feet on the side, shaped like pyramids. There
were thousands of them, placed in the water just offshore below high-
water line to prevent the landing craft from coming in. Mines were set
everywhere, on land and in the sea. They were still exploding every day.

While I was in Europe, I wanted to talk with the senior Air Force
officers about the reorganization of the Air Forces. During the war I had
greatly depleted my office by taking nearly all of my best personnel and
sending them to any theater that needed strengthening. Now I could not
carry the load in Washington any longer; someone else had to come in
and help.

General Giles, my deputy, was soon to leave for the Pacific. I had to
start collecting key people to carry the post European war Air Force task
in all theaters. The problems were: (1) To strengthen the Air Force
staff in Washington; (2) Bolster the Twentieth Air Force staff in the
Pacific so it could continue operations against Japan as efficiently as the
Eighth Air Force had operated against Germany; (3) To build up
Kenney's command as it moved northward. Kenney would need considerable reinforcement as he came closer and closer to Japan; (4) To
build up Wedemeyer's command in Burma and China.

The only source for such staff officers was the European Theater.
The task of the Eighth Air Force had eased up, so it should be possible
to take more and more men from there.

On April 13th, after I had gone to bed, my doctor, Colonel Marquardt,
came in and told me President Roosevelt was dead. The news was a great
shock, because Franklin Roosevelt was not only a personal friend, but
one of the best friends the Air Force ever had. He had supported me in
the development of the Air Force and in its global operations to an extent

that I little dreamed of a few years before, when I was in the doghouse. Many times he seemed more like a fellow airman than he did the Commander in Chief of all our Armed Forces, and I, one of his subalterns, in charge of aviation. I knew that we would miss him tremendously, but I had high hopes of President Truman's support of our future.

I prepared a message to Mrs. Roosevelt covering my feelings about President Roosevelt's death and sent it off right away.

Later in the evening, General Eaker, General Doolittle, General Spaatz, and I talked over the officers who should come to the United States to help build up the Army Air Forces Headquarters. Jimmy Doolittle told one of his typical stories about a B-17 which had come in all shot to pieces. It had been hit by a rocket and no one could understand how it had managed to stay together in the air. The tail surface was almost completely severed from the rest of the ship. Doolittle, in order to say something, and feeling a little overwhelmed, said to the tail gunner as he climbed out of the plane, "You were in that ship when it was hit?" The tail gunner, a tough, red-headed fellow, said, "Yes, sir. All the time."

After Doolittle had passed on, an officer heard the tail gunner say, "Where in hell did the bald-headed bastard think I was? Selling peanuts in Brooklyn?" One of the crewmen said, "That was General Doolittle!" The tail gunner replied, "I know; I've seen his pictures."

Next day, I sent for General Twining and General Cannon to fly up from Italy to report on their operations. General Beebe and Colonel Petersen arrived that day from a trip to England and Sweden.

That night, Assistant Secretary of War McCloy came for dinner. He told of finding some V-2's intact in an underground factory near Heidelberg. He said the factory was very extensive and there were no United States Air Force personnel at either the jet plant found underground or at the V-2 plant. I sent wires to Spaatz right away to have Air Force representatives sent to those establishments at once.

The following day, General Vandenberg came and we had a long talk on the reorganization that would come as a result of the developments in Europe, and went over some of the problems he would find when he came back to the United States. Vandenberg thought the time was right to announce that the air war in Europe was over. I thought so too, so I took the matter up with Spaatz to see if he thought it proper to make an immediate press release along that line. That was on April 16, 1945.

The next day I told General Eaker he was to come to Washington, and we all discussed the various things that had to be done there to build up the depleted staff. At times, the conference became very heated. One time, Ira Eaker said to me, "I didn't ask to go to Washington!" That made me explode, and I said, "Who in hell ever did ask to go to Washington? Do you think I ever asked to go there and stay for ten years? Someone has to run the Army Air Forces. We can't all be in command of combat Air Forces all around the world!" At that point, General Spaatz stepped in with a remark that calmed us both down.

I told Spaatz and Eaker that both General MacArthur and Admiral Nimitz wanted the Twentieth Air Force, but that it could not be under either one because we were operating beyond the battle area controlled by either of them—far beyond. Without a single over-all commander in the Pacific, MacArthur and Nimitz each visualized the operation of the Twentieth Air Force as being for the benefit of his particular campaign plans. Therefore, I must continue to hold on to the Twentieth Air Force myself until such time as there was a unified command out there. As there never was unified command in the Pacific, I retained command of the Twentieth Air Force until V-J Day.

One afternoon, I found a message from Air Marshal Tedder, asking me to come and see him. When his jeep arrived I followed it to his villa, a rather difficult place to find. Tedder, Lady Tedder, his daughter, and I had dinner together and talked about his visit with Stalin and about postwar aviation. Apparently the great Russian problem was transportation. Tedder said he believed the war in Europe would be over in another two months.

The only hitch in postwar aviation between Great Britain and the United States was the matter of carrying passengers by foreign air lines between the cities of any one country. I was under the impression that this phase of air transportation had been ironed out long ago. President Roosevelt and I had talked it over many times. The President was firm on the point that foreign lines should be able to cross the United States, picking up passengers in New York and San Francisco bound for foreign countries, but not picking up passengers in New York for San Francisco, or local points. These were the same principles that applied to steamship lines.

Tedder said "Stalin fully realizes he controls the German bread basket through his hold on Roumania, the Ukraine, Poland, and Hungary. Without these sources of food, Germany starves unless we, the United States and Great Britain, keep them alive, for Germany has not the production to support itself. That may well be a source of trouble in the future."

The areas for rest and recreation along the Riviera were administered with no requirements about such disciplinary things, as say, saluting. The men went to those areas and relaxed and did as they darned pleased. However, they did have separate hotels for the Air Force personnel and for the ground troops. I was inspecting one of the A.A.F. hotels, and had gone through a very elaborate, beautifully equipped dining doom and a splendid kitchen, when the noncommissioned officer in charge of the hotel asked if I would like to go up and see a typical room where the men slept. So, with my staff and the hotel staff of commissioned and noncommissioned officers, I was inspecting a room when we heard a commotion out in the hall. Quite obviously the officers who were stationed in the hotel were trying to stop two enlisted men from coming in to see me. It was also obvious that both enlisted men, who were little fellows, were slightly under the influence of liquor.

So I went out into the hall and asked, "What's the matter?" Whereupon, the conversation went like this:

Both soldiers: "Those fellows say we can't talk to you."

Arnold: "Sure you can talk to me. What's on your mind?"

Both soldiers: "They said we couldn't get near you."

Arnold: "Well here you are. What outfit are you with?"

Both soldiers: "101st Airborne."

Arnold: "That's a wonderful outfit. Did you jump in Holland?"

First soldier: "We sure did."

Second soldier: "You know we didn't."

First soldier: "The hell we did."

Second soldier: "You mean the first time or the second time?"

Arnold: "Well, didn't you make your first jump in the Arnheim section?"

Both soldiers: "Sure, we both jumped there."

Arnold: "And in Normandy?"

Both soldiers: "We jumped there too."

I said, "My heartiest congratulations! You did a wonderful job. Then both GI's said together: "We knew you'd let us talk with you," and one of them asked, "Can we take a picture?" I replied, "Well, let somebody else take the picture and you two fellows come over here and get in the picture with me." One of them asked, "You don't mind if I put my arm around you, do you?" I said, "Hell, no. Go ahead!" So the picture was taken that way, with the two men from the 101st Airborne Division standing with their arms around the Commanding General of the Army Air Forces. Then they saluted and said as they left, "Sir, you have done a grand job and you are a grand Joe."

After we finished inspecting the hotel, I went out the front door. Somehow, word had spread around that I was in the hotel, for there were soldiers by the hundreds blocking the street, standing at attention, some swaying slightly, some with smiles on their faces, but none saluting —except there, standing between the door of the hotel and my car, were the two GI's from the 101st, standing rigidly at attention, swaying from side to side, with their hands up in a full military salute, their chests expanded and battle jackets full of decorations.

By now my recovery was satisfactory and I was about ready to take the next step of my journey, through Italy and back to the United States by way of Brazil.

★ *30* ★

Our trip across the Mediterranean to Italy was unforgettable—the Alps to the north, with their snow-capped peaks, the towns and cities along the coast, the blue Mediterranean, all presented a beautiful picture. The south end of the German line where the French were fighting was not more than thirty miles away. We saw the north shore of Corsica, and then the Italian coast came through the broken clouds, with glimpses of the Italian towns, farms, rivers, and railroads. Finally, the city of Florence appeared through the undercast.

The people in Florence looked much better than those down south in Naples, or at Bari. There were no signs of lack of food; no thin children, nor, in fact, any thin adults.

While in Florence, I had an opportunity to talk with many of our boys who had been prisoners. They were extremely caustic about not getting supplies while they were in the concentration camps. In some cases, they didn't get any supplies at all from the Red Cross for a period of two months, and according to the boys who came back from Switzerland there were hundreds of tons of supplies piled up there that couldn't be sent through into Germany. This was probably because the war and our rapid advance had made transportation an uncertain quantity.

I went to Pisa from Florence to inspect the Brazilian Fighter Squadron under the command of Lieutenant Colonel Maura. The Brazilians, according to the commander, had shown themselves capable of being accepted as part of the Army Air Forces team. They lost 17 men in combat, and three to disqualification by the Flight Surgeon, or a total of 20. They were equipped with P-47's and they flew them very, very well. This, and Kenney's experience with the Mexican Squadron in the

Pacific, which had a splendid record, would seem to prove that it is quite possible to have a hemisphere Air Police Force.

Back in Florence, I saw General McNarney, who told me he was very worried about the attitude of the Russians. They had put so many restrictions on the activities of the Americans that we could do practically nothing in the Balkans or in the Vienna area. The head of our mission in Austria had to get permission twenty-four hours in advance to have his mechanic go out and work on his airplane! Neither McNarney, who was head of the American troops in the Mediterranean area, nor anyone else could land in the Vienna area without starting the wheels moving to get permission forty-eight hours ahead of the proposed flight. McNarney said the conditions were going to get worse, and he looked for trouble along that line with the Russians in the future.

General Spaatz and General Anderson, arriving from Germany that evening, reported that the destruction by bombers was so complete that Germany could not recover for years and years. Cities, towns, power plants, factories were all leveled to the ground—much worse than any of us had believed possible. Oil refineries, for instance, were completely wrecked. However, they brought out one point to which few of us had given serious thought. They said the Germans had built so many underground factories that we were really very lucky to catch them before they were completely in operation. We could not possibly have destroyed them, for the shops and warehouses were too far underground to be harmed by our bombs.

The following day I rode around Florence with Generals Clark and Truscott, both of whom agreed that the German Army in Italy was disorganized and broken. Both British and American troops were now across the Po, and Truscott said he would be in Verona "tonight," which was the 24th of April, and expected to be through the Brenner Pass, on the north side, by May 10th if he were permitted to. The following day marked the last bombing mission of the Eighth Air Force, against the Skoda works at Pilsen and the Salzburg marshaling yard in the heart of "the Redoubt."

While I was with Clark and Truscott I met the Polish General Anders, who had been captured by the Russians and held prisoner for a couple of years. When released he weighed only about 100 pounds. As soon as he was freed, he organized a new army and had it transported to Italy where he was doing excellent work with our forces there. Just when the morale of his troops was at its highest point, they heard of the Yalta Agreement that put the homes of practically every one of those loyal

Poles inside Russian territory. Anders did not know what to do, where to go, nor what to tell his men. They certainly did not want to live in Russian territory after the war was over. It was indeed a problem and no one seemed able to advise him. Our sympathy was with him and his men.

We went through the town of Bologna and saw an excellent example of our precision bombing. The railroad yards, the bridges, the airport, and the huge supply dump had all been destroyed, but little harm had been done to the city itself. The University, the oldest in the world, was only slightly damaged and could be easily repaired.

They had run out of targets for heavy bombing in southern Germany, Austria, and the Balkans. It looked as if the job of the Fifteenth Air Force, too, was about finished. Before long we could take them out of the European Theater and send them to the Pacific.

General Clark received a message on the 25th of April that Genoa had been captured, with about 54,000 prisoners. The Germans had no gasoline; tanks and trucks had been abandoned, and trucks were being pulled by horses and oxen. The Brenner Pass was out, all communication had been severed, and the enlisted men of the German Army were surrendering in large numbers. The war in Italy was finished.

I had a chance to talk to Field Marshal Alexander before I left Italy. He too was sure the war in Italy was about over, and believed we could be in Austria in two weeks if the high command wanted us to. He didn't think the Germans would continue fighting much longer. He thought Himmler would be the one to make the overtures for the surrender. In his opinion, Hitler had brain trouble and was hiding out somewhere— probably at some island in the Baltic. The report would come out that Hitler had been killed in the defense of Berlin, and in about five years, if conditions were right, he would suddenly reappear from the dead and become a hero to his people and a new threat to the world. I could not agree with Alexander, for after what I had heard and what I had seen of Germany, I didn't believe there was anything left in Hitler's "thousand year Reich" to provide a threat for a long, long time.

Alexander believed the Russians were jealous of the United States and the British, and that they were savages at heart. They had good high-level staff planning, but poor leadership in the staffs on the lower levels.

I went to Bari before taking off for Brazil, to have a conference with the commander and staff of the Fifteenth Air Force. At the various air bases around there, I talked to Air Force officers who told stories about Russian restrictions of our activities. We could go here; we couldn't go there. We couldn't do this; we couldn't do that. We could land here; we couldn't land there. We couldn't see the results of our bombing at this place or at that place. We couldn't go into this city, or land at that airport. Some day there would have to be a showdown. Spaatz, Alexander, and McNarney all said the same thing: The Russians had no fear of our Army or Navy, but they did fear our Air Force.

I inspected the 345th and 349th Groups at Foggia and found them in excellent shape—plenty of planes, crews, and spare parts. The Groups were all "raring to go," willing to leave in a short time and head for the Pacific to fight the Japanese. They didn't want to go home, particularly, until the entire war was over.

General McKee, from my office, caught up with me that night and I went over with him the plan for redeployment of the Air Force, and wrote a cable to be sent back to Washington covering the subject. I also sent a message to Eaker, telling him air supplies to Europe, except gasoline, should stop. There were enough supplies in the pipelines to fill all requirements.

While at Cannes I had received a very pessimistic letter from Bob Lovett. He thought the Army Air Forces were being ignored now, in the high-level conferences. Just what that meant I didn't know, but he wanted me to come back home as soon as I could. This business of ignoring the Army Air Forces had seemed to come and go. It had taken me a long time to build up President Roosevelt's confidence in me so that when he wanted to discuss air matters he would talk to me, instead of to a lot of other people not in the Air Force. Apparently, with a new President, it would be necessary to establish confidence all over again. Still, I was scheduled to go to Brazil. Finally, on the 29th, after talking things over with my doctor, I sent a message from Marrakech to General Marshall asking that I be notified when the Combined Chiefs of Staff would have their next meeting so that I could change my itinerary, if necessary.

We left Marrakech and went to Dakar, took off that same night and flew straight through to Brazil. We hit the shoreline at Natal and followed it down to the town of Recife. I was met by Colonel Bubb and found that Kay Francis, the movie actress, was there, visiting the various camps and putting on shows for the boys. General Wooten and General Walsh came in shortly thereafter and we had a chance to talk over conditions in Brazil. I went through the town of Recife by automobile, visited the market place, and found it to be a typical Portuguese tropical town. By the time I returned, Admiral Munroe had joined Walsh and

Wooten, and they were waiting for a conference. They wanted me to go down to Rio de Janeiro and make a public appearance.

In the afternoon I went, with Admiral Munroe, to see the excellent Navy Farm which had been cut out of the jungle. Here, with the assistance of the Brazilian Department of Agriculture, they produced vegetables, fruit, pigs, and fowl of various kinds for use by the Navy, with the first priority for the produce going to the Navy Hospital. And it had all started with four wild turkeys from South Carolina.

In Rio the next day I had a long talk with President Vargas about the development of aviation in the United States and in South America, particularly in Brazil; and about how our landing craft of various types could be used for exploring the deep interior of Brazil.

The following day, May 3rd, we flew to Galea to see the Brazilian Aviation Technical School and the aircraft plant where they were building Fairchild training planes. It was one of the first attempts the Brazilians had ever made to build airplanes and they were getting along very well. A couple of years before, I had sent Paul Riddle down to Brazil at their request to establish civilian aviation schools where they could train mechanics for their Air Arm.

In the evening at a dinner given by the Minister of Air, Salgado, General Dutra, the Minister of War, and General Gomes, both of whom were running for the next Presidency of Brazil, were present, as were the Minister of Marine and most of the senior officers in the Brazilian Army and Navy, Ambassador Berle, and members of our mission. Both Dutra and Gomes were expending every effort to prepare for the coming election. Gomes, as an air man, was closer to me than Dutra, and had an interesting background.

The next day, with Salgado and Paul Riddle, I went to inspect the plant at São Paulo. This is a city of a million and a half people, modern in every respect, with beautiful large houses and grounds, wide streets, fine parks, Poinsettia growing like trees, and flowers so large and colorful they made those in California look sick.

The technical school there had about 1800 students training as mechanics for the Army; it also trains Uruguayan students. Upon my arrival, they had assembled the band and the instructors. The ceremony was most effective, with the playing of the Brazilian National Anthem, the United States National Anthem; and a two-minute silence in honor of the war dead. Salgado and I both gave talks, followed by a review of all the students.

The school was operating efficiently and doing a grand job. All that was needed to develop Brazilian aviation was the necessary experienced personnel for the responsible jobs, and the necessary equipment, for they had the raw material from which they could make pilots and mechanics.

The following day I saw their flying schools—primary, basic, and advanced—where they had 1200 cadets and 1800 enlisted men for a three-year course. The young pilots, like ours, must be athletic in order to pass the test of physical fitness. They had the same type of obstacle course and swimming tests, but their physical fitness course was far more intensive than ours.

There again I had to give a talk to the officers and enlisted men in the school. A big review came as a surprise, and during it Salgado presented me with the "Order of Merit Aeronautic." There had been only one other such decoration issued and that had been to President Vargas. I was awarded the No. 2 article and was very much pleased.

In my ride back to town with General Gomes, I had an opportunity to talk with him about what he really wanted to do and what he would do if he were elected President. He came out with three fundamentals. He wanted to change the Constitution so it would: (1) Limit the term of the President; (2) Provide for a Congress; (3) Give better opportunity to aliens who came to Brazil to settle.

While I was in Rio, it became evident that the Armistice was going to be signed by the Germans, and as part of the higher echelon in the United States Armed Forces I had to make a speech for release on Armistice Day. Washington asked that in my talk I bring out the point that, whereas the fighting in Europe was over, we still had a big task ahead of us in the Pacific, and the war was yet to be won. Accordingly, I prepared such an address and dictated it onto a disk for broadcast back to the United States:

Fellow Americans: This is a day of rejoicing. A battle—a bloody and bitter battle, has been won. The men who won it—your sons, brothers and husbands—have triumphed over a host of relentless, desperate and powerful enemies. They have earned the deepest and most enduring gratitude of every civilized human being, in whatever country, for all time to come. They have indeed given the world a day for rejoicing.

The U.S. Army Air Force is proud of what it has done toward making this day possible. To provide air power needed for victory over the Axis partners in Europe, the Army Air Force had to travel a long way over an arduous road. Simultaneously, it had to initiate and supervise the production of more than 150,000 airplanes, train two and a half million men, and fight on a dozen potentially decisive fronts. On the night of December 7, 1941, the day war came to be, the Army Air Force found itself with less than 200 airplanes deployed against our enemies. Today's airplanes were either just beginning to come off the production line, or were just entering the blueprint stage. Our airmen were still in preflight training, or behind office or school desks—raw young civilians for the most part.

Remember too, if you will, the German Air Force, in the early days of this war. When the German Armies rolled into Poland, Norway, and France, they were spearheaded, covered and backed up by the pride of the Nazi militarism—the Luftwaffe. We knew that before our own Armies could come back; before we could mount a successful invasion of the European continent, this German Air Force would have to be shattered. The German Air Force was shattered. Our fighters and bombers ruined it in the air, as our strategic bombardment ruined the source of its strength on the ground. Together with the R.A.F. we disrupted the entire German economy. We forced them on the defensive and gave an air-tight cover to our invasion on D-Day.

When the time came, we paralyzed their transportation system to the point where the German ground forces were unable to execute the most desperately needed maneuvers. Air power was our margin of Victory. And the thing to remember on this, of all days, is that to give us this all-important margin, tens of thousands of the finest men who ever lived lie in nameless graves, scattered everywhere. We must never forget their sacrifice.

For many months now, scarcely a day has passed without our B-29's making their appearance over the Japanese homeland. The men in those airplanes know what their job is. The Japanese industry will have to be battered to the same chaos that engulfed Germany's military machine. That is a campaign barely begun. Daily, our air crews return to their work at the risk of death and capture by the Japanese. They have read the details of the Death March of Bataan as closely as you have. They know what and whom they are up against, and yet, they return to their targets, day after day, night after night, simply because they know that it must be done.

Remember those men on this day. Remember, although a great battle has been won, their war, and your war, goes on!

I prepared that speech, knowing that I would probably be en route to the U.S. at the time of the Armistice on May 7th. On May 6th, I went through a Brazilian Army hospital at Rio de Janeiro, which was much more modern and up to date than any hospital in any other tropical country I had ever seen. While I was there, I arranged with the Minister of Foreign Affairs and General Salgado for additional officers to be attached to our mission for duty, to help them out in the development of their aviation program.

We took off from Rio on the 6th of May, and continued, with one stop at Santa Cruz, to Georgetown, 2500 miles from Rio. While I was in the air between Santa Cruz and Borinquen the Armistice was declared in Europe.

We reached Miami on May 8th, after completing a trip of 17,900 miles. I found, upon landing: (1) A letter from President Truman in which he said he had complete confidence in me and would like to keep me on the job; (2) A newspaper clipping containing a story by one of our columnists, which said that because of my actions as Commanding General of the Army Air Forces, President Truman was going to ask for my resignation; (3) An item by a columnist who branded me as the hero of the air age; (4) Widespread reports that I was going to retire on account of my heart trouble and high blood pressure (Incidentally, I never had any high blood pressure). The doctors, after giving me an examination, told me I was better than I had been for ten years! Apparently, it was a case of you pays your money and you takes your choice.

As far as the Air Forces were concerned, we had anticipated the Armistice with Germany long before it happened, so we were not caught completely unprepared. We had made our plans for redeployment of the Air Forces in the Pacific. We had made our plans for modifying the B-29 to deliver the atomic bomb. We had prepared sufficient bases to take care of all the B-29's available. We hoped to put B-17's and B-24's on the landing fields at Okinawa and batter what remained of Japan to a pulp.

The Armistice with the Germans found us with about 700 B-29's in the Pacific. This number was to be increased to over 1000 during the last bombing operations prior to the end of the Japanese war in August.

We recognized that the big cry now would be: "Bring the boys home! The war is over!" We also realized there would be other problems— the helpless desolation of the conquered country and the matter of our Russian Allies, now to be dealt with along lines which our political leadership had apparently not prepared for.

Aside from the redeployment to the Pacific, one of our bigger jobs now was making preparations for handling the enlisted men and officers in the United States upon their return. They had to be processed through all kinds of offices in order to get complete records of each man's physical condition, and his war record, before his discharge to civilian life. This meant preparing centers in various parts of the United States.

After a fairly short stay in Washington, during which I became re-acquainted with President Truman and found him in complete accord with our Air Force plans and policies, I took off from Bolling Field, on June 6th, headed for the Pacific. On all my trips I had used the same.name for my airplane. It was always called the "Argonaut." I had started out with "Argonaut No. 1." The plane which we used on June 6th was the "Argonaut No. 4."

While in California, I drove to Sonoma and had the first view of our ranch, purchased two years before. Everything looked pretty good—the trees in the orchard were growing; the berries and the grapes seemed to be doing well; the garden looked fairly well; there were a couple of cows and calves, and a few chickens. But I found the deer were doing great damage to the garden, so I arranged to have a deer fence put around the orchard and the garden. I also had to buy enough hay, while the price was low, to fill the barn.

We took off for Honolulu on the evening of June 8th, and reached there the next morning. From General Richardson, the Army Commander, and his staff we got a complete story of the war in the Pacific from the Marshalls to Okinawa. Richardson was convinced that the Navy had been determined from the start to make and keep it a Navy war, under Navy control. Rigid Navy procedures must be followed and would not be changed. There would be no flexibility in operations, even though it meant complete disorganization of Army units. He had no criticism of Navy methods except that they did not permit getting maximum efficiency from Army units.

At first, the Navy opposed our B-29 operations, and opposed them violently; then they tolerated them, and then the whole Navy was back of them, but they wanted control of all the Superforts. I had a good chance to talk with Admiral Towers on June 10th, at which time his staff gave a presentation of the war in the Pacific from the Navy point of view. In two months Spruance's and Mitscher's carriers had lost 750 planes—250 in operations, 250 in combat, and 250 on ships as a result of the Japanese suicide attacks. The Navy, in turn, had made some 4300 sorties and had destroyed some 2400 enemy planes.

Later on, I had a conference with the Air Staff at Hickam Field and found that it was not always the Navy or the Army that stopped the Army Air Forces from getting things done. In connection with getting fighters up to Iwo Jima and Okinawa, everybody was blaming everybody else. As a matter of fact, the only thing that stopped them from getting the fighters up there was the "will to do."

During the conference it was brought out that we had 17 transport planes flying each way, every day, between Honolulu and Guam; seven between Guam and Okinawa; and four between Guam and Manila. There were 353 planes en route at that time from the United States to the Far East—181 C-54's and 172 C-47's. They were carrying an average of 270 casualties a day back to the United States.

That night I had dinner with General Richardson and a number of other people, including Moss Hart, the playwright, and Gertrude Lawrence, the actress. They came down to see us off. Much to the delight of the crew, while I was talking with General Richardson, Gertrude Lawrence, using a lipstick, drew a heart with an arrow through it on a paper plate, then put her initials, "G.L.," on it and placed it on the pillow in my bunk. The crew got a big kick out of that.

We took off that night on a 2457-mile flight to Kwajalein. We lost June 11th as we passed over the 180th meridian, so June 12th came up at midnight with clear but bumpy air. Next morning there were clouds and cloud shadows and sun spots on the water, looking like atolls; finally, real atolls; then nothing but more sun spots and more cloud shadows on the ocean, until we saw the sea breaking on a reef—unmistakably an atoll. It was Kwajalein, 80 miles in diameter. Inside the harbor were more ships than I had ever seen before. When we landed, I met General Ross, of the Marines; Admiral Harrill, of the Navy; and Commander Ben Wyatt, an old Navy pilot whom I hadn't seen since I was at San Diego back in 1920–24. It was like old home week.

All the airplanes going west went through Kwajalein. Ninety per cent of the operations at that time were Army; 10 per cent Navy. While I was there, 16 B-29's came through, headed for Guam. The hospital was small, but good—particularly good considering the fact that it was built on a veritable coral reef—and I had a wonderful opportunity to see the superior work our flight nurses were doing in the air evacuation of casualties from the combat areas to the United States.

While at Kwajalein, I saw a Japanese burial ground where our bulldozers had scooped holes in the ground, thrown the bodies in, and pushed the dirt over them. Then a sign was erected: "This is a Jap Burial Ground."

We took off for Guam, via Eniwetok, a distance of about 1630 miles. As we approached Eniwetok we saw the atoll and anchorage, about 50 miles square. Inside were maybe 200 ships all told. It was a sight that should have made a Japanese bombardier go crazy.

There was no doubt, the Navy was following out its approved policy with regard to the Pacific. Accordingly, we had to accept Navy control, command, and administration, when from a cold-blooded point of view, from a paramount interest point of view, and from the operational point of view, the Army should have had full control of some of the islands. Another thing—the War Department, for many years, had seemed to have the attitude that we shouldn't try to obtain unification of command in the Pacific. We must not bring the facts out squarely. We must not get the Navy mad at us right now. We must accept things as they were, even though we thought a change might be for the best; and we must not criticize the Navy. So we continued operating in our inefficient way, with first three, then two commands—MacArthur's and Nimitz'—both working toward the same end—the defeat of Japan, with overlapping lines of communication, overlapping air operations, overlapping sea operations, and, finally, overlapping land Army operations.

We landed at Saipan in the evening and had a conference with General Barney Giles, General LeMay, General Harmon, Admiral Whiting, and General O'Donnell about their B-29 setup. When we left for Guam, 120 miles away, I took General Giles with me. The Japanese were still on the Island of Rota, but as we flew over it we did not see any of them or any evidence of hostilities. We landed at Guam late in the evening and were met by Admiral Nimitz, General Kuter, and many of my old friends, including Colonel Shelmire, an old artilleryman with whom I had gone to school back in Pennsylvania, and who had joined up with the Air Forces and was doing a good job in the command at Saipan.

It seemed strange that although Saipan, Tinian, and Guam had been in our hands for many months, the Japanese were still being killed, still being brought in, walking and surrendering. Thirty had been killed the day I arrived at Guam. When I reached headquarters on June 13th, I received a radio from General Marshall which made me sit up and take notice. I had planned that General Spaatz would command all strategic bombers from a headquarters on Guam, regardless of whether they were B-29's or B-17's. Now, it seemed, the Navy wanted us to have only the Twentieth Air Force Headquarters on Guam. This I could not see.

We had planned on using Saipan, Tinian, and Guam as our three bases for the B-29's. By using all three, we had planned to take care of approximately 1000 B-29's. We hoped to get perhaps 1000 B-17's on Okinawa, where we could probably have a better strategic bombing headquarters than at Guam. The Navy's attitude of telling us what to do with our strategic bombing headquarters was, to me, intolerable. They certainly would not countenance the War Department's telling them where to locate the headquarters of their fleet units, and surely they had no strategic bombing experience.

Time was essential and we had to get things moving fast to get the maximum mass bombing of Japan started in the minimum of time. I thought the thing over and considered possibly calling off the idea of using Guam at all, and moving the Strategic Air Force Headquarters to Manila. Then I thought better of it, and sent a message to General Marshall saying I believed he should tell the Navy we would definitely put our strategic bombing headquarters at Guam and it would be there with the other B-29 units, period!

After I recovered from that brainstorm, I went down to Admiral Nimitz' headquarters and had a presentation of the Pacific War by the Navy Staff. It was very interesting as well as essential for me to have before I moved farther across the Pacific.

Back at LeMay's headquarters, I had them show me their plan for destroying the Japanese industrial facilities. Curt LeMay figured they could be destroyed by October 1st. In order to do this, he had to take care of some 30 to 60 large and small cities. With the destruction of these cities, Japan would have few of the things needed to supply her Army, Navy, and Air Force, and couldn't continue fighting. We had done the same thing in Germany with much more difficult targets and much more intense antiaircraft fire, not to mention the Luftwaffe's tough opposition.

LeMay, who had been a leading figure in that campaign, realized that incendiary bombs would have an even more terrible effect upon Japan than they had had on Germany, where 80 per cent of the damage done to the cities by the U.S.-R.A.F. air offensive was caused not by high explosives, but by fire bombs. In Germany, buildings and whole towns that from a distance seemed to be unscathed, were found, on closer approach, to be nothing but gutted, burned-out shells. In Japan there were so many old wooden buildings that a large load of incendiaries, with a strong wind, would normally destroy the major portion of a whole town with one attack. LeMay was taking advantage of this with bomb loads that stressed incendiaries.

Going back to my quarters, I found Lowell Thomas there and decided to take him up to Iwo Jima with me when I went up the following day. I had another conference that afternoon with LeMay and found he was operating under a very complicated organization. The Navy was ostensibly in command of everything, but we still had an Army command to control Army logistics and training. There were certain routines and procedures prescribed by the Navy, which were necessary to them, that the Army considered superfluous. The complications of the system, even if they involved only one inefficient individual somewhere down the line, made long delays in decisions a foregone conclusion. There had been delays and interference in operations because people assumed authority over Army Air matters that were really none of their business. A case in point came up with regard to hard standings for bombs. The Navy disapproved our request for 210,000 tons of bombs because of lack of hard standings for storing. This, in effect, told the Air Force how many bombs we would be able to drop in a month. Priority over the movement of the bombs and ammunition for B-29's was vested in Naval officers. In some cases, the interference resulted from consideration of what might happen, rather than what actually was happening.

Talking these things over with Admiral Nimitz later in the day, I found him very agreeable to every suggestion I made. He offered no objection to the Strategic Command's being at Guam, and was agreeable to having Spaatz command it. He also concurred in the principle of having both the Eighth and Twentieth Air Forces in the Strategic Command. He saw no conflict in the headquarters which could not be overcome, and was certain the advantages to his organization would outweigh the disadvantages. After this conference with Admiral Nimitz, it finally dawned on me that most of the Air Force problems, difficulties, and complications were a result of junior officers' magnifying something of relative unimportance and making it a great matter. Everything pointed to my getting my people together and giving them a talk.

Admiral Nimitz had a directive from the Joint Chiefs of Staff, stating that he was to command Okinawa and be Military Governor of Guam. Until these orders were rescinded nothing could be done about it. Accordingly, we in the Army must conform to his way of doing things, but he was perfectly willing to have Army Air Force officers on his staff. He agreed to a setup that would give us everything needed for the Strategic Air Force, and he welcomed having a representative of Spaatz' headquarters sit with his people to determine priorities in shipping and the changes that would have to be made to eliminate procedures that interfered with our operations. I couldn't see many difficulties left to be ironed out except such things as might arise after Spaatz' arrival, and I thought he and Nimitz could take care of those without any trouble. As far as I was concerned, people down along the line were making mountains out of mole hills.

That afternoon we went out to the 314th Group, a unit which had completed fourteen missions over Japan. I also talked to the 315th Group, from whose planes the armor and most of the guns had been removed, about the effect of the changes on their operations. Admiral Nimitz came over and joined us, and I introduced him to the assembled crews and officers, and to the plane that was to be christened "Fleet Admiral Nimitz."

So far on my trip across the Pacific, no one had hazarded the time for the defeat of Japan, except LeMay. Neither Admiral Nimitz nor General Richardson nor their staffs talked about when the war would be over. But while I was on Guam, I received the preliminary report of Francis d'Olier upon the strategic bombing in Germany, in which he said that bombing had not only hastened the end of the war there, but had had a most disastrous effect upon Germany's production. The attacks on oil and transportation, and the prevention of the movement of coal from the Ruhr had been in the words of Speer himself "tragic" and "a nightmare." I didn't see the whole report then, naturally, but reading that much of it caused me to do some serious thinking about Japan.

If our bombing did have that effect upon the national and industrial collapse of Germany, certainly the same amount of bombing, or perhaps less, would have a worse effect upon Japan.

The many cargo and personnel ships standing offshore at Tinian, Saipan, and Guam were a bomber's dream. Yet the Japanese planes had done comparatively little damage to these wonderful targets. Where was the Japanese Air Force? The Navy talked as if the Japanese Air Force still existed in large numbers, hiding and lurking behind something that couldn't quite be visualized, ready and waiting to come down and attack the Navy and all its ships when the opportunity offered. If the Japanese had actually had the airplanes they would certainly have made some effort to hit those concentrations of ships I had seen.

While I was at Saipan, I watched 520 B-29's take off for Osaka, carrying 3000 tons of bombs. It was quite a contrast to Doolittle's 18 planes, with their 15 tons, and the first B-29 mission a year ago with 68 planes and 181 tons.

That same day I received a cablegram from General Marshall in which he stated there would be a meeting of the Joint Chiefs of Staff, with the President, to discuss the subject, "Can we win the war by bombing?"

That was quite a subject—a question that meant a lot to the people at home. If we could win the war by bombing, it would be unnecessary for the ground troops to make a landing on the shores of Japan. Personally, I was convinced it could be done. I did not believe Japan could stand the punishment from the air that Germany had taken.

After thinking and talking it over, I was convinced LeMay probably had more information on the subject of "bombing Japan" than anyone else, so I proposed that he go to the meeting of the Joint Chiefs of Staff and make the presentation to the President. The Strategic Headquarters must be established at once and all the dilly-dallying must be stopped. The strategic bombing must be unhampered in its organization, administration, logistics, and operations. It must have a free hand to drop the greatest number of bombs in the shortest possible time. That meant the administrative delay in getting bombs, gasoline, and such things must be stopped. The Army and Navy must keep their hands off the actual bombing operations.

Meanwhile, I prepared and later sent off a cablegram to General Marshall, outlining my ideas.

1. Continue with our present plans and occupy Kyushu to get additional bases for forty groups of heavy bombers.

2. Give priority to B-29 attacks and the Kyushu operations so as to step up bombing attacks.

3. Make plans for complete destruction of Japan proper, using B-29's from the Marianas and Okinawa, heavy bombers and attacking planes from Kyushu, and carrier planes to cover areas not completely covered by other planes.

4. Give priority to, and take off all administrative restrictions to bombing efforts, and put all postwar activities into much lower priorities.

5. Continue plans for the main effort by ground troops for landing on Honshu, but keep it on a "live," but postponed, basis.

That settled, we continued on our trip with Lowell Thomas, General Giles, and his aide, Colonel Harry Chesley, to Iwo Jima, which was commanded by General Chaney. Iwo Jima is of volcanic origin and still has a live volcano at one end. Steam comes up through the runway. Approximately 1200 Japanese lived there, in prewar days, raising sugar cane, harvesting sulphur, and developing a plant from which they extracted the juice to make vanilla. When our Marines landed on Iwo Jima they bumped into 20,000 Japanese, with three divisions. The Marines lost about 3000 men. There were still about 200 Japanese soldiers there, hiding in caves and crevices, under debris and in wrecks of ships. Occasionally they came out, gave themselves up, or were killed. The night before we arrived, three were killed.

Sometime before, six had come out, prepared to fight, but on seeing some of our Negro soldiers were so surprised they surrendered. They had never seen any Negroes before. The Negroes searched the Japanese again and again and found nothing but their pistols, then took the Japanese to the mess tents to feed them. There was nothing in the kitchen but canned goods, which our men tried to open with their pocket knives, with no luck. Helpfully, one of the Japanese went deep into his trousers, pulled out a knife about a foot and a half long, and handed it to a couple of badly scared Negroes.

Iwo Jima was a wonderful supplementary supply base for our air operations against Japan. Up to that time 1200 crippled planes, or planes out of gasoline had landed there, many of them B-29's. In fact, of the 520 B-29's sent to bomb Osaka the day I was there, 43 had to land at Iwo either on the way up or on the way back.

Winning the war; winning the peace. Flying from Iwo to Manila, I thought of the many problems ahead, and I was convinced that, as much as the average American would prefer the diplomats to carry on the negotiations for a permanent peace, the military people would get along much better at the conference table than the diplomats ever had in the past. Every time peace conferences came up, the same things happened —diplomats sparred with each other and were not able to find an answer. Despite conflicting national aims and interservice rivalries, the Combined Chiefs of Staff, for all their arguing, had achieved both compromise and cooperative action. The measure of the agreement they had reached was to be seen now in the global victory.

Leaving Iwo Jima, we had gone through a front of heavy tropical rain squalls, but as we reached the east coast of Luzon, a break came in the clouds. We saw beneath us Mount Arajal, Pinatubo, Mariveles, Laguna De Bay, Corregidor, Manila Bay, the city of Manila, and then what used to be Nichols Field. There was little left of it. Manila itself, as I saw when I drove around it later, was a shambles. All the old landmarks were gone. The Manila Hotel, the Army & Navy Club, and the Elks Club were completely gutted by fire and explosives. Intra Muros was a wreck. The old wall was battered and breached in spots where our troops had forced their way in to rescue some 3000 Filipinos who were being held as hostages by the Japanese, finding most of them massacred.

I had a talk with General Stilwell, who was to start back to the U.S. the next day, General Stratemeyer, who was returning to the C.B.I. Theater, General Stone, and General Kenney about the unnecessarily hard way we went about fighting a war, with two commanders and two supply systems in the same theater, and in the afternoon, went to MacArthur's headquarters. We had a long and quite spirited conversation. He was in favor of an independent Air Arm, and was willing even that it should include the Air Force supporting the ground troops; furthermore, he was willing to organize the Army in the Pacific along those lines right then, and he would be satisfied, he said, with either Kenney or myself as Commanding General. He did not want a supreme commander, and accordingly was willing to sacrifice unity of command. My impression was that he believed the Navy would never relinquish any of its control; that it would be he who would have to give up everything necessary to achieve unity—hence, he had everything to lose and nothing to gain. He said he was satisfied with the Joint Chiefs of Staff directive as to command, but he resented the Navy's reluctance to turn over to him the islands and the supply system that he now, having advanced so far to the north, should control. Also, he felt that the Navy was now laying plans and completing facilities for building up its postwar organization.

In his opinion, our Strategic Air Command organization was wrong. It was all right if I kept the command; it was all right if Barney Giles was my deputy; but it was a complete mistake if the Strategic Command, under Spaatz, went to Guam. And while he believed bombing would do a lot to end the war, in the final analysis, he said, the doughboys would have to march into Tokyo. He had not entirely understood our plan for using B-29's to destroy 30, 40, 50, or 60 Japanese cities and their industries; for dropping 200,000 tons a month on targets in the invasion area, and 80,000 tons on invasion day, and was somewhat surprised at the maximum strength we planned for our B-29's. However, when I explained all this, he seemed to like it.

He recognized the Army's need to have its own supply system all the way from the United States to the front line, with no interruption by the Navy; but said he was not going to fight for control of island bases, even though they came within his area. That, he said, was a job for the Joint Chiefs of Staff. But when the subject arose of moving his headquarters to Guam for greater coordination and cooperation, the lid blew off! There was every reason why it should not be done and not one good reason for doing it! He could not see why there would be any better coordination with the Navy if his headquarters was on Guam than if it was at Manila.

Our conference lasted for about two and a half hours, and gave me a far better idea of MacArthur's line of thought and reasoning than I had ever had before.

The necessity for unity of command became more and more apparent to me. One of the main questions under consideration was Okinawa. When and if Okinawa was completely taken over by the United States, it would be under Navy control. MacArthur would have only domiciliary rights. The Navy Base Area Commander, with power to clear all ships in and out of the Okinawa area, would thus control all priorities into the island, and if the Navy wanted to give their own permanent construction on the island first priority, they could, and MacArthur couldn't do anything about it. That was not my idea of unity of command. Priorities should be dictated by the war situation, and not by the Army, Navy, or Air peacetime programs. There should be a shipping and supply priority clearing board. There was none—no central clearing point where Army, Navy, and Air all had their day at court.

Later I had my final talk with Stratemeyer and told him that if General Wedemeyer couldn't find a place for the Tenth Air Force in China, we should turn it over, lock, stock and barrel, to General Kenney because Kenney would find a place for it. Stratemeyer didn't like that, and said he would fix it up so that the Tenth would be taken care of in China.

I saw MacArthur again later that day and was shown a message from Admiral Nimitz on the Far East Air Force plan for coordinated bombing. Nimitz would not agree to having Kenney bomb ships or operate ten miles offshore; and he insisted the Navy must have first priority rights in the Japanese Island Sea.

In my opinion, that was one hell of a way to run a war—to have the power but not be able to use it because you were interfering with someone else's prerogatives! Fortunately, the war came to an end much sooner than any of us expected, so these problems never reached a point where they caused an open break between the Army and the Navy.

I went out to Fort McKinley and tried to find our old house, but very few of the old quarters were standing. I found what was left of our house: a set of concrete stairs leading from the street up to what used to be the front porch, and the foundation of the house proper. That was all. Then I went to look for General Marshall's house and found it was not so completely destroyed. The concrete steps leading up to the porch were still there, and the bathtub was still in place, with the hot water boiler. The Post Exchange had been destroyed, and the Parade Ground was grown over with grass and tropical plants. It looked almost like a jungle. It was hard to pick out the old landmarks where George Marshall and I had served as lieutenants some thirty years before.

We took off the next day, June 19th, and flew around Corregidor and El Fraile. Corregidor was badly battered; batteries were disabled, buildings destroyed, and all facilities completely gone. It was plain how Kenney had been able to use his airborne troops to take the Island at a small loss of life. When the Americans landed, they closed the tunnel, and today it is the burial ground of anywhere from 500 to 5000 Japanese. No one knows how many.

At Stotsenburg Kenney and Whitehead were waiting for us. The difference between Stotsenburg in 1941 and Stotsenburg in 1945 was decidedly marked. In 1941, we had not dared have an airplane visible anywhere—one visible meant one destroyed. In 1945, the Japanese Air Force was impotent and we had four, five, or six hundred fighters in the open on hard standings. Bombers, wing to wing, with no camouflage at all, stood on the various dispersal points around the field. There were about a thousand airplanes at that time at Clark Field.

When the Japanese took over Stotsenburg, they captured all the vehicles that were operating; apparently we didn't destroy any. The same thing happened down at Bataan. At the time of my visit, the Air Forces again were using the same vehicles; in a way, a hand-me-down from the Japanese. The car that was assigned to me had been captured by the Japanese and used by their commanding officer; now, it was back in the Army Air Forces, still in good condition.

We took off for Okinawa the next day with Kenney. The south section of the Island was still war-swept and we could see the firing going on beneath us as we flew over. Reportedly, they had about 2500 Japanese soldiers trapped in caves and there were still many left uncaptured, but organized resistance was about over. From what I saw as we flew around the Island, the Kamakaze suicide planes had an easy time finding targets when they came down to Okinawa because there were innumerable ships of all kinds everywhere. All the Japanese had to do, once near Okinawa, was to close their eyes and put the noses of their planes down, and they would be almost sure to hit a ship every time.

I was met at the airport by General Woods, the Marine Air Commander, and went with him to the Fifth Army Headquarters where I met General Geiger and Admiral Hill for a short conference on the air problems on the Island. It was obvious that to meet our B-17 demands, we must get more airfields without delay. To do this, we needed more engineers and more Seabees; more ports and post facilities. More troops must be unloaded; and a more energetic logistics policy put into effect. So I suggested, and they agreed, that a message be sent from the Army Commander to Admiral Nimitz, and I said I would also take the matter up with him on my way back.

General Buckner, an old friend of mine, who had been Commander of the U.S. Army troops on Okinawa, was killed just a short time before my arrival, while watching a tank attack in the southern part of the Island. The Japanese, apparently, had just one piece of artillery, which was located only about 300 yards away. The first shot they fired hit very near where Buckner was standing and a fragment went through his chest, killing him. Our country lost a wonderful soldier and leader.

While many of the high-ranking Navy, Marine, and Army officers were welcoming me in due form to Okinawa, a young man in a Marine uniform came up, stopped his jeep beside me, and without even getting out, called, "Hiya, Pop!" creating a terrific sensation among the officers, photographers, and everyone else. It was my son Bruce.

I went with him and made an inspection tour of his platoon. He had a fine camp and an excellent bunch of men with him. Like everybody else in battle, they had to fend for themselves to get essentials. For instance, it was easier for Bruce and his outfit to take a few of the relics and antiques they found in some sarcophagus or in a village which had been captured and trade them for uniforms and food with the Marines than it was to draw the routine supplies in accordance with administrative orders. That explained his Marine uniform, for he was a member of the Army Antiaircraft. I took him with me to dinner at the Tenth Army Headquarters, which I am sure he did not enjoy.

As I was saying good-by to him, we had an air alert. The Japanese were staging another small nuisance raid. There were flashings of guns and tracers, and the booming of artillery, but after many false alarms, the Japanese turned away without attacking.

Back on Guam, I had a conference with Admiral Nimitz and his Staff, General Stilwell and General Mandell of the Army, and Generals Giles and Coombs of the Air Force. I told Admiral Nimitz the information I had brought was merely that which I had obtained while at Okinawa and in the Philippines. I hadn't checked up on it, but the Army Supply officers were very much afraid that there would be a backlog of a million tons of shipping waiting to be unloaded at Okinawa by September, and there would not be enough bombs to carry out our program for destruction of Japanese industries, pre-invasion bombing, and support of an invading army. And the reason was that the docks at Okinawa would not be completed in time to permit unloading of supplies, although there were Seabees and engineer battalions awaiting shipment to Okinawa and facilities for taking them there as fast as they could be sent.

Admiral Nimitz assured me that all of these matters had been, or would be, taken care of. Engineers and Seabees were being sent as rapidly as available.

However, the bombing program was so important, from my point of view, that I asked Admiral Nimitz if it would be possible to have a representative of the Air Force, from General Giles' office, sit in with the Navy and make up progress reports periodically so the people at Okinawa would know what was going on and so they would not become all aflutter about something they feared was forgotten when it had already been taken care of. He agreed that would be a fine thing, and it was arranged right then and there.

Nimitz was worried about a message he had received relating to the employment of British engineers during these operations. I assured him their presence was just part of the general British plan to participate in the Pacific campaign and told him I would present his ideas on the subject to the Joint Chiefs of Staff. His ideas were:

1. The British engineers could come out at once if political heads said we must use the R.A.F.

2. The British engineers would be used in a pool on Okinawa, with Army engineers and Seabees.

3. As Kenney's Air Force units moved forward, the British could use such airdromes as required, if not needed by our very heavy bombers.

After lunch with General Giles, Lowell Thomas, and Giles' Staff, I went to the northwest airfield to see the B-29's return from the bombing of aircraft factories in Japan. Four hundred and eighty-four of them had taken off the preceding night. Four were lost—two on take-off and two over the target from phosphorous bombs which were dropped on them. I talked with many of the crews and they were convinced their targets had been hit and destroyed. The crews that had bombed were not tired, even after fifteen hours of flying, and their morale was high; while those that for one reason or another had not reached the target were weary, and their morale was low. One thing was certain—if there was any Japanese Air Force left in Japan it hadn't appeared to stop many of the 480 B-29's on that mission.

It was obvious from my talks there that we must build up our B-29 Depot Staff in Okinawa. I must have damned good air men on the staffs of both Nimitz and MacArthur, and a man on priorities with the Navy at Pearl Harbor who could look after our interests. And we must have men with the Navy on Guam for shipping and priorities.

We took off for Eniwetok next morning and landed in midafternoon after flying a distance of 1170 miles. As we approached Eniwetok, we passed four destroyers in line, hunting for a sub which had torpedoed, but had not sunk, an LST; then we passed several cargo ships headed from Eniwetok to Guam, and then a large convoy. Nearing the atoll, we could see for some forty miles away the large number of ships at anchor. Among them was the LST which had been hit by the sub the day before, apparently undamaged except for its rudder and one propeller, which were destroyed. We took off from Eniwetok that night, headed for Johnson Island.

Johnson Island is about 6500 feet long and not over 700 feet wide at any point. Coral reefs protect it from the sea. The island used to be only 4000 feet long, but had been built up by dredging. At that time it had a complete complement of buildings for its small garrison and from a distance it was very similar in appearance to a carrier. One wondered how our navigators were able to find such a small target in the middle of the Pacific, yet planes came in and out constantly—34 trips a day, both ways. Many times they came in with one engine out. Upon landing I found that most of the traffic going through at that time was bringing back wounded personnel, and the 34 daily trips eastward were to be built up to 64, the idea being to bring back as many evacuees as possible from the combat theater.

That same day we took off from Johnson Island and headed for the Hawaiian Islands, a distance of some 800 miles. It was an uneventful trip, with scattered clouds, and we remembered it was in that area that General Miff Harmon's plane had disappeared three months before. And three years before, to the northeast, Clarence Tinker's LB-30.

Upon landing at Honolulu, I met Admiral Towers, General Richardson, and General Ruffner and talked over the various matters that had come up during my trip; and learned that Admiral Nimitz had gone on east for a conference with Admiral King.

We took off that night from Honolulu and arrived at San Francisco, 2450 miles away, the next morning. As a matter of fact, I reached San Francisco on my birthday and learned that my wife, who was on the West Coast, had arranged a birthday party for me at our ranch. But I also learned that President Truman was to arrive a few minutes later for one of the earlier meetings of the United Nations Delegation. I thought it was essential that I report to him on my trip, and also meet with the United Nations representatives to determine, if I could, exactly what our plans for the future were. My birthday party was called off, and that night I had dinner with the United Nations representatives at the St. Francis Hotel.

After listening to our people who were present at the early meetings of the United Nations Council at San Francisco, I came unavoidably to the conclusion that, theoretically, the United Nations organization was sound—but so, also, was the League of Nations. Theoretically, the United Nations organization should prevent future wars, should take care of the disagreements and squabbles between nations, should iron out the difficulties and conflicts. But there was still the big question: Would it? Or would it be another organization with no power or teeth with which to enforce its decisions?

✯ *31* ✯

The major job of the Air Force at the end of June, 1945, was to get our heavy bomb groups into the Pacific area from the European Theater as rapidly as bases were available. It was the lack of bases that provided the bottleneck in that movement. The small islands which we captured soon became overcrowded with Army, Navy, and Air installations, and it was necessary to find additional sites. Many of the delays in doing this I believed would be eliminated after the discussions I had had with Admiral Nimitz and with General MacArthur. However, even under the best of conditions it would be several months before we would get landing fields in Okinawa capable of taking care of the hundreds of B-17's and the B-24's we could throw in there from Europe. In the meantime, we were building up our B-29's at a rapid rate, sending them over Japan with ever-increasing loads of explosives. It was certain, as General LeMay had said, that the interior of Japan would be a shambles by the 1st of October.

I could not see how Japan could stay in the war very long after the defeat of Germany, and the imminence of this final victory raised other questions, such as the future security of the United States; the creation of an organization that would prevent future wars; the future organization of the Army Air Force and its place in the world-wide air picture after the war. In general, these were matters for staff work; things to be studied carefully from all angles and tied in with our foreign policy, if we had any, so that when they were presented to higher authority—to the Combined Chiefs of Staff and our representatives at the United Nations' meetings—there would be no hit and miss conclusions.

I have always regretted two things about the war. One was not being able to accept an invitation from Goering to visit Germany before the war started. The other was not to have had a chance to talk with Goering after the war was over and he was a prisoner, and to ask him a few questions. The first I could not do, because of the disapproval of the War Department. The second was not possible because during my tour of Europe Goering had not yet been captured and later I was too busy to make a special trip to see him. I wanted particularly to ask him questions concerning things the German Air Force might have done, but did not do. Why did the German Air Force not continue the Battle of Britain when the R.A.F. was so badly battered? What made Goering overlook the obvious strategic power available in the development of his Air Force when he had such a wonderful start? Was it because Hitler dictated to Goering the policies for developing the German Air Force? Was it because the generals in the ground army had such influence over Hitler? Or was it because Goering himself just wasn't on the ball?

However, General Spaatz saw him. About the middle of May, I had received a letter from Tooey in which he outlined the interview he had had with Goering on May 10, 1945, three days after his capture. In that interview I found the answers to some of the questions in which I was interested; but whether they were offered truthfully or whether they simply represented Goering's effort to clear himself I could not determine.

For instance, Goering said that in 1940 Hitler began to interfere with Air Force operations by taking air fleets away from his (Goering's) planned operations. That, according to Goering, spelled the breakdown of the efficiency of the Luftwaffe. (Perhaps—perhaps not. He didn't say what the intended operations were; nor did he say how the air fleets Hitler took away were constructed, trained, or equipped.) He said one thing that showed to what extent the German Air Force had had to go down to the bottom of the barrel for replacements during the Battle of Britain: The JU-88 was primarily a commercial airplane which had to be adapted for use in the Battle of Britain, along with the He-111 "because we had nothing else. I was not in favor of engaging in the Battle of Britain at that time. It was too early. The He-177 (a four-engine bomber) was late in development."

That is a rather astounding statement, because by that time the German Air Force should have been at its peak, ready to lock horns with the R.A.F. under any and all circumstances. It was the thing for which the German Air Force presumably had been preparing for years. Why else did it exist? A few more months would not have helped the Luftwaffe to any great extent because the R.A.F. was beginning to reach its own peak, and the time had come when the two Air Forces must clash to see who was to have supremacy in the sky. The Battle of Britain was the real test of both the R.A.F. and the German Air Force.

When Goering was asked, "Did our bombing attacks affect your training program?" he gave an answer which we had known to be a fact long before I received Spaatz' letter. Said Goering, "The attacks on oil retarded the training, and our pilots could not get sufficient training before they were put in the air, where they were no match for your flyers."

We had planned it that way.

Another interesting question asked was, "Could Germany have been defeated by Air Power alone, using England as a base, without invasion?" Goering replied, "No, because German industry was going underground, and our counter measures would have kept pace with your bombing. But the point is, if Germany were attacked in her weakened condition, as now, *then the Air alone could do it*. That is, the land invasion meant that so many workers had to be withdrawn from factories, production, and even from the Luftwaffe."

When Goering was asked, "Which had the most effect on the defeat of Germany: Area bombing or precision bombing," his reply was, "The precision bombing, because it was decisive. Destroyed cities could be evacuated, but destroyed industries were difficult to replace."

Every time Goering was asked a question covering policies, he came out with the same answer: that he had been forced to do what he did by political dictates.

He was asked, "Why didn't you attempt to cut us off in North Africa, and send the Luftwaffe, which was then superior in the air, against our shipping and the concentration of our airplanes at Gibraltar?" Goering's reply was, "We had too few long-range airplanes, and then later, when you got to Algiers, the airfields in Italy were inadequate. You have no idea what a bad time we had in Italy. If they had only been our enemies instead of our allies we might have won the war." (That, also, was a remarkable statement, considering the amount of time the Germans spent in Italy, and the materials available which they might have used to improve the airdromes. We certainly had heavier airplanes than the Germans—planes that required longer runways. Yet, thanks to the rapid work of our aviation engineers, we were able to operate our Fifteenth Air Force from Italy with comparatively no trouble.)

"Why did you attack our airdromes on January 1, 1945?" Goering was asked. He replied, "Because every airdrome was loaded with airplanes." Then (to Goering): "Well, why didn't you come back? Why didn't you repeat?" Goering's reply, again typical, was, "Orders from higher headquarters. Hitler said it was no good to bomb American airplanes because more of them would come like bees."

Goering's interrogator then asked, "How would you contrast the Air Forces of the Allies?" He replied, "Well, the Russians are no good except on undefended targets. You need only three or four Luftwaffe airplanes to drive off a 20-plane Russian attack. The American airplanes are superior technically, and in production. As for personnel, English, Germans, and Americans are equal as fighters in the air."

He was asked, "In your opinion, in the tactical operations of our Air Force, the attacks on what targets were most damaging to you?" "The attacks on marshaling yards were most effective," he said. "Next came the low-level attacks on troops, then the attacks on bridges. The low-flying airplanes had a terror effect which caused great damage to our communications. Also demoralizing were the 'umbrella' fighters, which, after escorting the bombers would swoop down and hit everything, including the jet planes in the process of landing."

The question of whether he failed to build big bombers because he did not believe in strategic air power, or because the productive capacity was restricted to the production of tactical aircraft brought this reply: "I have always believed in strategic use of air power. I built the Luftwaffe as the finest bomber fleet, only to see it wasted on Stalingrad. I was always against the Russian campaign." (Perhaps there was some hindsight in that reply!)

It was a remarkable interview, but it didn't bring out all the information I should like to have obtained from Goering. I should like to have found out why the Luftwaffe carried out strategic air operations in the Polish campaign, and for a while in the Netherlands and the French campaigns, and thereafter appeared to be chained to the Army and did very little except troop support. Did the Germans ever really contemplate having a strategic air force? Did they have a full conception of what a strategic air force really was, and what was necessary to keep it operating? Did they really understand Air Power? Why did they not have a training and production program sufficiently large to take care of their combat losses? We had to do it in the United States to maintain a constant or ever-increasing strength in our battle areas. There were many other questions, the answers to which would have been interesting to me.

I had been very glad, during my trip in the Pacific, to see that the working staff of Francis d'Olier's Strategic Bombing Survey Committee, USSBS, was operating there. His report, made by disinterested men, always should be of extreme value to anyone who studies the future and is desirous of finding ways and means of minimizing the effect of bombardment.

The same general principles of bombing will apply in the Third World War. We may use different kinds of planes—jets instead of the orthodox, gasoline-engine type; we may use atomic bombs instead of normal, high-explosive type bombs, but the destruction carried out by bombing will have the same general effect. It may come much more quickly, and may be more decisive when it does come. Fundamentally, it will be the same.

On July 11th we took off, headed for the Potsdam conference, and after a stopover in Canada, where we had a day's fishing on the Mingan River (and caught nothing) we landed at Orly, a short distance from Paris, in the late afternoon of the 13th and drove straight to the Hotel Rafael.

As soon as the Rhine was crossed, our technical experts, moving through Germany with the advancing troops, began to obtain much detailed information from factories and experimental centers. After talking to the staff in Paris, it became apparent to me that our Air Intelligence was getting 100 per cent cooperation from the British and zero per cent from the Russians. Unfortunately, about 35 per cent of the German data was in Russian hands.

The Germans destroyed the original documents after making copies, then they hid the copies. In some instances, we were able to find the copies, and eventually to get a complete story of the German Air Force's technical development program for the future. For instance, we were able to send twenty-five Me-262's back to the United States. With one such jet, one German pilot claimed to have shot down forty-three of our heavy bombers.

I assembled the Air Staff and outlined my ideas for the future development of the United States Air Force. The war with Germany was over, and the war with Japan was in the bag, as far as creative work was concerned. I pointed out that there was little we could do other than see that planes, personnel and supplies got there. All our planning should now be directed toward the future. Accordingly, we must make accessible to the scientists all information available, from all sources, from all nations. We must have them see all gadgets, data, and drawings, so that they could give us a Buck Rogers program to cover the next twenty years. We must not let the American people down by slipping back into our 1938 position. Our program for the future, I said finally, must cover not only the technical development of materiél, but also the training of our personnel and of our units, and their technique of operations.

Some time back I had asked, through the Joint Chiefs of Staff, to have our diplomats secure permission from Norway, Denmark, France, and Italy for us to use their heavy bomber airdromes, so that we could operate heavy bombers radially around Germany. Just now we learned the diplomats were still considering the problem, and were taking it up through the various ambassadors. It looked as if we might have these airdromes in time for the next war, instead of for this one.

That afternoon, with General Cannon, I flew to Salzburg, over the ruins of Nuremberg and Munich, and while there learned that my son Hank had been transferred from the 106th Antiaircraft Battalion to the 45th Division staff, and was at Rheims or in that vicinity—or perhaps en route home. I immediately started the wheels turning to see if I could get him to meet me at Salzburg.

We set out for Berchtesgaden in Hitler's automobile, an open touring car with bullet-proof glass and armor plate. The hotel to which we were going was the Berchtesgadener Hof where Chamberlain, Mussolini, Prime Minister Schuschnigg of Austria, and others had waited to meet Hitler, and I learned, when we got there, that I was to have the suite that used to be occupied by Himmler.

Hank caught up with me that night, and next morning, July 14th, we left the hotel with General Tobin and General Cannon for Hitler's retreat, the "Eagle's Nest," located up a steep mountain road at an altitude of about five thousand feet. Actually, it was on the very top of a rocky crag, and commanded an exceptional view in all directions. The man who had run the elevator for Hitler was still on the job, and pointed with great pride to the seats where Hitler, Eva Braun, Goering, Goebbels, and Himmler had sat as they went up in the elevator together.

Thinking back about the Eagle's Nest now, it still seems to me fantastic beyond comprehension. It could have been of no value to anyone but Hitler and he actually had entered it only four times. Over 3000 people had worked for four years to build it and the amazing tunneled road up to it.

From the Eagle's Nest we drove to Koenigsee, a small town our U.S. Army had taken over, in which six hotels had been designated as recreational places for our enlisted men. The fraternization ban had been lifted at six o'clock the night before I arrived at Koenigsee. The ban was really a farce, for when American men have been away from home for a period of one, two, or three years, fighting all the time, they want to talk with someone besides soldiers and officers—to have companionship when the period of letdown and relaxation comes. The Germans and the French made no attempt to conform to this kind of prohibition, although it was supposed to be in effect in all Allied armies. Now our GI's were allowed to talk with the Germans and the Austrians in public. The night before the ban was lifted we had seen GI's sitting on benches, and German girls on adjacent benches, when we first drove by. When we returned a few minutes later, all had disappeared! So is fraternization prevented—by order!

We drove to a deserted resort hotel where Goering's art treasures were stored, loot from every great museum in Europe, as well as such private collections as Rothschild's. The rattling around on special trains before its capture by our 101st Airborne Division had not helped the collection any. Some of the statues had lost their heads and arms; many of the paintings were scarred, standing on the floor, on washstands, and on toilets. Three of the Raphaels were valued at two million dollars.

We left for Berlin the next day. I took Hank with me and hoped to have him with me when we flew back to the United States. We landed at Berlin in the late afternoon of July 15th and found that President Truman had landed just ahead of us. General Marshall was expected a few hours later. Admiral King had been there for two days. British and Russian soldiers lined the streets at intervals from the airport to Berlinerstrasse, Babelsberg, where General Marshall, Colonel McCarthy, Colonel Shepley, Major Sheffield, and I lived.

General Marshall and I called on the Secretary of War after Assistant Secretary McCloy and Mr. Bundy arrived, and had a long talk about the atomic bomb and when the first test would be held in New Mexico.

Babelsberg was the "Hollywood" of Germany. For some reason, when our bombers hit and destroyed most of Potsdam and Berlin they had missed Babelsberg. Accordingly, when the Potsdam conference was decided upon and it was necessary to find an area where a large number of high-ranking officers and their staffs and the secretariat could be accommodated, Babelsberg's comfortable houses, being practically unharmed, were an only too obvious choice. The suburban homes were in the Russian area, however, and that caused complications before we were settled.

As soon as the area was selected, the Russians used a very effective system for evacuation. They notified all Germans living in the district to get aboard trains bound for Russia that afternoon. If anyone complained it was just too bad. We were told there were few protests. There was the story, however, of a certain woman who refused to move. The Russians didn't fool with her. They shot her and buried her in her own front yard. There were no further complaints. The only things the people were allowed to take were such personal items as they could carry.

The British and the American delegates had areas side by side. The Russians had the rest of the city. The two zones were separated by a very heavy line of guards. All through the district there were Russian soldiers on duty as sentries and Russian soldiers directing traffic.

We had our first meeting on July 16th, and took up the agenda and procedure for the Combined Chiefs of Staff meeting which would be held that afternoon. We had a fifteen-minute talk with the President, and he agreed in principle to having a supreme commanding officer in the Pacific. He also accepted an AAF recommendation for handling matters brought up by the Prime Minister or Stalin with reference to operations in the Pacific.

Later I had a few minutes' talk with Portal. He called my attention to a bet I had made in 1942, that a bomb would land on Washington during the war. I lost, and hope I paid. We then made another bet, of a dinner. I bet the Japanese war would be over nearer to December, 1945, than Valentine's Day in 1946.

That afternoon, our Combined Chiefs of Staff meeting was a very peaceful one and went well, with no untoward incidents. I gave a résumé of the air situation in the Pacific, and after that, we talked chiefly about the Pacific war and what we could and could not do to bring it to a close sooner.

Marshall and I went to tea with the British Chiefs of Staff and then took a ride through Berlin. We saw Berlin and Potsdam in their terrible desolation, not a house standing, seemingly, for miles; not a building that had not been damaged or destroyed. Yet people, old and young, with no place to live but in the ruins—ruins with their stench and filth, the smell of rotting bodies and of broken sewers—were streaming into Berlin on bicycles and pushcarts. Baby buggies were piled high with all the household belongings they could carry.

The Chancellery was a wreck; Hitler's magnificent office with its marble floors was completely ruined; the Reichstag looked like a bad dream. We saw Iron Crosses, German Legion of Merit, and Honorable Service Medals strewn around by the thousands as a result of a direct bomb hit on the reserve supply of medals. Germans outside were selling anything and everything in order to get food. The streets were cleaned up, but everything else was a mess. Twenty-five, fifty years to get Berlin back as a city—who knows? My opinion was that a new site should be chosen and another city built. I really marveled at the destruction our Eighth Air Force and R.A.F. Bomber Command had done.

During our drive, we saw a Soviet troop train headed for Russia. It was filled with all manner of loot, most of which we in the United States would classify as junk—broken furniture, old tires, chandeliers, even livestock and bales of hay.

The Sieges Allee—Victory Way—with its once triumphant statues, was a complete wreck. Fighting had taken place in the Tiergarten, and statues, trees, and benches were all broken or destroyed. The benches still had signs on them reading, "Verboten für Juden." It was good to get out of the city and return to our house in the suburbs.

We had been invited to dinner with President Truman that night, and Marshall and I walked over together. As we entered the yard we were accosted by a Secret Service man. "Whom do you want to see?" he asked. We told him, "We were invited for dinner." He replied, "There is no one here and they won't be back until eight o'clock." We went into the house and found the mess boys setting the table. They had a seating arrangement chart with our names on it, but the official clock in the dining room said 6:45 and the dinner was progammed for 7:30. So back home we went.

It was a very small dinner, with just the President, the Joint Chiefs of Staff, the Secretary of War, and the Secretary of State. We were home by 9:30.

I find a note for the next day, which reads, "Hot water boiler exploded. No hot water for the entire house. General Marshall and all the rest of the occupants must get along with cold water shaves. Note: I wonder, can we blame the Russians for that?"

The story had reached us of how, the day before, Stalin had invited himself to lunch at President Truman's house. Stalin had arrived there about twelve o'clock, and when asked if pictures could be taken, replied, "After lunch." Until then, no one at the Truman house had known he was coming for lunch. But stay he did and the pictures were taken afterward.

While General Marshall and I had been having lunch the previous day, we had received word that the Secretary of War wanted to see us. We went over to Secretary Stimson's villa immediately and found Assistant Secretary McCloy and Mr. Bundy there. They showed us a cable stating that a successful test had been completed with the S-1, which was the atomic bomb, at Alamogordo, New Mexico, on July 16, 1945.

This did not come as a complete surprise to me, but I had thought the test was a week or two away. From the information we received, the scientists were very well pleased with the results. The sound, it was reported, could be heard fifty miles away, and the flash could be seen for over two hundred miles out in the desert north of El Paso.

An interesting postscript came to us later, with regard to this test: After all the years the scientists had been working on atomic fissure and to develop power and a bomb from that chain reaction, when the setup was finally completed, all component parts in place, electrical wiring for exploding the bomb ready, and they were only waiting to make sure, for safety's sake, that no one was within the danger area, one of those experts came up in the dark of the morning, grabbed General Leslie Groves by the arm and said, "General, for God's sake, don't explode that bomb!" When General Groves asked him why, he replied, "Because we do not know what will happen! We have no idea what it will do. It may tear off a corner of the earth. Don't, for heaven's sake, explode it!" That put General Groves in a very unhappy position, but he decided to go ahead, and the first of the atomic bombs was detonated. The results of that test proved conclusively that we had in our possession the means to wipe out completely large areas of an enemy country.

With Secretary Stimson and Mr. McCloy, General Marshall and I discussed the big questions: how soon would we be ready to use the bomb against Japan, and what should the targets be? I told them the best results would be obtained if we turned the matter of targets over to General Spaatz, who had planes ready and waiting out in the Pacific for the arrival of the bomb, and who knew the cities chosen for the test. This was accepted as the policy for the selection of targets, so I sent Spaatz a cable.

That afternoon, at a Combined Chiefs of Staff meeting, the British accepted our program for the remainder of the war in the Pacific, which meant that operations would remain under the control of the United States, regardless of whether the units were under MacArthur or Admiral Nimitz, or whether they were British or American. At a meeting of the Joint Chiefs of Staff that day, Admiral King agreed that Okinawa should be turned over to General MacArthur, though as far as logistics were concerned there were still strings attached which might and probably would lead to trouble.

At the end of the day's meetings, General Marshall, as host, took the Combined Chiefs of Staff to a review of the 2nd Armored Division in Berlin. Six hundred vehicles were lined up, hub to hub, for a mile and three-quarters along Unter den Linden. It was a most inspiring sight, and a terrific display of power.

The next day, after three days of clouds and slight rains, the sun came out over Berlin. Refugees were still flocking in by the thousands. The strangest kinds of conveyances were being used—three-wheeled wagons; trailers; horse-drawn vehicles; old automobiles; bicycles; baby carriages; horses pulling and horses pushing; men pulling two-horse wagons with straps over their shoulders; men, women and children hiking, with packs on their backs. There were about three women for every man, and the men either were quite old or very young, many of them wounded.

During the day, I talked with General Marshall about continuing in harness. Now that the war was about over, I did not believe we could continue to work with "our necks up in the collars" as we had for the past four years. We should let the next echelon of commanders have their chance. In short, I thought it was about time for us to retire. Marshall agreed with me, but I bet him five dollars he would still be in office six months after Japan capitulated. He took the bet. (Note: I haven't been paid yet. George Marshall was still on the job and working just as hard, if not harder, many months after V-J Day.)

In the afternoon, I had a long talk with Portal about how to reconcile the operations of our Air Forces, as well as of our commercial air lines in time of peace. It was not a simple problem, for we had conflicting ideas. We agreed we should both have bases throughout the world which the R.A.F. and the USAF could use, but the ways and means of securing these bases when operating under peacetime conditions stymied us, because our State Department and the Foreign Office in Great Britain had methods of doing things which were not conducive to helping the military in advance of a war.

We both believed our next enemy would be Russia, and a common line of thought emerged from our talk: The Russians understand manpower on the ground, and are confident they have the finest army in the world. They have no fear of any navy because they know no navy can get close enough to harm them. But one thing they fear and don't understand is strategic air power—long-range bombers. They have never had long-range bombers of their own and they apparently do not know the principles of employing them. Tomorrow, however, things may be different. To use our strategic Air Power successfully we must have bases so located around the world that we can reach any target we may be called upon it hit. On that, Portal and I both agreed.

I saw Eisenhower that same afternoon. As he would undoubtedly be the next Chief of Staff, I wanted to discuss with him whom he would like to have as his Chief of Air Force, for I would be ready to turn over the reins to somebody else in a few months. It was decided then and there that General Spaatz would take my place.

Later, General Marshall, Tom Sheffield, Frank McCarthy, Hank, and I went for a visit to Sans Souci, the Neues Palais, and the Orangerie, all of which were under Russian supervision. One would think that two five-star generals with their two aides would not find much difficulty getting into any place, Russian controlled or not, yet when we arrived at the entrance to Sans Souci the Russian sentry looked at us dumbly when we said we would like to go in and look around. As a matter of fact, he said there was not much he could do about it. Our aides told him who was in the car, but apparently it didn't make much of an impression. Finally he went to a telephone and called up somebody, somewhere. Then he reluctantly opened the gate and let us go inside. We went down to the fountains and were looking around when a Russian officer came up in an automobile, introduced himself in poor English, and asked us if we should like the fountains turned on. We said we should, so we were treated to a private exhibition of the gorgeous fountains of Frederick the Great. From then on we had no further difficulty in going through the rest of the Palace and the grounds. As a matter of fact, the Russians were not much interested in what we did or what we saw, just as long as we didn't take the Palace away with us.

I had noticed earlier in the day, during a drive to the Templehof Airdrome, that the Russians had set up trading posts all around the Reich Chancellery. They were using the American money they received from—well, the sources depended on whom you talked to. Some say our Treasury Department turned over to the Russians the plates from which they printed literally millions of American dollars. For the first time in five years, the Russian soldiers were paid, just before they came into Berlin. They had more American dollars than they knew what to do with, and since they could not take the money home, their main idea was to spend it. Exactly how many American dollars were available to the Russian soldiers will probably never be known. One thing is certain, the Russian soldier squandered his American dollars like nobody's business. He paid one U.S. dollar for one American cigarette; twenty U.S. dollars for a package of cigarettes; from two hundred to five hundred dollars for a watch. If it was a Mickey Mouse watch that ticked loudly, he paid anywhere from five hundred to six hundred dollars for it. One bar of chocolate usually cost the Russians about five dollars, but with that bar of chocolate he could get one woman. Rings, all kinds of household goods, silver knives, forks, and spoons were traded for bread or canned meat. These trading posts were countenanced by the Russian authorities, with hundreds of people patronizing them all day long.

Very naturally, our American soldiers soon became aware of this market and were taking advantage of it. They could get the desired articles from many sources, and even went so far as to have friends coming over from the States bring additional watches, cameras, etc., to sell to the Russians. The U.S. Finance Officers changed the Russian dollars into U.S. dollars as fast as the soldiers brought them in, and almost as fast as the Russians printed them. Then we, back in the States, redeemed them when the soldiers' letters of credit reached the States.

That night we had a dinner for rank at our house in Potsdam, and when I say "rank" I mean just that. With six officers present, we had a total of twenty-eight stars. There were five five-star generals or field marshals, and one three-star general—Field Marshal Montgomery, Field Marshal Alexander, Field Marshal Wilson, General Marshall, Lieutenant General Ismay, and myself.

At an R.A.F. concert later in the evening, we had a real galaxy of stars. They had the entire front row set off for the top-flight generals, field marshals, air marshals, and admirals. There were nine five-star generals, admirals or air chief marshals, one three-star general, and one two-star general—a total of eleven persons and fifty stars!

During the dinner, I had a chance to talk with Alexander and Montgomery. Both were worried over the troubles the forthcoming German winter must bring, with its lack of heat and food. There would be little medicine; an unsettled government; probably disease and epidemic. They also foresaw another war about twenty years hence. Sir Alan Brooke and Admiral Cunningham agreed with them.

On the 21st, it looked as if our work with the Combined Chiefs of Staff was about over. Portal and Brooke went off to Bavaria on a fishing trip. That night at dinner there were just five of us—Marshall, Sheffield, McCarthy, Shepley, and I. The following day, after a conference with the President, the Secretary of War called me in and again we talked over the atomic bombing of Japan—he from the standpoint of the political and economic factors involved, I from the standpoint of strategy;

that is, having in mind the targets whose bombing would most speedily spell the destruction of industrial Japan. Kyoto, the holy city, was again ruled out. Repeating my earlier recommendation that General Spaatz make the actual selection of targets and that Spaatz coordinate his decision with General Groves, I told General Marshall I would send Colonel Jack Stone back to Washington with a memorandum covering this matter. The Secretary agreed to this, and I dispatched Stone back to the United States at once.

That night, Secretary of State Byrnes, Averell Harriman, General Deane, and General Parks joined General Marshall and me for dinner. Jimmy Byrnes came out with something that struck me forcibly. He said what we must do now was not to make the world safe for democracy, but make the world safe for the United States. That seemed to me a very sensible way of looking at it.

After talking with Averell Harriman and General Deane, and with Echols, who was in Berlin and saw how the Russians operated, I could not help but feel that Russia was like a greedy kid, never satisfied, always wanting one more lollypop.

When the Russians went into Berlin and into other cities in its sectors, they took over all the money and other securities in the banks. They even opened safe-deposit vaults and confiscated all contents. That, with printing press marks, made it possible to practically sovietize that part of Germany. Then, having completely stripped the country, the Russians granted authority to the Germans to open their banks on a specified date. How the Germans were expected to open them with no money or securities, I do not know.

The French (and they can't be blamed after the way the Germans had treated them) were taking away all the livestock in their area and sending it to France, and they were living off the country. Obviously, they were increasing a condition which meant the Germans must be given outside aid to keep from starving. Certainly, the United States would be called upon to feed not only the French in France, but the Germans in Germany.

The next day, July 23rd, we had the Joint Chiefs of Staff and the Combined Chiefs of Staff meeting, and another meeting with the Secretary of War regarding the atomic bomb and its effect on Japan. We talked about the killing of women and children; the destruction of surrounding communities, the effect on other nations, and the psychological reaction of the Japanese themselves. We also discussed the possible effect of the weather and the topography on the explosion of the bomb.

There was no doubt that the effect of the atomic bomb would be much severer if it were exploded over an area in a valley, with high ridges on both sides to concentrate the effect of the blast, than if dropped over a coastal plain or over a large, flat area inland.

To me it seemed of the utmost importance, and I presented the idea, that we should try to find out what the explosive effect would be if an atomic bomb were dropped in a harbor. I thought that the explosion of such a bomb, sunk hundreds of feet in the mud beneath the water, might well destroy the surrounding area. I suggested that we evacuate a Japanese harbor after the war, put ships at dock and at anchor, and then try it. In that way we would learn what might happen to one of our land-locked harbors in case the same thing occurred to us when we least expected it. However, the test was never carried out.

That night we had dinner with the Prime Minister. It was a gala affair with the President, Mr. Churchill, Marshal Stalin, and their military staffs present. Three foreign secretaries were also at the table. The toasts were many, as usual. The Prime Minister, Stalin, and the President were all in good form. Stalin announced, with no attempt at secrecy, that now the war in Europe was over we had a common enemy in the Pacific, and "Here's to our next meeting in Toyko." That was the first time Stalin had ever come out in the open and talked about actually declaring war on Japan.

To me, that was good news, because it might mean closer air bases, from which we could literally rip Japan to pieces. However, I told Stalin, the Prime Minister, and the President that if our B-29's continued their present tempo there would be nothing left of Tokyo in which to have a meeting.

After the dinner was over, autograph collecting started. At previous dinners, Stalin had very reluctantly put his autograph on any of the menus. But this time, autograph seekers ran wild, and Stalin himself joined the throng and brought his menu around the table to have others sign it.

The R.A.F. band was present and gave us some excellent music, but as the music interfered with the toasts it was often stopped. Finally, the Big Three left the dining room and went into the music room where they could hear the concert without interruption. After the music was over, they came back, sat down at the table, and the toasts continued.

During the intervals before and after dinner, the British and the Americans were talking about the election in Great Britain and its probable results. The British were quite confident Churchill would be re-elected; the only question seemed to be how much of a majority he would receive. On that, there was a wide divergence of opinion. The Americans gave him a much greater majority than the British, looking upon him as the one real leader who had brought Britain through the war and who would naturally, therefore, receive the acclaim and plaudits of the people. We had numerous bets among us on how big his sweep would be. Needless to say, his defeat came as a great surprise not only to the Americans, but also to our British colleagues.

The next day we had a meeting with the Prime Minister, the President, the Combined Chiefs of Staff, Lord Leathers, and General Somervell, in which we discussed the work we had done at Potsdam and any future problems we thought might arise, including our Pacific operations and the transportation involved. After that meeting, the Secretary of War came to our house to talk with me again about the employment of the atomic bomb. I told him that as far as I could see, there was nothing more we could do until we heard from General Spaatz.

That night, Admiral King gave the Combined Chiefs of Staff a dinner. It was a fine party.

During our Combined Chiefs meeting, Lord Mountbatten gave us the Burma story. He gave full credit to the Army Air Forces, saying that the Burma Campaign would not have been possible except for the airlift. On an average, 30,000 tons a month had been flown in, monsoons or no monsoons, mountains or no mountains.

On the evening of the 25th, after a very full day, we received word that General Malin Craig, the ex-Chief of Staff, had died. He was one of my best friends and had helped me time and time again, making my various tasks much easier. However, he had been hopelessly ill, and it was a merciful thing that he passed away, although he would be greatly missed.

The next day we had a Combined Chiefs of Staff meeting with the Russians, who agreed to all our requests, and for the first time made decisions at the table with "Uncle Joe" absent. That was an innovation. The Russians present were Antinov, Chief of Staff; Fallalev, Chief of Air; and Kuznetsov, Chief of Navy. They even went so far, in this case, as to delegate responsibility to the local commander at Vladivostok regarding American dispositions in Manchuria.

One of the most important steps taken by the Combined Chiefs of Staff was the proclamation to the Japanese by the heads of the United States, the United Kingdom, and China. It made these points:

1. Japan should be given an opportunity to end the war.

2. Land, sea, and air forces of the United States, Great Britain, and China were poised to strike the final blows.

3. The futile and senseless German resistance to the might of the aroused free people of the world stood forth in awful clarity as an example to the people of Japan.

4. The complete destruction of the Japanese armed forces and of the Japanese homeland was inevitable.

5. The time had come for Japan to decide whether she would continue to be controlled by self-willed militaristic advisers, or whether she would follow the path of reason.

6. Our terms would not be changed. There would be no alternative, and we would brook no delays. There must be eliminated, for all time, the authority and influence of those leaders who had misled and deceived the people of Japan and embarked them upon world conflict. Irresponsible militarism must be driven from the world.

7. Until a new order was established, points in Japanese territory to be designated by the Allies should be occupied and held.

8. The terms of the Cairo Declaration would be carried out. The Japanese sovereignty should be limited to the islands of Honshu, Hokkaido, Kyushu, Shikoku, and such other minor islands as we determined.

9. The Japanese military forces, after being disarmed, should be permitted to return to their homes and lead peaceful and productive lives.

10. We did not intend that the Japanese should be enslaved as a race or destroyed as a nation, but stern justice would be meted out to all war criminals. Freedom of speech, of religion, and of thought, as well as respect of the fundamental human rights, would be established.

11. Japan would be permitted to maintain such industries as would sustain her economy and permit the exaction of reparations in kind, but not those which would enable her to rearm for war.

12. The occupying forces of the Allies would be withdrawn from Japan as soon as these objectives had been accomplished and there had been established, in accordance with the freely expressed will of the Japanese people, a peacefully inclined and responsible government.

13. We called upon the government of Japan to proclaim now the unconditional surrender of all Japanese armed forces and to provide proper and adequate assurance of their good faith in such action. The alternate for Japan was prompt and utter destruction.

We did not mention the atomic bomb.

By the 27th of July, the British members of the Combined Chiefs of Staff had gone to London and would not be back. The Prime Minister had also departed. The new Prime Minister, Mr. Atlee, was soon to come and pick up the load where the British people had caused Mr. Churchill to drop it. That left Stalin, Atlee, and the President to carry on.

The Joint Chiefs of Staff decided to leave right away. Admiral King was taking a trip to the ports and would meet Secretary of the Navy Forrestal; Secretary Stimson had already gone to Berchtesgaden and then was going on to Washington; Marshall and his party decided to go to Berchtesgaden for two or three days, and then to Washington; the President planned to leave for home the following Sunday.

With my son, Hank, who was returning to the United States with me, I took off from Paris at 10:00 o'clock on the 28th for the Azores, a distance of 1630 miles, and arrived there early in the morning.

Our next stop was Stevensville, 1855 miles distant, which we reached that night. Colonel Atkinson, the Commanding Officer, was waiting for me with the good news that a fishing trip was being arranged for us. Lee Wolfe, the local game garden, came in and we decided to go in a Navy amphibian to a lake 130 miles to the north. The rest would travel in cars to the Serpentine River and do some salmon fishing.

The lake was beautiful and the camp which had been established as a rest center for our soldiers was superb. The sky was overcast and rain was in the air; the prognostication for good fishing was bad. Two captains and some enlisted men had been out the day before and had caught many trout, a few salmon, but more grilse (a young salmon).

We fished the pools where the river runs into the lake. I had on rubber boots and slipped all over the rocks, and in due season went in up to my neck. Everything I had on was wet, my boots were full of water, and I had great difficulty in even getting back on my feet. I almost floated into the middle of the lake. However, I finally got to shore, took off the boots and my wet clothes and wrung them out. It was mighty cold, and I had just decided I would quit this salmon fishing business when I saw a pool nearby. I cast into it and a mass of trout rose to the fly, which was obviously too big—it was a salmon fly. With a smaller fly I landed ten trout, eight to fourteen inches long, out of that one pool (I had two more up on shore but missed them) and one grilse.

The weather soon changed to cold rain and it looked as though we might not be able to get back, so we returned to our plane. And then one engine caught fire. Finally, however, everything straightened out and we came back under a five-hundred-foot ceiling. I was still wet through, but a hot bath and a slug of Bourbon fixed me up all right.

Late in the morning of the next day we took off from Stevensville, reaching Washington that afternoon after covering a total distance of about ten thousand miles.

☆ 32 ☆

Redeployment demanded the closest possible teamwork between Army Engineers and Navy Seabees in the Pacific islands, and our own Air Force units. For instance, in the European Theater we had over 1800 heavy bombers of the B-17 and B-24 types, which we hoped to operate out of Okinawa, or out of Siberian bases if we could. All in all, we had a total of 10,378 airplanes in the ETO, and though we knew we could not use all of them in the Pacific, we wanted to use as many as possible. The bombers of the Eighth and the Fifteenth Air Forces had a very high destructive potential. Starting out, in 1942, by dropping about 6000 tons of bombs, in only four months of 1945 they had dropped a total of 445,000 tons. The combined Army Air Forces units in Europe had dropped a total of 1,554,000 tons of bombs against German targets. Though we might be able to use some of our 1100 European medium bombers from bases close to the Japanese mainland, I doubted if we needed very many of the 5000 fighters, because the Japanese air resistance had been reduced to a minimum by the time we returned from the Potsdam Conference, in August.

As soon as I could, I submitted a paper to the Joint Chiefs of Staff asking that the concept for employment of Air against Japan be changed. Before V-E day, the effect of strategic bombing upon the military German nation could not be thoroughly evaluated. Since then, we had acquired a definite knowledge of what it had accomplished. The interim report of Francis d'Olier stated: "The strategic air offensive, as developed and employed in the latter part of 1944, effectively paralyzed the German war economy and thereby contributed in a decisive measure to the early and complete victory which followed." Accordingly, with all of the Air Power available to us, I submitted to the Joint Chiefs of Staff the following:

I consider that our concept for operation against Japan should be to place, initially, complete emphasis upon strategic Air offensive, complemented by a Naval and Air blockade. While the presently-planned scale of air bombardment is expected to create conditions favorable to invasion of the Japanese homeland on November 1st, it is believed that an acceleration and augmentation of the strategic air program culminating in a land campaign, will bring about the defeat of Japan with a minimum loss of American lives. Estimates of the Joint Target Group indicate that the military and economic capacity of the Japanese nation can be destroyed by an effective dropping, on Japan, of 1,600,000 tons of bombs. This tonnage should disrupt industry, paralyze transportation and seriously strain the production and distribution of foods and other essentials of life. These effects might cause a capitulation of the enemy, and, in any event, will assure the success of the land campaign in Japan, and reduce the loss of American lives to a minimum.

This bombing program against Japan contemplated a total drop of 1,051,000 tons of bombs in 1945. In our opinion, it would make possible the complete destruction of interior Japan during that year.

In the meantime, General LeMay had taken hold of the Twentieth Air Force in a big way and had made a careful estimate of the results obtained by his bombing, and of his attendant losses. Not satisfied with either, he decided to make a radical departure from the previously employed technique of strategic bombing:

1. The bombing altitudes would be reduced from the higher altitudes, above 20,000 feet, to between 5000 and 8000 feet.

2. Only a small amount of armament and ammunition, if any at all, would be carried, and the size of the crews would be reduced;

3. Aircraft would attack individually, the attacks to be at night;

4. Tokyo, in spite of its antiaircraft defenses, would be the first target.

These changes made it possible for each B-29 to carry about eight tons of bombs against Tokyo, instead of six. With incendiaries that made a big difference, because they were small and the clusters broke up into many individual bombs. Further, this change enabled LeMay to expand the number of missions materially.

The percentage of airplanes completing their missions was increased, and so was the actual amount of damage. With the lowering of the altitude, fewer bombers had mechanical troubles, and night fighter interception was almost negligible. While ack-ack was heavy, it was relatively inaccurate. The weather was much better at night, and after the lead bomber had hit the target by the use of radar, and lighted the city with fires, the other B-29's were able to drop their bombs visually. Also, the bombing was far more accurate than it had been before.

Another task given to the Twentieth Air Force, in conjunction with the U.S. Navy submarines was that of bottling up the Japanese ships in their home waters. One Wing of the Twentieth Air Force was selected for this purpose and in the four days prior to the initial Okinawa landing, dropped more than 1000 tons of mines in the Shimonoseki Straits, closing the inland sea to all large vessels for ten days or two weeks. From then on, mines were dropped periodically in most of the important harbor entrances in southern Japan. By then, General Spaatz had taken over all strategic bombing in the Pacific, whether by B-17's, B-29's, or B-24's, and whether from the islands or from the mainland of Asia.

After August 1st, however, things moved at such a pace that the real deployment of the European Air Forces into the Pacific never had time to take place. On August 6th the world was astounded when the first atomic bomb fell on the city of Hiroshima. The effects were indescribable.

Nagasaki was hit by the second atomic bomb on August 8th.

The news of those two attacks came to me over the private wire which I had during the war, running from my home in Fort Myer to the White House. I awaited the reports at home, knowing it might be hours before I got them over the regular communication channels. Both times the private wire brought me the news within a few minutes after the bomb had been dropped.

Two days later we had a small reception for Air Marshal Harris at our home. Bits and pieces of information had started flowing through official channels during the day, and it was confirmed that the Japanese were about to ask for peace. At the party, General Marshall told Mrs. Arnold to listen over the radio for a special announcement that would be broadcast at seven o'clock. After the guests had gone, we heard the announcement that the Japanese Government had submitted an offer for surrender to the Allies.

That night we had no celebration, just a family dinner—or, at least, that's the way it started. Then Air Force generals and their wives began dropping in to extend their greetings and express gratitude that the war was over. General and Mrs. Hal George, and General and Mrs. Craig came in first—George who had done such a magnificent job in building up and running the Air Transport Command, and Craig, who had been one of the men so instrumental in planning and figuring out ways and means of making the "impossible" possible, in the Air war. Then General and Mrs. Fairchild rang our bell. Fairchild had been one of the strong men in building up our Air Organization, and in creating techniques for tactical and technical employment of our Air Forces. Soon, with Mrs. Streett, General St. Claire Streett arrived. He had been one of the men who had worked so hard to keep the General Staff of the Army on the beam with regard to Air Force employment and organization, and later did so well commanding the newly formed Thirteenth Air Force as it worked its way up through the South Pacific Islands from Morotai.

So the night passed, with Air Officers coming in and out. Presently someone suggested sending a message of congratulations to our Commander in Chief, the President of the United States, so I appointed a committee to go to the study and prepare it. After some difficulty they finally agreed on the wording and brought it to me for approval. I found parts that did not seem to fit the occasion, but after further attempts, and a bit of good brandy, a greeting was decided upon which seemed to fill the bill, and I dictated it over my private wire to a clerk at the other end in the White House. We were afterward told it was the first message of its kind the President had received.

The surrender of Japan was not entirely the result of the two atomic bombs. We had hit some 60 Japanese cities with our regular H.E. and incendiary bombs, and as a result of our raids, about 241,000 people had been killed, 313,000 wounded, and about 2,333,000 homes destroyed. Our B-29's had destroyed most of the Japanese industries and, with the laying of mines, which prevented the arrival of incoming cargoes of critical items, had made it impossible to carry on a large-scale war. We had destroyed 10,343 enemy airplanes, compared to the 29,900 destroyed in Europe. Accordingly, it always appeared to us that, atomic bomb or no atomic bomb, the Japanese were already on the verge of collapse.

Many of the Japanese leaders gave credit to the Superfortress attacks on interior Japan and Japanese industrial cities as the greatest single factor in forcing their surrender. Some of them went so far as to say we had reduced their military production by fully 50 per cent. Nevertheless, the abrupt surrender of Japan came more or less as a surprise, for we had figured we would probably have to drop about four atomic bombs, or increase the destructiveness of our B-29 missions by adding the heavy bombers from Europe.

With the surrender of Japan, my major mission was to carry out our demobilization as rapidly as possible. Congress and the American public wanted it that way, and we had to make our plans accordingly. To far too many people the question of the number of troops we should keep in Europe and in Japan, to insure an orderly peace, was apparently secondary. All that mattered was to get the boys home as soon as possible.

However, the Army, Navy, and Air leaders were still responsible for maintaining suitable training facilities in the United States, providing ways and means of getting the men home, and insuring that the occupational units overseas remained at least strong enough to perform their duties. Many of our men had been overseas a long time—two, three, or four years. It was their right to come home now, but trained men must replace them. For those of us who had to work all this out, the few months after V-J Day were hectic ones.

Another big job the Air Force had was to fly the wounded and other high-priority people home. We made plans to transport 30,000 passengers a month by air across the Pacific, and we just about met the figure.

When the war closed, we had in the Air Forces a total of about 2,300,-000 men and women, and about 72,000 airplanes, scattered all over the world. It was obvious our strength would be cut down to somewhere around half a million men, and the 72,000 airplanes would be cut down to about 10,000. Accordingly, we were faced with the problem of moving some 60,000 airplanes, and transferring some 1,800,000 people. That was a tremendous logistics problem. I turned it over to my Staff and to the Air Transport Command to work out, and they did it in a most satisfactory manner.

The question of what to do with surplus airplanes is one upon which no two people ever seem to agree. I announced at the time we were told to get rid of our planes that there was one way to do it properly. I was not in favor of trying to sell 60,000 airplanes. In the first place, there weren't that many buyers; and in the second place, by the time they were sold, many of them would be so obsolete, or would have so many defective parts, that the buyers would probably get into trouble with them. Furthermore, their sale certainly wouldn't help our aviation industry.

To me, the only solution, was to create an airplane crematory at some obscure place in the United States. With a big set of shears, cut the wings off, then throw the entire airplane into a press and crush it into a mass of metal. Then throw this mass of metal into a furnace and melt it. When it was melted, draw off the molten metal—first, the aluminum, or dural alloy, from the top; then the bronze and brasses from a second outlet; and from a third outlet, the steel; cast the metals into ingots; pile the ingots up out in the desert somewhere, like cord wood, and hold them until they were needed.

Apparently, my solution to the problem was too radical, and the Surplus Property people couldn't see it. The "melting" proposition was never seriously considered in the United States, though that procedure was followed in England.

Another vital problem which the Army never quite grasped, or was not allowed to do anything about, was the question of saving surplus supplies, when we had them, against the time when appropriations for maintenance of posts and buildings become hard to get. For some reason or other, the Army always empties its depots to the Surplus Property Disposal agencies; the Navy is more careful, or we might even say, frugal, in its definition of "surplus." After World War I, "surplus" Army paint, for instance, was sold to the public for fifty cents a gallon. The Army had to pay two dollars to get the same kind of paint, and Congress wouldn't appropriate the money to buy it. I tried to take the necessary action to prevent a recurrence of this situation; however, in 1948 I note that the Air Forces cannot get paint from the regular Army supply system. They need it badly, and what do they do? They trade for it, or beg it from the Navy, so that our Air Force buildings can be painted!

Another serious matter now to be dealt with was the technical development of the Air Forces: development of a better bombsight, for instance; development of the jet airplanes; the possibility of developing jet bombers; the question of whether we had the finest and the last word in bombs; whether we should switch to torpedoes; what should be done about fuses for our bombs; for our rockets; what we should do about the proximity fuse; what of fire control for supersonic airplanes; organization of our Air Arm; what was the province—the mission—of a modern air force; what must be done to prevent overlapping with the Army and Navy?

Nothing had definitely been decided yet about the Air. It had demonstrated that it was a strategic weapon which could be used far beyond the area occupied and controlled either by the land or by the sea units, and yet it was still a component part of the ground and sea forces. What should be done with it? Should it be made an independent arm? Or should it keep its prewar status? Fortunately, that problem has been solved, with the creation of a single Department of National Defense, with Land, Sea, and Air all on equal status.

There was that other question: what should we do to solidify the

Western Hemisphere? Did we have an obligation to the Western Hemisphere that had priority over our obligation to our European Allies? Should we create a military solidarity among all the Americas, with all of us using the same weapons, the same technique and type of training? Or, should we let that go while we continued to build up the facilities required for world-wide war operations? Or should we tie ourselves into a defensive alliance with the European Democracies?

In order to do the latter, we would have to have bases from which we could operate our airplanes. The B-29 was just a type—a type that demonstrated things to come. It had wonderful performance for its day, but other airplanes coming along at that moment, the B-35, the B-36, the B-50—with and without jet modifications—gave promise of revolutionary changes in aerial warfare. Security from foreign air attack meant a line of outposts, of antiaircraft defenses of the latest possible types, of equipment to intercept any surprise blow that might fall.

To win and maintain the good will of our hemispheric neighbors, we must let them in on our secrets, give them some of our equipment, let them use it and become acquainted with its techniques of operation, and help train their military students. This was anticipated in the Act of Chapultepec, signed by the American Republics during the Inter-American Conference on Problems of Peace and War at Mexico City in March, 1945.

With that in mind, I had long talks with President Roosevelt, and later with President Truman, on the advisability of starting such a program with the South American countries at once. In Brazil, the Air Forces had already started mechanics' training schools, supervised the training of Brazilian aviators, and helped in constructing buildings and securing machinery for the manufacture of airplanes and engines. Now we must carry the plan further, and do the same thing for other nations in South America. Why not, I thought, try Mexico?

At that point I began to run into diplomats. It is awfully hard for a practical soldier to understand the manner in which the minds of the diplomats work. I grant some exceptions. For instance, I was able all during the war to work smoothly and closely with Lord Halifax, the British ambassador to the United States. We exchanged news and views regularly and, as long as we were both in Washington, maintained a relationship that to me, at least, was of the greatest value. However, for the most part in any situation, they seem always to be looking for the little men who aren't there.

When, in the fall of 1945, I broached the subject of Air aid to the

Mexican officials in Washington, they were enthusiastic. Naturally, they took it up with their own government, and in due time I was invited, semi-officially, to visit Mexico City. The invitation included my wife and daughter.

The first person I saw when I arrived at the end of October was George Messersmith, our ambassador. I outlined my program for Mexico, and received his whole-hearted blessing. Then we called upon the Mexican Minister of Defense, General Urgueza, who was most interested and sympathetic. The only fly in the ointment was the absence of funds for the schools. He suggested an interview with President Avila Camacho the next day.

In talking the problem over with Ambassador Messersmith, it developed that it would not be as easy to establish aviation schools in Mexico as it had been in Brazil, for the situation was different in some respects. The first hurdle was money, and it might not be possible to put the entire project into effect. I had been instrumental in training and equipping a Mexican squadron for service in the Pacific, and knew their fine war record. They had done a splendid job working with our combat units against the Japanese. We could, in a pinch, continue to train their mechanics and pilots in limited numbers in our schools in the United States, and furnish them with our equipment for their operational training in Mexico. Messersmith thought that might be the solution.

The next morning, we went to the Palace, where I had a fine talk with President Avila Camacho. He was in accord with the principles involved, with the method of carrying out the program, but funds were the deciding factor as far as schools were concerned. Planes and other equipment could certainly be used as and when they were received.

When I added up the results of the trip after I returned to Washington, it was clear that our ambassador at Mexico City and the Mexican authorities were most enthusiastic over the plan for standardization of equipment and training—but what then? Where did we go from there? Meanwhile, I received invitations from Colombia, Peru, and Chile to confer with their leaders on the military air problems.

Some of my staff officers in Washington talked to the State Department to find out what assistance we might expect from it, and its attitude towards presenting to these Central or South American countries ways and means of putting the Chapultepec Agreement into effect, in so far as it pertained to the Air Forces. There was no doubt in my mind that this agreement was a completed document and had the approval of everybody concerned. The Latin Americans knew what was in it just as well as we did. However, after my staff officers had their preliminary conferences with the State Department officials at the lower levels, they told me that there would be no use in my going to South America unless I could get better cooperation from the diplomats. Apparently, some people in the State Department were not in accord with the provisions of the Chapultepec Agreement.

With this in mind, I went back and saw President Truman again. I told him that unless there was a change of attitude on the part of the State Department, it would do no good for me to go down to South America. He asked me why, and I told him of the preliminary talks and our present impasse. The President said he wanted me to go and he wanted me to do what I could to fix up with the South American countries some sort of an air force agreement in accordance with the Chapultepec plan. My reply was: "Mr. President, that's going to make the State Department very mad." He said, "It makes no difference. I want you to go anyhow." I told the President that before I went, I would make one last attempt to get the State Department's agreement. Then I would let him know what the score was, and start for South America.

Accordingly, I arranged a conference with Spruille Braden, and took General Walsh with me. Mr. Braden had three of the lower echelon State Department officials with him. They were probably all specialists in their lines. I give Spruille Braden credit for knowing more about South America, as a whole, and probably more about the individual South American countries, than I will ever know. That was his business. However, when it comes to some of the experts he had in his office, I can't say as much.

I outlined to Mr. Braden what I proposed to do: With the Chapultepec Agreement as a basis, work through the Ambassadors in each of the countries, starting with Colombia. For instance, our Ambassador would work out with the Colombian government details about the number of airplanes we could give them and the number they were ready to receive. Just how many they could handle at that particular moment was something to be decided locally. In the case of Colombia, for instance, our list included P-47's and advanced trainers. No objections were raised concerning the P-47's, but the words "advanced trainers" were hardly out of my mouth before one of the State Department officials told Mr. Braden we couldn't permit advanced trainers to go to Colombia.

Arnold: "Why not?"
State Department Official: "Because they can carry bombs."
Arnold: "What kind of bombs?"

S.D.O.: "It makes no difference what kind of bombs."

Arnold: "Why not?"

S.D.O.: "Because any kind of bombs they carry might be used in case of trouble with their neighbors and if any blood were shed it would be on our hands."

Arnold: "Do P-47's carry bombs?"

S.D.O.: "No."

Arnold: "What airplane do you suppose it was that destroyed most of the railroads in Italy, and many of the railroads in France and Germany; that destroyed the railroad bridges and the road bridges, and was used for all-around ground strafing?"

S.D.O.: "I don't know."

Arnold: "The P-47! Yet you say that we can give the P-47's to these South American countries, but you won't let me give them the advanced trainers! The P-47 fighter can carry a 1000-pound bomb!"

S.D.O.: "I didn't know that."

Then I turned to Mr. Braden and asked, "Isn't it possible, before we make these half-baked decisions, to know the facts in the case?"

Mr. Braden turned to his expert and said, "I don't know the answer to this, do you?" To which the State Department Official said, "We didn't know about that."

Then I said to Mr. Braden: "O.K. Now let's get down to cases. Why not let me go ahead and carry out my original plan and talk to our Ambassador at Bogotá, and let him make the arrangements for transfer of planes to that country? I won't do it. It won't come from the Air Forces. It will come from the State Department, through your Ambassador, and they will be able to create good will for themselves and for this country —something that should be done, and is sorely needed."

Mr. Braden agreed to this, but didn't want me to give away all the airplanes the Chapultepec Agreement contemplated in one fell swoop. I saw his point.

Early in January, 1946, Mrs. Arnold, my daughter, and I, in response to further invitations went to Bogotá. The Colombian Ambassador to the United States, Señor Santamaria, General Robert Walsh, my Aide, Major Sheffield, and Captain Jed Brown accompanied us.

The Columbians could not have been more hospitable. I believe we met most of the official families of the country at the various receptions and dinners given in our honor, and I never saw so many orchids in my life as were presented to Mrs. Arnold in the form of large floral pieces.

I finally told our Ambassador, John Wiley, what I had in mind—that he was to tell the President of Colombia and the Minister for Air that he had some airplanes to present to their country, the idea being that they would then have the same type of equipment we had, use the same technique of employment, and that we in the United States would supervise the training of such officers as they might select. Thus we could work together for the security of the Americas.

Ambassador Wiley said he thought it was one of the finest things he had ever heard of, and that it would do a lot toward directing the good will of the South American countries to the United States. I told him that sometime later, probably, the same thing would be done with other kinds of equipment. He said that would be wonderful!

Shortly thereafter, in a meeting with the President of Colombia, the Minister of Defense, and the Minister for Air, Mr. Wiley outlined to them exactly what he proposed to do. I had suggested to the Ambassador that he hold back a little bit so that if he needed a little additional "good will" at a future date, he would have something with which to bring it about. He agreed with that. But he did tell them he had airplanes available right now to give them. If they could let him know how many airplanes they were ready to receive and could properly employ, he would see that the planes were turned over to Colombia in a matter, not of months or years, but of a week. They were enthusiastic about the plan, and, when we left Bogotá for Lima, Peru, the next day everything seemed to be under control.

The altitude at Bogotá is very high, and is not good for anyone who has a bad heart. I got along all right as long as I watched my step and was careful to rest, but I felt the effects when I got down to Lima, where we were met by our Ambassador Pawley and by high-ranking officials of the Peruvian Government. I told Mr. Pawley we would have to slow up a bit in our various operations because of my health, and suggested he might modify our itinerary.

With that in mind, our party went out to the Country Club and stayed there, though I did, of course, call on the President and on the various Cabinet members. Like Mr. Wiley, Mr. Pawley thought my program was a wonderful idea. However, just about the time I thought we had everything under control, he called me up and said he had just received a telegram from Bogotá that I should read. It was from Ambassador Wiley, and paraphrased one that he had received from Washington—from the State Department—where I had had my conference before leaving the

United States. It said, in effect, to Ambassador Wiley: "By what authority have you promised these airplanes to the Colombian Government? It is not in accordance with State Department principles."

I explained to Ambassador Pawley what had taken place prior to this in Washington, and told him that this project of mine had the approval of the President of the United States, and that I had thought it had the approval of the State Department. Apparently, however, someone somewhere along the line in the State Department had thrown a monkey wrench into the machinery. I also told him I thought the next move was up to him. The President had told me to go ahead. Mr. Braden had given me his approval, and there was a definite number of airplanes available for him to give to the Peruvian Government at such time as he thought best. They could be delivered to Peruvian airfields whenever he so desired.

Ambassador Pawley's reply gave me every reason to believe he realized such conditions did exist in the State Department, and would continue to exist until there was a house cleaning.

The ceremonies and official functions in Peru were as strenuous as those in Colombia, and the people were just as interested in what we were doing in our country, and in what we could do to help them, as the Colombians had been. I regretted very much that the apparent misunderstanding in the State Department had made it impossible for me to go ahead in Peru, with Ambassador Pawley, as I had done in Colombia. Ambassador Pawley readily saw the need for it but after the rebuff Ambassador Wiley had received in Colombia, he was naturally a little hesitant.

In the meantime, my physical condition had become worse, so that we had to call off the part of the trip that would have taken us into Chile and probably across to Argentina and Brazil. We took the plane and headed back to Panama and from there to Miami, where I went into the hospital for a checkup.

While I was there, one of my best friends, and one of the most enthusiastic supporters of American Air Power, died. During a period of almost ten years, Harry Hopkins and I had worked together in building up the Army Air Forces and in seeing to it that our planes were used where they would do the most good. Our discussions took place constantly throughout the whole war, at breakfasts, lunches, and in the evenings. He was as much against dispersion of effort as I was. There had been many occasions when the British or our Navy would endeavor to divert combat units, particularly heavy bombers, from the Air Forces program already approved. If it were only a minor attack I could handle it myself, but if the top-flight personnel, like the Prime Minister, were brought into the picture, then I had to have help. Harry was always ready to assist with advice, or by ushering me into the President.

Sometimes those visits with the President would be in his bedroom before he had arisen. Other times they would be in his study. On a few occasions, they would occur at lunch with the President. Sometimes Harry would listen as I outlined my problem to Mr. Roosevelt, and would then withdraw, leaving me alone to thrash out the problem and get the decision.

Through Harry Hopkins, I became well acquainted with President Roosevelt. I always had a feeling that both the President and Hopkins understood my problems almost as well as I did. Many times either one or both would call me for a conference and I would find that they were thinking along new lines concerning the employment of our Air Forces. Such ideas might or might not have been previously given study by the Air Staff in the Pentagon.

I had not seen much of Harry after completing my previous tour in the hospital at Miami, in March, 1945. He had been sick and so had I. In addition, I had made several trips to the various war theaters. However, I did manage to pay him several visits. In December, 1945, I saw him in his hospital room in New York. Realizing his serious condition, I tried to cut the visit short, but Harry would not let me. He wanted to talk. He was working on his memoirs and asked me if I were going to write mine. I told him I did not know for sure just what I was going to write, but I felt that someone must write the history of the Air Force in such a manner that the real problems, the heartaches and the high-level troubles would be spread out for future Air leaders to read and heed.

Harry said, "You should write them, by all means! Incidentally, there is a lot of material that we will have in common."

While I was in Miami, I had a meeting with Winston Churchill, who was to make a speech at Fulton, Missouri. In the meantime, he was loafing at Miami Beach at the home of Colonel Clarke, who had so often been our host during the Quebec Conferences. I met Mr. Churchill on the beach and we talked of the war, of Hopkins, of President Roosevelt, and then of his proposed speech at Fulton. I gave it as my opinion that we must not forget the close association between the Chiefs of Staff of his country and the United States; that there was a means of insuring a military tie between the two countries that we must not lose—too much was at stake internationally. We had things that they needed, and they had things that we needed. The airplane had eliminated the Atlantic Ocean as a military barrier.

Mr. Churchill agreed that the principle was a sound one. Since then the entire international situation has become so involved that instead of merely a close tie between the United States and Great Britain, we are talking of the more widespread Atlantic Pact.

As soon as I finished my checkup, I returned to Washington and reported to the Secretary of War, the Chief of Staff, and to President Truman. I told them how useless it would be under the circumstances to continue my trip through South America. Until the State Department made up its mind what was going to happen, no one could do much good down there, whether he were an ambassador or a Service man.

The President was somewhat surprised, and although I didn't go into details for a solution of the problem, the general policy I talked over with Mr. Braden was later put into effect in the various South American countries. They are now getting, or were getting, surplus aviation equipment.

Early in the fall of 1945 I had made up my mind I should give up my job as Commanding General of the Army Air Forces. I had seen it grow from almost nothing into the mightiest Air Force the world had ever known. I had seen some of the world's finest airplanes developed, tested, and tried out in battle, and I had seen our Air Forces play their part with the R.A.F. and with the Naval Air Force in defeating the German Luftwaffe and the Japanese Air Force.

I was proud to have served as the leader of such an outfit. But I also saw that the future might not be as rosy as the past. There were plans that should be made during this period immediately following World War II which would be very important ten or fifteen years from now. It looked to me as if the time had come when the younger men who would have to carry out those plans, and who would have to continue to build up the Air Force, should be in the driver's seat. It was no place for the old fellows who had served their part and who should not be considered as even probable leaders in any new emergency.

With this in mind, on November 8, 1945, I wrote a memorandum to the Chief of Staff, as follows:

It is my judgment that I should retire from active service in the Armed Forces at an early date. The policies being established in the Army Air Force and by the Joint Chiefs of Staff will determine, to a large extent, the mission, composition, and over-all effectiveness of the

Armed Services of the United States for the indefinite future. I believe these policies should be formulated, as nearly as possible, by my successor, who will have the responsibility of carrying them out.

The whole-hearted and generous support that you gave to me throughout the war years contributed immeasurably to the accomplishment of the mission of the Army Air Forces. Your guidance on the many important matters that had to be solved was invariably sound and statesmanlike. The close and informal relationship that has existed between us for a good many years has been a source of deep satisfaction to me, and I feel it has borne fruit in the general spirit of harmony within the Army.

With your concurrence, I should like to request retirement from the Service. I should like to be separated from the Service and go on terminal leave.

H. H. ARNOLD
Commanding General, Army Air Forces.

That was not an easy memorandum to write. It would terminate forty-two years of service. It meant separation from the Army and it also meant separation from the Joint Chiefs of Staff and the Combined Chiefs of Staff, the only two agencies of their kind the United States had ever had. The President accepted my application for retirement and my wife and I left Washington on March 1, 1946, for Sonoma.

At the time of my retirement, some reporters at a National Press Club luncheon had asked me what I was going to do when I left Washington.

I replied, "I'm going out to my ranch in the Valley of the Moon, to sit under an oak tree. From there I'll look across the Valley at the white-faced cattle. And if one of them even moves too fast, I'll look the other way."

"You mean you're through with airplanes?"

"*Yes!* If one dares to fly low over my ranch house, I'll grab a rifle or something and shoot it down!"

By chance, many news dispatches carried that wisecrack, which later was to bounce back on me.

I forgot about it, but, apparently, other people didn't. There are usually planes somewhere in the air over the Valley of the Moon, what with Hamilton Field a few miles to the South, Sacramento not very far away, and the enthusiasm for private flying there is everywhere in California. But the planes all passed high, or in the distance. My wife and I could sit in the redwood chairs I had made in my workshop, drink in the quiet beauty of our valley, and watch the half-tame quail feed about our garden. On such calm, sunny afternoons you could almost imagine that the roar of four-engine bombers, the fiery flash of aerial battle, even the wrangles of diplomacy, had never existed.

One day, on just such a peaceful afternoon, I heard distinctly the sound of an airplane doing what it should not do, in a place where it should not be. I went outside and saw two training planes engaged in a lively dogfight. If the pilots were not intentionally putting on a demonstration for our benefit, they might as well have been. For a few apprehensive minutes, I watched the cavorting AT-6's. Then suddenly, they collided. As they separated, one started to limp back toward Hamilton, where, I learned later, it landed on its belly with the pilot uninjured. The second plane, however, had its tail sheared clean off. The pilot immediately bailed out, floating away to a safe landing on a near-by golf course. But his plane!

I had boasted often of the way our B-17's came home from Germany with important parts missing. In the early days I had flown planes myself that had started to come apart. But I never—not ever—had expected to see an airplane *with no tail* continue to fly right on, right down in malevolent spirals toward its objective!

And that objective was my house!

Down, down, but always flying just as if it were spiraling normally! This was it—the end of El Rancho Felíz! I knew what had to happen. It could only hit the house now, crash, cover it with gasoline, start the inevitable, disastrous fire!

It missed the roof by inches. Grazing the rose garden, it crashed in the south pasture, a few yards away, and exploded. The hole it made was thirty feet across and about six feet deep.

Fortunately, we have had no further interruptions of this kind at El Rancho Felíz. For the most part, our way of life in the Valley of the Moon is fairly quiet. During the last three or four years I have had plenty of time to think of the urgent and difficult war years and what preceded them.

But now, what of the future?

One thing stands out clearly against the background of my experience: the winning of Peace is much more difficult than the winning of even a global War. One look at the condition of the poor old world today, four years after the supposed ending of World War II, almost makes me gasp. Where is our Peace?

Theoretically, war gives the military man the clear-cut problem of creating his forces, and of so disposing them that if everything works out properly, the result will be the capitulation of the enemy. But even the fabric of wartime emergency, as this story may help to indicate, is really not quite that simple. The practical implication of any alliance, under even the most desperate conditions, is that even desperation will not keep any nation from endeavoring to guide world affairs in accordance with its own aims and ambitions.

Take, for instance, the recurring proposals for campaigns through the Caucasus, north through Greece and the Balkans, from Trieste, and the area northeast, to join the Russians; a drive through the mountains north of Italy, or a major offensive northward from southern France. Were they born of sound military thinking or of the ambitions of one or more of our European Allies?

There never was a doubt in my mind that the proper course to follow to defeat the Germans was to take the most direct line, the shortest line, to Berlin, knowing full well that in so doing we would meet and defeat the best Air Force and Armies, and be forced to pass through the most difficult defensive zone that the Germans had to offer. Long, weary hours of planning and talking were necessary before we had the full backing of our Allies for this plan.

Then too, we had troubles and differences in getting agreements on the composition, size, and employment of the military forces of our own country. The U.S. Navy for years had been thinking toward a state of readiness to lick the Japanese. They knew they could do it with little, if any, trouble—"with one hand tied behind them." Pearl Harbor came as a distinct shock to all of us, but to our Navy more than anyone. It upset years of their planning. It was only natural for them to figure on regaining their position in the sun. They must do everything possible to make the Pacific campaign not only the first-priority war theater, but also to make it a Navy war theater, run by the Navy. Hence, whenever a question of allocation of supplies and production arose, up came the argument of whether the critical items should go to the Pacific Theater or to other theaters. It required some time to iron out these difficulties.

Neither we nor the British helped the civilized world along the road to a permanent peace in 1945 by virtually agreeing that we could not get "tough" enough with the Germans and that the Russians should take over and run most of Germany. We agreed that Russia should occupy and govern central Germany and most of Berlin. We and the other Allied nations were to occupy small areas within Berlin—but only by sufferance. We must rely upon the good nature of Russia for corridors of entry and exit to our areas. Both Great Britain and America, and their leaders, knew what kind of people the Russians were. All knew the Russians had no compunction about breaking pacts, accords, and agreements. We should have foreseen trouble, but we didn't care to think of such things right then.

Then Russia got tough. It wasn't the United States, or Great Britain, or France. It was Russia who put the blockade on Berlin.

I have never thought that Russia would, under any circumstances during this postwar period, go to war. They were and are not ready for it. I am sure that had we taken a convoy, with tanks and armored cars, and headed for our section of Berlin, Russia would have "backwatered" and we would have broken the blockade. Instead, we chose to accept their restrictions and do things the hard way—supply Berlin by the airlift.

From June 26, 1948, until May, 1949, the eyes of the western world watched Operation VITTLES, first grimly, then with wonder. And not only the western world, including the 2,100,000 anxious Berliners cut off from normal fuel and food supplies by the Russian blockade—the eyes in Moscow and in the Soviet zone of Berlin watched too. By mid-winter, as the airlift, instead of slackening, flew in more and more tons, day after day and week after week in all kinds of weather, it was clear even to the Russians that they had bitten off more than they could chew. By April 16th, the 249th day of the blockade, when the "LeMay Coal & Food Co.," as boys called it after its founder, flew in, together with the R.A.F., 12,940.9 tons—"more," one awed correspondent pointed out, "than had ever been carried by a train from the west in a single day before the blockade"—it was plain that in the Cold War for Berlin the Russians were confronted by a thing which they could neither cope with nor even comprehend. In January, in direct connection with the airlift, J. Kingsbury Smith, European general manager of International News Service, had interviewed Stalin who now was reported as saying he would "be willing to discuss peace with President Truman." The State Department followed up this interview with interest in its official text of April 26th. At 12:01 A.M., May 12th, the Soviet blockade was officially lifted, though immediate aftermaths indicated it might be well not to disband the airlift organization too hurriedly. The Cold War for Germany lies ahead.

There were other factors, but no more dramatic evidence that "Air Power is Peace Power" could have been furnished. Some of the crews who carried Operation VITTLES out were too young to have been in the war, but to me the pattern was familiar. No longer did Chiang Kai-shek heckle for more tonnage over the Hump. Partly because of things deep in the soil of China, partly because of another aspect of the thing we were dealing with in Berlin, the Generalissimo had been made to vacate his power and move to a new address. The Hump itself had moved, from the Himalayas to Berlin. But as before, our crews carried with them not only the vital material but our national foreign policy. The link was made closer not only by the original presence of LeMay, who organized the airlift, but by the fact that the man who, as one paper put it, "increased its efficiency from the spectacular to the incredible" was the same Major General William H. Tunner who had been the executive in the ferrying of the supplies from India to China.

Words do not impress the Russians. They never have. Hence, the Atlantic Pact, by itself, means little. There must be force and power behind it to show the Russians that the nations in the Alliance mean business. There are several means of putting teeth in the Pact and of arming the nations whose safety and future security may depend upon such an alliance: first, we might send to the various nations the surplus arms and equipment we have on hand or are producing; second, we might send them anything—any kind of equipment they ask for; third, we might do a bit of advance planning and thinking to insure that each of the nations concerned had the kind of equipment it would need as a component part of a joint Allied force. There would then exist a unified command with the proper composition, strength, and equipment to deter any aggressor from war. At the very least, it would cause an aggressor nation to stop and think before making any hostile move.

These three points not only bring out the different ideas about furnishing equipment, but more important, make clear the necessity for a decision: Are we simply to waste funds and give away equipment; be a Santa Claus; or are we to make certain that if an emergency does arise, we will have the kind and type of equipment, the number and kind of trained units, and the composition of armed forces capable of meeting any onslaught in a modern way, instead of in a hit-and-miss fashion? Just sending tanks, guns, rifles, and ammunition overseas won't do the trick.

Take our own situation, for example: We no longer need an outpost line from Guam to Midway to Alaska, and along the Atlantic Coast to Puerto Rico and the Panama Canal. Modern war equipment has now made it necessary for us to have an outpost line of antiaircraft detectors and other devices from the Philippines to Okinawa to Japan to the Aleutians, across Northern Canada to England, and ending up in North Africa. Guided missiles, radar, sonic devices, jet fighters—all of the latest type and with the latest gadgets and developments—located along that line are the only protection we can build up against annihilating aerial attacks in the future.

Modern wars are different. I, for one, believe that devastating air attacks—probably with "A" bombs—on selected industrial cities in England, Holland, Norway, Belgium, and France—might disorganize movement and make it impossible for ground or sea forces, no matter how courageous, to carry out their prearranged plans for meeting an aggressor. If this happened, all the good intentions, pacts, agreements, we had with, and the equipment we had within those countries might be of little value to us in making a lodgement and driving the aggressor back beyond his frontiers.

I am not against the Atlantic Pact. I am for it, 100 per cent. But I am not for an indiscriminate armament of the member nations. Modern wars cannot be won that way. We must be matter-of-fact, and we must accept things as they really are. We should not try to write into the problem a lot of emotions, traditions, and hopes that have become an inherent part of all of us.

France is yelling: "We must be equipped first!" Maybe; or maybe not. The answer depends upon the probable intention of Russia. How would she go about carrying out that intention? And what could she use to do it with? What part will France play, and what kind of units and equipment will she need with which to play that part? The same line of reasoning should be applied to all nations that might become involved in the next war—which must not come.

We must stop "shoeing dead horses." We have been doing that far too long. We have, in the United States, been operating this Army station, or that Naval base, or that piece of equipment for years, because—well, because what? Well, any old reason. We did it because of Congressman or Senator "X"—we must have his support; he might lose votes, and so not support the Army, Navy, or Air Force Bill; or we have had this unit ever since the Revolution, and tradition is behind it, so we will keep it in being; or, some time or other there may be a use for this station, or that base, or some obsolete technique or pieces of equipment.

There is only one question that should be asked about these things: "Do they fit into the modern war picture?" Not the picture of 1918, nor of 1941, but of the war of the future. If they don't, we should be ruthless, and throw them out. For instance, who knows whether 70 groups of airplanes is the right or wrong number to prevent another war? Was not that number selected in relation to costs and expenditures, rather than with regard to the composition and strength necessary to our armed forces in the world picture? Do 70 groups have any relationship to our new foreign obligations? The proper number may be 47, 70, or even 170; but it should be based upon our foreign policy and the part we must take in the operations of the armed forces of the Alliance.

Do Russian capabilities provide a destructive threat against the Panama Canal, or has the picture there changed to danger of sabotage only? What does the present spread of Communism mean with regard to the Pacific islands? Does it mean large base forces and garrisons against invasion? Does it not mean we must change the military ideas about those areas that we have followed for the past thirty years?

The principles of yesterday no longer apply. Air travel, air power, air transportation of troops and supplies have changed the whole picture. We must think in terms of tomorrow. We must bear in mind that air power itself can become obsolete.

Duplications, obsolete construction projects, obsolete techniques and policies, overlapping in the armed services' operations and organizations must go by the boards. There is no place for two air forces today any more than there is for two ground forces, or two navies. Let us get smart, and, while we have a few years in which to reorganize, do it right. Let us give the people of the United States the best, the most efficient, the most modernly equipped armed forces possible, using as determining factors, our *foreign policy,* and the *capabilities and limitations of our probable enemies.*

Russia has no fear of an army; she thinks hers is just as good as, and bigger than, any in the world; she has no fear of a navy, since she cannot see how it can be employed against her; but she does fear our long-range Strategic Air Force, which she cannot as yet match, or as yet understand. In the Strategic Air Force, coupled with our atomic bomb, at this writing we hold the balance of power in the world.

INDEX

Help Us Help You

So that we can better provide you with the practical information you need, please take a moment to complete and return this card.

1. I am interested in books on the following subjects:
- ☐ architecture & design
- ☐ automotive
- ☐ aviation
- ☐ business & finance
- ☐ computer, mini & mainframe
- ☐ computer, micros
- ☐ other_____

- ☐ electronics
- ☐ engineering
- ☐ hobbies & crafts
- ☐ how-to, do-it-yourself
- ☐ military history
- ☐ nautical

2. I own/use a computer:
- ☐ Apple/Macintosh_____
- ☐ Commodore_____
- ☐ IBM_____
- ☐ Other_____

3. This card came from TAB book (no. or title):

_____

4. I purchase books from/by:
- ☐ general bookstores
- ☐ technical bookstores
- ☐ college bookstores
- ☐ mail

- ☐ telephone
- ☐ electronic mail
- ☐ hobby stores
- ☐ art materials stores

Comments _____

_____

_____

Name _____

Address _____

City _____

State/Zip _____

TAB BOOKS Inc.